T0211689

# Communications
# in Computer and Information Science     **616**

*Commenced Publication in 2007*
Founding and Former Series Editors:
Alfredo Cuzzocrea, Dominik Ślęzak, and Xiaokang Yang

More information about this series at http://www.springer.com/series/7899

Javier Bajo · María José Escalona
Sylvain Giroux · Patrycja Hoffa-Dąbrowska
Vicente Julián · Paulo Novais
Nayat Sánchez-Pi · Rainer Unland
Ricardo Azambuja-Silveira (Eds.)

# Highlights of Practical Applications of Scalable Multi-Agent Systems

## The PAAMS Collection

International Workshops of PAAMS 2016
Sevilla, Spain, June 1–3, 2016
Proceedings

 Springer

*Editors*
Javier Bajo
Departamento de Inteligencia Artificial
Universidad Politécnica de Madrid
Madrid
Spain

María José Escalona
Universidad de Sevilla
Sevilla
Spain

Sylvain Giroux
Faculté des Sciences
Université de Sherbrooke
Sherbrooke
Canada

Patrycja Hoffa-Dąbrowska
University of Poznan
Poznan
Poland

Vicente Julián
Universidad Politécnica de Valencia
Valencia
Spain

Paulo Novais
Department of Informatics
Universidade do Minho
Braga
Portugal

Nayat Sánchez-Pi
Fluminense Federal University
Rio de Janeiro
Brazil

Rainer Unland
Institute for Computer Science and Business
 Information Systems (ICB)
University of Duisburg-Essen
Essen, Nordrhein-Westfalen
Germany

Ricardo Azambuja-Silveira
Departamento de Informática e Estatístic
Universidade Federal de Santa Catarina
Florianópolis S.C.
Brazil

ISSN 1865-0929         ISSN 1865-0937 (electronic)
Communications in Computer and Information Science
ISBN 978-3-319-39386-5         ISBN 978-3-319-39387-2 (eBook)
DOI 10.1007/978-3-319-39387-2

Library of Congress Control Number: 2016939582

Printed on acid-free paper

This Springer imprint is published by Springer Nature
The registered company is Springer International Publishing AG Switzerland

# Preface

PAAMS Workshops complement the regular program with new or emerging trends of particular interest connected to multi-agent systems.

PAAMS, the International Conference on Practical Applications of Agents and Multi-Agent Systems, evolved from the International Workshop on Practical Applications of Agents and Multi-Agent Systems. PAAMS is an international yearly tribune to present, to discuss, and to disseminate the latest developments and the most important outcomes related to real-world applications. It provides a unique opportunity to bring multi-disciplinary experts, academics, and practitioners together to exchange their experience in the development of agents and multi-agent systems.

This volume presents the papers that were accepted in the workshops during the 2016 edition of PAAMS: Workshop on Agents and Multi-agent Systems for AAL and e-HEALTH; Workshop on Agent-Based Solutions for Manufacturing and Supply Chain; Workshop on MAS for Complex Networks and Social Computation; Workshop on Decision Making in Dynamic Information Environments; Workshop on Intelligent Systems for Context-Based Information Fusion; Workshop on Multi-Agent Based Applications for Smart Grids and Sustainable Energy Systems; Workshop on Multi-agent System-Based Learning Environments. Each paper submitted to PAAMS workshops went through a stringent peer review by three members of the international committee of each workshop. From the 77 submissions received, 37 were selected for presentation at the conference.

We would like to thank all the contributing authors, as well as the members of the Program Committees of the workshops and the Organizing Committee for their hard and highly valuable work. Their work contributed to the success of the PAAMS 2016 event. Thank you for your help, PAAMS 2016 would not exist without your contribution.

April 2016

Javier Bajo
María José Escalona

# Organization

## Workshops

**W1** – Workshop on Agents and Multi-agent Systems for AAL and e-HEALTH
**W2** – Workshop on Agent-Based Solutions for Manufacturing and Supply Chain
**W3** – Workshop on MAS for Complex Networks and Social Computation
**W4** – Workshop on Decision Making in Dynamic Information Environments
**W5** – Workshop on Intelligent Systems for Context-based Information Fusion
**W6** – Workshop on Multi-agent-Based Applications for Smart Grids and Sustainable Energy Systems
**W7** – Workshop on Multi-agent System-Based Learning Environments

## Workshop on Agents and Multi-agent Systems for AAL and e-HEALTH

### Program Committee Chairs

| | |
|---|---|
| Kasper Hallenborg (Co-chair) | University of Southern Denmark, Denmark |
| Sylvain Giroux (Co-chair) | University of Sherbrooke, Canada |

### Program Committee

| | |
|---|---|
| Juan M. Corchado | University of Salamanca, Spain |
| Javier Bajo | Technical University of Madrid, Spain |
| Juan F. De Paz | University of Salamanca, Spain |
| Sara Rodríguez | University of Salamanca, Spain |
| Valerie Camps | Paul Sabatier University of Toulouse, France |
| Cristian I. Pinzón | Technical University of Panama, Panama |
| Sigeru Omatu | Osaka Institute of Technology, Japan |
| Paulo Novais | University of Minho, Portugal |
| Luis F. Castillo | University of Caldas, Colombia |
| Florentino Fernandez | University of Vigo, Spain |
| Belén Pérez Lancho | University of Salamanca, Spain |
| Jesús García Herrero | Carlos III University of Madrid, Spain |
| Helena Lindgren | University of Umea, Sweden |
| Goretti Marreiros | Instituto Superior de Engenharia do Porto, Portugal |
| Gaetano Carmelo La Delfa | University of Catania, Italy |
| Tiancheng Li | Northwestern Polytechnical University, China |

# Workshop on Agent-Based Solutions for Manufacturing and Supply Chain

### Program Committee Chairs

| | |
|---|---|
| Pawel Pawlewski | Poznan University of Technology, Poland |
| Patrycja Hoffa | Poznan University of Technology, Poland |

### Program Committee

| | |
|---|---|
| Zbigniew J. Pasek | IMSE/University of Windsor, Canada |
| Paul-Eric Dossou | ICAM Vendee, France |
| Grzegorz Bocewicz | Koszalin University of Technology, Poland |
| Pawel Sitek | Kielce University of Technology, Poland |
| Izabela E. Nielsen | Aalborg University, Denmark |
| Joanna Kolodziej | Cracow University of Technology, Poland |
| Peter Nielsen | Aalborg University, Denmark |
| Allen Greenwood | Mississippi State University, USA |

# Workshop on MAS for Complex Networks and Social Computation

### Program Committee Chairs

| | |
|---|---|
| Vicente Botti | Universitat Politècnica de València, Spain |
| Miguel Rebollo | Universitat Politècnica de València, Spain |
| Elena Del Val | Universitat Politècnica de València, Spain |
| Alberto Palomares | Universitat Politècnica de València, Spain |
| Juan Miguel Alberola | Universitat Politècnica de València, Spain |

### Program Committee

| | |
|---|---|
| Daniel Villatoro | Vodafone, UK |
| Carlos Carrascosa | Universitat Politècnica de València, Spain |
| Vicente Julián Inglada | Universitat Politècnica de València, Spain |
| Guillem Martínez | Universitat de València, Spain |
| Francisco Grimaldo | Universitat de València, Spain |
| Katarzyna Musial-Gabrys | King's College London, UK |
| Juan José Ramasco | Institute for Cross-Disciplinary Physics and Complex Systems, IFISC, Spain |
| Stella Heras | Universitat Politècnica de València, Spain |
| Javier Palanca | Universitat Politècnica de València, Spain |

# Workshop on Decision Making in Dynamic Information Environments

### Program Committee Chairs

| | |
|---|---|
| Tiago Oliveira | University of Minho, Portugal |
| Jose Carlos Montoya | Universidad Carlos III de Madrid, Spain |

| | |
|---|---|
| Paulo Novais | University of Minho, Portugal |
| Ken Satoh | National Institute of Informatics, Japan |

## Program Committee

| | |
|---|---|
| Ângelo Costa | University of Minho, Portugal |
| Costin Bădică | University of Craiova, Romania |
| Claudia Schulz | Imperial College London, UK |
| Davide Carneiro | University of Minho, Portugal |
| Goreti Marreiros | Polytechnic of Porto, Portugal |
| Hiroshi Hosobe | Hosei University, Japan |
| Joe Steinhauer | University of Skövde, Sweden |
| José Neves | University of Minho, Portugal |
| Jason J. Jung | Chung-Ang University, South Korea |
| Javier Bajo | Technical University of Madrid, Spain |
| Kristijonas Čyras | Imperial College London, UK |
| Paulo Moura Oliveira | University of Trás-os-Montes e Alto Douro, Portugal |
| Pedro Henriques | University of Minho, Portugal |
| Philippe Roose | University of Pau and Pays de l'Adour, France |
| Randy Goebel | University of Alberta, Canada |
| Tony Ribeiro | Ecole Centrale de Nantes, IRCCyN, France |
| Vicente Julián | Valencia University of Technology, Spain |
| Brahim Ouhbi | University Ensam-Meknès, Morocco |
| Fábio Silva | University of Minho, Portugal |
| Nuno Silva | Polytechnic of Porto, Portugal |
| Igor Kotenko | Laboratory of Computer Security Problems, SPIIRAS, Russia |
| Antonio Fernández Caballero | University of Castilla-La Mancha, Spain |
| Vali Derhami | Yazd University, Iran |
| Florentino Riverola | University of Vigo, Spain |
| João Ferreira | High Institute of Engineering of Lisbon, Portugal |
| Jesus Capitan | University of Seville, Spain |
| Miguel Salido | Universidad Politécnica de Valencia, Spain |
| Mohammad Al-Zinati | Jordan University of Science and Technology, Jordan |
| Rosario Girardi | Federal University of Maranhão, Brazil |

# Workshop on Intelligent Systems for Context-Based Information Fusion

## Program Committee Chairs

| | |
|---|---|
| José Manuel Molina | Carlos III University of Madrid, Spain |
| Juan M. Corchado | University of Salamanca, Spain |
| Nayat Sánchez Pi | Universidade Federal Fluminense, Brazil |
| Jesús García Herrero | Carlos III University of Madrid, Spain |

Gabriel Villarrubia                    University of Salamanca, Spain
Javier Bajo                            Technical University of Madrid, Spain
Ana Cristina Bicharra García           Universidade Federal Fluminense, Brazil
Luis Marti                             Pontificia Universidade Catolica, Brazil
James Llinas                           State University of New York at Buffalo, USA

## Program Committee

Jesus Garcia Herrero                   Carlos III University of Madrid, Spain
James Llinas                           State University of New York at Buffalo, USA
Javier Bajo                            Technical University of Madrid, Spain
Juan F. De Paz                         University of Salamanca, Spain
Sara Rodríguez                         University of Salamanca, Spain
Fernando de la Prieta Pintado          University of Salamanca, Spain
Gabriel Villarrubia González           University of Salamanca, Spain
Antonio Juan Sánchez Martín            University of Salamanca, Spain
Miguel Angel Patricio                  Universidad Carlos III, Spain
Antonio Berlanga                       Universidad Carlos III, Spain
Lauro Snidaro                          University of Udine, Italy
Eloi Bosse                             University of Laval, Canada
Subrata Das                            Machine Analytics, Inc., USA
Vicente Julian                         Technical University of Valencia, Spain
Eugenio Oliveira                       University of Porto, Portugal
Florentino Fdez-Riverola               University of Vigo, Spain
Masanori Akiyoshi                      Osaka University, Japan
Luís Lima                              Polytechnic of Porto, Portugal
Andrew Campbell                        Darthmouth College, USA
Carlos Carrascosa                      Technical University of Valencia, Spain
Ana Cristina Bicharra Garcia           Universidade Federal Fluminense, Brazil
Nayat Sánchez Pi                       Universidade Federal Fluminense, Brazil
Luis Marti                             Pontificia Universidade Catolica, Brazil
Eleni Mangina                          University College Dublin, Ireland
Luís Correia                           University of Lisbon, Portugal
Cristian Iván Pinzón Trejos            Universidad Tecnológica de Panamá, Panamá
Luiz André Paes Leme                   Universidade Federal Fluminense, Brazil
José Viterbo Filho                     Universidade Federal Fluminense, Brazil
Marley Velasco                         Pontificia Universidade Catolica, Brazil
Lyudmila Mihaylova                     Lancaster University, UK
Joachim Biermann                       FKIE, Germany
Kellyn Rein                            FKIE, Germany
Eric Little                            Modus Operandi, USA

# Workshop on Multi-agent-Based Applications for Smart Grids and Sustainable Energy Systems

## Program Committee Chair

Rainer Unland                     University of Duisburg-Essen, Germany

## Steering Committee

Fernando Lopes                    LNEG National Research Institute, Portugal
Giancarlo Fortino                 Università della Calabria, Italy
Hugo Morais                       Denmark Technical University, Denmark
Rainer Unland                     University of Duisburg-Essen, Germany
Ryszard Kowalczyk                 Swinburne University of Technology, Australia
Zita Vale                         Polytechnic Institute of Porto, Portugal

## Program Committee

Alberto Fernández                 Universidad Rey Juan Carlos, Spain
Alberto Sardinha                  Technical University of Lisbon, Portugal
Andreas Symeonidis                University of Thessaloniki, Greece
Anke Weidlich                     Hochschule Offenburg, Germany
Benjamin Hirsch                   Etisalat BT Innovation Centre (EBTIC), UAE
Bo Nørregaard Jørgensen           Mærsk Mc-Kinney Møller Instituttet, Denmark
Christian Derksen                 Universität Duisburg-Essen, Germany
Christoph Weber                   Universität Duisburg-Essen, Germany
Costin Badica                     University of Craiova, Romania
David Sislak                      Gerstner Laboratory, Czech Republic
Fabrice Saffre                    Etisalat BT Innovation Centre, UAE
Frank Allgöwer                    Universität Stuttgart, Germany
Gauthier Picard                   ENS Mines Saint-Etienne, France
Georg Frey                        Universität des Saarlandes, Germany
Hanno Hildmann                    NEC Germany, Germany
Ingo J. Timm                      J.W. Goethe University of Frankfurt, Germany
Jan Sudeikat                      Hamburg Energie GmbH, Germany
Jan Treur                         Vrije Universiteit Amsterdam, The Netherlands
Juan A. Rodríguez-Aguilar         IIIA, CSIC, Spain
Koen Hindriks                     Delft University of Technology, Netherlands
Lars Braubach                     University of Hamburg, Germany
Lars Mönch                        Fernuniversität Hagen, Germany
Laurent Vercouter                 Graduate School of Engineering - Saint-Étienne,
                                  France
Marcin Paprzycki                  Polish Academy of Sciences, Poland
Maria Ganzha                      Warsaw Technical University, Poland
Massimiliano Giacomin             University of Brescia, Italy
Matthias Klusch                   DFKI, Germany
Miguel Ángel López Carmona        University of Alcalá de Henares, Spain

Paulo Leitão                    Polytechnic Institute of Bragança, Portugal
Paulo Novais                    Universidade do Minho, Portugal
Peter Palensky                  TU Delft, The Netherlands
Sascha Ossowski                 Universidad Rey Juan Carlos, Spain
Stamatis Karnouskos             SAP, Germany
Steven Guan                     Xian Jiatong-Liverpool University, China
Sudip Bhattacharjee             University of Connecticut, USA
Tiago Pinto                     Polytechnic Institute of Porto, Portugal
Witold Pedrycz                  University of Alberta, Canada
Wolfgang Ketter                 Rotterdam School of Management, The
                                Netherlands

## Workshop on Multi-agent System-Based Learning Environments

### Program Committee Chairs

Ricardo Azambuja Silveira       Universidade Federal de Santa Catarina, Brazil
Rosa Vicari                     Universidade Federal do Rio Grande do Sul, Brazil
Néstor Darío Duque Méndez       Universidad Nacional de Colombia, Colombia

### Program Committee

Néstor Darío Duque Méndez       Universidad Nacional de Colombia, Colombia
Ricardo Azambuja Silveira       Universidade Federal de Santa Catarina, Brazil
Rosa Vicari                     Universidade Federal do Rio Grande do Sul –
                                UFRGS, Brazil
Jose Cascalho                   Universidade dos Azores, Portugal
Cesar A. Collazos               Universidad de Cauca, Colombia
Ramon Fabregat Gesa             Universitat de Girona, Spain
Joao Carlos Gluz                UNISINOS, Brazil
Martin Llamas-Nistal            University of Vigo, Spain
Silvia Margarita Baldiris       Universitat de Girona, Spain
  Navarro
Demetrio Arturo Ovalle          Universidad Nacional de Colombia - Sede
  Carranza                        Medellín, Colombia
Carlos Vaz De Carvalho          ISEP, Portugal
Cecilia Dias Flores             Universidade Federal do Rio Grande do Sul, Brazil
Patricia Jaques                 UNISINOS, Brazil
Julian Moreno Cadavid           Universidad Nacional de Colombia, Colombia
Júlia Marques Carvalho          Instituto Federal do Rio Grande do Sul, Brazil
  Da Silva
Marta Bez                       Universidade Feevale, Brazil
Maria Rosangela Bez             I3C – Instituto Curiosidade Ciência e Criação,
                                Brazil

## Organizing Committee

| | |
|---|---|
| María José Escalona Cuaresma (Chair) | University of Seville, Spain |
| Javier Bajo (Chair) | Technical University of Madrid, Spain |
| Carlos Arevalo Maldonado | University of Seville, Spain |
| Gustavo Aragon Serrano | University of Seville, Spain |
| Irene Barba | University of Seville, Spain |
| Miguel Ángel Barcelona Liédana | Technological Institute of Aragon, Spain |
| Juan Manuel Cordero Valle | University of Seville, Spain |
| Francisco José Domínguez Mayo | University of Seville, Spain |
| Juan Pablo Domínguez Mayo | University of Seville, Spain |
| Manuel Domínguez Muñoz | University of Seville, Spain |
| José Fernández Engo | University of Seville, Spain |
| Laura García Borgoñón | Technological Institute of Aragon, Spain |
| Julian Alberto García García | University of Seville, Spain |
| Javier García-Consuegra Angulo | University of Seville, Spain |
| José González Enríquez | University of Seville, Spain |
| Tatiana Guardia Bueno | University of Seville, Spain |
| Andrés Jiménez Ramírez | University of Seville, Spain |
| Javier Jesús Gutierrez Rodriguez | University of Seville, Spain |
| Manuel Mejías Risoto | University of Seville, Spain |
| Laura Polinario | University of Seville, Spain |
| José Ponce Gonzalez | University of Seville, Spain |
| Francisco José Ramírez López | University of Seville, Spain |
| Isabel Ramos Román | University of Seville, Spain |
| Jorge Sedeño López | University of Seville, Spain |
| Nicolás Sánchez Gómez | University of Seville, Spain |
| Juan Miguel Sánchez Begines | University of Seville, Spain |
| Eva-Maria Schön | University of Seville, Spain |
| Jesús Torres Valderrama | University of Seville, Spain |
| Carmelo Del Valle Sevillano | University of Seville, Spain |
| Antonio Vázquez Carreño | University of Seville, Spain |
| Carlos Torrecilla Salinas | University of Seville, Spain |
| Ainara Aguirre Narros | University of Seville, Spain |
| Diana Borrego | University of Seville, Spain |
| Fernando Enríquez de Salamanca Ros | University of Seville, Spain |
| Juan Antonio Alvarez García | University of Seville, Spain |
| Antonio Tallón | University of Seville, Spain |

## PAAMS 2016 Sponsors

# Contents

## Workshop on MAS for Complex Networks and Social Computation (CNSC)

## Workshop on Decision Making in Dynamic Information Environments (DeMaDIE)

**Workshop on Intelligent Systems and Context Information Fusion (ISCIF)**

**Workshop on Multi-agent Based Applications for Energy Markets,
Smart Grids and Sustainable Energy Systems (MASGES)**

**Workshop on Multiagent System Based Learning Environments (MASLE)**

# Workshop on Agents and Multi-Agent Systems for AAL and e-HEALTH (A-HEALTH)

# Results of a Pilot Study with a Robot Instructor for Group Exercise at a Senior Living Community

Lundy Lewis[1], Ted Metzler[2(✉)], and Linda Cook[2]

[1] Computer Technology, Southern New Hampshire University, Manchester, NH, USA
l.lewis@snhu.edu
[2] School of Nursing, Oklahoma City University, Oklahoma City, OK, USA
{tmetzler,lcook}@okcu.edu

**Abstract.** We discuss the motivation, design, implementation, and pilot study of an agent-based exercise robot for five senior residents and five staff members in a senior living community. Our goals of the study were to evaluate the perform- ance of the resident group and the attitudes, acceptance, and opinions of both groups. The pilot study was performed on-site where senior participants were selected a priori by the staff. We use soft systems methodology as a guide to refine the requirements and to evolve the exercise protocol and robot behaviors over multiple exercise sessions. Based on a 30-min session with both groups combined, followed by focus sessions with each group individually, our findings suggest that senior residents moderately accept the robot as a group exercise leader and staff members are cautiously enthusiastic about the idea.

**Keywords:** Elder care · Quality of life · Robot · Entertainment · Exercise · Agent- based system

## 1 Introduction

Socially assistive robots (SARs) show promise for helping seniors cope with loneliness through conversation, articulating reminders of their tasks, assisting with routine daily activities which have become hard to perform, and generally taking on roles that are normally performed by caregivers. However, the predicted decrease in the number of caregivers in proportion to the increase in the number of seniors is problematic. The number of seniors is predicted to increase two-fold by 2050. To make matters worse, young students in psychology, sociology, nursing, and related disciplines are less inter- ested in elder care than in areas such as child development and disability management.

For these reasons, a current interest among researchers and entrepreneurs is to develop ways to integrate robots into senior living without human accompaniment but yet without diminishing the quality of life, yet better to augment the quality of life. The idea is worthy of pursuit, but it is a hard problem.

In this paper we are concerned with robot assistance for an important daily task of seniors – exercise. The work in Reference [1] is perhaps one of the best examples of a structured, controlled user study to evaluate the efficacy of an anthropomorphic robot coach for exercise. Although thorough and well-grounded in psychology research, that

© Springer International Publishing Switzerland 2016
J. Bajo et al. (Eds.): PAAMS 2016 Workshops, CCIS 616, pp. 3–14, 2016.
DOI: 10.1007/978-3-319-39387-2_1

study is performed in a lab outside the immediate personal environment of senior living. Further, the study involved seniors only, whereas the full integration of robots into senior living will involve staff members, caregivers, and family members. Next, the study was conducted with seniors in one-on-one coach-to-senior sessions for 20 min twice a week for a duration of two weeks, whereas group exercises are more motivating and typically meet weekly. Finally, the study involved only arm exercises.

The pilot study described here involves a 30-min session with the humanoid robot NAO serving as an exercise coach on the premises of the Golden Oaks Senior Living Community in Oklahoma, USA [2]. The participants include five senior residents selected by the staff of the facility and five staff members, two of whom were administrators and three were nurses. The robot's first routine is to introduce himself and play a "Tell me to do something" game to warm up the participants, e.g. to sing, dance, exercise, relax, wave, recite a poem, and tell a joke. Next, the robot initiates exercise routines involving arms, legs, hands, feet, eyes, and full body via a Tai Chi dance. The robot explains the exercise and encourages the group to follow along as he performs the exercises.

The paper is organized as follows: Sect. 2 discusses the importance of context in studies on the acceptance of robots as social assistants for the elderly. Section 3 describes our methodology, design principles, and implementation of behaviors into the NAO robot for the pilot study. Section 4 discusses the results of the study and our agenda for future work.

## 2   On the Importance of Contextual Studies in Elderly Care

While there have been several attempts in research literature and technology reviews to demonstrate the effectiveness of assistive robots towards independent living of the elderly, one of the major questions is "What are the circumstances in which elderly people adopt an assistive robot?" Despite advances in technology, the low rate of success in the use of assistive robots among seniors may be due to the lack of attention to the challenges that older people face. Some argue that while the concept of adoption is well-addressed, its use in the context of elderly care faces challenges due to the particular characteristics of the environment in which the elderly live [3].

To assess the attitudes of seniors towards the usefulness of robots, the first author conducted a one-and-half hour weekly workshop over five weeks at Rivier Institute for Senior Education [4]. An additional benefit of the workshop was brainstorming with a target audience on potential uses of robots. The participants were 55 years or older and were interested in the role of robotic technologies in assisting them in their everyday lives. Each senior elected to participate in the workshop. They were cognitively alert and physically able, e.g. they found their way to class like ordinary college students. The group picture in Fig. 1 will help contextualize the study for the reader.

Where possible, the instructor implemented prototype behaviors in the robot for further evaluation and critical analysis. Other activities included watching relevant videos, watching movies such as "Robot and Frank," reading articles, and demonstrating the capabilities of several off-the-shelf robots: the humanoid robot NAO, a tele-presence robot Double, and an animaloid robot Paro.

**Fig. 1.** Group picture of seniors participating in the workshop

The participants were given a questionnaire at the end of the workshop to gauge their attitudes after five weeks of activity with robots. The results showed that participants strongly agreed that robots as personal assistants and companions in the future was possible, strongly agreed that an older person in need of care would accept a robot as a companion, and strongly agreed that it's possible to bond with a robot as one might with another human. As an anecdote, at one point during the workshop the instructor was discussing the potential of conversational robots for the elderly to help alleviate problems of loneliness [5], whereupon one of the participants suggested that all one has to do is program the robot to raise its hands every five minutes and say "Tell me about the trip to Ohio!" Although amusing, there is some truth in it.

In a follow-on study, seven of the participants (range 67–86 years; Mean = 72.2; Male = 4) were interviewed a month after the workshop via a set of discussion questions. The interviews took an average of 36 min and were audio-recorded. An analysis of the interviews was performed using Alceste software. The analysis produced the following result: The elderly think that assistive robots can help them live independently by providing for their functional and psychological abilities, which in turn would give them increased capabilities towards independent living [3].

These results suggest a positive attitude towards the potential of robots for elderly care. However, the results are based on the participants' inherent interest in robots, hands-on experience with multiple robots during the workshop, and their further reflections after the workshop. To achieve authentic answers regarding the efficacy of robots' contributions to seniors' independent living, the next step is to place a functional robot in the elder's personal environment.

# 3   A Robot Instructor for Group Exercise at a Senior Living Community

## 3.1   An Iterative, Contextual Methodology: Soft Systems Methodology

The provision of assistive robots for elderly care is a hard interdisciplinary problem requiring collaboration among several kinds of person: seniors, caregivers, nurses, medical doctors, staff, robot designers, robot behavior designers, and robot operators. For these reasons, we selected soft systems methodology (SSM) as an aid to guide our study. Experience with SSM suggests that it is useful for problems in human affairs for which there are multiple stakeholders with different methods, mindsets, and views of the problem and during which a notional system is discovered and improved upon iteratively [6, 7].

Soft systems are unlike hard systems such as circuit boards and automobiles in which there is a well-defined specification for the system and it is the job of managers to direct engineering and manufacturing activities towards its realization. In contrast, SSM is designed for difficult problems in human affairs in which a vague, notional system is discovered and then improved upon iteratively in a cycle of inquiry and discovery. Figure 2. Shows the methodology.

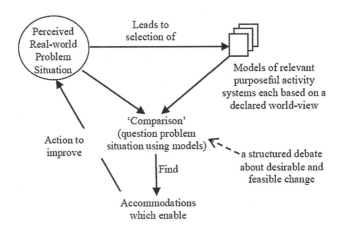

**Fig. 2.** The inquiring/learning cycle of SSM [6]

The underlying principles of SSM in relation to Fig. 2 are as follows:

- The real world is a complexity of relationships
- Relationships are to be explored via models of purposeful activity based on explicit world-views
- Inquiry is structured by questioning perceived situation using the models as a source of questions
- An 'Action to improve' is based on finding accommodations, i.e. versions of the situation which conflicting interests can live with

- The inquiry is in principle never-ending and is best conducted with a wide range of interested parties

The methodology is cyclic. In the initiating cycle, based on the authors' research and nursing experience in gerontology, our real-world problem situation is stated simply as "how to motivate and engage seniors in robot-led group exercise without human accompaniment." The problem led to various activities, including a literature review, an evaluation of socially assistive robots in elderly care and other domains, an evaluation and selection of a robot platform, design and implementation of robot behaviors for a first session, and a search for a suitable and willing facility in which to carry out the study. These activities are viewed as interactive subsystems which may produce emergent properties of the system as a whole.

After a number of meetings and debate, the authors agreed (i) to use the NAO commercial robot because it is comparatively easy to program innovative behaviors in the robot, conducive to achieving our goals, (ii) to carry out the study at Golden Oaks in Oklahoma, and (iii) to design and implement three routines for the first session of the study: An "Ask me to do something" routine to warm up the participants, an exercise routine in which the robot leads group exercises for the participants, and a routine in which the robot introduces the animaloid robot Paro and encourages the participants to interact individually with it. The latter routine is not a main concern of this paper.

## 3.2 Design Principles

As mentioned in the Introduction, we draw upon the work reported in [2] involving one-on-one coach-to-senior sessions. It is perhaps most similar to our coach-to-group sessions in a real setting. The authors posit five psychology-driven design principles for the robot during an episode of exercise coaching:

*Motivating.* Intrinsic motivation, in contrast to extrinsic motivation which is driven by external rewards, comes from within an individual and is based on pleasure derived from engaging in an activity. Specifically, the aim is for the robot to be capable of increasing the user's intrinsic motivation to perform the therapeutic task.

*Fluid and Highly Interactive.* A primary goal of coaching is to provide a fluid interaction which requires a robot to both perceive the user's activity and provide active feedback and guidance in real time, all with the aim of maintaining user engagement in the task. The robot must establish a clear set of goals combined with immediate and appropriate feedback.

*Personable.* The social interaction between the user and the robot is just as important as the task interaction for achieving success in healthcare interventions. Social interaction is the primary means of relationship building, including in therapeutic scenarios. Many social intricacies contribute to the foundation of a meaningful relationship, both in human-computer interaction and in human-robot interaction. These factors include empathy, humor, references to mutual knowledge, continuity behaviors, politeness, and trust, among others.

*Intelligent.* Trust is a key component to the success of any care-provider/user relationship, and one that is closely linked to the intelligence/helpfulness of the care provider as perceived by the user. Trust as a construct is determined by three components: perception of competence, perception of intentions, and capacity for trusting.

*Task-Driven.* The most important property of coach-to-senior interaction is that it be consistent in working to achieve the goals of the healthcare task, or in our case, in motivating exercise performance to achieve desired overall health benefits.

Since our study is iterative and thus requires frequent robot programming, we add a sixth design principle that is technology-driven rather than psychology-driven:

*Relatively Easy to Introduce New Behaviors and Modify Existing Behaviors.* The robot should be portable and programmable to the extent that it is possible to modify the exercise protocol in light of new requirements in a reasonable amount of time.

### 3.3   The Environment for the Study

The study was carried out in the facility's chapel where group activities take place. There were ten participants – five residents and five staff members. The residents were selected by the staff members with the goal of having seniors with varying cognitive and physical deficits, e.g. three of the residents were cognitively alert but physically challenged, one was both cognitively alert and physically able, and one was challenged both cognitively and physically. Figure 3 will help contextualize the study.

**Fig. 3.** Participants in the study interacting with robot

### 3.4   Design and Implementation of the Robot Behavior

The robot platform is the humanoid NAO robot. The robot is portable and offers multiple ways of behavior programming: (i) visual programming using pre-defined parameterized behavior boxes that can be linked together to provide increasingly complex behaviors, (ii) Python and C++ programming to implement behaviors not possible with behavioral boxes, (iii) choreographic programming in which complex movements are implemented much like a choreographer instructs a ballet dancer, and (iv) a conversational programming language QiChat which provides procedures for implementing intonation and nuance in the robot's speech-to-text and text-to-speech functions. We used each of the methods in our work and found that the approach contributes to the sixth design principle on robot programmability in a reasonable amount of time. Further, the robot comes off-the-shelf with a selectable Autonomous Life feature that gives the robot random fluid movements when listening or speaking to users, thus contributing to the first four design principles: motivating, fluid and highly interactive, personable, and intelligent.

We designed and implemented the behaviors in the robot using the agent perspective. We required that the agents be modular, be easily modifiable for future iterations of the methodology, be able to function independently of other agents, and be robust. For these reasons the design is based on the subsumption architecture. Agents reside on levels such that higher levels subsume lower levels. If higher-level agents become dysfunctional, the lower-level agents can continue to function albeit with less functionality than the system as a whole [8].

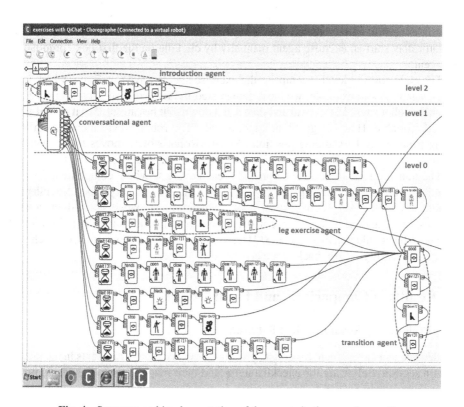

**Fig. 4.** Structure and implementation of the agents in the exercise routine

Specifically, we envisioned (i) an introduction agent whereby the robot describes himself and explains what he plans to do, (ii) a conversational agent to interact with the participants and to decide what actually to do, (iii) a multiplicity of lower-levels agents to do what was decided, and (iv) a transition agent to interact with participants at the end on an exercise and return control to the conversational agent. Communication among the agents is via message-passing between the output and input nodes of the agents. Both routines have this same structure. Figure 4 illustrates the design and implementation of the exercise routine. We have demarcated portions of the figure in red for purposes of explanation. The program in Fig. 4 is compiled, embedded into the robot, and executed such that the robot is autonomous.

The introduction agent on level 2 is passive. It speaks to the participants about the exercise agenda: "OK, let's do some exercises. We will exercise our head, arms, legs, hands, eyes, and feet. When you are ready we will try Tai Chi. First, let's get in the sitting position like I am now. Ready? OK, what would you like to do first? Head, arms, legs, hands, eyes, or feet?" After the introduction, control is passed to the conversational agent.

The conversational agent on level 1 has a reactive component and a deliberative component. The reactive component listens for audio input from participants and tries to detect a word it understands. The deliberative component is a simple rule-based system whereby the detection of a word routes control to a particular exercise. If the conversational agent doesn't detect an audio input within 5 s, it selects a random exercise and passes control to the selected exercise agent on level 0. If that doesn't work, a robot operator may start an exercise agent manually by clicking on the first box comprising the agent.

The eight rows in level 0 comprise the exercise agents, save row 7 row which is a "stop" agent. As an example, we have demarcated the leg exercise agent in row 3 in which the robot says "Let's stand and then squat down, but be careful. Try it only if you feel comfortable. Here we go. Watch me. Stand. (The robot slowly moves from the sitting position to the standing position). Squat. (Robot slowly moves to a squatting position.) Back up. (Robot moves to the standing position, and so on).

The transition agent on level 0 concludes each exercise with a compliment for the participants by randomly saying some synonym for "good," e.g. 'very good', 'excellent', 'beautiful', 'cool', 'very cool', 'most cool', 'splendid', or 'wonderful', then saying "Let's sit back and relax (at which point the robot goes into the sitting position), then saying "What would you like to do next? Head, arms, legs, hands, eyes, feet, or tai chi?", and finally passing control back to the conversational agent.

## 4   Results, a Comparison, and Future Work

### 4.1   Preliminary Results of the Pilot Study

We designed an engagement checklist by which to evaluate the participants in the initial 30-min session. Below are the checklist items and their mappings into the design principles discussed in Sect. 3.2.

| Attentive: | *Motivating* |
|---|---|
| Smiling: | *Motivating* |
| Head-nodding: | *Motivating* |
| Leaning forward: | *Motivating* |
| Cooperation: | *Fluid and Highly Interactive, Intelligent, Task-Driven* |
| Imitation: | *Fluid and Highly Interactive, Intelligent, Task-Driven* |
| Initiation: | *Fluid and Highly Interactive, Intelligent, Task-Driven* |
| Intensity: | *Fluid and Highly Interactive, Intelligent, Motivating* |

We studied the participants one-by-one as we viewed the video recording, with the exception of staff S3 whose visibility was obstructed. Each participant was scored on a scale of 1 to 10 with respect to each item. An additional category "Approval/Enjoyment" was a subjective overall assessment by the authors. The "Total Engagement" score reflects the number of engagement points out of 100. Table 1 shows the preliminary results.

The average total engagement score of residents is 46 and the average score of staff is 71.4, suggesting that residents are slightly less than perfectly ambivalent in their approval of the robot, while staffers strongly approve. Visual inspection shows that two of the residents highly approve, one is rather ambivalent, and two disapprove. We note that R5 appeared to be quite attentive during the session but was non-responsive overall. Thus it is difficult to determine R5's comprehension of the experience in general.

**Table 1.** Preliminary results

|  | R1 | R2 | R3 | R4 | R5 | S1 | S2 | S3 | S4 | S5 |
|---|---|---|---|---|---|---|---|---|---|---|
| Attentive | 7 | 10 | 10 | 8 | 10 | 10 | 10 | 10 | 10 | 10 |
| Smiling | 1 | 9 | 10 | 2 | 3 | 9 | 9 | 10 | 8 | 8 |
| Head-nodding | 0 | 0 | 3 | 0 | 0 | 0 | 3 | 10 | 0 | 0 |
| Leaning forward | 0 | 0 | 0 | 0 | 0 | 0 | 0 | 7 | 0 | 0 |
| Cooperation | 2 | 9 | 10 | 6 | 4 | 8 | 8 | 8 | 7 | 7 |
| Imitation | 0 | 10 | 9 | 7 | 0 | 8 | 8 | 8 | 7 | 7 |
| Initiation | 0 | 3 | 2 | 9 | 0 | 8 | 8 | 8 | 0 | 7 |
| Intensity | 0 | 10 | 10 | 7 | 0 | 8 | 8 | 8 | 8 | 8 |
| Participation | 3 | 10 | 10 | 7 | 1 | 10 | 10 | 10 | 10 | 10 |
| Approval/enjoyment | 1 | 9 | 9 | 5 | 4 | 9 | 10 | 10 | 8 | 9 |
| Total engagement | 14 | 70 | 73 | 51 | 22 | 70 | 74 | 89 | 58 | 66 |

The evidence thus far invites a number of questions and suggests some lessons learned that will influence the next cycle of our methodology. Inasmuch as the results show a stronger approval of the robots by staff than by residents, a number of potential factors causing the difference are possible. The difference may reflect one or more of the following kinds of differences separating the two groups: prior technological experience; experience with art forms such as movies involving robots; and the role differences in the Golden Oaks environment. One resident for example, demonstrated a passion for technology. Further, it is possible that head nodding should not be weighted equally with, say, level of participation. Adding relative weights to the scoring criteria might affect the staff-vs-resident gap in average scores.

The subsequent focus sessions with each group provided a wealth of suggestions to consider. The staff group was positive, enthusiastic, and creative in discussing the potential of robots on the premises, e.g. to recognize participants and call them by name, to take orders in the cafeteria, to escort residents from place to place, to play favorite songs, recite scripture, and so on. The resident group clearly enjoyed talking about the robot as well, evidenced by humor and laughter. Suggestions from the residents included talking to the robot, asking questions, and playing with it as one would play with a toy. One resident expressed a desire to have a robot to replace his wife.

## 4.2   Comparison

Developed at the University of Southern California (USC), Fig. 5 shows an exercise robot interacting with a senior [2]. In addition, there are reports in the popular press of RoboCoach, developed at Ngee Ann Polytechnic in Singapore and shown in Fig. 6. To our knowledge, there is no data on the design, operation, or evaluation of the RoboCoach robot.

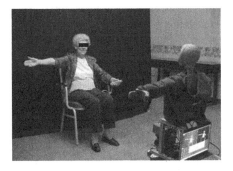

**Fig. 5.** Coach-to-senior robot at USC [2]

**Fig. 6.** RoboCoach [9]

The USC robot plays four exercise games: (i) a Workout Game in which the robot demonstrates arm exercises and asks the senior to imitate, (ii) a Sequence Game in which the robot demonstrates arm exercises for the senior to repeat a number of times, (iii) an Imitation Game in which the senior instructs the robot with arm exercises, and (iv) a Memory Game in which the senior tries to memorize a sequence of arm gesture poses. Communication is by (i) a two-button remote control held by the senior where one button transmits a "yes" to the robot and the other a "no" and (ii) a vision-based feedback system allowing the robot to determine the arm movements of the senior and provide feedback accordingly.

Seniors interacted with the robot one at a time over four sessions during two weeks. After the fourth session, participants filled out a questionnaire in order to evaluate the robot along multiple dimensions: enjoyableness of the interaction; value/usefulness of the interaction; companionship, helpfulness, intelligence, social attraction, and social presence of the robot; and potential as an exercise partner. The researchers compared the opinions of seniors interacting with the physical robot and also interacting with a virtual avatar-like version of the robot. Thus, the 33 seniors were divided into two study groups.

The results showed a strong preference for the physical robot over a virtual robot and showed that the participants engaged with the robot with high performance consistently throughout the interaction sessions. The participants rated the robot highly on enjoyableness and usefulness of the interaction, and highly in terms of helpfulness, social attraction, social presence, and companionship [2]. The seniors showed a more positive attitude toward the robot than those in our study. Some of differences between the studies may account for this. From an engineering perspective, the NAO robot (i) is a commercial, portable, and programmable robot; (ii) has a programmable vision system although we did not use it in this first pilot study; (iii) communicates verbally; and (iv) is agent-based. From a study perspective, our study (i) included seniors, caregivers, and administrators; (ii) involved group exercise with multiple routines, (iii) is incremental by design; and perhaps most important, (iv) was performed in the immediate environment of the seniors.

The innovations of our work are the use of soft systems methodology, the real-world setting in which the study was carried out, the agent perspective, and the evolutionary nature of the study in light of feedback from diverse participant groups.

## 4.3 Future Work

The pilot study at Golden Oaks has clear limitations. There is no control group. Senior residents were not profiled with respect to their cognitive and physical deficits. The evaluation was based only on video analysis, whereas a structured questionnaire at the end of the session could provide useful information for analysis.

However, the results thus far encourage us to continue this line of research. Following the methodology described in Sect. 3.1, for the next sessions at the facility we plan (i) to improve the behavior of the robot to make it more personal, (ii) improve our study evaluation criteria, (iii) program the robot so that it can learn to attach names to faces and thus identify participants by name, (iv) obtain more complete profile information on the participants in order to compare diverse population groups.

## References

1. Juan Fasola, J., Matarić, M.: A socially assistive robot exercise coach for the elderly. J. Hum.-Rob. Interact. **2**(2), 3–32 (2013)
2. www.goldenoaks.com. Accessed 17 Jan 2016
3. Talaei-Khoei, A., Lewis, L., Talaei-Khoei, T., Ghapanchi, A.: Seniors' perspectives on perceived transfer effects of assistive robots in elderly care: a capability approach analysis. In: International Conference on Information Systems, Fort Worth, Texas (2015)
4. www.rivier.edu/about.aspx?menu=142&id=1378. Accessed 17 Jan 2016
5. Lewis, L.: Using narrative with avatars and robots to enhance elder care (Chapter 14). In: Healthcare Informatics and Analytics: Emerging Issues and Trends. IGI Global, Pennsylvania (2014)
6. Checkland, P., Poulter, J.: Learning for Action: A Short Definitive Account of Soft Systems Methodology, and Its Use for Practitioners, Teachers and Students. Wiley, Hoboken (2007)
7. Checkland, P.: Soft systems methodology: a thirty year retrospective. Syst. Res. Behav. Sci. **17**(1), S11 (2000)
8. Brooks, R.: A robust layered control system for a mobile robot. IEEE J. Rob. Autom. **2**(1), 14–23 (1986)
9. www.np.edu.sg/sg50/events/Pages/20150101_npevents_robocoach.aspx. Accessed 17 Jan 2016

# FRIENDLY & KIND with your Health: Human-Friendly Knowledge-INtensive Dynamic Systems for the e-Health Domain

Federica Aielli[1]([✉]), Davide Ancona[2], Pasquale Caianiello[1],
Stefania Costantini[1], Giovanni De Gasperis[1], Antinisca Di Marco[1],
Angelo Ferrando[2], and Viviana Mascardi[2]

[1] Università Degli Studi Dell'Aquila, L'Aquila, Italy
{Federica.Aielli,Pasquale.Caianiello,Stefania.Costantini,
Giovanni.Gasperis,Antinisca.Marco}@univaq.it
[2] Università Degli Studi di Genova, Genova, Italy
{Davide.Ancona,Angelo.Ferrando,Viviana.Mascardi}@unige.it
http://www.disim.univaq.it, http://www.dibris.unige.it

**Abstract.** This paper presents our approach for addressing "Human-friendly Knowledge-INtensive Dynamic Systems" (FRIENDLY & KIND systems) from a methodological point of view, also providing tools and languages for their design, implementation and testing. FRIENDLY & KIND systems are an evolution of multiagent systems and represent a good option for engineering complex and dynamic applications like those in the e-Health domain. We will demonstrate the suitability of our approach by designing and implementing a Remote Monitoring System for oncological patients.

**Keywords:** Multiagent systems · Multi-context systems · Runtime verification · Computational logic · e-Health

## 1 Introduction and Motivation

As stated in the guidelines provided by the European Community[1], e-Health

1. *refers to tools and services using information and communication technologies (ICTs) that can improve prevention, diagnosis, treatment, monitoring and management;*
2. *can benefit the entire community by improving access to care and quality of care and by making the health sector more efficient;*
3. *includes information and data sharing between patients and health service providers, hospitals, health professionals and health information networks; electronic health records; telemedicine services; portable patient-monitoring devices, operating room scheduling software, robotized surgery and blue-sky research on the virtual physiological human.*

---

[1] http://ec.europa.eu/health/ehealth/policy/index_en.htm.

© Springer International Publishing Switzerland 2016
J. Bajo et al. (Eds.): PAAMS 2016 Workshops, CCIS 616, pp. 15–26, 2016.
DOI: 10.1007/978-3-319-39387-2_2

The American Telemedicine Association (ATA[2]) defines telemedicine as

*the use of medical information exchanged from one site to another via electronic communications to improve a patient's clinical health status.*

Telemedicine may exploit two-way video, email, smart phones, wireless tools and possibly many other sensor devices. Telemedicine services may include primary care and specialist online consultation (a specialist may interact either with a patient or the primary care physician in rendering a diagnosis, via data detected by dedicated devices) and Remote Patient Monitoring[3] (RPM),

*a technology to enable monitoring of patients outside of conventional clinical settings (e.g. in the home), which may increase access to care and decrease healthcare delivery costs.*

The features of an autonomous software agent, namely its situatedness, autonomy and flexibility [1], make the agent metaphor extremely suitable to describe, design, and implement RPM systems made up of Personalized Monitoring Agents (PMAs) in charge for the monitored patients. Each PMA should in fact be able to receive input from the sensors that the patient wears and from any device in the environment that may provide useful information (situatedness); it should quickly react to any change in the monitored environment that might be due to some critical situation (reactivity); it should achieve its long term goal of ensuring the patient's well being without distracting precious resources from the healthcare system: to this aim, it should monitor the patient suggesting suitable actions in non-critical situations and warning the doctor only when actually needed (proactivity and autonomy). Finally, the PMA should communicate with both the patient and the doctor, and possibly with other agents in the environment (social ability).

However, there are other features that must be taken into account for developing models, methodologies, and software infrastructures for RPM applications, and which are not considered "core" agent features by the agent-oriented software engineering research community:

**User friendliness:** the PMA should offer a user-friendly interface to the patient in order to make her feel comfortable with interacting with it.

**Knowledge-intensity:** a large amount of heterogeneous information and data must be retrieved, shared and integrated in order to reason on the patient's health status.

**System dynamics:** the high dynamics of the system, due to sensors and devices which may enter and exit it in any moment and to data sources which can change their reliability level over time, must be taken into account.

**Runtime monitoring ability:** the RPM system should continuously verify that the pattern followed by perceived sensory data is compliant with the expected medical protocol: in order to do so, it should implement a run-time verification mechanism.

---

[2] http://www.americantelemed.org/.

[3] https://en.wikipedia.org/wiki/Remote_patient_monitoring.

In this paper we propose an extension of MASs named FRIENDLY & KIND systems (Human-friendly Knowledge-INtensive Dynamic Systems).

FRIENDLY & KIND systems, F&Ks in the sequel, provide flexible access to dynamic, heterogeneous, and distributed sources of knowledge in a highly dynamic computational environment consisting of computational entities, devices, sensors, and services available in the physical environment, in the Internet, and in the cloud.

F&Ks are driven by terminological, bridge, and pattern rules. Terminological rules ensure interoperability among the F&K components by defining a common domain vocabulary. Bridge rules connect knowledge sources together and provide devices for selection, abstraction and conflict resolution among the underlying knowledge sources. Pattern rules can be verified at run-time to guarantee that the system actual dynamics conforms to the expected one. The high dynamism of the F&K computational environment requires models of trust, relevance, and preferences, and of their dynamics. Finally, an F&K must present a human-friendly interface.

The paper is organized as follows: Sect. 2 provides the necessary background to understand our proposal and discusses related works, Sect. 3 describes the proposal objectives and expected results in detail, Sect. 4 concludes and highlights the next steps we will undertake.

# 2 Background and Related Work

## 2.1 Background

From a technological point of view, F&Ks user-friendliness is achieved thanks to multilingual interfaces supporting natural language processing, knowledge heterogeneity is managed via the multi-context approach, and ontologies are used to allow for semantic interoperability among knowledge sources, users, and computational entities in the environment. On-the-fly composition of software services is a key requirement for F&Ks functioning as well as runtime verification techniques to monitor that the system behaves as expected. Models of trust and their dynamics must also be considered, as data sources can change their reliability over time. In our approach, computational logic is the basis for expressing terminological, bridge, and pattern rules which drive the F&K engineering and functioning.

*Ontology-driven and multilingual text classification.* Text classification is the task of assigning a document to one or more classes or categories. The most widespread approaches to text classification are based on machine learning, but alternative approaches based on domain ontologies, that do not require any training set, are also emerging. If the ontology is not hard-wired into the text classifier, it can work on many different domains just by changing the ontology. Also, if the ontology words can be translated on-the-fly into the text language by exploiting suitable resources like BabelNet[4], classification can work independently of the ontology and text languages. A working tool implementing this approach is described in [2] and is the basis for the F&Ks user-friendly interface.

*Multi-context systems.* In the Artificial Intelligence and Knowledge Representation fields, the Multi-Context Systems (MCS) approach [3–5] has been proposed to model information exchange among heterogeneous sources (contexts), which interact via bridge rules. The added value of the approach is to drop the assumption of making such sources homogeneous: rather, MCSs explicitly deal with different representation languages and semantics. MCSs are successful also in practical applications [6] as they aim at modeling real situations, where a number of sources distributed on the web can contribute to the solution of complex problems. MCSs have been extended to encompass multiagent systems equipped with ontologies and advanced communication capabilities in [7,8].

*Runtime verification and self-adaptivenness of multiagent systems.* Runtime verification of complex and distributed systems has been recently tackled by exploiting a powerful formalism named "trace expressions" [9] and an interpreter based on computational logic. This approach easily supports self-adaptivennes [10] and monitoring of fail-uncontrolled and ambient intelligence systems [11]. Meta-axioms for agents run-time self-checking and self-correction based upon a special interval temporal logic have also been studied (cf. [12] and the references therein).

*Models of trust.* Several models of trust exist in the literature, some based upon a third party authority, some on the elaboration of direct experiences and some others on game theory. A model of trust which combines the latter two approaches where trust level evolves in agents playing a game, with players of various typologies described by probabilistic strategies, is discussed in [13].

*Software engineering for integration systems.* The dynamic composition of software and services often requires to solve mismatch on service/component interface and their interaction protocols. In the last decade, the research community has devoted a significant effort to the synthesis of connectors/mediators that enable automatic software composition by solving such mismatches: a recent contribution is [14], tailored for environments characterized by a wide variety of heterogeneous systems that dynamically decide to interoperate to achieve some goal.

## 2.2   Related Wok

Our proposal follows the principles outlined in previous existing work, including [15,16]. In [15] the foundations for the development of agent-based platforms for the Tele-health domain are analyzed and discussed. Such platforms should

---

[4] http://babelnet.org/.

include different types of agents: user, reasoning, and sensor, where the agents role is to intelligently gather, understand and use relevant context. In [16] the construction of ontologies to be exploited in such systems is discussed.

A vast body of literature exists, discussing the application of ICT in general [17], and Artificial Intelligence in particular, to the e-Health field. Consider for instance:

- http://www.hhnmag.com/articles/6561-ways-artificial-intelligence-will-transform-health-care published in 2015 and
- http://www.fastcompany.com/3055256/elasticity/paging-dr-robot-the-coming-ai-health-care-boom published in 2016.

The relevance and the huge impact of this synergy is also claimed by IBM Watson that will implement the Health Platform, http://www.ibm.com/smarterplanet/us/en/ibmwatson/health. Differently from the envisioned Watson Health system, our FRIENDLY & KIND systems will be open and dynamic since sensors, devices, and knowledge sources will be able to enter and exit the system at run-time, hence requiring an on-the-fly interoperability among several sources of knowledge and services. The developed systems will be released under open source licenses making all the achieved results public.

We believe that e-Health tools should also provide personalized healthcare. In a set of seminal papers[5] ([18,19] and the references therein) it was argued that *"The development of ubiquitous systems for maintenance and control of treatment systems to assist individuals in managing their medical treatment plan would provide an improved system for home healthcare. Automation of knowledge base development for each individual patient would allow efficient personalization of each patients treatment plan and allow integration of the doctors individual diagnosis and treatment plan."* In particular, the authors advocate and present agent-based techniques so as to *"allow efficient development of individually tailored medical treatment knowledge bases"*.

A related area is that of correctness of knowledge based systems. Given the nature of medical opinions, for which such systems are unlikely to be deemed as "correct", truth maintenance of knowledge within an individual system is an important area, particularly when complete knowledge of a domain is unlikely to be achievable.

## 3   FRIENDLY & KIND with Your Health

The objectives of our proposal are the analysis, design, implementation and validation of methods and tools for engineering "human-friendly Knowledge-INtensive Dynamic systems" (FRIENDLY & KIND systems, F&K). The application of F&Ks to the e-Health domain is the major practical expected outcome. F&Ks (Fig. 1).

---

[5] Interrupted unfortunately in 2009 by the death of the main author.

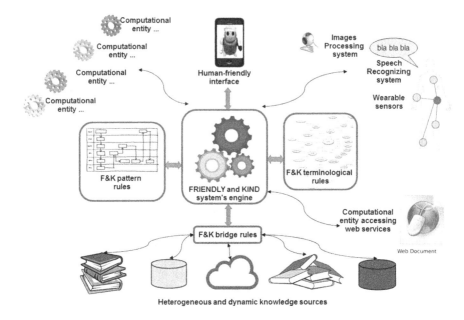

**Fig. 1.** General architecture of an F&K system.

1. access heterogeneous, distributed and dynamic knowledge sources;
2. integrate heterogeneous, distributed and dynamic computational entities;
3. reason on knowledge stored in sources and on information coming from the computational entities to infer new knowledge;
4. ensure that access to the knowledge sources and interactions among the computational entities follow safe patterns, to guarantee the application security;
5. present a human-friendly interface for accessing the F&K functionalities.

F&Ks operate in complex, open, and dynamic computational environments which include heterogeneous software components, physical devices and sensors including wearable health monitoring devices, intelligent software agents, third part services and data centers available on the Internet. F&Ks are designed and implemented for supporting Fog computing in the perspective of the Internet of Everything. To achieve their goals, F&Ks are driven by:

1. terminological rules to define the vocabulary common to knowledge sources and computational entities;
2. bridge rules to formulate complex queries by bridging the domain knowledge sources together;
3. pattern rules to state which event patterns are safe in the domain.

All these rules are customizable modules characterizing different F&Ks instances. In the e-Health domain, terminological rules will specify the meaning of technical terms related to a specific disease and their semantic relationships, bridge rules will bridge the databases containing patients' medical history and records with legacy knowledge bases and expert systems, and pattern rules will specify correct patterns of events related to the patient's privacy, real-time health conditions, and treatment according to existing medical protocols.

Another relevant F&K aspect is the system high dynamism:

- knowledge sources evolve in time: new knowledge will be discovered and bridge rules must evolve consistently;
- as new knowledge becomes available, the domain model may evolve as well;
- pattern rules might evolve to ensure the software system security and the physical system safety;
- as a consequence, measures of trust, relevance, and preferences can affect the interaction among computational entities and knowledge sources and may evolve in time according to the "performances" of the components participating to the system.

Since the actual instances of F&Ks are used by domain experts and by final users without specific technological background, a human-friendly user interface is provided for interacting with the application exploiting multimodal and multilingual modalities. Results concerning affective computing and theory of emotions in agents are taken into account to make the interface more agreeable to the user and more effective in collecting information and profiling user preferences. To demonstrate the feasibility of our approach, we will adopt a relevant real-world application in the field of e-Health, namely a Personalized Monitoring Agent tailored to oncological patients, as a testbed. The resulting F&K instance, named "e-Health FRIENDLY and KIND" (eHF&K), is presented in Fig. 2.

Competency on the medical domain is ensured by the domain experts[6], who will provide guidelines for the eHF&K features, provide data and knowledge bases for system testing, define and apply system evaluation criteria, and experiment eHF&K on real patients, in full respect of their privacy and comfort.

The objectives of our investigation are:

**O1**: Developing a software engineering methodology to engineer F&Ks.

**O2**: Developing models and formalisms for representing terminological, bridge and pattern rules, and for knowledge discovery and preferences/trust management.

**O3**: Developing software tools for managing and reasoning on terminological, bridge, and pattern rules, taking their dynamic nature into account, and for coping with knowledge discovery and preferences/trust management.

**O4**: Developing an integrated environment (F&K-IDE) for developing F&Ks.

**O5**: Implementing the e-Health FRIENDLY and KIND application (eHF&K) as a proof-of-concept of the proposed approach in the e-Health domain.

The results we expect from our research activities are in a one-to-one relationship with its objectives:

**R1**: The F&K characterization based on its architectural and functional features and the F&K software engineering methodology covering the life-cycle of an F&K.

---

[6] One of the authors of this paper is an oncological doctor.

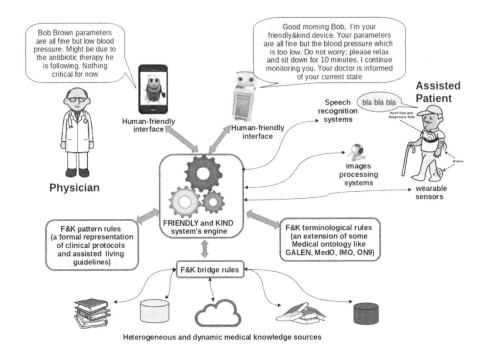

**Fig. 2.** The e-Health FRIENDLY and KIND system.

**R2**: Models and formalisms for representing terminological rules, bridge rules, and pattern rules, and for knowledge discovery and preferences/trust management.

**R3**: Software tools for terminological rules, bridge rules, and pattern rules, including verification of system and interaction properties, and for knowledge discovery and preferences/trust management.

**R4**: An integrated environment (F&K-IDE) for implementing F&Ks obtained by integrating results R2 and R3 above and coherent with the methodology resulting from R1.

**R5**: eHF&K, an F&K application in the e-Health domain.

Together with R1, R4 is the most relevant, original, and significant expected result from a scientific viewpoint. In fact results R2 and R3 might turn out to have a limited originality as models, formalisms, and working tools suitable for engineering F&Ks might be already available and others could appear: we might indeed discover that our needs can be satisfied, partly or "in toto", by bricks developed elsewhere. Nevertheless, putting such bricks together in an integrated software system that supports an engineering methodology is far from an easy task, and the originality of the result will be definitely greater than the sum of the bricks originality.

The most relevant practical result is instead R5. Consistently with the H2020 societal challenges, we will apply our approach in the e-Health domain by implementing eHF&K where:

1. Each patient is in charge of a Personal Monitoring Agent (PMA). This agent supervises the patient's welfare and health conditions and the correct administration of therapy according to suitable pattern rules created by the technological partners in collaboration with the domain experts. The PMA must be aware of all illnesses of the patient and manage their comorbidity. It manages the patient's medical history and records, is aware of the therapies and is able to supervise drugs administration according to prescription. The PMA interacts with the patient via an avatar able to communicate in natural language, in the patient's language: the vocabulary shared between the PMA and its user is specified by the eHF&K terminological rules. It is able to filter confusing inputs in order to determine the causes of the patient's distress with more accuracy. It employs Telemedicine techniques to collect data from medical devices the user is equipped with. In case of anomalous symptoms, the PMA exploits bridge rules to access knowledge bases for symptom interpretation, diagnosis and management treatment. The PMA interacts with either the patient or a human specialist or both (e.g., to request specific diagnostic tests), according with the eHF&K pattern rules.
2. Each doctor is provided with a notification system (e.g., a mobile app on smartphone) connected to the PMAs of its patients that send warnings in case the PMA identifies symptoms and side effects which require the doctor intervention.
3. The system provides a directory service so that PMAs are enabled to locate the needed components based upon components roles. The directory is equipped with knowledge discovery capabilities and manages preferences and trust.
4. The directory refers to a set of heterogeneous knowledge bases, expert systems or more generally services, either internal to the system and thus fully reliable, or external, whose reliability is to be evaluated.
5. Via bridge rules, the PMA can obtain pieces of knowledge by querying several sources and by integrating the returned results together. Queries can be positive (to assess that something is the case and/or retrieving/measuring quantities) or negative (to assess that something is not the case).
6. Sources interconnection must follow specific patterns which ensure safe interaction, and correct and complete interaction results. Such patterns rules must be well-defined and verifiable.

## 4    Conclusions and Future Work

In this paper we have described our proposal for analyzing, modeling, designing and implementing "FRIENDLY & KIND with your Health" systems. Our proposal will advance both the ICT research and the research in the e-Health field.

*Impact on ICT.* As virtually every application in the Fog Computing and Internet of Everything contexts can be conceptualized following the F&K metaphor, the body of knowledge, methods and tools resulting from our research activities will constitute a substantial advance to the Internet of Everything research field. A distinguishing characteristic of F&K is that of tackling practical applications from a neat formal perspective. This allows the interactions within the system to be clearly specified and verified, which is crucial in many application fields. F&Ks will be self-evolving, able not only to detect any anomalous behavior that should occur, but also to correct it at run-time so as to maintain the system parameters within the desired range. This is of particular importance for Cyber-Physical systems acting in critical situations. F&Ks can smoothly integrate Augmented Reality components, to provide advanced situational awareness. Therefore, other relevant application fields of F&Ks can be prevention, detection, response, and mitigation of the combination of physical and cyber threats to critical infrastructures, and smart cyber-physical systems.

*Impact on e-Health.* EHF&K systems, namely the instances of F&K systems configured and adapted for the e-Health domain, will provide a uniform, flexible and verifiable platform for implementing Remote Patient Monitoring applications with improved quality of the overall assistance, and with a better patient's satisfaction. EHF&K will in fact provide personalized patient support to locate, select, combine and evaluate the necessary services. EHF&K PMAs will be proactive, and thus able to take measures in consequence of the variations in patient's physical but also psychological conditions. PMAs will be able to consider objective reputation and reliability of sources, as well as the patient's personal preferences and experience. The ability of eHF&K concerning knowledge-sources dynamic retrieval, evaluation and comparison will represent another relevant feature of such systems, as the rapid expansion of the corpus of medical knowledge has made it more difficult than ever for the physician to stay up-to-date with the progress of medicine outside a narrow field. Consultation with a specialist is however not always possible, as it is often the case that expert opinion is either unavailable or not available in a timely fashion. EHF&K PMAs will help physicians to obtain specialist advice either from human consultants, or from trusted knowledge sources.

With respect to the patient care and efficiency, eHF&K will support new ways of delivering care by reducing the risk of medication errors. In fact, eHF&K will decrease the adverse drug events and interaction drugs due to politerapy prescribed by different specialists. Moreover, such eHF&K will assure a more intelligent monitoring of the patient since they will use integrated models of diseases implementing a holistic approach. Another advantage of eHF&K systems, is that they will reduce the inappropriate use of hospital resources since they will support the screening decisions on the basis of information collected during monitoring besides the good clinical practice.

*Future work.* Characterizing, modeling, and implementing a framework for F&K systems is the objective of a 3 years project proposal submitted to the Italian

Ministry of Education, University and Research (MIUR) under the "Scientific Research Programs with Relevant National Interest" 2015 call ("Programmi di Ricerca Scientifica di Rilevante Interesse Nazionale", PRIN 2015). The project consortium involves the University of Genova (with the "Consorzio Interuniversitario Nazionale per l'Informatica", CINI, as subcontractor) and the University of L'Aquila

The team involved in the project proposal is already working for addressing the ICT objectives, as they are scientifically relevant and coherent with the participants' background in the multiagent systems and computational logic fields. In particular, we started to experiment how trace expressions can be actually exploited to model medical protocols and how interaction driven by a medical ontology in multilingual natural language can take place. We are also devising suitable extensions and generalization of bridge rules so as to make them more flexibly applicable in real applications, and we are developing an implementation.

The e-Health scenario requires major resources so its implementation is part of our future plans, as it depends on the PRIN 2015 outcome.

# References

1. Jennings, N.R., Sycara, K.P., Wooldridge, M.: A roadmap of agent research and development. Auton. Agents Multi-Agent Syst. **1**(1), 7–38 (1998)
2. Leotta, M., Beux, S., Mascardi, V., Briola, D.: My MOoD, a multimedia and multilingual ontology driven MAS: design and first experiments in the sentiment analysis domain. In: Proceedings of the 2nd International Workshop on Emotion and Sentiment in Social and Expressive Media, pp. 51–66 (2015)
3. Brewka, G., Eiter, T., Fink, M.: Nonmonotonic multi-context systems: a flexible approach for integrating heterogeneous knowledge sources. In: Balduccini, M., Son, T.C. (eds.) Logic Programming, Knowledge Representation, and Nonmonotonic Reasoning. LNCS, vol. 6565, pp. 233–258. Springer, Heidelberg (2011)
4. Brewka, G., Eiter, T., Fink, M., Weinzierl, A.: Managed multi-context systems. In: Walsh, T. (ed.): IJCAI 2011, Proceedings of the 22nd International Joint Conference on Artificial Intelligence, IJCAI/AAAI, pp. 786–791 (2011)
5. Brewka, G., Ellmauthaler, S., Pührer, J.: Multi-context systems for reactive reasoning in dynamic environments. In: Schaub, T. (ed.): ECAI 2014, Proceedings of the 21st European Conference on Artificial Intelligence, IJCAI/AAAI (2014)
6. Velikova, M., Novák, P., Huijbrechts, B., Laarhuis, J., Hoeksma, J., Michels, S.: An integrated reconfigurable system for maritime situational awareness. In: Schaub, T., Friedrich, G., O'Sullivan, B. (eds.): ECAI 2014–21st European Conference on Artificial Intelligence. vol. 263 of Frontiers in Artificial Intelligence and Applications, pp. 1197–1202. IOS Press (2014)
7. Costantini, S.: Knowledge acquisition via non-monotonic reasoning in distributed heterogeneous environments. In: Calimeri, F., Ianni, G., Truszczynski, M. (eds.) LPNMR 2015. LNCS, vol. 9345, pp. 228–241. Springer, Heidelberg (2015)
8. Costantini, S.: ACE: a flexible environment for complex event processing in logical agents. In: Baldoni, M., Baresi, L., Dastani, M. (eds.) EMAS 2015. LNCS, vol. 9318, pp. 70–91. Springer, Heidelberg (2015). doi:10.1007/978-3-319-26184-3_5
9. Ancona, D., Ferrando, A., Mascardi, V.: Runtime verification with trace expressions and LTL. In: To appear in FdB60, Springer (2016)

10. Ancona, D., Briola, D., Ferrando, A., Mascardi, V.: Global protocols as first class entities for self-adaptive agents. In: Proceedings of the 2015 International Conference on Autonomous Agents and Multiagent Systems, AAMAS 2015, pp. 1019–1029 (2015)

11. Ancona, D., Briola, D., Ferrando, A., Mascardi, V.: Runtime verification of fail-uncontrolled and ambient intelligence systems: A uniform approach. Intell. Artif. **9**(2), 131–148 (2015)

12. Costantini, S., De Gasperis, G.: Runtime self-checking via temporal (meta-)axioms for assurance of logical agent systems. In: Bulling, N., van der Hoek, W. (eds.): Proceedings of LAMAS 2014, 7th Workshop on Logical Aspects of Multi-Agent Systems, held at AAMAS 2014. 241–255 Also, Proceedings of the 29th Italian Conference on Computational Logic, CEUR Workshop Proceedings, p. 1195 (2014)

13. Caianiello, P., Costantini, S., De Gasperis, G., Thakur, S.: Cooperating with trusted parties would make life easier. In: Gavanelli, M., Lamma, E., Riguzzi, F. (eds.) AI*IA 2015. LNCS, vol. 9336, pp. 128–135. Springer, Heidelberg (2015). doi:10.1007/978-3-319-24309-2_10

14. Marco, A.D., Inverardi, P., Spalazzese, R.: Synthesizing self-adaptive connectors meeting functional and performance concerns. In: Litoiu, M., Mylopoulos, J. (eds.): Proceedings of the 8th International Symposium on Software Engineering for Adaptive and Self-Managing Systems, SEAMS 2013, IEEE Computer Society, pp. 133–142 (2013)

15. Jørgensen, D., Hallenborg, K., Demazeau, Y.: Assessment of agent architectures for telehealth. In: Corchado, J.M., et al. (eds.) PAAMS 2014. CCIS, vol. 430, pp. 79–88. Springer, Heidelberg (2014)

16. Jørgensen, D.B., Hallenborg, K., Demazeau, Y.: Patient centric ontology for tele-health domain. In: Geissbühler, A., Demongeot, J., Mokhtari, M., Abdulrazak, B., Aloulou, H. (eds.) ICOST 2015. LNCS, vol. 9102, pp. 244–255. Springer, Heidelberg (2015)

17. Wildevuur, S.E., Simonse, L.W.: Information and communication technologyen-abled person-centered care for the big five chronic conditions: Scoping review. J. Med. Int. Res. **19**(3), e77 (2015)

18. Zhang, Y., Lee, M., Gatton, T.M.: Agent-based web healthcare systems for real-time chronic disease. In: 2009 IEEE Congress on Services, Part I, SERVICES I 2009, IEEE Computer Society, pp. 14–21 (2009)

19. Gatton, T.M., Lee, M.R., Kim, T., Lee, Y.-K.: Diagnostic knowledge acquisition for agent-based medical applications. In: Nguyen, N.T., Grzech, A., Howlett, R.J., Jain, L.C. (eds.) KES-AMSTA 2007. LNCS (LNAI), vol. 4496, pp. 626–635. Springer, Heidelberg (2007)

# Multi Agent Application for Chronic Patients: Monitoring and Detection of Remote Anomalous Situations

Daniel Hernández[✉], Gabriel Villarrubia, Alberto L. Barriuso,
Álvaro Lozano, Jorge Revuelta, and Juan F. De Paz

Department of Computer Science and Automation, University of Salamanca,
Plaza de la Merced, s/n, 37008 Salamanca, Spain
{danihiglesias,gvg,loza,jrevuelta,fcofds}@usal.es

**Abstract.** The clinical study of the most basic vital signs of a patient represents the simplest and most effective way to detect and monitor health problems. There are many diseases that can be diagnosed and controlled through regular monitoring of these medical data. The purpose of this study is to develop a monitoring and tracking system for the various vital signs of a patient. In particular, this work focuses on the design of a multi-agent architecture composed of virtual organizations with capabilities to integrate different medical sensors on an open, low-cost hardware platform. This system integrates hardware and software elements needed for the routine measurement of vital signs, performed by the patient or caregiver without having to go to a medical center.

**Keywords:** WNS · Home care · Healthcare sensors · PANGEA

## 1 Introduction

At present, there are over 860 million people with chronic disease [9]. It is estimated that 25 % of these patients could benefit immediately from solutions for monitoring their health from home [8]; another 50 % would benefit from integration existing medical resources [11, 13] into their phones and other devices. In Europe, there is a large group of people who suffer from some type of chronic disease such as diabetes or cardiovascular disease. These patients generate 80 % of healthcare spending in different countries of the European Union [3]. Moreover, they must regularly go to health centers to have their vital signs checked and determine whether they fall within the normal parameters or indicate an abnormality. In many cases, this process involves high costs and inevitable time spent transporting patients from their homes to medical centers, generating long queues, as the medical staff should check the vital signs manually and ensure that they fall within a normal range. In addition, it would be beneficial to monitor certain measurements over a period of time. For example, over a period of one week, an electrocardiogram can collect information about the behavior of the heart during daily physical activity of the patient, which would otherwise not be reproduced in a clinical trial at the medical center [15]. In most cases, the tests are simple and with a little training from medical staff, patients could perform these tests on their own from their homes [7]. This training along with appropriate medical tools could help patients maintain a continuous monitoring of their vital signs from the comfort of their homes. This paper presents a virtual architecture with embedded agents that can be assigned to each of the different medical sensors used, using a light communication protocol and a modular architecture that can self-adapt to the particular needs of the patient.

The use of sensor networks and the use of multi-agent systems can develop services that can be interesting and useful to society. Some existing studies, such as [16], proposed a solution based on Context Awareness, deploying a sensor network architecture in nursing homes. In the same context [4] proposes a system based on a multi-agent architecture for managing an intelligent environment nursing home. This paper proposes a system based on virtual organizations of agents deployed on an open hardware and low cost system. It is able to integrate up to nine medical sensors for measuring the vital signs of a user. The PANGEA [17] platform was used for the development of the system, as it facilitates the creation of virtual organizations of agents and their integration into different hardware devices. Specifically, the system integrates different virtual organizations to perform different tasks such as collecting data from various sensors, checking the maximum and minimum range for each collected value, and managing alerts or shipping information to the remote server that will be responsible for storing historical data.

The paper is organized as follows: Sect. 2 includes a collection of related work, Sect. 3 presents the proposed system, and Sect. 4 presents the results and conclusions.

## 2   Background

The current market contains various devices that monitor vital sign by using sensors connected through mobile devices with a wireless connection such as Bluetooth or WiFi. These devices, which include pulse sensors [5], connected glucometers such as the Wireless Blood Glucometer by iHealth, or blood oxygen sensors, are limited to showing the data obtained by the sensor to the user via the mobile device itself, and do not provide any type of information processing. Many studies focus on the development of new medical sensors, as in the case of Dr. Chris Rorden of the American University of South Carolina, who has developed a prototype system ECG (Fig. 1) based on the open source Arduino controller and a Bluetooth system [18].

**Fig. 1.** Prototype of South Carolina's college

In other works such as [12] the authors have implemented a data analysis system that collects health data from a user's home through the use of various sensors (heart rate, oxygen saturation and body temperature sensor). These sensors send the information wirelessly to the user's mobile phone and use accelerometers placed on the patient to monitor potential falls. The authors in [14] propose an architecture solution based on a wireless sensor network (WSN), focusing their use in a domestic environment and introducing non-intrusive sensors that can analyze the environmental conditions present in the user's daily life. This allows the authors to manage environmental information, which is useful when analyzing the health and potential risk factors in the environment. There are also several works that address the use of sensors and systems for Home Care in nursing homes [4], also called elderly care. Specifically, the authors in [2] stress the current need to create adaptive systems that adapt to the different needs of users.

It is also possible to find works applying multiagent architecture for managing Home Care environments, as in the case of [10]. In this paper the authors propose a multi-agent architecture for the home care of patients with heart failure. The system incorporates multiple processing modules based on statistics, standards and rules that apply to the medical data of patients, as well as learning ability based on previously performed medical procedures. The ultimate goal of this system is to monitor the health status of patients at home and notify medical staff, providing them with the data to assist them in making medical decisions. In [6] the authors analyze the important aspects of context-aware computing and determine how users interact with their environment. The architecture provides a new mechanism that integrates a task planning model based on the critical path method (CPM) [1] in intelligent agents. The CPM method connects a series of related activities in the most optimal way to achieve a specific objective.

## 3   Proposed Reasoning System

The system proposed in this paper aims to monitor and track the user's vital signs. When monitoring this data from the user's home an open and scalable hardware platform based on the Raspberry Pi board [20] was used, on which up to nine medical sensors can be placed. This device is connected to a central server where user data are processed, and also can provide an immediate response if a risk is detected. In order to implement efficient mechanisms to manage the different parameters collected by the medical sensors, and to monitor alerts, sending the data back to a central server, a MAS (multi-agent system) architecture-based on the PANGEA platform [17] was proposed for the Home Care scenario described in Fig. 2.

Then virtual organizations are as follows:

First we have the *Measuring Device* organization formed by the following agents: *alert*, *monitoring*, *visualization* and sub-organization *sensors*. This organization is deployed in the hardware system based on Raspberry Pi. The agent monitoring role will be responsible for analyzing the data obtained by the sensor array; if anomalous values are detected, this agent interacts with the agent responsible for managing alerts. The monitoring agent also provides the data to the visualization agent. The agent with the

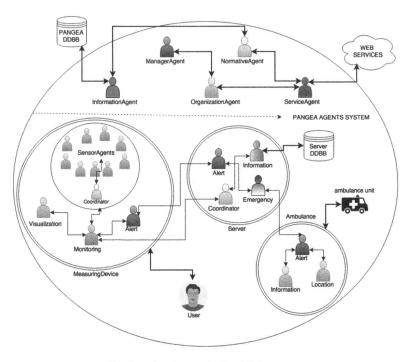

**Fig. 2.** Virtual organization of the system

alert role is responsible for sending alerts to the server to manage it efficiently. The visualization agent role is responsible for presenting the user data obtained through a monitor connected to the system. The sensor sub-organization includes the coordinator agent, who is responsible for collecting the data sent by each sensor and nine Agents, one for each sensor connected to the system. These agents may or may not be active or depending on whether the sensor is connected to the system.

The *Server* organization includes the following agents: *coordinator, alert, information*, and *emergency*. The coordinator agent role is responsible for managing the information coming from the measuring device. The information agent is responsible for storing user data in the database, while the alert agent analyzes different alerts coming from the measuring device. If these alerts require rapid intervention, the alert agent communicates with the emergency agent, which coordinates the dispatch of the nearest ambulance to the user's home. Finally, the *Ambulance* organization integrates the following roles: *alert, location* and *information*. The agent with the alert role, receives the alert notification from the server. The information relating to this alert will be managed by the information agent, along with the corresponding medical data that initiated the alert, to provide faster response and precise detailing. The information relating to the location and routes to reach the user's home is managed by the location agent.

## 3.1    Sensor System

The system for measuring the vital signs of the user is capable of integrating up to nine medical sensors, as previously mentioned. The system is able to adapt to the needs of the patient and set the sensors required to monitor their medical problems. There are nine medical sensors that make up the network of biometric sensors; the functionality of each is described below:

*Patient Position Sensor*: This sensor oversees five different patient positions (standing or sitting, supine, prone, left and right). In many cases, it is necessary to control body positions and movements performed because of a relationship with chronic diseases (sleep apnea or restless legs syndrome). Analyzing the movements during sleep can also help determine the quality of sleep and irregular sleep patterns.

*Glucose Sensor or Glucometer*: A medical device to determine the approximate concentration of glucose in the blood. A small drop of blood, obtained by pricking the skin with a lancet, is placed on a disposable test strip which is read by the meter and used to calculate the blood glucose level. The meter then displays the level in mg/dl or mmol/l.

*Temperature Sensor or Thermometer:* This sensor can measure body temperature. This data is of great medical importance as it can quickly determine if there are any health problems. In fact, a number of diseases are accompanied by characteristic changes in body temperature. Likewise, the course of certain diseases can be monitored by measuring body temperature, and the efficiency of a treatment initiated can be evaluated by the physician.

*Blood Pressure Sensor:* Blood pressure is the pressure of the blood in the arteries as it is pumped around the body by the heart. When the heart is beating, it contracts and pushes blood through the arteries to the rest of the body. This force creates pressure on the arteries. Blood pressure is recorded as two numbers—the systolic pressure (as the heart beats) over the diastolic pressure (as the heart relaxes between beats).

*Pulse and Oxygen in Blood*: Oxygen saturation is defined as the measurement of the amount of oxygen dissolved in the blood, based on the detection of Hemoglobin and Deoxyhemoglobin. Two different light wavelengths are used to measure the actual difference in the absorption spectra of $HbO2$ and $Hb$.

*Airflow Sensor:* Abnormal respiratory rates and changes in respiratory rate are a broad indicator of major physiological instabilities, and in many cases, respiratory rate is one of the earliest indicators of this instability. Therefore, it is critical to monitor respiratory rate as an indicator of patient status. AirFlow sensor can provide an early warning of hypoxemia and apnea.

*Sensor Skin Conductance:* Skin conductance, also known as galvanic skin response (GSR), is a method of measuring the electrical conductance of the skin, which varies according to its moisture level. This is significant because sweat glands are controlled by the sympathetic nervous system, so moments of strong emotion change the electrical resistance of the skin. Skin conductance is used as an indication of psychological or physiological arousal.

*Electrocardiogram Sensor (ECG):* The electrocardiogram (ECG or EKG) is a diagnostic tool that is routinely used to assess the electrical and muscular functions of the heart. The Electrocardiogram Sensor (ECG) has become one of the most commonly used medical tests in modern medicine. Its utility in the diagnosis of a myriad of cardiac pathologies ranging from myocardial ischemia and infarction to syncope and palpitations has been invaluable to clinicians for decades.

*Sensor Electromiógrafo:* An electromyogram (EMG) measures the electrical activity of muscles at rest and during contraction. Electromyography (EMG) is a technique for evaluating and recording the electrical activity produced by skeletal muscles. It can be used to identify neuromuscular disorders, and to evaluate lower back pain, motor system disorders, and kinesiology. An EMG is performed by using an instrument called an electromyograph to produce a record called an electromyogram. It detects the electrical potential generated by muscle cells when these cells are electrically or neurologically activated.

Each of the sensors that make up the architecture are low cost (less than 300€ per set). The chosen sensors are flexible and adaptable to the needs of the patient. The early-warning system and patient monitoring is described below.

### 3.2    Monitoring and Alert System

The alarm system is based on the detection of any anomalous values collected by any of the sensors that make up the platform. The system considers any value to be anomalous if it is outside normal limits previously defined in the system. These limits must be defined by a medical professional for each patient because the configuration can be different. Some of the elements that must be taken into consideration when defining these values are age, sex or weight. But these are not the only data that must be taken into account; to begin, it is essential to analyze the patient's health problems efficiently in order to set the normal range of data collected from each sensor and properly determine the alerts. For a healthy adult, without previous health problems, the range of correct values is described in Table 1.

**Table 1.** Normal levels of a user

| Sensor | Minimum value | Maximum value |
|---|---|---|
| Glucometer | 70 mg/dl | 100 mg/dl |
| Thermometer | 36.5 °C | 37.2 °C |
| Blood pressure | 100/60 mmHg | 140/90 mmHg |
| Pulsometer | 60 BPM | 100 BPM |
| Oximeter | 96 % $O^2$ in blood | 99 % $O^2$ in blood |
| Nasal airflow | 12 breath/min | 30 breath/min |
| Skin conductance | 1 μS | 10 μS |

In the case of the values given by the electrocardiogram and the electromyography, it is necessary to compare the values collected by these sensors in normal conditions to then determine the degree of difference from the monitored values to determine whether to launch an alert.

### 3.3    Alert System for Ambulances

The central server is responsible for evaluating the alerts that have been sent by the measurement system in the user's home (Fig. 3). An alert occurs if, while measuring the user's vital signs, the system records a value that has been marked outside the "normal" range for that user. This value, which is sent to the central server, is compared with the patient's historical data. If the data sent are not compatible with those on record, the system determines that it is an emergency. When this occurs, the system sends a notification to the ambulance nearest to the home user. Ambulances associated with the system have a mobile device with the emergencies application installed. This application receives geolocation information from home user and calculates the shortest route to get there.

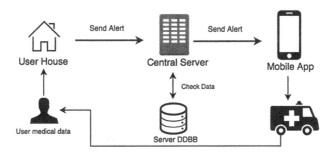

**Fig. 3.** Alerta sistem

## 4    Results and Conclusions

In order to validate the system, we selected a home in the town of Macotera (Salamanca, Spain) where a user voluntarily tested the system for 45 days. The user is a man of 25 years with heart problems who takes his vital signs twice daily. Figure 4 shows the user with various sensors placed on his person while performing a measurement and monitoring the results from a display connected to the device. The medical sensors included in the prototype are shown in Fig. 5, these sensors are manufactured by the company Cooking-hacks [19].

**Fig. 4.**  Real user testing the system

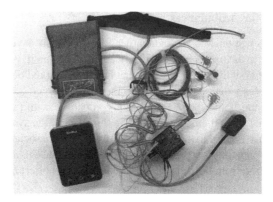

**Fig. 5.** Medical sensors

If any of the data recorded in the measurement fall outside the normal ranges established by the user, with the assistance of a medical professional, the system sounds an alarm and informs the user through screen, as seen in Fig. 6.

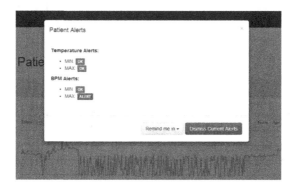

**Fig. 6.** Patient Alerts

While the user is notified of the alert, the notification arrives at the central server where it is analyzed together with the historical patient data. Having determined an emergency, the server proceeds to notify the nearest ambulance of the incident. The ambulance is notified of the alert via the mobile application installed. Figure 7(a) shows how the emergency notification arrives on the mobile device of an ambulance. In Fig. 7(b) we can observe how the notification includes the location coordinates of the patient as well as the shortest route to arrive.

In conclusion, this paper has proposed a multi-agent system based on the PANGEA platform to manage different medical data system. These data are captured by a hardware device equipped with nine medical sensors able to monitor a user's basic vital signs from home. This system also connects to a central server which manages and

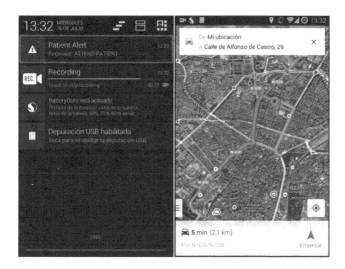

**Fig. 7.** Ambulance App. (a) Alert notification. (b) Route.

stores historical data, and serves as an emergency center in case of an anomaly in the data. The main advantages of the proposed system are:

- The low cost of the sensors.
- The analysis of the information for each patient, which can help predict a chronic illness well in advance.
- Save on travel time and eliminate different human errors that can occur when reading values.
- Monitor the patient 24 h and know their status at all times.
- Simultaneous monitoring of up to 9 vital signs.
- Ability to access all user tests and results from anywhere.
- Emergency system to detect problems in the data.

**Acknowledgements.** The research of Alberto L. Barriuso has been co-financed by the European Social Fund (Operational Programme 2014-2020 for Castilla y León, EDU/128/2015 BOCYL).

# References

1. Aquilano, N.J., Smith, D.E.: A formal set of algorithms for project scheduling with critical path scheduling/material requirements planning. J. Oper. Manage. **1**(2), 57–67 (1980)
2. van den Berg, N., et al.: Telemedicine and telecare for older patients–a systematic review. Maturitas **73**(2), 94–114 (2012)
3. Busse, R., et al.: Tackling chronic disease in Europe: strategies, interventions and challenges. Obs. Stud. **20**, 111 (2010)
4. Corchado, J.M., et al.: GerAmi: improving healthcare delivery in geriatric residences. IEEE Intell. Syst. **23**(2), 19–25 (2008)

5. Fezari, M., et al.: Ambulatory health monitoring system using wireless sensors node. Procedia Comput. Sci. **65**, 86–94 (2015)

6. Fraile, J.A. et al.: Context-aware multiagent system: planning home care tasks. Knowl. Inf. Syst. (2013)

7. Howe, A., Anderson, J.: Involving patients in medical education. BMJ **327**(7410), 326–328 (2003)

8. Huang, F.-H.: Explore home care needs and satisfaction for elderly people with chronic disease and their family members. Procedia Manuf. **3**, 173–179 (2015)

9. Knai, C., et al.: Systematic review of the methodological quality of clinical guideline development for the management of chronic disease in Europe. Health Policy **107**(2–3), 157–167 (2012)

10. Koutkias, V.G., et al.: Multi-agent system architecture for heart failure management in a home care environment. Comput. Cardiol. **2003**, 383–386 (2003)

11. Preuveneers, D., et al.: The future of mobile e-health application development: exploring HTML5 for context-aware diabetes monitoring. Procedia Comput. Sci. **21**, 351–359 (2013)

12. Varma, D., et al.: Development of home health care self monitoring system **4**(6), 252–255 (2015)

13. Varshney, U.: Mobile health: Four emerging themes of research. Decis. Support Syst. **66**, 20–35 (2014)

14. Virone, G., et al.: An advanced wireless sensor network for health monitoring. Transdiscipl. Conf. Distrib. Diagnosis Home Healthc. 2–5 (2006)

15. Wimmer, N.J., et al.: The clinical significance of continuous ECG (ambulatory ECG or Holter) monitoring of the ST-segment to evaluate ischemia: a review. Prog. Cardiovasc. Dis. **56**(2), 195–202 (2013)

16. Wood, A., et al.: Context-aware wireless sensor networks for assisted living and residential monitoring. IEEE Netw. **22**(4), 26–33 (2008)

17. Zato, C., et al.: PANGEA: a new platform for developing virtual organizations of agents. Int. J. Artif. Intell. **11**(13A), 93–102 (2013)

18. Chris Rorden's Neuropsychology Lab » Open source multi-channel EEG/ECG/EMG. http://www.mccauslandcenter.sc.edu/CRNL/tools/ads1298

19. Cooking Hacks - Electronic Kits, tutorials and guides for Makers and Education. https://www.cooking-hacks.com/

20. Raspberry Pi - Teach, Learn, and Make with Raspberry Pi. https://www.raspberrypi.org/

# Improving the Distribution of Services in MAS

Jesús A. Román[1], Sara Rodríguez[2(✉)], and Fernando de la Prieta[2]

[1] Department of Computer Science and Automatic, EPS of Zamora, University of Salamanca,
Avda. Cardenal Cisneros, 34, 49022 Zamora, Spain
zjarg@usal.es
[2] Department of Computer Science and Automatic, University of Salamanca,
Plaza de la Merced s/n, 37008 Salamanca, Spain
{srg,fer}@usal.es

**Abstract.** One way to reduce the computational load of the agents is the distribution of their services. To achieve this goal, the functionality of a MAS (multi-agent system) should not reside in the agents themselves, but ubiquitously be distributed so that allows the system to perform tasks in parallel avoiding an additional computational cost. The distribution of services that offers SCODA (Distributed and Specialized Agent Communities) allows an intelligent management of these services provided by agents of the system and the parallel execution of threads that allow to respond to requests asynchronously, which implies an improvement in the performance of the system at both the computational level as the level of quality of service in the control of these services. The comparison carried out in the case of study that is presented in this paper demonstrates the existing improvement in the distribution of services on systems based on SCODA.

**Keywords:** Multi-agent systems · Distributed services · Specialized communities · SOA

## 1 Introduction

The service-oriented computing (SOC) uses the services that allow the development of distributed applications quickly, operable, scalable and massive [15]. In this aspect, services are autonomous, independent of the platform and weakly coupled to the system that invokes these services. The key to carry out this paradigm are Service Oriented Architectures (SOA) [15]. SOA provides a set of guidelines, principles and techniques, through which the information and business processes, can be rearrange and distribute effectively raising the level of competitiveness [16]. The definition of service is crucial to the effectiveness of a service-oriented architecture, thus, a service can be defined as a function is clearly formulated, self-contained and independent of the context in which it is run [17]. The implementation of SOA is strongly linked to Web Services, these being a way to develop these architectures, but not the only [24, 32]. The development of multi-agent Systems (MAS) based on service-oriented computing[21], where the services rendered by the agents are executed in a distributed manner and on demand, endows these systems with greater levels of flexibility, scalability and a better distribution of computational load, which in centralized systems [5, 26, 31]. SCODA

© Springer International Publishing Switzerland 2016
J. Bajo et al. (Eds.): PAAMS 2016 Workshops, CCIS 616, pp. 37–46, 2016.
DOI: 10.1007/978-3-319-39387-2_4

(Specialized and Distributed Agent COmmunities) [22] uses distributed services so that its execution is optimized by the agents that make up this architecture. It also presents a high tolerance against faults with regard to the monitoring of the services it offers, in a way that provides a control added on these services, and therefore on the entire system. From the distribution of services proposed in SCODA is implemented an improvement in regard to the distribution of the computational load on the agents and services, as well as on its control. To demonstrate this improvement in the distribution of services is carried out a case of study in which proposes the prediction on different time series of demand for food products. The comparison is performed with a MAS (multi-agent system) in the same conditions of implementation and deployment that the system based on SCODA. In the MAS, the agents run the required services centrally and individually. The paper is structured as follow: the next section shows a background of services distribution in specialized intelligent communities; in Sect. 3 a case of study is detailed and the conclusions are described in Sect. 4.

## 2    Background

The idea that a MAS runs their services on a distributed has to take into account an effective communication between the agents and the services to run. That is why the philosophy of SOA is completely validated in its application to this type of systems. SOA proposes a model based on a set of services between which there is effective communication that can involve from a simple exchange of data, up to the possible coordination between these services [6]. This philosophy is desirable in the MAS which has distributed services, so that the coordination between the agents and the services allow a coordination and control over the same. In this aspect, the capacity that allows a multi-agent system to carry out a control of their distributed services is an advantage with regard to the solution of problems in this service, as a malfunction that service [22, 23].

Another very important aspect to take into account is the amount of replicas of a service required at run time required for the system to be able to attend to all the requests in an optimal way. This number of replicas of service can be calculated from the following formula:

$$N_R = \frac{N_S \times T_{MAX}}{P \times Th} \qquad (1)$$

Being: $N_R$, the number of replicas necessary; $N_S$, the number of services requested in a period of time P; $T_{MAX}$, the maximum execution time of service; P, a period of time; Th, the number of simultaneous threads on a service.

Depending on the number of existing replicas of a particular service, the system must have the ability to select the service that hold lower computational load, optimizing its operation.

All of these capabilities which are desirable in the MAS which runs their functions in a distributed manner are found in the SCODA components [22, 23], and especially in their SIC (Specialized Intelligent Communities), which perform their services in a distributed way and in the parameters established above.

In the SIC is present the ability to distribute and select your job in the smart way. They are composed of an controller agent (*CommunityController*), and a team integrated by a planner agent and another executor (*PlannerAgent* and *ExecutorAgent*), that are instantiated at run time when it is needed and released at the end of its work. The own internal architecture of the Community and the philosophy that was being pursued in regard to the instantiation and release of agents under demand implies that SCODA is considered as an efficient architecture in regard to the distribution of its services and the management of internal resources of the platform that runs it. These SIC run as autonomous systems, so that an implementation based on SCODA can be composed of one or several SIC and make use of the services they provide separately, or use multiple SIC and their services in a scaled way and coordinated, and thus to have the capacity to solve big problems in a collaborative way.

The services of the SIC represent the functionalities it offers any system based on SCODA, being these services to the communities where is the computational processing offered by the system. These systems are accessed in a distributed and ubiquitous way. These systems are accessed in a distributed and ubiquitous manner so that the agents of SCODA are released of computational load, so that, SCODA is considered as a lightweight architecture. The services of the Community are permanently assets to receive requests from its corresponding SIC and are designed for your access remotely via sockets, due to its ease of deployment and its good result in other jobs as they are [2, 9, 27]. The services are organized by categories in terms of their specialization, i.e. services relating to a particular functionality are grouped together for their access by the specialized community services that offers these, in this way the principal aim is to find the efficiency at the time of selecting the parameters required for a correct execution, as well as greater speed to find its location.

The services of the Community, as well as another type of distributed services such as Web Services and Services Oriented Architecture [15] must have mechanisms for publication and discoveries of services. Also have to possess an updated directory of the same so that they are accessible when you require [11, 17], this is the reason why SCODA has a flexible services directory, from where the services can be invoked, modified, added and deleted dynamically through the SIC that provide them, however, insertion, modification or elimination of the services of the Community is done manually for safety reasons [12].

The management of the quality of these services is done by one of the agents that provides SCODA, as is the *QualityAgent*. This agent has the ability to monitor at run time the operation of the services in a way that detects any abnormality in your operation. In addition this agent has the ability to restart a particular service if, in effect, detects that is inactive or that the requests that are made to this service are not answered correctly. From these capabilities offered by the SCODA architecture is carried out an improvement in the Quality of Service (QoS) at the level of fault tolerance on the services that they provide.

Another of the proposed improvements lies in the efficiency of the distribution of services that perform the SIC. This improvement will be demonstrated in the case of study that is presented in the following point.

## 3   Case of Study

There are various techniques used to predict time series, from traditional statistical models such as ARIMA and the transfer functions to nonlinear models based on artificial neural networks [30]. The prediction of values belonging to time series of various kinds is a widely discussed problem in the literature [1, 7, 8, 13, 14].

The use of one or the other technique has to do with the ability that it has to process the kind of temporary series selected, thus, in our case the time series corresponding to the demand of food products, is very diverse in terms of the type of product. If for example we take the time series of the orders daily that are performed a product "Product 1", we can see that the series has a periodicity in which their yearly maximum is reached at Christmas and Holy Week, however other products do not present or these maximums neither this periodicity, so it is necessary to use any technique that has a high capacity of generalization of non-linear series. In Fig. 1 presents the series of demand for three different products that are sold in the period between the 01/01/2009 until 30/09/2011.

As we can see in Fig. 1 the series of the demand for these three products is not linear. In addition, the first two have a character that is not newspaper and the product units defendant are completely different. It is observed in the three charts that there are a great variability of the data on the basis of the day of the year as the weekends and holidays, the demand for products is zero.

In view of these graphs can be deduced that there is a great difference between each one of the products that the company offers. It is also important to point out the difficulty that will be the time to predict the demand for the different products due to the nonlinear character and variability of these series, which implies that the selected technique has to have a high you capacity of generalization.

Within the non-linear techniques, the Multilayer Perceptron (MLP) has been widely used in the literature for the prediction of non-linear series, since they have the ability to approximate any continuous function defined in a compact domain, however, its specification is essentially based on heuristics criteria and expert judgment of modeler, so that, this process is based on a set of critical steps which affect the final result of the model, in terms of their adjustment to the historical data and its capacity of generalization in order to make predictions. In this way the prediction is realized by Support Vector Machines (SVM) [3, 4, 25, 28 – 30], due to its high capacity of generalization among other characteristics.

A comparison is presented at the structural level of SCODA with the MAS developed for the case. This comparison is made on the basis of a series of features that are related to the functionality of the architecture regardless of the platform for deployment. The MAS implemented consists of a *CoordinatorAgent* that exercises of coordinator, and an agent *ForecastAgent* that makes predictions and selects the appropriate model for this. Both systems are deployed on JADEX [18, 19] and on the same machine where the

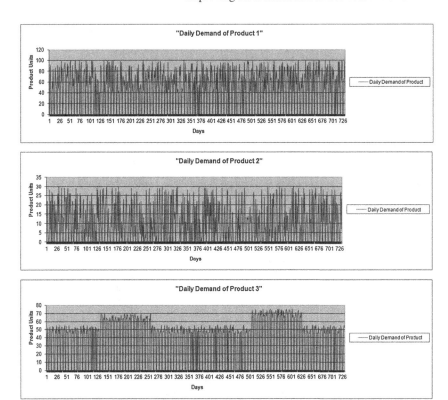

**Fig. 1.** Series of demand for different products

system is deployed with SCODA. Table 1 shows the differences at the structural level between the selected architectures for the resolution of the problem.

Analyzing the Table 1 the MAS implements an architecture based on centralized agents and on the contrary in SCODA are distributed. The advantage that offers a distributed architecture is the ability to allocate resources more efficiently. With regard to the protocols of communication used, both architectures use HTTP [20] as external communication and ACL [10] for internal communication between the agents. However, SCODA uses TCP/IP sockets for communication with external services, which implies that these services will be performed on different machines. Something to highlight is that the MAS is constituted of 2 permanent agents and SCODA of 3 + 2. In SCODA there is an agent that is responsible for carrying out the management of incidents and errors that occur at run time. SCODA enables complete management of incidents and has a high fault tolerance so that if one of the agents is not running properly, the system would not fall, is the agent which has the ability to boot at run time other agents which solves the error. This feature is absent in the MAS, forcing manually restart the agents that have undergone any interruption. In addition, SCODA provides a daily operations through that it is possible to monitor the operation of the system and manage the replication capability of services.

**Table 1.** Comparative of SCODA with a MAS system at the structural level

| Characteristics | MAS | SCODA |
|---|---|---|
| Type of architecture | Based on agents centralized | Based on agents distributed |
| Platform | JADEX | JADEX |
| Communication protocols | ACL<br>HTTP | ACL<br>HTTP<br>TCP/IP |
| Number of permanent agents | 2 | 3 + 2 |
| Programming language | JAVA | JAVA |
| Robustness | There is no incident management | Agent dedicated to incident management<br>Statistics of operation |
| Reuse of resources | Functionality built into the architecture | Reusable services<br>Reusable architecture |
| Resource distribution | Each agent performs a full-service | Distribution and replication of services<br>The agents perform specialized tasks<br>Instantiation at runtime |
| Computational load of the system | Centralized | Distributed |

In regard to the reuse and distribution of resources, the MAS developed integrates all the functionality in its architecture, so that the execution is performed centrally, thus using resources on the same machine where it is deployed its architecture, and forcing to reprogram the agents for any other development. On the contrary, SCODA distributes its resources, that implies that its architecture is standard on any problem, i.e. always consists of the same agents, and these agents always have the same structure. In addition to the distribution of services allows them to be reused in other developments individually or collaborative.

Finally is made reference to the computational load that exists in the implementation of both architectures. The architecture of the MAS is centralized, forcing consuming the resources needed on the machine where the system is running, and therefore, in operations that require a high consumption of resources covers a very high percentage of the same, not allowing the execution of another type of task. On the contrary SCODA distributes the computational load so that puts this computational load on external services. The existing burden on the machine where it is running SCODA is independent of whether the required tasks require an excessive use of resources, since the implementation of the same is done in a distributed manner and independent.

### 3.1 Results in the Case of Study

To realize a study of the efficiency of both systems are made a set of requests simultaneously on SCODA requesting the services of prediction provided and then perform the same operations on the MAS implemented in this case of study. In addition, it discusses several points on these requests by performing the following tests: (i) good requests; (ii) requests with faults in the input parameters; (iii) requests by eliminating one of the responsible agents; (iv) QoS at the level of control and correction of incidents in the system.

The Table 2 shows the response times of the MAS implemented against those of SCODA for requests of services of prediction for products of different typology. As noted, the time for a petition is around the 5000 ms in both cases, however as you increase the simultaneous requests SCODA responds more quickly due to the execution of requests are made through different threads, allowing you to manage more quickly the results of the requests. Something important is that from 21 simultaneous requests the MAS generates an error in the JADEX platform, which implies that the accumulation of such requests saturates the capacity of the agent.

**Table 2.** Response time (ms) for simultaneous requests in a MAS and in SCODA

| No requests | Response time MAS (ms) | Response time SCODA (ms) | Time by request MAS (ms) | Time by request SCODA (ms) |
|---|---|---|---|---|
| 1 | 5571 | 4958 | 5571 | 4958 |
| 5 | 26542 | 18125 | 5308,4 | 3625 |
| 10 | 50021 | 37521 | 5002,1 | 3752,10 |
| 21 | ERROR | 97327 | ERROR | 4634,62 |
| 36 | ERROR | 154025 | ERROR | 4278,47 |

As specified at the beginning of this point, the next test that is being performed is the perform of requests on the same terms as the previous test, but introducing various faults in the required parameters, services which do not exist, etc., randomly, to check the reaction of both systems. Table 3 shows that the results obtained follow the same line as in the previous case, which implies that at both systems the existence of errors does not vary virtually the response times.

**Table 3.** Response time (ms) for simultaneous requests in a MAS and in SCODA with errors

| No requests | Response time MAS (ms) | Response time SCODA (ms) | Time by request MAS (ms) | Time by request SCODA (ms) |
|---|---|---|---|---|
| 1 | 5471 | 5058 | 5471 | 5058 |
| 5 | 27534 | 18534 | 5506,8 | 3706,8 |
| 10 | 49929 | 37965 | 4992,9 | 3796,50 |
| 21 | ERROR | 97278 | ERROR | 4632,29 |
| 36 | ERROR | 155025 | ERROR | 4306,25 |

The following test that is performed on both systems is to eliminate one of the agents responsible for servicing the requests and compare the reaction of the systems. As soon as the MAS, directly removes the agent that implements the functionality of execute the predictions, implies that the request is not resolved and is returned an error because the agent cannot resolve the request.

In SCODA is deleted the *CommunityController* responsible for predictions and is the own architecture which has the ability to detect problems in the agents that comprise it and restart those agents. Therefore, the *CommunityController* is restarted and the request of the service runs correctly.

Finally the comparison between the two systems is by the management of the QoS to incident monitoring level and statistics of successes and failures in the system. In the second type of tests that were conducted by introducing faults in the input parameters, response times were similar, however the MAS does not give any information on the number of requests serviced properly, the type of failure that has occurred, etc., and however SCODA carries a complete control of the incidents that occurred in the system through the *QualityAgent*.

The tests performed and the proposed results above lead to demonstrate the existing improvement in the distribution of services that offers SCODA. With regard to its behavior in situations where it is required for an effective response, SCODA has obtained better results than the system MAS developed.

## 4   Conclusions

The distribution of services in multi-agent systems (MAS) allows to execute functionality that provide these systems more efficiently due to that the computational load required to perform this functionality does not reside in the agents as such, but in different locations in a distributed manner. The SCODA architecture provides its functionality in a distributed way by the Specialized Intelligent Communities (SIC). These functionalities are planned internally by the SIC and executed remotely by them. For each request, from the beginning of the process creates a thread so that these requests can be answered asynchronously and do not generate an overload to the agents.

On the basis of the comparative carried out between a MAS with ability to predict time series of food products and a system based on SCODA for the same work has been carried out a comparison on aspects of computational efficiency, as well as in the QoS in regard to the control and monitoring of communications and of the services offered by the both systems. Additionally, the architecture provides a mechanism for dynamically calculate the number of replicas of service necessary to respond to all the requests that are carried out in an optimal way.

**Acknowledgements.**   This work has been carried out by the project EKRUCAmI: Europe-Korea Research on Ubiquitous Computing and Ambient Intelligence. Ref. 318878. FP7-PEOPLE-2012-IRSES.

## References

1. Atiya, A., El-Shoura, S., Shaheen, S., El-Sherif, M.: A comparison between neural network forecasting techniques-case study: river flow forecasting. IEEE Trans. Neural Netw. **2**(10), 402–409 (1999)

2. Balaji, P., Bhagvat, S., Jin, H.-W., Panda, D.K.: Asynchronous zero-copy communication for synchronous sockets in the sockets direct protocol (SDP) over InfiniBand. In: International Parallel and Distributed Processing Symposium (IPDPS 2006) (2006)
3. Belousov, A., Verzakov, S., Von Frese, J.: A flexible classification approach with optimal generalisation performance: support vector machines. Chemometr. Intell. Lab. Syst. **64**, 15–25 (2002)
4. Burges, C.: A tutorial on support vector machines for pattern recognition. Data Min. Knowl. Discov. **2**(2), 121–167 (1998)
5. Camarinha-Matos, L.M., Afsarmanesh, H.: A comprehensive modeling framework for collaborative networked organizations. J. Intell. Manuf. **5**(18), 529–542 (2007)
6. Cerami, E.: Web Services Essentials Distributed Applications with XML-RPC, SOAP, UDDI & WSDL, 1st edn. O'Reilly & Associates Inc., Sebastopol (2002)
7. Corchado, J., Aiken, J.: Hybrid artificial intelligence methods in oceanographic forecasting models. IEEE SMC Trans. Part C **32**, 307–313 (2002)
8. Corchado, J., Lees, B.: A hybrid case-based model for forecasting. Appl. Artif. Intell. Int. J. **15**, 105–127 (2001)
9. Douglas, C., Pai, V.: Seekable sockets: a mechanism to reduce copy overheads in TCP-based messaging. In: International Parallel and Distributed Processing Symposium (IPDPS 2006) (2006)
10. FIPA. Foundation for Intelligent Physical Agents. http://www.fipa.org (2005). Accessed 14 Aug 2006
11. Leymann, F., Roller, D., Schmidt, M.-T.: Web services and business process management. IBM Syst. J. **2**(41), 198–211 (2002)
12. López, F., Luck, M., d'Inverno, M.: A normative framework for agent-based systems. Comput. Math. Organ. Theory **12**, 227–250 (2006)
13. Martín-Merino, M., Román, J.: A new SOM algorithm for electricity load forecasting. In: King, I., Wang, J., Chan, L.-W., Wang, D.L. (eds.) ICONIP 2006. LNCS, vol. 4232, pp. 995–1003. Springer, Heidelberg (2006)
14. Martín-Merino, M., Román, J.: Electricity load forecasting using self organizing maps. In: Kollias, S.D., Stafylopatis, A., Duch, W., Oja, E. (eds.) ICANN 2006. LNCS, vol. 4132, pp. 709–716. Springer, Heidelberg (2006)
15. Papazoglou, M.P., Traverso, P., Dustdar, S., Leymann, F.: Service-oriented computing: state of the art and research challenges. Computer **11**(40), 38–45 (2007)
16. Papazoglou, M., Georgakapoulos, G.: Introduction to the special issue about service-oriented computing. Commun. ACM **46**(10), 24–29 (2003)
17. Papazoglou, M., van den Heuvel, W.: Service-oriented design and development methodology. Int. J. Web Eng. Technol. **2**(4), 412–442 (2006)
18. Pokahr, A., Braubach, L., Lamersdorf, W.: Jadex: Implementing a BDI-infrastructure for JADE agents. In: EXP - In Search of Innovation (Special Issue on JADE), pp. 76–85 (2003)
19. Pokahr, A., Braubach, L., Walczak, A., Lamersdorf, W.: Jadex - engineering goal-oriented agents. In: Developing Multi-agent Systems with JADE, pp. 254–258. Wiley, Hoboken (2007)
20. RFC 2616. Hypertext Transfer Protocol – HTTP/1.1. The Internet Society (1999)
21. Ricci, A., Buda, C., Zaghini, N.: An agent-oriented programming model for SOA & web services. In: 5th IEEE International Conference on Industrial Informatics (INDIN 2007), pp. 1059–1064, Viena (2007)
22. Román, J., Rodríguez, S., Corchado, J.: Distributed and specialized agent communities. In: Pérez, J.B., et al. (eds.) Trends in Practical Applications of Agents and Multiagent Systems. AISC, vol. 221, pp. 33–40. Springer, Berlin (2013)

23. Román, J., Tapia, D., Corchado, J.: SCODA para el Desarrollo de Sistemas Multiagente. Revista Ibérica de Sistemas y Tecnologías de Información **8**, 25–38 (2011)
24. Rosen, M., Lublinsky, B., Smith, K., Balcer, M.: Applied SOA: Service-Oriented Architecture and Design Strategies. Wiley, Hoboken (2008)
25. Schölkopf, B., Smola, A.: Learning with Kernels. MIT Press, Cambridge (2002)
26. Shen, W., Norrie, D.H.: An agent-based approach for distributed manufacturing and supply chain management. In: Globalization of Manufacturing in the Digital Communications Era of the 21st Century, pp. 579–590 (1998)
27. Sunwook, K., Chanho, P., Seongwoon, K., Yongwha, C.: The offloading of socket information for TCP/IP offload engine. In: 11th International Conference on Advanced Communication Technology (ICACT 2009), vol. 1, pp. 826–831 (2009)
28. Vapnik, V.: The Nature of Statistical Learning Theory. Springer, New York (1995)
29. Vapnik, V., Golowich, S., Smola, A.: Support vector method for function approximation, regression estimation, and signal processing. Adv. Neural Inf. Process. Syst. **9**, 281–287 (1996)
30. Velásquez, J., Olaya, Y., Franco, C.: Predicción de Series Temporales usando Máquinas de Vectores Soporte. Ingeniare. Revista chilena de ingeniería **18**, 64–75 (2010)
31. Voos, H.: Agent-based distributed resource allocation in technical dynamic systems. In: Proceedings of the IEEE Workshop on Distributed intelligent Systems: Collective intelligence and Its Applications, pp. 157–162. IEEE Computer Society (2006)
32. Zimmermann, O., Schlimm, N., Waller, G., Pestel, M.: Analysis and design techniques for service-oriented development and integration. In: INFORMATIK, pp. 606–611 (2005)

# Workshop on Agents-Based Solutions for Manufacturing and Supply Chain (AMSC)

# A Multi-level and Multi-agent Approach to Modeling and Solving Supply Chain Problems

Jarosław Wikarek and Paweł Sitek$^{(\boxtimes)}$

Department of Information Systems,
Kielce University of Technology, Kielce, Poland
{j.wikarek, sitek}@tu.kielce.pl

**Abstract.** Supply chain problems cover several aspects at different levels and areas. There are decision on production allocation, resource allocation, production and inventory quantities, distributor selection, choice of transportation mode etc. There are many constraints in the supply chain problems. They concern the following areas (production, distribution, transport, etc.) and types (linear, non-linear, integer, logical, etc.). Therefore it is important effective modeling and solving constraints.

We consider a multi-level and multi-agent approach to modeling and solving supply chain problems using constraint and mathematical programming environments. Its efficiency results from the multi-level presolving and multi-agent architecture. An illustrative example presents effectiveness of the proposed approach. The presented approach will be compared with classical mathematical programming on the same data sets.

**Keywords:** Constraint logic programming · Mathematical programming · Multi-agent · Supply chain · Optimization

## 1 Introduction

The vast majority of decision and/or optimization models for supply chain problems have been formulated as the mixed integer programming (MIP) or mixed integer linear programming (MILP) problems and solved using the operations research (OR) methods [1]. Their structures are similar and proceed from the principles and requirements of mathematical programming (MP) [1].

Unfortunately, high complexity of decision-making models and their integer nature contribute to the poor efficiency of operation research methods. Therefore a new approach to solving these problems was proposed. This approach relies on the logical and functional division into smaller problems and the application of different modeling and programming paradigms in different levels of the whole problem. As the best structure for the implementation of this approach, multi-agent systems were chosen [2, 22].

The main contribution of this paper is the proposed new multi-level and multi-agent approach to the universal modeling and solving constrains in supply chain problems. The proposed approach is also characterized by the repeated application of the presolving methods.

© Springer International Publishing Switzerland 2016
J. Bajo et al. (Eds.): PAAMS 2016 Workshops, CCIS 616, pp. 49–60, 2016.
DOI: 10.1007/978-3-319-39387-2_5

The paper is organized as follows. In Sect. 2 the methods related to implementation multi-level approach have been reviewed. In Sect. 3 the concept of multi-level and multi-agent approach to modeling and solving supply chain problems, has been presented. Then, the general description of illustrative example has been discussed (Sect. 4). In Sect. 5 the implementation aspects of the presented approach were described. Finally test instances for illustrative example and some computational results were discussed in Sect. 6. The last section contains conclusions.

## 2 Methods

To modeling and solving constraints the most effective and most flexible are Constraint-based environments. They are much more efficient in modeling constraints than the methods of mathematical programming (MP).

Constraint-based environments are mostly based on CSPs (Constraint Satisfaction Problems) [3]. An instance of a CSP involves a set of variables $X = \{X_1, X_2,..., X_m\}$, a domain $Dom_j$ for each variable and a set of constraints $Cst = \{Cst_1, Cst_2,..., Cst_q\}$ s.t. $Cst_j \subseteq Dom_1 x Dom_2 x...x Dom_q$ which define feasible combinations of domain values. A CSP defined over a constraint network (Fig. 1) consists of finite set of decision variables, each associated with a domain of values and set of constraints.

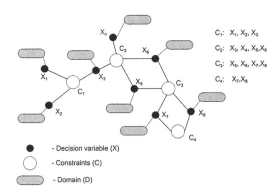

$C_1$:  $X_1, X_2, X_3$
$C_2$:  $X_3, X_4, X_5, X_6$
$C_3$:  $X_5, X_6, X_7, X_8$
$C_4$:  $X_7, X_8$

● - Decision variable (X)
○ - Constraints (C)
▭ - Domain (D)

**Fig. 1.** Constraint network (CSP)

CSP is to solve a problem by stating constraints representing all requirements about the solving problem and then, finding solutions satisfying all the constraints. CSP on finite domains are typically solved using a form of search (backtracking, constraint propagation, and local search). Constraint propagation process roughly amounts to choosing a small subset of a constraint set and to making some of its local constraints stronger by forbidding and eliminating some value assignment that would make the subset over constrained. The domain solution requires further solving process by backtracking search process. A backtracking search algorithm builds a partial solution by assigning values to decision variables one by one, if it finds a dead end in which the partial solution cannot be consistently extended, it withdraws a choice it made and tries another one etc. The backtracking search process is iterated until all possibilities (potential solutions) are tried or until solution is found. Backtracking search is a time-consuming procedure and may make CSPs NP-complete. The largest CSPs efficiency is obtained for binary constraints (which involve no more than two variables). For the constraints that bind a greater number of variables increases the number of backtrackings and thus it dramatically increases the time search for a solution. CSPs are frequently used in constraint programming (CP) [4, 7]. Constraint programming is the use of constraints as a programming language to encode and solve problems. Constraint logic programming (CLP) is a form of constraint programming, in which logic programming is extended to include concepts from constraint satisfaction. A constraint logic program is a logic program that contains constraints in the body of clauses [5, 6].

Both MP-based and CP-based environments involve decision variables and constraints. However, the types of the decision variables and constraints that are used, and the way the constraints are solved, are different in the two approaches [8]. MP-based method relies completely on linear equations and inequalities in integer variables, i.e., there are only two types of constraints: linear arithmetic (linear equations or inequalities) and integrity (stating that the variables have to take their values in the integer numbers). In CP-based methods, the constraint language is richer. In addition to linear equations and inequalities, there are various other constraints: nonlinear, disequalities, and symbolic (disjunctive, exclude, cumulative, all different, profile etc.) [5]. There is also a difference in the effectiveness of the two approaches to solve different types of constraints [9, 10].

Therefore, there have been many approaches of integration of CP and MP [11–13]. The authors also conducted research on the integration and hybridization of both environments [14, 15]. Our main direction of research in this area was the elimination mechanism for the distribution of variables and replace it with the MP methods. However, in previous studies we used single-level approach, modeling and solving the problem as a whole.

## 3   A Multi-level and Multi-agent Approach to Universal Modeling and Solving Constraints

The multi-level architecture results from the occurrence of constraints at various levels of the supply chain problems and need for universal modeling and effective solving of a variety of constraints. This approach based on the results of the previous studies on modeling and solving constraints [16, 17]. The concept of multi-level approach is shown in Fig. 2. In the first stage, the problem is modeled using CSPs for each functional sub-problem (e.g., production, distribution, sale, etc.) (Level 1). Then there are initially solved using the constraint propagation as presolving method (Level 2). In the next stage, the constraints (financial, environmental, transport etc.) that bind the sub-problems from first stage and the additional/auxiliary constrains (result from the user's specific requirements, the data instances, or ability to increase the effectiveness of the search for solutions) are modeled as CSPs (Level 3). They are also presolved (Level 4). But here as the presolving method is used transformation of the problem that has been presented, among others, in [14, 17]. It significantly changes the representation of the problem. Consequently, this allows the reduction and transformation of decision variables and constraints. The next step involves generating the ultimate MILP model. At this level, it is also introduced objective function that complements MILP model. Finally, the MILP model is solved using the mathematical programming environment (Level 5).

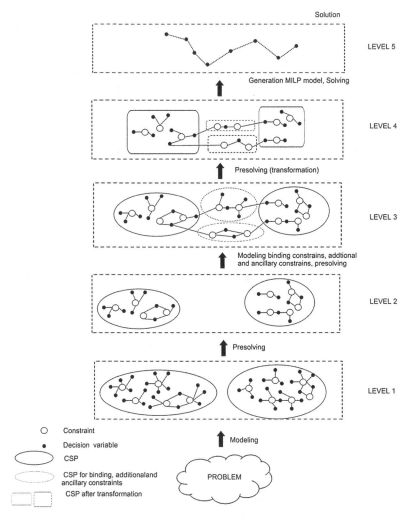

**Fig. 2.** The concept of multi-level approach to universal modeling and solving constraints for supply chain problems.

The multi-level approach also uses a hybrid approach concepts. Here, a hybrid approach involves the use CLP for modeling and presolving while MP to the final solution. Presolving in the presented approach occurs on many levels. It is an important feature that distinguishes the multi-level approach by the previous ones [14, 15]. In general, multi-level approach are the following presolving methods: constraint propagation, transformation, and both methods simultaneously. Presolving tasks include: narrowing the decision variable domains, reduction the number of decision variables, transformation of decision variables and the reduction and simplification of the constraints.

## 4 Illustrative Example

The example of practical use of the multi-level approach (Fig. 3) is based on the problem of supply chain optimization presented in [14, 17] including the production, distribution, retail/customers layers. All these layers are interconnected by multimodal transport, as shown in Fig. 3. Each layer has a specific set of constraints (production capacity, distribution centers capacity, timely execution of orders, transport capacity, etc.) presented in the form of CSPs, which essentially distinguishes presented model from the models previous published in [14, 17] where all constraints of the problem were modeled as a whole. The constraints that bind the layers (the number and capacity of transport means, environmental constraints, etc.) are also modeled as CSPs. The model for illustrative example in the form of CSPs for consecutive layers, connecting constraints, additional constraints is shown in Table 1. Description of decision variables and constraints that create CSPs for illustrative example is shown in Table 2. In this example, the objective function (Fc) is the sum of all costs for the entire supply chain (Table 2).

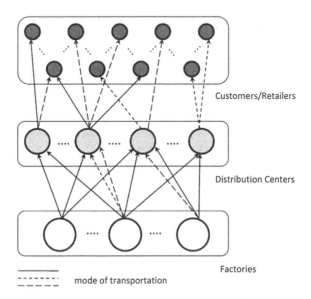

**Fig. 3.** The structure of supply chain with multi-modal transport.

**Table 1.** The model for illustrative example as a set of CSPs

| $CSP_s$ | Description |
|---|---|
| $CSP^0$ presolving, binarity and integrality | $CSP^0 = (C = \{C_1^0, C_2^0\}\}, X = \{Zx_n, Xp_{m,n}, Xs_{q,n}, Tc_q, Xb_{m,q,u},$ $Yb_{q,o,u}, Xa_{m,q,n,u}, Ya_{q,o,n,u}, Xk_{m,q,n,u}, Yk_{q,o,n,u}\}$ $D = \{D_{Zx}^0, D_{Xp}^0, D_{Xs}^0, D_{Tc}^0, D_{Xb}^0, D_{Yb}^0, D_{Xa}^0, D_{Ya}^0, D_{Xk}^0, D_{Yk}^0\})$ |
| $CSP^1$ for production | $CSP^1 = (C = \{C_1^1, C_2^1, C_3^1\}\}, X = \{Xp_{m,n}\}, D = \{D_{Xp}^1\})$ |
| $CSP^2$ for distribution centers | $CSP^2 = (C = \{C_1^2, C_2^2, C_3^2, C_4^2\}\}, X = \{Xs_{q,n}, Tc_q\}, D = \{D_{Xs}^2, D_{Tc}^2\})$ |
| $CSP^3$ for multi-modal transportation | $CSP^3 = (C = \{C_1^3, C_2^3, C_3^3\}\}, X = \{Xb_{m,q,u}, Yb_{q,o,u}\}, D = \{D_{Xb}^3, D_{Yb}^3\})$ |
| $CSP^4$ allows to link $CSP^3$ with $CSP^1$ | $CSP^4 = (C = \{C_1^4, C_2^4, C_3^4, C_4^4, C_5^4\}\},$ $X = \{Xb_{m,q,u}, Yb_{q,o,u}, Xa_{m,q,n,u}, Ya_{q,o,n,u}, Tc_q, Xk_{m,q,n,u}, Yk_{q,o,n,u},\},$ $D = \{D_{Xb}^4, D_{Yb}^4, D_{Xa}^4, D_{Ya}^4, D_{Tc}^4, D_{Xk}^4, D_{Yk}^4\})$ |
| $CSP^5$ allows to link $CSP^2$ with $CSP^3$ | $CSP^5 = (C = \{C_1^5, C_2^5, C_3^5, C_4^5\}\}, X = \{Xk_{m,q,n,u}, Yk_{q,o,n,u}, Xp_{m,n}, Xs_{q,n}\},$ $D = \{D_{Xk}^5, D_{Xk}^5, D_{Xp}^5, D_{Xs}^5,\})$ |

**Table 2.** Description of decision variables, constraint and objective function

| Decision variables | |
|---|---|
| $Xp_{m,n}$ | The production volume of the product $n$ in the factory $m$ |
| $Xs_{q,n}$ | The number of product $n$ that is handled at the distribution center $q$ |
| $Tc_q$ | If distribution center $q$ participates in deliveries, then $Tc_q = 1$, otherwise $Tc_q = 0$ |
| $Xb_{m,q,u}$ | The number of courses from factory $m$ to distribution center $q$ using mode of transportation $u$ |
| $Yb_{q,o,u}$ | The number of courses from distribution center $q$ to customer $o$ using mode of transportation $u$ |
| $Xk_{m,q,n,u}$ | Delivery quantity of product item $n$ from factory $m$ to distribution center $q$ using mode of transportation $u$ |
| $Yk_{q,o,n,u}$ | Delivery quantity of product item $n$ from distribution center $q$ to customer $o$ using mode of transportation $u$ |
| $Xa_{m,q,n,u}$ | If delivery product item $n$ is from factory $m$ to distribution center $q$ using mode of transportation $u$ then $Xa_{m,q,n,u} = 1$, otherwise $Xa_{m,q,n,u} = 0$ |
| $Ya_{q,o,n,u}$ | If delivery product item $n$ is from distribution center $q$ to customer $o$ using mode of transportation $u$ then $Ya_{q,o,n,u} = 1$, otherwise $Ya_{q,o,n,u} = 0$ |
| $Zx_n$ | Cumulative product item $p$ demand (values calculated) |
| Constraints | | |
| $CSP^0$ | $C_1^0$ | Determining the cumulative demand for particular products $n$ |
| | $C_2^0$ | Integrity and binarity |

(Continued)

**Table 2.** (*Continued*)

| Decision variables | | |
|---|---|---|
| $CSP^1$ | $C_1^1$ | Constraint ensures that the production capacity of the factory will not be exceeded |
| | $C_2^1$ | Constraint on the joint production capacity in the factory |
| | $C_3^1$ | Constraint ensures the execution of all customer orders |
| $CSP^2$ | $C_1^2$ | Constraint ensures that the quantity of products $n$ which result from the customer orders will be handled |
| | $C_2^2$ | Constraints ensures that the distribution center $q$ will be handled only those products $n$ that can it be supported |
| | $C_3^2$ | Constraint ensures that the total volume of handled products for each center is less than the capacity of the center |
| | $C_4^2$ | Constraint ensures that the total available capacity distribution centers $q$ is greater than total volume of handled products $n$ |
| $CSP^3$ | $C_1^3$ | Constraint ensures that the deliveries from the manufacturer $m$ to the distribution center $q$ are made along the used routes and permitted means of transport |
| | $C_2^3$ | Constraint ensures that the deliveries from the distribution center $q$ to the customer $o$ are made along the used routes and permitted means of transport |
| | $C_3^3$ | Constraint ensures that the transport is not used more means of transport than is available |
| $CSP^4$ | $C_1^4$ | Transportation from the factory $m$ only through working distribution centers $q$ |
| | $C_2^4$ | Transportation to the customer $o$ only from working distribution centers $q$ |
| | $C_3^4$ | Constraint ensures a suitable number of transport means $u$ for carrying products $n$ from factory $m$ to distribution center $q$ |
| | $C_4^4$ | Constraint ensures a suitable number of transport means $u$ for carrying products $n$ from distribution center $q$ to customer $o$ |
| | $C_5^4$ | Constraint ensures that the delivery was completed within the required deadline |
| $CSP^5$ | $C_1^5$ | Balance constraint - quantity produced in the factory $m$ equals the amount delivered to distribution center $q$ |
| | $C_2^5$ | Balance constraint - quantity delivered to distribution center $q$ equals the amount delivered to customer $o$ |
| | $C_3^5$ | Balance constraint - quantity delivered to a distribution center $q$ equals the amount handled in this center |
| | $C_4^5$ | Balance constraint - quantity delivered to customer $o$ equals the amount ordered by this customer |
| Fc - objective function | | The total cost of production, distribution, transport and environmental costs for the entire supply chain |

## 5  Multi-agent Implementation of Multi-level Approach

The best architecture to implement multi-level approach is multi-agent system. This is due to with parallel execution of CSPs and the need for communication between levels and specific CSPs. Each agent consists of a set of predicates in the CLP language. CLP predicate is a collection of clauses. The idea of clause is to define that something is true. Implementation of individual agents were made using ECL$^i$PS$^e$. This is a high-level modelling, control and declarative programming language, interfaces to third-party solvers and interfaces [18, 19]. The ECL$^i$PS$^e$ language is largely backward-compatible with Prolog and supports different dialects, including ISO Prolog. Thanks to its declarative nature, it can be used both as a modelling language for the description of problems and as a general purpose programming language.

There were several types of CLP agents. The first group includes the agents that implement the various CSPs (Table 1), and contain, among others, CLP predicates for specific constraints of those CSPs. The second group includes the agents used to presolving problem. Another group is a collection of agents to generation model in the form of MILP with the selected objective function. The last type of agent allows you to call external MP solver. In this implementation, as an external MP solver the LINGO system was used [18, 20]. The proposed implementation in the form of multi-agent system (Fig. 4) is characterized by: (a) high flexibility, (b) versatility (the problem can be modeled by adding or subtracting agents of the first group), (c) high efficiency (multiple use of agents to presolving problem).

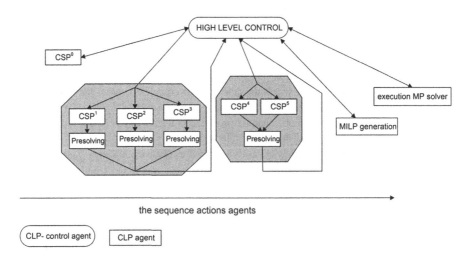

**Fig. 4.** Diagram of connections and sequence actions of agents for the implementation of multi-level approach.

## 6  Computational Experiments

In order to verify and evaluate the proposed approach and implementation, many computational experiments were performed for the illustrative example. All the experiments relate to the supply chain with ten factories $(m = 1..10)$, four distributor centers $(q = 1..4)$, ten customers $(o = 1..10)$, four modes of transportation $(u = 1..4)$, fifteen product items $(n = 1..15)$, and ten sets of orders $(S_1(10), S_2(20), S_3(30), S_4(50), S_5(60), S_6(80), S_7(100), S_8(150), S_9(175), S_{10}(200)$-$(N)$-the number of orders in set $Or_i)$.

The main purpose of the computational experiments was to study the efficiency of the proposed approach to mathematical programming and hybrid approach. The idea was to find answers for the two questions. Firstly, whether the modified method of modeling the problem and the introduction of multiple presolving method reduces the time to find a solution. Secondly, whether this approach allows solving problems of larger sizes. The obtained results (Table 3 and Fig. 5) give the most positive answers to these questions.

**Table 3.**  Results

| $S_i(N)$ | Mathematical programming | | | | Hybrid approach | | | |
|---|---|---|---|---|---|---|---|---|
| | Fc | T | V(Vint) | C | Fc | T | V(Vint) | C |
| 10 | 9000 | 45 | 113270(109846) | 67010 | 9000 | 6 | 3183(760) | 2032 |
| 20 | 9180 | 123 | 113270(109846) | 73410 | 9180 | 9 | 3287(862) | 2025 |
| 30 | 9460 | 234 | 113270(109846) | 79810 | 9460 | 34 | 3397(970) | 2027 |
| 50 | 10995* | 900** | 113270(109846) | 92610 | 10995 | 256 | 3596(1165) | 2040 |
| 60 | 14700* | 900** | 113270(109846) | 99010 | 14700 | 267 | 3637(1204) | 2033 |
| 80 | 18340* | 900** | 113270(109846) | 111810 | 17385 | 345 | 3680(1244) | 2031 |
| 100 | 25430* | 900** | 113270(109846) | 124610 | 20005 | 404 | 3703(1264) | 2030 |
| 150 | 25030* | 900** | 113270(109846) | 156610 | 24645* | 900** | 3828(1384) | 2035 |
| 175 | 28100* | 900** | 113270(109846) | 173510 | 27347* | 900** | 3891(1456) | 2037 |
| 200 | 28700* | 900** | 113270(109846) | 188610 | 28300* | 900** | 3988(1529) | 2040 |

| $S_i(N)$ | Multi-level approach | | | | |
|---|---|---|---|---|---|
| | Fc | T | V(Vint) | C | |
| 10 | 9000 | 1 | 666 (415) | 4491 | $S_i(N)$ - set of N orders |
| 20 | 9180 | 1 | 901(650) | 4967 | Fc - objective function |
| 30 | 9460 | 2 | 1136(885) | 5430 | T - time calculations in seconds |
| 50 | 10995 | 3 | 1604(1352) | 6343 | V(Vint) - the number of decision variables (integer decision variables) |
| 60 | 14700 | 3 | 1746(1495) | 6828 | |
| 80 | 17385 | 9 | 2022(1771) | 7775 | C – the number of constraints |
| 100 | 20005 | 29 | 2283(2032) | 8741 | ** - the calculation was stopped after 900 s |
| 150 | 24130 | 41 | 3992(2991) | 11070 | |
| 175 | 25056 | 37 | 4532(3546) | 12365 | * - the feasible value of the objective function after time T |
| 200 | 25660 | 26 | 4942(4391) | 13380 | |

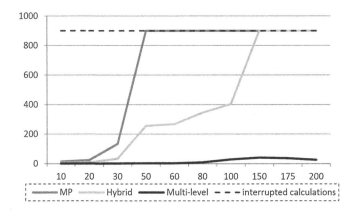

**Fig. 5.** Computation times (vertical axis in seconds) for each instance of data (horizontal axis) using a multi-level approach, hybrid approach and mathematical programming.

## 7  Conclusions

The concept of multi-level and multi-agent approach is flexible in terms of modeling and highly effective computationally (Sect. 6). The presented solution is a development of the hybrid method [14, 15], both in the area of modeling (modeling problem as separate CSPs for different areas, linked CSPs, additional CSPs etc.) and solving (the presolving methods).

Our approach allows you to find the optimal solution for the same instance of data by two orders of magnitude faster than the other approaches. Moreover, for larger data instances within an acceptable time (T = 900 s) other approaches provide only feasible solutions.

Hence, the use of multi-level and multi-agent approach for illustrative example allowed the optimal solutions to the problems are much larger (more than 200 orders while a hybrid approach for 100 orders and mathematical programming only for the 30 orders).

Therefore, the multi-level and multi-agent approach is recommended for real optimization problems occurring in supply chains such as optimization of the total cost, choice of transport fleet, the location of distribution centers, optimizing the storage size and so on. Further work will run in three directions.

Firstly, we introduce the paradigm of fuzzy logic [21] to the Multi-level approach. Secondly, due to the applied multi-agent architecture, implementation will be done in the cloud [24]. Thirdly, we would like to propose a multi-level approach applied to eco-innovative economy (manufacturing, logistics, product, etc.) [23].

## References

1. Schrijver, A.: Theory of Linear and Integer Programming. Wiley, New York (1998). ISBN 0-471-98232-6
2. Barbati, M., Bruno, G., Genovese, A.: Applications of agent-based models for optimization problems in a literature review. Expert Syst. Appl. **39**, 6020–6028 (2012)

3. Tsang, E.: Foundation of Constraint Satisfaction. Academic Press, London and San Diego (1993)
4. Benhamou, F., Jussien, N., O'Sullivan, B.A.: Trends in Constraint Programming. Wiley, New York (2007). ISBN 978-1-905209-97-Wiley-ISTE
5. Rossi, F., Van Beek, P., Walsh, T.: Handbook of Constraint Programming. Foundations of Artificial Intelligence. Elsevier Science Inc., New York (2006)
6. Apt, K., Wallace, M.: Constraint Logic Programming Using Eclipse. Cambridge University Press, Cambridge (2006)
7. Bocewicz, G., Banaszak, Z.: Declarative approach to cyclic steady states space refinement: periodic processes scheduling. Int. J. Adv. Manuf. Technol. **67**(1–4), 137–155 (2013)
8. Bzdyra, K., Banaszak, Z., Bocewicz, G.: Multiple project portfolio scheduling subject to mass customized service. In: Szewczyk, R., Zieliński, C., Kaliczyńska, M. (eds.) Progress in Automation, Robotics and Measuring Techniques. AISC, vol. 350, pp. 11–22. Springer, Heidelberg (2015)
9. Bockmayr, A., Kasper, T.: Branch-and-Infer: a framework for combining CP and IP. In: Milano, M. (ed.) Constraint and Integer Programming. Operations Research/Computer Science Interfaces Series, pp. 59–87. Springer US, New York (2004). doi:10.1007/978-1-4419-8917-8_3
10. Achterberg, T., Berthold, T., Koch, T., Wolter, K.: Constraint integer programming: a new approach to integrate CP and MIP. In: Trick, M.A. (ed.) CPAIOR 2008. LNCS, vol. 5015, pp. 6–20. Springer, Heidelberg (2008)
11. Bistarelli, S., Montanari, U., Rossi, F.: Semiring-based constraint satisfaction and optimization. J. ACM **44**(2), 201–236 (1997). doi:10.1145/256303.256306
12. Hooker, J.N.: Logic optimization, and constraint programming. J. Comput. **14**(4), 295–321 (2002)
13. Milano, M., Wallace, M.: Integrating operation research in constraint programming. Ann. Oper. Res. **175**(1), 37–76 (2010). doi:10.1007/s10479-009-0654-9
14. Jain, V., Grossmann, I.E.: Algorithms for hybrid MILP/CP models for a class of optimization problems. INFORMS J. Comput. **13**(4), 258–276 (2001)
15. Sitek P., Wikarek J.: A hybrid method for modeling and solving constrained search problems. In: Proceedings of 2013 Federated Conference on Computer Science and Information Systems, FedCSIS, pp. 385–392 (2013)
16. Sitek, P., Wikarek, J.: A hybrid framework for the modelling and optimisation of decision problems in sustainable supply chain management. Int. J. Prod. Res. **53**(21), 6611–6628 (2015). doi:10.1080/00207543.2015.1005762
17. Sitek, P., Wikarek, J., Grzybowska, K.: A multi-agent approach to the multi-echelon capacitated vehicle routing problem. In: Corchado, J.M., Bajo, J., Kozlak, J., Pawlewski, P., Molina, J.M., Gaudou, B., Julian, V., Unland, R., Lopes, F., Hallenborg, K., Teodoro, P.G. (eds.) PAAMS 2014. CCIS, vol. 430, pp. 121–132. Springer, Heidelberg (2014)
18. Sitek P.: A hybrid CP/MP approach to supply chain modelling, optimization and analysis. In: Federated Conference on Computer Science and Information Systems, pp. 1385–1392 (2014)
19. Eclipse: Eclipse - The Eclipse Foundation open source community website (2015). www.eclipse.org. Accessed 4 May 2015
20. Lindo Systems INC: LINDO™ Software for Integer Programming, Linear Programming, Nonlinear Programming, Stochastic Programming, Global Optimization (2015). www.lindo.com. Accessed 4 May 2015
21. Relich, M.: Identifying relationships between eco-innovation and product success. In: Golinska, P., Kawa, A. (eds.) Technology Management for Sustainable Production and Logistics, pp. 173–192. Springer, Heidelberg (2015)

22. Sudo, Y., Kurihara, M., Mitamura, T.: Extending fuzzy constraint satisfaction problems. J. Adv. Comput. Intell. Intell. Inf. **10**(4), 465–471 (2006)
23. Grzybowska, K.: Selected activity coordination mechanisms in complex systems. In: Bajo, J., Hallenborg, K., Pawlewski, P., Botti, V., Sánchez-Pi, N., Duque Méndez, N.D., Lopes, F., Vicente, J. (eds.) PAAMS 2015 Workshops. CCIS, vol. 524, pp. 69–79. Springer, Heidelberg (2015). doi:10.1007/978-3-319-19033-4_6
24. Deniziak, R., Bąk, S., Czarnecki, R.: Synthesis of real-time cloud applications for internet of things. Turk. J. Electr. Eng. Comput. Sci. **7719**, 35–49 (2013)

# Supply Chain Logistics Platform as a Supply Chain Coordination Support

Katarzyna Grzybowska[1(✉)] and Brigita Gajšek[2]

[1] Chair of Production Engineering and Logistics, Faculty of Engineering Management,
Poznan University of Technology, Strzelecka 11, 60-965 Poznan, Poland
katarzyna.grzybowska@put.poznan.pl
[2] Faculty of Logistics, University of Maribor, Mariborska Cesta 7, 3000 Celje, Slovenia
brigita.gajsek@um.si

**Abstract.** Modern logistics platform paradigm positively effects development of enterprises. Over time several types of logistics platforms have developed. One of them is supply chain logistics platform, which is essential to reduce the overall cost of logistic activities between supply chain partners, to improve the overall efficiency of logistics and to integrate social resources. Superficially said, it is a general information exchange platform, which applies computer, internet and communication system, and other modern information technology [1]. With the purpose of integrating social resources, it reduces the threshold of the logistics informatization and provides all kinds of accurate, timely, shared information for each participant in logistics activities [2]. Logistics platforms represent a modern approach aimed towards fostering and facilitating logistics activities and business exchange with associated flows in a specific geographic area. We examined whether stakeholders of logistics system in various types of organizations in Slovenia and Poland understand information communication system and joint interactive portal as parts of supply chain's logistics platform. With a case study, we demonstrated that implementation of common information solution is a step on a way to contemporary and comprehensive logistics platform. Additionally, common information solution should not be simply equated with the concept of supply chain's logistics platform. Given the important role of IT solutions in the field of supply chains, this paper proposes a novel operation procedure for coordination of supply chain actions for validation and further research.

**Keywords:** Coordination · Communication · Information technology · Logistics platform · Supply chain

## 1 Introduction

Literature on supply chain management emphasises the importance of co-ordination mechanisms to manage logistics processes successfully across supply networks [3]. Coordination between agencies during multi-agency emergency responses, although a key issue, remains a neglected research area [4]. Coordination between the different agencies (enterprises) involved is a major challenge. We can recognize three alternative

© Springer International Publishing Switzerland 2016
J. Bajo et al. (Eds.): PAAMS 2016 Workshops, CCIS 616, pp. 61–72, 2016.
DOI: 10.1007/978-3-319-39387-2_6

perspectives: (1) single-person perspective, (2) team perspective, and (3) nexus-of-contract perspective of organization. According to the single-person perspective of organization, a system is managed by a single decision maker who has access to all information. The team perspective of organization complements the single-person perspective by highlighting the cooperative coordination among multiple parties. The team perspective underscores the existence of multiple parties who take different roles in the operation. Each party has limited information and action sets, so they need to communicate and coordinate their activities to achieve the global objective. The coordination takes place in full cooperation among the team members. By contrast, the nexus-of contract perspective of organization follows the tradition of agency theory [5] in which an organization is a nexus of contracts among self-interested "agents", each maximizing his or her personal objective [6].

This article provides a discussion of selected coordination mechanism of supply chain systems. We focus on coordination mechanism that can align the objectives of individual supply chain members.

The article consists of several parts. The first part discusses the most important issues regarding coordination theory. The second part discusses activity coordination problem in complex systems, multi-agent systems. In the third part, we present selected activity coordination mechanism and the Reference Model: the Electronic Bulletin Board (EBB) or the logistics platform (LP). In the next part we present concept of logistics platform. The fifth part is dedicated support the supply chain through logistics platform and Electronic Bulletin Board. The article is concluded with a summary.

## 2   Coordination Problems in the Supply Chain

Supply chains (SCs) are a system with "multiple actors". The supply chain is commonly seen as a collection of various types of companies (raw materials, production, trade, logistics, transport, etc.) working together to improve the flow of products, information and finance. As the words in the term indicate, the supply chain is a combination of its individual links in the process of supplying products (material/products and services) to the market [7]. SCs are complex systems, dynamic, dispersed and open. Those elements together with other factors (e.g. multiple subjects, independence of cooperating enterprises) determine difficulties in the field of management, or more broadly, of coordination of commonly take up and independently realized actions. The discussed systems are affected, as a whole, by a lack of internal rationality, unverified information and insufficient knowledge. The problem is also posed by uncertainty and a lack of precision [8, 9], indispensable in the realized projects and complex undertakings. Supply chain management (SCM) is defined as "the systemic, strategic coordination of the traditional business functions and the tactics across these business functions within a particular company and across businesses within the supply chain, for the purposes of improving the long term performance of the individual companies and the supply chain as a whole" [10].

Coordination defined as the process of managing dependencies among activities. Starting with the individual activity it is easily recognized that the industrial reality contains a multitude of various activities. When focusing solely on individual activities, these might seem to have a generic value, for example considering a production or exchange activity [11, 12]. Cooke [13], for example, defines SCM as "successful coordination and integration of all those activities associated with moving goods from the raw materials stage through to the end user, for sustainable competitive advantage. This includes activities like systems management, sourcing and procurement, production scheduling, order processing, inventory management, transportation, warehousing, and customer service" [13]. But the higher level of specialisation, standardisation and formalisation reduces the flexibility of the organizational structure [14, 15].

Multi-agent systems is a typical collective behavior in networked systems with a group of autonomous mobile agents [16–18]. Multi-agent systems heavily rely on the communication and cooperation between the involved agents. The socio-technical nature of supply chain problems, however, motivates an alternative modelling paradigm: agent-based models. The actions of each actor – represented as an agent – and the interactions between them are explicitly represented in such models, and in consequence the behaviour of the entire system emerges [19].

Agents to have certain properties and attributes, as follows [20]:

- **Autonomy.** An agent is autonomous and self-directed. An agent can function independently in its environment and in its interactions with other agents. When we refer to an agent's behavior, we refer to a general process that links the information the agent senses from its environment and interactions to its decisions and actions.
- **Modularity.** Agents are modular or self-contained. An agent is an identifiable, discrete entity with a set of characteristics or attributes, behaviors, and decision-making capability.
- **Sociality.** An agent is social, interacting with other agents.
- **Conditionality.** An agent has a state that varies over time. Just as a system has a state consisting of the collection of its state variables, an agent also has a state that represents its condition, defined by the essential variables associated with its current situation. An agent's state consists of a set or subset of its attributes and its behaviors. The state of an agent-based model is the collective states of all the agents along with the state of the environment. An agent's behaviors are conditioned on its state. As such, the richer the set of an agent's possible states, the richer the set of behaviors that an agent can have. Agents often have additional properties, which may or may not be considered as requisite properties for agency. An agent may have explicit goals that drive its behavior, not necessarily objectives to maximize as much as criteria against which to assess the effectiveness of its decision and actions. An agent may have the ability to learn and adapt its behaviors based on its experiences.

The division of the responsibilities between particular parties engaged in assuring safety [21].

# 3   Supply Chain Logistics Platform

The LP concept is one of the contemporary concepts in business strategies, which has attracted broader attention in the last decade. The Abrahamsson et al. [22] were probably the first scientists who proposed the definition of LPs. They used several terms in their definition which made it very broad and, as such, covers almost everything and touches on several areas of business [23]. Aldin and Stahre [24] revealed that an LP is a homogenous part of the logistics system, centrally controlled and designed by focal organizations, and is a resource-base for new marketing channel positions. Cambra and Ruiz [25] presented LP as a source of competitive advantage, but Gajšek and Rosi [23] stated that they do not reveal the stakeholders involved, the exact constituents and how to accomplish the implementation of the concept. Leal and Salas [26] defined an LP as a specialized area with the infrastructure and services required for co-modal transportation, with the added value of the products making use of the infrastructure. According to Váncza et al. [27] the main idea behind the concept is to provide ways to integrate information flows between partners in line with relevant system design architecture. The LP's definition focuses on the information visibility that is essential to streamlining SC operations. Almotairi [28] defined a model of integrated LP in connection with an area of research that has recently been the focus of studies – port logistics. He observed that the provision of distribution and value-added logistics activities within the gateway position of major seaports had become a source of competitive advantage and an important business model, and that an integrated LP is one of the strategies that aim to integrate sea/land interfaces with the inland logistics equation.

Generally, we can divide LPs into business (micro level) and regional (meso and macro level). Business LPs divide on company and supply chain's logistics platforms (SCLPs) [29]. Our focus will be on SCLPs, because they might form a solid frame for implementation of EBB.

We reviewed 23 peer reviewed scientific articles on all kind of LPs incurred between 1995 and 2015. Causally we have extracted the particularities of each LP type and the general characteristics of all [23]. Below we expose only the findings regarding SCLPs.

SCLP is developed and built for realization of clearly defined material flow between several companies forming SC but more often than not only one manages and controls events. This particular central SC player firstly defines SC logistics system, than develops the conceptual framework of LP and runs management and coordination mechanism. Defined logistics system comprises all or only a defined number of companies forming SC, organization and logistics processes that run between them. Because operation of management and coordination mechanism a set of private owned resources is developed and gathered. In doing so, some of sources can be more important or leading and will be developed before all other. As such, they will influence on development and design of the rest. In case of SC, we assume that IT resources can be the one of major impact. We will try to prove that bellow with case study.

One part of scientists emphasizes the importance of technical and infrastructural resources [25, 26, 30–34] in evolving set of resources and other part of researchers emphasizes the importance of informational resources [27, 28, 34] in evolving set of resources. Gajsek and Rosi [23] combine mentioned two research streams within the LP general definition, which includes all the resources necessary for the implementation of logistics activities in given logistics system. They proposed a general definition of LPs, which covers all definitions given above. They considered that each LP consists of the management and coordination mechanism for directing the development and operation of previously defined logistics system and consequently custom assembled or developed set of constituents that appears because of the previously mentioned management and coordination mechanism.

# 4    Case Study on Supply Chain Logistics Platform

To learn more about SCLPs' set of resources we considered a case from practice. We wanted to know what constitutes SCLP and if there is regarding to our assumption a specific resource of major impact on all other. More specifically, whether the information solutions are part of SCLP.

SC is built around successful European company that develops innovative engines und units. With around 4,000 employees they are one of the world's leading independent manufacturers of diesel engines. As a company with an international orientation, they are looking for qualified, high-performance suppliers all over the world.

Central player in SC has decided to deploy LP in order to optimise coordination between suppliers, logistics service providers and all of their dislocated units. Established service supports all parties participating in the supply chain with their work and expands their possibilities for controlling the logistics processes.

About the benefits of using LP senior vice president for logistics stated: "In our company we trust in LP as the tool for management of our 260 global suppliers and intermediaries, of which about 200 are working on LP. Currently runs more than 80 percent of all orders via LP in the cloud. Involving partners through the LP has led to greater oversight of the SC and optimizing processes. All freight units now arrive uniformly marked. We have less empty runs. Faxes and e-mails for operational work are rear. We managed to reduce logistics costs for 20,000 dollars per year. Furthermore, we approached to process mapping and standardization of processes, which will ultimately reduce waiting and unloading times. We also saved 1.5 million Euros, because we did not need to invest in new warehouses."

LP implementation was the solution that ultimately led the SC's central player to the realization of its strategy: communication with all suppliers in the same way from one single database, regardless of where their production capacity are located. The observed SC equates centrally managed LP with information system supporting SC logistics activities and connecting partners in order to supply production plants on cost-effective manner. At the same time, however, it tends to standardization and continuous improvement processes. The system also enables immediate detection of undesirable deviations in processes and requires immediate solving. Naming of the information system for cooperation between partners in SC with phrase LP has grown into a concept, which indicates much broader context than just IT solution. B2B business activities between SC partners base on modern IT solution, which the manufacturer names logistics platform. IT solution implementation interconnects SC companies and causally requires standardization of processes and use of by attributes comparable and compatible technical, technological and human resources, all of which together form the SCLP. IT solutions is like a first domino that overturns rest in a series.

Furthermore, SC partners tend with the implementation of SCLP (a kind of IT solution) to:

- Transparent monitoring of processes,
- Automated detection of incidents, delays, interruptions, cancellations, etc.,
- Capture the data required for analysis and reporting,
- Fair and transparent evaluation of suppliers and other companies in the SC,
- Detect bottlenecks in the process,
- Continuous improvement,
- Use data necessary for the simulation and prediction of events,
- Reduce administrative tasks, especially the number of double entries,
- Quick adding/removal of SC partners.

In the analyzed company, they also recognize some negative effects of transition to SCLP. They need to inform all new suppliers with IT solution. Later they have to monitor supplier's compliance with the safety requirements and provide 8/24/365 support to them. However, benefits of using the SCLP prevail over negative effects. Companies still do not trust completely to cloud solution. They feel dependent on IT solutions provider and are afraid of intrusions into information systems and fraud. The central company must find a way to quick introduction of new SC partner in SC operating and features of IT solution. Newcomer must be fully familiar with the system functionality to gain optimal operational costs.

## 5   ICT Support as Important Part of Supply Chain Logistics Platform

In this part, we will answer the question whether stakeholders of logistics system understand information communication system (ICT logistics support) and join interactive portal as parts of SCLP. If following quantitative study will give a positive answer, not only the case study above, this would mean that the development of new IT solutions has a great sense. In previous chapter we have showed that SCs can benefit a lot from a kind of IT support that contribute to the unification of working methods, shortening processing times and cuts costs. SCLP we described through theory review and case study as a mean for contemporary operation of logistics and transportation activities that require strong IT support.

The survey concerned itself with four types of stakeholder in Slovenia and Poland, these being [35]: logistics companies, production companies, branch associations/states agencies/chambers, and educational institutions. Slovenia represents an excellent research context for a survey on a practical understanding of the concept of LP. Whilst Poland is investing heavily in development, Slovenia is better at talking about it. When comparing both states' transport indicators in the UNECE region in 2010, a total of 14 times more t/km was carried out by road and by rail in Poland.

The questionnaire, excluding the demographics section, consists of several questions, with sub-questions. The answers were provided in the form of a five-point scale. The survey was web-based. The data were collected stepwise in Slovenia in November 2011 and Poland in April 2012, each over a three-week period, yielding a total of 184 completed surveys: 89 in Slovenia and 95 in Poland. The second question is concerned with the 12 basic constituents of LPs proposed in the general LP model [29] and their centrality to the concept in the eyes of stakeholders. 12 basic LP constituents are geographical position, business environment, traffic infrastructure, logistics infrastructure, logistics technological equipment, logistics technology, ICT logistics support, logistics specialists, logistics organisations, regulation, joint interactive portal and organized group of stakeholders. This question is composed of thirteen sub-questions, twelve being 'closed' and one 'open'. The latter allowed the entry of a constituent, which we might have overlooked. For this article, only two constituents are interesting, namely ICT logistics support and common interactive portal for shared marketing and information services. The key finding is that all proposed constituents are included in written and oral sources from which respondents informed themselves about SCLP. Respondents added no additional constituent.

Slovenian organizations had on average (Mean value 3.14) less strongly connected the basic constituent elements with LP in comparison with their Polish colleagues (Mean value 3.77). This can be associated with a lower level of familiarity with the concept and the resulting uncertainty in decision-making. Neither ICT logistics support nor joint interactive portal were not foremost and prevalent logistics platform constituents.

**Table 1.** Correlations between constituents and SCLP

| Constituents/A set of resources | SCLP |
| --- | --- |
| Geographical position | 0,157 |
| Business environment | 0,063 |
| Traffic infrastructure | 0,20 |
| Logistics infrastructure | .276* |
| Logistical technological equipment | −0,013 |
| Logistics technology | 0,033 |
| ICT logistics support | .346* |
| Logistics specialists | ,247* |
| Logistics organisations | 0,101 |
| Regulation | 0,079 |
| Joint interactive portal | −0,1 |
| An organized group of stakeholders | −0,118 |

SCLP – supply chain logistics platform
\* - significant at 0.05 (2-tailed)
\*\* - significant at 0.01 (2-tailed)

Bivariate correlation was used, namely the Spearman correlation coefficient, to verify correlations concluded from the literature review and case study between 12 proposed LP's constituents and areas in which LPs are implemented (company, supply chain, region, country, European Union). In the paper, we only report on the correlations between the 12 constituents and the scope of supply chain, Table 1.

Slovenian and Polish organizations perceive a weak link between SCLP and ICT logistics support (rs = 0.346, p < 0.05). Respondents do not observe a statistically significant correlation between SCLP and joint interactive portal for shared marketing and information services. Consequently, we can only partially confirm our guesses based on review of scientific articles and case study. We can once more conclude that ICT support to logistics activities is the important part of SCLP but not the only one. In our opinion, it is not reasonable to equate SCLP with any kind of IT solution or model. However, ICT support to logistics activities is an essential part of SCLP, according to which the rest of constituents is selected and profiled.

In addition, Slovenian and Polish organizations perceive a weak link between SCLP and logistics infrastructure (rs = 0.276, p < 0.05). Logistics infrastructure comprises all kind of real estate used for logistics purposes. Respondents also observed a weak link between SCLP and logistics specialists (rs = 0.247, p < 0.05). Human resources with logistics competences are indispensable for the establishment of the management and coordination mechanism for directing the development and operation of previously defined logistics system. They will be able to design and implement needed IT solutions and to assemble or develop a set of custom LP constituents.

Respondents did not observe any other statistically significant correlation between SCLP area and the constituents proposed.

## 6    Support Mechanisms for Coordination – Reference Model: The Electronic Bulletin Board, Logistics Platform

We suggest that the use of the Electronic Bulletin Board is maintaining the coordination and supervision of all of the works in two variant. Large organisations, particularly transnational ones build their own models, which are used as benchmark tools [36, 37] and complementarity of processes [38, 39]. In analyzing first variant, one can indicate the so-called distance – the distance between one cell and the remaining ones. In the presented example, Fig. 1(A) presents 5 enterprises (cells) and 4 channels (connections). Cells A and E are in the worst situation. They communicate directly with the sole closest cell. In the second coordination variant (Concentrated nature), cell D, who is the main ordering party, has the most advantageous position, having the full coordination of the activities and control over the completion of the order (Fig. 1(B)).

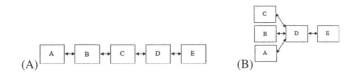

**Fig. 1.**  (A) Orderly nature, (B) Concentrated nature [40]

The presentation of processes in the form of a map inherently reflects the steady-state (e.g., static behavior) of a process [42]. Execution of the model provides measures of system performance under varying conditions that provide the basis for analysis that ultimately supports decisions and actions. Of course, the quality of the results depends on the quality of the input – the definition and specification for the model [43]. The applied mechanism of coordination of actions (Concentrated nature), called "Approving with application of an Electronic Bulletin Board (EBB)", encompasses serial presence of two roles - the commissioner (receiver) and the contractor (supplier). It is a task role, assumed consciously, regarding the performed actions, and resulting from the ascribed task. The same enterprise may (regarding the business processes that take place), play a role of both a supplier and a receiver. This results from the complexities of the actions realized within the SC. The commissioner (of the first degree), decomposes the primary requests into sub-requests. They also allocate those sub-requests to the verified contracting parties that they cooperate with. What is more, they use their own (most often closed) database of subcontractors and a so called EBB [41]. The role of the contractor is complementary towards the role of the commissioner. They perform sub-requests directly or commission the task to another entity. They change their role into the commissioner of a lower rank (second degree).

## 7    Conclusions and Future Works

SCs are systems with multiple completely different actors who need to communicate with each other. They are complex systems, dynamic, dispersed and open. Those elements together with other factors, like multiple subjects, independence of cooperating enterprises, determine difficulties in the field of management, or more broadly, of coordination of commonly take up and independently realized actions. Modern communication is electronic, supported by computers and software by minimizing the need to integrate human.

The LP concept is one of the contemporary concepts in business strategies that often appears in scientific literature as a magic bullet that can solve majority of inter-organizational problems. Although the scientific literature generally equates SCLP to IT solutions and models this is not a case. With the survey, we could confirm that ICT support to logistics activities is the important part of SCLP but unfortunately, it is not the only one. Slovenian and Polish organizations perceive also a weak links between SCLP and firstly the logistics infrastructure and secondly the logistics specialists. In our opinion, it is not reasonable to equate SCLP with any kind of IT solution or model. However, ICT support to logistics activities is an essential part of SCLP, according to which the rest of constituents is selected and profiled.

With a case study, we demonstrated that information solution is a first part of each contemporary comprehensive logistics platform, and that it should not be simply equated with the concept of supply chain's logistics platform. Given the important role of IT solutions in the field of SC, this paper proposes a novel operation procedure for coordination of SC actions for validation and further research.

The research results regarding the assessment and the modelling of factors impacting the diverse cooperation and integration of the companies cooperating within the multi-agent systems, indicate that sharing information and coordination are the most important. A good logistics information platform can not only integrate the material flow and the information flow together, but also play key role in the aspects of optimizing resources allocation and integrating logistics resources [44]. With the development of logistics information platform, the intelligent business and financial services are needed to expand new functions to meet the needs for a certain custom [45]. Moreover, building a competitive edge over market competitors entails creating propitious internal conditions [46].

**Acknowledgement.** Presented research works are carried out under the project – WIZ - DS 2016 Poznan University of Technology.

# References

1. Xu, L., Haijun, M., Yumin, L.: Changzhou Modern Logistics Development Plan. College of Transportation, Southeast University, Nanjing (2002)
2. Xu, L., Song-zheng, Z., Wei Yang, J.: Based on regional research capabilities logistics information platform architecture. J. Inf. **7**, 9–12 (2008)
3. Romano, P.: Co-ordination and integration mechanisms to manage logistics processes across supply networks. J. Purchasing Supply Manag. **9**, 119–134 (2003). doi:10.1016/S1478-4092(03)00008-6
4. Chen, R., Sharman, R., Rao, H.R., Upadhyaya, S.J.: Coordination in emergency response management. Commun. ACM **51**(5), 66–73 (2008)
5. Jensen, M., Meckling, W.: Theory of firm: managerial behavior, agency cost, and capital structure. J. Financ. Econ. **3**, 305–360 (1976)
6. Whang, S.: Coordination in operations: a taxonomy. J. Oper. Manag. **12**(3–4), 413–422 (1995)
7. Sitek, P.: A hybrid CP/MP approach to supply chain modelling, optimization and analysis. In: Federated Conference on Computer Science and Information Systems (FedCSIS), pp. 1345–1352 (2014). doi:10.15439/2014F89
8. Relich, M.: Identifying relationships between eco-innovation and product success. In: Golinska, P., Kawa, A. (eds.) Technology Management for Sustainable Production and Logistics, pp. 173–192. Springer, Heidelberg (2015)
9. Relich, M.: Using ERP database for knowledge acquisition: a project management perspective. In: Proceedings of International Scientific Conference on Knowledge for Market Practice, Olomouc, Czech Republic, pp. 263–269 (2013)
10. Grzybowska, K., Awasthi, A., Hussain, M.: Modeling enablers for sustainable logistics collaboration integrating Canadian and Polish perspectives. In: Ganzha, M., Maciaszek, L., Paprzycki, M. (eds.) Proceedings of the 2014 Federated Conference on Computer Science and Information Systems, ACSIS, vol. 2, pp. 1311–1319 (2014). doi:10.15439/2014F90
11. Bankvall, L.: Activity coordination from a firm perspective-towards a framework. In: Proceedings IMP-Conference in Uppsala, Sweden (2008)
12. Kałkowska, J., Kozlov, A.V.: Decision making process for the knowledge based enterprise: Fuzzy sets theory application to the strategic management. In: Proceedings of the International Conference on Information Systems Architecture and Technology, pp. 135–146 (2015)

13. Cooke, J.A.: In this issue. Supply Chain Management Review, 1 (1), 3 (1997)
14. Pawlowski, E.: Size of an enterprise and organizational innovations. In: Proceedings of the 5th International Conference on Applied Human Factors and Ergonomics (2014)
15. Pawlowski, E., Pawlowski, K.: A framework of organizational structure designing for Agile Enterprises. In: AHFE International Conference (2008)
16. Sitek, P., Wikarek, J.: A hybrid method for modeling and solving constrained search problems. In: Federated Conference on Computer Science and Information Systems (FedCSIS 2013), pp. 385–392 (2013)
17. Cao, Y., Ren, W.: Distributed coordinated tracking with reduced interaction via avaiable structure approach. IEEE Trans. Autom. Control 57(1), 33–48 (2012)
18. Pawlewski, P.: DES/ABS approach to simulate warehouse operations. In: Bajo, J., Hallenborg, K., Pawlewski, P., Botti, V., Sánchez-Pi, N., Duque Méndez, N.D., Lopes, F., Vicente, J. (eds.) PAAMS 2015 Workshops. CCIS, vol. 524, pp. 115–125. Springer, Heidelberg (2015)
19. van Dama, K.H., Adhitya, A., Srinivasan, R., Lukszo, Z.: Critical evaluation of paradigms for modelling integrated supply chains. Comput. Chem. Eng. 33(10), 1710–1726 (2009)
20. Macal, Ch.M., North, M.J.: Introductory tutorial: agent-based modeling and simulation. In: Jain, S., Creasey, R.R., Himmelspach, J., White, K.P., Fu, M. (eds.) Proceedings of the 2011 Winter Simulation Conference. Institute of Electrical and Electronics Engineers, Inc, Piscataway, New Jersey, pp. 1456–1469 (2011)
21. Mrugalska, B., Arezes, P.M.: An investigation of safety design practices of metal machines. Work: J. Prev. Assess. Rehabil. 51(4), 747–755 (2015)
22. Abrahamsson, M., Aldin, N., Stahre, F.: Logistics platforms for improved strategic flexibility. Int. J. Logistics: Res. Appl. 6(3), 85–106 (2003)
23. Gajsek, B., Rosi, B.: Stakeholder differences in the understanding of inter-organizational concept content as a risk factor: the case for a logistics platform. Int. J. Logistics Manag. 26(1), 107–127 (2015)
24. Aldin, N., Stahre, F.: Electronic commerce, marketing channels and logistics platforms – a wholesaler perspective. Eur. J. Oper. Res. 144, 270–279 (2003)
25. Cambra, F.J., Ruiz, B.R.: Advantages of intermodal logistics platforms: insights from a Spanish platform. Supply Chain Manag.: Int. J. 14(6), 418–421 (2009)
26. Leal, E., Pérez Salas, G.: Logistic platforms: conceptual elements and the role of the public sector. In: UN ECLAC Bulletin FAL - Facilitation of Trade and Transport in Latin America and the Caribbean, issue 274, no. 6, pp. 1–9 (2009)
27. Váncza, J., Egri, P., Karnok, D.: Planning in concert: a logistics platform for production networks. Int. J. Comput. Integr. Manuf. 23(4), 297–307 (2010)
28. Almotairi, B.: Integrated logistics platform – the context of the port relational exchanges and systematic integration. Thesis for the degree of Doctor of philosophy, Department of Technology Management and Economics. Chalmers University of Technology, Göteborg (2012)
29. Gajsek, B.: Logistics platforms in theory and practice. Faculty of Logistics, University of Maribor, Celje (2014)
30. Lin, C.Y., Ho, Y.H.: RFID technology adoption and supply chain performance: an empirical study in China's logistics industry. Supply Chain Manag.: Int. J. 14(5), 369–378 (2009)
31. Sanchez, O., Villalobos, J.R.: Design of a logistics platform for the distribution of fresh produce. In: The INFORMS Annual Meeting 2007, Seattle, WA, 4–7 November 2007
32. Nunez-Carballosa, A., Guitart-Tarres, L.: Third-party logistics providers in Spain. Ind. Manag. Data Sys. 111(8), 1156–1172 (2011)
33. Mangan, J., Lalwani, C.: Port-centric logistics. Int. J. Logistics Manag. 19(1), 29–41 (2008)

34. Lieb, R., Bentz, B.A.: The North American third party logistics industry in 2004: the provider CEO perspective. Int. J. Phys. Distrib. Logistics Manag. **35**(8), 595–611 (2005)
35. Gajšek, B., Grzybowska, K.: Across-county contextual comparison of the understanding of the term logistics platform in practice. Res. Logistics Prod. **3**(2), 85–108 (2013)
36. Butlewski, M., Misztal, A., Jasiulewicz-Kaczmarek, M., Janik, S.: Ergonomic and work safety evaluation criteria of process excellence in the foundry industry. Metalurgija **53**, 701–704 (2014)
37. Górny, A.: The elements of work environment in the improvement process of quality management system structure. In: Advances in Human Factors, Ergonomics, and Safety in Manufacturing and Service Industries, pp. 599–606 (2011)
38. Kałkowska, J., Włodarkiewicz-Klimek, H.: The susceptibility of organizations' potential on identifying the opportunities in the knowledge based-economy. In: 2015 10th International Workshop on Robot Motion and Control (RoMoCo). IEEE Conference Publications, pp. 207–212 (2015). http://ieeexplore.ieee.org, doi:10.1109/RoMoCo.2015.7219736
39. Mrugalska, B., Akielaszek-Witczak, A., Aubrun, C.: Towards product robust quality control with sequential D-optimum inputs design. Chem. Eng. Trans. **43**, 2137–2142 (2015). doi:10.3303/CET1543357
40. Grzybowska, K.: Selected activity coordination mechanisms in complex systems. In: Bajo, J., Hallenborg, K., Pawlewski, P., Botti, V., Sánchez-Pi, N., Duque Méndez, N.D., Lopes, F., Vicente, J. (eds.) PAAMS 2015 Workshops. CCIS, vol. 524, pp. 69–79. Springer, Heidelberg (2015)
41. Grzybowska, K.: Reference models of selected action coordination mechanisms in the supply chain. LogForum **11**(2), 151–158 (2015). doi:10.17270/J.LOG.2015.2.3
42. Pawlewski, P.: Multimodal approach to modeling of manufacturing processes. Procedia CIRP **17**, 716–720 (2014). Variety Management in Manufacturing — Proceedings of the 47th CIRP Conference on Manufacturing Systems
43. Greenwood, A., Pawlewski, P., Bocewicz, G.: A conceptual design tool to facilitate simulation model development: Onject flow diagram. In: Pasupathy, R., Kim, S.-H., Tolk, A., Hill, R., Kuhl, M.E. (eds.) Proceedings of the 2013 Winter Simulation Conference (2013)
44. Jijun, Ch., Shiyu, G., Fudon, Z.: Research on the development prospects for logistics public information platform. Logistics Technol. **1**, 128–131 (2010)
45. Jie, Z., Bin-Bin, F., Heng-Liang, T., Chun-Lin, Z.: A research on normalized construction of logistics information platform. In: International Conference on Management Science and Management Innovation, pp. 638–643 (2014)
46. Górny, A.: Ergonomics aspects of CRS in system shaping the quality of work environment. In: Advances in Social and Organizational Factors, pp. 541–550 (2012)

# A Multi-agent Framework for Cost Estimation of Product Design

Marcin Relich[1(✉)] and Pawel Pawlewski[2]

[1] Faculty of Economics and Management, University of Zielona Gora, Zielona Gora, Poland
m.relich@wez.uz.zgora.pl
[2] Faculty of Engineering Management, Poznan University of Technology, Poznan, Poland
pawel.pawlewski@put.poznan.pl

**Abstract.** This paper presents the use of a multi-agent framework for evaluating parameters of new products and estimating cost of product design. Companies often develop many new product projects simultaneously. A limited budget of research and development imposes selection of the most promising projects. The evaluation of new product projects requires cost estimation and involves many agents that analyse the customer requirements and information acquired from an enterprise system, including the fields of sales and marketing, research and development, and manufacturing. The model of estimating product design cost is formulated in terms of a constraint satisfaction problem. The illustrative example presents the use of a fuzzy neural network to identify the relationships and estimate cost of product design.

**Keywords:** Multi-agent system · Fuzzy neural network · Constraint programming · New product development · Decision support system

## 1 Introduction

Decreasing product life cycles, increasing variety of products, and quick adjustment to market trends require the successful new product development (NPD) that is one of the most important factors in maintaining company's competitiveness. New product success depends on customer satisfaction that is related to utility, quality and price of a product [1–3]. Incorporating customer requirements in a new product incur expenditures during the NPD phases such as product design, prototype manufacturing and testing. The expenditure budget in research and development (R&D) is often limited, and company has to select the most promising NPD projects according to the criteria such as the expected profitability and R&D cost of a new product. Consequently, cost estimation for the NPD projects is needed.

The product design phase includes design reusability and engineering design, and it precedes phases such as product manufacturing and commercialisation. The poor product design raises many categories of cost relates to special equipment or modifications, inefficient assembly, excessive part proliferation, difficulties with part fabrication and product reliability, and finally, customer dissatisfaction [4, 5].

© Springer International Publishing Switzerland 2016
J. Bajo et al. (Eds.): PAAMS 2016 Workshops, CCIS 616, pp. 73–84, 2016.
DOI: 10.1007/978-3-319-39387-2_7

Today's enterprise information systems support the user in managing different phases of the NPD process, and also register and store the performance of the previous NPD projects (e.g. customer requirements, design parameters, product manufacturing). More and more companies are using solutions such as customer relationship management (CRM), computer-aided design (CAD), computer-aided engineering (CAE), computer-aided manufacturing (CAM), and enterprise resource planning (ERP) system. The data stored in an enterprise system can be used to identify the key factors influencing cost of a particular phase of the NPD process, and finally, improve the performance of the current NDP projects and the product success.

Product design involves many individuals and groups, including customers, analysts, project managers, R&D employees, chief marketing, production officers, etc. The product design process can be supported through an integrated business information system that combines the different agents and enables their communication. A multi-agent approach can replace the conventional centralized systems (for manufacturing, product design etc.) with a network of agents that are endowed with a local view of its environment and the ability to respond locally to that environment. As a result, the overall system performance is not globally planned, but emerges through the dynamic interactions between agents in real time [6].

Despite increasing popularity and applications of agent-based technology in the business domain, there is still a lack of unifying framework that would used the multi-agent paradigm to cost estimation of product design. This study aims to develop an agent-based framework for estimating cost of product design providing a foundation for conceptual analysis. The proposed multi-agent system includes client agent, marketing agent, research and development agent and data mining agent that identify variables suspected of significant impact on the cost of past products. Relationships between the cost of past products and variables influencing the cost are sought with the use of a fuzzy neural network that is able to discovered complex nonlinear relations and is suitable tool for estimating the cost.

The cost estimation model is formulated in term of a constraint satisfaction problem (CSP) as a set of variables, their domains, and constraints linking and limiting the variables. CSP can be treated as a knowledge base that includes the identified patterns and expert knowledge, and enables formulating routine questions such as what is the cost of product design, what is the most promising NPD project portfolio, or what values should have the parameters of a NPD project to fulfil the cost expectations. Knowledge base formulated as CSP can be effectively implemented in constraint programming environment that is an emergent software technology for a declarative CSP description and can serve as a pertinent framework to develop a decision support system [7, 8].

The remaining sections of this paper are organised as follows: Sect. 2 presents the use of multi-agent approaches in new product development. Section 3 presents a model of cost estimation of product design in terms of constraint satisfaction problem. The proposed multi-agent framework for evaluating parameters of new products and estimating the cost of product design is shown in Sect. 3. An illustrative example of the proposed approach is presented in Sect. 4. Finally, some concluding remarks are contained in Sect. 5.

## 2    Multi-agent Systems in New Product Development

Multi-agent systems (MAS) are systems with multiple agents and are suitable for complex problems that have alternative problem solving techniques, involve reasoning with multiple models at different levels of abstraction and representations, and usually involve distributed knowledge sources [9]. MAS are intelligent distributed approach suited for applications that are modular, complex, and changeable, for example, in product design. These systems have capabilities such as autonomy, integration, reactivity and flexibility, and they are an emerging sub-field of artificial intelligence that is concerned with a society of agents interacting in order to solve a common problem [10]. The paradigm of MAS provides a very suitable architecture for a design and implementation of integrative business information systems. The complex information systems development can be supported with the use of agent-based technology in the context of natural decomposition, abstraction and flexibility of management for organisational structure changes [11].

Agent technology is a result of convergence of many technologies within computer science such as object-oriented programming, distributed computing and computational intelligence [12]. Recently, an increasing number of approaches related to computational intelligence, including neural networks and fuzzy logic has been used to multi-agent applications. For instance, the artificial neural networks have been used to the output regulation problem of the nonlinear multi-agent systems [13], create a machine agent who determines the appropriate machine in order to fulfil clients' requirements [14], form a classifier agent team [15], MAS that incorporates a case-based reasoning system and automates the business control process [16], or create a multi-agent identifier in order to identify the dynamics of the plant [17].

The use of fuzzy logic-based approaches in the context of MAS includes the fields such as modelling the controller that regulates the number of agents in MAS [18], designing fuzzy model for supply chain modelling based on agents [19], developing the agent-based negotiation process for e-commerce [20], or making decision rules [21]. There are also hybrid approaches based on fuzzy neural network structures that can be used to intelligent task planning and action selection in MAS [22] or modelling the controller in multi-agents [23].

Design is a complex knowledge discovery process in which information and knowledge derives from various sources. Complex design combines automated software components with human decision makers. Software agents provide the necessary support for keeping humans in the loop, and multi-agent framework combines various sources of information and reasoning [24]. The use of the MAS paradigm in the context of knowledge management includes tasks such as [25]: knowledge search, acquisition, analysis and classification from diverse data sources; information given to human and computing networks once usable knowledge is ready to be consulted; negotiation on knowledge integration or exclusion into the system; explanation of the quality and reliability which are related to the system integrated knowledge; and learning progressively all along the knowledge management process.

Product design strongly impact on assembly planning enabling reduction of manufacturing cost and enhancing production efficiency and product quality. Zha [26] presented advantages of a multi-agent framework for developing the integrated design and assembly planning system. Chu et al. [27] considered the effectiveness of multi-agent technologies to implement a collaborative three-dimensional design system. A multi-agent system has also been used to identify the variables influencing the product success and select portfolio of new product development project [28].

Knowledge acquisition in the field of new product development is of significant importance for a contemporary organisation taking into account potential increment of technology and infrastructure. As in the knowledge discovery process is not possible to eliminate a human dimension, a multi-agents approach seems to be a suitable framework to model the problem of identifying a set of variables influencing the cost of product design and evaluating the parameters of a new product. This type of information and knowledge is needed to estimate the cost of product design, and support the project managers in selecting the most promising NPD project portfolio and conducting what-if analysis.

## 3    Model of Estimating Product Design Cost

Specifications of the past NPD projects, including design parameters, product portfolios, and customer requirements are registered and stored in an enterprise information system that includes e.g. CAD, CRM and ERP system. If new product development is related to slight modification of previous products, then enterprise database may be used to identify the factors influencing the cost of designing previous products, and estimating the cost of a new design. The presented model is formulated in terms of CSP and consists of a set of decision variables, their domains, and the constraints that refer to the company's resources and performance indicators. The model description encompasses the limitations of a company, parameters of new products and a set of routine queries formulated in the framework of CSP. The structure of the constraint satisfaction problem may be described in the following form [29]:

$$CSP = ((V, D), C)$$

where:

- $V$ is a finite set of variables,
- $D$ is a finite set of discrete domains of variables,
- $C$ is a finite set of constraints.

The presented model of estimating product design cost contains the following variables:

- Number of interviewed clients to survey client's requirements
- Number of client's requirements for a new product
- Number of client's requirements translated into product specification
- Number of ideas for a new product
- Number of components in a new product
- Number of modified components in a new product
- Number of project team members

The constraints include the total number of team members directly involved in a NPD project $C_{1,t}$ and financial means $C_{2,t}$ in the $t$-th time unit ($t = 0, 1,\ldots, T$). The decision criterion for product portfolio selection is minimisation of the cost of product design by the given constraints.

The constraint satisfaction problem can be considered in the context of a knowledge base that is a platform for query formulation and obtaining answers [7, 30]. The model formulation in terms of CSP integrates technical parameters, available resources, identified patterns (rules) and user requirements in the form of knowledge base, and facilitates the development of a decision support system. The problem solution is related to seeking the answer to the following questions:

• What is the product design cost and what products should be selected to the product portfolio to obtain the minimal cost of NPD projects by a fixed amount of resources?
• What values should have the parameters of NPD projects to fulfil the cost expectations?

Constraints satisfaction problems can be solved with the use of constraint programming that seems to suit very well for modelling decision problems [31]. Constraint programming techniques have embedded ways to solve CSP with greatly reduction of the amount of search needed [32]. This reduces the processing time of calculations, what is especially important for extensive search space, and it is sufficient to solve many practical problems such as supply chain problem [33–35] or scheduling problem [36, 37].

A multi-agent approach can be successfully used to solve constraint satisfaction problems, for example, $n$-queen problems and coloring problems. In solving a CSP with this approach, each agent can represent a variable and its position corresponds to a value assignment for the variable. The environment for the whole multi-agent system contains all the possible domain values for the problem. The conducted research shows that the performance of a multi-agent approach in solving CSPs for approximate solution is time-efficient [38].

# 4   The Proposed Multi-agent System for Estimating Product Design Cost

The design parameters of past products are routinely registered and stored in an enterprise information system. The big amount of data and easiness of data retrieval from an enterprise system increases an opportunity to acquire valuable information, and finally, improve cost estimation of product design. To automate the process of analyzing huge amount of data and discovering nontrivial and potentially useful patterns, data mining techniques are used. One of data mining techniques is a fuzzy neural network that can identify complex nonlinear relationships and is a suitable tool for modelling, simulating, and estimating [3].

In the case of product customization, cost estimation of product design can be based on information obtained from customers and the parameters of past products. The product design process can be divided into a few sub-processes, such as identification of the customer requirements, seeking the relationships between different variables suspected of the impact on the cost of NPD projects, evaluation of NPD projects, and selection of the most promising NPD portfolio. To successful performance, these sub-processes require cooperation and communication between the agents involved. Figure 1 illustrates a multi-agent system for estimating cost of product design.

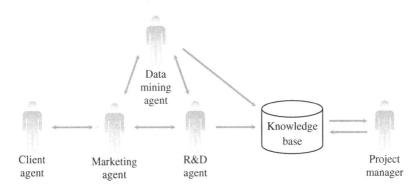

**Fig. 1.** Multi-agent system for estimating product design cost

In the phase of identification of the customer requirements, a marketing agent communicates with customers to investigate their needs for a new product. In the next phase, a marketing agent communicates with an R&D agent to specify the customer requirements for a new product. An R&D agent determines the expected time of new product development and the range of the customer requirements translated into product specification, and sends these parameters to a marketing agent who in turn investigates customer acceptance of a new product. A data mining (DM) agent identifies variables suspected of significant impact on the cost of past products and sends the requests of the expected values of these variables for a new product to a marketing agent and an R&D agent. Finally, an R&D agent and DM agent store the identified rules in knowledge base that is used to estimate the cost of new products, conduct what-if analysis on the basis of the parameters specified by the project manager, and select the most promising NPD portfolio. Apart from rules, knowledge base stores the facts related to the constraints such as the NPD project budget, a number of project team members, the expected time-to-market for a new product.

The agents have the various objectives and constraints that concern the specific area of the product design process. Consequently, the cooperation between the agents is needed to adjust their local tasks and improve the estimating quality of product design cost. Table 1 presents an example of information that is specified in the messages between the agents.

The negotiation algorithm between a marketing agent and R&D agent is executed until the specification of a new product meets the customer requirements in the agreed range. The customer requirements are verified in the context of available technology and the cost that the company can incur to obtain the required materials, components and technology.

**Table 1.** An example of message description

| Item | Description |
|------|-------------|
| Sender | Marketing agent |
| Receiver | R&D agent |
| Message type | Product design specification |
| Message task | Specifying customer requirements |
| Deadline | Time by which the R&D agent has to respond |
| Content | The description of the customer needs and requirements for a new product |

Relationships between the cost of previous products and variables influencing the cost are sought with the use of a fuzzy neural network that includes advantages of both neural networks (e.g. learning abilities, optimization abilities and connectionist structures) and fuzzy systems (e.g. if-then reasoning, simplicity of incorporating expert knowledge). A fuzzy neural network identifies if-then rules that are further used to cost estimation of product design. In this study, the adaptive neuro-fuzzy inference system (ANFIS) has been used. The parameters of a new product (values of input variables) are specified by a marketing agent and R&D agent and led to the ANFIS that estimates the cost of product design. As the NPD cost is criterion of product portfolio selection, the most promising set of the NPD projects can be determined.

In this study, the knowledge base is formulated as a constraint satisfaction problem that can be effectively implemented in constraint programming (CP). CP is an emergent software technology for a declarative CSP description and can serve as a pertinent framework to develop a decision support system [7, 8]. The next section illustrates the use of a fuzzy neural network to identify relationships among data, develop knowledge base and estimate the cost, and the use of CP to seek the admissible solutions according to a user request.

## 5 Example

An illustrative example consists of two parts. The first part concerns the use of the ANFIS to identify relationships and estimate the NPD cost. In turn, the second part illustrates the use of constraint programming to seek the possible solutions (if there are any) for the constraints specified by the user.

### 5.1 Cost Estimation with the Use of ANFIS

Cost of product design (CD) has been estimated on the basis of the following variables: number of interviewed clients (CS), number of client's requirements for a new product (CR), number of client's requirements translated into product specification (CRT), number of ideas for a new product (INP), number of components in a new product (CNP), number of changed components in a new product (CCP), and number of project team members (PTM). The ANFIS uses data of previous projects and identifies the relationships (in the form of if-then rules) between input variables and the cost of past product.

In studies, the ANFIS has been learnt according to subtractive clustering method implemented in the Matlab® software, with the following parameters: range of influence – 0.3, squash factor – 1.25, accept ratio – 0.5, reject ratio – 0.15. The membership functions are specified for each input variables and the identified if-then rules that are further used to estimate the cost of product design. Figure 2 illustrates the membership functions of 10 rules identified by the ANFIS.

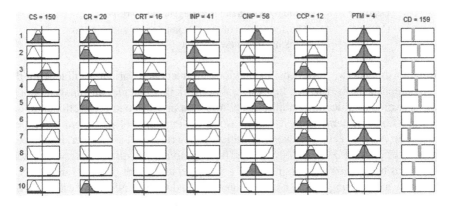

**Fig. 2.** The use of ANFIS to cost estimation of product design

The forecast of product design cost is calculated after inputting the expected parameters of a new product to the learnt ANFIS. The values of two input variables (number of interviewed clients and number of client's requirements for a new product) are specified by the marketing agent. In turn, the values of five input variables (number of client's requirements translated into product specification, number of ideas for a new product, number of components in a new product, number of changed components in a new product, and number of project team members) are specified by the R&D agent. In the presented example, the forecast of product design cost (CD) equals 159 monetary units (m.u.) for the following input variables: CS – 150, CR – 20, CRT – 16, INP – 41, CNP – 58, CCP – 12, and PTM – 4. The identified rules are stored in knowledge base and can be further used to feasibility study of the NPD projects and selecting the most promising projects for development.

### 5.2    Fulfilling Cost Expectations with the Use of CP

If the NPD cost exceeds the project budget, the project manager can need information about the conditions to fulfil cost expectations. In this case, such values of input variables are sought that fulfil the project budget. Let us assume that the budget of product development is limited to 100 m.u., and the range of the selected variables is as follows: CNP from 45 to 75, CCP from 8 to 18, and PTM from 3 to 6. A large number of admissible solutions imposes the use of techniques that enable the reduction of the amount of search needed, such as constraint programming. The considered problem has been implemented in the Oz Mozart programming environment that includes constraint programming paradigms. The number of admissible solutions equals 10 instances by the minimal cost of product design reaches 93 m.u. Figure 3 presents the explored search tree for the considered case.

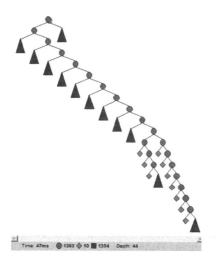

**Fig. 3.** The use of CP to seek admissible solutions

The search tree illustrates choice nodes as purple circles and solution nodes as green diamonds. The fully explored subtrees, which do not contain solution nodes, are presented as a single red triangle.

# 6    Conclusion

The new product development process involves many agents in the field of customers, marketing, research and development, manufacturing, etc. As in new product development is required knowledge acquisition from the different local areas and communication between these areas, the use of a multi-agent framework seems to be a pertinent framework to evaluate the parameters of product design, and finally, estimate its cost. The proposed approach takes a global perspective concerning product design and presents a mechanism of interaction between agents. As an enterprise information system stores the data related to the various areas of business, including customer requirements for a new product and specification of the past NPD projects, enterprise database can be used to seek the relationships between the cost and variables suspected of influencing cost. In this study, a fuzzy neural network has been used to identify potential relationships that can also be used to feasibility study and selecting the most promising NPD project portfolio.

The characteristics of the presented approach includes the use of expert domain knowledge to select variables used in the knowledge discovery process, fuzzy neural network to seek the relationships and their description in the form of if-then rules, and framework of constraint satisfaction problem to specify a knowledge base. This knowledge base includes the facts (e.g. R&D budget), rules identified by fuzzy neural network or/and an data mining agent, and it allows the project managers to obtain an answer to the routine questions such as what is the cost of product design, what is the most promising set of NPD projects or what values should have the parameters of NPD projects to fulfil the cost expectations. The use of constraint programming environment solves CSP in an effective way and enables creating an interactive task-oriented decision support tool.

Advantages of the presented approach can be considered in the context of placing product design in a global perspective that involves the external (customers) and internal (employees) actors of the NPD process, the low effort of data retrieval to analysis because the data are stored in an enterprise system, the possibility of sensitivity and what-if analysis, as well as the selection of the most promising product portfolio according to the project manager's preferences. Drawbacks of using the proposed approach are connected with constructing the stop criterion in the negotiation algorithm between client and marketing agent, collecting enough amounts of data of the past similar NPD projects, and specifying several parameters to build and learn a fuzzy neural network.

**Acknowledgements.** Presented research works are partially carried out under the project – status activities of Faculty of Engineering Management DS 2016 Poznan University of Technology.

# References

1. Cooper, R., Edgett, S.: Maximizing productivity in product innovation. Res. Technol. Manag. **51**(2), 47–58 (2008)
2. Spalek, S.: Improving industrial engineering performance through a successful project management office. Eng. Econ. **24**(2), 88–98 (2013)
3. Relich, M., Bzdyra, K.: Knowledge discovery in enterprise databases for forecasting new product success. In: Jackowski, K., et al. (eds.) IDEAL 2015. LNCS, vol. 9375, pp. 121–129. Springer, Heidelberg (2015). doi:10.1007/978-3-319-24834-9_15
4. Ulrich, K.T., Eppinger, S.D.: Product Design and Development. McGraw-Hill, Boston (2011)
5. Anderson, D.M.: Design for Manufacturability: Optimizing Cost, Quality and Time-to-Market. CIM Press, Cambria (2001)
6. Yan, Y., Kuphal, T., Bode, J.: Application of multiagent systems in project management. Int. J. Prod. Econ. **68**, 185–197 (2000)
7. Bocewicz, G., Nielsen, I., Banaszak, Z.: Iterative multimodal processes scheduling. Annu. Rev. Control **38**(1), 113–122 (2014)
8. Relich, M., Swic, A., Gola, A.: A knowledge-based approach to product concept screening. In: Omatu, S., et al. (eds.) Distributed Computing and Artificial Intelligence. AISC, vol. 373, pp. 341–348. Springer, Heidelberg (2016)
9. Madhusudan, T.: An agent-based approach for coordinating product design workflows. Comput. Ind. **56**, 235–259 (2005)
10. Fazel Zarandi, M.H., Ahmadpour, P.: Fuzzy agent-based expert system for steel making process. Expert Syst. Appl. **36**, 9539–9547 (2009)
11. Kishore, R., Zhang, H., Ramesh, R.: Enterprise integration using the agent paradigm: foundations of multi-agent-based integrative business information systems. Decis. Support Syst. **42**(1), 48–78 (2006)

12. Tweedale, J., Ichalkaranje, N., Sioutis, C., Jarvis, B., Consoli, A., Phillips-Wren, G.: Innovations in multi-agent systems. J. Netw. Comput. Appl. **30**, 1089–1115 (2007)
13. Liu, J., Chen, Z., Zhang, X., Liu, Z.: Neural-networks-based distributed output regulation of multi-agent systems with nonlinear dynamics. Neurocomputing **125**, 81–87 (2014)
14. Lopez-Ortega, O., Villar-Medina, I.: A multi-agent system to construct production orders by employing an expert system and a neural network. Expert Syst. Appl. **36**, 2937–2946 (2009)
15. Quteishat, A., Lim, C., Tweedale, J., Jain, L.: A neural network-based multi-agent classifier system. Neurocomputing **72**, 1639–1647 (2009)
16. Borrajo, L., Corchado, J., Corchado, E., Pellicer, M., Bajo, J.: Multi-agent neural business control system. Inf. Sci. **180**, 911–927 (2010)
17. Lopez-Franco, M., Sanchez, E., Alanis, A., Lopez-Franco, C., Arana-Daniel, N.: Decentralized control for stabilization of nonlinear multi-agent systems using neural inverse optimal control. Neurocomputing **168**, 81–91 (2015)
18. Olajubu, E., Ajayi, O., Aderounmu, G.: A fuzzy logic based multi-agents controller. Expert Syst. Appl. **38**, 4860–4865 (2011)
19. Hanafizadeh, P., Sherkat, M.: Designing fuzzy-genetic learner model based on multi-agent systems in supply chain management. Expert Syst. Appl. **36**, 10120–10134 (2009)
20. Huang, C., Liang, W., Lai, Y., Lin, Y.: The agent-based negotiation process for B2C e-commerce. Expert Syst. Appl. **37**, 348–359 (2010)
21. Doskocil, R., Doubravsky, K.: Decision-making rules based on rough set theory: creditworthiness case study. In: Proceedings of the 24th International Business Information Management Association Conference, pp. 321–327, Milan (2014)
22. Jolly, K., Kumar, R., Vijayakumar, R.: Intelligent task planning and action selection of a mobile robot in a multi-agent system through a fuzzy neural network approach. Eng. Appl. Artif. Intell. **23**, 923–933 (2010)
23. Vatankhah, R., Etemadi, S., Alasty, A., Vossoughi, G.: Adaptive critic-based neuro-fuzzy controller in multi-agents: distributed behavioural control and path tracking. Neurocomputing **88**, 24–35 (2012)
24. Liu, H., Tang, M.: Evolutionary design in a multi-agent design environment. Appl. Soft Comput. **6**, 207–220 (2006)
25. Monticolo, D., Miaita, S., Darwich, H., Hilaire, V.: An agent-based system to build project memories during engineering projects. Knowl.-Based Syst. **68**, 88–102 (2014)
26. Zha, X.F.: A knowledge intensive multi-agent framework for cooperative/collaborative design modelling and decision support for assemblies. Knowl. Based Syst. **15**, 493–506 (2002)
27. Chu, C., Wu, P., Hsu, Y.: Multi-agent collaborative 3D design with geometric model at different levels of detail. Robot. Comput.-Integr. Manuf. **25**, 334–347 (2009)
28. Relich, M., Pawlewski, P.: A multi-agent system for selecting portfolio of new product development projects. In: Bajo, J., Hallenborg, K., Pawlewski, P., Botti, V., Sánchez-Pi, N., Duque Méndez, N.D., Lopes, F., Vicente, J. (eds.) PAAMS 2015 Workshops. CCIS, vol. 524, pp. 102–114. Springer, Heidelberg (2015)
29. Rossi, F., van Beek, P., Walsh, T.: Handbook of Constraint Programming. Elsevier Science, Philadelphia (2006)
30. Relich, M.: A knowledge-based system for new product portfolio selection. In: Rozewski, P., et al. (eds.) New Frontiers in Information and Production Systems Modelling and Analysis. ISRL, vol. 98, pp. 169–187. Springer, Heidelberg (2016)
31. Sitek, P., Wikarek, J.: A hybrid approach to the optimization of multiechelon systems. Mathematical Problems in Engineering **2015**, Article ID 925675 (2015). doi: 10.1155/2015/925675

32. Van Roy, P., Haridi, S.: Concepts, Techniques and Models of Computer Programming. Massachusetts Institute of Technology, Cambridge (2004)
33. Sitek, P.: A hybrid CP/MP approach to supply chain modelling, optimization and analysis. In: Federated Conference on Computer Science and Information Systems (FedCSIS), pp. 1345–1352 (2014)
34. Grzybowska, K.: Selected activity coordination mechanisms in complex systems. In: Bajo, J., Hallenborg, K., Pawlewski, P., Botti, V., Sánchez-Pi, N., Duque Méndez, N.D., Lopes, F., Vicente, J. (eds.) PAAMS 2015 Workshops. CCIS, vol. 524, pp. 69–79. Springer, Heidelberg (2015)
35. Grzybowska, K.: Application of an electronic bulletin board, as a mechanism of coordination of actions in complex systems – reference model. LogForum **11**(2), 151–158 (2015)
36. Bocewicz, G., Nielsen, I., Banaszak, Z.: Automated guided vehicles fleet match-up scheduling with production flow constraints. Eng. Appl. Artif. Intell. **30**, 49–62 (2014)
37. Baptiste, P., Le Pape, C., Nuijten, W.: Constraint-Based Scheduling: Applying Constraint Programming to Scheduling Problems. Kluwer Academic Publishers, Norwell (2001)
38. Liu, J., Jing, H., Tang, Y.Y.: Multi-agent oriented constraint satisfaction. Artif. Intell. **136**, 101–144 (2002)

# How to Simulate Transportation Disturbances in the Logistic Process?

Patrycja Hoffa-Dabrowska[(✉)]

Poznan University of Technology, ul. Strzelecka 11, 60-965 Poznań, Poland
patrycja.hoffa@doctorate.put.poznan.pl

**Abstract.** The paper presents a description of modelling the supply chain including disturbances by using simulation software. In order to make the best representation of reality, the route, the lorry's speed and various types of disturbances are taken into account. The purpose of this article is to demonstrate how disturbances can be modeled and to present benefits of using the simulation programs to plan a route and time of transport.

**Keywords:** Disturbances · Creation of special objects in simulation · Supply chain

## 1 Introduction

The paper presents author's work about how can be modeled a supply chain including different disturbances occurring in transport processes. Because of wide range aspects involved in a supply chain, author concentrates on transport area. Networks in supply chain can be modeled in different ways, like by using Petri net, or algorithm Dijkstra and Floyd-Warshall algorithms or by using simulation. In this article author wants to show the use of simulation to modeling the supply chain. Moreover, method of modeling one disturbance (bed weather) is described. In presented case study, the lorry's route is defined at the beginning. This route includes different variables, as: a vehicle speed and some disturbances like severe weather conditions and breaks in driver works. This model was created by using a modern software FlexSim, that allows build models of various degrees of complexity [24]. Author integrated Discrete Event Simulation (DES) with an Agent Based Simulation approach (ABS) to model disturbances. Disturbance is represented by own created object.

The main aim of this article is to present a way of modeling transport route including some disturbances. Author tries to improve prediction of delivery time performance using simulation. The route is being modeled with some assumptions like vehicle's speed and some disturbances. In this case author considers two disruptions – bad weather conditions and breaks in driver working time. Author describes in detail how one of these disturbances is created in simulation model, not only in theoretical way. Moreover, by doing different experiments, user can see what will change in process, and how it will affect to whole process.

An article consists of 5 parts. Section 2 contains a literature background about a supply chain - complexity of this issue, methods of route modeling, and the aspect of

© Springer International Publishing Switzerland 2016
J. Bajo et al. (Eds.): PAAMS 2016 Workshops, CCIS 616, pp. 85–97, 2016.
DOI: 10.1007/978-3-319-39387-2_8

occurrence the disturbances in transport. In Sect. 3 author presents mathematical description of the supply system model and general information about created simulation model. In Sect. 4 author presents model of selected route for realization transport task. Here, detailed description of created disturbance is included. Besides, in this part were described carried out experiments and results of them. The final conclusions are stated in Sect. 5.

## 2 The Supply Chain Issue and Aspect of Occurrence Disturbances in Supply Chain

### 2.1 The Complexity of the Supply Chain Issue

When people hear "supply chain", they think about transport goods from point A to point B. But the issue is more complexity. Analyzing the transportation process, it is important to see a broader range of this activity, not only the moving of goods. Of course, the main role of the supply chain is a transportation of products from one point to the other, but many other aspects should be considered, such as: ensuring adequate quality services at the lowest cost, finding the best mode of transport, the management of different entities involved in whole process,... In order to confirm the complexity of aspects in supply chain, few definition about them are presented. Recalling Umeda: "A supply chain system is a chain of processes from the initial raw materials to the ultimate consumption of the finished product spanning across multiple supplier-customer links. It provides functions within and outside a company that enable the value chain to make products and provide services to the customers" [20]. According to the dictionary of logistics terminology, a supply chain is "the organizational structure of the group of companies, implementing joint actions necessary to meet the demand for certain products" [9].

At present, supply chains are dispersed systems [17, 21]. What makes, that the next problem is how to manage links and the structure of the whole chain in order to achieve the best results (in strategical and financial dimension). Therefore, people pay more and more attention to issue of modeling the supply chains and management of them by using various computer programs. The network can be described and modeled in few ways – the most known are: modeling transport routes by using different type of network, for example Petri net [18]; by using algorithm like Dijkstra and Floyd-Warshall algorithms [8]; in mathematical description [22]; and by using simulation software [26].

In this article, for the purposes of modeling the processes in the supply chain two methods are used: Discrete-Event Simulations (DES) and Agent-Based Simulation (ABS). First method is a good option when we deal with well-known processes, for which the situations of uncertainty are defined using statistical distributions. DES models are characterized by the process approach – they focus on modeling the system in detail, not on the independent units [3]. Second method focuses on individual elements and their behaviors [13]. Referring to the supply chain – the individual chain participants (companies, manufacturers, wholesalers and retailers) can be treated as agents who have their own goals and skills, and their common goal is to produce and deliver a product to a specific customer [23]. Agent-Based Simulation is discussed in more detail in [2, 7, 13]. There are also numerous articles dedicated to agent modeling and multi-agent modeling in the transport and supply chains [4, 5, 14, 16].

### 2.2 The Aspect of Occurrence the Disturbances in Supply Chain

Analyzing transportation process, it is important to see a broader range of this activity, not only the moving of goods. As in any other process, the presence of various types of interference in the realization of activities should be taken into account.

Many articles about transporting hazardous materials and risk associated with this transport can be found in the literature [6, 10, 19]. Other popular aspect are car accidents [1, 15].

Author focuses on the transport area in supply chain, and on the aspect of realization transport task on time. Author distinguished various disturbances in this area, and now is trying to determine how they affect to realization of whole process and time of it [12]. Such disturbances in transport operations have been distinguished [11]:

(1) related with means of transport, like the failure of vehicle,
(2) related with the route, like: the traffic congestion, the road accident, weather conditions, the fee payment in Toll Collection Point,
(3) resulting from the fault of the sender and receiver, like: no enough free ramps for loading/unloading,
(4) related with the driver, like: the driver working time,
(5) and other.

## 3 Problem Definition

During the analysis of the literature about various disturbances in transport, author noticed that exists a little number of articles about way of modeling of these disturbances. Therefore, author decided to concentrate on the modeling the disturbances with the determination of the influence of these disturbances on the transport process, on time of transport.

On the first step, author presents mathematical description of the supply system model. Next, shows simulation model of the supply chain.

### 3.1 The Supply System Model – Mathematical Description

Author presents general description of the supply system model (Fig. 1). This is a theoretical description of the supply system, it is an introduction to research problem, connected with the occurrence of disturbances and their influence on the time of the transport process.

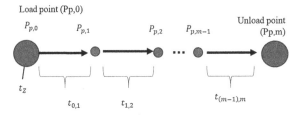

**Fig. 1.** The supply system model.

A supply system model (Fig. 1) is defined as:

$$SD = (P, D, T) \qquad (1)$$

Where:

$P$ - a transport route, defined as a sequence of:

$$P = \left(P_{p,0}, P_{p,1}, \ldots, P_{p,i}, \ldots, P_{p,(m-1)}, P_{p,m}\right) \qquad (2)$$

$P_{p,i}$ - $i{-}th$ intermediate point, where disturbances are considered,

$m$ - a number of intermediate points,

$P_{p,0}$ - a starting point (load point),

$P_{p,m}$ - an unload point.

Intermediate points – these are locations where interference may occur in the delivery. Disturbances have affect to the delivery time.

$D$ - a sequence of distances between intermediate points:

$$D = \left(d_{0,1}, d_{1,2}, \ldots, d_{(i-1),i}, \ldots, d_{(m-1),m}\right) \qquad (3)$$

$d_{(i-1),i}$ - a distance between the point $P_{p,(i-1)}$ and point $P_{p,i}$,

$T$ - a sequence of transit times between intermediate points:

$$T = \left(t_{0,1}, t_{1,2}, \ldots, t_{(i-1),i}, \ldots, t_{(m-1),m}\right) \qquad (4)$$

$t_{(i-1),i}$ - a travel time from the point $P_{p,(i-1)}$ to $P_{p,i}$ counted in contractual units of time [c.u.t.], $t_{(i-1),i} \in R$. The travel time is defined as a random continuous variable, for which it probability density function $g_{(i-1),i}(t)$ is known. The probability density function is different for every type of disturbance.

For the supply system modeled by the SD (1), the total time of delivery is defined as $T_{proc}$.

$$T_{proc} = \sum_{i=1}^{L_{pal}} T_{Z_i} + \sum_{i=1}^{m} t_{i,(i+1)} \qquad (5)$$

where:

$T_{Z_i}$ - a time of loading of i-th pallets [c.u.t.],

$L_{pal}$ - a number of pallets.

The total time of realization the delivery $T_{proc}$ determines a date of unloading $Ra_o$:

$$Ra_o = Z_0 + T_{proc} \tag{6}$$

where:

$Z_0$ - a date of loading [c.u.t], $Z_0 \in R$,

$Ra_o$ - an expected date of unloading, $Ra_o \in R$.

For presented system, the research problem can be defined as: there is a supply system (SD), for which it is known latest and earliest delivery time (interval $(Ra';Ra)$).

Author looks for answer for this question: Is there a time of starting the loading $Z_0$, which ensures, with the specified probability (Pd), that the delivery will end at defined interval $Ra_o \in (Ra';Ra)$?

$$(Z = ?) \Rightarrow \left[ P\left( Ra_o \in \left( Ra';Ra \right) \right) \geq Pd \right] \text{ dla } SD, \left( Ra';Ra \right) \tag{7}$$

### 3.2    The Simulation Model of Supply Chain – General Information

In order to show how can be used simulation to model different processes in the supply chain, an example of transport route was created. This simulation model was built using FlexSim software. Using FlexSim is very simple by build-in tool and objects [24].

This route includes travel from Komorniki city to Żary city, both of them are located in Poland. The distance is equal 167 km. The planned route includes journey using national road No. 32 and 27. Figure 2 presents this route.

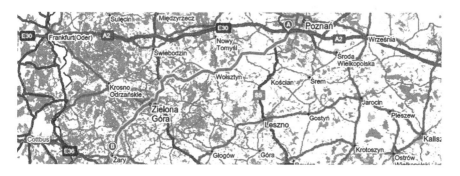

**Fig. 2.** Komorniki-Żary route. Source [27].

During build the simulation model, in order to present reality in the best way, some assumptions were made. One of them is vehicle's speed at national routes, which is equal 70 km/h (+ − Acceleration/Deceleration). This speed is intentionally not a

random value, because author wants to clearly show the influence of various disturbances to the modeled route - on the time of realization the transport order.

The purpose of presented simulation model is to show the possibility of modeling
the transport route, which will includes some disturbances. By made few experiments
on this model, it will be possible to define the time, which is needed to travel this route.
This will be shown at next part in this article.

## 4    Case Study

This section provides an example of modeling the transport route, which includes some
disturbances. Author took into account only two disruptions, because wants to show,
influence of them on the whole process. Moreover, wants to present in detail how
disturbances can be modeled. Analyzing the transport order, it is important to focus on
the transportation time from the start to the final point.

Building a simulation model, containing certain assumptions (for example speed)
and including disturbances, will simplify the observation and analysis of the individual
activity in the whole process. By addition of the randomness of emergence of disturbances, and then running a series of experiments, it is possible to get an answer about
the travel time from point A to B (containing defined assumptions). When we will add
the real data into the model, we will get a good tool, which can improve the transportation planning in the company.

In this model, author included two disturbances:

(1) Weather conditions – author treats severe weather conditions like downpour,
    blizzards, high winds, as disturbances. The occurrence of these phenomena is
    associated with reduction of a travel speed. And, of course, it has an impact of the
    time of realization the transport order. A detailed description of the method of
    modeling of this disturbance is included in further part of this article.
(2) Driver's working time - in conjunction with the applicable provisions [25] author
    decided to consider time of driver's working. This disruption is certain - we exactly
    know when the driver should have a break and how long. Of course it makes that
    travel time will be longer. Author considered one option of driver working time -
    4.5 h of driving/work, then 45 min of break, then 4.5 h of driving/work and then a
    11 h of break. Author does not take into account other cases of breaks in work,
    because on the market exist many programs to manage of time of driver working.
    In created model, this disturbance has function as a reminder that the driver must
    have breaks! In the present model, the time of driver's working starts at time, when
    vehicle received the message about new transport order. So, loading and unloading
    operations are included in time working.

### 4.1    Breaks in the Weather – Description and Method of Modeling

Severe weather conditions (downpour, blizzards, high winds) make, that travel by car is
harder, sometimes impossible. Because of this disturbance, the running speed will be

reduced, what have an impact of the extension of the travel time. Of course, collection the data about weather condition is difficult problem, but not impossible. Based on the historical data and information obtained from the weather maps, it is possible to determine the likelihood of severe weather conditions in the analyzed area. Besides, based on a data on current weather conditions at certain points (which are available on the Internet -for example [28]), new data to the model can be introduced, in order to take into account them in the experiments. Moreover, based on these data, it is possible to create a base of weather conditions - for example it can be defined places where rain is rare phenomenon or place where is often windy.

This disturbance can be modeled in two ways. Both of them, in theoretical way are described in [11]. In presented case study, this disturbance is modelled according to method 1 described in the above mentioned article. Difficult weather is represented by an agent with two specified ranges of action (Fig. 3).

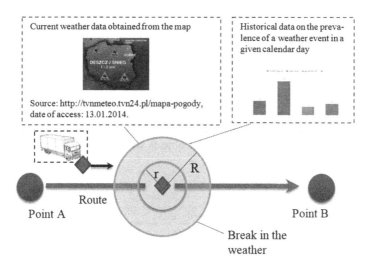

**Fig. 3.** A break in the weather represented by an agent – way 1. Source [11].

First area (smaller) – is a center of change, the second – is a ring, which forms the area surrounding the center. The agent representing disturbance, checks (in specified units time), whether in his area there is another agent representing a means of transport. If there is one, agent sends information to the vehicle about an occurring disturbance (message about reducing speed to defined value). The vehicle, after receiving this message, changes the traveling speed according to the given information.

Author created his own object with special label. Each bad weather condition has been mapped on a single object named Bad_Weather. Author created this object with using TaskExecuters Object in FlexSim. Author used this type because it has additional function – definition of collision and possibility to check if other objects are in collision area. Range of this disturbance is expressed by two circles. Radius of bigger circle is defined by modeler, by using normal statistical distribution (with a mean, a deviation, and with a minimum and a maximum value). The radius of smaller circle (center of weather change) has been set as 0.3 radius of a bigger circle. The same situation is about a truck's speed – speed in the surrounding area is defined by modeler (in labels), while speed in center is converted as 0.7 speed value.

Created Bad_Weather object has 14 labels (Fig. 4):

- Labels 1–4 - contain information about a mean, a deviation, a minimum and a maximum value of a speed in a bigger area of the disturbance (in the ring, which forms the area surrounding the center). These information have to be defined by the modeler.
- Labels 5–8 - include information about a radius of a bigger area. These information have to be defined by the modeler.
- Label 9 - contains information about a speed outside (in ring), which is defined based on labels 1–4.
- Label 10 - includes information about a speed in a center of the disruption, is equal as 0,7*speed_outside.
- Label 11 - contains information about an outside radius (the whole radius of the disruption), which is defined based on labels 5–8.
- Label 12 - includes information about a center radius, is equal as 0,3*radius_outside.
- Label 13 - presents a number of stream, it is changeable in this model.
- Label 14 - includes a table of information about a type of active collision (in center or in a surrounding area) and the name of truck, which is in this area. Based on this information, it is possible to manage of objects which are in range of disturbance, and change their speed.

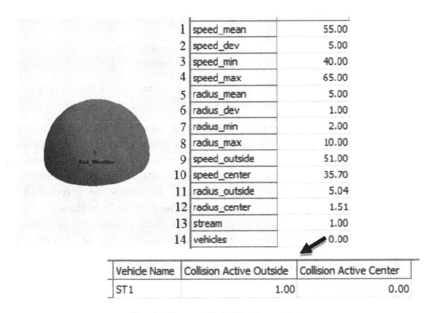

| 1 | speed_mean | 55.00 |
| 2 | speed_dev | 5.00 |
| 3 | speed_min | 40.00 |
| 4 | speed_max | 65.00 |
| 5 | radius_mean | 5.00 |
| 6 | radius_dev | 1.00 |
| 7 | radius_min | 2.00 |
| 8 | radius_max | 10.00 |
| 9 | speed_outside | 51.00 |
| 10 | speed_center | 35.70 |
| 11 | radius_outside | 5.04 |
| 12 | radius_center | 1.51 |
| 13 | stream | 1.00 |
| 14 | vehicles | 0.00 |

| Vehicle Name | Collision Active Outside | Collision Active Center |
|---|---|---|
| ST1 | 1.00 | 0.00 |

**Fig. 4.** Created Bed_Weather object.

For presenting bed weather disturbance 3D simulation program was used. This is a reason, why a surrounding area of this disturbance in Fig. 4 is in 3D, while in reality two dimensions are sufficient (in accordance to the present description).

When the bad weather condition will occur, an area of effect is defined by a normal distribution with parameters stored in object labels. The value of speed decrease is defined in the same way. Described object checks, in certain time interval, if there is another object in range. When an object (truck) is detected, its travel speed is decreased to specific value, firstly speed is adequate to speed at surrounding area (case 2 at Fig. 5), then to speed for center area (case 3 at Fig. 5) and then again at speed for surrounding area (case 4 at Fig. 5). When this object leaves area, its speed is set back to original value (case 5 at Fig. 5). Time interval is relative small (currently 0.01 time unit). It provides, that moment when the vehicle has left the disturbance is quickly noticed. Figure 5 shows described situations.

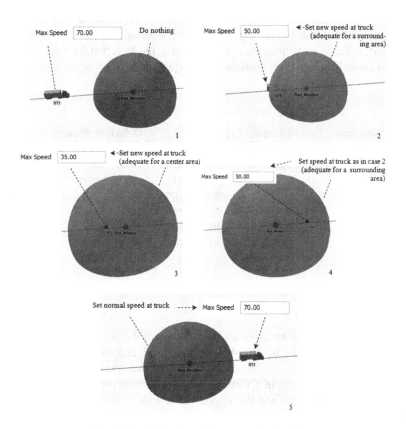

**Fig. 5.** Bed_Weather object – mode of action.

## 4.2    Description of Simulation Experiments

For presented simulation model in point 3.2, four experiments (4 scenarios) were made. Each experiment was made 10 times (10 replications) to show the influence of a random value setting in the disturbance. Experiments were made by using built-in experimenter tool in FlexSim. Author intentionally presents only 4 simple experiments to show clearly the influence of the disturbances on analyzed process.

In every experiments, main variables for a weather disturbance were changed, to show how this disruption affects to the time of realization the transport process. In present case author does not take into account a possibility of a detour – the alternative route. The issue of seeking a new route, because of occurrence of disturbances, is not the aim of this study. The main goal is to show various times needed to realize the transport task. This time depends on random values in disturbances (like radius of this disruption or truck's speed in an area of this disruption). To show relations between the process time versus disturbances, author made some simplifications. Firstly: only two disruptions are considered in this model. Secondly: acceleration and deceleration aspects are not taken into account in this model. Information about experiments are summarized in Table 1. An important information is the fact, that the travel time from point A to point B without any disturbance is equal an 2.38 h.

**Table 1.** Definition of simulation experiment.

| Exp. no | Take into account the driver's working time | Definition of speed | | | | Definition of range | | | |
|---------|---------|---------------------|---|---|---|---------------------|---|---|---|
| | | Mean value of speed | Dev of speed | Min value of speed | Max value of speed | Mean value of radius | Dev of radius | Min value of radius | Max value of radius |
| 1 | Yes | 55 | 5 | 40 | 65 | 5 | 1 | 2 | 10 |
| 2 | Yes | 60 | 10 | 40 | 65 | 10 | 2 | 2 | 15 |
| 3 | Yes | 55 | 10 | 40 | 67 | 10 | 3 | 2 | 15 |
| 4 | Yes | 40 | 15 | 30 | 55 | 10 | 5 | 2 | 15 |

## 4.3    Result of Experiments

The main purpose of these experiments was to present the transportation time, which depends on random values in disturbances, as speed and radius. Table 2 presents results of these experiments. As we can see, the minimal transportation time is at an experiment 1, because values in a weather disturbance have only a small influence on process. The smallest speed, and the largest radius of this disruptions was defined at scenario 4, which is reflected in the obtained results.

By using built-in experimenter tool in FlexSim, we can get information about interval of values of the analyzed time for 90, 95 or 99 % confidence.

**Table 2.** Results of simulation experiments. Source: results obtained from FlexSim model.

Transportation time [h]

|            | Rep 1 | Rep 2 | Rep 3 | Rep 4 | Rep 5 | Rep 6 | Rep 7 | Rep 8 | Rep 9 | Rep 10 |
|------------|-------|-------|-------|-------|-------|-------|-------|-------|-------|--------|
| Scenario 1 | 2,48  | 2,46  | 2,46  | 2,44  | 2,45  | 2,51  | 2,46  | 2,44  | 2,44  | 2,48   |
| Scenario 2 | 2,61  | 2,52  | 2,65  | 2,50  | 2,57  | 2,60  | 2,47  | 2,48  | 2,52  | 2,46   |
| Scenario 3 | 2,59  | 2,46  | 2,47  | 2,51  | 2,51  | 2,53  | 2,47  | 2,53  | 2,49  | 2,61   |
| Scenario 4 | 2,72  | 2,56  | 2,75  | 2,72  | 2,91  | 2,91  | 2,55  | 2,47  | 2,45  | 2,75   |

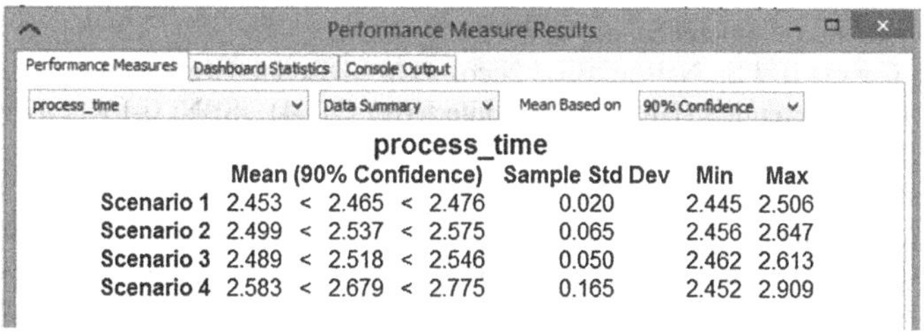

**Fig. 6.** Confidence interval for analyzed time. Source: results obtained from FlexSim model.

Figure 6 presents results for 90 % confidence interval. Referring to description of model of supply system and specified there question about an existence of the time $Z_0$, we can say- that it exists and it can be defined by using Experimenter tool in FlexSim software.

## 5   Conclusion and Further Investigations

The presented approach to modeling a supply chain enables a precision analysis of processes and impact of each of them at the transport process. Thanks to using the simulation, an observation and analysis of process is possible. In addition, including aspect of disturbances, a useful tool to determine the time required for transport is created. Author in a detailed description presents a way of modeling the processes in supply chain and disturbances. In order to show the use of the described aspects, the simulation model for the sample transport routes have been created. By performing a number of experiments, a relationship between "the disturbance's strength" and times of transport realization was shown. Obviously, there is an opportunity for a further development of the proposed work: modelling next disturbances in described way (with combining ABS and DES approach) and checking relation between them and time of realization the transport task. By creating library with disturbances, fast building of simulation model will be possible. Next step is "play" with the simulation model and definition of time of analyzed process, with using build-in experimenter tool.

**Acknowledgement.** Presented research works are carried out under the project - 503215/11/140/DSPB/4134 Poznan University of Technology.

# References

1. Alteren, B., Hokstad, P., Moe, D., Sakshaug, K.: A barrier model for road traffic applied to accident analysis. In: Spitzer, C., et al. (eds.) Probabilistic Safety Assessment and Management, pp. 3603–3608. Springer, Heidelberg (2004)
2. Bae, J.W., Lee, G., Moon, I.: Introductory tutorial: agent-based modeling and simulation. In: Winter Simulation Conference, pp. 3809–3820 (2012)
3. Banks, J., Carson II, J.S., Nelson, B.L., Nicol, D.M.: Discrete-Event System Simulation, 4th edn., pp. 68–86. Prentice Hall, Upper Saddle River (2004). ISBN: 0-13-144679-7
4. Baykasoglu, A., Kaplanoglu, V.: A multi-agent approach to load consolidation in transportation. Adv. Eng. Softw. **42**, 477–490 (2011)
5. Bocewicz, G., Nielsen, P., Banaszak, Z., Dang, Q.V.: Multimodal processes cyclic states scheduling. In: Corchado, J.M., et al. (eds.) PAAMS 2013 Workshops. CCIS, vol. 365, pp. 73–85. Springer, Heidelberg (2013)
6. Brussaard, L.A., Kruiskamp, M.M., Oude Essink, M.P.: The Dutch model for the quantitative risk analysis of road tunnels. In: Spitzer, C., et al. (eds.) Probabilistic Safety Assessment and Management, pp. 2660–2665. Springer, Heidelberg (2004)
7. Chan, W.K.V., Son, Y., Macal, C.M.: Agent-based simulation tutorial – simulation of emergent behavior and differences between agent-based simulation and discrete-event simulation. In: Winter Simulation Conference, pp. 135–150 (2010)
8. Chen, S., Peng, H., Liu, S., Yang, Y.: A multimodal hierarchical-based assignment model for integrated transportation networks. J. Transp. Syst. Eng. Inf. Technol. **9**(6), 130–135 (2009)
9. Fertsch, M.: Słownik Terminologii Logistycznej, p. 95. Instytut Logistyki i Magazynowania, Poznań (2006)
10. Gheorghe, A., Birchmeier, J., Kröger, W.: Advanced spatial modelling for risk analysis of transportation dangerous goods. In: Spitzer, C., et al. (eds.) Probabilistic Safety Assessment and Management, pp. 2499–2504. Springer, Heidelberg (2004)
11. Hoffa, P., Pawlewski, P.: Agent based approach for modeling disturbances in supply chain. In: Corchado, J.M., et al. (eds.) PAAMS 2014. CCIS, vol. 430, pp. 144–155. Springer, Heidelberg (2014)
12. Hoffa, P., Pawlewski, P.: Models of organizing transport tasks including possible disturbances and impact of them on the sustainability of the supply chain. In: Pawlewski, P., Greenwood, A. (eds.) Process Simulation and Optimization in Sustainable Logistics and Manufacturing. Eco Production, pp. 141–151. Springer, Heidelberg (2014). Environmental Issues in Logistics and Manufacturing
13. Kim, S.-H., Robertazzi, T.G.: Modeling mobile agent behavior. Comput. Math. Appl. **51**, 951–966 (2006)
14. Krejci, C.C., Beamon, B.M.: Modeling food supply using multi-agent simulation. In: Winter Simulation Conference, pp. 1167–1178 (2012)
15. Orlandelli, C.M., Vestrucci, P.: Development of a road transportation risks data base for Italy: methodology, models and results. In: Spitzer, C., et al. (eds.) Probabilistic Safety Assessment and Management, pp. 2269–2274. Springer, Heidelberg (2004)

16. Pawlewski, P.: DES/ABS approach to simulate warehouse operations. In: Bajo, J., Hallenborg, K., Pawlewski, P., Botti, V., Sánchez-Pi, N., Duque Méndez, N.D., Lopes, F., Vicente, J. (eds.) PAAMS 2015 Workshops. CCIS, vol. 524, pp. 115–125. Springer, Heidelberg (2015)
17. Sitek, P., Wikarek, J.: A hybrid approach to supply chain modeling and optimization. In: Federated Conference on Computer Science and Information Systems, pp. 1223–1230 (2013)
18. Skorupski, J.: Sieci petriego jako narzędzie do modelowania procesów ruchowych w transporcie. Prace Naukowe Politechniki Warszawskiej, Transport, z.78, pp. 69–84 (2011)
19. Tixier, J., et al.: Development of a risk knowledge platform dedicated to accident of dangerous goods transportation. In: Guedes Soares, G., Zio, E. (eds.) Safety and Reliability for Managing Risk, pp. 117–122. Taylor & Francis Group, London (2006)
20. Umeda, S.: Simulation analysis of supply chain systems with reverse logistics. In: Winter Simulation Conference, pp. 3375–3384 (2013)
21. Wieland, A., Wallenburg, C.M.: Supply-Chain-Management in Stürmischen Zeiten. Universitätsverlag der TU, Berlin (2011)
22. Wilhelm, T., Hollunder, J.: Information theoretic description of networks. Phys. A **385**(1), 385–396 (2007)
23. http://www.anylogic.com/agent-based-modeling. Accessed Jan 2014
24. https://www.flexsim.com/. Accessed Jan 2015
25. http://isap.sejm.gov.pl/. Accessed Jan 2015
26. http://www.llamasoft.com/supply-chain-simulation-software.html. Accessed Mar 2015
27. https://mapa.targeo.pl/. Accessed Mar 2015
28. http://www.traxelektronik.pl/pogoda/lokalizacja.php?RejID=8&B=1366&H=728. Accessed Mar 2015

# An Approach to Represent Material Handlers as Agents in Discrete-Event Simulation Models

Allen G. Greenwood[✉]

Poznan University of Technology, ul. Strzelecka 11, 60-965 Poznań, Poland
allen.greenwood@put.poznan.pl

**Abstract.** This paper introduces an initial approach to represent human-driven, industrial-truck material handlers as agents in discrete-event simulation models of manufacturing systems. The approach is network based and involves material handlers creating work tasks for themselves based on the current states of the system, such as inventory in a production area and material availability in a supply area. The material handler integrates other work tasks with supporting the production lines. The approach leverages constructs currently available in simulation software and is implemented in *FlexSim*. An illustrative example is provided and the agent-based results are compared to traditional means for modeling material handling.

**Keywords:** Material handling · Agents · Simulation · Manufacturing systems

## 1 Introduction

Material handling is a key activity in any manufacturing/production system. In many industries it contributes a significant portion of total manufacturing cost. As such, the design and operation of material handling processes have a significant effect on overall system performance.

Since material handling is a key part of production systems, it is commonly a major part of discrete-event simulation (DES) modeling and analysis. In fact, it is oftentimes the focus of simulation projects, such as those that analyze and assess alternative material handling methods in order to identify the best option in terms of cost and service. Many simulation models involve the transport of material between locations by automated and non-automated means. The focus of this research is on non-automated means; in particular, the movement of materials over large distances within a facility by human-operated industrial-trucks, such lift trucks, pallet jacks, platform trucks, etc.

Modeling and analyzing manufacturing systems using agent technologies have a long history as noted in Monostori et al. [8] and Shen et al. [12], to name a few. However, the major focus is on manufacturing control systems. In contrast, other general sources on agents do not mention manufacturing as an application area. For example, neither Allan [1] nor Macal and North [7] mention manufacturing and logistics as an application of agent-based modeling. Macal and North [7] note "agent-based modeling is being applied to many areas, spanning human social, behavioral, cultural, physical, and biological systems."

© Springer International Publishing Switzerland 2016
J. Bajo et al. (Eds.): PAAMS 2016 Workshops, CCIS 616, pp. 98–109, 2016.
DOI: 10.1007/978-3-319-39387-2_9

One reason that agent-based modeling is not as widely applied in manufacturing systems may be due to the many well-defined processes that exist in manufacturing systems. While manufacturing systems are highly complex – they are dynamic, stochastic systems that contain a large number of elements and processes with significant dependencies – many aspects are well defined and procedural. In fact, in order to develop DES models, processes, flows, routings, etc. must be explicit and well defined. Various simulation model development tools, e.g., those proposed by Greenwood and Pawlewski [3] and Pawlewski [9], are designed to define operational processes in very structured ways in order to enable the system to be represented in simulation software. However, some aspects of manufacturing systems, such as the case of material handlers defined in this paper, lend themselves to other modeling paradigms besides a process representation, such as agent-based modeling.

Macal and North [6] define agent-based systems as "a computational framework for simulating dynamic processes that involve autonomous agents. An autonomous agent acts on its own without external direction in response to situations the agent encounters during the simulation." Macal and North [7] define agent-based modeling in terms of following three basic elements.

(1) Agents, which contain the following properties and attributes:
    a. Autonomy, acting independently, being self directed.
    b. Modularity, being self contained.
    c. Sociality, interacting with other agents, e.g. contention for space, collision avoidance, communication and information exchange.
    d. Conditionality, having a state that varies over time with behaviors conditional upon its state.
(2) Agent Relationships, methods of interaction; networks are a common topology for interaction among agents.
(3) Agents' Environment, functioning and interacting with their surroundings.

The approach proposed in this paper for representing material handlers as agents in DES of manufacturing systems meet all of the conditions above.

The objective of this paper is to provide an approach for more realistically representing material handling activities in DES models in order to improve their effect on the analysis of alternative production rates, stocking rates, material-handling resource type, availability, policies, etc. To this end, the paper provides an initial approach for representing material handlers as agents in DES models. As agents they interact with other objects in the model, but are not directly driven by them; they are driven by the resulting behavior of the other objects. Another objective is to develop the modeling approach by leveraging capabilities that are currently available in DES modeling and analysis software. As Chan et al. [2] posit, DES has already developed a rich set of theories and practices; in contrast, agent-based simulation is still in its infancy stage of developing modeling techniques. Similarly, Siebers et al. [11] find that there is considerable interest in agent-based simulation in academia and industry, but most people do not know how to apply it and there is no established frameworks or methodologies to guide researchers and analysts through the agent-based modeling and simulation process.

This paper is organized as follows. Section 2 defines the material handling function in manufacturing systems. Section 3 describes the proposed approach for modeling material handlers as agents. Through an illustrative example, Sect. 4 discusses implementation of the approach in simulation software (*FlexSim*) and compares the agent-based approach to a traditional modeling approach for material handling. Section 5 provides conclusions and plans for further research.

## 2   Material Handling in Manufacturing Systems

The Material Handling Institute provides the following taxonomy of material handling equipment [13] for the movement and storage of material within a facility.

(1) Transport Equipment moves material from one location to another. Major subcategories are: conveyors, cranes, and industrial trucks, but material can be transported manually with no equipment.
(2) Positional Equipment handles material at a single location so that it is correctly positioned for subsequent activities.
(3) Unit Load Formation Equipment restricts material to maintain integrity when handled as a single load.
(4) Storage Equipment holds or buffers material over time.
(5) Identification and Control Equipment collects and communicates information to coordinate the flow of materials.

This research focuses on the first category, the use of transport equipment to move material from one location to another. The transport activity is defined such that it includes the following tasks: traveling from a current location to the source location of a material, loading material at the source, travelling from the source to the destination location, and unloading at the destination. In our case, the transport is made by a sociotechnical system, an industrial truck (e.g. lift truck) driven by a human. The truck handles the physical aspects of the transport and the human provides the cognitive aspects, e.g. deciding what activity to perform and when to perform it based on a set of guidelines and current conditions. The combination of the truck and person is referred to as the material handler.

As indicated above, material handling involves more than just physically moving material between locations A and B. It involves deciding what to move and when; e.g., checking production lines to identify which one(s) need material, deciding when to check, and deciding what to do if a needed material is not available at its storage location. These activities are typically performed by the human component of the material handler.

Simulation software conducts material handling activities in different ways; however, there are two typical approaches:

(1) Material at a storage location is "pushed" to a production line as it becomes available and there is capacity for it at the production line.
(2) Material is "pulled" from a storage location by a production line's needs.

In both cases, the material handler is called to move the material when both the storage and production areas are ready for it to move. The calls involve a sequence of tasks that need to be performed by the material handler and are queued by the material handler, or at a central controlling object, and performed in a specified order, e.g. priority, distance, FIFO. The material handler makes no decisions; it just mechanistically reacts to instructions from the production system.

Now, consider a common material handling situation where a material is supplied from storage, say at location A, to production, e.g., at location B, when the inventory level at production falls below a threshold (referred to as a reorder point). Once the threshold is reached, a request for material is made from production (B) to storage (A); i.e., it is pulled. However, a request for transport is not made until sufficient quantity is available at A, then it is pushed to B. It is not until all of these conditions are met that the material handler is called to transport it.

In many operations there are no direct communications between locations A and B. Instead, a material handler checks (oftentimes a visual scan) the inventory levels in the production area and notes those location(s) needing materials. If material is needed, the material handler travels to the storage area to obtain the materials and bring them to the production area; if no material is needed, the material handler does other work. Since the other work is performed in other areas of the facility, the checks of the production area are done according to guidelines, e.g. about every 30 min, and not at precise intervals or on a schedule. In addition, the material handler typically notes several production locations that need resupply in case the desired material is not available, thus avoiding wasted travel time. Breaks are guidelines as well, e.g., about 20 min every two hours - the material handler does not just stop every two hours, especially if in the middle of a task. Thus, the material handler gathers the needed information and decides what to transport, and when, based on guidelines. Therefore, the material handler acts as an agent.

## 3    Agent-Based Representation of Material Handling in DES

There are obviously many possible approaches to modeling material handling as an agent-based system. One main demarcation is to consider the material hander as a single agent, with all or most of the behaviors contained and managed in one object, or as a distributed system of agents. One example of an encapsulated approach is described by Pawlewski [10] for the order-picking process in a warehouse. The approach developed in this paper uses a distributed approach where material handling behavior is partitioned, packaged, and distributed based on function, such as move, check, decide, control, etc. and where the functions occur in the system. Thus, material handling is considered as a multi-agent system.

It is possible in future research that the current approach may be encapsulated similar to [10]. However, distributing agent functionality is not uncommon. For example, Kasaie and Kelton [4] note that in general, "the distinguishing characteristic of agent-based systems is based on decentralization of a system into its constituent components, and representing it through a collection of agents and their environment."

The reason for taking the distributed multi-agent approach is two-fold. Since this is an initial approach, defining and separating the various behaviors makes the approach easier to develop and understand. The second reason is to leverage and re-use, or use differently, existing capabilities in simulation software, thus reducing development and testing time. As noted earlier, *FlexSim* provides the basic capabilities to develop an agent-based approach in DES models.

The functions are distributed through a static network and mobile transporters. Macal and North [7] note that networks are a common topology for interaction among agents. A network contains a set of nodes that are connected in pairwise fashion with other nodes by edges. The nodes that form the travel paths are referred to as basic travel nodes and are not considered as agents.

By adding functionality to these basic travel nodes, they are transformed into special nodes that act as agents. One special node is referred to as a decision node agent since most of a material handler's other activities, besides transport, involves decision making – what to move, when to move, etc. Another type of special node is an interface node that provides links to other objects in the model, primarily for information. The interface node has more capability than a basic network node, but is not considered an agent.

Figure 1 provides a conceptual representation of the proposed constructs for introducing material handling agents into DES models using a function-based distributed approach. The approach leverages existing capabilities found in DES software, such as path networks, basic task execution, transporters, network nodes, etc.

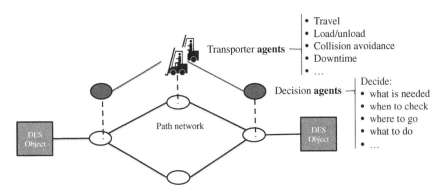

**Fig. 1.** Conceptual representation of the distributed agent approach.

The basic agent constructs defined in Fig. 1 are used in a DES model to represent the physical topology of a facility. An example is provided in Fig. 2. The agents and network nodes are arranged in a manner similar the physical system. Storage locations and production lines are shown as "black box" submodels.

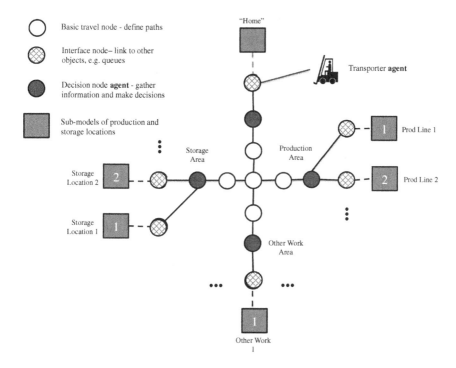

**Fig. 2.** Objects used to represent material handlers as agents.

The basic functions of a material handler that are distributed to agents (mobile transporters and static decision nodes) as well as basic network nodes and interface nodes are defined in Table 1.

### 3.1 Transporter Agent

The transporter agent, sometimes referred to in general as a task executer, is a mobile, dynamic resource that moves from location to location performing tasks as a simulation model executes. The tasks are often bundled; e.g., a resupply bundle might include the set of tasks: travel to source (storage), load material, travel to destination (production), unload. Tasks are queued and processed in a defined order, such as FIFO, priority, distance. Basic attributes of a transporter include speed and acceleration, carrying capacity, and size. Transporters typically move on a path network that defines the locations of the other objects that it must interact with and records distance traveled. They also maintain information on the tasks performed, time since last inventory check, current production line it is serving, if any, and are always spatially aware of their location in the environment.

This work leverages the basic task executer construct, but enables the transporter to create and manage its own tasks based on information obtained from the environment and/or in collaboration with decision-node agents. The decision-making functionality is distributed throughout the network to areas where it physically occurs.

Transporters can become unavailable due to planned and unplanned downtimes, such as operator breaks, battery recharging, malfunction requiring repair.

**Table 1.** Material handling functions mapped to agents and nodes.

| | Functions | Transporter agent | Decision node agent | Interface network node | Basic network node |
|---|---|---|---|---|---|
| 1 | Move between locations | | | | |
| | a with material | ✓ | | | ✓ |
| | b without material, empty | ✓ | | | ✓ |
| 2 | Check inventory level | | | | |
| | a at Production to determine which lines needs material | | ✓ | | |
| | b at Storage to determine if needed material is available | | ✓ | | |
| 3 | Decide what to move | | | | |
| | a at Production, the one or two lines with the highest need | | ✓ | | |
| | b at Storage, the one or two lines with the highest need | | ✓ | | |
| 4 | Decide where to move | ✓ | ✓ | | |
| 5 | Transfer material | | | | |
| | a at Production, from material handler to line | ✓ | | ✓ | |
| | b at Storage, from location to material handler | ✓ | | ✓ | |
| 6 | Avoid collisions | ✓ | | ✓ | |
| 7 | Downtime | ✓ | | | |

## 3.2 Decision-Node Agent

Decision-node agents are basic travel nodes that include logic to gather information and make decisions in the proximity to where they would be made in a real system, such as near a production or storage area. Distribution of the decision function is intended to reduce agent complexity. As shown in the example in Fig. 2, the decision-node agents form gateways to the Storage and Production Areas; and, are used at the Home and Other Work Areas. They link one or more basic travel nodes to each interface node for an area, e.g., a production line or storage location.

**Decision-Node Agent at the Production Area.** If a transporter enters a decision node in the Production Area carrying material, it just passes through since it is destined for a delivery to a production line.

If a transporter enters a decision node empty, the decision node and transporter collaborate to check the inventory level of all production lines and notes the time the check is made. If any material is needed, the location(s) of the needs are noted and the transporter travels to the Storage Area. If no material is needed, the transporter travels to the Other Work Area.

**Decision-Node Agent at the Storage Area.** The logic is similar to that used in the Production Area. If a transporter enters a decision node in the Storage Area carrying material, it just passes through since, it is destined for a delivery to a production line.

If a transporter enters a decision node empty, the decision node and transporter collaborate to check the inventory level of all Storage Locations where material is needed. If any one is available, the transporter proceeds to the specific Storage Location. If no material is available, the transporter travels to the Other Work Area.

**Decision-Node Agent at the Other-Work Area.** There may be multiple other-work locations, all connected to the Other Work Area decision node. This is similar to the structure in the production and storage areas.

On each pass through the decision node, the node and transporter collaborate to see if the inventories in the Production Area need to be checked – the time since the last check is compared to a guideline threshold, e.g. the Production Area should be checked at least every 30 min. If the time is below the threshold, the other work time is determined; the transporter travels to the work area; and, then returns to the Other Work Area decision node when finished. If the time is above the threshold, the transporter travels to the Production Area decision node to check inventories.

**Decision Node Agent at the Home Area.** The decision node is similar to the one in the Other Work area. There may be multiple locations where the operator takes breaks, the truck battery is recharged, etc., but they are all connected to the Home Area decision node in the network.

For operator breaks, e.g., 20 min every two hours, the material handler travels to the home area as soon as its current task is finished. Break times start when the transporter reaches home. At the end of the break, the material handler travels to the Production Area to check inventory levels; however, if it is awaiting material for a production line, it travels to the Storage Area to check the material availability.

### 3.3   Supporting Network Nodes

To complete the functionality of the network, two other types of nodes are used. One is a basic travel node; the other is a travel node but provides links to other objects.

**Basic Travel Network Node.** The combination of nodes and edges form a network. All nodes have the basic capability of managing edges that connect a node to other nodes. Transporters move from object to object over the paths defined by the network. Each node knows the distance to each node connected to it. Edges between nodes may be uni- or bi-directional, but are assumed to be bi-directional – transporters can travel in either direction between nodes. Edges between nodes can permit transporters to pass or not; no passing is assumed for safety reasons.

**Interface Network Node.** Interface network nodes are basic travel nodes but include logic that link the transporter to other objects in the simulation model. Production lines and the means in which storage locations are filled are often complex processes that require significant modeling. The interface node separates that complexity from the transporter by treating these areas as "black boxes" and provides only the information needed by the material handler to make its decisions, such as whether the material inventory at the production line is low enough to need supply or whether the needed material is available in its storage location. Another use of the interface node is to move material between a transporter agent and a storage location or a production line.

## 4   Illustrative Example - Implementation and Comparison

Using an example, this section describes implementation of the proposed approach in the simulation software *FlexSim* and compares the operational performance of the agent-based approach to modeling material handling with a traditional approach.

### 4.1   Description of the Example

The overall structure of the example system is similar to Fig. 2 – each of two production lines require a single, but different, material. A single material handler transports both materials. The material handler's speed is 200 m/min and is always available except during breaks that occur for 20 min every two hours. When no material needs to be transported, the material handler does other work, which is always available. The time to perform each other-work task is triangularly distributed (in minutes: minimum 8, maximum 12, and most likely 10).

The system is balanced; i.e., the process time for each unit in production is exponentially distributed with a mean of 10 min and material in the storage area is made available according to the same distribution. The reorder point for each material is three units; and, at startup, each line has an initial inventory of eight units. The transfer quantity between the storage and production areas is eight units.

Each scenario is simulated for 40 h and replicated 20 times. Common random numbers are used for variance reduction.

## 4.2   Implementation in FlexSim

*FlexSim* provides a powerful, open, object-oriented simulation environment that contains all of the basic constructs needed to represent material handling as an agent-based system in a discrete-event simulation model.

One major change from the basic application of *FlexSim* is that the transporter acts as an agent and creates its own tasks based on the status of the system (agent's environment). Typically, other objects send tasks and a queue of tasks are maintained and processed in a specified sequence, e.g., priority, distance, FIFO. The agent transporter interfaces with other modeling objects (agent's environment) and a decision-node agent to decide what to do next. This includes getting the current amount of material in inventory at each production line, determining whether the needed material is available in the storage location, etc. The agent transporter still maintains a queue of tasks to perform but it is short and self-derived. It is still possible for other objects in the model to push tasks to the agent transporter, but in the current implementation the agent transporter creates all tasks.

The material handler is represented as collaborating agents distributed on a network and satisfies Macal and North's [7] definition. It is autonomous (self directed), modular (self contained), conditional (state depends on other agents and the environment), and social (interacts with other agents). Sociality is achieved by interaction between the transporter and decision-node agents and between transporters. The inter-transporter collaboration occurs with the no-passing condition on the network (faster transporters cannot pass slower ones traveling in the same direction on the same network edge) and with collision avoidance. *FlexSim* provides collision avoidance for its task executers so the material handlers contend for space on the network.

The initial implementation of the material handler as agents in *FlexSim* is shown in the simple model in Fig. 3; the topology is the same as that shown in Fig. 2. The snapshot of the simulation shows a transporter moving material from Storage Location 2 to Production Line 2.

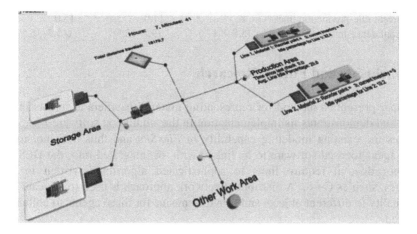

**Fig. 3.**  Example implementation of an agent-based approach to material handling in *FlexSim*.

The production and storage areas are shown as "black boxes"; i.e., the include logic for a simple production line and fill process in the storage area. These can be any production or storage system since they link to the material handler through the Interface network node.

### 4.3 Comparison with Traditional Modeling Approach

For the traditional case, when the reorder point is reached at production, material is immediately requested from storage. Once the requested quantity is available at storage, the material handler is requested to transport it to production. Requests for transport are queued on a first-in, first-out basis. Also, operator breaks occur as soon as they are scheduled – no completing the current task and no travel to a break area.

For the agent case, the material handler checks the inventory level in the production at least every 30 min (60 min is considered as an alternative). The operator goes on break after a task is finished and the break time begins when the operator reaches the break area.

Table 2 summarizes the comparison in terms of total distance traveled and the percentage of time the production area is idle due to lack of material. While the agent-based approach indicates poorer operational performance, it is considered more realistic; thus, the traditional approach would overstate performance and could be misleading. Also, the table indicates the importance of how often the material handler checks the inventory levels in the production area – longer times between checks result in less distance traveled, but more downtime in production.

**Table 2.** Operational performance comparison – traditional versus agent-based modeling

|  | Traditional | Agent-based | |
|---|---|---|---|
| Time between inventory checks | N/A | 30 | 60 |
| Avg. distance traveled, meters per hour (95 % confidence interval) | 1250.5 (1226.7–1274.4) | 1936.5 (1878.6–1989.3) | 1504.2 (1472.3–1536.1) |
| Avg. percent idle-production lines (95 % confidence interval) | 6.8 (5.8–8.1) | 11.0 (9.5–12.5) | 15.0 (13.5–16.5) |

## 5    Conclusion and Future Research

This paper presents a method for representing material handlers as agents in DES models and demonstrates its implementation in the simulation software *FlexSim*. It leverages the existing modeling capability in *FlexSim* and thus does not require special agent-focused software to be linked with, or integrated into, the DES software, nor does it require links to sophisticated algorithms written in other languages, such as C++,. A distributed network approach is used to allocate agent functionality to different objects and provides means for those agents to collaborate as needed.

Since this paper provides initial results, future work will further develop and expand the functionalities of the agents. Also, the basic distributed network premise will be tested. As such, one area for future research is to attempt to integrate the capabilities that are currently distributed into a single agent. If the integration is successful, it will provide the basis for comparison between the distributed and fully self-contained paradigms in terms of ease of use, maintainability, type of models that can utilize the two agent approaches, etc.

**Acknowledgements.** Support for this research has been provided by the Faculty of Engineering Management DS. 2016 Poznan University of Technology.

# References

1. Allan, R.: Survey of agent based modeling and simulation tools. STFC 2008–2009, pp. 1–28 (2009)
2. Chan, W.K.V., Son, Y., Macal, C.M.: Agent-based simulation tutorial – simulation of emergent behavior and differences between agent-based simulation and discrete-event simulation. In: Winter Simulation Conference, pp. 135–150 (2010)
3. Greenwood, A.G., Pawlewski, P., Bocewiecz, G.: A conceptual design tool to facilitate simulation model development: object flow diagram. In: Winter Simulation Conference (2013)
4. Kasaie, P., Kelton, K.W.: Guidelines for design and analysis in agent-based simulation studies. In: Winter Simulation Conference, pp. 183–193 (2015)
5. Law, WSC
6. Macal, C.M., North, M.J.: Introductory tutorial: agent-based modeling and simulation. In: Winter Simulation Conference, pp. 362–376 (2013)
7. Macal, C.M., North, M.J.: Introductory tutorial: agent-based modeling and simulation. In: Winter Simulation Conference, pp. 6–20 (2014)
8. Monostori, L., Váncza, J., Kumara, S.: Agent-based systems for manufacturing. Ann. CIRP **55**, 697–720 (2006)
9. Pawlewski, P.: Multimodal approach to modeling of manufacturing processes. In: Variety Management in Manufacturing — Proceedings of the 47th CIRP Conference on Manufacturing Systems, Procedia CIRP, vol. 17, pp. 716–720 (2014)
10. Pawlewski, P.: DES/ABS approach to simulate warehouse operations. In: Bajo, J., Hallenborg, K., Pawlewski, P., Botti, V., Sánchez-Pi, N., Duque Méndez, N.D., Lopes, F., Vicente, J. (eds.) PAAMS 2015 Workshops. CCIS, vol. 524, pp. 115–125. Springer, Heidelberg (2015)
11. Siebers, P.O., Macal, C.M., Garnett, J., Pidd, M.: Discrete-event simulation is dead, long live agent-based simulation. J. Simul. **4**(3), 201–210 (2010)
12. Shen, W., Hao, Q., Yoon, H.J., Norrie, D.H.: Applications of agent-based systems in intelligent manufacturing: an updated review. Adv. Eng. Inform. **20**, 415–431 (2006)
13. http://www.mhi.org/cicmhe/resources/taxonomy. Accessed Jan 2016

# Using DES/ABS Approach to Model and Simulate Bus Assembling Process

Pawel Pawlewski[(✉)] and Kamila Kluska

Poznan University of Technology, ul.Strzelecka 11, 60-965 Poznań, Poland
pawel.pawlewski@put.poznan.pl,
kamila.kluska@student.put.poznan.pl

**Abstract.** This paper presents the results of the project, which goal is to analyze the production process capability after reengineering the assembly process due to expansion of a bus production plant. The verification of the designed work organization for the new configuration of workstations on new production hall is necessary. The simulation model is the best tool for visualization and verification of the work organization based on individual workteams which are supporting particular workstations. Owing to the simulation it is possible to define the imperfections of this conception and elaborate improvements which will minimize the idleness of workers and downtime occurring in the assembly process. The objective of performed activities is to provide assurance that the new organization of assembly process will lead to maximum utilization of production capacity in the company. To solve described problems authors propose a method based on mixing DES (Discrete Event Simulation) and ABS (Agent Based Simulation) approach. DES was used to model the main process – material flow (buses), ABS was used to model assembling operations of teams of workers.

**Keywords:** Agent based modeling · Simulation · Assembling · Production plant

## 1 Introduction

The authors of the article conducted research in a bus production plant. Due to the increasing number of orders and the diversity of bus types, the assembly organization which has been applied so far does no longer meet the new requirements. Therefore, the reorganization of the assembly process is necessary. The factory employees have a radical idea for changing the organization of the assembly process. Their idea is to transition from one assembly line to three parallel assembly lines. As a result, such a change can be considered as the reengineering of the assembly process [6].

The main goals, which the enterprise wants to achieve, are the elimination of "bottle necks" and the increase in the production process efficiency. In the reengineering project the company staff designed the arrangement of workstations in the new production hall and the work organization of workteams, which perform various operations for many different types of buses. Then the simulation model was made to verify the described concept. The scope of the project includes:

© Springer International Publishing Switzerland 2016
J. Bajo et al. (Eds.): PAAMS 2016 Workshops, CCIS 616, pp. 110–121, 2016.
DOI: 10.1007/978-3-319-39387-2_10

– building a simulation model, which presents the new assembly line in the factory, taking into account the arrangement of workstations and workteams in the new production hall as well as the transport between workstations,
– presenting work organization of workteams and division of individual workers' labour (who belongs to a particular workteam and performs operations on buses in a particular workstation) in order to determine the best allocation of tasks and the optimum size of individual workteams,
– determining the effect of assembly interferences on the work of particular workteams and the efficiency of the whole production system,
– defining the efficiency of the designed assembly lines and proposing changes aimed at the quality improvement of the created conception.

Another problem, which we needed to analyse simultaneously, was the question of verifying the efficiency of the designed workstations system, especially when the factory produces such types of buses which are the most labour-intensive for employees.

In the course of research and creation of the simulation model there were a lot of difficulties. They were mostly related with the need to understand the specific vision of the company's employees, as well as with the visualization and verification of the new work organization and the appropriate use of data about operations in the simulation model. After the selection of data, separate lists of operations for each workteam were created. These lists determined, among other things, sequences and execution times of operations for different types of buses. The lists of operations were organized in a such way that operations were carried out in accordance with the technological route (used in the factory) and the actual state of affairs in the production plant. A big challenge was to present the work organization of various workteams in individual workstations.

The model was created with use of LogABS technology [10] and FlexSim Simulation Software.

The main goal of the paper is to present a method based on mixing DES (Discrete Event Simulation) and ABS (Agent Based Simulation) approach where DES was used to model the main process – material flow (buses) and ABS was used to model assembling operations of teams of workers.

The article consists of 6 sections. The first section provides an introduction. Literature review is the subject of the second section. The third section defines the problem. The fourth section discusses the DES and ABS approaches. Implementation of Agent Base Simulation, structure of agents and possible analysis are described in section five. Conclusions and plans for further work are the subject of the sixth section.

## 2    The Literature Review

The problem described in the previous section refers to balancing the production line. It is a technique applied in factories which use production lines or group technologies by elaborate objective systems [4]. It depends on assigning work to workstations, which are connected in a series, while we should focus on minimizing the number of workstations and reduce the total idle time for all workstations (e.g. changeovers, unplanned maintenance activities [7]) for a given level of production [5]. In theory, when all workstations have the same amount of work which must be done, the production line is perfectly balanced. In reality, however, most of production lines are unbalanced, because the actual amount of work done by individual workstations is different. The problem of proper balance of production lines is one of the most common issues raised by engineers – production organizers. It is a multi-step decision-making process, which is related to allocation of a specific permissible group of operations to workstations on an assembly line, at particular discrete points in time called the assembly cycles. Due to the criterion of optimization, the problem concerns two types of tasks: minimizing the quantity of assembly positions with a constant cycle, or minimizing the duration of the production cycle with a constant quantity of workstations. According to the classical method of balancing the production line for a set cycle time, tasks should be assigned to workstations in such a way so that the time losses (idle time of machines) are as short as possible [2]. The balance problem is related to a much wider group of production lines. However, taking the constraints into account, the solution in each case is supposed to minimize the idleness of workstations. The applied methods can be classified into two groups [11]:

– exact methods, discrete linear programming, dynamic programming, division and restrictions,
– heuristic methods, serialization and division algorithms, approximation methods (one and many heuristics, relapse, limited time to obtain an optimal solution).

The examples of heuristic methods are as follows [13]:

– RPW- Ranked Positional Weight,
– RRPW- Reversed Ranked Positional Weight,
– Kilbridge's and Wester's,
– Hoffman's Sequence Array Method,
– IUFF – Immediate Update First Fit.

In the industrial environment, the most commonly used solutions are the very simple ones. Employees create graphs on boards, in the form of magnetic panels or sheets (the size of a sheet is proportional to the time it takes to perform an individual activity), which show Gantt charts. In this case, Excel Spreadsheets are the most commonly used IT support. Usually, such solutions are sufficient to organize work in one workstation for several workteams.

However, simple solutions like, for example, magnetic boards with Gantt charts cannot solve complex problems and take into account uncertain execution times of operations which are extremely important in this case (usually execution times are changeable, they oscillates around particular values). It is also necessary to take into account the distance travelled by workers during the passing between several workstations - it is important factor in case of the assembly of large objects such buses. Considering issues listed above we decided to use simulation technology for modeling work organization of workteams. The available simulation software allows building complex models [3] in a relatively easy way. Moreover many simulation programs offers tools, which supports the preparation of schedules.

The most commonly used software is DES (Discrete Event System). DES has been the main way for the process simulation of manufacturing and logistics for about four decades.

This is adequate for problems that consist of queuing simulations and a variability is represented through stochastic distributions [12]. This approach is applicable in simulating the manufacturing and supply chain processes. DES models are characterized by a process oriented approach (the focus is on modeling the system in detail, not the entities) [8]. They are based on a top-down modeling approach and have one thread of control (centralized). They contain passive entities (i.e. something is done to the entities while they move through the system) and intelligence (e.g. decision making) is modeled as part of the system. In DES, queues are the crucial element; a flow of entities through a system is defined; macro behavior is modeled and input distributions are often based on collected/measured (objective) data.

In case of assembling operations we think that the process approach is insufficient. Workers are task executers. It means that they have the list of tasks to do. The worker decides what he will do next based on this list. So we think about worker as an agent. To do it we use approach based on ABS (Agent Based Systems). ABS modeling seems to be useful for modeling operators and forklifts, which have their own "intelligence", where the intelligence means the ability to complete changeable task lists (in our case – the picking list). In this case, an operator must have the ability to receive and send messages to the adoption of a task list, and to send a message about the execution or termination of the implementation of the task list. In the literature this approach is also referred to as Task Driven [3]. In some papers can find different opinion about using agent based simulation for manufacturing:

– Not recommended for example in [1],
– Recommended in [1].

Authors based on their research propose to mix DES and ABS approaches.

## 3   Problem Definition

The topic of the project is reengineering of the assembly process and the analysis of assembly process efficiency in an expanded production hall, in one of the biggest bus production plants in Poland. Due to the rapid development of the company there is a need for investment. In recent years the number of contracts won by the company has been steadily growing and their products have been conquering the European market. The assembly line must be more efficient, because imperfections of the current work organization are becoming a problem for the company employees and directly affects financial results of the company. The current work organization does not allow to take full advantage of labour force and it is impossible to realize the necessary number of procurements.

Currently, work is performed spontaneously. Data about the time and sequence of performing operations are not standardized. Employees are often not able to perform all operations in one cycle of work. Workers perform them in the next workstation or continue operations when other workteams have already finished working on a bus. The potential of many workers is not used in the right way, while others are overworked. That is why, the company management have decided to expand the production plant by building a new production hall and changing the work organization. The purpose of these actions is to reduce the time and distance travelled by workers during the assembly process and, therefore, help the company save both time and money.

The defined task is to visualize and verify the work organization so that we can design precise arrangement of workstations and workteams. The aim of the analysis performed with the simulation model is to confirm or reject the designed organization of the production process and identify imperfections of the created conception. These activities will help the company to improve the project before it is put into practice and also avoid time-consuming and expensive verification or solving problems which may appear.

The main change is to transition from a single assembly line to three parallel assembly lines, which work with a delay, but their work is synchronized. This is a complex problem because it is necessary to describe each phase of the process, which involves completion of more than 2700 operations for many types of buses by over 200 workers, who work in 20 workstations.

The model presents groups of workstations called: ST0, ST1, ST2, ST3, ST4, ST5, ST6. These workstations support three parallel production lines (Fig. 1).

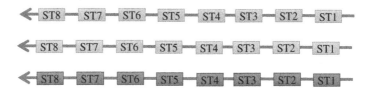

**Fig. 1.** Material flow by three parallel production lines

The workstations are supported by many workteams, which have different names, different sizes and various lists of operations which must be performed in consecutive cycles of work. Information about individual workteams is presented in Table 1. The work organization in workstations St1–St6 differs significantly from the work organization in St0 workstation. St0 workstation is supported only by B1 workteam, which performs operations on a bus continuously over the period of 300 min. Other workstations are supported by at least three workteams. Every workteam works in a workstation for 150 min and then passes to the next production line within a given workstation. The way of changing workstations by B2, B3 and B4 workteams in time is shown in the Fig. 2.

**Table 1.** Summary of the information about the workteams.

| Workteams name. | B1 | B2 | B3 | B4 | B5 | B6 | B7 | B8 | B9 | B10 | B11 | B12 | B13 | B14 | B15 | B16 |
|---|---|---|---|---|---|---|---|---|---|---|---|---|---|---|---|---|
| The number of members. | 15 | 12 | 12 | 11 | 11 | 11 | 11 | 13 | 12 | 10 | 11 | 12 | 12 | 14 | 10 | 13 |
| Supported workstations | ST0 | ST1 | ST1 | ST1 | ST2 | ST2 | ST3 | ST3 | ST2, ST3, ST4 | ST4, ST5 | ST2, ST3, ST4 | ST4 | ST5 | ST6, ST7, ST8 | ST6 | ST5, ST6 |

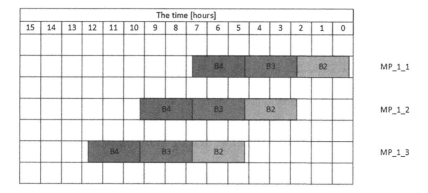

**Fig. 2.** Work organization of a workteam.

Buses pass through several workstations within the same assembly line. In the consecutive workstations buses are operated by other workteams. Employees from several workteams perform operations on buses in a sequence and time defined by global tables. Therefore, it is possible to carry out activities in accordance with the technological route and the work reality in the factory.

The data obtained from the company:

– information about the number of staff in each workteam, with their assigned workstations, supported by a several workteams,
– the list of all operations carried out during the production process,
– the duration of each operation, depending on the bus type,
– the project of the new production hall,
– the locations and names of workstations,
– the layout of operator workplaces in a workstation.

The assumptions of the project:

– The speed of workers is 37 m/min.

Each workteam consists of a specified number of employees. Each workteam is assigned a list of operations and workstations, which is necessary for the work. B1 workteam works in accordance with a specific algorithm, which is different than work organization of the other workteams. B9, B10, B11 and B16 workteams work in many workstations at the same time. Takt time of the production line for St0 workstation is 300 min, while for St1, St2, St3, St4, St5 and St6 workstations it is 450 min. After 300 min (which each bus spends at the St0 workstation) or 450 min (in case of others workstations) a bus is moved to the next workstation within a given production line.

Six major zones are designated in each workstation, depending on the stage of production. These zones are the destinations for workers, who have to execute their assembling operations. The division of the workplace into zones is shown in Fig. 3. Zones are marked with the numbers 1 to 6, which means respectively: 1- front, 2- interior, 3- back, 4- side, 5- roof, 6- chassis of the bus. The employees also carry out the subassembling operations in the dedicated zone of the production hall.

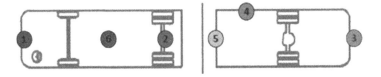

**Fig. 3.** The division of a workplace into various zones.

## 4   DES/ABS Concept to Model Work of Workteams

As mentioned earlier – Sect. 2, authors propose to mix DES and ABS approach to model work of workteams. Typically simulation tools use a process driven approach where the flow of the parts between processes cause the demands on resources, i.e. a part moves to a machine and demands a resource to complete the operation. Whilst this methodology is fine for some applications it does not allow for situations where the resources have tasks to complete which are not flow related – in. In these situations a task driven approach ensures that jobs can be undertaken in a realistic manner, e.g. an operator (mobile resource) has the job of performing a set of inspections of idle equipment when not otherwise engaged in process work. The task based approach allows for the creation of activities for an operator (mobile resource) which are totally independent of any processing activities and allows him to become engaged in a set of tasks which may require him to travel, acquire tools and remain "busy" for a period of time. Furthermore, using a task driven approach, resources can incorporate their own 'intelligence' to decide what jobs to do and when.

Many discrete events simulation programs available on market offer these possibilities. For the performed projected we choose FlexSim due to the following features [3]:

– ease of use in a real size with drag and drop technology,
– loading an .dwg file from the layout directly to a model,
– objects ASRS vehicle, Crane, Robot, Elevator,
– extended possibilities to model conveyors,
– fitting the shape of trucks and their parameters – in real values,
– integrating built-in experimenter tool with OptQuest,
– **including task sequence technology**.

Flexsim Simulation Software is a powerful analytical tool, which allows building three-dimensional computer models of systems as well as studying and analyzing their performance at a significantly lower cost than in case of real-time simulations. Moreover constructed model must be easy to use and understandable for its future users, because it takes into account all their requirements for the verification of the designed process and also helps them to understand it.

The bus assembling process is characterized by this feature that the bus is moving from station to station every cycle time (450 min) and on the station some workteams of operators work. Their work depend on task lists not on flow. So natural way is to model flow of buses using standard process approach (offered by DES program – in this case by FlexSim) and to model work of operators grouped in workteams using task driven approach. FlexSim offers one of more developed task driven approach on the market, but it is still not enough for complex model of human works. We need more general concept/idea, more "smarter" object which break the restrictions of FlexSim's tasksequence concept. Approach based on ABS offers it.

## 5    Implementation

This section presents the main idea to implement ABS in discrete event simulation program. We prepared the solution in environment of FlexSim. This program offers the tasksequence mechanism to model mobile resources. The modeler has possibilities to prepare the list of tasks for execution using special functions. The set of tasks includes following activities: travel, load, unload, break, utilize. FlexSim offers the special object called dispatcher to manage the set of operators. We extended this concept. We define agents based on taskexecuters from FlexSim – we add intelligence it means that our agent (extended FlexSim taskexecuter object) can make decision and he prepares based on order for him, his own list of tasks to do with possibilities to change this list. The defined agent has following characteristics according to [9]:

- is identifiable, a discrete individual with set of characteristics and rules governing its behaviors and decision-making capabilities,
- is autonomous and self-directed,
- is situated, living in environment with it interacts with other agents – has protocols for interaction with other agents,
- is goal directed – having goals to achieve,
- is flexible – having the ability to learn and adapt its behaviors based on experiences.

To solve problem of modeling and simulation work of many workteams for assembling, we defined two special agents:

- base agent – contractor,
- team agent.

Contractor is agent build based on taskexecuters from FlexSim, but his set of skills is extended in comparison with original taskexecuter from FlexSim – Table 2.

Team agent is the agent which has following rules:

- to prepare the goals for agents from team based on order (main task list),
- to control – it means to select, prepare and activate agents in team,
- to control time.

The protocols for communications between agents and team agents are defined – Fig. 4.

**Table 2.**  Summary of the information about the workteams.

| Feature | FlexSim taskexecuter | Agent contractor |
|---|---|---|
| Making decision | No | Yes |
| Possibility to check and evaluate the situation | No | Yes |
| Base skills | Travel, load, unload, utilize | Travel, load, unload, park, ready, check, check and load, call (other agent), free, reorganize, work |
| Where is represented intelligence? | Outside taskexecuter | Inside - Intelligence is represented within each individual entity |

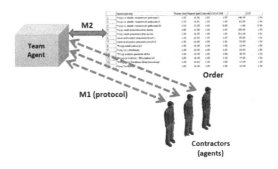

**Fig. 4.**  Information flow between agents

Orders (list of activities to perform) are built based on an excel file obtained from bus company. The structure of this file is as follow:

– a row in a table – one activity from the location indicated by columns,
– columns contain the name of the activity, number of station (Fig. 1), number of zone (Fig. 3), time of activity depend on type of bus – if time is 0 it means that this activity is not valid for this type of bus.

The Team Agent prepares the list of tasks based on the set of rows from Order table (M2 arrow from Fig. 4) and sends this list to Contractors (M1 arrows from Fig. 4). The Team Agent works as an answer to a request from the assembling line Fig. 5 – big arrows with "Requests" starting from ST1. When the bus enter to station the requests are sent to Team Agents which are assigned to this station. Team Agent has to perform the list of all activities in cycle time (150 min) using all Contractors assigned to team.

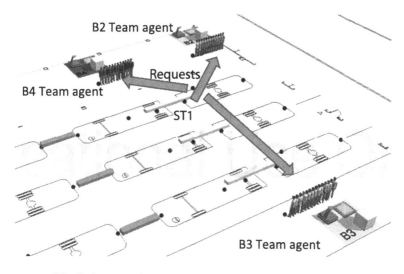

**Fig. 5.** Requests for work from assembling line to team agents

Described mechanism was implemented in FlexSim (Fig. 6). The model includes 20 stations – 2 special stations in the beginning of process and 18 stations in three parallel lines (Fig. 1). The work of 23 workteams was modeled. It is possible to change the number of members of workteams and to define new type of bus. The model enables to perform experiments with following reports:

- workteam conflicts – situation when the workteam finish his work after end of the cycle time,
- list of operations which cannot be performed because the time to the end of cycle is shorter than time of operation,
- list of idle time by workteam at the end of cycle – to evaluate the team work.

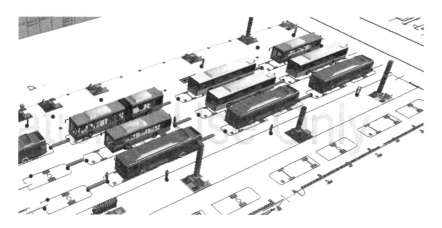

**Fig. 6.** View of bus assembling line in FlexSim

## 6   Conclusions

The paper presents the research results performed for bus company. The research focus on building the simulation model of workteams work in finish assembling line. To build the model we use mixt DES/ABS approach. As base the DES simulation program FlexSim was used and in this environment we developed our own agent base simulation tool. To do it we extended standard FlexSim taskexecuters and tasksequence mechanism. The model and prepared tools were implemented in bus company to analyse new assembling process. Thanks it company can short the time to make decision about workteam work organization. This tool can be used in two levels:

– design level – when new layout and new organization of works are designed,
– operational level – where finding the best solution is needed because of absence of workers or sudden disturbances in assembling process.

The paper presents first build model. Model was accepted by bus company so we define the possibilities to extended it by:

– skills matrix of workers – Team agent assign workers to activity based on skills of workers which are saved in this matrix,
– introducing special Contractor Agent – Jumpers – workers which can be shared by many workteams,
– introducing tools which will enable to define optimization task to find the best assigning.

**Acknowledgement.**   Presented research works are carried out under the project – status activities of Faculty o Engineering Management DS 2016 Poznan University of Technology.

## References

1. Allan, R.: Survey of agent based modeling and simulation tools. In: STFC 2008–2009, pp. 1–28 (2009)
2. Bartkowiak, T., Gessner, A.: Modeling performance of a production line and optimizing its efficiency by means of genetic algorithm. In: ASME 2014 12th Biennial Conference on Engineering Systems Design and Analysis - Volume 3: Engineering Systems; Heat Transfer and Thermal Engineering; Materials and Tribology; Mechatronics; Robotics Copenhagen, Denmark (2014)
3. Beaverstock, M., Greenwood, A., Lavery, E., Nordgren, W.: Applied Simulation: Modeling and Analysis Using Flexsim. Flexsim Software Products, Inc., Canyon Park Technology Center, Orem, USA (2011)
4. Bozarth, C., Handfield, R.B.: Introduction to Operations and Supply Chain Management, 3rd edn. Prentice Hall, Upper Saddle River (2012)
5. Cox, J.F., Blackstone, J.H.: APICS Dictionary, Alexandria, VA, APICS (2002)
6. Hammer, M., Champy, J.: Reengineering the Corporation: A Manifesto for Business Revolution. HarperBusiness (1993)

7. Jasiulewicz-Kaczmarek, M., Drożyner, P.: Maintenance management initiatives towards achieving sustainable development. In: Golinska, P., et al. (eds.) Information Technologies in Environmental Engineering Environmental Science and Engineering, pp. 707–721. Springer, Berlin (2011)

8. Korytkowski, P., Karkoszka, R.: Simulation based efficiency analysis of an in-plant milk-run operator under disturbances. Int. J. Adv. Manuf. Technol. **82**(5), 827–837 (2016)

9. Macal, Ch.M., North, M.J.: Agent-based modeling and simulation: desktop ABMS. In: Henderson, S.G., Biller, B., Hsieh, M.H., Shortle, J., Tew, D.J., Barton, R.R. (eds) Proceedings of the 2007 Winter Simulation Conference

10. Pawlewski, P.: DES/ABS approach to simulate warehouse operations. In: Bajo, J., Hallenborg, K., Pawlewski, P., Botti, V., Sánchez-Pi, N., Duque Méndez, N.D., Lopes, F., Vicente, J. (eds.) PAAMS 2015 Workshops. CCIS, vol. 524, pp. 115–125. Springer, Heidelberg (2015)

11. Scholl, A., Becker, C.: A survey on problems and methods in generalized assembly line balancing. Eur. J. Oper. Res. **168**(3), 694–715 (2003)

12. Siebers, P.O., Macal, C.M., Garnett, J., Buxton, D., Pidd, M.: Discrete-event simulation is dead, long live agent-based simulation! J. Simul. **4**(3), 204–210 (2010)

13. Zemczak, M.: Zagadnienie balansowania linii montażowej i szeregowania zadań w systemach produkcji mixed-model. Informatyczne systemy zarządzania: tom 4: (Wybrane zastosowania)/red. nauk. Marcin Relich., Wydawnictwo Uczelniane Politechniki Koszalińskiej (2013)

# Workshop on MAS for Complex Networks and Social Computation (CNSC)

# Overview of Case Studies on Adapting MABS Models to GPU Programming

Emmanuel Hermellin[(✉)] and Fabien Michel

LIRMM - CNRS University of Montpellier,
161 Rue Ada, 34095 Montpellier, France
{hermellin,fmichel}@lirmm.fr

**Abstract.** General-Purpose Computing on Graphics Units (GPGPU) is today recognized as a practical and efficient way of accelerating software procedures that require a lot of computing resources. However, using this technology in the context of Multi-Agent Based Simulation (MABS) appears to be difficult because GPGPU relies on a very specific programming approach for which MABS models are not naturally adapted. This paper discusses practical results from several works we have done on adapting and developing different MABS models using GPU programming. Especially, studying how GPGPU could be used in the scope of MABS, our main motivation is not only to speed up MABS but also to provide the MABS community with a general approach to GPU programming, which could be used on a wide variety of agent-based models. So, this paper first summarizes all the use cases that we have considered so far and then focuses on identifying which parts of the development process could be generalized.

**Keywords:** MABS · GPGPU · GPU delegation

## 1 Introduction

Multi-Agent Based Simulation (MABS) rely on directly modeling and simulating the interactions of micro-level entities, namely agents [15]. In this scope, when a large number of agents have to be modeled, the simulation process may require a lot of computing resources, which often represents a major issue with respect to the experimentation [17].

Considering this issue, General-Purpose Computing on Graphics Units (GPGPU) is a High Performance Computing (HPC) solution which is interesting because it allows to use the massively parallel architecture of the graphics cards of usual computers for accelerating general-purpose computations in a very efficient way[1] [5,6]. However, GPGPU is strongly related with the highly specialized architecture of Graphics Processing Units (GPU) and thus implies a specific programming approach to be used efficiently. In particular, a MABS

---

[1] e.g. https://developer.nvidia.com/about-cuda.

© Springer International Publishing Switzerland 2016
J. Bajo et al. (Eds.): PAAMS 2016 Workshops, CCIS 616, pp. 125–136, 2016.
DOI: 10.1007/978-3-319-39387-2_11

model cannot take advantage of the GPU power without being adapted to the GPU programming paradigm.

Still, it turns out that adapting a MABS model to GPU programming is a difficult task which is generally done only for the sake of efficiency, in an adhoc way, and especially without considering the accessibility nor the reusability of the produced software [20]. Indeed, to be GPU compliant, the problem must be represented by distributed and independent data structures and usual object oriented features, which are common in MABS, are no longer available using GPGPU [16]. Therefore, most of the works that use GPGPU for developing MABS are hardly accessible and thus not reusable outside of the context for which they have been designed. So, a lot of development efforts are lost and the use of GPGPU still represents a marginal approach in the scope of MABS despite its increasing success as an HPC solution.

Among the research works that tackle the use of GPGPU for MABS from a software engineering perspective, most of them propose solutions that hide GPU programming, thus making its use completely transparent (e.g. [12,25]). However, because of the heterogeneity of multi-agent models, such solutions only focus on some particular type of MAS models and cannot be easily generalized.

Instead of tackling accessibility and reusability by means of transparency, [14] proposes a design guideline which promotes and eases the direct use of GPU programming when adapting and developing MABS models in a GPGPU context, namely the GPU environmental delegation principle. More specifically, this approach relies on identifying which parts of the MAS model could be implemented using GPU programming. So far, we have used this approach on six different use cases [9,10,14] and obtained interesting results both from a performance point of view and from a software engineering perspective. This paper first summarizes these different works and their results before discussing the practical lessons learned from these experiments. Especially, based on the idea that there is a need for a methodology for adapting MABS to GPU programming, we show that we have been able to identify a recurrent development pattern which could be generalized.

The paper is organized as follows. Section 2 presents GPGPU basics and the evolution of the use of GPGPU in MABS. Section 3 describes and summarizes all the experiments done with the GPU delegation principle. Section 4 presents a first generalization of the approach toward the creation of a methodology dedicated to GPGPU for MABS. Section 5 concludes the paper and outlines some related perspectives.

## 2    Related Works and Motivations

### 2.1    GPGPU-Based MABS

Initially designed for graphics rendering, GPU are now composed of hundreds of ALU (Arithmetic Logic Units) forming a highly parallel structure able to perform general-purpose computations. The programming paradigm associated consists in executing simultaneously a series of operations on a dataset. When the data structure is suitable (and only if), the massively parallel architecture of the GPU provides very high performance gains (thousands of times faster).

In the context of MABS, empirical results from various experiments show that high simulation speeds can be achieved with very large agents populations (e.g. [7]). Nonetheless, this excellent speedup comes at the expense of modularity, ease of programmability and reusability [20]. This was especially true at the beginning of GPGPU because there was no specialized programming interface and one had to hack the GPU graphical functions to achieve GPGPU-based simulations [23].

Still, despite the evolution of GPGPU, and especially the release of specialized programming frameworks such as CUDA[2] and OpenCL[3], the current GPGPU-based MABS solutions remain difficult to use and it is worth noting that the majority of the new works start from scratch and still put all the focus on acquiring the best computational gains without considering accessibility, reusability nor modularity (e.g. for the study of flocking [8], crowd [24], traffic simulations [27] or autonomous navigation and path planning algorithms [4]).

Before 2011, most of those works were based on an approach that consists in executing completely the model on the GPU (called *all-in-GPU* here). This approach is useful when the main objective is only to accelerate the simulation's execution but, from a software engineering point of view, this approach is not satisfying because all the development efforts are lost due to the specificities of GPU programming: The optimization which is required eventually produces code that cannot be easily understood nor reused outside of the scope of a particular experiment.

That is the reason why hybrid approaches, that is sharing the execution of the MABS between the CPU and the GPU, begin to appear in 2011. Even if they are by design less efficient than all-in-GPU implementations, they exhibit two main advantages [9]: (1) They allow to implement more complex MABS because they do not longer need to be entirely compliant with GPGPU (see e.g. [13]) and (2) they naturally promote modularity and thus ease the development process thanks to a more concrete separation of concerns, for instance by enforcing the distinction between the agent model and the environment model (see e.g. [14,18]).

## 2.2   The Need for a Methodology for Porting MABS on GPU

Not surprisingly, research works that address software engineering issues in the scope of GPGPU-based MABS are now all based on an hybrid approach. However, it is worth noting that most of them rely on hiding the use of GPGPU through predefined programming languages or interfaces which are based on specific agent and environment models (e.g. [22]). Even though they represent concrete solutions for easing the use of GPGPU for MABS, such approaches cannot take into account the wide variety of MABS which can be conceived because they rely on predefined software structures and conceptual models.

---

[2] Compute Unified Device Architecture, https://developer.nvidia.com/what-cuda.
[3] Open Computing Language, http://www.khronos.org/opencl.

Consequently, instead of hiding GPGPU, we here argue on the idea that it would be interesting to provide the MABS community with a methodology that would concretely help to adapt and implement a MABS model using directly GPU programming. This would allow to take into account a largest number of models because such an approach would not rely on a predefined agent model and implementation. Therefore defining such a methodology is one of our main long-term goals.

## 3    Experimenting GPU Environmental Delegation

In this section, the GPU environmental delegation principle (*GPU delegation* for short) is introduced. Then, all the works we have done using this approach are described and their outcomes presented from both a performance and a practical perspective. Then, we show that the design guideline promoted by GPU delegation can be a starting point for the definition of a methodology dedicated to the modeling and the developing of MABS models in a GPGPU context.

### 3.1    The GPU Environmental Delegation Principle

Proposed in [14], the GPU environmental delegation principle is based on the fact that it is very difficult to deport the entire MABS model on graphics cards.

Inspired by an Agent-Oriented Software Engineering (AOSE) trend which consists in using the environment as a first class abstraction in MAS [1,28], GPU delegation has to be related to other research works that reify parts of the agents' computations in external structures. Examples of this trend are EASS (Environment As Active Support for Simulation) [2], IODA (Interaction Oriented Design of Agent simulations) [11], the environment-centered approach for MABS proposed in [19] and artifact approach [21].

GPU delegation thus relies on an hybrid approach which divides the execution of the MAS model between the CPU and the GPU. Especially, this principle consists in making a clear separation between the agent behaviors, managed by the CPU, and environmental dynamics, handled by the GPU. To this end, one major idea underlying this principle is to identify agent computations which can be transformed into environmental dynamics and thus implemented into GPU modules (called kernel, these modules contain the computations executed on the GPU). Originally, the GPU Environmental Delegation Principle was first stated as follows [14]: *Any agent perception computation not involving the agent's state could be translated to an endogenous dynamic of the environment, and thus considered as a potential GPU environment module.*

So, the two main design guidelines underlying this principle are: (1) Compliant environmental dynamics must be transformed into GPU modules and (2) agent computations which are compliant with the previously stated criterion should be translated in environmental dynamics and thus implemented as GPU modules.

## 3.2   GPU Delegation Case Studies

**Multi-Level Emergence.** [14] GPU delegation was first used for developing a model of Multi-Level Emergence (MLE) of complex structures inspired by [3]. This very simple model relies on a unique behavior which allows to generate complex structures which repeat in a fractal way[4]. The corresponding agent behavior is extremely simple and based on the reaction of agents to pheromones. So, in this work, two GPU modules dedicated to the perception and the spread of pheromones were proposed.

From a performance point of view, this experimentation shows that the use of GPU modules have decreased the overall execution time for each time step of the simulation. So, an acceleration gain up to x5 have been achieved, according to the hardware configuration. Figure 1 summarizes the coefficient gains obtained for three size of environment[5]: 500, 1000 and 1600.

From a practical perspective, this work had two objectives which were successfully fulfilled [14]: (1) Keeping the programming accessibility of the agent model in a GPU context (the original agent model was not modified) and (2) being able to scale up both the number of agents and the size of the environment. Moreover, this experiment showed that GPU delegation suggests a fine grained and modular approach for designing and integrating GPU modules which eases the development and maintenance tasks. Especially, this experiment shows that GPU delegation allows to tackle the genericness issue by promoting the reusability of the created GPU modules because, as they represent endogenous environmental dynamics, they deal with computations which are entirely independent from agent behavioral models. So, they could be easily reused in other contexts.

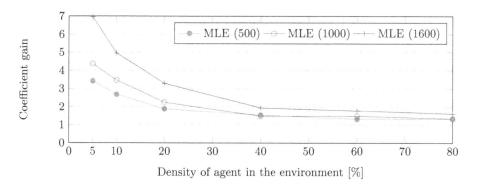

**Fig. 1.** Performance gains between CPU and CPU+GPU versions

**Reynolds's Boids** [9]. To further trial GPU delegation, a second experimentation was proposed in [9] and described how the principle has been used and eventually modified to implement a classic MABS, namely Reynolds's Boids[6].

---

[4] See http://www.lirmm.fr/~fmichel/mle for some videos of this experiment.
[5] In all these experiments, the environment is as a 2D square grid discretized in cells.
[6] See www.lirmm.fr/~hermellin/Website/Reynolds_Boids_With_TurtleKit.html.

In this model, each agent moves by taking into account the orientation and the speed of the others. So, applying GPU delegation, a GPU module dedicated to the computation of average orientations in each part of the environment was proposed, thus freeing the agents from doing the computation related to this perception.

To achieve this, it is worth noting that the original GPU delegation criterion had to be modified and extended so that it can be applied on this use case. Indeed, there was no agent computation fulfilling the original criterion but this experiment showed that it was in fact possible to apply GPU delegation after a slight modification of the underlying criterion. So, this latter evolved and is now stated as follows: *Any agent perception computation not **modifying** the agent's state could be translated into an environmental dynamics computed by the GPU.*

From a performance point of view, the experiment confirmed that, using GPU delegation, it is possible to increase both the size of the environment and the number of agents while obtaining an interesting speedup (up to 25 % according to the chosen parameters: Size of the environment and population density). Figure 2 summarizes the coefficient gains obtained for two size of environment: 256 and 512.

Apart from the extension of the GPU delegation criterion, from a practical perspective, this experiment also shows that the resulting agent implementation was easier to understand, thanks to the delegation of computations which are not part of the agents' deliberation.

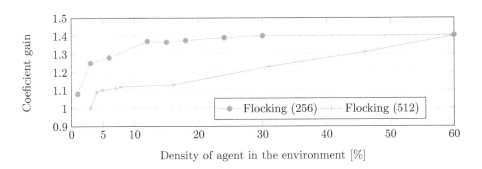

**Fig. 2.** Performance gains between CPU and CPU+GPU versions

**Game of Life, Schelling's segregation, Fire and DLA** [10]. To gain more experience on the benefits and limits of GPU delegation, it has been used to develop four different MABS simultaneously. So, [10] describes the adaption and implementation of four models: Conway's Game of Life, Schelling's segregation, Fire and DLA (diffusion-limited aggregation), the last two being taken from the NetLogo library [26][7].

---

[7] Detailed descriptions and computation kernels are available online: http://www.lirmm.fr/~hermellin/Website/GPGPU_MABS_Methodology.html.

In this work, three GPU modules have been created. The first one, for the Game of Life model, consists in computing for each cell of the environment its state for the next step of the simulation, according to the Game of Life rules. The second one, for Schelling's segregation, computes the happiness of each agent at each time step. The third one, for the Fire model, computes the heat diffusion in the environment. Finally, the DLA model reuses the GPU module from Game of Life (only the data structure sent to the GPU have been adapted to fit with this module) to search for the nearest neighbors in the vicinity of each agent.

From a performance point of view, Fig. 3 shows that performance gains vary significantly depending on the simulated model and the size of the environment: The gain can reach x14 but is more likely between x2 and x5.

From a practical perspective, this experiment highlighted again that GPU delegation promotes reusability by producing generic GPU modules which could be used across different MABS. Moreover, thanks to its modularity, the simplicity of the defined GPU modules shows that this approach offers a good accessibility to GPGPU because GPU delegation eventually produces simple kernels (a few lines of code are required in most cases).

Overall, beyond performance gains, this last experiment has confirmed the advantages of the approach considering software engineering aspects such as accessibility, reusability and genericity. Still, it also highlights some open questions such as the difficulty of implementation for a new GPGPU user or the types of models on which GPU delegation could be applied.

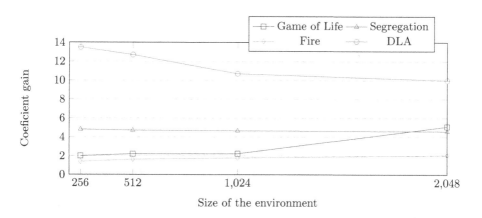

**Fig. 3.** Performance gains between CPU and CPU+GPU versions

## 4    Highlighting a Recurrent Development Pattern

From a software engineering perspective, the main objective of GPU delegation is to offer a generic approach which can be applied on a wide variety of MABS models and eases the use of GPGPU. Especially, as previously mentioned, our goal is to capitalize on our experiments to eventually produce a methodology which could be used on any kind of MABS. So, in this section, we present the different parts of the development process which we have been found as recurrent during our experiments. This enumeration is thus a first step toward a comprehensive methodology relying on GPU delegation.

With respect to the workflow that we have applied for adapting and developing the previous MABS, applying GPU delegation on a model can be divided into four main phases. The first step consists in identifying in the model all the computations which are required by the agents' behaviors or the environmental dynamics. Once these computations are referenced, the second step consists in selecting which ones could be modeled and implemented as an environmental dynamics according to the GPU delegation criterion. The third step relies on analyzing the selected computations for choosing which ones could bring interesting performance gains once translated into GPU modules. Finally, the fourth step consists in applying GPU delegation on the identified computations for developing the related GPU modules. Figure 4 summarizes this development pattern.

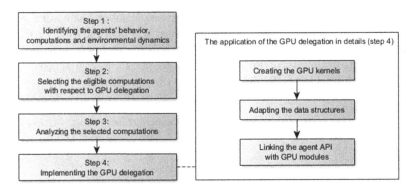

**Fig. 4.** Recurrent steps for the implementation of the GPU delegation

**Step 1: Identifying.** This phase of identification consists in decomposing the agents' behaviors to individualize as much as possible all the computations that they require. For instance, each perception process should be linked with a reified computation. The same approach holds for the environmental dynamics which are present in the model. The more the model is decomposed in simple computations, the more GPU delegation could be then successfully applied.

**Step 2: Selecting the Compatible Computations.** The selection of computations is an essential step because it relies on deciding which ones could benefit from GPGPU. If no part of the model is compliant with the principle, it is therefore useless to go further because, in such a case, the gains brought by GPGPU could be insignificant or even negative [13].

So, for now, in our experiments the selection of computations has been made according to the following workflow and specific criteria:

1. Considering the environment:
    - If no computations or environmental dynamics have been identified in step 1, proceed to the agents' behaviors.
    - If the environment is discretized into a 2D grid and contains computations or environmental dynamics which are applied on a large part of the cells, the delegation of these computations to GPU modules could be possible and highly relevant. Indeed, in those cases, the computations are independent from the agent's states and thus agree to the GPU delegation principle (see Sect. 3.1).
2. Considering the agents' behaviors:
    - If computations made within the behavior of the agent do not involve nor modify the agent's states, they could be translated into environmental dynamics.

**Step 3: Analyzing the Selected Computations.** Before applying GPU delegation on the selected computations, one must consider the performance benefits that these computations can bring. So, it is necessary to verify that (1) computations are performed by a large number of agents or applied on a lot of cells (for the environment). Because of the very high data transfer costs, if computations are rarely used, triggering a GPU computation could be not efficient even if their are compatible with the principle. Moreover, (2) the data structures used by these computations must be independent and adapted to the GPU architecture. If this is not the case, one has to check that the data can be adapted. Indeed, if the data do not match the highly specialized GPU architecture, this will impact the overall performance of the model (see [5] for more information on this aspect).

**Step 4: Applying GPU Delegation.** Implementing GPU delegation can be divided into three parts for each selected computation:

1. Creating the GPU kernel;
2. Adapting the data structures;
3. Linking the agent API with the GPU module.

(1) Applying GPU delegation starts with the creation of the GPU kernel, that is the GPU programming version of the selected computation. Thanks to the decomposition which have been done in the identifying step, little GPGPU knowledge is required and the produced kernels are easy to implement through a few lines of code (see e.g. [10]). (2) Then, the data structures need to be adapted to the new GPU module. This adaptation is based on the nature of both the computations and the environment model (arrays fitting the discretization of the environment are mostly used). Finally, these new elements must be integrated and linked with the CPU part of the model. So, new functions must be created to allow the agents and the environment to collect and use the data computed by the GPU module.

## 5    Summary and Future Works

Using GPGPU in the context of MABS remains difficult and the spreading of this technology in the MABS community is still limited, mainly because of accessibility and reusability issues.

In this context, this paper has proposed an overview of several case studies on using the GPU delegation principle for adapting MABS models to GPU programming and discussed related practical results. Especially, our experiments showed that this approach is an original and relevant solution toward the direct use of GPU programming for developing MABS. Notably, GPU delegation not only allows to obtain performance gains but also embeds a software engineering perspective that promotes GPGPU accessibility together with the resusability and genericity of the produced software modules.

This paper has then presented how the workflow which has been used in our experiments could be generalized. To this end, we described all the steps that we followed for modeling and adapting the models used in our experiments so that they can benefit from GPU programming. The underlying idea of this work is to eventually define a comprehensive methodology relying on GPU delegation. From a higher perspective, we argue on the idea that such a contribution would be crucial because it would allow to handle a wider range of models and thus contribute to the spreading of the GPGPU technology in the MABS community.

To this end, our next objective is thus to formalize the different steps and criteria which have been identified and presented in this paper to define a first version of such a methodology.

## References

1. Weyns, D., Michel, F. (eds.): E4MAS 2014. LNCS (LNAI), vol. 9068. Springer, Heidelberg (2015)
2. Badeig, F., Balbo, F., Pinson, S.: A contextual environment approach for multi-agent-based simulation. In: ICAART 2010, 2nd International Conference on Agents and Artificial Intelligence, pp. 212–217, Spain, June 2010
3. Beurier, G., Simonin, O., Ferber, J.: Model and simulation of multi-level emergence. In: ISSPIT 2002, April 2008
4. Bleiweiss, A.: Multi agent navigation on the GPU. In: Games Developpement Conference (2009)
5. Bourgoin, M., Chailloux, E., Lamotte, J.-L.: Efficient abstractions for GPGPU programming. Int. J. Parallel Program. **42**(4), 583–600 (2014)
6. Che, S., Boyer, M., Meng, J., Tarjan, D., Sheaffer, J.W., Skadron, K.: A performance study of general-purpose applications on graphics processors using CUDA. J. Parallel Distrib. Comput. **68**(10), 1370–1380 (2008)
7. D'Souza, R.M., Lysenko, M., Rahmani, K.: SugarScape on steroids: simulating over a million agents atinteractive rates. In: Proceedings of Agent 2007 Conference (2007)
8. Erra, U., Frola, B., Scarano, V., Couzin, I.: An efficient GPU implementation for large scale individual-based simulation of collective behavior. High Perform. Comput. Syst. Biol. **2009**, 51–58 (2009)

9. Hermellin, E., Michel, F.: GPU environmental delegation of agent perceptions: application to reynolds' s boids. In: Gaudou, B., et al. (eds.) MABS 2015. LNCS, vol. 9568, pp. 71–86. Springer, Heidelberg (2016)

10. Hermellin, E., Michel, F.: Toward a methodology for developing MABS using GPU programming. In: Proceedings of the International Conference on Autonomous Agents and Multiagent Systems, AAMAS, Singapore (2016)

11. Kubera, Y., Mathieu, P., Picault, S.: IODA: an interaction-oriented approach for multi-agent based simulations. Auton. Agent Multi-Agent Syst. **23**(3), 303–343 (2011)

12. Laville, G., Mazouzi, K., Lang, C., Marilleau, N., Herrmann, B., Philippe, L.: MCMAS: A toolkit to benefit from many-core architecure in agent-based simulation. In: an Mey, D., et al. (eds.) Euro-Par 2013. LNCS, vol. 8374, pp. 544–554. Springer, Heidelberg (2014)

13. Laville, G., Mazouzi, K., Lang, C., Marilleau, N., Philippe, L.: Using GPU for multi-agent multi-scale simulations. In: Omatu, S., Paz Santana, J.F., González, S.R., Molina, J.M., Bernardos, A.M., Rodríguez, J.M.C. (eds.) Distributed Computing and Artificial Intelligence. AISC, vol. 151, pp. 197–204. Springer, Heidelberg (2012)

14. Michel, F.: Translating agent perception computations into environmental processes in multi-agent-based simulations: a means for integrating graphics processing unit programming within usual agent-based simulation platforms. Syst. Res. Behav. Sci. **30**(6), 703–715 (2013)

15. Michel, F., Ferber, J., Drogoul, A.: Multi-agent systems and simulation: a survey from theagents community's perspective. In: Uhrmacher, A., Weyns, D., (eds.) Multi-Agent Systems: Simulation and Applications, Computational Analysis, Synthesis, and Design of Dynamic Systems, pp. 3–52. CRC Press - Taylor & Francis, June 2009

16. Owens, J.D., Luebke, D., Govindaraju, N., Harris, M., Kruger, J., Lefohn, A.E., Purcell, T.J.: A survey of general-purpose computation on graphics hardware. Comput. Graph. Forum **26**(1), 80–113 (2007)

17. Parry, H., Bithell, M.: Large scale agent-based modelling: a review and guidelines for model scaling. In: Heppenstall, A.J., Crooks, A.T., See, L.M., Batty, M. (eds.) Agent-Based Models of Geographical Systems, pp. 271–308. Springer, Heidelberg (2012)

18. Pavlov, R., Müller, J.P.: Multi-agent systems meet GPU: deploying agent-based architectures on graphics processors. In: Camarinha-Matos, L.M., Tomic, S., Graça, P. (eds.) DoCEIS 2013. IFIP AICT, vol. 394, pp. 115–122. Springer, Heidelberg (2013)

19. Payet, D., Courdier, R., Sébastien, N., Ralambondrainy, T.: Environment as support for simplification, reuse and integration of processes in spatial MAS. In: Proceedings of the 2006 IEEE International Conference on Information Reuse and Integration - Heuristic Systems Engineering, 16–18 September, Waikoloa, Hawaii, USA, pp. 127–131. IEEE Systems, Man, and Cybernetics Society (2006)

20. Perumalla, K.S., Aaby, B.G.: Data parallel execution challenges and runtime performance of agent simulations on GPUs. In: Proceedings of the 2008 Spring Simulation Multiconference, pp. 116–123 (2008)

21. Ricci, A., Piunti, M., Viroli, M.: Environment programming in multi-agent systems: an artifact-based perspective. Auton. Agent Multi-Agent Syst. **23**(2), 158–192 (2011)

22. Richmond, P., Coakley, S., Romano, D.M.: A high performance agent based modelling framework on graphics card hardware with CUDA. In: Proceedings of The 8th International Conference on Autonomous Agents and Multiagent Systems, AAMAS 2009, vol. 2, pp. 1125–1126. International Foundation for Autonomous Agents and Multiagent Systems, Richland, SC (2009)

23. Richmond, P., Romano, D.M.: Agent based GPU, a real-time 3d simulation and interactive visualisation framework for massive agent based modelling on the GPU. In: Proceedings International Workshop on Super Visualisation, IWSV 2008 (2008)

24. Richmond, P., Romano, D.M.: A high performance framework for agent based pedestrian dynamics on GPU hardware. In: European Simulation and Modelling (2011)

25. Richmond, P., Walker, D., Coakley, S., Romano, D.M.: High performance cellular level agent-based simulation with FLAME for the GPU. Briefings Bioinform. **11**(3), 334–347 (2010)

26. Sklar, E.: NetLogo, a multi-agent simulation environment. Artif. Life **13**(3), 303–311 (2007)

27. Strippgen, D., Nagel, K.: Multi-agent traffic simulation with CUDA. In: High Performance Computing Simulation, HPCS 2009, pp. 106–114, June 2009

28. Weyns, D., Van Dyke Parunak, H., Michel, F., Holvoet, T., Ferber, J.: Environments for multiagent systems state-of-the-art and research challenges. In: Weyns, D., Van Dyke Parunak, H., Michel, F. (eds.) E4MAS 2004. LNCS (LNAI), vol. 3374, pp. 1–47. Springer, Heidelberg (2005)

# Holonic Multiagent Simulation of Complex Adaptive Systems

Rafik Hadfi$^{(\boxtimes)}$ and Takayuki Ito

Department of Computer Science and Engineering,
Nagoya Institute of Technology, Gokiso, Showa-ku, Nagoya 466-8555, Japan
{rafik.hadfi,ito.takayuki}@nitech.ac.jp

**Abstract.** We propose a holonic multiagent simulator that can simulate any complex urban environment. We focus on traffic simulation within any geographic area on earth, subject to any weather conditions. We adopt an agent-based approach for the different beahviors of the vehicles, drivers, and pedestrians. The proposed driving behavioral models can realistically emulate driving behaviors of humans. The resulting simulator can handle all the complexities of such environments in accordance with the laws of physics.

**Keywords:** Multiagent simulation · Holonic system · Traffic simulation · Geographic information system · Mobility generation · Weather simulation

## 1 Introduction

Multiagent systems have inspired an increasing number of researchers from different domains. The need for adequate tools for the simulation of complex systems has motivated much of the agent-related research. The main goal of a multiagent system is to model the real world in terms of autonomous agents that can purposely interact with their external environment [18]. An agent can basically gather information from the environment using sensors, while attempting to execute its objectives using effectors [16].

In the context of complex adaptive systems simulation, it is possible to use a multiagent system to reduce the complexity of the simulation by breaking it into several subtasks. For instance, simulating a complex system could be divided into parallel simulations that can handle different subdomains.

Traffic in an open environment is an example of complex adaptive system. It is therefore practical to adopt a multiagent approach for such simulation. Multiagent traffic simulation has been extensively studied since traffic and transportation management require autonomic, collaborative, and reactive agents [1]. It is therefore possible to implement automated traffic control management systems thanks to the fact that agents can operate without centralized control. Furthermore, multiagent systems can connect to distributed subsystems, and can be extended to large-scale multiagent simulation.

© Springer International Publishing Switzerland 2016
J. Bajo et al. (Eds.): PAAMS 2016 Workshops, CCIS 616, pp. 137–147, 2016.
DOI: 10.1007/978-3-319-39387-2_12

In this paper, we propose a multiagent simulator that is suitable for complex adaptive systems. In particular, we focus on simulating traffic as well as the weather conditions that affect its environment. An inherent feature of complex systems is their hierarchical structure and the nested levels of detail that compose them. Therefore, adopting a multiagent agent approach for complex systems modeling will have to acknowledge this organization. Holonic multiagent systems [6] are a practical way for a recursive modeling of autonomous agents, by allowing a dynamic reorganisation of the whole system. Our main motivation is to build a scalable holonic simulator that can emulate traffic as well as any environmental factor that effects traffic flow, routing, and even $CO_2$ emission. Being able to simulate weather is a novel way to approach traffic simulation since it allows the reproduction of real-world scenarios like traffic in natural disaster situations. Such simulator can become a testbed for general-purpose computational intelligence and can be used for the benchmarking of routing algorithms. Additionally, our multiagent approach to behavioral modeling ensures the reproduction of realistic driving behaviors. To this end, we will model our simulator in terms of multiple independent layers. Each layer processes a particular aspect of the simulation through the interactions of its internal elements, or simply, agents. A layer will therefore be represented by a complex network of interacting agents that can communicate within that layer and possibly with other layers. The idea behind our simulation architecture is to adopt a holonic multiagent architecture coupled to a behavioral-based agent simulation. This is in fact a way to refine both the microscopic and the macroscopic aspects found in many traffic simulators. In fact, the availability of data collected via sensors and mobile devices allows us to better model human behaviors. For instance, this allows for the analysis of driver behaviors and the underlying decision-making mechanisms [3,13–15]. As a result, we can build large-scale simulations by embedding the social interactions and by elaborating fine-grained human behaviors [10]. The resulting multiagent social simulation [2] is well suited to any social context due to its ability to simulate pro-active behaviors, parallel computations [12], and dynamic micro scenarios [7,9]. It is within this perspective that we propose our holonic multiagent simulator.

The paper is structured as following. In Sect. 2, we provide the architecture of the simulator. In Sect. 3, we cover the behavioral models used by the different agents. In Sect. 4, we provide the results. In Sect. 5, we conclude and highlight the future work.

## 2   Simulator Architecture

### 2.1   Description

Our idea is to represent the whole complex system as a superposition of layers, as shown in Fig. 1. Each layer operates autonomously with all its internal threads, agents, graphical objects, etc. The holonic aspect resides in the fact that the content of each layer is a hierarchy in itself and that all the components of the layers can interact according to the dynamics of the simulation. For instance, the

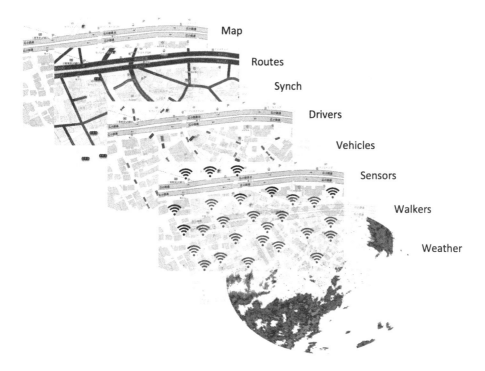

**Fig. 1.** Multilayered representation of a complex system

vehicles (Vehicles layer) are driven by drivers (Drivers layer) according to traffic lights (Synch layer), while interacting with routes, map, sensors and possibly pedestrians (Walkers). The whole is affected by the weather layer that embodies the physical conditions (precipitations) that affect the whole system.

We note that the layers should be as independent as possible so that the complexity of the simulation does not affect the communication between the different layers. Additionally, there should be a separation between the vehicles and the map in the sense that the way the vehicles navigate their space?should not be?specific to one particular Geographic Information System (GIS). In the following we adopt OpenStreetMap [8] as referential.

## 2.2   Architecture

The architecture of the simulator is illustrated in Fig. 2. As mentioned in the previous section, we should lower the coupling between the layers of the simulator. Specifically, there should be independence between the actual simulation (**Behavioral Models** and **Physical Engine**) and the corresponding OpenStreetMap rendering. This is important when the renderer is complex, that is, when we are not only rendering vehicles, but rendering pedestrians, weather data, snow, etc. This separation obeys the Dependency Inversion Principle in the sense that physical simulation acts as a high-level, abstract, objective, mathematical

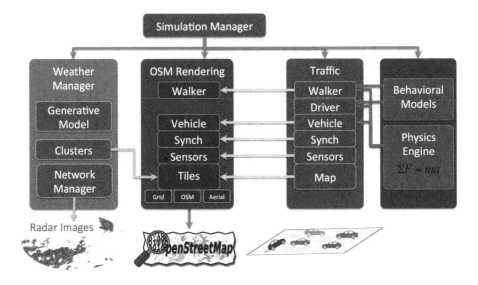

**Fig. 2.** Architecture

representation of the phenomena we want to simulate, while the OpenStreetMap rendering is one possible way of rendering the simulation. The renderer could easily be exchanged by another one. In the following, we provide a brief description of the components of the architecture.

**Physics Engine and Behavioral Models.** The Physics Engine component provides an approximate simulation of the physics that underly traffic, motion and the interactions between the agents. This component performs the simulation in real-time before rendering the result. The Behavioral Models describe the scenarios that govern the motion of the vehicles and the pedestrians.

**Traffic Tier** is composed of the following agent components:

1. **Walker**. Pedestrians are implemented as artificial agents that perform random walks. In particular, an agent performs mobility generation within a closed polygon, or as a random itinerary on the map. Additionally, such agents can predict collisions with other agents.
2. **Driver**. A vehicle is driven by an agent that can also perform collision detection, traffic lights and lanes assessment.
3. **Vehicle**. A vehicle is in fact an agent that modulates the forces acting on a graphical vehicle object. Such forces include the acceleration, direction, location, friction, velocity, and breaking.
4. **Synchronization**. We distinguish a set of agents that update the states of the traffic lights according to the intervals $\Delta_r$, $\Delta_o$, and $\Delta_g$.
5. **Sensors**. A sensor network is built on top of the map and allows the detections of the vehicles motion.

**Weather Manager.** The weather simulation is in fact the generation of precipitation as if it is detected by a weather surveillance radar (WSR). Additionally, it is possible to download this data in real-time and render it directly onto the map. The weather radars are capable of detecting the motion of rain droplets in addition to the intensity of the precipitation. Both types of data can be analyzed to determine the structure of storms and their potential to cause severe weather.

The simulation of the weather is a mapping between a precipitation vector field onto the geographic tiles, represented as weather clusters. This mapping is computed dynamically since the tiles are loaded as a function of the simulation location.

**OpenStreetMap Rendering.** The rendering of the geographic map relies on downloading and updating a hierarchy of OpenStreetMap tiles. Such tiles correspond to a specific area of the map and are loaded dynamically, depending on where the simulation is being run. Herein, we use two different maps. The first map (core map) is assigned to the physics engine and is used to run the simulation in real-time so that the result is later rendered onto the second map. The second map represents a real-world referential (OpenStreetMap in our case). The mapping from the core map to the OpenStreetMap map converts absolute references into latitude/longitude references. This conversion is required since it is difficult to manipulate latitudes and longitudes within a small area due to floating-point inaccuracies (E.g. manipulating vectors with latitudes in $\{136.892649, 136.909015, 136.909011\}$). To this end, we use the conversion function (1), where $x$ and $y$ are the coordinates in the core map, $x'$ and $y'$ are the latitude and longitude, $w$ and $h$ are the dimensions of the core map, and $x_-$ (resp. $y_-$) and $x_+$ (resp. $y_+$) are the minimal and maximal latitudes (resp. longitude).

$$x' \leftarrow \frac{x - x_-}{x_+ - x_-} \times (h - 1) \tag{1a}$$

$$y' \leftarrow \frac{y - y_-}{y_+ - y_-} \times (w - 1) \tag{1b}$$

## 3  Behavioral Modeling

The behavioral models govern the agents mobility as well as the range of actions allowed within the simulator. We distinguish three types of behavioral models for drivers, pedestrians, and vehicles.

### 3.1  Driving Behavioral Model

The main feature that reflects the driving behavior of a human is the velocity. However, we also need to look at how this velocity changes as function of the turns. In fact, turns are important indicators of the driver's mastery and control of the steering wheel (with angle $\lambda$) and its physical effect on the vehicle. We can look at the turning angle $\theta$ comprised between the velocity and the direction of the current itinerary. For instance, driving in a straight line corresponds to $\theta = 0$ while a right turn corresponds to $\theta = \pi/2$.

Let us assume that the minimal and maximal velocities of the vehicle are respectively $v^-$ and $v^+$, and that $v$ fluctuates in $[v^-, v^+]$. This interval refers to the driver's spectrum of physically allowed velocities. A behavioral model is therefore a specific way of mapping the turning angle $\theta$ to a specific velocity $v$, illustrated in function (2).

$$v_\theta : [0, \pi] \rightarrow [v^-, v^+] \tag{2}$$

Figure 3 shows three behavioral models. Model $v_1$ corresponds to what is perceived as a reckless driver since he barely decelerates when performing right turns. Model $v_2$ shows a conservative driver since he decelerates drastically when reaching right turns. Finally, $v_3$ shows a standard driver. We assume that a behavior is invariant beyond $\pi$ (U-turn), and thus, choose to limit the angular interval to $[0, \pi]$.

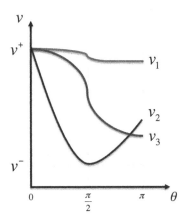

**Fig. 3.** Behavioral models $v_1$, $v_2$, and $v_3$

### 3.2 Pedestrian Behavioral Model

A pedestrian (walker) is modeled as an agent that moves within a closed polygonal space. The polygonal space is in fact a block on the map.

### 3.3 Vehicle Behavioral Model

For a vehicle, the act of moving from point $A$ to point $B$ is reduced to the execution of set of operations that could be summarized as following.

1. Updating the forces that act upon the vehicle.
2. Updating the acceleration $a$.
3. Updating the velocity $v$.
4. Updating the direction $d$.
5. Updating the location $x$ of the vehicle.

These actions are described as following:

**Updating direction** $d$ according to (3). Here, $\lambda$ is the steering wheel angle, $L$ is the vehicle wheelbase, $t_r$ is the turning radius, $u_m$ is the number of units per meter, $p$ is the simulation step, $\alpha_d$ is the angle of direction $d$, and $\alpha_s$ is the angular speed.

$$t_r \leftarrow L/sin(\lambda \times \frac{\pi}{3}) \tag{3a}$$

$$\alpha_s \leftarrow (\|v\| \times u_m)/t_r \tag{3b}$$

$$d \leftarrow \alpha_d + \alpha_s \times p \times \frac{180}{\pi} \tag{3c}$$

**Updating velocity** $v$ according to (4), with $a$ being the acceleration.

$$v \leftarrow d \times \|v\| + a \times p \tag{4}$$

In case $|\alpha_v - \alpha_d| > \frac{\pi}{2}$, $v$ is nullified. $\alpha_v$ being the angular velocity.

**Setting direction** as function of $\theta$ as in (5).

$$\theta' \leftarrow \theta \times \frac{\pi}{180} \tag{5a}$$

$$d \leftarrow \left( \cos(\theta'),\ \sin(\theta') \right) \tag{5b}$$

**Updating acceleration** based on Newton's second law ($\sum f = ma$) as in (6). The motive force of the vehicle is $F_m$, the friction force is $F_f$, and $m$ is the vehicle's mass.

$$a \leftarrow \frac{F_m + F_f}{m} \tag{6}$$

**Updating all the forces**, which requires updating the friction force whenever the driver breaks. This is done according to (7). $a_{max}$ is the maximal acceleration.

$$F_f \leftarrow d \times -a_{max} \tag{7}$$

**Updating the location** $x$ according to (8).

$$x \leftarrow x + v \times u_m \times p \tag{8}$$

## 4    Results

The interface of the simulator is shown in Fig. 4. The default view is the Open-StreetMap view. However, it is possible to show different perspectives that illustrate the superposed weather and traffic simulations as shown in Fig. 5. The user can macroscopically switch between the views (Aerial view, OpenStreetMap view, Grid view) of the simulation by altering the opacity of the layer.

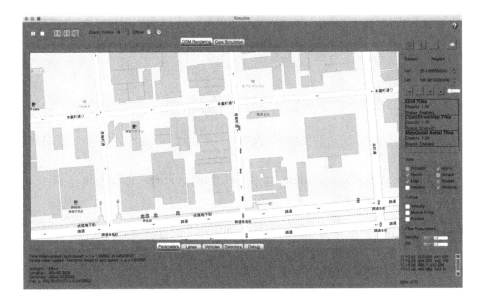

**Fig. 4.** Simulator main interface

The separation between the layers allows the simulations to be scalable in the number of vehicles and pedestrians, despite the complexity of their behaviors. Furthermore, running the physical simulations within one monolithic components allows us to render all the results faster than if each layer had to perform complex physical computations separately. The simulator can additionally generate rich datasets relative to the vehicles, the pedestrians, the drivers' actions, and the weather effect of the simulation map.

## 5    Related Work

In the context of traffic simulation, the multiagent approach is well suited to build traffic simulators and reproduce the dynamic and complex phenomena that are hard to express using purely mathematical models. In the mathematical approach, we tend to reproduce the vehicles streams from car-following dynamics obtained empirically from data collected at different operating road sections [11].

(a) Weather Simulation: Aerial View

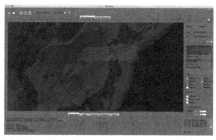

(b) Weather Simulation: OpenStreetMap View

(c) Macroscopic Traffic View

(d) Microscopic Traffic View

**Fig. 5.** Weather and traffic views

However, such mathematical approaches are only suited for simple traffic analysis since they are not realistic and do not offer accurate traffic flow for high density traffic.

As opposed to this mathematical approach, we find the behavioral approach, which is more coherent with the multiagent paradigm. Such approach relies on the interaction between various agents, such as vehicles, drivers, pedestrians, traffic lights, sensors, and so forth. The simulation is therefore an emergent phenomena of all these interactions. An example of such multiagent behavioral simulator is Archsim [5]. Such simulator allows a realistic coupling between the driving simulation and the traffic simulation. Another similar approach attempts to realistically model road junctions [4]. This approach is based on opportunistic individual behaviors that can detect critical circumstances.

Another family of simulators rely on Stochastic Cell Transmission Model (SCTM) [17], and has been proposed as a macro traffic simulation model of high accuracy. SCTM can represent the uncertainty of the traffic states as well as the changing travel demand and supply conditions. So far, SCTM has only been applied to freeways and simple networks that are one-to-one origin-destination networks.

# 6    Conclusion

We proposed a holonic multiagent simulator that can reproduce traffic as well as the weather conditions of the underlying geographic area. The proposed architecture ensures a low coupling of the different hierarchies of the multiagent system, which allows a realistic reproduction of traffic as well as the behaviors of the drivers and pedestrians.

As future directions, we think of distributing the multiagent system so that the different simulations are assigned to different clusters. This would allow us to add more computational intelligence by improving the behavioral models of the pedestrians and adding argumentation between the vehicles. Another direction is to adopt a 3D renderer instead of the 2-dimensional OpenStreetMap rendering. Most importantly, we think of deploying different routing algorithms on the simulator and evaluating the evolution of traffic congestion.

**Acknowledgement.** This work has been partially supported by the project "Multi-agent Future Traffic Prediction to Relieve Traffic Congestion" in the issue "Research and Development on Applications of Social Big Data".

# References

1. Chen, B., Cheng, H.: A review of the applications of agent technology in traffic and transportation systems. IEEE Trans. Intell. Transp. Syst. **11**, 485–497 (2010)
2. Davidsson, P.: Multi Agent Based Simulation: Beyond Social Simulation. Springer, Heidelberg (2001)
3. Dia, H.: An agent-based approach to modelling driver route choice behaviour under the influence of real-time information. Transp. Res. Part C: Emerg. Technol. **10**(5–6), 331–349 (2002)
4. Doniec, A., Mandiau, R., Piechowiak, S., Espie, S.: A behavioral multi-agent model for road traffic simulation. Transp. Res. Part C: Emerg. Technol. **21**(8), 1443–1454 (2011)
5. Espie, S.: Archisim, multi-actor parallel architecture for traffic simulation. In: Proceedings of the Second World Congress on Intelligent Transport Systems, vol. 4 (1995)
6. Fischer, K., Schillo, M., Siekmann, J.H.: Holonic multiagent systems: a foundation for the organisation of multiagent systems. In: Mařík, V., McFarlane, D.C., Valckenaers, P. (eds.) HoloMAS 2003. LNCS (LNAI), vol. 2744, pp. 71–80. Springer, Heidelberg (2003)
7. Gilbert, N.: Computer Simulation of Social Processes. Number 6. Social Research Update, Department of Sociology, University of Surrey, UK (1994)
8. Haklay, M.M., Weber, P.: Openstreetmap: user-generated street maps. IEEE Pervasive Comput. **7**(4), 12–18 (2008)
9. Harding, A.: Microsimulation and Public Policy. Elsevier, Amsterdam (1996)
10. Hattori, H., Nakajima, Y., Yamane, S.: Massive multiagent-based urban traffic simulation with fine-grained behavior models (2011)
11. Lieberman, E., Rathi, A.: Traffic flow theory. Trans. Res. Part C: Emerg. Technol. (1997)

12. Misra, J.: Distributed discrete-event simulation. ACM Comput. Surv. (CSUR) **18**, 39–65 (1986)
13. Nagel, K., Marchal, F.: Computational methods for multi-agent simulations of travel behaviour. In: Proceedings of International Association for Travel Behavior Research (IATBR), Lucerne, Switzerland (2003)
14. Rossetti, R.J., Bordini, R.H., Bazzan, A.L., Bampi, S., Liu, R., Vliet, D.V.: Using BDI agents to improve driver modelling in a commuter scenario. Trans. Res. Part C: Emerg. Technol. **10**(5–6), 373–398 (2002)
15. Rossetti, R.J., Liu, R., Cybis, H.B., Bampi, S.: A multi-agent demand model. In: Proceedings of the 13th Mini-Euro Conference and the 9th Meeting of the Euro Working Group Transportation, pp. 193–198, Bari, Italy (2002)
16. Russell, S., Norvig, P.: Artificial intelligence: a modern approach (1995)
17. Sumalee, A., Zhong, R., Pan, T., Szeto, W.: Stochastic cell transmission model (SCTM): a stochastic dynamic traffic model for traffic state surveillance and assignment. Trans. Res. Part B: Methodol. **45**(3), 507–533 (2011)
18. Wooldridge, M., Jennings, N.R.: Intelligent agents: theory and practice. Knowl. Eng. Rev. **10**(02), 115–152 (1995)

# Multiagent Social Influence Detection Based on Facial Emotion Recognition

Pankaj Mishra$^{(\boxtimes)}$, Rafik Hadfi, and Takayuki Ito

Department of Computer Science and Engineering, Nagoya Institute of Technology,
Gokiso, Showa-ku, Nagoya 466-8555, Japan
{pankaj.mishra,rafik}@itolab.nitech.ac.jp, ito.takayuki@nitech.ac.jp

**Abstract.** There has been an increasing interest in information diffusion within social networks and the usage of multiagent systems for knowledge discovery. In this paper, we build a multiagent system that can track the social correlations within a group of people based on video data. Our information diffusion system targets small groups of people, possibly composed of office workers, meeting attendees, etc. Adopting a multiagent architecture to study the influential correlations in a social network is an adequate choice since it maintains the scalability and robustness of the system. The correlation amongst the nodes of the social network is built on the basis of facial emotions. We evaluated the method in a social network with scripted discussions. Our results show that the emotion propagation was effectively reflected in the predicted social influence correlation.

**Keywords:** Multiagent system · Facial feature extraction · Knowledge discovery · Emotion diffusion · Social network · Social correlation

## 1 Introduction

Detecting and tracking multiple people in real-world environments is a challenging task. Moreover, any social gathering possesses a number of social influences between the individuals. We propose a multiagent system that can analyse a social network, node-by-node, to track the emotions diffusion in the network. This allows the discovery of influential correlations amongst the nodes by studying the change in facial expressions (emotions). In any workgroup, people have the tendency to come together and form virtual groups and then, the actions of the influential person are propagated to others in this virtual group. The analysis of the ways in which these group members induce their actions (emotion, speech, etc.) to other members is the goal behind our work.

In order to study the social behaviours propagation in a social network, many works integrated social theories with computational methods. For instance, [4] proposed a system to analyse the social interactions in real working environments by tracking the human location and head pose. Similarly, [25] analyses the behaviours of the participants in a meeting by tracking their speaking and

© Springer International Publishing Switzerland 2016
J. Bajo et al. (Eds.): PAAMS 2016 Workshops, CCIS 616, pp. 148–160, 2016.
DOI: 10.1007/978-3-319-39387-2_13

writing patterns. Moreover, the propagation of influence in huge social networks, like Twitter or Facebook, are extensively studied by tracking online activities [1,23].

In the existing works, the analysis of social correlation focuses only on pose detection, such as head pose, shoulder pose, hand pose, etc. However, very less attempt was given to the analysis of social correlation on the basis of the facial emotions. In this paper, we are more interested in tracking the facial emotions in small groups of people, such as colleagues, business meeting attendees, etc. In such gatherings, the chances of groupings are done on the basis of concepts like homophilia, cofounding or influence. Homophilia and cofounding concepts are based on the background information of people, such as profession, knowledge of the topic of discussion, age, etc. However, the analysis of influence is purely based on tracking the actions and the corresponding reaction among the participants in the network. The action can be a pose, speech, emotion, etc. In our work, we focus on tracking the emotion and speech of all the participants to analyse the influence among them. A facial emotion is considered as one of the important actions for human communication as well as for the understanding the social relationship between humans. Hence, our work is more inclined towards human emotions to understand their correlation.

Multiagent architectures are largely adopted for knowledge discovery in social networks as it maintains scalability and robustness [21]. Although our considered networks are not huge, the length and width may vary. Therefore, our system has two main functionalities, that is, emotion detection and social influence detection, which is also embedded in a multiagent architecture. Herein, emotion detection was based on the deformable model, Active Appearance Model (AAM) [5]; for features extraction and these features were classified to emotion labels, by training the binary class scalar vector machine (SVM) [20]. Later, social influence detection was done, based on the proposed algorithms which is discussed in the later sections. Briefly, we propose a scalable multiagent system, integrated with machine learning algorithms to discover the knowledge of the influential correlation among all the participants in the network. These knowledge find many applications such as, negotiation, viral marketing, surveys, etc.

In this paper, we have made two main contributions. Firstly, an emotion diffusion parameter was introduced, which defines the strength of the emotion induction between two nodes at each instance of time. Another contribution was the calculation of influence in terms of weights of weighted graph, which is also associated with the sign '−' or '+'; which represents the direction of the induced emotion. Apart from this, the frontal video dataset of a scripted discussion, which was used in this paper as testing dataset can also be adopted to build a similar baseline system.

The rest of the paper is organised as following. Section 2 provides the agent architecture along with data pre-processing and the facial emotion detection. Section 3 explains the influence analysis module in detail and its different steps are discussed. Section 4 presents the experimental results that validate our proposed algorithm. Finally, we conclude and provide the future work in Sect. 5.

## 2    Agent Architecture

The overall architecture of the system is depicted in Fig. 1, which consist of two main modules: the facial emotion detection and the influence detection. A homogenous and autonomous agent is associated with every participant in the considered network. These agents interact with modules independently and gather informations to finally build the social correlation amongst all the agents. Our multiagent system was implemented in JADE [3] framework. In Fig. 1, we depict the interactions of two agents (participants), $A_1$ and $A_2$ interacting with the two modules and finally a weighted graph representing the influence amongst the agents is built. In the later sections we discuss the whole methodology divided into three steps namely, Data processing, Facial emotion detection and Social Influence detection.

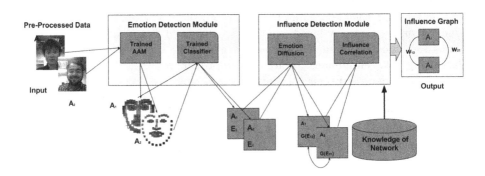

**Fig. 1.** Architecture

### 2.1    Data Pre-processing

In the proposed work, the system requires a frontal video data[1] of the participants. Wherein, change in one's emotion being induced on other's emotions can be observed. This video data is firstly need to be pre-processed. The pre-processing includes framing of the video and later locating and cropping the frontal image in all the frames, by using Viola-Jones algorithm [12]. These, processed frontal frames for all the participants along with the actions of all the participants in each frame is recorded; where the actions include, emotion, speech or both based on the metadata. Later, each instantiated agents for all the participants is activated by its stream of frames and actions carried by the frame. The further stages of an activated agent is discussed in the next sections.

### 2.2    Facial Emotion Module

In this section, we will discuss the steps required to detect the emotions of each agent in the frame. All the agents will go through these steps for all the stream

---

[1] Cameras focused on the faces.

of frames they carry. The whole process in divided into two steps, feature extraction in the frames and classify these frames into emotion labels, based on the extracted features. Firstly, we will discuss the facial features extraction from a frame. In order to extract the facial features from each frontal frames, first step is to locate the positions of the facial features points, such as nose, eyes, mouth, etc. Then, around these detected facial points, we extract the shape and appearance feature vectors. The shape feature vector denotes the co-ordinates of all the facial features, whereas appearance features can be Gabor descriptor, Local Binary Pattern (LBP) descriptor, etc. as discussed in [9]. However, most of the past works like, [2,5,15], are based on the deformable model named Active appearance model (AAM). AAM is a computer vision algorithm to track the facial feature points on human face. Additionally, AAM provides a compact statistical representation of the shape and the appearance variation of the human face. Therefore, we choose a trained AAM to align the face, and later to extract the shape and the appearance features. The appearance features are scale-invariant feature transform (SIFT) [14] descriptors. AAM implementation was based on the Menpo [17] python libraries, and AAM was trained using the two publicly available database, FERA database [24] and LFPW database [19]. Further, this trained AAM is used to track the face, and to extract the three types of holistic[2] features are extracted around the 68 tracked landmark points. These three holistic features are, similarity normalised shapes (s-pts), similarity normalised appearance (s-app) and canonical appearance (c-app) [2].

In our final AAM implementation, the landmarks of the current frame is initialised with the landmarks of the previous frame, which reduces the fitting iteration. These extracted features are used for the detection of emotions in the facial frames by training the classifier. Basically, emotion is recognised by the presence of one or more specific Facial Action Units (FACS) [6]; whereas the combination of these FACS defines one of the 8 basic emotions namely, happy, sad, disgust, anger, contempt, surprise and fear. In order to detect the presence of FACS in the frames, we train the binary class SVM with the extracted feature vectors and FACS labels. Therefore, the emotion detection module comprises of a trained AAM model and a trained SVM classifier. We summarise all the frames, and consider emotion labels for each second in order to build the social correlation amongst the agents.

## 3   Influence Analysis Module

In this section, we would discuss the steps to build the social graph, where each agent represents the nodes in the graph. Later, on the basis of the emotion labels carried per second by each agents and proposed algorithms, we analyse the influential correlation among them in terms of weights of the graph. The overall analysis of social influence correlation amongst the agent is based on the detected emotion per seconds (E), the tracked action per second (A) and the knowledge database (D). Whereas, D includes the information about the

---

[2] Herein, holistic means that the whole face is considered.

agents/participants in the network. These information can be age, gender, profession, seniority, etc. Based on information in D, we calculate the node centrality ($\gamma$) (importance of an agent) in the network. Although, there are many different methods to calculate the value of $\gamma$ in a network, as discussed in [22]. However, in the considered domain, mentioned methods do not suffice our purpose to rank the agents. Therefore, we decide it on the basis of these information in D. The intuition behind the value of $\gamma$ is, if one of the agent has the superior knowledge in the topic of discussion, or is the senior member, then this agent's opinion will be most likely choice of the others. However, mere $\gamma$ value does not contribute to the influential characteristics of a person. Because, an influential character depends on many factors such as speech, expression, way of conveying, background knowledge, etc. So we use $\gamma$ value just to locate the path to influential node, but do not consider it as an influential node. Therefore, it can be said that, higher the $\gamma$ value, higher is the chances of the agent to be influential. The whole process of social influence detection is divided in two basic steps (i) Emotion diffusion tracking and (ii) Social influence calculation, as discussed in the next subsections.

### 3.1    Emotion Diffusion Tracking

In any given social graph, emotion propagates among the nodes of the graph. This knowledge of emotion propagation helps to find the influential correlation amongst all the nodes. This is done by analysis of, change in one's emotion or action causing change in the emotions of others. Further, in our work, we consider emotions induction in two ways, firstly action induces emotion ($a \rightarrow e$) and the other, emotion induces emotion ($e \rightarrow e$). The $a \rightarrow e$ correlation is said to have occurred, if the action of an agent has influenced the emotion of the other agents. Whereas, $e \rightarrow e$ correlation is said have occurred when the emotion of an agent influences the emotions of the other agents. The diffusion of emotions in the scenarios can be represented by an emotion diffusion parameter ($\Delta E$), calculated using the Eq. 1,

$$\Delta E = \frac{\tau_e \times \omega_e}{T} \tag{1}$$

where $\tau_e$ is the time interval of emotion $e$, and $\omega_e$ is an agent's emotion coefficient of $e$. $T$ is the total frame considered for emotion diffusion calculation $\Delta E$. The value of $\omega_e$ is calculated using Eq. 2, which is pre-calculated for all the agents for every emotion. $t_e$ is the total time instance for which agent has an emotion $e$ and $N_e$ is the total number of time instance when all the agents has emotion $e$.

$$\omega^e = \frac{\gamma \times t^e}{N^e} \tag{2}$$

Other than this, we define the direction of the emotion diffusion by $\delta$, which can have be 1 or $-1$ given the orientation of the carried emotion. The $\delta$ values for all the considered emotion is listed in the Table 2, which is based on the discussion in [8]. The emotion diffusion in both the scenarios is calculated using the Algorithms 1 and 2. Let us first discuss the Algorithm 1 for $a \rightarrow e$ scenario, which accepts the list of passive (agent with action: emotion or no emotion) agents for every active (agent with action: speech or both) agents, and gives $\Delta E^1$ and $\delta^1$ for all combinations of passive and active agents as output. In the equation on line 8, we calculate the $\Delta E^{1e}$ values for each emotion $e$ carried by the agent p for time $\tau^e$, during the interval $T_a$, for which the agent $a$ was active. Then, the final $\Delta E^1$ value is the maximum value in set $\Delta E^{1e}$. Thus finding that emotion $e$ was induced by an agent $a$ on agent p. Later final $\delta^1$ is calculated by multiplying the $\delta$ value of $a$ and e, which gives the direction of the emotion induction. Similarly, in Algorithm 2, emotion diffusion $\Delta E^2$ and $\delta^2$ are calculated for all the pairs of nodes, irrespective of the active agent, where $T = 1$. At the end of this step, we get four values, $\Delta E^1$ and $\Delta E^2$ denote the emotion diffusion parameters and $\delta^1$ and $\delta^2$ denote the direction of emotion diffusion values for all the pairs of agents. Later, we build the influential correlation among the agents, as discussed in the next subsection.

---

**Algorithm 1.** Emotion Propagation $(a \rightarrow e)$

---

1: **procedure** EMOTION GRADIENT
2:     **Input:** $a$ Active agent
3:     $P$ List of passive agent
4:     **Output:** $\Delta E^1$ and $\delta^1$ for all passive agent
5:     // where $\delta$ is $-1$ or $1$
6:     **for** all $p$ enumerate(P) **do**
7:         **for** all $e$ Emotion E **do**
8:             $\{\Delta E^{1e}{}_{ap}\} \leftarrow \frac{\tau^e{}_{ap} \times \omega^e{}_p}{T_a}$
9:             // Maximum of $\Delta E^{1e}$ is final $\Delta E^1$
10:            // $\delta^e$ is emotion having maximum for $\Delta E^{1e}$
11:            $\Delta E^1{}_{ap} \leftarrow max(\{\Delta E^{1e}{}_{ap}\})$
12:            $\delta^1{}_{ap} \leftarrow \delta_a \times \delta^e{}_p$
13:     **End**

---

### 3.2 Social Influence Calculation

From the Algorithms 1 and 2, we get the emotion diffusions $\Delta E^1, \Delta E^2$, $\delta^1$ and $\delta^2$ for both the scenarios. Finally, we calculate the influence of each agent on the other agents, based on the Algorithm 3. The objective is to find the social influence amongst all the agents in the network, in terms of weight of the weighted graph. The input to this algorithm is list of $\Delta E^1$, $\Delta E^2$, $\delta^1$ and $\delta^2$ for all the pairs of agents. Based on these values, the weight $W_{ij}$ between agent i and j is calculated using the equation on line 7. Where, summation of $\Delta E^1$ and $\Delta E^2$ for i and j is divided by summation of $\Delta E^1$ for all the neighbouring nodes of j and j. Finally the orientation of the influence is associated with the $W_{ij}$, by multiplying $\delta_{ij}$. Thus, as a output we get a weighted graph, where weight represents the influence and sign '$-$' and '$+$' represents the orientation of the influence being induced.

**Algorithm 2.** Emotion Propagation $(e \rightarrow e)$

---

1: **procedure** EMOTION GRADIENT
2:   **Input:** $A$ List of all agent
3:   $B$ List of all agent
4:   **Output:** $\Delta E^2$ and $\delta^2$ for all pair of nodes
5:   // where $\delta$ is $-1$ or $1$
6:   **for** all $a$ enumerate(A) **do**
7:     **for** all $b$ enumerate(B) **do**
8:       **for** all $e$ Emotion E **do**
9:         $\{\Delta E^{2e}{}_{ab}\} \leftarrow \frac{\tau^e{}_{ab} \times \omega^e{}_b}{T}$ // where $T$ is 1
10:        // Maximum of $\Delta E^{2e}$ is final $\Delta E^2$
11:        // $\delta^e$ is emotion having maximum for $\Delta E^{2e}$
12:        $\Delta E^2{}_{ab} \leftarrow max(\{\Delta E^{2e}{}_{ab}\})$
13:        $\delta^2{}_{ab} \leftarrow \delta_a \times \delta^e{}_b$
14: **End**

---

**Algorithm 3.** Influence Calculation

---

1: **procedure** INFLUENCE
2:   **Input:** $\Delta E^1$ and $\Delta E^2$ for each pair of nodes
3:     $\delta^1$ and $\delta^2$ for each pair of nodes
4:   **Output:** $W$ weight for each pair of nodes
5:   **for** each pair of node $i$ and $j$ **do**
6:     $\delta_{ij} \leftarrow \delta^1{}_{ij} \times \delta^2{}_{ij}$
7:     $W_{ij} \leftarrow \frac{\Delta E^1{}_{ij} + \Delta E^2{}_{ij}}{\sum^k_{N(j)} \Delta E^1{}_{kj}} \times \delta_{ij}$
8:     // $N(j)$ neighbours of node $j$
9: **End**

---

## 4    Experimental Results and Discussion

In this section, we describe the evaluation of the baseline system to analyse the social influences in the network on the basis of change in the extracted facial expressions. In order to test our proposed algorithm, we need the frontal video data of small networks to detect the emotions. However, similar datasets were not available, therefore we recorded a scripted discussion of three of our colleagues, namely, agent A, B and C. Moreover, the $\gamma$ values of all the three agents were decided on the basis of two parameters, seniority and the knowledge about the topic. Assuming agent A being the senior among the three, and agent B having higher knowledge on topic of discussion. On the basis of these assumptions, $\gamma$ values for the agents were defined as 4, 5, and 2 for agent A, B and C respectively. Similarly, the calculation of $\gamma$ values for larger network can be done by comparing the basic information of all the agents. Additionally, the video data should be able to showcase the influence caused by emotion and action (speaking). Therefore, we structured the script where each participants does the action (speaks) for approximately 120 s in a sequence, yielding a total of 360 s video. Once an agent corresponding to each person is instantiated, these agents interact

**Table 1.** Detected Emotion per seconds

| Person | Neutral | Happy | Surprise | Angry | Sad |
|--------|---------|-------|----------|-------|-----|
| A | 100 | 20 | 100 | 45 | 95 |
| B | 22 | 190 | 75 | 33 | 40 |
| C | 27 | 140 | 80 | 53 | 60 |

**Table 2.** Emotion Orientation ($\delta$) and FACS

| Label | Emotion | $\delta$ | FACS |
|-------|---------|----------|------|
| 1 | Neutral | +1 | null |
| 2 | Happy | +1 | 6+12 |
| 3 | Surprise | +1 | 1+2+4+25 |
| 4 | Sad | −1 | 1+4+15 |
| 5 | Angry | −1 | 4+7+23+25 |

with the different modules to extract the facial expression and analysis of social influence in the network, as shown in Fig. 1.

### 4.1 Results

The input video of length 360 s is first converted into frames and other pre-processing steps are done. This results into frontal frames, which are then aligned with the trained AAM, in order to extract three different feature vectors, namely, s-pts, s-aap and c-aap. Next these feature vectors are used to detect the set of FACS present in the frames and later detect the emotion on the basis of combination of these detected FACS. In our experiment, we considered only 5 emotions, namely neutral, happy, surprise, sad and angry. Therefore, we end up considering 10 FACS; combination of which represents these emotions. The chosen FACS are 1, 2, 4, 6, 7, 12, 15, 23 and 25 as shown in the Table 2. The classification of these FACS in the frames were done using the binary class linear SVM for each FACS, therefore we trained 10 SVM classifiers. Training was done using the CK+ dataset [15], considering s-pts and c-app feature vectors only, because it gives the best results as discussed in [15]. Moreover, the trained classifiers were cross validated and accuracy of all the classifiers range between 75 % to 95 %. Finally, we consider emotion per seconds, and Table 1 represents the emotions detected per second for all the agents. Further, the social influential correlation was done on the basis of these change in emotion labels for every second, considering both the scenarios. The calculated values of $\Delta E^1$ and $\Delta E^2$ are listed in the Tables 3 and 4. In the end, we calculate the influence in network, based on the Algorithm 3. Finally, we represent the results in a weighted graph, as shown in Fig. 2. The discussion about the results and validation of our work is discussed in the next subsection.

### 4.2 Discussion

We have proposed an algorithm to analyse the diffusion of emotion and finding the influential correlation in a small social network. Further, in order to demonstrate the validity and accuracy of our proposed methods, we compared the diffusion of emotion in the script with the final experimental results.

**Table 3.** Emotion Diffusion $\Delta E^1$

| Agent | A | B | C |
|-------|---|---|---|
| A | 0 | 1.8 | 0.9 |
| B | 2.5 | 0 | 2.2 |
| C | 0.8 | 1.5 | 0 |

**Table 4.** Emotion Diffusion $\Delta E^2$

| Agent | A | B | C |
|-------|---|---|---|
| A | 0 | 2.5 | 1.2 |
| B | 2.8 | 0 | 2.5 |
| C | 1.2 | 0.8 | 0 |

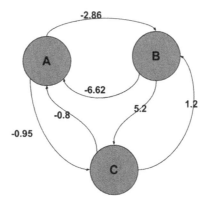

**Fig. 2.** Social influence graph

Firstly, the emotion diffusion amongst the 3 participants in the fed video was plotted for better analysis. Figures 3 and 4 represents the emotion diffusion in scenarios $a \rightarrow e$ and $e \rightarrow e$ respectively. Wherein, y-axis depicts emotions normalised along the axis for better representation and x-axis represents the time in seconds. Beginning with the emotion diffusion in scenario $a \rightarrow e$, in Fig. 3, it can be briefly concluded that, agent B induces agent C in a positive sense more often. Whereas, agent B induces agent A in negative sense; that is agent A would be happy when agent B gets upset. However, considering these short interval emotion induction during which only one agent is active, may lead to false judgement of an influential node. Therefore, we also considered the overall emotion induction during the whole 360 seconds. That is by considering the scenario, $e \rightarrow e$, and its emotion diffusion is depicted in the Fig. 4. From this graph, it can be briefly said that agent B induces emotion on agent C and agent A. Additionally, induction of emotion in reverse sense is not reciprocated from both the scenarios. Therefore, from the script, it can be said that agent B induces C in positive sense and agent A in negative sense more often. Now considering the final experimental result, which is a weighted graph in Fig. 2. From the Fig. 2, B induces emotion on C with 5.2 weight and induces emotion on A with $-6.62$ weight. The sign '$-$' denotes the emotion induced in the opposite direction. Furthermore, A has the least influence on C, and C has less influence on B compared to the influence of B on C. We think that the weighted graph in

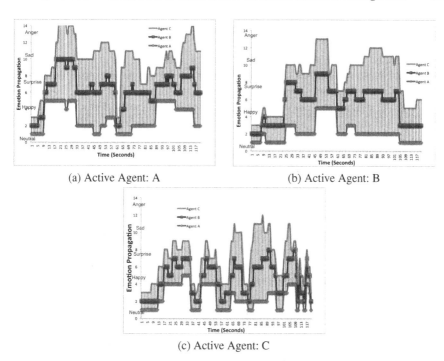

(a) Active Agent: A                    (b) Active Agent: B

(c) Active Agent: C

**Fig. 3.** Emotion propagation with 3 active agents

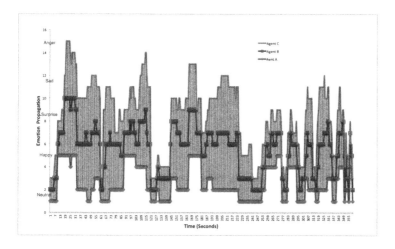

**Fig. 4.** Overall emotion propagation

Fig. 2 follows the emotion diffusion in the scripted discussion. Therefore it can be said that our proposed algorithm can effectively measure the influence in the considered network.

## 5    Conclusion

We introduced a multiagent system that can track the emotions diffusion in a social network, which can help in extracting the social influence correlation among the nodes of the network. Intuitively, the measure of social correlation gives an idea of how the change of emotions of one person affects the emotions of another person. If any particular node in the network brings a high degree of emotional change in the network, it can be said that this node is an influential node in the network. Facial emotions were classified by training an SVM on the basis of the facial features extracted using a trained deformed model AAM. After detecting the emotions of all the nodes in the network, the influence of change in emotions was measured using the proposed algorithms. We also introduced the term emotion diffusion parameter, which defines the degree of emotions being induced by one node on the others. Finally, we represent the influence in the network in the form of weighted graph, where weight denotes the influence and the associated sign denotes the orientation of the induced emotion. The proposed method was tested against the scripted discussion video in our laboratory. The final experimental results were validated by comparing the final correlation results with the emotion diffusion in the scripted discussion. It was found that the calculated correlations follows the actual emotion diffusion in the discussion.

As future work, we think of extending our method to larger real-life networks and incorporating emotions from voice data along with facial emotions. The resultant emotions can depict human correlation in a more accurate fashion. We also plan on investigating how social associations can be build based on any anonymous network using social network mining techniques.

**Acknowledgements.** This work has been partially supported by the project "Large-scale Consensus Support System based on Agents Technology" in the research area "Intelligent Information Processing Systems Creating Co-Experience Knowledge and Wisdom with Human-Machine Harmonious Collaboration" of JST CREST projects.

## References

1. Anagnostopoulos, A., Kumar, R., Mahdian, M.: Influence and correlation in social networks. In: Proceedings of the 14th ACM SIGKDD International Conference on Knowledge Discovery and Data Mining, pp. 7–15. ACM (2008)
2. Ashraf, A.B., Lucey, S., Cohn, J.F., Chen, T., Ambadar, Z., Prkachin, K.M., Solomon, P.E.: The painful face-pain expression recognition using active appearance models. Image Vision Comput. **27**(12), 1788–1796 (2009)
3. Bellifemine, F., Bergenti, F., Caire, G., Poggi, A.: Jadea java agent development framework. In: Multi-Agent Programming, pp. 125–147. Springer, New York (2005)
4. Chen, C.W., Ugarte, R.C., Wu, C., Aghajan, H.: Discovering social interactions in real work environments. In: 2011 IEEE International Conference on Automatic Face & Gesture Recognition and Workshops (FG 2011), pp. 933–938. IEEE (2011)
5. Cootes, T.F., Edwards, G.J., Taylor, C.J.: Active appearance models. IEEE Trans. Pattern Anal. Mach. Intell. **6**, 681–685 (2001)

6. Ekman, P., Rosenberg, E.L.: What the Face Reveals: Basic and Applied Studies of Spontaneous Expression using the Facial Action Coding System (FACS). Oxford University Press, New York (1997)
7. Finin, T., Labrou, Y., Mayfield, J.: KQML as an agent communication language. In: Software Agents. MIT Press, Cambridge (1995)
8. Ghamen, K., Caplier, A.: Positive and negative expressions classification using the belief theory. Int. J. Tomogr. Stat. **17**(S11), 72–87 (2011)
9. Happy, S., Routray, A.: Robust facial expression classification using shape and appearance features. In: 2015 Eighth International Conference on Advances in Pattern Recognition (ICAPR), pp. 1–5. IEEE (2015)
10. Hinton, G.E., Osindero, S., Teh, Y.W.: A fast learning algorithm for deep belief nets. Neural Comput. **18**(7), 1527–1554 (2006)
11. Hsu, C.W., Chang, C.C., Lin, C.J., et al.: A practical guide to support vector classification (2003)
12. Jensen, O.H.: Implementing the viola-jones face detection algorithm (2008)
13. Li, X., Wang, L., Sung, E.: Adaboost with SVM-based component classifiers. Eng. Appl. Artif. Intell. **21**(5), 785–795 (2008)
14. Lowe, D.G.: Object recognition from local scale-invariant features. In: Proceedings of the Seventh IEEE International Conference on Computer Vision, vol. 2, pp. 1150–1157. IEEE (1999)
15. Lucey, P., Cohn, J.F., Kanade, T., Saragih, J., Ambadar, Z., Matthews, I.: The extended cohn-kanade dataset (ck+): a complete dataset for action unit and emotion-specified expression. In: 2010 IEEE Computer Society Conference on Computer Vision and Pattern Recognition Workshops (CVPRW), pp. 94–101. IEEE (2010)
16. McPherson, M., Smith-Lovin, L., Cook, J.M.: Birds of a feather: homophily in social networks. Annu. Rev. Sociol. **27**, 415–444 (2001)
17. Alabort-i Medina, J., Antonakos, E., Booth, J., Snape, P., Zafeiriou, S.: Menpo: A comprehensive platform for parametric image alignment and visual deformable models. In: Proceedings of the ACM International Conference on Multimedia, MM 2014, pp. 679–682. ACM, New York (2014). http://doi.acm.org/10.1145/2647868.2654890
18. Ruiz, A., Van de Weijer, J., Binefa, X.: From emotions to action units with hidden and semi-hidden-task learning. In: Proceedings of the IEEE International Conference on Computer Vision, pp. 3703–3711 (2015)
19. Sagonas, C., Tzimiropoulos, G., Zafeiriou, S., Pantic, M.: 300 faces in-the-wild challenge: the first facial landmark localization challenge. In: 2013 IEEE International Conference on Computer Vision Workshops (ICCVW), pp. 397–403. IEEE (2013)
20. Simon, T., Nguyen, M.H., De La Torre, F., Cohn, J.F.: Action unit detection with segment-based SVMS. In: 2010 IEEE Conference on Computer Vision and Pattern Recognition (CVPR), pp. 2737–2744. IEEE (2010)
21. Stone, P., Veloso, M.: Multiagent systems: a survey from a machine learning perspective. Auton. Robots **8**(3), 345–383 (2000)
22. Sun, J., Tang, J.: A survey of models and algorithms for social influence analysis. In: Aggarwal, C.C. (ed.) Social Network Data Analytics, pp. 177–214. Springer, New York (2011)
23. Tang, J., Sun, J., Wang, C., Yang, Z.: Social influence analysis in large-scale networks. In: Proceedings of the 15th ACM SIGKDD International Conference on Knowledge Discovery and Data Mining, pp. 807–816. ACM (2009)

24. Valstar, M.F., Jiang, B., Mehu, M., Pantic, M., Scherer, K.: The first facial expression recognition and analysis challenge. In: 2011 IEEE International Conference on Automatic Face & Gesture Recognition and Workshops (FG 2011), pp. 921–926. IEEE (2011)
25. Zhang, D.: Probabilistic graphical models for human interaction analysis. Technical report IDIAP (2006)
26. Zhu, Y., De la Torre, F., Cohn, J.F., Zhang, Y.J.: Dynamic cascades with bidirectional bootstrapping for action unit detection in spontaneous facial behavior. IEEE Trans. Affect. Comput. 2(2), 79–91 (2011)

# Self-regulation of Social Exchange Processes: A Model Based in Drama Theory

Renata G. Wotter[✉], Diana F. Adamatti, and Graçaliz P. Dimuro

Centro de Ciências Computacionais, Universidade Federal do Rio Grande,
Rio Grande, RS, Brazil
renata.wotter@gmail.com

**Abstract.** This paper presents a dramatic model for self-regulation of social exchange processes in multiagent systems, based on the concepts of Drama Theory. The model has five phases of dramatic resolution, which involve feelings, emotions, trust and reputation. Agents with different social exchange strategies interact each other in order to maximize their strategy-based fitness functions. The objective is to obtain a more natural model than the ones existing in the literature, which are based on (partially observable) Markov decision processes or in game theory, so that it can be applied in real-world applications. We aim at promoting more balanced and fair multiagent interactions, increasing the number of successful social exchanges and, thus, promoting the continuity of social exchanges.

**Keywords:** Drama theory · Social exchange processes · Regulation of interactions

## 1 Introduction

The Piaget's Social Exchanges Theory [1] has been used as the basis for the analysis of interactions in Multiagent Systems (MAS). Such interactions are called services exchanges, which are evaluated by the agents when interacting, creating the concept of social exchange values, that are qualitative and subjective values [2–5]. A fundamental problem that has been discussed in the literature is the regulation of social exchanges [6–12], in order to allow, for example, the emergence of balanced exchanges along time, leading to social equilibrium and stability [1] and/or fairness behaviour [13,14]. In particular, this is a difficult problem when the agents, adopting different social exchange strategies, have incomplete information on the other agents' exchange strategies. This is a crucial problem in open agent societies (see [8,9]).

In previous works (e.g., [6,8,9]), Dimuro et al. and Pereira et al. have introduced different models (e.g., centralized/decentralized control, internal/external control, closed/open societies) for the social exchange regulation problem, developing different hybrid agent models. In particular, Macedo et al. [15] introduced the first step towards the self-regulation of the social exchanges processes. The

© Springer International Publishing Switzerland 2016
J. Bajo et al. (Eds.): PAAMS 2016 Workshops, CCIS 616, pp. 161–172, 2016.
DOI: 10.1007/978-3-319-39387-2_14

problem was tackled in a game theory context, given a new interpretation, in terms of material[1] exchanges, to the special kind of interaction described by the evolutionary spatial ultimatum game discussed by Xianyu [14]. Considering an agent society organized in a complex network, the paper analyzed the evolution of the agents' exchange strategies along the time considering the influence of their social preferences on the emergence of the equilibrium/fairness behavior. However, long-term aspects of the interaction and other concerns that exchange processes may involve were not considered in this simplified model.

In [11], Dimuro et al. introduced the Game of Self-Regulation of Social Exchange Processes (GSREP), where the agents, possessing different social exchange strategies, considering both the short and long-term aspects of the interactions, evolve their exchange strategies along the time by themselves, in order to promote more equilibrated and fair interactions, guaranteing the continuation of the exchanges. In [12], Von Laer et al. analysed the problem of the self-regulation of social exchange processes in the context of a BDI-based[2] MAS, adapting the GSREP game to Jason [17] agents and introducing a cultural aspect, where the society culture, aggregating the agents' reputation as group beliefs, influences directly the evolution of the agents' exchange strategies, increasing the number of successful interactions and improving the agents' outcomes in interactions.

In Game Theory [18–20], usually, a game is defined by fixing the preferences and opportunities of the players. In 1991, Nigel Howard created the Drama Theory [21,22], a game theory extension, where the preferences and choices of the characters (players) may change under the pressure of the pre-game negotiations. Game theory tries to predict the outcome of a game with "rational" players. However, the theory of drama shows how aspiring players, communicating each other before a game, build not only the game that they will play, but also the result that they expect of it, without the need to predict an outcome. Furthermore, the drama theory challenges the theoretical concept of "rational" game. After analysing the pre-game communication, it is discarded the hypothesis that the players know what they want, what others want, and what they and others can do about it, and that all these things are fixed [22].

This objective of the present paper is to propose a dramatic model for the self-regulation of social exchange processes, applying the concepts of the drama theory to GSREP game, adding feelings and expressions of emotions based on the OCC model [23], in order to obtain a natural model that approximates the reality and sp that it can be applied on real world applications.

The paper is organized as follows. Section 2 summarizes the theoretical basis of this work: the main concepts of social exchanges and of drama theory. Section 3 presents the definition of dramatic model and Sect. 4 is the Conclusion.

---

[1] Material exchanges are concerned just with the short-term aspects of the interaction, involving only exchange values generated immediately after the interaction. [2].

[2] BDI stands for "Beliefs, Desires, Intentions", a particular cognitive agent model introduced in [16].

## 2    Theoretical Basis

### 2.1    Social Exchange

According to Piaget [1], a social exchange is any sequence of actions among two agents, such that one of them, to realize his/her actions, provides a service to another, with the immediate individual qualitative evaluation of the services provided. That is, the agent assigns a value to its investment in the realization of a service to another agent and the latter assigns a value of satisfaction for having received such a service. Such values are called material exchange values. In a social exchange process, debt and credit values are also generated, which allow the realization of future exchanges. Debt and credit are called virtual values.

A social exchange among agents involves at least two agents, $X$ and $Y$, in two exchanges steps/stages, as shown in Fig. 1. In **Step I** the agent $X$ performs a service to the agent $Y$ and, in **Step II**, the agent $X$ requests to the agent $Y$ a payment for the service previously performed for it. In each step, the following exchange values are generated:

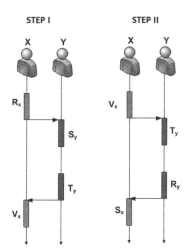

**Fig. 1.** Steps of a social exchange process among two agents [24].

– **Step I**:
   1. $r_x$: *Investment* value of agent $X$.
   2. $s_y$: *Satisfaction* value of agent $Y$.
   3. $t_y$: *Debit* value of agent $Y$.
   4. $v_x$: *Credit* value of agent $X$.

In this way, the agent $X$ performs a service with some investment value ($r_x$) to the agent $Y$. The agent $Y$ generates for the services received a satisfaction value

$(s_y)$ and an acknowledgement value $(t_y)$ or debt for the satisfaction to received service of $X$. At the end of this step, the agent $X$ finished with a virtual value $(v_x)$, that is, a credit related to the action performed to the agent $Y$.

- **Step II**:
    1. $v_x$: *Credit* value of agent $X$.
    2. $t_y$: *Debit* value of agent $Y$.
    3. $r_y$: *Investment* value of agent $Y$.
    4. $s_x$: *Satisfaction* value of agent $X$.

Similar to **Step I**, there is a possible charge debt from the agent $X$ to agent $Y$, where the agent $X$ collect of agent $Y$ a service relative to its credit virtual value $(v_x)$, acquired in **Step I**. The agent $Y$ has on its conscience a debit value $(t_y)$, and it will perform an offer with investment value $(r_y)$ to the agent $X$, which will generate a satisfaction value $(s_x)$ to $Y$ offer.

So, in both steps (**Step I** and **Step II**), $r_{agent}$ and $s_{agent}$ are material values generated while performing/receiving a service, and $t_{agent}$ and $v_{agent}$ are virtual values that can be traded in the near future and will enable the choice of future agents' decisions. Importantly, there is no order in the occurrence of the steps **I** and **II** in repeated processes of social exchanges [6].

The social equilibrium is obtained when the balance of the values for each agent are around an acceptable value for the agent society, in general, around zero.

## 2.2   Drama Theory

Differently from Game Theory, which considers that a game is defined by previously fixed preferences and opportunities for the players, Drama Theory [21,22,25,26] is a theory of how the game itself may change: how a game $G$ can be transformed into other game $G'$, which, in its turn, may be transformed to a game $G''$, and so on. These transformations result from the fact that the players may put pressure on others during the pre-game negotiations, since they exchange threats, promises, emotional persuasion and rational arguments.

Drama theory helps to identify transformations caused by internal dynamics of pre-game negotiations. Such transformations describe rational and irrational processes of human development and self-realization, rather than just the rational choice of a given end.

While game theory exposes the rational behaviour, based on goals, drama theory shows how, in the course of an interaction, people change and evolve. Rationality is still important, but no longer dominates.

## 3   The Dramatic Model of Self-regulation Social Exchange Processes

The dramatic model of self-regulation of social exchange processes proposed is based in the five phases of dramatic resolution of Drama Theory, that are represented in Fig. 2.

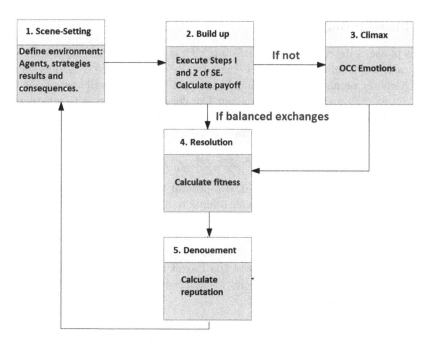

**Fig. 2.** Phases of dramatic resolution.

## 3.1   Phase 1: Scene-Setting

At this phase, the environment is defined with the actors (agents), agents' social exchange strategies, results and consequences.

The agents' social exchange strategies that are considered in this paper are altruism, weak altruism, selfishness, weak selfishness and rationality. For example, an agent with selfishness strategy is more likely to devalue the received service and overvalue an offered service, which impacts on debt and credit values; the rational agent plays just for the Nash Equilibrium[3]. The social exchange strategies are determined by various factors, as we explain in the following, but, in particular, by the maximal investment value $r^{max}$ that the agents are willing to have for a service performed for another agent, and the minimal satisfaction value $s_{min}$ they are willing to accept, with $r, s \in [0, 1]$.

The consequence is represented by a function $Q : X \rightarrow X$ , where $X$ is the set of the individual results of the characters or agents, i.e., their strategies. Individual results are a pair composed of aspiration (a particular future we would like to achieve) and a position (a future that it proposes to others).

In the dramatic model, the result of an agent is represented by the investment proposed ($r^{prop}$), i.e., the future it proposes to other agents; and the satisfaction expected ($s^{esp}$), i.e., the desire, a particular future that it would like to achieve.

---

[3] See [11] for a discussion on the Nash Equilibrium of the Game of Social Exchange Processes.

## 3.2   Phase 2: Build up

At this phase, a determinate frame $F = (Q, P)$ is selected, where, $Q$ is the result set of each agent and $P = (P_i | i \in C)$ is a family of preference relations, one for each character or agent $i$ at casting $C$, defined along of results set $X$. In this game, $(x, y) \in P_i$ means that "the agent $i$ prefers the strategy $x$ to strategy $y$".

After selecting the frame, the steps **I** and **II** of the social exchange are executed, as shown in Sect. 2.1. A social exchange strategy of an agent $\lambda = ij$, is defined by the tuple:

$$(r_\lambda^{prop}, s_\lambda^{esp}, k_\lambda^{\rho t}, k_\lambda^{\rho v}), \tag{1}$$

where $r_\lambda^{prop} \in [0, 1]$ and $s_\lambda^{esp} \in [0, 1]$ represent the proposed investment value that the agent $\lambda$ will have for a service offered to another agent, and the satisfaction value that agent $\lambda$ expects for received services, respectively; $k_\lambda^{\rho t}, k_\lambda^{\rho v} \in [0, 1]$ are, respectively, the factors of depreciation ($\rho = d$) or overvaluation ($\rho = o$) of debit and credit values that define each exchange strategy.

In this phase, they are calculated the Payoff Supposed (*payoffSup*) and the Payoff Effective (*payoffEfet*) of social exchange between the agents $i$ e $j$, with the respective exchange strategies:

$$(r_i^{max}, r_{ij}^{prop}, r_{ij}^{efet}, s_i^{min}, s_i^{esp}, k_i^{\rho t}, k_i^{\rho v}) \text{ e } (r_j^{max}, r_{ji}^{prop}, r_{ji}^{efet}, s_j^{min}, s_j^{esp}, k_j^{\rho t}, k_j^{\rho v})$$

The *payoffSup* obtained by an agent $i$ in this interaction is evaluated by function $p_{ij}^{sup} : [0, 1]^4 \to [0, 1]$, defined by.

$$p_{ij}^{sup} = \begin{cases} \dfrac{1 - r_{ij}^{prop} + s_{ij}^{esp}}{2}, & se(r_{ij}^{prop} \leq r_i^{max} \wedge s_{ji}^{esp} \geq s_j^{min}) \wedge (r_{ji}^{prop} \leq r_j^{max} \wedge s_{ij}^{esp} \geq s_i^{min}) \\ \dfrac{1 - r_{ij}^{prop}}{2}, & se(r_{ij}^{prop} \leq r_i^{max} \wedge s_{ji}^{esp} \geq s_j^{min}) \wedge (r_{ji}^{prop} > r_j^{max} \vee s_{ij}^{esp} < s_i^{min}) \\ 0, & se(r_{ij}^{prop} > r_i^{max} \vee s_{ji}^{esp} < s_j^{min}) \wedge (r_{ji}^{prop} > r_j^{max} \vee s_{ij}^{esp} < s_i^{min}) \end{cases} \tag{2}$$

The *payoffEfet* obtained by an agent $i$ in this interaction is evaluated by function $p_{ij}^{efet} : [0, 1]^4 \to [0, 1]$, defined by:

$$p_{ij}^{efet} = \begin{cases} \dfrac{1 - r_{ij}^{efet} + s_{ij}^{esp}}{2}, & se(r_{ij}^{efet} \leq r_i^{max} \wedge s_{ji}^{esp} \geq s_j^{min}) \wedge (r_{ji}^{efet} \leq r_j^{max} \wedge s_{ij}^{esp} \geq s_i^{min}) \\ \dfrac{1 - r_{ij}^{efet}}{2}, & se(r_{ij}^{efet} \leq r_i^{max} \wedge s_{ji}^{esp} \geq s_j^{min}) \wedge (r_{ji}^{efet} > r_j^{max} \vee s_{ij}^{esp} < s_i^{min}) \\ 0, & se(r_{ij}^{efet} > r_i^{max} \vee s_{ji}^{esp} < s_j^{min}) \wedge (r_{ji}^{efet} > r_j^{max} \vee s_{ij}^{esp} < s_i^{min}) \end{cases} \tag{3}$$

The *payoffSup* and the *payoffEfet* of $j$ agent are defined analogously.

Considering an environment composed of the cast $C = 1, ..., m$ of $m$ agents, each agent $i \in C$ interacts with the others $m - 1$ neighbours agents $j \in C$, such that $j \neq i$. In every interaction cycle, each agent $i$ evaluates its material results of local social exchange with each neighbour agent $j$, using the local *payoffSup* and *payoffEfet* functions, given in the Eqs. (2) and (3). Then, the full *payoffSup* and *payoffEfet* received by each agent are calculated after each agent has performed the two-step exchange with all its neighbours. For $p_{ij}^{sup}$ and $p_{ij}^{efet}$

calculated by Eqs. (4) and (5), the allocation of total *payoffSup* and *payoffEfet* of a neighbourhood of $m$ agents, is given by :

$$X^{sup} = x_1^{sup}, ..., x_m^{sup}, \text{where } x_i^{sup} = \sum_{j \in C, j \neq i} p_{ij}^{sup} \tag{4}$$

$$X^{efet} = x_1^{efet}, ..., x_m^{efet}, \text{where } x_i^{efet} = \sum_{j \in C, j \neq i} p_{ij}^{efet} \tag{5}$$

After calculating the payoff effective of exchanges, the balance of these exchanges is analysed. Ideally, a balanced exchange is when the difference between the payoffs of all exchanges is zero. However, in practice, this divergence occurs around zero. This divergence between the payoffs are calculated according to Eq. 6:

$$D_i = \frac{1}{(m-1)} \sum_{i \neq j}^{j=[1..m]} |x_i - x_j| \leq \alpha \tag{6}$$

where, $m$ is the total number of agents and $\alpha$ is the divergence factor.

Therefore, it is considered balanced exchanges when $D_i \leq \alpha$ for all exchanges.

## 3.3   Phase 3: Climax

If, in phase 2, all the exchanges occur in a balanced way, the phase 3 is ignored and the game moves on to the phase 4, where the emotions will have null weight in the calculus of the *fitness* value, denoted by $F_i(X^{efet})$ of an agent $i$.

If a of exchanges is not balanced, all agents migrate to the phase 3. We considered four types of emotions of the OCC model [23], namely, gratification, gratitude, regret and anger, represented by $a_\lambda, b_\lambda, c_\lambda$ and $d_\lambda$, respectively. Observe that in the OCC model there are three aspects that change the world reactions: events, agents and objects. The events are interesting because we may analyse its consequences, the agents because we may analyse their actions, and objects because the aspects and properties of those objects are analysed. The chosen emotions are part of a group that focuses on the action of an agent and the consequences of the events [27].

A *spatial social exchange strategy* of an agent $\lambda, \lambda = 1, ..., m$ is defined by the tuple:

$$(r_\lambda^{prop}, r_\lambda^{efet}, s_\lambda^{esp}, a_\lambda, b_\lambda, c_\lambda, d_\lambda, k_\lambda^{pt}, k_\lambda^{pv}), \tag{7}$$

where $a_\lambda, b_\lambda, c_\lambda, d_\lambda$ reflect the influence of the emotions in the fitness value $F_i(X^{efet})$ of an agent $i$, in the following way:

– **Gratification** $(a_i)$

$$F_i(X^{efet}) = x_i^{efet} + \frac{a_i}{(m-1)} \sum_{i \neq j} \max(x_j^{efet} - x_j^{sup}, o)$$

where $X^{efet}$ is the total payoff effective allocation of agent $i$.

*Gratification* is a positive feeling generated in the agent itself who proposed the exchange when the *payoff effective (payoffEfet)* of the agent that received the service $(x_j^{efet})$, obtained by effective investment, is greater than the *payoff supposed (paypffSup)* it was supposed to receive $(x_j^{sup})$. This means that practising a value greater than the promised value, the agent feels more confident and also generates a reciprocal feeling of gratitude on the other agent.

– **Gratitude** $(b_i)$

$$F_i(X^{efet}) = x_i^{efet} + b_i + \max(x_i^{efet} - x_i^{sup}, 0)$$

where $X^{efet}$ is the total payoff effective allocation of agent $i$.

Gratitude is a positive feeling generated in the agent that received the service when the *payoff effective (payoffEfet)* of the agent that has practised the exchange $(x_i^{efet})$ is greater than the *payoff supposed (payoffSup)* it was supposed to receive the group $(x_i^{sup})$. When receiving a greater value than the one promised, the agent is grateful to the agent who performed the service, generating a good reputation of this agent, since it comply with what it promised.

– **Regret** $(c_i)$

$$F_i(X^{efet}) = x_i^{efet} - \frac{c_i}{(m-1)} \sum_{i \neq j} \max(x_j^{sup} - x_j^{efet}, o)$$

where $X^{efet}$ is the total payoff effective allocation of agent $i$.

*Regret* is a negative feeling generated in the agent itself who proposed the exchange when the *payoff effective (payoffEfet)* of the agent that received the service $(x_j^{efet})$ is less than the *payoff supposed (payoffSup)* that it was supposed to receive $(x_j^{sup})$. This feeling generated a reciprocal feeling of anger at another agent, and consequently it will get a bad reputation of this other agent, since it did not comply with what it promised.

– **Anger** $(d_i)$

$$F_i(X^{efet}) = x_i^{efet} - d_i + max(x_i^{sup} - x_i^{efet}, o)$$

where $X^{efet}$ is the total payoff effective allocation of agent $i$.

*Anger* is a negative feeling generated in the agent who received the service when the *payoff effective (payoffEfet)* of the agent who practised the exchange $(x_i^{efet})$ is less than the *payoff supposed (pauoffSup)* it was supposed to receive $(x_i^{sup})$.

Therefore, it is clear that an equilibrated balance is achieved when the antagonistic emotions are annulled.

### 3.4   Phase 4: Resolution

After execution of the steps **I** and **II** of the social exchange process in the build up phase, if there is an equilibrated balance, the game progresses to phase 4. At this phase, considering the payoff obtained in phase 2, the agent $i$ calculates its adaptation degree through its *fitness* function $F_i : [0,1]^m \to [0,1]$, defined by:

$$F_i(X^{efet}) = x_i^{efet}$$

where $X^{efet}$ is the total payoff effective allocation of agent $i$.

If the phase 3 has been executed, the emotions generated are added to the fitness function, representing the influence of these emotions on the results of the total agents' payoff effective.

Let $X$ be the allocation of total *payoffEfet* of a neighbourhood of $m$ agents. The general definition of the fitness function, based on exchange strategy of an agent $i$, is given by:

$$F_i(X^{efet}) = \tag{8}$$
$$x_i + \frac{a_i}{(m-1)} \sum_{i \neq j} \max(x_j^{efet} - x_j^{sup}, o) + b_i + \max(x_i^{efet} - x_i^{sup}, 0)$$
$$- \frac{c_i}{(m-1)} \sum_{i \neq j} \max(x_j^{sup} - x_j^{efet}, o) - d_i + max(x_i^{sup} - x_i^{efet}, o)$$

### 3.5   Phase 5: Denouement

After obtaining the value of *fitness* function, the phase 5 is executed. At this phase, the reputation of agents is calculated. For the social sciences, reputations are defined as a collective of beliefs and opinions that influence the actions of individuals in relation to their peers. The reputation can still be seen as a social tool in order to reduce uncertainty to interact with individuals of unknown attributes. To [28], reputation is generally defined as the amount of confidence inspired by a particular person in an environment or specific area of interest.

In computer science, reputation and trust it has gained growing evidence in last years, especially in the *Distributed Artificial Intelligence* (DAI) area, where Multiagent Systems are included. Trust and Reputation are used as a way of search for partners. The reputation has the power to propagate trust and can prevent unnecessarily agents interact. See [29–32]

Rodrigues and colleagues [33] developed a reputation model based on models such as REGRET [34] and Hübner [35]. The analysis of Reputation is divided into three dimensions: Social Dimension, Single Dimension and Ontological Dimension, as proposed in REGRET model. On the Social Dimension is analysed the effectiveness of the agent to its social group. In the Single Dimension is analysed the direct exchanges among agents. Finally, there is the Ontological Dimension, where social and individual dimensions are combined for a final analysis.

To our dramatic model, we used the reputation model proposed by [33], considering only the single dimension at the moment. At this phase 5, the *payoffs* obtained in phase 3 through social exchanges will be stored in a list of size $v$.

The calculation of the reputation is given by:

$$Rep = \frac{\sum_{j \in C, j \neq i} p_{ij}}{size(v)} \tag{9}$$

With the obtained information in the denouement phase, the game return to phase 1, where it will redefine the environment from new strategies, i.e., from the calculated reputation, the agents will choose new partners to execute the social exchange, and start the second round of the game.

## 4    Conclusion

This introduced the model of a dramatic game of self-regulation of social exchange processes.

In the real world, the social exchanges not happen exclusively in a rational way, frequently involving feelings and emotions. In this way, the possibility of applying the drama theory to the game of self-regulation of social exchange processes has emerged.

Applying the concepts of drama theory and improving the trust and the reputation model to the developed dramatic model, we aim at the application in a simulation game of social exchanges in an environment that approximates the real world, that is, a world where the exchanges relations are based on emotions, feelings, trust and reputation.

The model will be implemented in NetLogo, an simulations with different compositions of the agent society and scenarios will be conducted to study the development of the strategies and social exchange processes through time.

**Acknowledgments.** This work was partially supported by the Brazilian funding agencies CAPES and CNPQ, under Processes 481283/2013-7, 306970/2013-9 and 232827/2014-1. G.P. Dimuro is in a sabatic year at Departamento de Automática y Computación, Universidad Pública de Navarra, under the Brazilian Program of Science without Borders, CNPq/Brazil.

## References

1. Piaget, J.: Sociological Studies. Routlege, London (1995)
2. Dimuro, G.P., Costa, A.C.R., Palazzo, L.: Systems of exchange values as tools for multi-agent organizations. J. Braz. Comput. Soc. **11**, 27–40 (2005)
3. Rodrigues, M.R., da Rocha Costa, A.C.: Using qualitative exchange values to improve the modelling of social interactions. In: Hales, D., Edmonds, B., Norling, E., Rouchier, J. (eds.) MABS 2003. LNCS (LNAI), vol. 2927, pp. 57–72. Springer, Berlin (2004)
4. Rodrigues, M.R., Costa, A.C.R., Bordini, R.: A system of exchange values to support social interactions in artificial societies. In: Proceedings of the 2nd International Conference on Autonomous Agents and Multiagents Systems, AAMAS 2003, Melbourne, pp. 81–88. ACM Press (2003)

5. Grimaldo, F., Lozano, M.A., Barber, F.: Coordination and sociability for intelligent virtual agents. In: Sichman, J.S., Padget, J., Ossowski, S., Noriega, P. (eds.) COIN 2007. LNCS (LNAI), vol. 4870, pp. 58–70. Springer, Heidelberg (2008)
6. Dimuro, G.P., da Rocha Costa, A.C., Gonçalves, L.V., Hübner, A.: Centralized regulation of social exchanges between personality-based agents. In: Noriega, P., Vázquez-Salceda, J., Boella, G., Boissier, O., Dignum, V., Fornara, N., Matson, E. (eds.) COIN 2006. LNCS (LNAI), vol. 4386, pp. 338–355. Springer, Heidelberg (2007)
7. Pereira, D.R., Gonçalves, L.V., Dimuro, G.P., Costa, A.C.R.: Towards the self-regulation of personality-based social exchange processes in multiagent systems. In: Zaverucha, G., da Costa, A.L. (eds.) SBIA 2008. LNCS (LNAI), vol. 5249, pp. 113–123. Springer, Heidelberg (2008)
8. Dimuro, G.P., Costa, A.R.C., Gonçalves, L.V., Pereira, D.: Recognizing and learning models of social exchange strategies for the regulation of social interactions in open agent societies. J. Braz. Comput. Soc. **17**, 143–161 (2011)
9. Dimuro, G.P., da Rocha Costa, A.C.: Regulating social exchanges in open MAS: The problem of reciprocal conversions between POMDPs and HMMs. Inf. Sci. **323**, 16–33 (2015)
10. Rodrigues, M.R.: Social techniques for effective interactions in open cooperative systems. Ph.D. thesis, University of Southampton, Southhampton (2007)
11. Macedo, L.F.K., Dimuro, G.P., Aguiar, M.S., Coelho, H.: An evolutionary spatial game-based approach for the self-regulation of social exchanges in MAS. In: Schaub, T., Friedrich, G., O'Sullivan, B., (eds.) ECAI 2014–21st European Conference on Artificial Intelligence, Proceedings in Frontier in Artificial Intelligence and Applications, vol. 263, Netherlands, pp. 573–578. IOS Press (2014)
12. Von Laer, A., Dimuro, G.P., Adamatti, D.F.: Analysing the influence of the cultural aspect in the self-regulation of social exchanges in MAS societies: an evolutionary game-based approach. In: Pereira, F., Machado, P., Costa, E., Cardoso, A. (eds.) EPIA 2015. LNCS, vol. 9273, pp. 673–686. Springer, Heidelberg (2015)
13. Rabin, M.: Incorporating fairness into game theory and economics. Am. Econ. Rev. **86**(5), 1281–1302 (1993)
14. Xianyu, B.: Social preference, incomplete information, and the evolution of ultimatum game in the small world networks: An agent-based approach. J. Artif. Soc. Soc. Simul. **13**, 2 (2010)
15. Macedo, L.F.K., Dimuro, G.P., Aguiar, M.S., Costa, A.C.R., Mattos, V.L.D., Coelho, H.: Analyzingthe evolution of social exchange strategies in social preference-based MAS throughan evolutionary spatial approach of the ultimatum game. In: 2012 Third BrazilianWorkshopon Social Simulation, BWSS 2012, Los Alamitos, pp. 83–90. IEEE (2012)
16. Rao, A.S., Georgeff, M.P.: Modeling rational agents within a BDI-architecture. In: Fikes, R., Sandewall, E. (eds.) Proceedings og the 2nd International Conference on Principles of Knowledge Representation and Reasoning, pp. 473–484. Morgan Kaufmann, San Mateo (1991)
17. Bordini, R.H., Hübner, J.F., Wooldrige, M.: Programming Multi-agent Systems in AgentSpeak Using Jason. Wiley Series in Agent Technology. John Wiley & Sons, Chichester (2007)
18. von Neumann, J., Morgenstern, O.: Theory of Games and Economic Behavior. Wiley, New York (1944)
19. Luce, R.D., Raiffa, H.: Games and Decisions: Introduction and Critical Survey. Dover, New York (1989)

20. Leyton-Brown, K., Shoham, Y.: Essentials of Game Theory: A Concise, Multidisciplinary Introduction. Morgan & Claypool, San Rafael (2008)
21. Howard, N.: Drama theory and its relation to game theory. part 1: Dramatic resolution vs. rational solution. Group Decis. Negot. **3**(2), 187–206 (1994)
22. Howard, N.: What is Drama Theory? (2016). Acessed January 2016
23. Ortony, A., Clore, G.L., Collins, A.: The Cognitive Structure of Emotionsn. Cambridge University Press, Cambridge (1988)
24. Rojas, Y.E.L., Adamatti, D.F., Dimuro, G.P.: Trust transference on social exchanges among triads of agents based on dependence relations and reputation. In: Proceedings of 2nd International Workshop on Smart Simulation and Modelling for Complex Systems at 24th Internacional Joint Conference on Artificial Intelligence, IJCAI 2015, Buenos Aires (2015)
25. Howard, N.: Soft game theory. Inf. Decis. Technol. **16**, 215–227 (1990)
26. Howard, N.: Drama theory and its relation to game theory. part 2: Formal model of the resolution process. Group Decis. Negot. **3**(2), 207–235 (1994)
27. Adamatti, D.F., Bazzan, A.: Afrodite - ambiente de simulação baseado em agentes com emoções. In: Proceedings of ABS 2003 - Agent Based Simulation, Montpellier (2003)
28. Marsh, S.: Formalising Trust as a Computational Concept. Ph.D. thesis, University of Stirling (1994)
29. Sabater, J., Sierra, C.: Review on computational trust and reputation models. Artif. Intell. Rev. **24**(1), 33–60 (2005)
30. Sabater, J., Sierra, C.: Reputation and social network analysis in multi-agent systems. In: Proceedings of the First International Conference on Autonomous Agents and Multiagents Systems, AAMAS 2002, pp. 475–482. ACM (2002)
31. Huynh, T.D., Jennings, N.R., Shadbolt, N.R.: An integrated trust and reputation model for open multi-agent systems. Auton. Agent. Multi-Agent Syst. **13**(2), 119–154 (2006)
32. Yu, H., Miao, C., An, B., Shen, Z., Leung, C.: Reputation-aware task allocation for human trustees. In: Proceedings of the 13th International Conference on Autonomous Agents and Multiagent Systems, AAMAS 2014, New York, pp. 357–364. IFAAMAS/ACM (2014)
33. Rodrigues, H.D.N., Adamatti, D.F., Dimuro, G.P.: Modelagem de agentes BDI-Fuzzy submetidos ao processo de reputação. In: X Workshop-Escola de Sistemas de Agentes, seus Ambientes e Aplicações, p. 143. UFF, Niterói (2015)
34. Sabater, J., Sierra, C.: Regret: A reputation model for gregarious societies. In: Proceedings of the Fourth Workshop on Deception Fraud and Trust in Agent Societies, pp. 61–70 (2001)
35. Hübner, J.F., Vercouter, L., Boissier, O.: Instrumenting multi-agent organisations with artifacts to support reputation processes. In: Hübner, J.F., Matson, E., Boissier, O., Dignum, V. (eds.) COIN@AAMAS 2008. LNCS, vol. 5428, pp. 96–110. Springer, Heidelberg (2009)

# JGOMAS 2.0: A Capture-the-Flag Game Using Jason Agents and Human Interaction

Luis Hernandez, Sergio Esparcia$^{(\boxtimes)}$, Vicente Julian, and Carlos Carrascosa

Departamento de Sistemas Informáticos y Computación (DSIC),
Universitat Politècnica de València, Camino de Vera s/n, Valencia, Spain
{lhernand,sesparcia,vinglada,carrasco}@dsic.upv.es

**Abstract.** Over the last few years educators have increasingly incorporated game simulations into higher education computer science curricula. Experiences have proved that students respond enthusiastically to these courses. According to this, this paper presents an evolved version of the JGOMAS simulator, which is a simulation game where students design and implement different types of agents and strategies in order to win the game. This new version allows students to practice different technologies related to the multi-agent paradigm as coordination, cooperation or decision-making.

**Keywords:** Multi-Agent Systems · Simulation games · Education

## 1 Introduction

The use of game design elements for teaching and learning computer science subjects has provided a number of advantages in recent years [1]. Developing computer games involves many aspects of computing, including computer graphics, artificial intelligence (AI), human-computer interaction, security, distributed programming, simulation... In this sense, there is a growing evidence of the effective use of games and game elements across Higher Education contexts and concretely in Computer Science degrees.

During different academic years, the toolkit JGOMAS 1.0 [2] has been used as a part of the learning process of students in a subject named Intelligent Systems of the Bachelor's Degree of Computer Science Engineering in the *Universitat Politècnica de València*. JGOMAS 1.0 is a simulation game where students can design and implement different types of agents and test different coordination strategies in order to win the game. Moreover, the toolkit allows the students to organize competitions between the developed teams. During the last years, the use of this toolkit notably improved the motivation of the students due to their interest in new areas such as behavior design, artificial intelligence, or the creation of multiplayer games. All these areas are covered by the JGOMAS toolkit.

Nevertheless, the first version of JGOMAS has different aspects that may be improved: (i) the user may observe the evolution of the game from different

© Springer International Publishing Switzerland 2016
J. Bajo et al. (Eds.): PAAMS 2016 Workshops, CCIS 616, pp. 173–184, 2016.
DOI: 10.1007/978-3-319-39387-2_15

points of view (several render engines may be attached to the same game), but cannot interact with the game to dynamically change its evolution. The experience can be dramatically improved including some kind of immersion of the students during the simulation; (ii) JGOMAS 1.0 is based on the JADE platform [3] and all their agents are implemented as JADE agents. This is not a problem by itself, but the use of any AI approach or sophisticated coordination techniques must be implemented from scratch. This problem can be solved by integrating existing, more complex, agent architectures into the toolkit; and (iii) current supported renders do not allow an optimal user experience since they do not support complex graphics.

Taking into account all these aspects, this paper presents an evolution of the JGOMAS toolkit. This new version allows students to work with heterogeneous teams of agents, being able to deal not only with JADE agents but also with JASON [4] agents. This new agent architecture allows students to create agents with a more sophisticated decision-making engine. Moreover, the toolkit has introduced the human in the execution cycle, so a student may interact with his team in a transparent way for the agents, which see him as other agent. Finally, a new render based on UNITY[1] has been also implemented.

The rest of the paper is structured as follows: Sect. 2 presents the background of the proposal; Sect. 3 introduces the new version of the JGOMAS toolkit; finally, some conclusions are commented in Sect. 4.

## 2    Background

This section describes the two works that are the background for the proposal of this paper. First, the Jason agent programming language is described. Second, JGOMAS, the framework for teaching agent programming, is described.

### 2.1    Jason

Jason [4] is an agent programming language based on AgentSpeak [5]. This language is based on the BDI (Beliefs-Desires-Intentions) architecture for defining cognitive software agents. In this approach, an agent is an entity composed of a set of beliefs, representing the current state of an agent and knowledge about the environment in which it is situated, a set of goals, which corresponds to tasks the agent has to perform/achieve, and a set of plans which are courses of actions, either internal or external, triggered by events, and that agents can dynamically compose, instantiate and execute to achieve goals. Jason extends AgentSpeak with different features, being the most important one the addition of speech-act based inter-agent communications. Other new features include: strong negation; handling of plan failures; support for developing Environments; support for MAS organizations and agents that reason about them; a library of essential "internal actions"; or an IDE in the form of a jEdit or Eclipse plugin.

---

[1] http://unity3d.com/.

## 2.2    JGOMAS

JGOMAS (Game Oriented Multi-Agent System based on JADE) [2] is a Multi-Agent System (MAS) for social simulation based on JADE [6] that has been developed to meet different purposes. Its main purpose is to serve as a starting point for studying the feasibility of the integration between Multi-Agent Systems (MAS) and Computer Graphics, including applications such as Virtual Reality.

Thus, JGOMAS adds a 3D rendering engine that depicts in real-time the execution of the MAS running in the background. This can be used to qualitatively evaluate and validate the implementation of the MAS.

As a test for the developed MAS, a capture-the-flag (CTF) game has been developed. In this kind of games, two teams compete against each other. Each team has a base, with a flag located inside it. The objective of the teams is to capture the flag from the base of the opponent and to bring it to its own base to score a point or to win the game. This type of game was firstly introduced in 1984 by the game *Bannercatch*, and is now a standard multiplayer mode for the first- and third-person shooters since it was made popular when it was first introduced as a modification to the *Quake* videogame. It is intuitive to implement a CTF game using a MAS because a player (i.e. a member of the team) can be modeled as an agent. Moreover, it is also interesting for studying agent cooperation, since each player has to collaborate with his teammates to achieve the objective of the game.

However, the JGOMAS version of CTF is slightly different. The two represented teams are the Allies and the Axis, each one having a base, but only the Axis have a flag. The objective of the Allies is to reach the Axis base, capture the flag and get it to their own base. If they reach the base within the established game limit, the Allied team wins. The objective of the Axis is to defend their base from the Allies. If the time expires and the Allies did not captured the flag, the Axis wins the game.

A domain like CTF enables a simple and entertaining way to establish a testbed either for algorithms and optimizations individually on each agent and for competitive and cooperative strategies, within and between teams.

After working with this first version of JGOMAS in both research and education domains, some aspects have been detected to be improved. These improvements will enhance the user experience and the possibilities offered by the second version of JGOMAS. The following section describes JGOMAS 2.0.

# 3    JGOMAS 2.0

## 3.1    Agents Description

As has been stated in the previous section, JGOMAS is primarily composed of two subsystems. On the one hand, there is a multi-agent system with two different kinds of agents. One of these types of agents handles the game logic, while the others belong to one of the two teams, and play the game.

Actually, this subsystem is a layer that runs on top of a multi-agent plat-form (specifically, JADE) and can take advantage of all the services provided by JADE.

JGOMAS 2.0, which is the current version of the JGOMAS platform allows the use of Jason agents to form teams of agents.

On the other hand, a new ad-hoc Render Engine to display a 3D virtual envi-ronment has been developed. According to the specific requirements of graphic applications (e.g., high computational cost for short periods), this engine has been designed as an external module (not as an agent). It has been written in UNITY 3D (Fig. 1 shows an example of a JGOMAS game displayed with this new render engine).

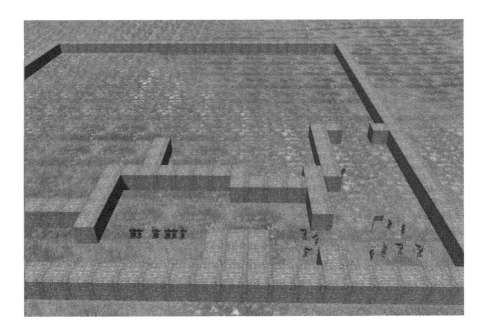

**Fig. 1.** JGOMAS render engine view

Figure 2 shows a JGOMAS architecture where all components and their rela-tionships can be seen: the JADE platform as support for JGOMAS Multi-Agent System, which is comprised of agents, one of them acting as a controller for other agents, and as an interface for the Render Engine.

The Multi-Agent System JGOMAS can be viewed as a kernel (basic package), which provides an interface for the Render Engine to connect to the current game.

**Agent Taxonomy.** The following taxonomy of agents within JGOMAS accord-ing to their functionality may be established:

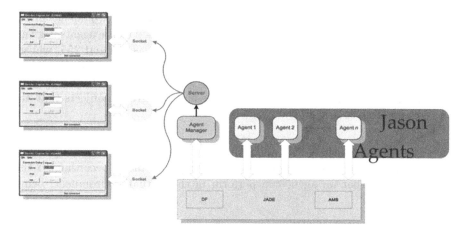

**Fig. 2.** JGOMAS 2.0 architecture

– Internal agents: are those which form themselves the JGOMAS management
  platform. Their behaviors are predefined, and the user cannot change them.
  These agents are JADE agents, and there exist the following types:
  • Manager: This is a special agent. Its main objective is to coordinate the
    current game. In addition, it answers requests from other agents. Another
    task that it is responsible for is to connect the game with the Render
    Engine.
  • Pack: There are three different types of packs, the medic packs (used to
    give health to agents), ammo packs (used to give ammunition to agents)
    and the objective pack, i.e. the flag to capture. All these agents are dynam-
    ically created and destroyed with the exception of the flag (there exists
    only one flag throughout the game and cannot be destroyed).
– External agents: They are the players. They have a predefined set of basic
  behaviors that the user can modify or even add new ones. These agents are
  developed in JADE or Jason. An agent can play a unique role in the current game. There are three roles defined, but the user can define new, each
  providing a unique service. Thus, these agents (also known as troop agents),
  specialize in the following three roles:
  • Soldier: provides a backup service (the agent goes to help its teammates).
  • Medic: provides a medic service (the agent goes to give medic packs).
  • FieldOps: provides an ammo service (the agent goes to give ammo packs).

External agents are integrated into the virtual environment, allowing the
interaction between them (through the perception of nearby peers and enemies)
which can lead to cooperation and coordination with teammates. Also, since
agents are located in this virtual environment, they must take into account the
features of the terrain where they are located (mainly walls). All the communication that takes place between the agents in the platform is performed by
passing messages according to protocols established by the FIPA ACL [7].

**Maps.** JGOMAS uses different maps to define the virtual environment. These maps, by default, are of size $256 \times 256$, so that the position of the agents is given by its coordinates (x, y, z), where x, z take values between 0 and 255, whilst, in the maps supplied, y is always equal to 0 (these maps do not have height). Each agent has partial access to the map where the game is played, since despite having access to static information about it, can only perceive objects that are at a certain distance (within the "cone of vision").

**Tasks.** A task is something that an agent has to perform in a particular position of the virtual environment. There are various types of tasks, according to the different actions that an agent can perform in the virtual environment, being the main ones:

- TASK_GIVE_MEDICPAKS: A medic must generate packets of medicine in a particular place (the position of the agent which requested it and which has agreed to go to give them).
- TASK_GIVE_AMMOPAKS: A fieldops must generate packets of ammo in a particular place (the position of the agent which requested it and which has agreed to go to give them).
- TASK_GIVE_BACKUP: A soldier should go to help a teammate to a particular place (the position of the agent which requested it and which has agreed to give it go).
- TASK_GET_OBJECTIVE: The agent, from the ALLIED team, must go to the starting position of the flag for it. If it manages to grab the flag, this task becomes going back to their home base.
- TASK_GOTO_POSITION: The agent must go to a specific location.

A task is associated to its type, the agent that causes the task (the agent itself or the agent which requested it), the position where it should be performed, priority and any possible additional contents. Always the task with the highest priority is launched. Users can redefine the priority of each type of task. Only the agent can add tasks to the list of active tasks, not the user. In Jason, a plan is used to add a task: add_task

```
!add_task(task(TaskPriority, TaskType, Agent, Position, Content)),
                              or
        !add_task(task(TaskType, Agent, Position, Content))
```

Such objectives trigger the plan creating the task. The second one assigns the priority defined by the agent.

**Execution Loop.** Each JGOMAS external agent executes a Finite-State Machine (FSM) as the one in Fig. 3:

- STANDING: The agent does not have any triggered task.
- GO_TO_TARGET: The agent has triggered a task and it is moving to the position where it has to do it.

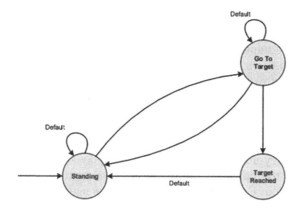

**Fig. 3.** FSM defining JGOMAS external agents behavior

– TARGET_REACHED: The agent has reached the position where it has to perform the triggered task, and it is performing the actions related to it.

**Interface (API).** The interface (API) for working with JGOMAS is composed of .asl files written in Jason that contain the different agents (each one with its own beliefs, goals, and behaviors). Inside these files, *jgomas.asl* includes the non-modifiable behaviors of the agent. To modify the behavior of the agent the files with a name following the pattern *jasonAgent_TEAM_TYPE.asl* have to be modified, where TEAM refers to the side of the agent (ALLIED, AXIS), and TYPE is the type of the agent (SOLDIER, MEDIC, FIELDOPS).

Regarding agent beliefs, the main ones are:

– tasks(task_list): Contains the list of active tasks of the agent.
– fovObjects(object_list): Contains the list of objects currently seen by the agent.
– state(current state): This belief is used to indicate the state of the agent in its state machine: *standing*, selecting which task to do or waiting; *go_to_target*, going to its next target; *target_reached*, it has reached the target; quit, has to finish.
– my_health(X): Stores the health of the agent. The initial, and maximum, value is 100. When this value reaches 0, the agent dies.
– my_ammo(X): Stores the amount of bullets of the agent. The initial value is 100.
– my_position(X,Y,Z): Stores the last position known by the agent.

The different plans of the agents that can be modified by the users are:

– !perform_look_action: This objective is invoked when the agent looks around and updates the list of surrounding objects *fovObjects(L)*. It would be necessary to implement the plan associated to the creation of this event to be able to look what is around.

- `!perform_aim_action`: This objective is triggered if there is an enemy to aim, which can be used to take a decision about what to do with the aimed agent. A simple implementation of the plan is available.
- `!get_agent_to_aim`: This objective is invoked after *!perform_look_action*, and it would be used to decide if there is any enemy to aim. A simple implementation that can be extended or modified of the associated plan is available.
- `!perform_no_ammo_action`: This objective is triggered when the agent shoots and has no ammo. It is necessary to implement the associated plan to take a decision. For example, to run away.
- `!perform_injury_action` This objective is triggered when the agent is shot. It is necessary to implement the plan associated to the creation of this event to take a decision. For example, run away if the agent has a low life value.
- `!performThresholdAction`: This objective is triggered when the agent has less life or bullets than the thresholds *my_ammo_threshold(X)* and *my_health_threshold(X)*. A simple implementation of the associated plan is available, which asks for help to medics or fieldops of its team.
- `!setup_priorities`: This objective is triggered during agent initialization to fix agent task priorities. Each agent has its own priorities. A simple implementation is available. It is interesting to modify it to add new tasks or modify the priorities to have agents that behave in a different way.
- `!update_targets`: This objective can be used to update the tasks and its priorities. It is invoked when the agent changes to the *standing* state and has to choose a new task among the available ones. It is necessary to implement the plan associated to the creation of this event.

**Communication.** In JGOMAS 2.0, communication is used by agents for registering services and for promoting coordination between them. It is necessary to highlight that an agent plays only one role during the whole game. For example, if an agent A1 is created as a soldier of the type Soldier and belong to the AXIS team, it will be for the rest of the game.

Each role has different features and offers specific basic services that can be improved. Indicating the role and the basic services offered by an agent is carried out at the initialization, using a process known as Registration. Nevertheless, an agent can add new services during the development of the game.

*Registration.* A role has to register a service to allow other roles to request it. Registration is carried out using the internal action: `.register(''JGOMAS'', ''type'')`

Once an agent has registered a service, it is possible for an agent of its same team to check which agents of its team offer a specific service.

*Coordination.* JGOMAS is provided with mechanisms that allow agent coordination. It can be of one of these two types:

- No communication (implicit): It is achieved by sensing the environment. When an agent looks around itself the objective `!perform_look_action` is triggered. By rewriting the associated plan it can be decided what to do according to the perception.

- With communication (explicit): In this case it is used the message passing using the following internal action:

    .send_msg_with_conversation_id (Rec, Perf, Cont, ConvId)

  where:

    • Rec: receiver of the message (could be a list)
    • Perf: performative (tell, untell, achieve...)
    • Cont: content
    • ConvId: Conversation Id (used in JADE)

### 3.2    Immersing the Human in JGOMAS

One of the new features of JGOMAS is the interaction with the user. Now, a user can take the control of an agent and give orders directly. The motivations for this interaction are:

- Improve the ability to test the behavior of JGOMAS agents, test strategies, etc. The direct control of an agent allows the user to perform specific actions (like shooting a particular agent or follow a certain path) and see the reaction of the other agents (both enemies and friends) to these decisions. In previous versions, it was necessary that the game reaches this situation by its own evolution to assess its performance.
- From an educational point of view, involvement of the students in the development of agents increases. The students can now validate their designs easier.

This user-JGOMAS interaction is achieved by means of the UNITY engine used in this release. UNITY has allowed not only the improvement in the rendering as discussed above but also to develop the user-JGOMAS interface. Aside from allowing rendering the game, the UNITY render engine gives support to program all aspects of the game including game management, artificial intelligence, etc. In our case, these aspects are developed by JGOMAS code in Java in the JADE architecture or in Jason to implement the agents. However, UNITY can be used for the interface between user and JGOMAS. This way, the user will interact with UNITY which will contact with JGOMAS to communicate user decisions. This communication is done through the JGOMAS messaging system as UNITY is seen as another agent for JGOMAS.

As stated above, the user gives commands via the interface to the agent, but the agent retains its properties. The agent can be any Jason-based agent of the system, and the user does not control it. It sends orders to the agent that are translated to FIPA-ACL messages. These messages are received by the agent and translated into the highest priority intentions, so it may seem that the user controls it, but if the user stops to send orders to the agent, it will still work.

The game may have multiple users each one controlling an agent. One consequence of this is an increasing immersion of the user. The user does not know if the agents he is fighting against (or collaborating with) are under the control of

AGENT:A2 SOLDIER ALLIED
HEALTH:92
AMMO:92
ANGLE:1.570796
POS:21.2065 28.5

A2 SELECTED

**Fig. 4.** Human immersed in one JGOMAS soldier

another user or not. Also it can be considered double immersion because it also acts on the system side: the agents do not know which agents are under computer control or under the control of external users. The agents act according to their beliefs and perceptions and the subsequent reasoning based on them, not considering the nature of the other agents. To make this interaction, the user selects an agent by means of the mouse. The user can take the control of this agent by pressing the key B. From that moment the user can control the agent through a series of keyboard commands and the view is centered in this agent's viewpoint (see Fig. 4). Table 1 summarizes user commands. The choice of the keys did not follow naming criteria but the keyboard layout.

One of the most interesting options with respect to validation is the action associated to the P key. This key sends a message from the user-controlled agent to another agent. The user only has to implement the Jason code as the receiving agent wants to respond to that message. Another option to note is the activation of the first-person camera that further enhances the user's immersion in the game.

**Table 1.** User commands

| Key | Action |
|-----|--------|
| B | Control agent selected |
| I | Move agent in the current direction |
| J | Turn the agent to the left |
| L | Turn the agent to the right |
| K | Turn the agent 180 degrees |
| V | Shot |
| C | Call for medical |
| X | Call for ammo |
| Z | Call for backup |
| T | Select the upper camera |
| M | Toggle to the first person camera |
| N | Toggle to the third person camera |
| G | Show controlled agent info |
| P | Send a message to another agent |

## 4    Conclusions and Future Work

This paper has presented JGOMAS 2.0, which is a simulation game where students design and implement a group of agents and test different coordination strategies in order to win the game. This new version improves different aspects regarding the first version. Concretely includes the possibility to develop Jason agents allowing students to integrate BDI-oriented strategies in the decision-making of the agents. Moreover, the new version has introduced the human in the execution process allowing the student to interact with his/her developed team. This interaction includes sending messages or participating as another member of the team. As future work, emotional states will be included in the agent's model. These emotional states will change according to changes in the environment and the agent's personality. Emotional values may be used by the students in order to improve the decision making of the agent's team during the game.

**Acknowledgments.** Work partially supported by Spanish Government through the project iHAS (grant TIN2012-36586C03-01).

## References

1. Overmars, M.: Teaching computer science through game design. Computer **37**(4), 81–83 (2004)
2. Barella, A., Valero, S., Carrascosa, C.: JGOMAS: New approach to AI teaching. IEEE Trans. Educ. **52**(2), 228–235 (2009)

3. Bellifemine, F.L., Caire, G., Greenwood, D.: Developing Multi-Agent Systems with JADE. Wiley Series in Agent Technology. John Wiley & Sons, New York (2007)
4. Bordini, R.H., Hubner, J.F., Wooldridge, M.J.: Programming Multi-Agent Systems in AgentSpeak using Jason. J. Wiley, Chichester, Hoboken (2007)
5. Rao, A.S.: Agentspeak(l): Bdi agents speak out in a logical computable language. In: Perram, J., Van de Velde, W. (eds.) MAAMAW 1996. LNCS, vol. 1038, pp. 42–55. Springer, Heidelberg (1996)
6. Bellifemine, F., Poggi, A., Rimassa, G.: Developing multi-agent systems with JADE. In: Castelfranchi, C., Lespérance, Y. (eds.) ATAL 2000. LNCS, vol. 1986, pp. 89–103. Springer, Berlin Heidelberg (2001)
7. O'Brien, P.D., Nicol, R.C.: Fipa towards a standard for software agents. BT Technol. J. **16**(3), 51–59 (1998)

# Workshop on Decision Making in Dynamic Information Environments (DeMaDIE)

# An Immune Multi-agent Based Decision Support System for the Control of Public Transportation Systems

Salima Mnif[1(✉)], Sabeur Elkosantini[2], Saber Darmoul[2], and Lamjed Ben Said[1]

[1] SOIE Laboratory, High Institute of Management of Tunis, University of Tunis, Tunis, Tunisia
mnifsalima@yahoo.fr, lamjed.bensaid@isg.rnu.tn
[2] Department of Industrial Engineering, King Saud University, Riyadh, Kingdom of Saudi Arabia
{selkosantini,sdarmoul}@ksu.edu.sa

**Abstract.** Public Transportation Systems (PTSs) are always subjected to disturbances and need a real time monitoring and control to maintain its performance at acceptable levels. In PTS, several types of disturbances can affect buses such as accidents, delays and traffic jams that can also affect schedules so dramatically that these schedules could become useless. Consequently, it becomes a necessity to develop a Decision Support System (DSS) able to help human regulator in managing PTS efficiently, and to provide users with high quality services, in terms of punctuality, frequency and productivity. In this paper, a reactive and decentralized DSS is developed for the control of PTS based on the biological immune theory. This DSS is an artificial immune system, which presents many interesting capabilities, including identification, learning, memory and distributed parallel processing. Through experimental validation, we show that this exploratory approach seems to be promising.

**Keywords:** Multi-agent system · Biological immune system · Artificial immune system · Negative selection theory · Immune memory · Public transport control

## 1 Introduction

Public Transportation Systems (PTSs) are always subjected to disturbances and need real time monitoring and control to maintain the system performance at acceptable levels. Several types of disturbances can affect buses such as bad weather, absence of personnel, traffic congestion and accidents that can also affect schedules so dramatically that these schedules can become useless. These disturbances cause pre-established time-tables to be delayed or to become obsolete, which affects service quality and reliability. For these reasons, the development of a Decision Support System able to help transportation agencies to monitor the good execution of the timetables becomes a necessity. Such systems are referred to in this paper as Public Transportation Control System (PTCS). PTCS should monitor the PTS and propose corrective decisions as early as possible to prevent passenger dissatisfaction and performance degradation.

Many PTCS were developed using different approaches based on from artificial intelligence paradigms. The agents' paradigm is widely used in the control of PTS. A complete review on the use of Multi-Agent System (MAS) in transportation can be found in [1].

© Springer International Publishing Switzerland 2016
J. Bajo et al. (Eds.): PAAMS 2016 Workshops, CCIS 616, pp. 187–198, 2016.
DOI: 10.1007/978-3-319-39387-2_16

Authors pointed out that 64 % of the research conducted in the field of transportation focused on the use of the agent paradigm to design DSS. Although the ability of MAS to distribute control, 30 % of research papers used MAS to develop centralized PTCS.

Authors in [2] developed a PTCS combining Case Based Reasoning (CBR) and agents to deal with disturbances. In this system, some agents are associated with vehicles and other associated with stops. They communicate and cooperate to identify the consequences of a detected disturbance. Two other types of agents are created to manage a detected disturbance, namely incident and zoneint agents. Authors in [3] presented a PTCS combining Petri nets and MAS for an agent oriented PTCS considering the interaction with the human regulator to monitor the PTS. [4] presented an agent-based PTCS named SATIR that monitors the network activity in real-time and thus assists the bus network regulator under normal and disrupted conditions. Using a "Disturbance Model", the system measures qualitatively the seriousness of a delay and considers its context and its consequences on the activity of the PTS. Authors in [5] also designed a MAS based PTCS named SMAST that aims at regulating a multimodal PTS. The system is able to manage and diagnose some types of disturbances. Although the number of developed approaches for reactive decision making in PTCS, there is still a lack of generic approaches, able to deal, simultaneously, with a variety of disturbance types and causes, while at the same time not requiring great customization each time a new disturbance type or cause is considered.

This paper focuses on the development of a reactive and decentralized control of PTS. Only the bus network is considered in this paper. Furthermore, this paper is not interested in the elaboration of bus time tables from scratch. It suggests a control system, which is more focused on the adaptation of bus schedules based on corrective decisions applied to pre-established time tables. The main contribution of the paper is the development of a set of immune knowledge models and mechanisms for disturbance management in public transportation systems for the decentralized and reactive decision making.

In this paper, we consider the properties of the biological immune system to develop new techniques and mechanisms for distributed control. In fact, this paper establishes and shows the effectiveness of using an analogy between the biological immune system and the bus network. It has been demonstrated in [6] that the immune system has the capability to recognize new patterns, learn, classify, memorize and process information. In addition, the immunity, which is the feature of recovering and maintaining a status of good health, can be preserved even in the face of a dynamically changing environment. The biological immune system can recognize different patterns and generate selective immune responses. A previous investigation work was already conducted in [7] and suggested a first analogy with the public transportation systems. Authors have suggested a decision support system using the immune clonal selection theory. In this paper, we investigate other immune mechanisms combining Negative Selection and the immune memory. These mechanisms are integrated in a MAS based PTCS. Section 2 presents the biological immunity key concepts and mechanisms and the suggested analogy with PTS. Section 3 presents developed models and techniques inspired from immunity. Section 4 presents the architecture of the suggested PTCS. Finally, Sect. 5 illustrates an implementation of the system.

# 2 Biological Immunity for the Control of PTS

## 2.1 Biological Immune Systems

The Biological Immune System – BIS – is a robust complex system. The BIS reacts to adverse environmental changes, internal and/or external stimuli to the organism by discovering and eliminating foreign pathogens, called "antigens" or non-self, such as viruses, bacteria, and other parasites. These antigens are recognized by the body as foreign which stimulates an immune response. The biological immune system develops a strategy aimed at neutralizing the detected antigen. Indeed, when an antigen enters into the body, it stimulates a subset of immune cells, called "lymphocytes", to produce special molecules, called "antibodies" or self. Antibodies bind to antigens, block them and thereby lead to their elimination [8]. In BIS, an antibody can identify antigens using its receptors, called "paratopes" that cover its surface in order to recognize and neutralize them. Furthermore, an antibody is not activated unless its receptors bind to the antigen with an affinity that exceeds an affinity threshold. Thus, the body is based on the self-nonself discrimination principle to distinguish between antigens (non-self) and anti-bodies (self). Such a principle is called the negative selection mechanism.

As soon as a non-self-cell such as an antigen is detected, the body activates the immune response. Then, lymphocytes are generated and are divided into two main types of cells: effector cells and memory cells [9, 10]. Effector cells have a short lifetime and are created for the immediate defense of the organism. Memory cells are long-lived cells that circulate through the host organism. This concept is called the immunological memory. When confronted with the presence of an antigen that was previously recognized, memory cells are able to launch a rapid and effective response. Usually, Artificial Immune Systems – AISs – often use the idea of memory cells to retain good solutions to the problem under consideration. In our case, we rely on immune memory, and on the mechanism of affinity to control traffic at intersections.

Many concepts and mechanisms have been abstracted from the biological immune system and applied to create effective computational solutions to complex problems in a wide range of domain areas [11]. However, to the best of authors' knowledge, few research works have been conducted to investigate BIS in the field of the public transportation.

## 2.2 Analogy Between PTS and BIS

Let us remember that the primary focus of this paper is to investigate how the human BIS can be an inspiration for the development of a PTCS to help human operators to react in a timely way to disturbances affecting transportation schedules. A PTCS should protect the PTS from disturbances affecting pre-established schedules, just as the biological immune system protects the body from disease causing elements threatening its normal functioning. In this paper, an antigen represents a disturbance that affects the transportation network, such as a bus delay, a technical problem or successive buses. An antibody represents an elementary corrective decision that could be recommended to regulate the system, such as "hold stations" or "skip stations". The immune response must determine the best set of actions (B-cells) that will regulate the network using an

Immune memory based algorithm, as a response strategy, and the affinity between the action and the disturbance (Table 1).

**Table 1.** Analogy between biological and public transportation network.

| Biological immune system | Public transportation system |
|---|---|
| Body | Public transportation network |
| Self-cells | Buses with normal behavior |
| Infected cells | Disturbed buses |
| Antigens (non-self-cells) | Disturbances affecting a bus |
| Antigenic determinant (or epitope) | An attribute that characterizes a special feature of a disturbance |
| Antibodies | Unitary control decisions |
| Paratope | A feature triggering a decision control |
| B-cells | Control decisions |
| T helper cells (or Th-cell) | Control strategy |
| Memory cells | Data base |
| Negative Selection | Bus network monitoring and disturbance detection |
| Response strategy | Immune memory based algorithm |

## 3   Immune Concepts for Disturbance Management

The suggested PTCS have to deal with different types of knowledge, capturing, using, and storing them. In order to be effective, such knowledge needs to be structured using knowledge models. In the following subsections, we introduce a set of models for structuring and representing knowledge related to disturbances and decisions based on the proposed analogy (see Sect. 2.2).

### 3.1   A Self-cell Representation

According to our analogy, cells represent the normal situation of the buses of the network. In this paper, we suggest a model to represent and structure knowledge related to normal situations. The model includes four attributes as presented in (1):

$$SC = \langle B_i, L_i, \{(St_i, StE_i)\}, TrE, \{(St_j, StDj), TrD\}\rangle \qquad (1)$$

Where: $B_i$ is the disturbed bus; $L_i$ is the bus line, Li $\{(St_i, StE_i)\}$ is a set that details the amount of earliness $StE_i$ at each stop station $St_i$ subject to earliness; $TrE$ is the cumulated earliness of a trip; $\{(St_j, StD_j)\}$ is a set that details the amount of delay $StD_j$ at each stop station $St_j$ subject to a delay; $TrD$ is the cumulated delay of a trip.

## 3.2 Antigen Representation

In this work, a disturbance is any kind of event that affects a single bus. Therefore, if there are several disturbed buses, an antigen will be created for each one. In this paper, we characterize a disturbance as a vector with 10 antigenic determinants, also called epitopes, each one characterizing a specific feature of a disturbance. The antigen includes all important knowledge describing the affected bus (kind of the disturbance, charge of the bus, etc.) and the disturbance itself:

$$Ag = \langle AD_1 = B_i, AD_2 = L_i, AD_3 = C, AD_4 = D, AD_5 = P,$$
$$AD_6 = N_{db}, AD_7 = N_{fb}, AD_8 = R, AD_9 = WP, AD_{10} = S \rangle \tag{2}$$

Where $C$ is the cause of the disturbance (1 for accident or technical problem, 2 for traffic congestion, 3 for absence of driver, and 4 for the cause bad weather), $D$ is its duration (0 is for short and 1 for long period), $P$ is the period of the duration (1 for rush hour and 0 for a off-peak hour), $N_{db}$ is the number of passengers in the disturbed bus while $N_{fb}$ is the number of passengers in the following bus, $R$ is the availability of a bus, $WP$ is the number of waiting passengers in the next station while $S$ describes the state of the bus (0 is for behind the schedule and 1 for delay).

## 3.3 Antibody Representation

Antibodies represent different types of actions or decisions. An antibody is an elementary action which can be combined with others in order to neutralize a disturbance. In this paper, we consider five different kinds of actions which are listed below:

- Half-turn online (HTOL): it consists in eliminating a part of the trip. The vehicle will continue in the opposite direction.
- Skip stations (SS): speeding up buses by skipping stations (one or several)
- Hold at a station (HS): delaying the bus, at a given station, if it is are ahead of its planned timetable
- Injection of a bus (IB): it consists in injecting a new bus in the network to strengthen the number of buses in the network.
- Exchange of a bus (EB): it consists in replacing an existing bus that is not able to continue its trip.

## 3.4 B-cell Representation

According to the suggested analogy, B-cells represent control decisions applied to a disturbed bus. Hence, the system must create a B-cell for each detected antigen. Equation 3 illustrates our definition of B-cells. Indeed, the Paratopes part of B-cells, which represent the receptor of the cells, is a precondition that has the same structure as the antigen as described above (see Eq. 2).

$$Bcell = \langle Paratopes, Antibodies \rangle \tag{3}$$

In the suggested model, an action can take 0 or 1 as a value. If an antibody is activated, it is assigned the value 1; otherwise it is assigned the value 0. Th-cell representation. In case of the occurrence of many disturbances affecting many buses, the PTCS should build a control decision for each bus. The set of control decisions, represented by B-cells, are called a control strategy. Indeed, a control strategy is an aggregation of one or several control decisions (antibodies) aimed at reacting to the occurrence of a disturbance. Based on our analogy, we introduce a Th-cell to define a control strategy that is able to recognize and neutralize the detected antigens. Thus, the control strategy is presented by Eq. 4.

$$Thcell = \langle Bcell_1, Bcell_2, \ldots, Bcell_j \rangle \quad j = 1 \ldots m \tag{4}$$

Where $m$ is the number of disturbed buses. It is worth noting that some coordination is required to fix a control strategy for each disturbed vehicle and to insure coherence and efficiency of the overall reaction to a disturbance.

### 3.5 A Negative Selection Algorithm (NSA) for PTS Monitoring

The detection of disturbances is the first step in the process of disturbance management. In this paper, an adaptation of the negative selection algorithm is presented to monitor and detect disturbances. Initial concepts of the negative selection theory are presented in [12]. The algorithm aims to recognize self-cells and identify non-self-cells. In this paper, we define self-cells as normal situations of the network which need to be protected. We define the set $S$ including the self-cells (see Subsect. 3.1 and Eq. 1) representing the acceptable level of performance of the network. This set should be specified by experts or human regulators. We also define another set $R$, named set of patterns, including a set of non-self-cells representing abnormal situations or disturbances. Initially, the set $R$ is empty and it should be completed by cells using a simulation based learning mechanism as it will be detailed in the Sect. 3.6. The objective of this algorithm is to build the set $R$ using a learning mechanism based on simulation and the self-non-self-discrimination concept (see Sect. 2), inspired from the negative selection theory. The algorithm is constituted by the following steps: Learning and Monitoring.

The objective of the first step, the learning, is to produce a set of non-self-cells by periodically comparing the state of the network and normal situations (self-cells). We define the matching rate to measure the distance between a given situation (using collected data), denoted by SC, and elements of the set S, denoted $S_i$, in order to check their similarities. The matching rate is calculated by Eq. (5).

$$Mat(S_i, SC) = \frac{100}{8} \times \sum_{i=1}^{8} \delta_i \tag{5}$$

Where Mat($S_i$, SC) is the rate of the matching (in %); $S_i$ is one of the normal situations of the set $S$; SC is a situation. Values of attributes are collected from a simulation software (see Sect. 4); $\delta_i$ is defined as in (6):

$$\delta_i = \begin{cases} 1 & \text{if } SC^j = S_i^j \\ 0 & \text{otherwise} \end{cases} \tag{6}$$

Where $SC^j$ is the $j^{th}$ attribute of a situation $SC$ and $S_i^j$ is the $j^{th}$ attribute of the $i^{th}$ situation from the set $S$. If the matching rate is less than a fixed threshold $th_1$, then the situation is considered to be abnormal and then added to the set of patterns $R$. The set $R$ is then used in the next step to detect disturbances.

In the second step, the monitoring, the developed PTCS will continuously read values from the PTS and compares them with abnormal situations of the set $R$. The Eq. 5 is used to determine the matching rate between a situation and all abnormal stations from the set $R$. If there is a situation from $R$ which is very similar to the current situation (i.e. the matching rate is greater than a fixed threshold $th_2$), then, a disturbance is detected and an antigen is created. The PTCS will then activate the reaction response which is presented in the next section.

### 3.6 B-cell/Antigen Affinity

The affinity refers to the similarity degree between the disturbance and a control decision. This measure function is similar to the biological affinity between the epitopes part of a B-cell and the antigenic determinant (epitope). In this paper, the Manhattan distance measure is adopted. This measure is an important element in measuring the affinity between an antibody and an antigen in biological immunity. According to [13, 14], the Manhattan distance is more efficient than Euclidean distance in parallel and distributed systems. Moreover, Manhattan distance has demonstrated a better performance in presence of noisy data which is always the case in public transportation systems [13]. Authors in [15] noted also that a single error in the value of one of the antigenic determinants or of a paratope of an antibody can be considerably amplified by the Euclidean distance. Hence, the Manhattan distance is more suitable for our PTCS. The affinity is then determined using Eq. (7):

$$Affinity(Bcell, Ag) = \frac{\sum_{i=1}^{Length(Ag)} \delta_i}{Length(Ag)} \tag{7}$$

Where

$$\begin{cases} \delta_i = 1 & \text{if Bcell.Paratope.AD}_i = Ag.AD_i \\ \delta_i = 0 & \text{otherwise} \end{cases} \tag{8}$$

### 3.7 Immune Memory Algorithm (IMA)

In this paper, we introduce also an Immune Memory Algorithm (IMA) to build a reaction strategy for detected disturbances. Similarly to biological immune systems, the suggested PTCS memories a set of control decisions for some disturbances that the system is able to recognize. Indeed, the BIS is able to memorize encountered antigens and the used B-cells to neutralize them. Such cells are named memory B-cell and have the same structure as B-cells. Such response, named the primary immune response, allows the immune system to respond more rapidly and effectively to antigens that have been encountered and recognized previously. In this work, we introduce an Immune Memory DataBase (IMDB) including a set of memory B-cells. The suggested IMA works according to the following steps:

- Step 1 – Read and collect data: the algorithm performs measurement data acquisition from the network. In this paper, measurement data is related to the number of passengers in the disturbed bus, the number of passengers in the following bus, the availability of a bus and difference between the scheduled timetable and exact position of the bus.
- Step 2 – Data analysis: the algorithm analyzes collected data in order to detect possible disturbances based on the negative selection algorithm presented in the previous section.
- Step 3 – Selection of the appropriate control decision: the algorithm selects from the database (the immune memory) the control strategy (B-cell) that can deal with the disturbance (antigen). To that end, the algorithm calculates the affinity measure between the detected disturbance and memory B-cells stored in the IMDB to determines appropriate control decision for detected disturbance using the affinity measure (see Sect. 3.6). Thus, the algorithm selects the control decision with the highest value of affinity. The considered affinity measure in this paper is the Manhattan presented in the Sect. 3.6.
- Step 4 – the control decision (B-cell) with the highest affinity degree will be considered as a preliminary decision to the disturbed bus. As outlined in Sect. 3.5, a coordination is required to insure coherence and efficiency of the overall reaction to a disturbance.
- Go to step 1 for data acquisition.

Steps 1 to 4 are repeated each T (sampling period) seconds. It is worth noting that data acquisition is performed at the beginning of a sampling period, while the determined control decision is applied at the beginning of next sampling period.

To create the initial Immune Memory DataBase (IMDB), we adopted a Simulation Optimization (SO) technique. Indeed, a first run of a simulation is required to create the set of patterns $R$ (see Sect. 3.6) including most representative antigens. Then, we use SO to determine the optimal combination of antibodies that can minimize total delay of buses for each antigen of the set $R$. Finally, both obtained antigens of the set $R$ and antibodies constitutes the memory B-cells of the IMDB.

# 4   The Immune Multi-agent PTCS

## 4.1   An Overview of the Architecture

The use of multi-agent systems for the development of PTCS seems to be an interesting approach for many reasons. Indeed, agents have capabilities to perform reasoning on a specific problem more effectively than a decentralized decision support system [16]. In addition, the PTS has a distributed nature which encourage using MAS. PTCS is also characterized by dynamic interaction between vehicles, stop-stations, DSS or decisions makers which fit with MAS paradigm.

Accordingly, we design the architecture of a MAS based PTCS to control PTS based on immune concepts and mechanisms presented in Sect. 3. Then, we developed a prototype artificial immune decision support system able to monitor PTS and build decision in a distributed way. The system includes two types of agents: Bus Agent (BA) and Bus Line Agent (BLA). One BA is associated with each bus and one BLA is associated with each bus line. The objective of BA is to monitor the execution of the predefined timetable of one bus, detect disturbances and develop a control decision. BLA aims at insuring a coherent, integrated and consistent control strategy that is able to neutralize several disturbances. In the suggested system, we adopted a hierarchical MAS organizations which includes different levels with some agents in a given level. Agents of the lower level, the BAs, should send their decisions to agents of upper level, the BLAs, in order to coordinate and synchronize the communication between agents. Consequently, BA depend on BLA and BLA may even be in partial or full control of agent of BA. The most important advantage of such hierarchical structure is the significant reduction in the amount of communication between agents.

### 4.2 Bus Agents (BA) Behavior Model

The goal of the Bus Agents (BA) is to monitor the performance of buses, analyze collected data, detect disturbances and make appropriate decisions to tackle them. According to the theory of MAS, this agent should has a representation of its environment. In this paper, we used models presented in Sects. 3.1–3.4 to represent and structure knowledge related to the agent's environment.

As presented in the state-transition diagram of Fig. 1, the BA has different states. For example, the agent has to explore its surrounding environment using sensors implemented in buses. Then, the BA agents have to monitor the performance of buses and detect abnormal situations using the immune Negative Selection Algorithm (NSA)

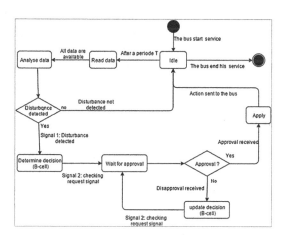

**Fig. 1.** State-transition diagram

presented in Sect. 3.6. As soon as a disturbance is detected, the agent creates a signal to activate the first immune response corresponding to the Immune Memory Algorithm (IMA) and which is detailed in Sect. 3.7. Consequently, the IMA generates the control decision B-cell that can tackle the detected disturbance. The BA creates and sends another signal, referred to *checking request signal*, to the Bus Line Agent (BLA) in order to check if the selected B-cell is coherent and consistent with decisions (B-cells) taken by other BA for different buses. The BA should wait for approval or disapproval signal from the BLA (see Sect. 4.3).

### 4.3   Bus Line Agents (BLA) Behavior Model

The main function of this agent is to insure a consistent and coherent control strategy especially in case of the occurrence of many disturbances affecting different buses in the same line. Indeed, BA can generate sometimes non-feasible control decisions, due for example to the selection of contradictory B-cells, or to the selection of decisions that are not coherent with the disturbance.

For illustration purpose, let us take the example of a first bus which is subjected to an accident at station number 5 and the associated BA has selected the Half-turn online (HTOL) as control decision of the B-cell, by setting the value 1 to the corresponding antibody. This means that the bus will stop serving other stations and will continue its route in the opposite side. Let us also consider a second bus that the same line is also disturbed at station number 10 and the associated BA has also selected the Half-turn online (HTOL) as a control decision of the B-cell, by setting the antibody corresponding at the value 1. This means that the second bus will also stop serving other stations and will continue its route in the opposite side. In this case, the control strategy Th-cell constituted by these two B-cells means that the two buses will continue in the opposite side and, as consequence, passengers from station no. 5 until the end of the line will have a long waiting time which can affect the quality of service of the system. Such Th-cell is considered to be inconsistent. To avoid such a control strategy, BAs will send *checking request signal* to BLA to check the inconsistency of the control strategy. The BLA uses a set of IF...THEN rules to detect incoherence within the th-cell. In case of a problem, the BLA will send a *change B-cell request* to one of the Bas, to change its B-cell. The choice of the B-cell to change is based on data included in the paratope part of B-cells. Moreover, these rules allow the detection of antagonistic decision actions such as HTOL with another HTOL or HTOL with SS. Such rules can be specified by experts.

## 5   Implementation and Test

In this section, we present the implementation of the PTCS and discuss preliminary results. The proposed PTCS is implemented with Python programming language. We used also the SPADE, a multi-agent platform developed with Python, to implement agents. To evaluate the system, a bus network is simulated using PTV VISSIM 7, a traffic simulation software. We simulated a line with 10 stations and 9 buses. Initially, the time interval between buses is 20 min and the time spent by buses to reach next station in normal conditions is

10 min. The first bus is injected in the network at 7am. To build the set S, we used 10 self-cells to represent normal situations in which we accepted delays less than 2 min. We have also used 15 rules for BLA. We have simulated a scenario in which we simulated a traffic congestion starting from station no. 3 to station no. 4 after 42 min from lunching the simulation. This disturbance has affected the timetable of two successive buses (no. 1 and no. 2). Bus no. 1 is affected near station no. 3 and bus no. 2 is affected near station no. 4. Bus no. 3 is not affected by the disturbance as it leaved the first station after 40 min. The theoretical timetable of this bus in presented in Fig. 2.

| position | 1 | 2 | 3 | 4 | 5 | 6 | 7 | 8 | 9 | 10 |
|----------|-----|-----|-----|-----|-----|-----|-----|-----|-----|-----|
| Bus1 | 7 :00 | 7 :10 | 7 :20 | 7 :30 | 7 :40 | 7 :50 | 8 :00 | 8 :10 | 8 :20 | 8 :30 |
| Bus2 | 7 :20 | 7 :30 | 7 :40 | 7 :50 | 8 :00 | 8 :10 | 8 :20 | 8 :30 | 8 :40 | 8 :50 |
| Bus3 | 7 :40 | 7 :50 | 8 :00 | 8 :10 | 8 :20 | 8 :30 | 8 :40 | 8 :50 | 9 :00 | 9 :10 |

**Fig. 2.** Prescheduled timetable of buses no. 1, no. 2 and no. 3.

As soon as BAs associated with buses no. 1 and no 2. detected disturbances using the NSA, the IMA is activated. The same control decision is activated by BAs as they implement the same IMDB including similar B-cells. The initial considered control decision is to skip 3 stations. The first bus has to skip stations 3 to 5 and the second bus has to skip stations 4 to 6. A control strategy (Th-cell) is then created with these two decisions and is sent to BLA for evaluation. The BLA evaluates the Th-cell using the 15 created rules and considers it as inconsistent since passengers waiting from station 3 to 6 have to wait until the arrival of bus no. 3. BLA sends a disapproval for the BA associated with bus no. 1 asking him to ignore this disturbances. By the end, bus no. 2 will continue to serve stations from station no. 7 without delays and the system will accept the delay for bus no 1 to avoid the long waiting time of passengers.

# 6   Conclusion

In this paper, a set of concepts, inspired from biological immunity, are introduced for knowledge representation. We also introduced mechanisms also inspired from biological immunity for PTS monitoring and decentralized decision making. These concepts and mechanisms are integrated in a multi-agent systems. The combination of Negative Selection, Immune Memory mechanisms and multi-agent systems offers to the system the ability to recognize disturbances and select appropriate decisions in a decentralized way. To the best of authors' knowledge, no such integrated decision support system was developed in the scientific literature.

In order to enhance the system described in this paper, first, an in-depth performance analysis of the suggested concepts and mechanisms should be conducted to assess the developed PTCS. Other concepts inspired by the biological immune system such as danger theory can be investigated to consider the influence of a disturbed bus on the whole network. Furthermore, the system will be compared to other public transportation regulation systems. Finally, the proposed PTCS will be extended to consider multimodal public transport network including subways and streetcar.

**Acknowledgments.** This work was supported by NSTIP strategic program number (12-INF2820-02) in the Kingdom of Saudi Arabia. The authors would like to thank all personnel involved in this work.

# References

1. Davidsson, P., Henesey, L., Ramstedt, L., Törnquist, J., Wernstedt, F.: An analysis of agent-based approaches to transport logistics. Transp. Res. Part C **13**, 255–271 (2005)
2. Bouamrane, K., Tahon, C., Beldjilali, B.: Decision making system for regulation of a bimodal urban transportation system, associating classical and multi-agent approaches. INFORMATICA **16**(3), 1–30 (2005)
3. Ezzedine, H., Trabelsi, A., Kolski, C.: Modeling of an interactive system with an agent-based architecture using Petri nets, application of the method to the supervision of a transport system. Math. Comput. Simul. **70**, 358–376 (2006)
4. Balbo, F., Pinson, S.: Using intelligent agents for transportation regulation support system design. Transp. Res. Part C Emerg. Technol. **18**(1), 140–156 (2010)
5. Rahal, D.D., Rahal, F., Chekroun, M.R.: Multi-agent system for modeling transport systems. European J. Sci. Res. **46**, 80–89 (2010). ISSN 1450-216X
6. Dasgupta, D., Ji, Z., Gonzalez, F.: Artificial immune system (AIS) research in the last five years. In: The Congress on Evolutionary Computation (CEC 2003), vol. 1, pp. 123–130 (2003)
7. Darmoul, S., Elkosantini, S.: Artificial immunity to control disturbances in public transportation systems: concepts, mechanisms and a prototype implementation of a knowledge based decision support system. Int. J. Knowl.-Based Syst. **58**, 58–76 (2014)
8. Hightower, R., Forrest, S., Perelson, A.: The Baldwin effect in the immune system: learning by somatic hypermutation. In: Mithchell, M., Belew, R. (eds.) Adaptive Individuals in Evolving Populations: Models and Algorithms. Addison-Wesley, Boston (1996)
9. Hofmeyr, S.A.: An interpretative introduction to the immune system. In: Cohen, I., Segel, L.A. (eds.) Design Principles for the Immune System and Other Distributed Autonomous Systems. Oxford University Press, Oxford (2000)
10. Perelson, A.S., Weisbuch, G.: Immunology for physicists. Rev. Mod. Phys. **69**(4), 1219–1267 (1997)
11. Kim, J., Bentley, P.: The human immune system and network intrusion detection. In: 7th European Conference on Intelligent Techniques and Soft Computing, Aachen (1999)
12. Forrest, S., Perelson, A.S., Allen, L., Cherukuri, R.: Self-nonself discrimination in a computer. In: 1994 IEEE Computer Society Symposium on Research in Security and Privacy, 1994, Proceedings, pp. 202–212, 16–18 May 1994
13. Freitas, A.A., Timmis, J.: Revisiting the foundations of artificial immune systems: a problem-oriented perspective. In: Timmis, J., Bentley, P.J., Hart, E. (eds.) ICARIS 2003. LNCS, vol. 2787, pp. 229–241. Springer, Heidelberg (2003)
14. de Castro, L.N., Timmis, J.: Artificial Immune System: A New Computation Intelligence Approach. Springer, Berlin (2002)
15. Lau, H.Y.K., Wong, V.W.K.: An immunity-based distributed multiagent-control framework. IEEE Trans. Syst. Man Cybern. Part A Syst. Hum. **36**(1), 91–108 (2006)
16. Taghezout, N., Ascar, B., Bessedik, I.: An agent based decision support system for spunlace nonwovens production management: case study of INOTIS Enterprise. In: Decision Support Systems, pp. 411–422 (2012)

# Argumentation-Based Reasoning
# with Preferences

Kristijonas Čyras[(✉)]

Imperial College London, London, UK
k.cyras13@imperial.ac.uk

**Abstract.** One of the main objectives of AI is modelling human reasoning. Since preference information is an indispensable component of common-sense reasoning, the two should be studied in tandem. Argumentation is an established branch of AI dedicated to this task. In this paper, we study how argumentation with preferences models human intuition behind a particular decision making scenario concerning reasoning with rules and preferences. To this end, we present an example of a common-sense reasoning problem complemented with a survey of decisions made by human respondents. The survey reveals an answer that contrasts with solutions offered by various argumentation formalisms. We argue that our results call for advancements of approaches to argumentation with preferences as well as for examination of the type of problems of reasoning with preferences put forward in this paper. Our work contributes to the line of research on preference handling in argumentation, and it also enriches the discussions on the increasingly important topic of preference treatment in AI at large.

**Keywords:** Argumentation · Preferences · Reasoning

## 1 Introduction

Preferences are quotidian phenomena. They appear in everyday reasoning problems, within utterances such as "I prefer Brownie over Almond cake". Since AI is inherently concerned with human type-of reasoning, preferences are of natural interest to the AI community. Lately, dealing with preference information has increasingly become of great interest in areas of AI that involve reasoning under uncertainty (see e.g. [13,18,26,34] for discussions).

Argumentation (as overviewed in [34]) is by now an acknowledged branch of AI that is particularly concerned with reasoning with incomplete, uncertain and conflicting information. It is widely used in areas such as multi-agent systems, common-sense reasoning, decision making (see e.g. [2,15,26,29,34]). Preferences in argumentation, as well as in AI on the whole, are used to, for example, qualify the uncertainty of, or discriminate over, information. A principal issue, however, is the lack of consensus on how preferences should be accounted for (see e.g. [26] for a relatively recent overview). Hence the variety of formalisms of argumentation with preferences: e.g. [1,3,5,6,9,12,21,22,24,27,30,32,33,36,37].

© Springer International Publishing Switzerland 2016
J. Bajo et al. (Eds.): PAAMS 2016 Workshops, CCIS 616, pp. 199–210, 2016.
DOI: 10.1007/978-3-319-39387-2_17

In this paper we propose a simple common-sense reasoning scenario concerning decision making in the presence of preference information. The scenario is accompanied by a social experiment, i.e. a survey, that indicates the intuitive decision that people make when faced with the problem in question. By investigating how current approaches to argumentation with preferences handle the scenario, we find they yield different outcomes than human intuition dictates.

The scenario is described as follows.

*Example 1 (Cakes).* There are three pieces of cakes on a table: a piece of Almond cake, a Brownie, and a piece of Cheesecake. You want to get as many cakes as possible, and the following are the rules of the game.

(a) You can take cakes from the table in two 'rounds':
   1. In the first round you can take at most two cakes;
   2. In the second round you can take at most one cake.
(b) If you take Almond cake and Cheesecake in the first round, Brownie will not be available in the second round. (Nothing is known about other possible combinations.)

Finally, very importantly, suppose that you *prefer* Brownie over Almond cake. (No other preferences.)

Which pair(s) of cakes would you choose in the first round?

This example falls into the family of reasoning (or, decision making) problems that involve reasoning with *rules* and *preferences*. In this case, there is essentially a single rule, namely that taking Almond cake and Cheesecake removes Brownie.[1] There is also only one preference, namely that Brownie is preferred over Almond cake. Given this information, what could be the reasoning outcome?

Obviously, {Almond cake, Cheesecake} is not a good option, because it prevents one from getting the Brownie. Meanwhile, among pairs {Almond cake, Brownie} and {Brownie, Cheesecake}, both result into the desired outcome. In addition, neither of the two is in conflict with the preference information: on the one hand, since there are no preferences involving Cheesecake, {Almond cake, Brownie} does not violate the preference of Brownie over Almond cake; on the other hand, {Brownie, Cheesecake} satisfies the preference too, as along Cheesecake, the more preferred item is chosen instead of the less preferred one.

So both choices {Almond cake, Brownie} and {Brownie, Cheesecake} seem to be equally good, or 'rational', in the sense that both lead to the desired outcome of obtaining all the cakes and both satisfy the preference relation. As a decision, one could thus randomly choose between the two pairs.

However, upon the inception of the problem, it felt as if the {Brownie, Cheesecake} choice is somehow more intuitive, or preferred. We have therefore posed the question, as formulated in Example 1, to our colleagues and friends, and, perhaps somewhat surprisingly though not unexpectedly, the answer "Brownie and Cheesecake" dominated. With the hypothesis in mind

---

[1] Since all three cakes are wanted, condition (a) simply indicates that the first round decision is pivotal and involves basically only one rule expressed in condition (b).

that {Brownie, Cheesecake} is more often the preferred choice, we have then conducted an anonymous survey with precisely the formulation as in Example 1. There were four possible answers:

- {Almond cake, Brownie}
- {Brownie, Cheesecake}
- Indifferent between {Almond cake, Brownie}, and {Brownie, Cheesecake}. (I.e. randomly choose one of the two pairs.)
- Other

The three concrete answer choices were randomized for each respondent, while the 'Other' choice, which allowed for a specification, was always the last one.

In the survey, out of total 84 participants, 41 (i.e. 48.81 %) chose "Brownie and Cheesecake", and only 12 (11.90 %) chose "Almond cake and Brownie", while among the rest, 32 (38.10 %) participants said they were indifferent between the two pairs, and 1 (1.19 %) person suggested taking Almond cake and Cheesecake.[2] So, not only that {Brownie, Cheesecake} dominated more than four times {Almond cake, Brownie}; it also got 10 % more responses than the option of being indifferent between the two pairs. This suggests that Brownie and Cheesecake is the more 'intuitive' choice in this problem.

There may presumably be multiple explanations for the mismatch between the results of the survey and the 'rational' solution delineated above. We are, however, not going to speculate on this issue. Rather, we will attempt to present formalizations of the problem in question in various approaches to argumentation with preferences. The analysis will reveal that current formalisms opt mostly for the normative 'rational' solution (i.e. either of the two pairs), rather than the observed 'intuitive' one (Brownie and Cheesecake).

## 2   Cakes Example in Argumentation

In argumentation information is represented via *arguments* and *attacks* among them. For instance, abstract argumentation (AA) [20] frameworks are tuples $(Args, \rightsquigarrow)$ with a set $Args$ of arguments and a binary attack relation $\rightsquigarrow$ on $Args$: for $A, B \in Args$, we say that A attacks B iff $A \rightsquigarrow B$. Whereas in AA the internal structure of arguments is unknown, structured argumentation (see e.g. [7] for a recent overview) allows for more granularity in defining arguments and attacks. Usually, a formal language for representing knowledge is assumed, and arguments are constructed as deductions from premises to conclusions, with attacks constructively defined.

For both abstract and structured argumentation, *semantics* is an essential procedure for designating sets $E \subseteq Args$ of arguments, called *extensions*,

---

[2] The survey results can be found at https://www.surveymonkey.com/results/ SM-GLNNBZ8Q/. We have surveyed PhD students at the Department of Computing, Imperial College London. Invitations to take the survey were distributed by email via the Department's PhD students' mailing list. 79 responses were obtained in a single day. We do not claim any statistically significant findings.

which can be deemed collectively acceptable. For example, stable semantics [20] requires that for no arguments $A, B \in E$ it holds that $A \rightsquigarrow B$, and that for each $A \notin E$ there is $B \in E$ with $B \rightsquigarrow A$; e.g. if $Args = \{A, B\}$ and $B \rightsquigarrow A$ is the only attack, then $\{B\}$ is a unique stable extension. Many different argumentation semantics have been investigated (see e.g. [4, 34] for overviews). Broadly speaking, they represent different modes of reasoning with respect to certainty of information, i.e. more sceptical, or more credulous. For the purposes of this paper, we will focus on stable semantics, as other semantics do not yield significantly different outcomes with respect to our Cakes example.

A commonality of majority of argumentation formalisms that deal with preference information is to use preferences to modify the attack relation: attacks from less preferred arguments are discarded, i.e. if $B$ is less preferred than $A$ (in symbols, $B \lhd A$), then $B \rightsquigarrow A$ fails; see e.g. [1, 6, 9, 12, 21, 22, 24, 27, 33]. Some formalisms (e.g. [36, 37]) employ preferences to select among extensions the most 'preferred' ones, or even combine the two uses (e.g. [3]). In what follows we select several representatives of the broad family of approaches, and show that in modelling the Cakes problem, they do not yield the 'intuitive' answer to choose Brownie and Cheesecake. This, we believe, illustrates that the task of capturing human reasoning in argumentation calls for novel approaches to preference handling. Complete specifications of different formalisms are omitted due to space constraints, but simplified expositions sufficient for our purposes are given.

### 2.1  Deductive Argumentation

We begin with a well known formalism called Deductive Argumentation [8, 9] in which classical logic is commonly used as a basis. Deductive Argumentation can be seen as a representative of those formalisms that employ forms of propositional, first-order, conditional or temporal logics, e.g. [1, 8, 9, 22, 25].

Assume classical propositional logic (PL) with atoms $a, b, c, \ldots$, connectives $\neg, \wedge, \rightarrow$ (including falsum $\perp$) and the classical consequence relation $\vdash$. A knowledge base is a set $\Delta$ of (PL) formulas. Given $\Delta$, for $A \subseteq \Delta$ and a formula $\alpha$, $\langle A, \alpha \rangle$ is an *argument* if $A \vdash \alpha$, $A \nvdash \perp$, and there is no $A' \subsetneq A$ with $A' \vdash \alpha$. We say $\langle A, \alpha \rangle$ *attacks* $\langle B, \beta \rangle$, written $\langle A, \alpha \rangle \rightsquigarrow \langle B, \beta \rangle$, if $\alpha \vdash \neg b$ for some $b \in B$. Given a preference relation (strict partial order) $\lhd$ over arguments, we say $\langle A, \alpha \rangle$ *defeats* $\langle B, \beta \rangle$, written $\langle A, \alpha \rangle \hookrightarrow \langle B, \beta \rangle$, if $\langle A, \alpha \rangle \rightsquigarrow \langle B, \beta \rangle$ and $\langle A, \alpha \rangle \ntriangleleft \langle B, \beta \rangle$.

Deductive Argumentation is completely modular with respect to preference relations $\lhd$ over arguments and is not concerned how they are obtained. Thus, given a preference relation $<$ over, say, atoms, one has to lift it up to the argument level. This is known as preference aggregation. For instance, we can employ versions of the well known Elitist and Democratic ordering principles (see e.g. [32]), respectively called Disjoint Elitist and Disjoint Democratic orders, denoted by $\lhd_{DE}$ and $\lhd_{DD}$, and defined as follows:

$$\langle S, \sigma \rangle \lhd_{DE} \langle S', \sigma' \rangle \text{ iff } \exists s \in S \setminus S' \text{ such that } \forall s' \in S' \setminus S \text{ we have } s < s';$$
$$\langle S, \sigma \rangle \lhd_{DD} \langle S', \sigma' \rangle \text{ iff } \forall s \in S \setminus S' \text{ it holds that } \exists s' \in S' \setminus S \text{ with } s < s'.$$

Let us see how Deductive Argumentation equipped with these preference relations copes with our Cakes example.

*Example 2 (Cakes in Deductive Argumentation).* Suppose that atoms $a, b, c$ stand for the different pieces of cake, namely Almond cake, Brownie, Cheesecake, respectively. The rule that taking Almond cake and Cheesecake in the first round kicks out Brownie in the second one, can be represented as $a \wedge c \rightarrow \neg b$. Finally, the preference of Brownie over Almond cake is specified as $a < b$. We thus have the knowledge base $\Delta = \{a, b, c, a \wedge c \rightarrow \neg b\}$ with preference $a < b$. The following arguments can then be constructed:[3] $A = \langle\{a\}, a\rangle$, $B = \langle\{b\}, b\rangle$, $C = \langle\{c\}, c\rangle$, $A_1 = \langle\{a, b\}, a \wedge b\rangle$, $A_2 = \langle\{a, c\}, a \wedge c\rangle$, $A_3 = \langle\{b, c\}, b \wedge c\rangle$, $X = \langle\{a, c\}, \neg b\rangle$. Comparing relevant arguments, we have: $A_2 \lhd_{DE} A_3$; $X \lhd_{DE} A_3$; $A_2 \lhd_{DD} A_3$; $X \lhd_{DD} A_3$. Consequently, regarding both defeat relations $\hookrightarrow_{DE}$ and $\hookrightarrow_{DD}$ (with respect to the orderings $\lhd_{DE}$ and $\lhd_{DD}$), the same argument framework $(Args, \hookrightarrow)$ (where $\hookrightarrow = \hookrightarrow_{DE} = \hookrightarrow_{DD}$) results. It can be represented graphically as follows (in this and further illustrations of argument frameworks, nodes hold arguments and directed edges indicate defeats).

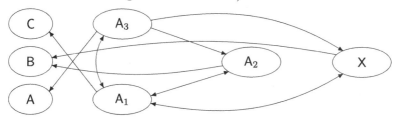

The sets $E = \{B, C, A_3\}$ and $E' = \{A, B, A_1\}$ are the only stable extensions of $(Args, \hookrightarrow)$, representing that one can choose either Brownie and Cheesecake ($E$), or Almond cake and Brownie ($E'$). This is the 'rational' solution.

## 2.2 ASPIC+

We turn to a well established structured argumentation formalism ASPIC+ [14, 32, 33]. It is a widely used expressive approach representative of the use of *defeasible* rules[4] and preference aggregation in argumentation (see e.g. [21, 31–33]).

Lengthy details on ASPIC+ frameworks must be omitted, but the following suffices for our purposes (see [32] for details). Assume a logical language $\mathcal{L}$ closed under negation $\neg$. Specify a set $\mathcal{R}_s$ of (strict) rules and a set $\mathcal{K}_p$ of premises. To satisfy certain rationality criteria [14], impose contraposition (also called transposition) on rules: whenever $\varphi_1, \ldots, \varphi_n \rightarrow \psi \in \mathcal{R}_s$, we have $\varphi_1, \ldots, \varphi_{i-1}, -\psi, \varphi_{i+1}, \ldots, \varphi_n \rightarrow -\varphi_i \in \mathcal{R}_s$ too, for all $i$.[5]

---

[3] By definition, there are infinitely many arguments, but it suffices to consider only a finite number of them, as they represent the essential information; see [9] for details.

[4] Two types of rules are commonly used in argumentation: *strict* rules, whose consequent necessarily follows from the antecedent; and *defeasible* rules, whose consequent *normally* (e.g. unless there are exceptions to the rule) follows from the antecedent.

[5] For $\varphi \in \mathcal{L}$, its *complement* $-\varphi$ is: $\neg\psi$ if $\varphi = \psi$; and $\psi$ if $\varphi = \neg\psi$.

Arguments are then constructed as deductions from premises using rules; attacks ($\rightsquigarrow$) are obtained by deducing complements of premises; an attack A $\rightsquigarrow$ B succeeds as a defeat only if A $\not\vartriangleleft$ B. ASPIC$^+$ offers two particular argument ordering principles, namely Elitist and Democratic, denoted by $\vartriangleleft_E$ and $\vartriangleleft_D$ respectively. For our purposes, given a preference relation $<$ over premises, they can be defined as follows: for $S, S' \subseteq \mathcal{K}_p$,

$S \vartriangleleft_E S'$ iff $\exists \mathsf{s} \in S$ such that $\forall \mathsf{s}' \in S'$ it holds that $\mathsf{s} < \mathsf{s}'$;
$S \vartriangleleft_D S'$ iff $\forall \mathsf{s} \in S$ it holds that $\exists \mathsf{s}' \in S'$ such that $\mathsf{s} < \mathsf{s}'$.

We next formalize the Cakes example in ASPIC$^+$.

*Example 3 (Cakes in ASPIC$^+$).* Assuming language $\mathcal{L} = \{\mathsf{a}, \mathsf{b}, \mathsf{c}, \neg\mathsf{a}, \neg\mathsf{b}, \neg\mathsf{c}\}$, we have the (strict) rules $\mathcal{R}_s = \{\mathsf{a}, \mathsf{c} \rightarrow \neg\mathsf{b}, \quad \mathsf{a}, \mathsf{b} \rightarrow \neg\mathsf{c}, \quad \mathsf{b}, \mathsf{c} \rightarrow \neg\mathsf{a}\}$ and premises $\mathcal{K}_p = \{\mathsf{a}, \mathsf{b}, \mathsf{c}\}$ (which stand for cakes), together with preference $\mathsf{a} < \mathsf{b}$. We can construct arguments $\mathsf{A} = [\mathsf{a}]$, $\mathsf{B} = [\mathsf{b}]$, $\mathsf{C} = [\mathsf{c}]$, $\mathsf{A}_1 = [\mathsf{A}, \mathsf{B} \rightarrow \neg\mathsf{c}]$, $\mathsf{A}_2 = [\mathsf{A}, \mathsf{C} \rightarrow \neg\mathsf{b}]$, and $\mathsf{A}_3 = [\mathsf{B}, \mathsf{C} \rightarrow \neg\mathsf{a}]$, and obtain the following attacks: $\mathsf{A}_1 \rightsquigarrow \mathsf{C}, \mathsf{A}_2, \mathsf{A}_3$; $\mathsf{A}_2 \rightsquigarrow \mathsf{B}, \mathsf{A}_1, \mathsf{A}_3$; $\mathsf{A}_3 \rightsquigarrow \mathsf{A}, \mathsf{A}_1, \mathsf{A}_2$. Comparing argument premises yields (among other relationships) $\mathsf{A}_2 \vartriangleleft_E \mathsf{B}$, but $\mathsf{A}_2 \not\vartriangleleft_D \mathsf{B}$. Hence, $\mathsf{A}_2 \not\hookrightarrow_E \mathsf{B}$, but $\mathsf{A}_2 \hookrightarrow_D \mathsf{B}$, while other attacks succeed as defeats. Therefore, under the Elitist comparison, $\{\mathsf{B}, \mathsf{C}, \mathsf{A}_3\}$, $\{\mathsf{A}, \mathsf{B}, \mathsf{A}_1\}$ and $\{\mathsf{A}, \mathsf{B}, \mathsf{C}, \mathsf{A}_2\}$ are stable extensions (representing the 'rational' choice, and the impossible choice of all three cakes). whereas under the Democratic comparison, $\{\mathsf{B}, \mathsf{C}, \mathsf{A}_3\}$, $\{\mathsf{A}, \mathsf{B}, \mathsf{A}_1\}$ and $\{\mathsf{A}, \mathsf{C}, \mathsf{A}_2\}$ are stable extensions ('rational' choice, and an additional arguably unintuitive choice). The two argument frameworks are drawn below.

$(Args, \hookrightarrow_E)$                    $(Args, \hookrightarrow_D)$

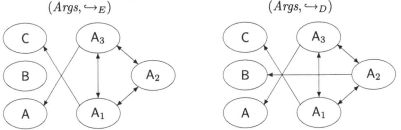

## 2.3  p_ABA

We next investigate *Assumption-Based Argumentation Equipped with Preferences* (p_ABA) [37], which is an extension of the well studied structured argumentation formalism Assumption-Based Argumentation (ABA) [10,35]. While ABA itself does not possess a mechanism to deal with explicit preferences, to the best of our knowledge p_ABA is the only structured argumentation formalism to use preferences on the extension level to discriminate among extensions.

ABA frameworks are tuples $(\mathcal{L}, \mathcal{R}, \mathcal{A}, \overline{\phantom{x}})$ with $\mathcal{L}$ a language, $\mathcal{R}$ a set of rules, $\mathcal{A} \subseteq \mathcal{L}$ a distinguished set of *assumptions*, and a total mapping $\overline{\phantom{x}} : \mathcal{A} \rightarrow \mathcal{L}$ giving *contraries* of assumptions. Similarly to ASPIC⁺, arguments are constructed as deductions from sets of assumptions using rules, and the attacks are directed at assumptions by deducing their contraries (consult e.g. [35]).

p_ABA frameworks $(\mathcal{L}, \mathcal{R}, \mathcal{A}, ^-, <)$ generalize ABA frameworks by adding a preference ordering $<$ over $\mathcal{L}$. This ordering then induces an ordering over arguments, which in turn induces an ordering $\sqsubseteq$ over extensions of the underlying ABA framework. For two extensions $E$ and $E'$ of $(\mathcal{L}, \mathcal{R}, \mathcal{A}, ^-)$, $E \sqsubseteq E'$ essentially requires that there is a consequence $\varphi$ of $E'$ but not $E$, for which among consequences of $E$ but not $E'$ there is $\psi$ but not $\psi'$ with $\psi < \varphi < \psi'$.[6] p_ABA then selects those extensions $E$ that are not strictly less preferred than any other extension $E'$ (i.e. $E \not\sqsubseteq E'$ for any $E'$), subsequently called $\mathcal{P}$-extensions.

Our Cakes example can be cast in p_ABA as follows.

*Example 4 (Cakes in p_ABA).* We have a p_ABA framework $(\mathcal{L}, \mathcal{R}, \mathcal{A}, ^-, <)$ with language $\mathcal{L} = \{a, b, c, \bar{a}, \bar{b}, \bar{c}\}$, rules $\mathcal{R} = \{\bar{b} \leftarrow a, c\}$, assumptions $\mathcal{A} = \{a, b, c\}$ (standing for cakes) and preference $a < b$. We construct arguments $A : \{a\} \vdash a$, $B : \{b\} \vdash b$, $C : \{c\} \vdash c$, and $X : \{a, c\} \vdash \bar{b}$. The only attack is $X \rightsquigarrow B$, so the underlying ABA framework $(\mathcal{L}, \mathcal{R}, \mathcal{A}, ^-)$, as depicted below, has a unique stable extension $\{A, C, X\}$ (choice of Almond cake and Cheesecake).

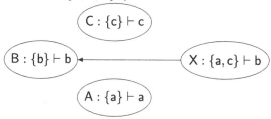

Since the ABA extension is unique, in p_ABA preferences do not play a role and $\{A, C, X\}$ is a unique stable $\mathcal{P}$-extension of $(\mathcal{L}, \mathcal{R}, \mathcal{A}, ^-, <)$.

## 2.4   Abstract Argumentation

We finally consider AA with preferences. While originally [20] it did not incorporate preference handling mechanism, there are many proposals on how to extend AA with preference information, e.g. [1,3,5,6,12,22,27,30]. Those approaches follow essentially the same guideline that an attack succeeds only if the attacker is not less preferred than the attackee. We therefore employ, following e.g. [27], a generic representative approach where given an AA framework $(Args, \rightsquigarrow)$ and a preference relation $\lhd$ over arguments, the defeat relation $\hookrightarrow$ is obtained from the condition $A \hookrightarrow B$ iff $A \rightsquigarrow B$ and $A \not\lhd B$.

Consider our attempt to render the Cakes problem in AA with preferences.

---

[6] For simplicity, we omit the precise definitions of the consequence operator as well as the relation $\sqsubseteq$; see [35,37] for details.

*Example 5 (Cakes in AA).* Let a, b and c stand for taking a piece of Almond cake, the Brownie and a piece of Cheesecake, respectively. Every combination of a, b and c thus represents a choice of cakes, e.g. $\{b, c\}$ typifies the choice of Brownie and Cheesecake. For simplicity, since taking all three pieces of cakes at once is not permitted, we can disregard the choice $\{a, b, c\}$; similarly, not taking anything, i.e. $\emptyset$, can be discarded.[7] So let $Args = \wp(\{a, b, c\}) \setminus \{\emptyset, \{a, b, c\}\} = \{\{a\}, \{b\}, \{c\}, \{a, b\}, \{a, c\}, \{b, c\}\}$ be the set of arguments.

We can then stipulate the attack relation as follows: for $S, S' \in Args$, let $S \rightsquigarrow S'$ stand for 'if you want the cakes from $S$, do not choose $S'$'. For example, if Brownie and Cheesecake is wanted, then do not take Almond cake and Cheesecake, and vice versa, i.e. $\{b, c\} \rightsquigarrow \{a, c\}$ and $\{a, c\} \rightsquigarrow \{b, c\}$. Similarly, if you want Brownie and Cheesecake, then do not choose Almond cake, i.e. $\{b, c\} \rightsquigarrow \{a\}$; yet if Almond cake is desired, then it is not a problem to take Brownie and Cheesecake, i.e. $\{a\} \not\rightsquigarrow \{b, c\}$. This way, due to the rule that taking Almond cake and Cheesecake prevents getting Brownie, we have (among others) an attack $\{b\} \rightsquigarrow \{a, c\}$.

Preference information tells us that a < b. To account for this we can employ the Elitist and Democratic ordering principles, as well as their Disjoint counterparts, defined in previous sections. Then $S \hookrightarrow S'$ iff $S \rightsquigarrow S'$ and $S \not\lhd S'$, where $\lhd \in \{\lhd_E, \lhd_D, \lhd_{DE}, \lhd_{DD}\}$. Relevant to the attacks, we find: $\{a, c\} \lhd_E \{b\}$; $\{a, c\} \lhd_{DE} \{b, c\}$; $\{a, c\} \lhd_{DD} \{b, c\}$. So we obtain that $\{a, c\} \not\hookrightarrow_E \{b\}$, $\{a, c\} \not\hookrightarrow_{DE} \{b, c\}$ and $\{a, c\} \not\hookrightarrow_{DD} \{b, c\}$. The following graphically depicts the argument frameworks in question.

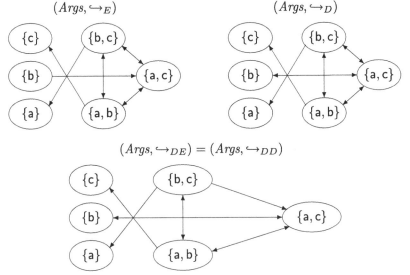

$$(Args, \hookrightarrow_E) \qquad\qquad (Args, \hookrightarrow_D)$$

$$(Args, \hookrightarrow_{DE}) = (Args, \hookrightarrow_{DD})$$

---

[7] With the attack relation specified next, this simplification is meant purely to make the argument framework easier to read.

In $(Args, \hookrightarrow_E)$, $(Args, \hookrightarrow_{DE})$ and $(Args, \hookrightarrow_{DD})$, the sets $E = \{\{b\}, \{c\}, \{b, c\}\}$ and $E' = \{\{a\}, \{b\}, \{a, b\}\}$ are the only stable extensions (corresponding to the 'rational' choice), whereas $(Args, \hookrightarrow_D)$, in addition to $E$ and $E'$, admits $E'' = \{\{a\}, \{c\}, \{a, c\}\}$ as a stable extension.

We note that in *Preference-based Argumentation Frameworks* (PAFs) [3], the preference relation $\lhd$ over arguments is used to *reverse*, rather than discard attacks. However, in Example 5 such attack reversal would result into already existing attacks, so the outcome would be the same.

# 3   Related Work and Discussion

We briefly discuss a few distinguished formalisms, namely Extended Argumentation Frameworks (EAFs) [30,31], Argumentation Frameworks with Recursive Attacks (AFRA) [5] and Defeasible Logic Programming (DeLP) [23,24]. Both EAFs and AFRA are generalizations of AA that allow for attacks to be directed at attacks, as well as at arguments. The intuition is that an attack on an attack A ⤳ B expresses a preference for B over A. However, if a preference relation among arguments is not explicitly given, as in the Cakes example, then it is not trivial to figure out what additional attacks on attacks should be introduced.

DeLP, on the other hand, is another structured argumentation formalism that relies on defeasible rules (see Sect. 2.2), and in addition involves the concept of negation as failure [16] from Logic Programming. To represent any non-factual information DeLP employs defeasible rules, and if negation as failure is used, then attacks succeed irrespective of the preferences, like in ABA.

In terms of modelling the Cakes problem from Example 1 in the formalisms considered, we concede that different representations are possible. We chose a natural way to represent a single (strict) rule and a single preference involving two alternatives, and believe that other representations would come at the expense of perspicuity and generality.

We have seen that among the selected formalisms of argumentation (both abstract and structured) with preferences none opt exclusively for the 'intuitive' answer "Brownie and Cheesecake" when modelling the Cakes problem. In Deductive Argumentation (Sect. 2.1) the normative 'rational' solution of choosing indifferently between {Almond cake, Brownie} and {Brownie, Cheesecake} was obtained. ASPIC$^+$ (Sect. 2.2) yielded other choices (such as {Almond cake, Cheesecake}) in addition to the 'rational' one. Preference information in p_ABA (Sect. 2.3) did not really play a role, and just like ABA, the formalism generated a unique choice {Almond cake, Cheesecake}. Finally, AA with preferences (Sect. 2.4) produced either the 'rational choice', or additionally the one afforded by p_ABA too.

The fact that current approaches do not opt exclusively for the 'intuitive' solution in the Cakes example does not mean those argumentation formalisms are ill-suited to handle preferences. Each formalism has been shown to satisfy some desirable properties and adhere to certain intuitions. Some approaches may also aim for being more normative systems, in the sense of complying with certain rationality standards, rather than mimicking human intuition at the expense of rationality. Indeed, common-sense reasoning and human decision making are not necessarily rational endeavours (see e.g. [28]). However, as argumentation is a technique to model common-sense reasoning, it is natural to demand of formalisms that aspire to this goal to be able to accordingly model common-sense reasoning scenarios such as the one considered in this paper.

## 4    Conclusion and Future Work

In this paper we investigated whether and how existing approaches to argumentation with preferences model human intuition behind common-sense reasoning scenarios involving rules and preference information. To this end, we proposed an example of a decision making problem that assumes essentially a single strict rule and a single preference. The example was supplemented with both an informal solution to the problem, referred to as the 'rational' choice, and a survey, results of which indicated a solution, referred to as the 'intuitive' choice, that human respondents have opted for most often. We rendered the problem in several representative formalisms of argumentation with preferences, and saw that they produce either the 'rational' or some other choices, but not exclusively the 'intuitive' one. As argumentation is used in areas such as common-sense reasoning and decision making among others, the results, we argue, call for a deeper analysis of how to adequately represent in argumentation the type of problems as the one considered here. Still further, our investigation opens up space for discussions on how to deal with such reasoning problems involving preferences in argumentation-based approaches to, for instance, multi-agent systems, as well as in AI more generally.

Recently, we have proposed a novel formalism, $ABA^+$ [17], to account for preferences in argumentation. $ABA^+$ extends the established structured argumentation formalism Assumption-Based Argumentation [10,35] with an explicit preference relation over assumptions and integrates an attack reversal mechanism (as proposed for abstract argumentation in Preference-based Argumentation Frameworks [3]) based on preference information. In particular, preferences in $ABA^+$ are incorporated into the attack relation, dispensing with preference aggregation techniques on either argument or extension level. Preliminary analysis indicates that such a method yields the 'intuitive' solution to the Cakes problem discussed in this paper, and we will investigate further.

Additionally, we plan to study scenarios as in the Cakes Example themselves and their treatment in AI. In particular, it would be interesting to see what existing reasoning techniques (e.g. constraint logic programming, Event Calculus) would capture human intuitions in such scenarios. This research direction also includes enquiry into the meaning of preferences and their relation to, for example, rules. In addition, it involves exploring what formal properties regarding preferences can be conceived, as in e.g. [11]. It furthermore means designing and running more surveys to get a better grasp behind human intuitions. Such research is essential to understanding preferences and approaching common-sense reasoning problems from the argumentation perspective in particular, and from the point of view of AI in general.

In AI at large there is much debate on how to manage preferences (see e.g. [19,26]). Our work contributes to this line of research by presenting a simple example of reasoning with preferences, opening up space for discussions on how to cope with such common-sense reasoning scenarios in argumentation, and challenging the existing and potential argumentation formalisms to model the human intuition behind them.

# References

1. Amgoud, L., Cayrol, C.: A reasoning model based on the production of acceptable arguments. Ann. Math. Artif. Intell. **34**(1–3), 197–215 (2002)
2. Amgoud, L., Prade, H.: Using arguments for making and explaining decisions. Artif. Intell. **173**(3–4), 413–436 (2009)
3. Amgoud, L., Vesic, S.: Rich preference-based argumentation frameworks. Int. J. Approximate Reasoning **55**(2), 585–606 (2014)
4. Baroni, P., Caminada, M., Giacomin, M.: An introduction to argumentation semantics. Knowl. Eng. Rev. **26**(04), 365–410 (2011)
5. Baroni, P., Cerutti, F., Giacomin, M., Guida, G.: AFRA: argumentation framework with recursive attacks. Int. J. Approximate Reasoning **52**(1), 19–37 (2011)
6. Bench-Capon, T.: Persuasion in practical argument using value based argumentation frameworks. J. Logic Comput. **13**(3), 429–448 (2003)
7. Besnard, P., García, A., Hunter, A., Modgil, S., Prakken, H., Simari, G., Toni, F.: Introduction to structured argumentation. Argument Computat. **5**(1), 1–4 (2014)
8. Besnard, P., Hunter, A.: A logic-based theory of deductive arguments. Artif. Intell. **128**(1–2), 203–235 (2001)
9. Besnard, P., Hunter, A.: Constructing argument graphs with deductive arguments: a tutorial. Argument Computat. **5**(1), 5–30 (2014)
10. Bondarenko, A., Dung, P.M., Kowalski, R., Toni, F.: An abstract, argumentation-theoretic approach to default reasoning. Artif. Intell. **93**(97), 63–101 (1997)
11. Brewka, G., Eiter, T.: Preferred answer sets for extended logic programs. Artif. Intell. **109**(1–2), 297–356 (1999)
12. Brewka, G., Ellmauthaler, S., Strass, H., Wallner, J., Woltran, S.: Abstract dialectical frameworks revisited. In: Rossi, F. (ed.) Proceedings of the 23rd International Joint Conference on Artificial Intelligence (IJCAI), pp. 803–809. IJCAI/AAAI, Beijing (2013)
13. Brewka, G., Truszczynski, M., Niemelä, I.: Preferences and nonmonotonic reasoning. AI Mag. **29**(4), 69–78 (2008)
14. Caminada, M., Amgoud, L.: On the evaluation of argumentation formalisms. Artif. Intell. **171**(5–6), 286–310 (2007)
15. Carrera, Á., Iglesias, C.: A systematic review of argumentation techniques for multi-agent systems research. Artif. Intell. Rev. **44**(4), 509–535 (2015)
16. Clark, K.L.: Negation as failure. In: Gallaire, H., Minker, J. (eds.) Logic and Data Bases, pp. 293–322. Springer, Heidelberg (1978)
17. Čyras, K., Toni, F.: ABA+: assumption-based argumentation with preferences. In: Principles of Knowledge Representation and Reasoning: Proceedings of the Fifteenth International Conference (KR), to appear. Cape Town (2016)

18. Delgrande, J., Schaub, T., Tompits, H., Wang, K.: A classification and survey of preference handling approaches in nonmonotonic reasoning. Comput. Intell. **20**(2), 308–334 (2004)
19. Domshlak, C., Hüllermeier, E., Kaci, S., Prade, H.: Preferences in ai: an overview. Artif. Intell. **175**(7–8), 1037–1052 (2011)
20. Dung, P.M.: On the acceptability of arguments and its fundamental role in non-monotonic reasoning, logic programming and n-person games. Artif. Intell. **77**, 321–357 (1995)
21. Dung, P.M.: An axiomatic Analysis of Structured Argumentation with Priorities. Artif. Intell. **231**, 107–150 (2016)
22. Dunne, P., Hunter, A., McBurney, P., Parsons, S., Wooldridge, M.: Weighted argument systems: basic definitions, algorithms, and complexity results. Artif. Intell. **175**(2), 457–486 (2011)
23. García, A., Simari, G.: Defeasible logic programming: an argumentative approach. Theor. Pract. Logic Program. **4**(2), 95–138 (2004)
24. García, A., Simari, G.: Defeasible logic programming: DeLP-servers, contextual queries, and explanations for answers. Argument Comput. **5**(1), 63–88 (2014)
25. Gorogiannis, N., Hunter, A.: Instantiating abstract argumentation with classical logic arguments: postulates and properties. Artif. Intell. **175**(9–10), 1479–1497 (2011)
26. Kaci, S.: Working with Preferences. Less is More. Springer, Heidelberg (2011)
27. Kaci, S., van der Torre, L.: Preference-based argumentation: arguments supporting multiple values. Int. J. Approximate Reasoning **48**(3), 730–751 (2008)
28. Kahneman, D., Tversky, A.: Prospect theory: an analysis of decision under risk. Econometrica **47**(2), 263–291 (1979)
29. Kakas, A., Moraitis, P.: Argumentation based decision making for autonomous agents. In: The Second International Joint Conference on Autonomous Agents and Multiagent Systems (AAMAS), pp. 883–890. ACM Press, Melbourne (2003)
30. Modgil, S.: Reasoning about preferences in argumentation frameworks. Artif. Intell. **173**(9–10), 901–934 (2009)
31. Modgil, S., Prakken, H.: Reasoning about preferences in structured extended argumentation frameworks. Front. Artif. Intell. Appl. **216**(9–10), 347–358 (2010)
32. Modgil, S., Prakken, H.: A general account of argumentation with preferences. Artif. Intell. **195**, 361–397 (2013)
33. Modgil, S., Prakken, H.: The ASPIC+ framework for structured argumentation: a tutorial. Argument Comput. **5**(1), 31–62 (2014)
34. Rahwan, I., Simari, G.: Argumentation in Artificial Intelligence. Springer, Heidelberg (2009)
35. Toni, F.: A tutorial on assumption-based argumentation. Argument Comput. **5**(1), 89–117 (2014)
36. Wakaki, T.: Preference-based argumentation built from prioritized logic programming. J. Logic Comput. **25**(2), 251–301 (2013)
37. Wakaki, T.: Assumption-based argumentation equipped with preferences. In: Dam, H.K., Pitt, J., Xu, Y., Governatori, G., Ito, T. (eds.) PRIMA 2014. LNCS, vol. 8861, pp. 116–132. Springer, Heidelberg (2014)

# Almost Fair: Conjoint Measurement Theory and Score-Based Bargaining Solutions

Joe McCool$^{(\boxtimes)}$ and Isaac Davis

Carnegie Mellon University, Pittsburgh, USA
jmccool@andrew.cmu.edu

**Keywords:** Bargaining theory · Multi-attribute utility · Nash bargaining

## 1  Introduction

A bargaining problem is a cooperative game in which players are permitted to negotiate before the game is played. Bargaining theory can be used to economic interactions such as union negotiations, international trade agreements, and duopolies. A general theory of bargaining games thus has a wide application to many areas of economics and political science. There are several specifications of bargaining games and their solutions, the most prominent of which is the Nash Bargaining problem. These bargaining theories identify unique points in the bargaining space that satisfy some axiomatic or constraint-based notion of "fairness" and "efficiency". In this paper, we introduce a score-based method for identifying bargaining solutions, that not only identifies the unique point satisfying a notion of fairness, but assigns a numerical "score" to each possible option in the bargaining space. This measure can then be used to numerically evaluate how much better or worse one potential solution is than another, and imposes a total preference ordering over the bargaining space.

In this section we present some background on bargaining theory and the standard Nash bargaining solution. In the Sect. 2, we introduce multi-attribute utility theory and conjoint measurement functions, and demonstrate how they can be modified to handle bargaining problems. In Sect. 3 we demonstrate how our method can be applied to two canonical bargaining solutions, the Nash and Shapley solutions. In the final section, we discuss some applications of this theory and outline future work.

### 1.1  Bargaining Problems

For this paper we will borrow our notation from R. Duncan Luce and Howard Raiffa's *Games and Decisions-Introduction and Critical Survey*. Formally, we assume that players may send messages to each other without distortion, all negotiated agreements are binding, and a player's evaluation of outcomes are not affected by these negotiations. Additionally, we must assume a reliable and consistent measure of each player's utility over the available payouts.

© Springer International Publishing Switzerland 2016
J. Bajo et al. (Eds.): PAAMS 2016 Workshops, CCIS 616, pp. 211–223, 2016.
DOI: 10.1007/978-3-319-39387-2_18

In a general bargaining game with two players, we assume each player has a discrete set of choices-the options or "moves" a player may make-and to each pair of choices the two players can make, we associate a pair of payouts. We will refer to this set of moves and payout pairs as the "menu" or "pure strategies". Additionally, a player may choose a "mixed strategy", whereby the player randomizes between two pure strategies available to her. Thus if a player has two pure strategies $A$ and $B$, the player may generate a mixed strategy $C$ by playing $A$ with some probability $p$ and $B$ with some probability $1 - p$. Suppose we treat each pair of strategies $(x, y)$ as a point in a two-dimensional plane, where each player's payout utility is represented by an axis. We refer to the region containing payout pairs for all possible strategy pairs, including these mixed strategies, as $R$. By allowing for cooperation, however, we can expand the region of possible payout pairs to include payouts attainable only through correlated mixed strategies. To illustrate this, consider the following simple game:

|            | $\beta_1$    | $\beta_2$    |
|------------|--------------|--------------|
| $\alpha_1$ | $(2, 1)$     | $(-1, -1)$   |
| $\alpha_2$ | $(-1, -1)$   | $(1, 2)$     |

Suppose player $A$ must choose strategy $\alpha_1$ or $\alpha_2$ and player $B$ must choose strategy $\beta_1$ or $\beta_2$. Player $A$ may play a mixed strategy by randomizing between $\alpha_1$ and $\alpha_2$ with probability $1/2$, and player $B$ may do the same with strategies $\beta_1$ and $\beta_2$. This gives a $1/4$ probability of any of the four possible pairs of payouts being realized, leading to an expected payout of $(1, 1)$. If, however, the two players are permitted to negotiate before choosing their strategies, they can achieve an expected payout of $(3/2, 3/2)$ by correlating their mixed strategies: with probability $1/2$ the two players choose $(\alpha_1, \beta_1)$, and with probability $1/2$ they choose $(\alpha_2, \beta_2)$. Thus, by introducing cooperation, we add an expected payout of $(3/2, 3/2)$ to the payout region $R$, which was not possible without allowing prior agreements between the players. Thus we see that allowing for cooperation will in general expand the payout region of a game, as cooperation enables players to jointly randomize between pairs of strategies, rather than each player individually randomizing between individual strategies.

## 1.2    The Nash Bargaining Problem

With this established, the role of bargaining theory is to determine a "fair" outcome for a cooperative game. The question is, then, how does one mathematically formalize the notion of "fairness?" There are a number of mathematical formulations that have been proposed, but the most common and perhaps canonical bargaining problem is due to Nash. The standard Nash bargaining problem specifies a particular payout pair as the status quo, or "walkaway" point. This is taken to be the payout the players will receive in the event that no agreement is reached.

A Nash bargaining game is fully specified by the region $R$ of possible payout pairs and the status quo point $(u^*, v^*) \in R$. A bargaining solution, then, is a function $F$ that selects, for each game $[R, (u^*, v^*)]$, a particular payout pair from $R$ as the "best", or "fairest" solution.

Intuitively, the Nash solution for a bargaining game $[R, (u^*, v^*)]$ is obtained by maximizing the product of each player's surplus utility over their status quo utility. This function can be computed by first rescaling each player's utility function so that the status quo point $(u^*, v^*)$ is transformed into $(0, 0)$, and applying the same transformation to the region $R$, obtaining the transformed region $R'$. We then find the unique point $(u'_0, v'_0) \in R'$ that maximizes the product $u'_0 v'_0$. Note that because $R'$ is scaled so as to transform $(u^*, v^*)$ into $(0, 0)$, maximizing the product $u'_0 v'_0$ over all $(u'_0, v'_0) \in R'$ is equivalent to maximizing the product $(u_0 - u^*)(v_0 - v^*)$ over all $(u_0, v_0) \in R$, which is precisely the product of each players' surplus over their status quo payouts.

Formally, Nash derives this solution by proposing four constraints to characterize a "fair" bargaining solution, and demonstrating that the function described above uniquely satisfies the four constraints. The constraints Nash establishes are as follows:

1. Invariance to Equivalent Utility Representations: The bargaining solution should be independent of the scale and origin used for each player's utility measure. That is, suppose bargaining problems $[R_1, (u_1^*, v_1^*)]$ and $[R_2, (u_2^*, v_2^*)]$ differ only in the units and origins of the utility functions. Then the solutions to the two games should differ only by the same transformation in units and origins.

2. Symmetry: Suppose a bargaining problem $[R, (u^*, v^*)]$ is symmetric, in the sense that $u^* = v^*$ and $(u, v) \in R$ if and only if $(v, u) \in R$. Then the bargaining solution $u_0, v_0$ must satisfy $u_0 = v_0$. Intuitively, this asserts that if each player has the same set of possible payouts and the same status quo payout, then both players should receive equal payout.

3. Independence of Irrelevant Alternatives: Suppose $[R_1, (u^*, v^*)]$ and $[R_2, (u^*, v^*)]$ are bargaining games with the same status quo point such that $R_1 \subset R_2$. If $(u_0, v_0)$ is the solution to $R_2$ and $(u_0, v_0) \in R_1$, then $R_1$ must also have solution $(u_0, v_0)$. Intuitively, this asserts that if an option is not used in constructing the solution, then a smaller sub-game not containing that option must have the same solution.

4. Pareto Efficiency: A solution $(u_0, v_0)$ to bargaining game $[R, (u^*, v^*)]$ must satisfy $u_0 \geq u^*$, $v_0 \geq v^*$. Furthermore, If there exists a point $(u, v) \in R$ such that $u \geq u_0$ and $v \geq v_0$, then $(u, v) = (u_0, v_0)$.

With the above axioms established, we can formally characterize the Nash solution to the general bargaining game $[R, (u^*, v^*)]$ as

$$f[R, (u^*, v^*)] = \underset{(u,v) \in R}{\mathrm{argmax}}[(u - u^*)(v - v^*)] \tag{1.1}$$

This is the unique function satisfying all of the above constraints.

### 1.3   Constraint-Based Versus Score-Based Bargaining Solutions

The Nash bargaining solution constructs a unique point in the outcome space which satisfies the notion of fairness and efficiency, as defined by the axioms. For this reason, we refer to these solutions as "constraint-based". However, there is much more information that can be extracted from a bargaining problem than a single solution point. In this paper, we establish a method for defining a total ordering over the full outcome space. While our solution will still identify a single point as optimal (the same point identified in each bargaining solution), our method also allows us to judge between any two potential points in the outcome space. In full, we want to be able to say of any two points which is the "better" solution, by how much, and how far off it is from the optimal solution. In order to achieve this, we use conjoint measurement theory (explained in more detail below) to construct a function that assigns a real-valued score to any point in the outcome space, with which we can gauge their relative desirability. For this reason, we refer to our methods as "score-based" solutions.

Like Nash, we limit our treatment to two player bargaining problems. To achieve our total ordering over bargaining outcomes, we introduce a third hypothetical "player", the *impartial arbitrator*, whose only concern is that the bargaining outcome be fair and efficient. Our total ordering over bargaining solutions will be derived from our arbitrator's utility function over the outcomes, which is a multi-attribute utility function in which each of the first two players' utilities is a distinct attribute.

## 2   Multi-Attribute Measurement Systems

### 2.1   Multi-Attribute Utility Theory

Multi-attribute utility theory is a refinement of standard univariate theories (e.g. von Neumann and Morgenstern's Expected Utility theory) which permits decision makers to make fine-grained distinctions between possible "rewards" in the outcome space. We do this by breaking each reward into $n$ distinct attributes, then comparing each reward on $n$ dimensions. For example, if deciding which of two apartments to rent, your attributes might be *floor space*, *windows*, and *distance from the nearest bus stop*. The utility a decision maker would derive from any given apartment then becomes a function of *floor space* (measured in square meters), *total window surface-area* (measured in square meters), and *distance from the nearest bus stop* (measured in meters).

Suppose our decision-maker, Brock's, "apartment utility" is increasing in *floor space* and *window area*, and decreasing in *bus stop distance*. The simplest comparisons between two apartments are those where one apartment dominates another in all attributes (i.e. bigger, more windows, and closer to bus stop). Multi-attribute functions are interesting in cases where some attributes are better while the others are worse. In such cases, it becomes necessary to define tradeoffs between attributes. Suppose, for example, that Brock is viewing his second apartment for the day. He knows all the details for apartment 1, and everything about apartment 2 except for the distance to the nearest bus stop, as illustrated in the following table:

|             | Floor space | Window area | Bus stop distance |
|-------------|-------------|-------------|-------------------|
| Apartment 1 | 75          | 10          | 300               |
| Apartment 2 | 75          | 8           | ?                 |

A multi-attribute utility function allows us to fill in the distance which would make Brock indifferent between the two apartments. Since Brock's utility is increasing in *window area* and decreasing in *bus stop distance*, we can infer that apartment 2 would need to be closer to a bus stop to make up for the loss in *window area*, though the magnitude will be dependent on Brock's utility function. The implications should be clear. We are introducing a fourth score, *utility*, with which we are able to define tradeoff values between any pair of attributes. Let us say that Brock would be indifferent between the two apartments if the apartment is 260 meters from a bus stop. From this, we can say that from the reference point of apartment 1, cutting his walk to the bus stop by 40 meters is worth 2 square-meters of window space to Brock *in terms of his utility*.

### 2.2   Conjoint Measurement Functions and Bargaining Problems

Notice that we have just qualified a tradeoff between two seemingly incommensurable things: windows and walking distance. This is the strategy we employ, by imposing a scoring system over our outcome space in 2-person games which allows us to directly compare utilities. As such, we can make claims to the effect of: "from the reference point of bargaining outcome $(x, y)$, a gain of 40 utils to player 1 is worth a gain of 100 utils to player 2 in terms of an *impartial arbitrator's* utility".

The general functional form that we will be using for each of our bargaining solutions is a conjoint measurement function. Formally, suppose a measurement involves $n$ attributes, so that each object can be represented as a point in some $n$-dimensional attribute space $A = A_1 \times \ldots \times A_n$. Suppose furthermore we have a weak ordering $\succeq$ defined over $A$. A conjoint measure consists of a set of one-place functions $\phi_1 : A_1 \to \mathbb{R}, \ldots, \phi_n : A_n \to \mathbb{R}$, and an $n$-place function $F : \mathbb{R}^n \to \mathbb{R}$, such that for all $a = (a_1, \ldots, a_n), b = (b_1, \ldots, b_n) \in A$, $a \succeq b$ if and only if $F(\phi_1(a_1), \ldots, \phi_n(a_n)) \geq F(\phi_1(b_1), \ldots, \phi_n(b_n))$. Intuitively, each $\phi_i$ is a measurement function over a single attribute, mapping that attribute value to a measurement in $\mathbb{R}$. The $F$ function combines the measurements from each attribute into a single measurement over the whole space.

An example of a conjoint measurement function is density. Measuring the density of an object involves two attributes, *mass* and *volume*. Suppose you are calculating the density of a block of wood. Let $a_1$ represent *mass* and $a_2$ *volume*. Then $\phi_1(a_1)$ and $\phi_2(a_2)$ map *mass* and *volume* to appropriate units, and density is defined by the conjoint measurement function $F(\phi_1(a_1), \phi_2(a_2)) = \frac{\phi_1(a_1)}{\phi_2(a_2)}$.

We have two attributes, then, with separate effects on the total score (density) which contribute non-additively. This means that while increasing mass and decreasing volume both increase density, the effect on density of increasing mass depends entirely on the volume of the block of wood. For example, adding two kilograms to a block of wood that is 10 $cm^3$ (by, say, drilling a hole and pressing in a piece of iron) will increase the density of that block of wood much more than if you add 2 kg to a block of wood measuring 1 $m^3$ in volume.

Generally, we wish to allow the distinct attributes to have separate influences on the final output of the conjoint measurement function. For the purpose of this paper, "separate" means decomposable. Decomposable functions can have interdependencies among attributes, but the kinds of interactions are restricted. Intuitively, a decomposable function preserves the qualitative ordering over the attribute space (in our case preferences over outcomes). Formally, decomposability is defined as follows:

**Definition 2.1 (Decomposability).** *Suppose that $\succeq$ is a binary relation on $A = A_1 \times \ldots \times A_n$. For $a_1, a_2 \in A$, let $a_1 \sim a_2$ denote indifference between $a_1$ and $a_2$ (i.e. $a_1 \succeq a_2$ and $a_2 \succeq a_1$). Then the structure $\langle A_1 \times \ldots \times A_n, \succeq \rangle$ is decomposable if and only if the following conditions hold:*

1. *$\succeq$ is a weak ordering over $A$. That is, $\succeq$ is a transitive and reflexive relation such that for all $a_1, a_2 \in A$, either $a_1 \succeq a_2$ or $a_2 \succeq a_1$.*
2. *$A \backslash \sim$ has a countable order-dense subset. This axiom serves as to force $F$ to be a real-valued function.*
3. *$\sim$ satisfies the following condition: for all $1 \leq i \leq n$, all $a_i, a_i' \in A_i$, and all $b = (b_1, \ldots, b_n), c = (c_1, \ldots, c_n) \in A$,*

$$(b_1, \ldots, b_{i-1}, a_i, b_{i+1}, \ldots, b_n) \sim (b_1, \ldots, b_{i-1}, a_i', b_{i+1}, \ldots, b_n)$$

*if and only if*

$$(c_1, \ldots, c_{i-1}, a_i, c_{i+1}, \ldots, c_n) \sim (c_1, \ldots, c_{i-1}, a_i', c_{i+1}, \ldots, c_n)$$

The last condition is called *substitutability*. To illustrate the substitutability axiom, suppose we consider our preferences over cars, treating cars as bundles of attributes (i.e. engine size, number of doors, etc.). Substitutability requires that, if I am indifferent between two cars that are identical except that one has a turbocharged V6 engine and the other has a naturally aspirated V8, then I should also be indifferent between any two cars that are identical except that one has a turbocharged V6 engine and the other a V8.

With these three axioms established, we can state the following representation theorem:

**Theorem 2.2** *Suppose $\succeq$ is a binary relation on $A = A_1 \times \ldots \times A_n$. The structure $\langle A_1 \times \ldots \times A_n, \succeq \rangle$ is decomposable if and only if there exist real valued functions $\phi_1 : A_1 \to \mathbb{R}, \ldots, \phi_n : A_n \to \mathbb{R}, F : \phi_1(A_1) \times \ldots \times \phi_n(A_n) \to \mathbb{R}$ such for all $a, b \in A$,*

$$a \succeq b \text{ if and only if } F(\phi_1(a_1), \ldots, \phi_n(a_n)) \geq F(\phi_1(b_1), \ldots, \phi_n(b_n))$$

In the context of this paper, the attribute space will have two dimensions, each attribute corresponding to the utility of one player (though this can be extended to handle $n$-player games). The goal will be, for a given bargaining problem and bargaining scheme (e.g. Nash, Shapley) to construct a conjoint measurement function $F(\phi_1(x_1), \phi_2(x_2))$ such that the optimal value $(x_1^*, x_2^*)$ of $F$ is achieved when $(x_1^*, x_2^*)$ is the bargaining solution for that particular scheme. Once the conjoint measurement function is constructed, we can derive the preference ordering over bargaining outcomes from this function.

## 2.3    Decomposability in Bargaining Problems

Any measurement function must be "anchored" to some empirical observations. Returning to our density example, an object must have both *some* mass and *some* volume in order for it to be capable of having density. Assuming that "no mass" is represented by a value of 0, and "no volume" has a measurement of 0, we refer to $(0, 0)$ as the anchor point for density. With density, this anchor point is universal. Universal in this context means that no set of empirical conditions will return this same anchor point once *unit* and *scale* are established, and the empirical ordering will be preserved among all objects.

For example, suppose that we have two solid blocks of iron, one twice the volume of the other. Supposing that the increased volume means there is twice as much iron, the mass increases proportionally. It is easy to see that objects with different masses and different volumes will have the same density. In a multi-attribute problem, we would say that these two blocks of iron lie on the same indifference curve. Two blocks of pine, for example, would lie on a lower indifference curve (indicating lower density), while two blocks of lead would lie on a higher indifference curve. Given unit, scale, and our universal anchor point of "no mass, no volume", these indifference curves will not change.

For our score-based bargaining solution, on the other hand, we have no such universal anchor point. Even with a fixed origin and scale for the two agents' utility functions, two identical bargaining outcomes can vary greatly in terms of fairness and efficiency. This is because our anchor point may *move* depending on the menu. If our anchor point were universal, then we could express some universal utility score for our arbitrator for any given outcome, as long as we hold the scale and origin for each player's utility fixed. This consequence is absurd, however. Consider, for example, a bargaining problem in which Rob and Kasey, college roommates, are deciding how to divide the $200 cost of a ping pong table for their apartment. Suppose each has $180 available (meaning that if Rob and Kasey do not agree on a division, they do not get the table), and the least preferred option for both of them is that no table is purchased. Splitting the costs 50/50 seems reasonable in this case, and it is likely that the impartial arbitrator's utility function would be maximized near a 50/50 split.

Now suppose that several months after the ping pong table purchase, Kasey asks Rob if he would like to get a video game console for their living room. Again, the cost is $200 and they each have $180. Suppose Kasey argues for purchasing the console on the basis that it can both play games *and* DVDs, both of which appeal to both roommates. Suppose, however, that Rob already has a DVD player in his room, though he would additionally like to be able to play games.

In this case, the "walkaway point" is much better for Rob than for Kasey, since with or without Kasey's cooperation, Rob can watch movies in their apartment, but Kasey is left with neither. For Rob, the least preferred option is paying $180 and getting the console is, meaning that Rob prefers not getting the console at all to paying the full $180. In this case, it does not seem fair for Kasey to demand a 50/50 split since Kasey wants to reach an agreement more than Rob does, and Rob would likely reject such a demand out of hand. Our impartial arbitrator's utility function would, in this case, be maximal with Rob paying less. With the same agents, the same costs, and even if we allow for identical payouts in utility between the two bargaining problems, we will reach a much different bargaining solution.

To explain this context-dependent multi-attribute utility function, we introduce the concept of *game-specific anchor points* in order to be able to apply a modified conjoint measurement function. Our anchor points uniquely determine the arbitrator's utility function (and therefore indifference curves) up to scale and origin of the players' utility functions, which commits us to the fact

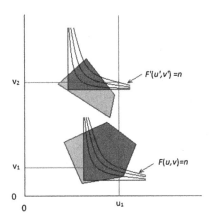

**Fig. 1.** Two sub-games with different status quo points depicted in the same bargaining space

that our function, unqualified, will violate substitutability. We claim that our modification of certain bargaining models (e.g. Nash, Shapley) are *conditionally decomposable*, meaning that if we take features of the bargaining problem as our empirical anchoring point, the resulting function is decomposable. All bargaining problems with identical scale and origin for the bargaining agents' utility functions and an identical *game-specific anchor point*, can treat the impartial arbitrator's utility function as a *decomposable structure* Fig. 1.

In the following diagram, we demonstrate the necessity of these additional qualifications. Specifically, the issue with treating the whole space of bargaining outcomes as tied to some universal anchoring point will violate substitutability, and therefore decomposability:

The above figure depicts a single bargaining space and two sub-games, each with a distinct status quo point. The utility functions for players 1 and 2 are presumed to be fixed in scale and origin. Given that each sub-game has different anchoring points, we can see that points $(u_1, v_1)$ and $(u_1, v_2)$ are on indifference curves which share the same score from the arbitrator's point of view. By substitutability, it must be the case that for any other $u$, $(u, v_1) \sim (u, v_2)$, meaning that $F(u, v_1) = F(u, v_2)$. Clearly, this will not be the case. Notice that as the $u$ value decreases while holding value $v_1$ constant, the arbitrator's utility drops more quickly in the lower sub-game than in the upper one. However, it is the case that if we take as given a game-specific anchor point (or walk-away point) similarly to the $(0, 0)$ used in the density example, then our functions will satisfy all three axioms of decomposability, and we can treat it as a conjoint measurement function. Each bargaining problem makes use of a single anchor point, which is derived from features of the menu of strategies available to each player.

# 3 Solving Bargaining Problems with Conjoint Measurement Functions

## 3.1 The Nash Solution

Recall that for a bargaining problem with outcome region $R$ and walk-away point $(u^*, v^*) \in R$, the Nash solution is defined to be

$$(u_0, v_0) = \underset{(u,v)\in R}{argmax}(u - u^*)(v - v^*) \tag{3.1}$$

Using the above expression, we construct the multi-attribute utility function for our impartial arbitrator. We define this function with respect to a specific class of bargaining problems. In this case, the class is determined by the utility scale for each player and the walk-away point. So, suppose $U$, $V$ are the sets of possible payouts to players 1 and 2, respectively. We first define $\phi_1 : U \to \mathbb{R}$ and $\phi_2 : V \to \mathbb{R}$ as $\phi_1(u) = u - u^*$, $\phi_2(v) = v - v^*$. These functions rescale each player's utility measure so that the status quo payoff is assigned a utility of 0. We then define the conjoint measurement function $F : \mathbb{R}^2 \to \mathbb{R}$ as $F(a, b) = ab$.

Composing these two components gives us a function for computing the "score", or the arbitrator's utility, of any payout pair $(u, v)$, as

$$F(\phi_1(u), \phi_2(v)) = \phi_1(u)\phi_2(v) = (u - u^*)(v - v^*) \tag{3.2}$$

This leaves us with the expression from (3.1) with the *argmax* term removed, so optimizing $F(\phi_1(u), \phi_2(v))$ over all $(u, v) \in R$ will produce the Nash solution to this bargaining problem. Furthermore, we can now define an ordering of all potential outcomes in $R$ by asserting, for all $(u_1, v_1), (u_2, v_2) \in R$: $(u_1, v_1) \succeq (u_2, v_2)$ if and only if $F(\phi_1(u_1), \phi_2(v_1)) \geq F(\phi_1(u_2), \phi_2(v_2))$. It is important to note that any point which is not the maximal value of this function fails to be efficient and/or fails to be fair by Nash's criteria, since his four bargaining axioms, as defined in the previous section, are not satisfied. Our bargaining scheme uses a score-based method for tracking degrees efficiency and fairness.

To illustrate this, consider a simple two-player bargaining game in which the agents must divide a dollar. Each player's utility is linear over the available monetary payouts, and the arbitrator's utility is a function of the two players' payouts in terms of their utilities. Figure 2 depicts this bargaining game with a budget line drawn (i.e. the total amount of goods to be divided), and contours representing the arbitrator's indifference curves. Each such curve can be derived by choosing a fixed value $z_0$ for the arbitrator's utility, and drawing all points $(x, y)$ such that the arbitrator's utility of outcome $(x, y)$ equals $z_0$. The efficiency constraint requires the Nash Solution, labeled in Fig. 3, to lie on the budget line. Points labelled $A$ and $B$ represent two other outcome pairs in the payout region. Note that point $B$ also lies on the budget line, which means that $B$ is an efficient solution (though not necessarily a fair one). Moving from point $A$ to point $B$ therefore increases the efficiency of the solution, while moving down the budget line from $B$ to the Nash solution increases "fairness", but has no effect on Pareto efficiency. Furthermore, for any point in the payout region, the arbitrator's score function will increase most steeply in the direction from that point to the Nash solution.

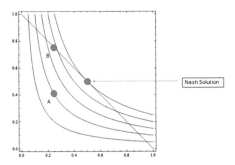

**Fig. 2.** Budget line is shown, contours represent arbitrator's indifference curves over payouts

## 3.2   The Shapley Value

The Shapley method offers an arbitration scheme for a non-strictly competitive game. For two player games, the Shapley method is quite similar to the Nash bargaining solution, but there is an extra step involved: a general non-strictly competitive game does not have a specially identified status quo point. Instead, the Shapley value is obtained by calculating each player's security value (payout from his or her maximin strategy), and using this pair of security payouts as a status quo point for the purpose of solving a Nash bargaining problem.

Formally, the game is specified exactly as a Nash bargaining game, but without the status quo point. Given the menu of pure strategy options, each player can find his or her maximin strategy as a randomization of the available pure strategies. Let the pair of maximin strategies be $(a', b')$, and suppose the corresponding utility pair in $R$ is $(u', v')$. We can now consider this as a Nash bargaining game with status quo point equal to $(u^*, v^*)$. Let $(s_0, t_0)$ denote the Shapley solution of the $R$. This is exactly the Nash bargaining solution of the game $[R, (u', v')]$, namely

$$(s_0, t_0) = \underset{(u,v) \in R}{argmax}[(u - u')(v - v')]$$

Since this is identical to the Nash solution for a game with payout space $R$ and status quo point $(u', v')$, constructing a joint measurement function that recovers the same solution is equally immediate. Simply define $\phi_1(u) = u - u'$, $\phi_2(v) = v - v'$, and $F(x, y) = xy$. Then the point ranked highest by measurement function $F$ is

$$\underset{(u,v) \in R}{argmax}[F(\phi_1(u), \phi_2(v))] = \underset{(u,v) \in R}{argmax}[\phi_1(u)\phi_2(v)] = \underset{(u,v) \in R}{argmax}[(u - u')(v - v')]$$

which is precisely the Shapley value for the two-person game $R$.

# 4   Applications and Future Work

The applications of a score-based bargaining scheme are wide-ranging. We outline two such applications here:

## 4.1   Streamlined Bargaining

One application is to streamline a two-player bargaining game, as we can now formalize utility tradeoffs between individuals in a meaningful way where we previously could not. Furthermore, we can provide a real number to gauge how much better one solution is than the other.

The tradeoffs between individual utilities can be derived from the arbitrator's score function. Suppose for a particular bargaining problem the score function we derive is some $F(\phi_1(u), \phi_2(v))$. The *impartial arbitrator* will prefer outcome $(u_1, v_1)$ over $(u_2, v_2)$ if and only if $F(\phi_1(u_1), \phi_2(v_1)) \geq F(\phi_1(u_2), \phi_2(v_2))$.

J. McCool and I. Davis

This implies that the arbitrator will be indifferent between any two outcomes such that $F(\phi_1(u_1), \phi_2(v_1)) = F(\phi_1(u_2), \phi_2(v_2))$. Thus, for a fixed value $C$, the equation $C = F(\phi_1(u), \phi_2(v))$ defines a relation between the outcome utilities of player 1 and player 2. In the case of Nash, for example, the score function is $(u - u^*)(v - v^*)$, where $(u^*, v^*)$ is the walk-away point. Thus for any fixed $C$, we can derive the relation $(u - u^*) = \frac{C}{v - v^*}$, which gives a rule for trading off utility from player 1 to utility from player 2, while maintaining the same score. In this way, our framework allows us to draw meaningful comparisons between agents' utilities where previously no such relation was permitted.

By giving both agents a formal shared scale with which they can measure the efficiency and fairness of any bargaining outcome, we can efficiently identify a smaller subset of $R$ that is "sufficiently close", however we choose to define "close", to the ideal bargaining solution. This formal scale removes much of the ambiguity surrounding the notion of fairness, and reduces the influence of bargaining skill by letting unskilled negotiators know how badly they are getting fleeced. Additionally, this shared scale can be used to evaluate the performance of the arbitrator on an objective scale.

## 4.2 Bargaining over Multiple Attributes

Suppose two agents are engaged in a Nash bargaining problem over several different bundles of goods. For instance, consider two brothers dividing an inheritance, consisting of a guitar collection and a plot of land. The brothers could use this scheme to identify how to trade "fairly" between land and guitars. This game would have multiple rounds, allowing for each player to make concessions and demands in a way that is formally supported by our framework. This game would proceed as follows: first, each brother computes his utility scales for both land and guitars. Once the utilities have been computed, the brothers can construct a Nash bargaining problem for only the first attribute (guitars), and reach an agreement for the guitar-game. The brothers then construct the Nash bargaining problem for only the second attribute (land). Now, given the agreement the brothers reached in the guitar game, they can compute the "score" of the outcome they arrived at, and the "score" of the ideal Nash solution. If the agreed upon outcome for the guitar game is not the ideal Nash solution, the brother who's payout is sub-optimal is entitled to compensation in the land game. The amount of compensation he is owed can be computed by identifying the difference between the actual outcome score and the ideal outcome score. This difference, converted into land, is the amount over the optimal outcome for land to which the brother is entitled.

## 4.3 Conclusions and Future Work

In this paper, we introduce a score-based method for solving bargaining problems that offers more information and tools than traditional score-based bargaining solutions. We demonstrate how this method can be used for two of the more prominent bargaining theories, those due to Nash and Shapley. It remains to be determined which other bargaining theories may be adapted to our framework. Other bargaining solutions, such as that due to Kalai-Smordinsky, which maximizes the ratio of maximal gains, or Braithwaite, which relies on security values and threat potential, differ significantly from the standard Nash theory. While we have no a priori reason to believe that these bargaining solutions cannot be adapted to our framework, it remains to be seen how these solutions may be expressed in the language of conjoint measurement theory. More generally, we wish to exhaustively characterize which classes of bargaining solutions can be adapted to this framework, and how those adaptations might work mathematically. We intend to pursue these questions in future work.

# References

1. Krantz, D., Luce, R., Suppes, P., Tversky, A.: Foundations of Measurement, vol. 1. Dover Publications Inc., Dover (1971)
2. Shapley, L.S.: A Value for N-Person Games No. RAND-P-295. Rand Corp, Santa Monica (1952)
3. Nash Jr., J.F.: The bargaining problem. Econometrica J. Econometric Soc. **18**, 155–162 (1950)
4. Luce, R.D., Raiffa, H.: Games and Decisions: Introduction and Critical Survey. Wiley, New York (1957)

# Tracking Users Mobility at Public Transportation

Nuno Baeta, Agnelo Fernandes, and João Ferreira[✉]

ADEETC at ISEL, Lisbon, Portugal
njbaeta@gmail.com, jferreira@deetc.isel.ipl.pt

**Abstract.** In this research work we propose a new approach to estimate the number of passengers in a public transportation or determinate the users' route path based on probe requests of users mobile device through collected data in wireless access point. This data is manipulated to extract the information about the numbers of users with mobile devices and track their route path and time.

**Keywords:** Wi-Fi · Mobile device · Tracking · GPS

## 1 Introduction

With the proliferation of mobile devices among the population, wireless sensor networks have recently received a lot of attention due to a diversity of applications such as objects or persons tracking. Access Points (AP) allows passive tracking and this collected big data can be mined to extract useful knowledge about persons tracking movements. Location-Based Services (LBS) is increasing the number of publication and available related services [1] and the use of Wi-Fi network of mobile devices is increasing rapidly. More and more public places are offering (free) Wi-Fi, which enables people to use their location sensitive smartphones and several business opportunities raises with this reality [2]. One of these success applications is the track of shoppers in a shopping centre, which shops they visited, through their phones. They only need the Wi-Fi turned on, which are instantly picked by the system, which logs the unique ID of the phone. These unique IDs to phones are similar to fingerprints. It is common policy at commercial areas for users to use free Wi-Fi, they are asked to hand over information. To sign in, they are encouraged to use social media services such as Facebook, and agree to give Wi-Fi access to elements of their Facebook account, including their email address and likes. This information can then be used to target bespoke emails. This allows users identification and other business opportunities like advertisement at users Facebook posts about shopping. On this research work we propose to apply this concept to public transportation because it is important to get users mobility patterns to optimize public transportation offers. In 2015 the number of mobile phone users is around 4.5 billion [3], the majority of apps in the store have access to the list of routers around you (scanned every 20 s) and the Android smartphone by default scans for Wi-Fi routers even if you disable Wi-Fi. Also based on Wi-Fi it is possible to count people [4] and pattern tracking [5]. The collected data is very important to several entities from city planners, public transportation operator, business owners and police, interested in crowd control to civilians both as a form of intelligence-gathering or everyday problem relief. This mobility

© Springer International Publishing Switzerland 2016
J. Bajo et al. (Eds.): PAAMS 2016 Workshops, CCIS 616, pp. 224–235, 2016.
DOI: 10.1007/978-3-319-39387-2_19

patterns are collected passively without user intervention based on the probe request of mobile devices. These probes request are send periodically broadcasting packets, which contain the unique MAC address of the client and (sometimes) the name of a network to which it has previously connected. This can be used to determine the owner of mobile device in a range of an AP. We propose a passive Wi-Fi tracking system based on AP in each public transportation mean (e.g. bus in our study) and a central tracking cloud server. The focus of this research is on the collection and processing of Wi-Fi probe request detections, like the identified in Fig. 1, used to identify the number of persons with mobile devices and find their route path and timing in a public transportation. This approach is integrated in a bus fleet program management Xtran of a Portuguese Company Tecmic [6], so this data can be combined with other like the information of bus door (open/close), location (GPS) and day/time. Unfortunately, passive Wi-Fi detection is an unreliable and highly noisy source of location information by modern localization standards. Phones are unmodified, and thus transmit at their discretion. Wi-Fi transmissions from a mobile device may range up to 300 m, or may be too faint to detect at 20 m range depending on transmit power, path loss and fading effects. Figure 2 gives a general overview of the passive Wi-Fi tracking system for public transportation integrated with XtraN.

```
*Mar 1 00:27:04.675: 000357, 008, -11b, ffff.ffff.ffff, bcd1.d344.a696 SSID: NULL
*Mar 1 00:27:44.347: 0002AF, 008, -11b, ffff.ffff.ffff, bcd1.d344.a696 SSID: Casa-BAMJ
*Mar 1 00:27:44.351: 0002AF, 008, -11b, ffff.ffff.ffff, bcd1.d344.a696 SSID: NULL
*Mar  1  00:28:11.367:  0001C1,  008,  -11b,  ffff.ffff.ffff,  98d6.f79a.9875  SSID: FON_ZON_FREE
```

**Fig. 1.** Debug probe request on AP in monitor mode

Another work contribution is the field application, because this approach is one of the first applications in public transportation and the output (number of passengers in a bus and user's route path and time) are important information for public transportation operator to enable them to tune their offer to users' needs. Number of passengers in a bus can be used for bus drivers' fuel consumption ranking in an Eco-Driving program, because the number of passengers is related with weight and time in idle at bus stops, details of this can be found in [7]. Mobility user patterns have been widely studied [8–10]. The majority of the work in this area relies on GPS information available from users' mobile devices. Wi-Fi monitoring detects the signal that Wi-Fi-enabled devices send out all the time in their search for a Wi-Fi access point (AP). The user is not actively involved in this a kind of passive localization. The information that can be derived from these signals can be useful for crowd control, marketing purposes or real time monitoring of public space use. Most of these approaches are based on a series of Wi-Fi monitors deployed in the region of interest and users mobile devices sends their Wi-Fi probe request. The server processes data from the monitors to reproduce the device most likely trajectory, which is exported in the form of a second by second location trace. Alternatives to this approach are Bluetooth based on mobile device signal receive from beacon, working in a low energy mode (BLE). Basically this BLE have the advantage of no installation need, working in a simple configuration, but Wi-Fi have the advantage of providing more user interaction. Example of this BLE is the work [11] in partnership with the public transportation operator of Funchal in Madeira Island, who explored the Bluetooth technology for passenger counting.

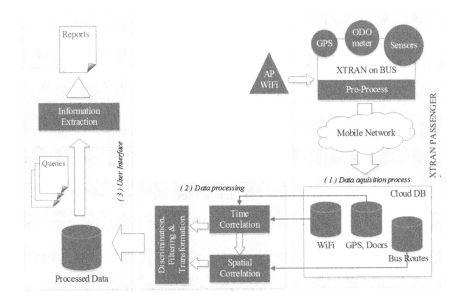

**Fig. 2.** Proposed system, (1) Data acquisition, (2) Data process at cloud server, (3) User interface for information access

## 2   Developed System

As illustrated in Fig. 2, our approach is split in three steps: (1) data collection, (2) data processing, and (3) user interface to show the results and available reports.

### 2.1   Data Collection

For the WiFi sensor we installed an AP Cisco series 1250, but no AP with monitor capability could be used. Due to commercial reason (because the project is connected to a company) we have used Cisco, but with other brands the process is less complex because Cisco blocks without payment or without additional equipment some AP's features. This is the case for obtaining the Received Signal Strength Indicator (RSSI) from every client's Probe Requests, which requires a Wireless LAN Controller (WLC).

The AP1250 series can be controlled from the WLC versions from 5 to 8. We used the 7.3.101.0 version, graciously borrowed from Cisco during 90 days, which matched the AP version 15.2(2).

For the sake of cost reduction, the intention is to use only one Access Point, so the project was developed to find the best results with only the counting from Probe

Requests. Later we added the received signal information from the WLC as one option to improve the results.

From XtraN, we use GPS data, sensor information door open/close, date and time.

The information from each sensor device is sent to XTraN controller module via Syslog. This module wraps all the log files that are produced by each trip with some identifiers like bus_id, route_id, route_way, trip_nbr, etc., so they can be tracked after being sent to the cloud server database. All events from the XTraN sensor devices are also referenced by a timestamp value.

## 2.2    Pre-processing

Wi-Fi data is aggregated and filtered to reduce the amount of information to be sent to the database server. The Wi-Fi log file has several entries per second for each client for a single scanning event due to the private SSID list saved on each terminal – it sends a probe request message for each saved SSID. All this entries can be aggregated to a single one, reducing information volume. If information about RSSI is present, an average value can be saved. Data from XTraN sensors are also filtered to pass only relevant fields. Table 1 shows GPS data with information or door open/close.

**Table 1.**  Excerpt of a pre-processed GPS log file

| Bus_Id | Trip | Bus# | Door | Date-time | Lat | Long |
|---|---|---|---|---|---|---|
| 536 | 8 | 702 | Open | 06-08-2015 12:09:36 | 38,73068 | 9,17321 |
| 536 | 8 | 702 | Close | 06-08-2015 12:01:31 | 38,73238 | 9,17183 |
| 536 | 8 | 702 | Open | 06-08-2015 12:02:27 | 38,73465 | 9,17021 |
| 536 | 8 | 702 | Open | 06-08-2015 12:03:52 | 38,73316 | 9,16900 |

There is no direct link between the MAC address and the user, that identifies, but it is possible to extract information regarding the individual's habits and potential social connections. Crossing this information obtained temporally with other information (basically from logins through mobile devices in social network), it is possible to identify the user through his terminal's MAC. To avoid this we perform a hash function on each MAC before we store the information, see Table 2.

**Table 2.**  Colected user MAC address transformed by a Hash function for privacy issues

| Timestamp | Hash_mac |
|---|---|
| 07-09-2015 19:01:40 | e29eb50b762d4b7bcdf2cd1c4635f641 |
| 07-09-2015 19:01:41 | b7bcb467ef889408315b9c7cd4183a5c |

## 2.3    Data Processing at Cloud Server

AP data from client probe request and XtraN data are sent to a SQL database in a cloud environment. All that data will be processed and related to produce a single table with summarized data. This process of data correlation consists on the following steps:

XTraN data from GPS and Door sensors are correlated in the time domain so that a GPS position can be added for each door open/close event.

With the identified position, more information is added relating it with the static XTraN data about the BUS routes and its stops, so we can identify the name and number of that bus-stop (Fig. 3).

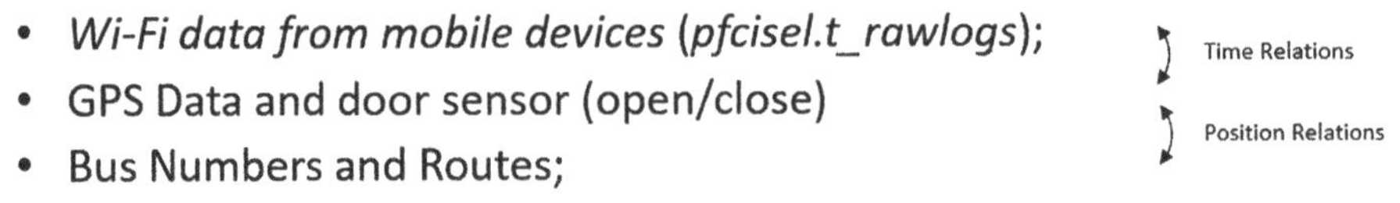

- *Wi-Fi data from mobile devices (pfcisel.t_rawlogs);*    ⟩ Time Relations
- GPS Data and door sensor (open/close)    ⟩ Position Relations
- Bus Numbers and Routes;

**Fig. 3.**  Data correlation based on time and position

The WiFi data was previously filtered and has now one event per probe request and per terminal, consisting basically from a hash code and a timestamp. This data will be sampled in a timely manner and related with GPS and Door sensor events.

The advantage of this method is that practically we have a way of tracking individual passenger's routes and count them stop by stop. The chosen method for the counting is by sampling WiFi data segment by segment. One segment is the distance in time or space between consecutive stops. This distance gives the longest time sampling duration, which is necessary to increase terminal detection chances, because of the unpredictable probe request nature of the terminal WiFi scanning method. The drawback is when the bus reaches the bus-stop where many passengers may be waiting for the bus and can be counted as inside the bus (false positives). To solve this problem, several sampling and filtering functions were implemented as described below.

Figure 4 resumes several use cases of passengers in and out of the bus among with the two main sampling functions:

- by segment (from stop to stop, triggered by open door event), represented with blue ellipses
- by location (bus stop area, centered on its GPS position), represented with orange ellipses

Those functions were merged into one (intersection of the two) in order to avoid the bus stop region. Two new variants functions were implemented in order to compare the results, namely:

- Function A: sampling by segment minus a time-delta.
  - time-delta is a user definable function parameter, in seconds, which will subtract the time of door open event, avoiding the stop region in some cases. This method is easy to implement and works even if no access to GPS information.
- Function B: sampling by segment until reaching the stop zone.
  - stop zone is a user definable function parameter, radius in meters, from the stop position center. The time of a matching bus GPS position is used as the sampling end time, avoiding the stop region in all cases. This method works for all cases but needs precise GPS information.

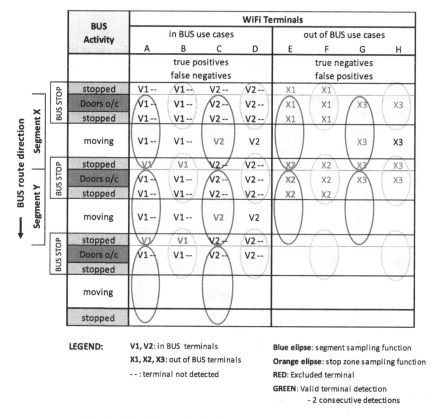

**Fig. 4.** Sampling terminals use cases (Color figure online)

The Fig. 4 represents a subset of theoretical use cases we found initially to be problematic to this project. The figure is split into three parts: bus state, WiFi terminals in and out of the bus. For the WiFi terminals, we can have true or false detections and/or true or false exclusions depending on when the terminal was detected regarding the bus state and its position. For the outside of bus terminals, we are admitting that some can be moving along with the bus – G and H use cases.

WiFi terminals are represented with "V" for the ones that in fact are in the bus and with "X" for the ones that are out of the bus. The double dash "--" means that the terminal did not sent any probe request for that sampling period. This exercise explores tow sampling methods: by segment, between each door open activity (blue ellipses) and by position, when the bus arrives and leaves the bus stop zone (orange ellipses). We are representing with color letter green/red when a probe request is counted. Considering that the main rule for a detection is having two consecutive counts, we represent a true/false detection in green and a true/false exclusion in red. The presented use cases (which do not address all possibilities) tries to explore the limits for a true and false detection/exclusion which was very useful for the design of the sampling and filtering functions.

## 3   Case Study

We performed tests during a week period in a series of buses. We chose buses with few passengers to facilitate the manual counting and the manual identification of each route path performed by each passenger. These requirements were made because we wanted to evaluate our current proposal with real metrics. We chose routes with loops and nearby stops (separated by a straight distance around 150 m), as the example of bus 400 shown in Fig. 5.

**Fig. 5.**  Bus route 400, bus stops and route path representation

In Fig. 6, we show a small extract of data collected by XtraN regarding GPS data and door sensor. Process started with data collection, cleaning and store in a SQL database. Data is available from the probe requests in AP, XtraN sensors door (open/close), timestamps and

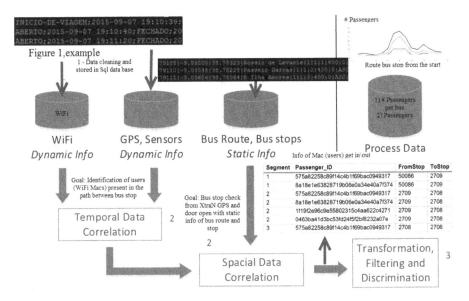

**Fig. 6.**  Data collected through XtraN regarding bus stop, GPS position, door sensor, Wifi data after cleaning is sent to data base, then correlation process (special and temporal) and last process is the transformation, filtering and discrimination towards final number of passengers in a bus or their route path.

GPS, bus route schedule and route information. Second process step is the temporal and spatial correlation, where the output are hashed mobile device MAC address with information about the stop he gets in and out. Last process is the manipulation of this data towards the information (number of passengers and route path of passengers).

### 3.1  Main Problems

Several field tests have been performed; we will highlight some of the major findings:

- Unpredictable nature of the terminal WiFi scanning for networks;
- Bus routes with route loops;
- Crowded areas near bus-stops.

There is no standard for active scanning for wireless networks. Each manufacturer implements their method of WiFi scanning which may differ among operating system software versions, device models, etc. Although we found that the majority of devices make a probe each second in average, if the terminal is in active state (with active processes which need internet access). In other modes like battery save mode or sleep mode, or if all processes and applications that needs internet communication are disabled (email, social networks, weather forecast, etc.) then it is most likely that the terminal will not scan for WiFi networks even if WiFi interface is enabled. This pointed us into the way of sampling the probe messages between stops, which gave us the maximum time for terminal detection without compromising counting precision.

Nearby stops because route loops, as the example showed in Fig. 7, where the stops identified by the numbers 7805 (8) and 2511 (10) are in a distance around 150 m.

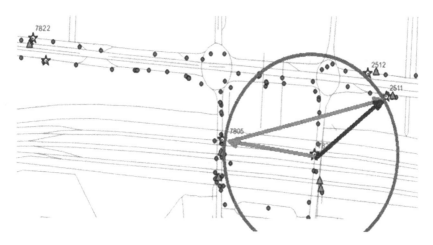

**Fig. 7.** BUS route and stops at Oriente station (GPS data) (Color figure online)

To overcome these problems we used an algorithm based on the vector distance between three consecutive stops which detects this kind of situations. If the sum vector (dark green in Fig. 7) is smaller than a pre-defined distance - we used the minimum distance between stops of 300 m – it signals the system to use an extra segment to the next stop. Based on this information, we apply the best filter: with 2 or 3 obligatory and consecutive segments, at which a passenger must be detected to be considered inside the bus.

Crowded areas near bus-stops are a big problem because they can introduce many erroneous counting for bus passengers. It was clearly a zone to avoid and so we decided to change the sampling function to anticipate the stop time. Two alternatives were implemented and can be used exclusively, for instance:

- If GPS information is present and precise, we register the time when the bus enters on the bus-stop zone, defined by a radius of 100 m. This time will be used as the sampling end period - function B referenced in 3.3;
- If no precise GPS information is available, we use a fixed time interval of 10 s, which subtracts the bus-stop open door time. This time will be used as the sampling end period - function A referenced in 3.3.

### 3.2  Main Results

Figure 8 represents passenger counting for each segment of a route path (route no. 400, ascending way). There are plotted 4 different curves, each one is the result for different combinations of segmentation and filtering functions:

- Function A: sampling by segment minus a time-delta (10 s).
- Function B: sampling by segment until reaching the stop zone (100 m radius).
- 2 segment Filter: passenger valid only if present on 2 consecutive segments.
- 3 segment Filter: passenger valid only if present on 3 consecutive segments.

Figure 8 shows clearly that trying to avoid the stop zone does not help much on crowded places, especially on a circular route path (stops 7 to 10). On the other hand, applying the correct filter on this particular case - filter with 3 segments (light blue and light green curves) - will help to discriminate the outlier terminals, filtering-out about 20 units. From the manual counting process, results from the table above shows an average precision of 61 %, although the overall precision from all tests reached up to 70 %. Precision was defined by:

$$Precision = 1 - \frac{|Real\ Counts - Inferred\ Counts|}{Real\ Counts} \tag{1}$$

Comparing the inferred counts with the real ones, we noted that there were terminals that were not detected. This is probably caused by terminals in sleep mode or with its WiFi interface disconnected. It could also be caused because in the sampling period the terminal did not sent any probe request: since there is no standard in terms of frequency of probe request messages – for each manufacturer, for each model and device version, the behavior can be different. Another reason can be the exclusion of terminals that eventually made only a few scarce probe requests, which did not comply with the required filter parameters.

Table 3 shows exactly the same information, in a tabular format, where we identify the number of passengers per segment and associated precision.

The fact of choosing a route with too few passengers (necessary for manual counting) implies that one unit error makes a big precision decrease.

Knowing the fact that not all people have smartphones, nor all smartphones have Wi-Fi interface active, the results of this simple system based purely on passive terminal Wi-Fi detection from an AP in monitor reached a precision of 70 %. This result was possible to achieve thanks to the sampling and filtering methods used. The sampling functions used maximises the detection time, so a probe request message can be detected and counted.

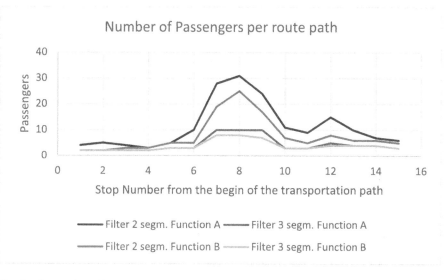

**Fig. 8.** Comparing different filters and segmentation functions for passenger counting (Color figure online)

Also the filtering algorithms used were very effective to eliminate outlier terminals that were not in the bus. This type of data collected anonymously represents huge data sets that with correct data pre-processing and cleansing it is possible to extract for free important user mobility patterns in a city. This approach on buses allows to collect public transportation mobility data, times, day and route occupancy rate, identify route with few passengers. This information is very important towards a public transportation and towards user needs. Connectivity allows new opportunities as collaboration towards traffic and bus arrival times and allows transport operators to deliver information messages on time to their target population (passengers). We think this year we will be able to run a large scale application at a public transportation operator at Lisbon.

**Table 3.** Comparing different filters and segmentation functions for passenger counting

| # Stop | BUS-STOP origin | Filter function | | | | Real count | Precision |
|---|---|---|---|---|---|---|---|
| | | 2 segm. | 3 segm. | 2 segm. | 3 segm. | | |
| | | Sampling function | | | | | |
| | | A | A | B | B | | |
| 1 | Rossio de Levante | 4 | 2 | 2 | 2 | 4 | 50 % |
| 2 | Passeio Garcas | 5 | 2 | 2 | 2 | 4 | 50 % |
| 3 | R. Ilha Amores | 4 | 2 | 3 | 2 | 4 | 50 % |
| 4 | Cais Olival | 3 | 2 | 3 | 2 | 4 | 50 % |
| 5 | Cais Olival | 5 | 3 | 5 | 3 | 6 | 50 % |
| 6 | Av. Boa Esperanca | 10 | 3 | 5 | 3 | 8 | 38 % |
| 7 | Av. D. Joao II | 28 | 10 | 19 | 8 | 8 | 100 % |
| 8 | Oriente Station | 31 | 10 | 25 | 8 | 4 | 0 % |
| 9 | Oriente Station | 24 | 10 | 17 | 7 | 4 | 25 % |
| 10 | R. Caribe | 11 | 3 | 7 | 3 | 3 | 100 % |
| 11 | Av Mediterraneo | 9 | 3 | 5 | 3 | 3 | 100 % |
| 12 | Oceanario | 15 | 5 | 8 | 4 | 3 | 67 % |
| 13 | Av Fernando Pessoa | 10 | 4 | 6 | 4 | 3 | 67 % |
| 14 | H. Descobertas | 7 | 4 | 6 | 4 | 3 | 67 % |
| 15 | Parque Nacoes Sul | 6 | 3 | 5 | 3 | 3 | 100 % |
| | | **172** | **66** | **118** | **58** | **64** | **61 %** |

# 4    Conclusions

We described a passive tracking system to acquire users' habits in public transportation. This approach applied to public transportation is new with several problems associated, like the need for a significant number of users with Wi-Fi interface on, problems with bus stops in route loops, and the problematic timing or scarcity of the probe request messages. An approach to solve the false positive counting was introduced with adaptive filtering techniques based on the detection of route loops. Also for maximizing the passenger detection chances, the WiFi probe sampling was made between stops - segment by segment. Our findings revealed that the proposed system has some drawbacks due to the passive nature of probing adopted, which are very dependant to the terminal WiFi probe frequency: short trips are difficult to detect and the system may incur on low precision for the exact origin and destination stop. The main advantage of the proposed solution is a very scalable and low cost implementation that gives medium-high precision of passenger habits to the bus route planners. Alternative methods will be introduced to complement this approach, like the Bluetooth low emissions beacons and the count based on camera image process. This last method is already in place in some buses and was already been tested. This solution has a high precision and is very expensive, but can be used to complement the proposed solution. This information and the estimation of passengers in a public transportation are important information for a better planning towards users' effective needs. Wi-Fi can be also used to send information to passengers and all this collected data, if processed correctly, creates useful information about users' mobility patterns. We are aware that this passive approach cannot give the exact number of passengers but the information extracted is very useful.

# References

1. Ogawa, K., Verbree, E., Zlatanova, S., Kohtake, N., Okhami, Y.: Towards seamless indoor-outdoor applications: developing stakeholder-oriented location based services. Geo-spatial Inf. Sci. **14**(2), 109–118 (2011)
2. Chon, J., Cha, H.: LifeMap: a smartphone-based context provider for location-based services. IEEE Pervasive Comput. **10**(2), 58–67 (2011). doi:10.1109/MPRV.2011.13
3. Number of mobile phone users worldwide. http://www.statista.com/statistics/274774/forecast-of-mobile-phone-users-worldwide/. Accessed May 2015
4. Hou, Y.-L., Pang, G.K.: People counting and human detection in a challenging situation. IEEE Trans. Syst. Man Cybern. Part A Syst. Hum. **41**(1), 24–33 (2011). doi:10.1109/TSMCA.2010.2064299
5. Bonné, B., Barzan, A., Quax, P., Lamotte, W.: WiFiPi: involuntary tracking of visitors at mass events. In: IEEE 14th International Symposium and Workshops on a World of Wireless, Mobile and Multimedia Networks (WoWMoM), pp. 1–6 (2013)
6. Tecmic website. www.tecmic.pt. Accessed May 2015
7. Ferreira, J., Almeida, J., Silva, A.: The impact of driving styles on fuel consumption: a data warehouse and data mining based discovery process. IEEE Trans. Intell. Transp. Syst. Mag. Intell. Transp. Syst. **16**(5), 2653–2662 (2015). doi:10.1109/TITS.2015.2414663
8. Van der Spek, S., Van Schaick, J., De Bois, P., De Haan, R.: Sensing human activity: GPS tracking. Sensors **9**(4), 3033–3055 (2009)
9. Musa, A.B.M., Eriksson, J.: Tracking unmodified smartphones using WiFi monitors. In: SenSys 2012, Toronto (2012)
10. McArdle, G., Demšar, U., van der Spek, S., McLoone, S.: Classifying pedestrian movement behavior from GPS trajectories using visualization and clustering. Ann. GIS **20**(2), 85–98 (2014)
11. Kostakos, V.: Wireless detection of passenger trips on public transport buses. LabUSE, University of Madeira, Carnegie Mellon University (2008)

# Energy Planning Decision-Making Under Uncertainty Based on the Evidential Reasoning Approach

Hamza Sellak[1(✉)], Brahim Ouhbi[1], and Bouchra Frikh[2]

[1] LM2I Laboratory, ENSAM, Moulay Ismaïl University, Meknes, Morocco
hamza.sellak@yahoo.com, ouhbib@yahoo.co.uk
[2] LTTI Laboratory, ESTF, Sidi Mohamed Ben Abdellah University,
Fez, Morocco
bfrikh@yahoo.com

**Abstract.** In the last two decades, energy planning decision-making (EPDM), especially the evaluation and prioritization of renewable energy sources (RES), has attracted significant attention. The decision-making process is aligned with several sources that can be uncertain, including incomplete information, limited domain knowledge from decision-makers, and failures to provide accurate judgments from experts. In this study, the Evidential Reasoning (ER) approach is developed to manage the expanding complexities and uncertainties in assessment problems. The ER approach is employed as a multiple criteria framework to assess the appropriateness regarding the use of different renewable energy technologies. A case study is provided to illustrate the implementation process. Results show that using the ER approach when assessing the sustainability of different RES under uncertainty allows providing robust decisions, which brings out a more accurate, effective, and better-informed EPDM tool to conduct the evaluation process.

**Keywords:** Renewable energy sources · Assessment problems · Uncertainty · Evidential reasoning approach · Multiple criteria decision-making

## 1 Introduction

The efficient, clean, and renewable energy was distinguished as the key success to strongly activate the sustainability vision for future life. The last two decades have seen an important increased use of renewable energy sources (RES). Recently, resources such as solar energy, wind power, hydropower, geothermal power, and biomass started to effectively replace the conventional sources and to provide better resources use, better cost-effectiveness, better efficiency, and better environment [2]. Despite the obvious advantages of RES, they present considerable drawbacks, such as the discontinuity of generation, as most RES depend on the climate. This is one of many reasons why their exploitation requires complex design, planning, and control optimization methods [3].

Energy planning, exploitation, and management have attracted the attention of decision makers for a long time. Typically, energy planning endeavor involves decision makers investigating the exploitation of RES in a particular area to meet energy demand

© Springer International Publishing Switzerland 2016
J. Bajo et al. (Eds.): PAAMS 2016 Workshops, CCIS 616, pp. 236–249, 2016.
DOI: 10.1007/978-3-319-39387-2_20

in an optimal manner. A great deal of research has already devoted to designing techniques that aid in handling this set of energy planning decision-making (EPDM) problems. Particularly, to support the sustainability vision of energy, scholars have proposed several decision-making tools. The latest advancements taking place in information and communication technologies, decision support systems (DSSs) using multiple criteria decision-making (MCDM) methods occupied the big part of the literature. According to earlier literature reviews [4–7], MCDM methods have been applied to deal with the complexity of renewable energy planning and policy, RES evaluation and prioritization, projects selection, and environmental considerations. Decision-making for sustainable energy planning and development requires methods that allow to handle complexities of specific management situations, and to address uncertainties of long-term consequences. EPDM involves many sources of uncertainty due to internal and external factors. Long time frame planning, financial issues, as well as unknown future conditions need to be considered [1]. In addition, EPDM problems especially decision makers judgments are usually vague and prone to a high degree of uncertainty. In general, it is difficult for decision makers to provide exact values in the evaluation data depending on different criteria. Moreover, ambiguity, experts' knowledge, and decision makers' preferences might be inadequate for a particular decision problem, which often lead to biased and uncertain decisions with respect to the evaluated alternatives and criteria [1, 2, 9]. Fuzzy techniques have been used recently for predicting the importance of energy sources/systems under uncertainty [10]. During the past two decades, fuzzy approaches such as fuzzy AHP, fuzzy ANP, and fuzzy VIKOR, and fuzzy TOPSIS have been strongly used to deal with uncertainty in decision-making problems, especially to examine the RES assessment problem [11–13].

Although much work has been done for RES assessment problem, the following four practical issues were not fully addressed in literature and deserve more considerations. (1) Incomplete and imprecise information exist in evaluation data. Reasons are mainly: (i) the inability of decision makers to provide judgments with confidence due to the lack of required knowledge, and (ii) the complexity of providing the exact statistics of optimal RES. (2) Evaluation data could be in various forms, including quantitative information (e.g., statistics, interval ranges, and probability distributions), and human qualitative judgments (e.g., linguistic variables or grades). A complete assessment might include all these forms of information. As a result, a comprehensive method is needed to deal with these various forms in a unified format [14]. (3) To explore the relationship between evaluation criteria and alternatives in EPDM problems, most existing works are classical DSSs usually employed to only provide a final decision. Specifically, none of the proposed models takes into consideration concrete knowledge about the relationship between decision-makers preferences, the certainty of experts' assignments, the selection of criteria factors, and final decisions. (4) Fuzzy based MCDM (FMCDM) approaches are now being used in a wide range of applications in the renewable energy sector (e.g., energy systems, smart grid and micro-grid management applications, demand side management, etc.). However, these solutions are classified as "complex" [10]. They require specialists to run the process and to interpret the results. Besides, the application of FMCDM in EPDM problems is questionable. The fact that dealing with a sensitive strategic sector such as energy planning that requires allocating huge funds, time, and resources with the decision-making tools based on only linguistic terms is an unsafe call.

Furthermore, outcomes based on these decision models might be undesirable. They should be referred as decision aid tools rather than decision-making tools.

Accordingly, for improved energy planning outcomes and optimal utilization of RES under uncertain environment, and in view of all shortcomings discussed above, this study proposes the application of a recently developed decision-making approach. We propose to use the Evidential Reasoning (ER) approach [18] to assess potential RES in a given area including explicitly dealing with incomplete information and under ignorance, fuzziness, and vagueness. This paper is a step towards initiating a new generation of intelligent, robust, and effective decision-making tools to deal with the complexity of EPDM and to fully exploiting potentials from RES [19].

The rest of the paper is organized as follows. Section 2 gives the basic description and identification of the RES assessment problem. Then, the ER approach will be fully investigated in Sect. 3, including the identification of assessment attributes, the determination of their weights, the ER distributed modeling framework, the description of the recursive ER algorithm, and the utility based ER ranking method. Section 4 presents the examination of a real case study with real data using the proposed approach. The paper is concluded in Sect. 5 with both discussions about features of the ER approach and future works.

## 2   Problem Identification

In light of strong incentives for investment, technical potentials, and environmental restrictions, the evaluation and selection of RES are multiple criteria analysis (MCA) problems. One of the most challenging tasks in this area of research is how to rationally handle various types of uncertainties, incomplete information in evaluation data, and the subjectiveness in-group judgments [20].

To manage the expanding complexity and uncertainties in assessment problems, the ER approach for multiple attribute decision analysis (MADA) is developed based on evidence theory [21] and belief decision matrix [14]. Compared with other MCDM methods, the ER approach is able to deal with the uncertainty and diversity originally due to the deployment of the belief decision matrix to model the multiple criteria problems. In a belief decision matrix, the performance of an alternative on a given criterion is represented by a distribution instead of a single value as in a conventional decision matrix [20]. For example, several experts were asked to assess different sources of energy with respect to the relevant criteria in Turkey. Based on the evaluation of the participants, the performance of "oil" option on the criterion "National economic benefits" can be modeled by the following distribution [9]:

$$\{(verylow, 22\%), (low, 44\%), (medium, 33\%), (high, 0\%), (veryhigh, 0\%)\} \quad (1)$$

Using a conventional decision matrix to model this assessment problem means that the above distribution is most likely to be estimated by a single value such as "low", which means that performance distributions of "oil" alternative on all other criteria may also need to be estimated to single values. Such approximations introduce information loss or distortion. Moreover, the accumulated imprecisions may impact the whole assessment analysis process to become unreliable. As a consequence, decision makers may lose confidence in and become less committed to the decisions made on the basis of such approximated or distorted evaluation values. Instead of a conventional decision matrix, the belief decision matrix can deal with the above shortcomings, for modeling MCA problems. The subsequent research on the ER approach demonstrates that the use of the belief decision matrix also provides several additional advantages [14, 17, 18, 20, 22–24]. For instance, the belief decision matrix provides a novel structure to model MCA problems, by assessing each alternative based on a two-dimensional variable (i.e., as explained above, assessment grades and their associated degrees of belief) while dealing with both quantitative and qualitative criteria with uncertainties, fuzziness, and even incomplete evaluation values.

The ER approach, as outlined in the following section, is designed to fully use information in data from different sources with different type of uncertainties to generate rational, reliable, and informative decisions. The ER approach is discussed in details in [18].

# 3    The Evidential Reasoning Approach for RES Assessment

The ER approach was proposed and developed to model various uncertainties on the basis of decision theory and the Dempster–Shafer (D–S) theory of evidence [15–18]. ER approach allows mapping different formats of attributes using a unified distributed modeling framework. The distributed assessment concept enables various types of information to be incorporated into a decision-making process without pre-aggregation, in contrary to the single assessment value approaches [27]. As a consequence, a belief decision matrix concept was conceived. Each attribute is characterized by a set of collectively exhaustive assessment grades and probabilistic uncertainty. Then, the D–S combination rule of evidence is modified and used to aggregate the assessment attributes. The ER approach has been widely used in various areas such as motorcycle evaluation [18], bridge condition assessment [23], nuclear waste repository assessment [20], environmental impact assessment [22], weapon system capability assessment [14], and recently in a combined medical quality assessment [24]. Due to the distributed modeling capability and belief structure, we chose the ER to model the RES assessment problem. This consists of five main parts: (1) the selection of assessment attributes (2) the determination of weights and assessment grades for each attribute (3) the identification of the distributed modeling framework (4) the application of the recursive ER analytical algorithm for aggregating multiple assessment attributes and finally, (5) the prioritization of RES in terms of their overall assessment performances using the concept of expected and interval utility based ranking method. The following sections discuss the previous five main components of the ER approach.

## 3.1    Identification of RES Assessment Attributes

A set of criteria or generally referred as attributes need to be first investigated and carefully identified. These attributes enable a comparison of the alternatives from different perspectives. Several examples from studies in the literature have already tried to capitalize all existing attributes used to compare different RES (e.g. [5]). However, only a few works proposed to deal with both quantitative and qualitative criteria under uncertainty [8]. For comparison reasons and as a basis for formulating the attributes and evaluation data, we chose [8]. Eleven renewable energy technologies have been identified from the Scottish Government's 2020 route map for renewable energy [26] including onshore wind, offshore wind, hydropower, wave power, tidal power, geothermal power, photovoltaic, solar thermal, dedicated biomass, energy-from-waste, heat pumps. The evaluation data used in this study represents the maturity scores assigned to each technology and these have been determined based on literature information and through dialogue with relevant stakeholders as explained in [8]. Nine attributes are selected comprising three different levels of assessment: technical, environmental and socio-economic. The selected attributes are summarized in Table 1. The values and associated ranges for each selected attribute assigned to the different renewable technologies are given in detail in [8].

**Table 1.** Overview of the selected attributes [8].

| Attribute | Level | Unit | Optimize* |
|---|---|---|---|
| Potential total power generation | Technical | TW h/yr | Maximize |
| Technology maturity | Technical | Qualitative (1-5) | Maximize |
| Reliability of energy supply | Technical | Qualitative (1-5) | Maximize |
| Greenhouse gas emissions | Environmental | g $CO_2$ eq/kW h | Minimize |
| Impacts on amenity | Environmental | Qualitative (1-5) | Maximize |
| Area requirements | Environmental | $m^2$/kW | Minimize |
| Leveled energy cost | Socio-economic | £/MW | Minimize |
| Contribution to economy | Socio-economic | Qualitative (1-5) | Maximize |
| Social acceptability | Socio-economic | Qualitative (1-5) | Maximize |

* Optimize refers to whether a high or a low value for a given attribute is preferred.

## 3.2 Determination of Weights and Assessment Grades

The identified attributes usually have different importance and play different roles in the assessment process of RES. Some of them are crucial, some of them are very important, some of them are important but not very important or crucial compared with the others. In this study, we assume that all attributes are equally important and they have therefore been assigned uniform weights [8]. We should notice that the focus here is specifically on the uncertainty in attributes performance values not on the applied weights, as in [8]. On the other side, assessment standards or generally known as evaluation grades need to be defined. There were several evaluation grades examples proposed and defined depending on the domain problem. Some studies have used 0 or 1 (i.e., yes or no) as a rating concept, some used good and worst to describe the performances, whilst others used three assessment grades: good, fair, and poor. What kind of standards should be used depends on the requirement from the problem at hand. The most used and preferred evaluation grades in the literature are: worst (W), poor (P), average (A), good (G), and excellent (E) (see e.g. [24]). So, for simplicity reasons, we propose to use the same set of evaluation grades in this study.

## 3.3   The ER Approach

After identifying assessment attributes, weights, and grades, we are qualified now to employ the ER approach to aggregate evaluation data. Firstly, suppose we have $N$ alternatives $A$ $(A_1, A_2, \ldots, A_N)$ that need to be appraised or ranked based on $L$ attributes or criteria $C$ $(C_1, C_2, \ldots, C_L)$, the $l$th attribute $C_l$ $(l = 1, 2, \ldots, L)$ can be either quantitative or qualitative, and each attribute $C_l$ can be assessed through a set of $M$ assessment grades $G$ $(G_1, G_2, \ldots, G_M)$ which are assumed to be collectively exhaustive and mutually exclusive. As mentioned in Sect. 3.2, the attributes may be of different importance, and attribute weight $\omega_l$ $(l = 1, 2, \ldots, L)$ can be used to denote such unequal importance if it exists. In addition, these weights should meet the condition of $\omega_l \geq O$ and $\sum_{l=1}^{L} \omega_l = 1$. $\beta_{ml}$ $(m = 1, 2, \ldots, M; l = 1, 2, \ldots, L)$ denotes the degree of belief in the $m$th assessment grade $G_m$ on assessment of the $l$th attribute $C_l$, it can either be subjective if it quantifies a "personal belief" or objective if it is a computed probability on the basis of recorded data [24]. Next, a belief decision matrix can be used to represent the performance assessment of the given problem modeled by the ER approach as shown in Table 2 [18]. Based on the belief decision matrix, the ER algorithm can be used to aggregate the distributed assessments of all attributes and generate an overall assessment of each alternative. The recursive ER algorithm as follows [16, 18]. First, transform the degrees of belief $\beta_{ml}$ $(m = 1, 2, \ldots, M; l = 1, 2, \ldots, L)$ into basic probability mass by combining the relative weights and the degrees of belief using the following equations:

$$m_{m,l} = \omega_l \beta_{ml} \tag{2}$$

$$m_{G,l} = 1 - \sum_{m=1}^{M} m_{m,l} = 1 - \omega_l \sum_{m=1}^{M} \beta_{ml} \tag{3}$$

$$\bar{m}_{G,l} = 1 - \omega_l \tag{4}$$

$$\tilde{m}_{G,l} = \omega_l \left(1 - \sum_{m=1}^{M} \beta_{ml}\right), \tag{5}$$

where $m_{G,l} = \bar{m}_{G,l} + \tilde{m}_{G,l}$ for all $l = 1, \ldots, L$ and $\sum_{l=1}^{L} \omega_l = 1$. $m_{m,l}$ represents the basic probability mass of $C_l$ being assessed to the assessment grade $G_m$. Furthermore, the probability mass assigned to the grade set $G$, which is unassigned to any individual attribute, is the sum of two parts: $\bar{m}_{G,l}$ caused by the relative importance of the $l$th attribute $C_l$ and $\tilde{m}_{G,l}$ which reflects the importance of the $l$th attribute $C_l$. Then, all the $L$ attributes are aggregated to generate the combined degree of belief in each possible grade $G_m$. Suppose $m_{m,S(l)}$ is the combined degree of belief in $G_m$ by aggregating the first $l$ attributes $(C_1, C_2, \ldots, C_l)$, and $m_{G,S(l)}$ is the remaining degree of belief unassigned to any grade. Let $m_{m,S(1)} = m_{m,1}$ and $m_{G,S(1)} = m_{G,1}$. Then, the overall combined degree of belief $\beta_m$ in $G_m$ is calculated as follows:

$$\{G_m\} : m_{m,S(l+1)} = K_{S(l+1)}[m_{m,S(l)}m_{m,l+1} + m_{m,S(l)}m_{G,l+1}$$
$$+ m_{G,S(l)}m_{m,l+1}], l = 1, 2, \ldots, L - 1 \, m_{G,S(l)} = \bar{m}_{G,S(l)} \tag{6}$$
$$+ \tilde{m}_{G,S(l)}, l = 1, 2, \ldots, L$$

$$\{G\} : \tilde{m}_{G,S(l+1)} = K_{S(l+1)}[\tilde{m}_{G,S(l)}\tilde{m}_{G,l+1} + \bar{m}_{G,S(l)}\tilde{m}_{G,l+1}$$
$$+ \tilde{m}_{G,S(l)}\bar{m}_{G,l+1}], l = 1, 2, \ldots, L-1 \tag{7}$$

$$\{G\} : \bar{m}_{G,S(l+1)} = K_{S(l+1)}[\bar{m}_{G,S(l)}\bar{m}_{G,l+1}], l = 1, 2, \ldots, L-1 \tag{8}$$

$$K_{S(l+1)} = \left[1 - \sum_{m=1}^{M}\sum_{\substack{t=1\\t\neq m}}^{M} m_{m,S(l)}m_{t,l+1}\right]^{-1}, l = 1, 2, \ldots, L-1 \tag{9}$$

$$\{G_m\} : \beta_m = \frac{m_{m,S(L)}}{1 - \bar{m}_{G,S(L)}}, m = 1, 2, \ldots, M \tag{10}$$

$$\{G\} : \beta_G = \frac{\tilde{m}_{G,S(L)}}{1 - \bar{m}_{G,S(L)}} \tag{11}$$

$\beta_G$ represents the remaining belief degrees unassigned to any $G_m$. It has been proven that $\sum_{m=1}^{M}\beta_m + \beta_G = 1$ [18]. As a result, the aggregated assessment can be denoted by $O(C_l, l = 1, 2, \ldots, L)) = \{(G_m, \beta_m), m = 1, 2, \ldots, M, l = 1, 2, \ldots, L\}$. The ER approach gives the opportunity to identify weak areas together with strengths for each alternative based on the distributed assessment of each attribute. In addition, to rank alternatives based on one or all attributes, a single score to represent the performance of each alternative is given. The distributed assessment results discussed above may not be directly used for ranking purpose. To do so, the concept of expected utility to generate a numerical value from each distributed assessment was proposed [18]. The next sub section describes the concept of the expected and utility interval.

**Table 2.** A belief decision matrix of the ER approach.

| Evaluation grades | Belief degrees | | | | |
|---|---|---|---|---|---|
| | $\omega_1(C_1)$ | $\omega_2(C_2)$ | ... | $\omega_l(C_l)$ | ... | $\omega_L(C_L)$ |
| $G_1$ | $\beta_{11}$ | $\beta_{12}$ | ... | $\beta_{1l}$ | ... | $\beta_{1L}$ |
| $G_2$ | $\beta_{21}$ | $\beta_{22}$ | ... | $\beta_{2l}$ | ... | $\beta_{2L}$ |
| ⋮ | ⋮ | ⋮ | ... | ⋮ | ... | ⋮ |
| $G_m$ | $\beta_{m1}$ | $\beta_{m2}$ | ... | $\beta_{ml}$ | ... | $\beta_{mL}$ |
| ⋮ | ⋮ | ⋮ | ... | ⋮ | ... | ⋮ |
| $G_M$ | $\beta_{M1}$ | $\beta_{M2}$ | ... | $\beta_{Ml}$ | ... | $\beta_{ML}$ |

## 3.4 Alternatives Ranking

As aforementioned in Sect. 3.3, there may be situation where distributed assessments are not sufficient to demonstrate the difference between two alternatives. The concept of expected utility is used to overcome such problematic. As defined in [18], we suppose that $u(G_m)$ is the utility of the grade $G_m$ with:

$$u(G_{m+1}) > u(G_m) \ if \ G_{m+1} \ is \ preferred \ to \ G_m \tag{12}$$

If all assessments are complete and precise, then $\beta_G = 0$ and the expected utility of the attribute $y$ can be used for ranking the alternatives, and given as follows:

$$u(y) = \sum_{m=1}^{M} \beta_m u(G_m) \tag{13}$$

An alternative $a$ is preferred to another alternative $b$ on $y$ if and only if $u(a) > u(b)$. On the other side, if any assessment for the attribute is incomplete, it will be proven that $G_H > 0$. This means that the likelihood to which $y$ may be assessed to $G_m$ is not unique and can be a value in the interval $[\beta_m, (\beta_m + \beta_G)]$. In such circumstances, [18] define three measures to characterize the assessment for $y$, namely the minimum, maximum and average expected utilities. If all assessments $O(C_l)$ are complete, then $\beta_G = 0$ and $u(y) = u_{min}(y) = u_{avg}(y) = u_{max}(y) = 0$. Interested readers may refer to [18] for more details about the concept of expected and interval utility and the ranking of alternatives.

# 4   Results

The ER approach as explained above allows solving the RES assessment problem. As already mentioned in Sect. 3.1, we chose [8] as basis for data collection and comparison.

## 4.1   Analysis

We conducted the data aggregation using the ER approach step by step as follows.

Step 1: Transform numerical values from quantitative attributes to assessment grades with a belief structure.

To transform numerical values to distribute assessments with belief degrees, [24] proposed to calculate the benchmark values of E, G, A, P, and W grades for each attribute. For this purpose, they proposed a pragmatic method for transforming numerical values to assessment grades with a belief structure. Based on the data evaluation from [8], we should compute the minimum (denoted by $a$), the 25th percentile ($b$), the 50th percentile ($c$), the 75th percentile ($d$) and the maximum ($e$) for each attribute. As Table 1 indicates, there are both attributes to maximize and others to minimize. In [24], authors proposed to work only with minimizing attributes. In our case, we will explain briefly how to transform maximizing values to assessment grades with a belief structure. To do so, bigger attributes values mean better performance. Then the set of computed $a, b, c, d$, and $e$ values for each attribute are used as benchmark values at E, G, A, P, and W grades respectively. Let $z$ be a numerical value of an attribute and $\alpha, \beta, \gamma, \delta$ and $\theta$ represent the degrees of belief in E, G, A, P and W grades respectively after transforming numerical value z to assessment grades. For instance, if z is less than the benchmark value at W grade ($z < e$), then the attribute can be definitely assessed as W grade, and $z$ can be transformed to assessment with belief degree of 1 ($\theta = 1$) associated with worst. Belief degrees assigned to other grades: E, G, A, and P are all set to be 0 ($\alpha = 0, \beta = 0, \gamma = 0, \delta = 0$). Another illustrative example is: if $z$ is equal or greater than the benchmark value for the W grade and less than the benchmark value for the P grade ($e \leq z < d$), then $z$ can be transformed to assessment with belief degrees ($\theta = (d - z)/(d - e)$) and ($\delta = 1 - \theta$) associated with the W and P grades respectively. Belief degrees assigned to the other grades: A, G, and E ($\alpha = 0, \beta = 0, \gamma = 0$). This process continues until we transform each numerical value on a belief degree structure. Finally, we should notice that all assessments in this study are complete.

Step 2: Apply the ER approach to aggregate attributes.

Before data aggregation, we assigned equal weights to all attributes as mentioned in Sect. 3.2. The Java SE environment was used to develop a computerized program to calculate and aggregate all attributes automatically. Moreover, as already mentioned, the ER has the ability to assess the performance of alternatives while taking into consideration each evaluation level separately. Figure 1 shows overall performances of the eleven alternatives while considering each level separately. After aggregating evaluation performances from all attributes in the three levels (i.e., technical, environmental, and socio-economic), we obtain distributed assessments about each renewable energy technology as shown in Table 3.

Step 3: Rank the eleven renewable technologies.

To rank different renewable technologies, it is necessary to generate numerical values that reflect the overall performances from the distributed assessments. As a consequence, the utilities of individual assessment grades need to be defined first [18]. More specifically, we assigned a performance score of 100 to excellent, 80 to good, 55 to average, 30 to poor, and 0 to worst. In this way, a distributed assessment can be transformed to a performance score (see Fig. 2). Finally, we present in Fig. 3 the final ranking of the renewable technologies on the basis of the computed scores.

## 4.2   Discussion

Figure 1 shows the distributed assessments of the eleven alternatives on each level separately. When considering each level separately this might help decision makers to obtain a clear vision of each alternative based on different perspectives. In addition, these results allow the decision-maker to directly examine with increased confidences which of the alternatives are the best or worst options given the selected level. For instance, considering the technical level, it is obvious that the hydro-power, geothermal, and solar thermal are the technologies with the most interesting technology potentials whilst the energy-from-waste (EfW), biomass, tidal, and wave are immature choices. Moreover, the environmental level confirms that all the eleven renewable technologies are green and clean energies since all results are positive, with a small

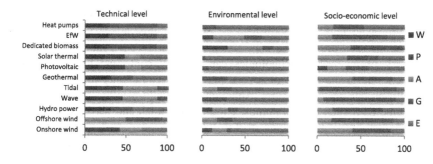

**Fig. 1.** Distributed assessments for each level separately (Color figure online).

**Table 3.** Overall performances of the eleven renewable technologies.

| Renewable technology | Distributed assessment |
|---|---|
| Onshore wind | (W, 0.00%), (P, 16.88%), (A, 28.69%), (G, 14.96%), (E, 39.46%) |
| Offshore wind | (W, 0.00%), (P, 0.00%), (A, 27.02%), (G, 46.65%), (E, 26. 31%) |
| Hydro power | (W, 7.08%), (P, 6.01%), (A, 10.78%), (G, 31.42%), (E, 44.68%) |
| Wave | (W, 4.50%), (P, 9.61%), (A, 15.54%), (G, 43.93%), (E, 26.40%) |
| Tidal | (W, 4.54%), (P, 9.68%), (A, 20.54%), (G, 40.65%), (E, 24.57%) |
| Geothermal | (W, 9.07%), (P, 0.37%), (A, 11.59%), (G, 35.12%), (E, 43.82%) |
| Photovoltaic | (W, 4.43%), (P, 13.11%), (A, 12.22%), (G, 9.83%), (E, 60.38%) |
| Solar thermal | (W, 6.98%), (P, 6.92%), (A, 16.58%), (G, 11.62%), (E, 57.86%) |
| Dedicated biomass | (W, 5.52%), (P, 12.58%), (A, 25.39%), (G, 45.88%), (E, 10.61%) |
| Energy-from-waste | (W, 8.32%), (P, 4.21%), (A, 16.30%), (G, 50.37), (E, 20.78%) |
| Heat pumps | (W, 6.46%), (P, 2.15%), (A, 5.21%), (G, 36.46%), (E, 49.70) |

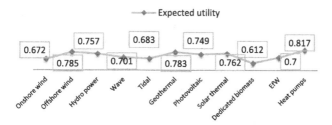

**Fig. 2.** Expected utilities of the eleven renewable technologies

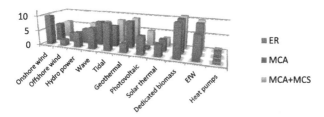

**Fig. 3.** Ranking of the eleven renewable technologies (Color figure online)

superiority for solar thermal, PV, heat pumps, and geothermal energy. The EfW and biomass are extending low performances even for this level. Furthermore, the socio-economic level presents the same conclusion as in the environmental level since the majority of renewable technologies can strongly contribute to the economic development and to the benefit of several parts, from community members, governments, until private sector investors. Although, we should mention the slight superiority of some RES such as heat pumps, photovoltaic, tidal, and wave. Moreover, the aggregated distributed assessments in Table 3 and the expected utilities in Fig. 2 confirm the analysis explained above (i.e., analysis based on each level separately). Heat pumps and offshore wind are the best options, whilst biomass and EfW are the least preferred options. However, it is still difficult to distinguish which alternative is the best or the worst without using the expected utility of each alternative as a numerical score to rank them (since all assessments are complete). Figure 3 represents the ranking provided by three different approaches: the ER approach implemented in this study, the MCA using the best estimate criteria values from [8], and MCA using 10,000 Monte Carlo simulations (MCSs) to deal with uncertainty in attributes values variations over the estimated ranges from [8] too. Attribute values were defined by probability distributions and MCS has been used to run the MCA [8]. We note that there is a strong consensus between the ranking provided by the ER approach and the one using the 10,000 MCSs. When all attributes are considered equally important heat pumps, offshore wind, PV, and solar thermal are all the best options, while biomass and EfW are the least favored options based on the selected nine attributes. Thus, there is a complete disagreement on the rank considered for geothermal in both approaches. The MCS ranked the geothermal as the 9th best option while the ER approach ranked it as the 3th best option, which seems more reasonable due to the good performances of this renewable technology as discussed above in all the three levels. In addition, this result agrees well with the findings from a recent MCA study by [25] in which it is concluded that geothermal is one of three RES that offer the most overall benefits. However, when using the MCA based MCSs as indicated in [8], within the range of possible attributes values, almost any ranking of the eleven technologies is possible, which is confirmed when all of the technologies have been found to be the most and the least favored option in some of the simulations, which is not the case when using the ER approach, only a single ranking scenario is provided. The objective when using the MCS approach is, however, to show the uncertainty in the ranking explicitly not to explicitly deal with this uncertainty. Thus, proposing to overcome this uncertainty in attribute values while producing another uncertainty issue is not reasonable. This is what explicitly explained by [8] authors: "Multi-criteria decision-making models, like the one developed here, can be used to assess, compare and rank different renewable energy technologies ... Such models can therefore be useful for informing the selection of the most suitable renewable energy technology for a given area or location ... However, the results from this study also demonstrate a clear limitation in the use of MCA for assessing and comparing the sustainability of different energy technologies and/or schemes due to the many uncertainties involved." The distributed assessment framework which is the core of the ER approach eliminates such uncertainties to arise, from the first step which is the selection of assessment attributes until the final one which is the prioritization and ranking of alternatives.

# 5   Conclusion

The ER approach using belief structure and belief decision matrix can provide an appropriate and transparent MCDM approach not only for the selection and evaluation of available resources of energy but also for renewable energy management and other EPDM activities in general. Even if it will rarely be possible to obtain exact rankings of RES due to the large uncertainties associated with the evaluation data, the ER approach in contrast to existing MCA approaches is, therefore, applied to careful drawing conclusions and to explicitly address the associated uncertainties and sensitivities. In this paper, we have developed an (ER) approach as a multiple criteria framework to assess the appropriateness regarding the use of different renewable energy technologies and to manage the expanding complexities and uncertainties in assessment problems. A case study illustrates the implementation process. Results show that using the ER approach when assessing the sustainability of different RES under uncertainty allows providing robust decisions, which brings out a more accurate, effective, and better-informed EPDM tool to conduct the evaluation process.

In our future research, an intelligent web decision-making system will be developed, to automatically assist decision makers in EPDM problems using the ER approach. This tool might also be used to extract attributes and their associated weights, acquire expert judgments, collect decision-makers views and appreciation via an interactive user-friendly platform, and to finally produce in a representative form the assessment results.

# References

1. Başar, Ö., Uğurlu, S., Kahraman, C.: Assessment of green energy alternatives using fuzzy ANP. In: Cavallaro, F. (ed.) Assessment and Simulation Tools for Sustainable Energy Systems. Green Energy and Technology Series, vol. 129, pp. 55–77. Springer, London (2013)
2. Oberti, P., Muselli, M., Haurant, P.: Photovoltaic plants selection on an insular grid using multi-criteria outranking tools: application in Corsica Island (France). In: Cavallaro, F. (ed.) Assessment and Simulation Tools for Sustainable Energy Systems. Green Energy and Technology Series, vol. 129, pp. 27–54. Springer, London (2013)
3. Banos, R., Manzano-Agugliaro, F., Montoya, F.G., Gil, C., Alcayde, A., Gómez, J.: Optimization methods applied to renewable and sustainable energy: a review. Renew. Sustain. Energy Rev. 15(4), 1753–1766 (2011). Elsevier
4. Pohekar, S.D., Ramachandran, M.: Application of multi-criteria decision making to sustainable energy planning—a review. Renew. Sustain. Energy Rev. 8(4), 365–381 (2004). Elsevier
5. Wang, J.J., Jing, Y.Y., Zhang, C.F., Zhao, J.H.: Review on multi-criteria decision analysis aid in sustainable energy decision-making. Renew. Sustain. Energy Rev. 13(9), 2263–2278 (2009). Elsevier
6. Taha, R.A., Daim, T.: Multi-criteria applications in renewable energy analysis, a literature review. In: Daim, T., Oliver, T., Kim, J. (eds.) Research and Technology Management in the Electricity Industry, pp. 17–30. Springer, London (2013)

7. Strantzali, E., Aravossis, K.: Decision making in renewable energy investments: a review. Renew. Sustain. Energy Rev. **55**, 885–898 (2016). Elsevier

8. Troldborg, M., Heslop, S., Hough, R.L.: Assessing the sustainability of renewable energy technologies using multi-criteria analysis: suitability of approach for national-scale assessments and associated uncertainties. Renew. Sustain. Energy Rev. **39**, 1173–1184 (2014). Elsevier

9. Kabak, Ö., Cinar, D., Hoge, G.Y.: A cumulative belief degree approach for prioritization of energy sources: case of Turkey. In: Cavallaro, F. (ed.) Assessment and Simulation Tools for Sustainable Energy Systems, pp. 129–151. Springer, London (2013)

10. Suganthi, L., Iniyan, S., Samuel, A.A.: Applications of fuzzy logic in renewable energy systems–a review. Renew. Sustain. Energy Rev. **48**, 585–607 (2015). Elsevier

11. Kaya, T., Kahraman, C.: Multicriteria renewable energy planning using an integrated fuzzy VIKOR & AHP methodology: the case of Istanbul. Energy **35**(6), 2517–2527 (2010). Elsevier

12. Tasri, A., Susilawati, A.: Selection among renewable energy alternatives based on a fuzzy analytic hierarchy process in Indonesia. Sustain. Energy Technol. Assessments **7**, 34–44 (2014). Elsevier

13. Shafiee, M.: A fuzzy analytic network process model to mitigate the risks associated with offshore wind farms. Expert Syst. Appl. **42**(4), 2143–2152 (2015). Elsevier

14. Jiang, J., Li, X., Zhou, Z.J., Xu, D.L., Chen, Y.W.: Weapon system capability assessment under uncertainty based on the evidential reasoning approach. Expert Syst. Appl. **38**(11), 13773–13784 (2011). Elsevier

15. Yang, J.B., Sen, P.: A general multi-level evaluation process for hybrid MADM with uncertainty. IEEE Trans. Syst. Man Cybern. **24**, 1458–1473 (1994). IEEE

16. Yang, J.B., Singh, M.G.: An evidential reasoning approach for multiple attribute decision making with uncertainty. IEEE Trans. Syst. Man Cybern. **24**, 1–18 (1994). IEEE

17. Yang, J.B., Wang, Y.M., Xu, D.L., Chin, K.S.: The evidential reasoning approach for MCDA under both probabilistic and fuzzy uncertainties. Eur. J. Oper. Res. **171**, 309–343 (2006). Elsevier

18. Yang, J.B., Xu, D.L.: On the evidential reasoning algorithm for multiple attribute decision analysis under uncertainty. IEEE Trans. Syst. Man Cybern. Part A Syst. Hum. **32**(3), 289–304 (2002). IEEE

19. Sellak, H., Ouhbi, B., Frikh, B.: Towards an intelligent decision support system for renewable energy management. In: The 15th International Conference on Intelligent systems Design and Applications. IEEE, Marrakesh (2015)

20. Xu, D.L.: Assessment of nuclear waste repository options using the ER approach. Int. J. Inf. Technol. Decis. Making **8**(03), 581–607 (2009). World scientific

21. Shafer, G.: A Mathematical Theory of Evidence, vol. 1. Princeton University Press, Princeton (1976)

22. Wang, Y.M., Yang, J.B., Xu, D.L.: Environmental impact assessment using the evidential reasoning approach. Eur. J. Oper. Res. **174**(3), 1885–1913 (2006). Elsevier

23. Wang, Y.M., Elhag, T.M.: Evidential reasoning approach for bridge condition assessment. Expert Syst. Appl. **34**(1), 689–699 (2008). Elsevier

24. Kong, G., Xu, D.L., Yang, J.B., Ma, X.: Combined medical quality assessment using the evidential reasoning approach. Expert Syst. Appl. **42**(13), 5522–5530 (2015). Elsevier

25. Stein, E.W.: A comprehensive multi-criteria model to rank electric energy production technologies. Renew. Sustain. Energy Rev. **22**, 640–654 (2013). Elsevier

26. Scottish Government: 2020 Renewable Route Map for Scotland—Update. Scottish Government, Edinburgh (2012)
27. Zhang, Z.J., Yang, J.B., Xu, D.L.: A hierarchical analysis model for multiobjective decision making. In: Analysis, Design and Evaluation of Man–Machine System 1989 (Selected Papers from the 4th IFAC/IFIP/IFORS/IEA Conference, Xian, PR China, September 1989), Pergamon, Oxford, UK, 1990, pp. 13–18 (1989)

# Orientation System Based on Speculative Computation and Trajectory Mining

João Ramos[1(✉)], Tiago Oliveira[1], Ken Satoh[2], José Neves[1], and Paulo Novais[1]

[1] Department of Informatics, Algoritmi Centre, University of Minho, Braga, Portugal
{jramos,toliveira,jneves,pjon}@di.uminho.pt
[2] National Institute of Informatics, Hitotsubashi, Chyoda-ku, Tokyo, Japan
ksatoh@nii.ac.jp

**Abstract.** Assistive technologies help users with disabilities (physical, sensory, intellectual) to perform tasks that were difficult or impossible to execute. Thus, the user autonomy is increased through this technology. Although some adaptation of the user might be needed, the effort should be minimum in order to use devices that convey assistive functionalities. In cognitive disabilities a common diminished capacity is orientation, which is crucial for the autonomy of an individual. There are several research works that tackle this problem, however they are essentially concerned with user guidance and application interface (display of information). The work presented herein aims to overcome these systems through a framework of Speculative Computation, which adds a prediction feature for the next move of the user. With an anticipation feature and a trajectory mining module the user is guided through a preferred path receiving anticipated alerts before a possible shift in the wrong direction.

## 1 Introduction

Cognitive disability is a broad concept which includes different intellectual or cognitive deficits. These deficits may be present from birth (like birth defect) or may be acquired later (like traumatic brain injury). More precisely, this term is used to define a person who has more difficulties in one or more types of mental tasks when compared to an ordinary person [17]. A disability may be present in several levels of incidence, varying from mild to extreme. An individual with severe or extreme cognitive disabilities needs constant assistance throughout his

J. Ramos—This work has been supported by COMPETE: POCI-01-0145-FEDER-007043 and FCT Fundação para a Ciência e Tecnologia within the Project Scope: UID/CEC/00319/2013. The work of João Ramos is supported by a doctoral the FCT grant SFRH/BD/89530/2012.
T. Oliveira—The work of Tiago Oliveira is also supported by the FCT grant with the reference SFRH/BD/85291/2012.

© Springer International Publishing Switzerland 2016
J. Bajo et al. (Eds.): PAAMS 2016 Workshops, CCIS 616, pp. 250–261, 2016.
DOI: 10.1007/978-3-319-39387-2_21

everyday life whereas a mild to moderate disabled person may be capable of having an independent life, only requiring some assistance in certain activities.

Assistive technology aims to increase, maintain or even improve functional capabilities of a person with disabilities [1]. A mental task commonly affected is orientation, which is imperative for an independent life. Thus, it is necessary to have technologies that assist the user during his travel between home and office/school. Using an orientation device the user is sufficiently autonomous to travel between his current location to a predefined destination. Current approaches focus essentially on the guidance activity, giving more attention to the information display and to the communication with a caregiver [5,9,11].

This work proposes an orientation system that, besides guiding the user, tries to anticipate possible mistakes. An alert is triggered when the user is expected to make a wrong turn in his path. In order to adapt the system to the user it is also included an trajectory mining feature so it is possible to calculate a path that is preferred by the user (which may not be the shortest one).

This paper is organized as follows. Section 2 briefly presents related work concerning orientation systems for people with cognitive disabilities. Section 3 provides a description of the orientation system giving emphasis to new developments on the Speculative Module and Trajectory Mining Module. The Speculative Module that hosts the framework for Speculative Computation is explained in Sect. 4. On Sect. 5 the Trajectory Module used to get a path according to the user's preferences is described . Finally, conclusions are drawn and future work considerations are made in Sect. 6.

## 2    Related Work

The works described in [5,9,11] are examples of three different orientation methods for people with cognitive disabilities. In these examples the main goal is to guide a person outdoors from the current location to a predefined destination. The difference between them resides in how this is done, but all are particularly focused on the user interface. Thus, they lack the predictive capabilities which would allow them to anticipate wrong user actions and apply necessary measures to avoid them, and the capability of adjusting the path to user preferences.

The technological development of smartphones brought more portability to the user since it became possible to execute applications in small and portable devices. These devices are specially important to people with cognitive disabilities since it is through them that the user may contact his caregiver. In order to execute an application to guide the user, the developers have to pay special attention to the interface [8].

With the goal of guiding cognitive disabled people and considering the systems interface, Carmien et al. [5] developed an application that enables the user to travel using a public transportation system reducing the effort needed to understand complex transportation maps. While the user is travelling, a personal travel assistant ensures that the user has taken the correct bus, alerting him otherwise.

Liu *et al.* [11] focused their research on the display of instructions. They used static pictures with overlaid arrows (or highlighted areas in an image), audio and/or visual messages to guide the user. Their objective was finding the best way of providing the directions to the user using either static pictures reflecting user perspectives with landmarks that are easy to find or visual/audio messages whenever an image is not available.

A different approach was used by Fraunhofer Portugal in the AlzNav orientation system [9]. This system used an arrow that resembles a compass to guide the user. Thus, the user has to interpret the information presented on the device's screen. Besides the compass, the user has also information about the street he is and the distance he should travel in the calculated direction. This systems has also a monitoring system enabling caregivers to know the current position of the user through a SMS.

The previously presented approaches tackle some important aspects of orientation systems for people with cognitive disabilities. However there are some features that should be considered in order to make the system adaptable to the user and not the other way around. Predicting user steps is a big advantage for this type of system since it is possible to identify critical points in a certain path and alert the user before he makes a mistake. If the system is able to predict when an error will occur, it can issue an alert to the user reinforcing the right path. Another important feature is the ability to adjust the path to the user since he may prefer to travel for a longer but preferred path instead of taking the shortest one. These are the kind of features proposed in this work. The goal is to develop an orientation system that adapts to the user, maximizing his autonomy and consequently his independence.

## 3   System Description

CogHelper is an ongoing project [14–16] with two main goals: provide an efficient orientation system for people with cognitive disabilities and provide a tracking system for caregivers. The former is accomplished through an augmented reality interface so users only need to align the mobile device with the correct travelling path in order to see a green arrow indicating the right direction. The latter enables caregivers to know in any time the current position of the person with disabilities.

The orientation method under development is conceived for outdoors which has been fully described in [13]. The core of the system is considered to be fully developed, *i.e.*, both applications for caregivers (mobile and web), the webservices (running on the server) needed in order to assure communications between applications, the database, and finally the mobile application for the person with cognitive disabilities. At this point this application uses augmented reality for the orientation and the selected path is the shortest one (not being adapted to the user as proposed in this paper).

The primary target of CogHelper system is people with cognitive disabilities. Thus the mobile application intended to this audience is composed by four layers (see Fig. 1), each with specific functions. The *Information Layer* stores the information for the normal execution of the application (like user data and his contacts). In the *Localization Layer* the current user position is retrieved from the GPS module of the device (or from the network) and is used by the *Navigation Algorithm*. To this information is added data gathered from the device sensors, like the camera, magnetic sensor and accelerometer (enabling the system to compute the device's direction), which are used by the decision algorithm to ensure the user is travelling in the correct path. All information is then presented to the user through the user interface (under the *System input/output*). A detailed description of previously cited modules is done in [14]. Being an ongoing project, CogHelper is being improved with new modules in order to give the system an adaptability feature. The *Trajectory mining* and *Speculative Module* components (depicted in Fig. 1) are responsible for the adaptability of the system to the user.

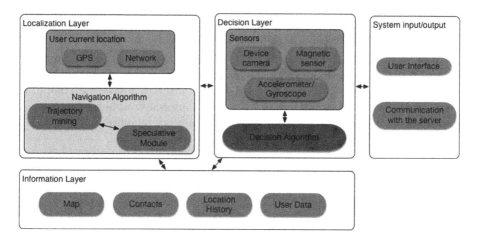

**Fig. 1.** Information layers of the CogHelper module for people with cognitive disabilities

The *Trajectory mining* component generates a path that is preferred by the user (which may not be the shortest one), *i.e.*, the path is calculated according to the preferences of the user (historic data from previous uses of the application). The *Speculative Module* ensures that the user is travelling in the correct path alerting him otherwise. These modules are described in more detail in Sects. 5 and 4, respectively.

Moreover, one cannot exclude the development of additional features, such as the ones described in [6], in order to detect other user activities, namely fall detection.

## 4    Speculative Module for Users with Cognitive Disabilities

The Speculative Module under the mobile application for people with cognitive disabilities has the objective of predicting the next step of the user (when using the orientation system) and use that prediction to set the information that should be displayed to the user (alert/warning or acknowledge messages). The execution of the Speculative Computation resembles an interface between the rules with the instructions for the correct path, the set of default values (predictions about user travels from one location to another), and real information returned by information sources (informing the real journey of the user).

Through the use of this module the system continues its execution using a default value (whenever the real information is missing) or using the real one (returned from the information sources). Thus, the system does not enter an idle state when there is missing information. It tries to generate a tentative solution for the problem, which is revised when the real information is received (to verify if the default value is consistent with the real one).

For the execution of the Speculative Computation module the computation changes between its normal execution phase (*Process Reduction Phase*) and temporarily to a revision phase (*Fact Arrival Phase*) to revise the computation according to the received values. The initial information, before execution, represented in the Speculative Computation framework includes:

1. All the possible paths between two points, in the form of connections between intermediary points, as facts in the knowledge base;
2. The transitions between points usually performed by the user as default values;
3. Information of whether a point is included or not in the recommended path as default values;
4. A set of rules that structure the derivation of the path the user is likely to follow given the information during execution and the issuing of alerts/warnings in case of a potential mistake;

At the beginning of the computation, when there is no information regarding the actual position of the user and his transitions between the most relevant points, the defaults are used in the *Process Reduction Phase* to build the most likely path, step by step, and issue the warnings for potential mistakes or acknowledgements of correctly taken steps. A warning is issued whenever a user is likely to take the wrong path, which may happen when the defaults tell the computation that the user will make a transition to a point not included in the correct path. Through *Fact Arrival*, the GPS sensor and a recognizer inform the Speculative Module of the actual transitions of the user and whether the points are indeed part of the correct path or not. If the user actually moves to a point not included in the correct path, the recognizer re-calculates the path to the destination and a point previously out of the correct path may suddenly become part of the new path. *Fact Arrival Phase* is the mechanism through which this information is updated and the tentative paths produced for a user are adjusted and improved.

Items 1, 2, and 3 from the list above are obtained from a Trajectory Mining Module. Item 1 corresponds to the calculation of the possible paths between two points, producing a reduced graph, with only the most relevant points an the connections between them. Item 2 is obtained from the pattern mining of the trajectories usually taken by the user, reflecting his walking habits. Finally, item 3 corresponds to the calculation of the recommended path between the point of origin and the destination, expressed in the form of intermediary points included in the route. It is also stated which points are not included in this route. As an example, one can consider the graph of Fig. 2, in which the objective is for the user to move from node 1 to node 3. From the Trajectory Mining Module it is possible to know that the user usually moves from 1 to 2, from 2 to 3, but also from 3 to 4, from 4 to 5, from 5 to 6, and from 6 to 3. Additionally, it is possible to determine that nodes 1, 2, and 3 are part of the shortest path, while node 4 is obviously not. However, since the user, when in node 2, usually moves to 4, this is identified during *Process Reduction* as a point where a mistake may happen and, as a result, a warning is issued. If, during *Fact Arrival*, it is confirmed the user indeed moves to 4, this node becomes now part of the route and the alternative path including 5 and 6 is selected. Although simple, this example illustrates the role of the Speculative Module in producing instructions for the user and preventing mistakes in his path.

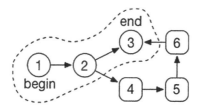

**Fig. 2.** Possible ways to travel between locations 1 and 3.

Below there is a logic program that represents the formalization of the problem depicted in Fig. 2 and the situation described above according to the Speculative Computation Framework for Users with Cognitive Disabilities. Its components include: $\Sigma$, a representation of existing system modules responsible for providing information; $\mathcal{E}$, the predicates which represent the necessary information to derive the path of the user; $\Delta$ is the default answer set and consists in a set of default values; $\mathcal{A}$, a set of abducible predicates; and $\mathcal{P}$ is a logic program with a set of clauses. In the logic program given below the literal $path(a, b)$ denotes that there is a physical connection between the locations $a$ and $b$, thus the user may travel between them. The literal $show\_next\_point$ is used to indicate that the system must show the next location to which the user should travel. This location may be an intermediate point or the final destination.

Whenever the user travels in the wrong direction the literal *show_user_warning* is activated indicating to the system that it must alert the user. In the set $\mathcal{E}$ there are the predicates *user_travel(a, b)* (which states that the user will travel from location *a* to location *b*) and *included(a)* (to indicate if a location *a* is part of the route). The values for these predicates are asked from the information sources *gps_sensor* and *recognizer*, respectively. The former verifies if the user is travelling from point A to B. The latter checks if point B is included in the set of valid locations.

- $\Sigma = \{gps\_sensor, recognizer\}$
- $\mathcal{E} = \{user\_travel, included\}$
- $\Delta = \{user\_travel(1, 2)@gps\_sensor, user\_travel(2, 3)@gps\_sensor,$
  $user\_travel(2, 4)@gps\_sensor, user\_travel(4, 5)@gps\_sensor,$
  $user\_travel(5, 6)@gps\_sensor, user\_travel(6, 3)@gps\_sensor,$
  $included(1)@recognizer, included(2)@recognizer,$
  $included(3)@recognizer, \sim included(4)@recognizer$
  $included(5)@recognizer, included(6)@recognizer,$
- $\mathcal{A} = \{show\_next\_point, show\_user\_warning\}$
- $\mathcal{P}$ is the following set of rules:
  $guide(A, A) \leftarrow .$
  $guide(A, B) \leftarrow$
  $\qquad path(A, F),$
  $\qquad show\_next\_point(F),$
  $\qquad user\_travel(A, F)@gps\_sensor,$
  $\qquad guide(F, B).$
  $guide(A, B) \leftarrow$
  $\qquad path(A, F),$
  $\qquad user\_travel(A, F)@gps\_sensor,$
  $\qquad show\_user\_warning(F),$
  $\qquad guide(F, B).$
  $path(1, 2) \leftarrow .$
  $path(2, 3) \leftarrow .$
  $path(2, 4) \leftarrow .$
  $path(4, 5) \leftarrow .$
  $path(5, 6) \leftarrow .$
  $path(6, 3) \leftarrow .$
- $\mathcal{I}$ denotes the following set of integrity constraints or invariants:
  $\perp \leftarrow$
  $\qquad show\_next\_point(F),$
  $\qquad \sim included(F)@recognizer.$
  $\perp \leftarrow$
  $\qquad show\_user\_warning(F),$
  $\qquad included(F)@recognizer.$

## 5    Trajectory Mining Module

Advances in mobile computation (*e.g.*, smartphones) and in location-acquisition methods (*e.g.*, GPS module) enabled the gathering of massive spatial trajectory data, which, in turn, has raised the interest of researchers in trajectory data mining [19]. According to [7] there are three important attributes when considering Behavioural Pattern Mining: location, trajectory and behaviour. The first attribute considers the extraction of important user locations (like home or office). The second one considers the trajectory modeling through the extraction of regular routes. The last attribute emphasizes the extraction of behavioural patterns. Thus the system may be able to predict the user's destination through his current path.

Through active recording (the user location is logged only when the application is running) it is possible to obtain the position of the user. However there are a few steps that precede the trajectory pattern mining like trajectory data preprocessing and trajectory data management [19].

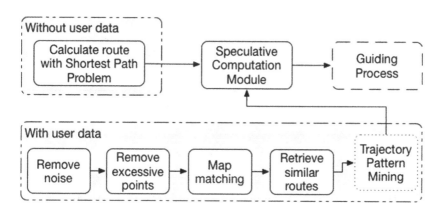

**Fig. 3.** Generation of default values schema

For the mining module operation it is important to consider the existence of user historic data. When the user is using CogHelper for the first time (thus, there isn't any information about his travelling habits) the system calculates the shortest path and uses it as input for the speculative computation module in order to guide the user. When there is available information about the user, the mining module extracts similar routes according to the current user location and the intended destination and use them for the trajectory pattern mining. Ending this process the data is sent to the speculative computation module (as default values) so the system is able to guide the user. Before applying the pattern mining the retrieved data need to be preprocessed. An illustration of this process is presented in Fig. 3.

## 5.1   Data Preprocessing

In a first step (trajectory data preprocessing) it is important to remove the noise from each collected position (Fig. 4a is an example of raw data collected during a travel). There may be points that may appear outside the travelled route (due to a bigger GPS error), which should not be considered for the trajectory data mining (Fig. 4b). Then, since collected locations represent a large number of samples, it is important to remove excessive data, *i.e.*, points that do not bring useful information like intermediate points in roads without intersections.

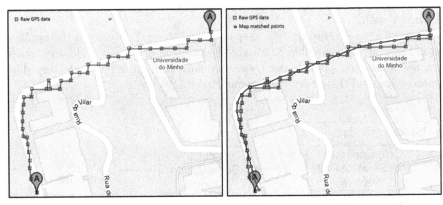

(a) Route obtained from database raw data

(b) Error removal from raw data

**Fig. 4.** Trajectory data processing

After this process, the remaining data should represent locations on a map that may appear slightly outside the road. Thus, a map matching process is necessary in order to align the collected data with the existing real maps.

Ending this preprocessing stage and before starting the trajectory data mining process, the system has to obtain similar routes (*e.g.*, travel paths with the same destination and a similar starting point). Thus, instead of using all routes for this stage, the system selects the similar routes (or similar route parts) through similarity/distance functions. When, for a user, there is no route for an intended destination the system selects the shortest path.

## 5.2 Trajectory Mining

Finally, the trajectory data mining may begin. For this process there are different types of pattern mining. The described process may be considered as a standard for the use of trajectory data mining, however there might be some derivations of it. According to its own proposes an author may adapt this standard for his algorithm or system.

In [10] the authors consider a trajectory pattern as a set of individual trajectories which share an identical sequence of visited places. For their trajectory pattern mining in an initial stage the authors try to get a set of regions of interest (which is possible by different approaches) and then the authors try to define the trajectory patterns. Giannotti *et al.* intend to apply their trajectory pattern mining in the analysis of traffic flows. An extension of this work is presented in [12] in which the authors make use of all trajectories saved on the database to construct a predictive model in order to be able to predict the user's (or object's) next move (*e.g.*, predict where the user will be when the GPS module is temporarily unavailable).

A different approach is applied in [2]. Here the aim is to automatically obtain the frequent moves, neglecting the time at which their occur. To the authors a trajectory is an ordered list of stops and moves, *i.e.*, the user moves between to places (considered as stops) in which he stays for a given time interval. For their purpose the authors intend to discover the pattern of moves between two places usually done by the users regardless the intermediate points (*e.g.*, the streets or roads used). Using this data Alvares *et al.* could obtain answers for questions like the most frequent stops during a period of time, which stops have a duration higher than a predefined threshold, among others.

Chen, in [7], propose a model in which after the geo-coordinates extraction, a tree-based hierarchy graph is built. Through this the author intends to apply hierarchy density clustering algorithms like OPTICS [18] to find patterns in the recorded data. The OPTICS algorithm [18] has been used for mining people's life pattern using GPS log data. This is an algorithm that tries to find density-based clusters in the spatial data [4]. For this process a distance metric between location points is required in order to group the data into clusters.

Considering the different models and their application our goal is to define the best strategy to apply in CogHelper. According to our research and considering the goal for each method/algorithm, we consider that OPTICS will be the most appropriated for our system.

# 6   Conclusions and Future Work

This work proposes a trajectory mining method which produces a set of default values. These values are considered the predictions for the directions that the user should follow in order to travel between his current location to the intended destination. The trajectory mining module process uses data from previous executions of the system, which are used to obtain the best travelling path (according to user preferences) and critical points, such as intersections in which the user may take the wrong turn. Through this set of default values the Speculative Computation module is used as a mechanism that determines if it is necessary to issue an alert or not. The integration of these two modules are the main contribution of this work. The speculative framework is independent of how the trajectory mining is achieved using the calculated values to ensure the correct travel. A structured reasoning method is provided through the combination of these modules. After preprocessing the data, it is possible to apply different trajectory mining techniques. Our future goal is to determine the most appropriate one for the problem.

In order to better perceive the advantages and disadvantages of CogHelper, a comparison with different systems (presented in Sect. 2) should be conducted.

However this may not be an easy task since CogHelper has an adaptability feature that is not present in other systems. These last are mainly focused on the user interface (on how the information should be available to the user) and do not adapt the travelling path to user preferences.

As future work, user privacy issues will be considered taking into account the work developed in [3].

# References

1. Alper, S., Raharinirina, S.: Assisitive technology for individuals with disabilities: a review and synthesis of the literature. J. Spec. Educ. Technol. **21**(2), 47–64 (2006)
2. Alvares, L.O., Bogorny, V., Antonio, J., Fernandes De Macedo, J.A., Moelans, B., Spaccapietra, S.: Dynamic modeling of trajectory patterns using data minig and reverse engineering. In: ER 2007, pp. 149–154 (2007)
3. Andrade, F., Neves, J., Novais, P., Machado, J., Abelha, A.: Legal security and credibility in agent based virtual enterprises. In: Camarinha-Matos, L.M., Afsarmanesh, H., Ortiz, A. (eds.) IFIP TC5 WG 5.5. IFIP, vol. 186, pp. 503–512. Springer, New York (2005)
4. Ankerst, M., Breunig, M.M., Kriegel, H.P., Sander, J.: Optics: ordering points to identify the clustering structure. ACM Sigmod Rec. **28**(2), 49–60 (1999)
5. Carmien, S., Dawe, M., Fischer, G., Gorman, A., Kintsch, A., Sullivan, J.F.: Socio-technical environments supporting people with cognitive disabilities using public transportation. ACM Trans. Comput.-Hum. Interact. **12**(2), 233–262 (2005)
6. Castillo, J.C., Carneiro, D., Serrano-Cuerda, J., Novais, P., Fernández-Caballero, A., Neves, J.: A multi-modal approach for activity classification and fall detection. Int. J. Syst. Sci. **45**(4), 810–824 (2014)
7. Chen, Z.: Mining individual behavior pattern based on significant locations and spatial trajectories. In: 2012 IEEE International Conference on Pervasive Computing and Communications Workshops, PERCOM Workshops 2012, pp. 540–541 (2012)
8. Dawe, M.: Desperately seeking simplicity: how young adults with cognitive disabilities and their families adopt assistive technologies. In: Proceedings of the SIGCHI Conference on Human Factors in Computing Systems, CHI 2006, pp. 1143–1152. ACM (2006)
9. Portugal, F.: AlzNav (2012). http://www.fraunhofer.pt/en/fraunhofer_aicos/projects/internal_research/alznav.html
10. Giannotti, F., Nanni, M., Pinelli, F., Pedreschi, D.: Trajectory pattern mining. In: Proceedings of the 13th ACM SIGKDD International Conference on Knowledge Discovery and Data Mining, KDD 2007, pp. 330–339. ACM (2007)
11. Liu, A.L., Hile, H., Borriello, G., Kautz, H., Brown, P.A., Harniss, M., Johnson, K.: Informing the design of an automated wayfinding system for individuals with cognitive impairments. In: Proceedings of Pervasive Health 2009, vol. 9, p. 8 (2009)
12. Monreale, A., Pinelli, F., Trasarti, R.: WhereNext : a location predictor on trajectory pattern mining. In: Proceedings of the 15th ACM SIGKDD International Conference on Knowledge Discovery and Data Mining - KDD 2009, pp. 637–645 (2009)
13. Ramos, J., Costa, A., Novais, P., Neves, J.: Interactive guiding and localization platform. Int. J. Artif. Intell. (IJAI) **12**(1), 63–78 (2014)

14. Ramos, J., Novais, P., Satoh, K., Oliveira, T., Neves, J.: Speculative orientation and tracking system. Int. J. Artif. Intell. (IJAI) **13**(1), 94–119 (2015)
15. Ramos, J., Oliveira, T., Novais, P., Neves, J., Satoh, K.: An alert mechanism for orientation systems based on Speculative computation. In: 2015 International Symposium on Innovations in Intelligent SysTems and Applications, Innovations in Intelligent Systems and Applications (INISTA), pp. 1–8. IEEE (2015)
16. Ramos, J., Satoh, K., Novais, P., Neves, J.: Modelling an orientation system based on speculative computation. In: Omatu, S., Bersini, H., Corchado Rodríguez, J.M., González, S.R., Pawlewski, P., Bucciarelli, E. (eds.) Distributed Computing and Artificial Intelligence 11th International Conference. AISC, vol. 290, pp. 319–326. Springer, Heidelberg (2014)
17. Spitzer, R.L., Gibbon, M., Skodol, A.E., First, M.B.: DSM-IV Casebook: A Learning Companion to the Diagnostic and Statistical Manual of Mental Disorders, 4th edn. American Psychiatric Association, Arlington (1994)
18. Ye, Y., Zheng, Y., Chen, Y., Feng, J., Xie, X.: Mining individual life pattern based on location history. In: Proceedings - IEEE International Conference on Mobile Data Management, pp. 1–10 (2009)
19. Zheng, Y.U.: Trajectory data mining : an overview. ACM Trans. Intell. Syst. Technol. **6**(3), 1–41 (2015)

# The Effect of Decision Satisfaction Prediction in Argumentation-Based Negotiation

João Carneiro[1,2(✉)], Diogo Martinho[1], Goreti Marreiros[1], and Paulo Novais[2]

[1] GECAD – Knowledge Engineering and Decision Support Group,
Institute of Engineering – Polytechnic of Porto, Porto, Portugal
{jomrc,1090557,mgt}@isep.ipp.pt
[2] ALGORITMI Centre, University of Minho, Braga, Portugal
pjon@di.uminho.pt

**Abstract.** Supporting group decision-making is a complex process, especially when decision-makers have no opportunity to gather at the same place and at the same time. Besides that, finding solutions may be difficult in case representing agents are not able to understand the process and support the decision-maker accordingly. Here we propose a model and an algorithm that will allow the agent to analyse tendencies. This way we intend that agents can achieve decisions with more quality and with higher levels of consensus. Our model allows the agent to redefine his objectives to maximize both his and group satisfaction. Our model proved that agents that use it will obtain higher average levels of consensus and satisfaction. Besides that, agents using this model will obtain those higher levels of consensus and satisfaction in most of the times compared to agents that do not use it.

**Keywords:** Group decision support systems · Argumentation · Decision satisfaction · Automatic negotiation · Multi-Agent systems

## 1 Introduction

The future and success of organizations depend greatly on the quality of every decision made. It is known that most of the decisions in organizations are made in-group [1]. To support this type of decision, the Group Decision Support Systems (GDSS) have been widely studied throughout the last decades [2, 3]. However, in the last ten/twenty years, we have seen a remarkable change in the context where the decision-making process happens, especially in large organizations [4, 5]. With the appearance of global markets, the growth of multinational enterprises and a global vision of the planet, we easily find chief executive officers and top managers (decision-makers) spread around the world, in countries with different time zones. In order to provide an answer and operate correctly in this type of scenarios the traditional GDSS have evolved to what we identify today as Ubiquitous Group Decision Support Systems (UbiGDSS). The UbiGDSS support the decision-making process by using the main characteristics of ubiquity ("anytime" and "anywhere") [6, 7].

There are some works in the literature that address the term of UbiGDSS [7]. The UbiGDSS may present different levels of complexity. They can provide information

© Springer International Publishing Switzerland 2016
J. Bajo et al. (Eds.): PAAMS 2016 Workshops, CCIS 616, pp. 262–273, 2016.
DOI: 10.1007/978-3-319-39387-2_22

about decision-maker preferences and other simple statistical information [8]. They can also follow the entire decision-making process using agents that represent decision-makers. These agents can use automatic negotiation models to solve problems, finding consensual alternatives that provide a high level of satisfaction [9, 10]. However, most of published works address the decision in a completely different perspective. In literature, we find many proposed works that deal with the topic of decision-making through the use of agents, argumentation models, heuristics, etc. [11, 12]. However, the type of the decision and how it is oriented in those works is completely different from the decision-making context where organizations make use of UbiGDSS. For instance, in most of works in the literature that use agents to perform automatic negotiation tasks, they will be either fully competitive or fully collaborative. In order to support decision-making groups that represent an entire organization while using automatic negotiation mechanisms it is necessary to pay close attention to some details. The system will be used by humans, it is necessary to involve the decision-maker in the decision-making process, it is very important that the decision-maker understands the logic behind such suggestions and it is essential to find solutions which result from the exchange of knowledge and the creation of intelligence [13, 14]. In this type of context, it is not the right approach to take advantage of the agent's lack of knowledge just to place him in a better position to accept a certain request. We are dealing with a context where there will be a combination of both competition and collaboration.

In this work, we study how the decision-making group can obtain higher levels of consensus and satisfaction by giving agents the ability to predict the final level of satisfaction, which theoretically should lead to decisions with more quality. For that, we propose a model and an algorithm that will allow agents to identify an alternative tendency and that will result in the agent redefining objectives and obtaining a higher level of satisfaction compared to the case where he does not make that redefinition.

The model is structured in two parts. In the first part, whenever the agent identifies an alternative tendency he will verify if new alternatives should be added to his objectives. In the second part, the agent will analyse and select the best alternative from his objectives to make a request at a certain time.

The hypotheses which we intend to analyse in this work are: (h1) intelligent agents are capable to understand the context and show flexibility to make better decisions, (h2) agents able to predict the final level of satisfaction make decisions easier (achieve higher level of consensus) and (h3) agents able to predict the final level of satisfaction make more satisfactory decisions (the perception of quality level of the agent is higher). To test the proposed model and algorithm we have used an argumentation model adapted to the context of this work and that has been introduced before. Several experiments were performed in two simulation environments with different levels of complexity. The goal was to compare agents with the ability to analyse tendencies with agents without the same ability. We have anticipated that agents able to analyse tendencies and redefine objectives, and therefore being more flexible, will be able to achieve decisions with more quality and with higher levels of consensus.

The rest of the paper is organized as follows: in the next section our approach is presented, where the model and the algorithm are described. In the Sect. 3 we present the evaluation done to our work and report the obtained results. Finally, some conclusions are taken in Sect. 4, along with the work to be done hereafter.

## 2  Methods

Being able to predict the final level of satisfaction may have a great impact on the final level of satisfaction of the decision-maker, the decision group and in the decision quality. We can only make such statement due to the relation existing between the satisfaction and the perception of the decision quality [15]. It is considered that the final satisfaction of a decision-maker or a group of decision-makers reflects the perception of quality and other things [6, 10]. In order to measure satisfaction some aspects can be considered such as: the results, the process, the defined behaviour or the strategy towards a certain problem, the interactions, etc. [10]. In order to predict satisfaction (in a human way) it is first necessary to have the sensitivity to do so and secondly it is necessary to have the knowledge about the context (which sometimes may not be possible).

As introduced in literature the satisfaction can be used as a metric (effective and efficient) to validate the quality of negotiation models, group decision support systems, etc. [10]. It is important to note that the satisfaction is widely used in literature as a metric for many other things, such as: life satisfaction [16], job satisfaction [17], etc.

In many existing negotiation models, agents will send requests hoping that other agents will accept them. They use arguments that can justify requests and also persuade other agents [18, 19]. Besides that, it is very common to see agents that use algorithms to identify moments when they can accept a certain request [20]. In this work, we study a new branch, which is the agent's ability to analyse tendencies, and how that will affect the final satisfaction and the ability to reach consensus. We will consider that a decision-maker, within a scale [0...1] will do the alternatives' appreciation of {[Alt1, 0.89], [Alt2, 0.54], [Alt3, 0.34], [Alt4, 0.11]}. To simplify our scenario we assume that the final satisfaction level is equivalent to the appreciation done to the chosen alternative, which we have a type of meeting that selects the winning alternative with the highest level of consensus after 10 rounds or the first alternative to reach a consensus greater than 75 % of all the participants. Let us suppose that an agent have an accepting range of 0.20, which would allow him to accept all the alternatives (according to his preferred alternative) that vary between 0.89 and 0.69. This means that in this situation the agent would never be in conditions to accept any requests. This also means that even in case that only one more acceptance is needed for Alt2 and Alt4 to reach the 75 %, the same agent would still seek Alt1 as his only objective for that meeting. This way the agent would be losing a clear opportunity to reach a final satisfaction level of 0.54, while only reaching a satisfaction level of 0.11. Besides this, even if the acceptance range would allow the agent to accept Alt2, if that alternative was never requested to him, he would never consider it as an objective. Given that agents must demonstrate a social behaviour equivalent to human beings, and that they should demonstrate and generate intelligence, this does not seem to be the best approach.

The goal of this work is to prevent these situations from happening. Therefore the main idea is to provide an agent with the ability to identify tendencies and to be able to redefine his objectives. This way we believe that it is possible to maximize the satisfaction of every agent as well as the entire group, which will result in decisions with much higher quality.

Our model is very simple and is based in the Algorithm 1 (written in pseudocode):
Algorithm 1

```
Let Ag1 be the agent.
Let AltsNP be the list of all alternatives still not pre-
ferred by the Ag1.
Let altTendency be the alternative of the tendency.
Let AltsObj be the list of all alternatives which can be
considered as an objective to Ag1.
Let altPref be the preferred alternative to Ag1.
Let newAlt be the new alternative to be added to AltsObj.
Start
  resultNewAlt = 0
  resultTendency ← Result(altTendency)
  resultPref ← Result(altPref)
  If(resultTendency > resultPref)
    For each alt ∈ AltsNP Do
      resultAlt ← Result(alt)
      If((preference(alt) > preference(altTendency)) and
(resultAlt > resultTendency) and (resultAlt > resultNe-
wAlt))
        resultNewAlt = resultAlt
        newAlt = alt
      End If
    End For
    If(resultNewAlt != 0)
      AltsObj.add(newAlt)
    End If
  End If
End
```

The model is based mainly in two parts. In the first part, a tendency is identified and the agent will verify if there are any conditions that allow him to add another alternative (different from his initial preferred alternatives) to his list of objectives. Every time an agent saves the knowledge about a new alternative preference for another agent he will use the formula (1) in order to measure the tendency result for that new alternative (in pseudocode it is equivalent to the Result() tag). In case he verifies that tendency already has a higher result compared to his preferred alternative (once again using formula (1)), he will analyze all the alternatives that are still not part of the list of his objectives and verify if there is any alternative with a preference greater than the tendency. From the list of all possible alternatives that fit this condition he will select the one which provides the highest result and add it to his list of objectives. The agent will then be able to choose that alternative for future requests.

The second part is related with how the agent chooses, from his list of objectives, which alternative should be used for a request. For that, he will use the formula that measures the 'result' and only considering alternatives from his list of objectives. It is assumed that the initial preferred alternatives by the agent are also included in his list of objectives. The formula (1) is used to measure the result for each alternative in the list of objectives.

$$A_{Result_{Alt_x}} = \frac{Alt_x * CS + \left(\frac{NS}{ND}\right) * CO}{CS + CO} \tag{1}$$

Where:

- $Alt_x$ is the assessment done to the alternative for which the result is being measured;
- $CS$ is the value of Concern for Self [1–3];
- $NS$ is the current number of agents supporting $Alt_x$;
- $ND$ is the total number of participating agents;
- $CO$ is the value of Concern for Others [1–3].

In case an agent without a defined behaviour is being considered, the formula can also be used by giving the same value to $CS$ and $CO$ variables (for example "1") for that agent. The alternative that provides the highest $A_{Result}$ will be chosen whenever the agent makes a new request. This formula will allow the agent to define his objectives according to the importance of the alternatives and how likely they are to be chosen at a certain time during the discussion.

## 3  Evaluation and Results

The considered scenario involves agents' negotiation in order to solve the problem of choosing a desktop monitor for an organization that wants to purchase 200 new desktop monitors to one of its subsidiaries. Each agent intends to represent one member of the organization administration board. Each alternative has been classified according to five criteria: Size (numerical, without value), Resolution (numerical, maximization), Hz (numerical, maximization), Ms (numerical, minimization) and Price (numerical, minimization).

In Table 1, all specifications are presented for each considered alternative.

The satisfaction and the level of consensus are used as metrics to evaluate the overall performance of the different scenarios. The satisfaction metric is used to understand the quality perception (of the decision-maker that is represented) towards the chosen alternative or the alternative supported by most agents at a certain time. For that, the notion of satisfaction that is used is the one proposed in [10]. The satisfaction is measured in two parts (for agents without a defined behaviour only the first part is considered). It is first measured objectively through the formulas (2), (3) and (4).

**Table 1.** Multi-criteria problem

| Alternatives | Size | Resolution | Hz | Ms | Price |
|---|---|---|---|---|---|
| Asus 27" ROG SWIFT PG278Q | 27 | 2560*1440 | 144 | 1 | 699,99€ |
| BenQ 27" XL2720Z | 27 | 1920*1080 | 144 | 1 | 489,00€ |
| AOC 24" E2476VWM6 | 24 | 1920*1080 | 60 | 1 | 154,90€ |
| BenQ 24" XL2430T | 24 | 1920*1080 | 144 | 1 | 399,00€ |
| LG 27" 27MP37VQ-B | 27 | 1920*1080 | 60 | 5 | 210,80€ |
| Asus LED 21.5" VS228HR | 21,5 | 1920*1080 | 60 | 5 | 129,90€ |
| Samsung LED 22" S22C570H | 22 | 1920*1080 | 60 | 5 | 179,90€ |
| BenQ 24" LED BL2420PT | 24 | 2560*1440 | 60 | 5 | 399,90€ |
| Asus LED 24" VG248QE 144 Hz 3D | 24 | 1920*1080 | 144 | 1 | 288,90€ |
| Samsung 24" Curvo LED S24E500C | 24 | 1920*1080 | 60 | 4 | 199,90€ |

$$D_{Lost} = Alt_F - Alt_P \tag{2}$$

$$A_{Conversion} = 2Alt_F - 1 \tag{3}$$

$$D_{Satisfaction} = \left(1 - |A_{Conversion}|\right) * D_{Lost} + A_{Conversion} \tag{4}$$

Where:

- $D_{Lost}$ is the loss of decision maker's satisfaction based in the difference between the assessments made for the alternative chosen by the group and for his preferred alternative. The loss is zero when the chosen alternative is the same as his preferred alternative;
- $Alt_F$ is the assessment made by the participant for the final alternative, alternative chosen by the group;
- $Alt_P$ is the assessment made by the participant for his preferred alternative;
- $A_{Conversion}$ is the conversion of the assessment made by the participant in the range $[-1..1]$.

The second part relates the $D_{Satisfaction}$ and the behaviour defined by the decision-maker. In this second part, the satisfaction is measured according to the values of the agent's defined behaviour (agent's with defined behaviour follow the work proposed in [21]) for concern for self and concern for others dimensions. So, the $D_{Satisfaction}$ is remeasured using formula (5).

$$D_{Satisfaction} = \frac{D_{Satisfaction} * CS + OAAD_{Satisfaction} * CO}{CS + CO} \tag{5}$$

Where:

- $CS$ is the value of Concern for Self $[1–3]$;
- $OAAD_{Satisfaction}$ is the average satisfaction of all the remaining agents;
- $CO$ is the value of Concern for Others $[1–3]$.

The level of consensus is measured with the value of the alternative that gathered more supporters, at the time t, during iteration i, or round r.

In order to evaluate our model, three simulation environments have been considered (12 Agents and 5 Alternatives; 12 Agents and 10 Alternatives; 40 Agents and 10 Alternatives). In each simulation environment, three experiments have been performed and the average satisfaction and consensus levels were measured. Each experiment was performed 100 times, in 900 simulations. For each simulation environment the information used in the configurations will be the same for the three experiments so that the results can be compared. However, these configurations (such as the agent's defined behaviour and its preferences) have been randomly generated. In the first experiment, agents are given the ability to forecast tendencies. In this first experiment, the agents use the first part of the model proposed in Sect. 2 (make use of Tendency Forecast but never change the requested alternatives). In the second experiment, agents use the model proposed in Sect. 2. This way, agents will have the ability to forecast tendencies and change their preference towards which alternative should be used in the request. In the third experiment, agents use the argumentation model without what is proposed in this work. This means that the agents do not have the ability to forecast tendencies.

In the first simulation environment, we ran 100 simulations for each of three experiments. The level of consensus achieved in the experiments of "Tendency Forecast + Request" and "Without Tendency Forecast" are very high (good). On the other hand, the level of consensus obtained by the experiment of "Tendency Forecast" is quite low. The average values of consensus for the experiments "Tendency Forecast", "Tendency Forecast + Request" and "Without Tendency Forecast" are respectively 0.36, 0.67 and 0.64. In our point of view, the experiment of "Tendency Forecast" has the lowest average level of consensus because even though agents are capable to identify tendencies and accept new alternatives that they consider to be advantageous, they still only send requests for alternatives initially preferred by the decision-maker. In practice, agents with just "Tendency Forecast" will not make true use of their ability to analyse tendencies. Agents have social skills and if they do not report nor show or make use of their change of opinion that will reflect negatively on the achieved results. Besides this, both agents with "Tendency Forecast" and "Tendency Forecast + Request" choose the alternative that they used in the last request (before the decision-making process ended) which will lead to agents with "Tendency Forecast" never using their social skills. This situation was always verified in the three simulations environments (see Figs. 1 and 3), and because of that the results analysed were mainly focused in the experiments "Tendency Forecast + Request" and "Without Tendency Forecast". In these 2 experiments it was achieved very close average level of consensus, in fact, in 62 % of the times the same exact level of consensus was achieved. In 25 % of the times, agents with "Tendency Forecast + Request" achieved a higher level of consensus and in the remaining 13 % of the times, agents "Without Tendency Forecast" achieved a higher level of consensus. The average satisfaction level obtained in the three experiments is very similar. Experiments with the same satisfaction level are differentiated by the level of consensus that is achieved. It is important to note that the satisfaction is measured according to the alternative that the agent considered as his final choice at a time (t) and the alternative that at the same (t) gathered the highest consensus from all the agents.

Another important point is that in practice the group satisfaction always tends to value 0. This happens mainly because only one iteration or one round is being simulated, and because of that no user reconfigurations will be made based on the information reported to the decision-maker. Therefore, this satisfaction evaluation is always related to the very first problem configuration. The average satisfaction level in the first simulation environment for "Tendency Forecast", "Tendency Forecast + Request" and "Without Tendency Forecast" are 0.09, 0.17 and 0.09 respectively. In this case, we can consider that there is a slight advantage for agents that use "Tendency Forecast + Request". One interesting fact is that agents with "Tendency Forecast + Request" and agents "Without Tendency Forecast", in 90 % of the times, have achieved a consensus towards the same alternative which can tell us that the model here presented may not be too relevant in terms of finding the "best" solution. However, agents with "Tendency Forecast + Request" obtained a higher satisfaction compared with agents "Without Tendency Forecast" in 96 % of the times. This means that agents achieved usually a consensus towards the same alternative (besides sharing the same argumentation model) due to the fact that we are considering a problem with a very low complexity level (12 agents and 5 possible alternatives).

Both Figs. 1 and 2 are related to the second simulation environment, where 12 agents aim to choose an alternative from a set of 10 possible alternatives. Compared to the previous simulation environment it is clear that the complexity of the problem is much greater.

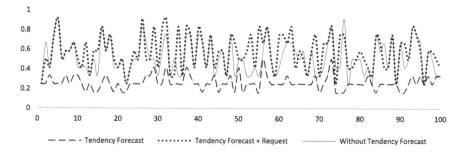

**Fig. 1.** Second simulation environment – consensus

The level of consensus achieved by the experiments of "Tendency Forecast + Request" and "Without Tendency Forecast" is still very positive. Similar to the first simulation environment the level of consensus obtained by the experiment of "Tendency Forecast" is quite low. The average values of consensus for the experiments "Tendency Forecast", "Tendency Forecast + Request" and "Without Tendency Forecast" are 0.26, 0.57, and 0.51 respectively. This means that compared to the first simulation environment there was a loss of 0.1, 0.1 and 0.13 respectively. This allows us to assume that not only do agents that use "Tendency Forecast + Request" achieve better results for satisfaction and level of consensus; they also have the ability to deal with more complex problems better than agents "Without Tendency Forecast". Anyway, now, this is something that needs more evidence in order to be proved and that is the reason why the third and last simulation environment was considered, where 40 Agents e 10 Alternatives will be used so that the problem complexity can be even greater.

In this second simulation environment, agents with "Tendency Forecast + Request" obtained the same level of consensus of agents "Without Tendency Forecast" in 53 % of the times (less 9 % compared to the first simulation environment). More importantly in this simulation environment (more complex) agents with "Tendency Forecast + Request" achieved a higher level of consensus 37 % of the times against only 10 % of the times where agents "Without Tendency Forecast" achieve a higher level of consensus.

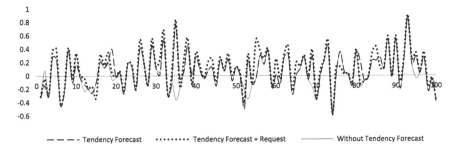

**Fig. 2.** Second simulation environment – satisfaction

Figure 2 shows the results obtained for the agents' average satisfaction level in the second simulation environment. Once again, the average satisfaction level obtained is very similar in both three experiments. The average satisfaction levels for "Tendency Forecast", "Tendency Forecast + Request" and "Without Tendency Forecast" are now 0.07, 0.12 e 0.04 respectively. There is still a slight remarkable advantage for agents that use "Tendency Forecast + Request". A very interesting fact compared with the first simulation environment is that now agents only achieved a consensus towards the same alternative 82 % of the times. Knowing that agents that use "Tendency Forecast + Request" achieved the highest average satisfaction level, this may mean that when we are consider more complex problems agents with "Tendency Forecast + Request" will achieve better decisions. It is also important to note that in 92 % agents with "Tendency Forecast + Request" achieved a higher average satisfaction level against 7 % of the times where agents "Without Tendency Forecast" achieve a better average satisfaction level and only in 1 % of the times the same average satisfaction level was achieved in both situations.

Both Figs. 3 and 4 are related to the last simulation environment, where 40 agents attempt to achieve a consensus for an alternative from a set of 10 possible alternatives, and therefore will be the most complex scenario from the three studied in this work.

The level of consensus achieved for the experiments of "Tendency Forecast + Request" and "Without Tendency Forecast" is 0.18, 0.47, and 0.40 respectively (Fig. 3). This means that compared to the first simulation environment there was a loss of 0.18, 0.20 and 0.24 respectively. This allows us to assume that agents that use "Tendency Forecast + Request" obtain better results for the level of consensus in either less or more complex problems.

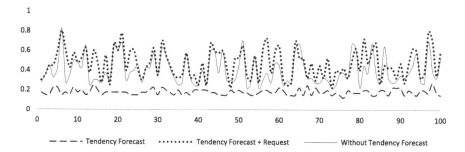

**Fig. 3.** Third simulation environment – consensus

In this last simulation environment, agents with "Tendency Forecast + Request" obtained the same consensus level as agents "Without Tendency Forecast" in only 23 % of the times (less 39 % compared to the first simulation environment). More importantly, it is in this simulation environment (the more complex) that agents with "Tendency Forecast + Request" have achieved a level of consensus greater in 65 % of the times against only 12 % of the times where agents "Without Tendency Forecast" will achieve a higher level of consensus. This shows that as the problem becomes more complex agents with "Tendency Forecast + Request" will also become better at achieving higher levels of consensus and at more times compared with other agents.

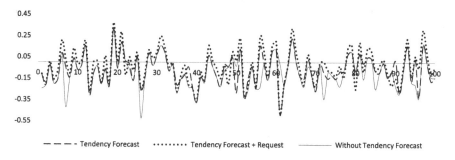

**Fig. 4.** Third simulation environment – satisfaction

Figure 4 shows the results for the average satisfaction levels obtained in the last simulation environment. Once again, the average satisfaction level obtained in three experiments is very similar. The average satisfaction levels obtained for "Tendency Forecast", "Tendency Forecast + Request" and "Without Tendency Forecast" are now −0.06, −0.02 and −0.09 respectively. This allows us to understand that agents that use "Tendency Forecast + Request" will always have the higher satisfaction levels, even if the problem is more or less complex. Once again, it was possible to identify a drop in the percentage where agents with "Tendency Forecast + Request" and agents "Without Tendency Forecast" achieve a consensus for the same decision, only happening 79 % of the times. In 93 % of the times, agents with "Tendency Forecast + Request" achieved a higher satisfaction level compared with agents "Without Tendency Forecast".

# 4 Conclusions and Future Work

In this work, we propose a tendency analysis model with the goal to make GDSS that use negotiation models more intelligent. Our model has the main goal to improve the quality of the decision that is made as well as the group capacity to achieve a consensus. For that, agents that represent decision-makers must analyse the alternatives tendency and use the proposed algorithm to identify situations where they should reformulate their objectives.

To test our model and algorithm a case of study was performed with three different simulation environments that represent three different levels of complexity. We were able to conclude that agents that use the tendency analysis model manage to achieve in average higher levels of consensus when compared to agents that under the same circumstances do not use it. Besides this, agents that use the proposed model also manage to achieve higher levels of satisfaction. We also concluded that has the context's level of complexity increases, the tendency model becomes even more important. In the most complex simulation environment that we testes, agents with the ability to analyse tendencies were able achieve a higher consensus 65 % of the times while agents that did not use this model were only able to achieve a higher consensus only 12 % of the times. When measuring the level of satisfaction in the same environment agents with the ability to analyse tendencies achieved a higher level of satisfaction in 93 % of the times. By combining both measures in the same study (satisfaction and consensus), it clearly shows the importance of providing agents with the ability to analyse tendencies in order to obtain decisions with higher quality in the context of this work.

As future work, we intend to expand our model. More precisely, we want to include in our model the analysis of credibility. Credibility (in a very simple way) can be important for situations when a decision-maker considers another to be credible it might make sense to support his opinion even if that was not part of initial preferences. This way we think to be possible (together with automatic negotiation mechanisms) to achieve solutions with more quality as well as with higher levels of consensus, with the system always informing the decision-maker properly about each step of the negotiation process and the reasons behind suggestions that are given to him.

**Acknowledgements.** This work has been supported by COMPETE Programme (operational programme for competitiveness) within project POCI-01-0145-FEDER-007043, by National Funds through the FCT– Fundação para a Ciência e a Tecnologia (Portuguese Foundation for Science and Technology) within the Projects UID/CEC/00319/2013, UID/EEA/00760/2013, and the João Carneiro PhD grant with the reference SFRH/BD/89697/2012 and by Project MANTIS - Cyber Physical System Based Proactive Collaborative Maintenance (ECSEL JU Grant nr. 662189).

# References

1. Luthans, F.: Organizational Behavior. McGraw-Hill, Boston (2005)
2. DeSanctis, G., Gallupe, B.: Group decision support systems: a new frontier. ACM SIGMIS Database **16**, 3–10 (1984)

3. Desanctis, G., Gallupe, R.B.: A foundation for the study of group decision support systems. Manage. Sci. **33**, 589–609 (1987)
4. Grudin, J.: Group dynamics and ubiquitous computing. Commun. ACM **45**, 74–78 (2002)
5. Marreiros, G., Santos, R., Ramos, C., Neves, J.: Context-aware emotion-based model for group decision making. IEEE Intell. Syst. **25**, 31–39 (2010)
6. Carneiro, J., Santos, R., Marreiros, G., Novais, P.: UbiGDSS: a theoretical model to predict decision-makers' satisfaction. Int. J. Multimed. Ubiquit. Eng. **10**, 191–200 (2015)
7. Kwon, O., Yoo, K., Suh, E.: UbiDSS: a proactive intelligent decision support system as an expert system deploying ubiquitous computing technologies. Expert Syst. Appl. **28**, 149–161 (2005)
8. Shim, J.P., Warkentin, M., Courtney, J.F., Power, D.J., Sharda, R., Carlsson, C.: Past, present, and future of decision support technology. Decis. Support Syst. **33**, 111–126 (2002)
9. Paul, S., Seetharaman, P., Ramamurthy, K.: User satisfaction with system, decision process, and outcome in GDSS based meeting: an experimental investigation. In: Proceedings of the 37th Annual Hawaii International Conference on System Sciences (HICSS 2004)-Track 1, vol. 1, pp. 10037–10032. IEEE Computer Society (2004)
10. Carneiro, J., Marreiros, G., Novais, P.: Using satisfaction analysis to predict decision quality. Int. J. Artif. Intell.™ **13**, 45–57 (2015)
11. Muller, J., Hunter, A.: An argumentation-based approach for decision making. In: 2012 IEEE 24th International Conference on Tools with Artificial Intelligence (ICTAI), pp. 564–571. IEEE (2012)
12. Marey, O., Bentahar, J., Khosrowshahi-Asl, E., Sultan, K., Dssouli, R.: Decision making under subjective uncertainty in argumentation-based agent negotiation. J. Ambient Intell. Humanized Comput. **6**, 307–323 (2015)
13. Dennis, A.R.: Information exchange and use in small group decision making. Small Group Res. **27**, 532–550 (1996)
14. Hill, G.W.: Group versus individual performance: are N + 1 heads better than one? Psychol. Bull. **91**, 517 (1982)
15. Higgins, E.T.: Making a good decision: value from fit. Am. Psychol. **55**, 1217 (2000)
16. Schimmack, U., Oishi, S., Furr, R.M., Funder, D.C.: Personality and life satisfaction: a facet-level analysis. Pers. Soc. Psychol. Bull. **30**, 1062–1075 (2004)
17. Judge, T.A., Heller, D., Mount, M.K.: Five-factor model of personality and job satisfaction: a meta-analysis. J. Appl. Psychol. **87**, 530 (2002)
18. Ramchurn, S.D., Jennings, N.R., Sierra, C.: Persuasive negotiation for autonomous agents: a rhetorical approach (2003)
19. Ito, T., Shintani, T.: Persuasion among agents: an approach to implementing a group decision support system based on multi-agent negotiation. In: International Joint Conference on Artificial Intelligence, pp. 592–599. Citeseer (1997)
20. Kraus, S., Sycara, K., Evenchik, A.: Reaching agreements through argumentation: a logical model and implementation. Artif. Intell. **104**, 1–69 (1998)
21. Martinho, D., Carneiro, J., Marreiros, G., Novais, P.: Dealing with Agents' Behaviour in the Decision-Making Process. In: SOOW (2015)

# Experiments with Multiple BDI Agents with Dynamic Learning Capabilities

Amelia Bădică[1](✉), Costin Bădică[1], Maria Ganzha[2], Mirjana Ivanović[3], and Marcin Paprzycki[2]

[1] University of Craiova, A.I.Cuza, 200530 Craiova, Romania
ameliabd@yahoo.com, cbadica@software.ucv.ro
[2] Polish Academy of Sciences, Systems Research Institute, Warszawa, Poland
{Maria.Ganzha,paprzyck}@ibspan.waw.pl
[3] Faculty of Sciences, Novi Sad, Serbia
mira@dmi.uns.ac.rs

**Abstract.** In this paper we show how multiple BDI agents, enhanced with temporal difference learning capabilities, learn their utility function, while they are concurrently exploring an uncertain environment. We focus on the programming aspects of the agents using the Jason agent-oriented programming language. We also provide experimental results showing the behavior of multiple agents acting in a Markovian grid environment. We consider agents with the perception function affected by the intermittent faults and Gaussian noise, as well as agents for which their action function is not always successful.

**Keywords:** BDI agent · Reinforcement learning · Agent-oriented programming

## 1 Introduction

Our research is focused on narrowing the gap between agent-oriented programming and learning. Agents, acting in an uncertain and dynamic environment, can use reinforcement learning (RL, hereafter) to either learn their utility function in passive learning, or an optimal policy that maximizes their utility in active learning. RL assumes that an agent is using observed rewards (also known as reinforcements) that are perceived from the environment to measure its welfare following its actions in an uncertain and dynamic environment [11].

Agent-oriented programming (AOP, hereafter) is concerned with the development of better programming models for the engineering of multi-agent systems (MAS, in what follows). Currently AOP is a hot research topic that resulted in quite a large number of proposed AOP languages [1]. The AgentSpeak(L) programming language, represented by its Jason incarnation, based on the Java platform, can be considered as the *de facto* standard of AOP [4].

Temporal Difference Learning (TDL, hereafter) is a passive RL method that can be used by an agent to learn its utility function, while it is acting according

© Springer International Publishing Switzerland 2016
J. Bajo et al. (Eds.): PAAMS 2016 Workshops, CCIS 616, pp. 274–286, 2016.
DOI: 10.1007/978-3-319-39387-2_23

to a given policy in an uncertain and dynamic environment. In [2] we reported our initial approach and results for modeling and implementation of the TDL using Jason. Here we expand the research in the following directions:

- We consider multiple agents acting concurrently and asynchronously, Each agent gets individualized percepts in the environment, while agent actions are processed concurrently by the environment.
- We consider agents with the perception function affected by intermittent faults and Gaussian noise.

## 2   Background

### 2.1   Agent-Oriented Programming

**Brief Overview of AgentSpeak(L).** The software agent paradigm was proposed about two decades ago to capture the new model of a "computer system situated in some environment that is capable of flexible autonomous action in order to meet its design objectives" [7]. Historically, agent-oriented programming, here understood as computer programming based on the agent paradigm, was firstly proposed more than 20 years ago as "a new programming paradigm, one based on cognitive and societal view of computation" [10].

AgentSpeak(L) is an abstract AOP language firstly introduced in [8]. Jason is a Java-based implementation, as well as an extension of the AgentSpeak(L) [4,6]. AgentSpeak(L) follows the paradigm of practical reasoning, i.e. reasoning directed towards actions, and it provides an implementation of the belief-desire-intention (BDI, hereafter) architecture of software agents [8]. According to this view, an agent is a software module that (i) provides a software interface with the external world, and (ii) contains three components: belief base, plan library and reasoning engine.

The agent's external world consists of the physical environment, as well as possibly other agents. Consequently, the agent interface provides three elements: sensing interface, actuation interface and communication interface. The agent uses its sensing interface to get percepts from its physical environment. The agent uses its actuation interface to perform actions on its physical environment. Finally, the agent uses its communication interface to interact by exchanging messages with other agents.

The *belief base* defines what an agent "knows" or "believes" about its environment at a certain time point. The BDI architecture does not impose a specific structuring of the belief base other than as a generic container of beliefs.

The *plan library* defines the agent's "know-how" and it is structured as a set of behavioral elements called plans. A plan follows the general pattern of event-condition-action rules and it is composed of three elements: triggering event, context and body. The *plan body* specifies a sequence of agent activities. AgentSpeak(L) provides three types of activities: actions, goals, and belief updates. Actions define primitive tasks performed by the agent either on the environment (external actions) or internally (internal actions). Goals represent complex tasks. AgentSpeak(L) distinguishes between test goals and achievement goals. Belief updates represent the assertion $+b$ or the retraction $-b$ of a belief $b$ from the belief base.

The *plan context* is represented by a conjunction of conditions that define the context, in which a plan can be applied. The *triggering event* specifies the event that can trigger the selection of the plan for execution. The plan is actually selected for execution if and only if its context logically follows from the belief base.

Each Jason agent contains a component called a "reasoning engine" that controls the agent execution by "interpreting" the Jason code. The reasoning engine performs a reasoning cycle that consists of a fixed sequence of steps. Basically, each agent performs the following sequence of steps during the reasoning cycle: the agent perceives the environment, updates its belief base, receives communication from other agents, selects an event, selects an applicable plan and adds it to its agenda, selects an item (called intention) for execution (from the agenda) and, finally, executes the next step of the partially instantiated plan that represents the top of the currently selected intention. We can think of each intention as a stack of partially instantiated plans (somehow similar to a call stack) that represents an agent execution thread. The agent agenda is organized as a list of stacks representing the agent intentions. Each stack represents one focus of attention of the agent. Using this approach an agent can execute concurrent activities to manage multiple focuses of attention [4].

The behavior of the reasoning engine is parameterized according to several selection functions that represent nondeterministic choice points of the agent interpreter: $S_M$ (message selection), $S_E$ (event selection), $S_O$ (option selection), and $S_I$ (intention selection).

**Engineering Jason Agents.** Jason programming language and system [6] is an implementation, as well as an extension of the AgentSpeak(L) that allows programmers to build experimental MAS. Jason is based on Java. The agent program is written in Jason, while the environment, including the management of the environment state, the agent percepts and the effect of agent actions must be programmed in Java. Additionally, the programmer can customize the agent class, as well as the agent architecture to alter the default behavior of selection and perception functions of the Jason interpreter. This approach has the following advantages: (i) the clean separation of the agent logic from the environment logic; (ii) the extensibility of the agent sets of percepts and actions to match a specific environment that is the most suitable for the problem in hand; (iii) the customization of the agent interpreter to match more specific application requirements.

*Agent Code.* The agents are programmed in Jason following the BDI metaphor. The basic constructs of Jason are beliefs and plans, as has been described above.

*Environment Code.* Environment implementation is realized in Java, by extending the *Environment* class. Usually the programmer has to provide an implementation for the *init* method, to initialize the environment, as well as the *executeAction* method, to update the environment state after the execution of each agent action. Percepts are represented using a *Literal* class and they are added to the environment state using method *addPercept* of class *Environment*. An agent action is a structured term represented using the *Structure* class that provides methods for checking its functor and its arguments.

*Agent Class and Architecture Code.* The agent class can be customized to overwrite the default behavior of selection functions. This can be achieved by subclassing the *Agent* class of the Jason package to overwrite the definition of the selection Java methods.

The architecture of an agent is responsible with the agent interface with the middleware layer. Basically this is concerned with the agent ↔ middleware software interfaces for perceiving and acting, as well as for sending and receiving messages. These interfaces can be customized for example to simulate faults in the effector-sensorial and / or communication subsystem of an agent. The update of the agent architecture can be achieved sub-classing the *AgArch* class to overwrite perception, action, and communication Java methods.

## 2.2 Temporal Difference Learning in Markovian Environments

In RL, the agent is using the observed rewards (known also as reinforcements) which are part of its percepts, to learn an optimal policy for acting in an uncertain and dynamic environment [11]. RL assumes that the agent environment is uncertain and dynamic, thus leading to the nondeterminism of agent actions. Therefore, the RL adopts a Markovian model of the environment.

Specifically, for a Markovian environment $E$, we denote with $p(e'|e, a)$ the probability of the environment to transit into state $e'$ given its current state is $e$ and the agent executes action $a$. Obviously, $\sum_{e' \in E} p(e'|e, a) = 1$ for all $e \in E$ and $a \in Ac$. In practice many of the values $p(e'|e, a)$ will be 0, as taking action $a$ in the current state $e$ possibly reaches only few neighboring states of $e$ from $E$.

In each state $e$ of the environment the agent receives a reward $R(e)$ represented by a positive or negative real number. Thus, an agent percept is a pair $(e, R(e))$. The agent must decide what to do for each perceived state $e$ of the environment, using its private strategy. This is called a policy and it is defined by a function $\pi : E \rightarrow Ac$, with $\pi(e)$ denoting the action recommended by policy $\pi$ to the agent in state $e$.

The agent utility depends on the sequence of rewards received on each state of the environment history. Usually the agent horizon for decision making is considered infinite, while the utility function is additive with discounted rewards: $U_h([e_0, e_1, e_2, \dots]) = \sum_{i \geq 0} \gamma^i R(e_i)$, where $\gamma \in (0, 1]$ is the discount factor.

While the environment is Markovian, many different environment histories are possible, starting from a given initial state $e_0 = e$, for the same agent policy. Therefore, it is natural to define the true utility of a state $e$ as the expected utility of all environment histories $H(e) = [e_0 = e, e_1, e_2, \dots]$ starting with $e$. Basically, each such environment history $H(e)$ can occur with a given probability that depends on the stochastic model of the environment, so the utility $U^\pi(e)$ for the given agent policy $\pi$ is the weighted average of the utilities of each possible environment history, i.e. $U^\pi(e) = \mathbb{E}[U_h(H(e))]$, where $\mathbb{E}[\cdot]$ denotes the expected utility.

It can be easily shown that $U^\pi$ satisfies a Bellman system of equations for a given policy $\pi$, i.e. $U^\pi(e) = R(e) + \gamma \sum_{e' \in E} p(e'|e, \pi(e)) U^\pi(e')$ for all $e \in E$. So, at least in principle, $U^\pi(e)$ can be determined by solving the Bellman equations. However, in a realistic agent system this is not possible, as the agent does not know the model of the environment. In an extreme scenario, the agent does not even know the set $E$ of states. In fact, the agent discovers the elements of $E$ while it explores the environment.

The agent can use a passive RL method to learn $U^\pi$. Methods of passive RL include direct utility estimation, adaptive dynamic programming and temporal difference learning – TDL [9]. In this paper we are considering TDL, due to its simplicity. Nevertheless, the approach can also be extended to other RL methods, either passive or active.

The idea of TDL is to use each observed transition $e \rightarrow e'$ to adjust the value of $U^\pi(e)$, so that it better approximates the Bellman equations. The updated value of $U^\pi(e)$ is $U^\pi(e) + \alpha(R(e) + \gamma U^\pi(e') - U^\pi(e))$. As can be noticed, TDL uses a very simple mathematical equation and it does not need to estimate the stochastic model of the environment (i.e. the probability distribution $p(e'|e, a)$).

## 3    Experiments

The starting point of our experiments was the initial implementation of the TDL, using the Jason platform that was reported in [2]. Here, we consider only the updates that were necessary to adapt the setup for running concurrently multiple agents with altered perceptual functions.

### 3.1    Experimental Setup

We consider a MAS comprising a team of BDI agents that explore the $3 \times 4$ rectangular grid firstly introduced in [9], as shown in Fig. 1, using a statically defined policy. The goal of each agent is to compute the utility value of each state. The actions available to agents are: *up, down, left* and *right*. When a trial is finalized, i.e. an agent reached a goal state, a new trial must be prepared by generating a new initial state. For this purpose we introduce a special agent action called *null*.

The effect of a normal agent action is uncertain. If the agent attempts to move in a certain direction it will succeed with probability 0.8 or it will fail by changing direction to the left or to the right of the intended direction with probabilities equal to 0.1. Grid squares are represented as pairs of integers $(row, column)$ with $row \in \{1, 2, 3\}$ and $column \in \{1, 2, 3, 4\}$. The grey square from position $(2, 2)$ defines an obstacle. Also the grid walls are considered obstacles. An attempt of the agent to move in the direction of an obstacle will fail, leaving the agent in the initial position. States $(2,4)$ and $(3,4)$ are goal states such that $(3,4)$ is a successful goal state, where the agent receives a positive reward of $+1$, while $(2,4)$ is a failure goal state, where the agent receives a negative reward of $-1$. For each of the other states the agent receives a small negative reward of $-0.04$ with the meaning of the small energy consumed to take an action. We consider the agent policy specified in Fig. 1. For example, in state $(1,1)$ the agent takes the action *up*, while in state $(3,2)$ the agent takes the action *right*.

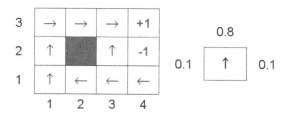

**Fig. 1.** Sample environment and agent policy.

We are using the same application model as in [2]. The model was updated to accommodate the execution of multiple concurrent and possibly different agents that are sharing the same grid environment. In what follows we are only focusing on these updates. For the other details concerning our experimental setup, the reader should consult [2]. Basically the updates were:

(i) Definition of multiple agents;
(ii) Expanding the environment implementation to support the execution of multiple concurrent agents with individualized perception;
(iii) Altering the agent perception function to simulate agents sensing faulty percepts, by updating the agent architecture.
(iv) Altering the agent action function to simulate agents performing unsuccessful actions, by updating the agent architecture.

The Jason platform provides facilities for developing software agents that act concurrently in a shared environment programmed in Java. The Java code that defines the environment, is based on introducing the class *MDPEnvN*, while the Java code that defines the agent architecture is based on introducing the class *TDLAgentArch*. Using these definitions, the script that defines a MAS composed

```
MAS team {
    infrastructure: Jade
    environment: MDPEnvN
    agents: tdlAgent agentArchClass TDLAgentArch #4;
}
```

**Fig. 2.** Script that defines a MAS composed of 4 agents of type *tdlAgent*.

of 4 agents is shown in Fig. 2. Node that, according to this definition, the agents are using the JADE [3] infrastructure for exchanging information.

We have updated the environment Java code introduced in [2] that defines the environment *MDPEnvN* class, as follows:

(i) We added two member variables that define the number of agents, as well as the root of the name of our agents. By default, an agent member of our *team* MAS has the name composed of the given name `"tdlAgent"` (see Fig. 2) and a counter (taking values from 1 to 4 for the MAS defined in Fig. 2).

(ii) We added a member variable representing the array of agent names.

(iii) We added a member variable representing the map that associates each agent to its current location on the grid. The association is using the agent name as key.

(iv) We updated the *updatePercepts* and *executeAction* methods that perform individualized perception and action, by adding a parameter to represent the agent name.

(v) We added a constructor of the *MDPEnvN* class for initializing the array of agent names and the mapping of agent names to their initial locations.

(vi) We updated the code of the *init* method to initialize the agents' percepts.

The code that describes these updates is presented in Fig. 3. Note that only a part of the Java code of the *executeAction* method is presented. We have shown the fragment that determines the current agent position and that sets the next agent position, after the execution of the agent action.

## 3.2 Experiments with Agents with Faulty Perception

We considered two kind of faults in the agents' perception function: (i) perception affected by intermittent faults (IF faulty perception) and (ii) perception affected by Gaussian noise (GN faulty perception). We ran an experiment with 4 agents such that the first agent had IF faulty perception, the second agent had a GN faulty perception, while the third and fourth agent were not faulty.

We followed the hints from [4] for the simulation of faulty perception, by overwriting the *perceive* method of the agent architecture class. In order to simplify the coding, we developed a single agent architecture class that was named *TDLAgentArch*. This class provides different implementations of the *perceive* method, depending on the agent type (here represented by the agent id). The code of the *perceive* method is shown in Fig. 4.

For the agent with IF faulty perception, we altered the reward perceived between the 2000-th and the 2010-th perception by adding a value of 100. For the agent with GN faulty perception we always added to the perceived reward a Gaussian signal with mean 0 and standard deviation 1.0 (see Fig. 4).

We have reused the experimental context from [2]. The Jason program was not altered for the experiments with faulty perception. So basically we have reused the static policy that defines agents' actions in each state and the learning factor (the same for all agents).

```
public class MDPEnvN extends Environment {
    // ...
    final int nAgents = 4;
    final String agName = new String("tdlAgent");
    String agentsNames[] = new String[nAgents];
    Map<String,AgentPosition> agentsPositions =
        Collections.synchronizedMap(new HashMap<String,AgentPosition>(1));

    public MDPEnvN() {
        // Initialize the array of agents names
        for (int i=0;i<nAgents;i++) { agentsNames[i] = agName + (i+1); }
        // Set initial position of each agent to (agentStartRow,agentStartColumn)
        for (int i=0 ; i<nAgents ; i++) {
            agentsPositions.put(agentsNames[i],
                new AgentPosition(agentStartRow,agentStartColumn));
        }
    }

    public void init(String[] args) {
        for (int i=0;i<nAgents;i++) { updatePercepts(agentsNames[i]); }
    }

    private void updatePercepts(String agent) {
        int agentRow,agentColumn;
        // Remove previous percepts of the agent
        clearPercepts(agent);
        // Determine the agent's current position
        AgentPosition ap = agentsPositions.get(agent);
        agentRow = ap.getRow();
        agentColumn = ap.getColumn();
        // Determine the literal percept and add it to the list of agent's percepts
        double r = rewards[agentRow][agentColumn];
        String agentPos = new String("pos(");
        agentPos += agentRow; agentPos += ",";
        agentPos += agentColumn; agentPos += ",";
        agentPos += r; agentPos += ",";
        agentPos += (isExitState(agentRow,agentColumn) ? "t" : "n");
        agentPos += ")";
        addPercept(agent,Literal.parseLiteral(agentPos));
    }

    public boolean executeAction(String ag, Structure action) {
        // ...
        int agentNewRow,agentNewColumn;
        int agentRow,agentColumn;
        AgentPosition ap = agentsPositions.get(ag);
        agentRow = ap.getRow(); agentColumn = ap.getColumn();
        // ...
        if (! walls[agentNewRow][agentNewColumn]) {
            agentsPositions.replace(ag,new AgentPosition(agentNewRow,agentNewColumn));
        }
        updatePercepts(ag); // update the agent's percepts for the new
                            // state of the world (after this action)
        return true;        // all actions succeed
    }
}
```

**Fig. 3.** Updates of the environment Java code.

We ran 100000 iterations for each agent. Taking into account that the environment is Markovian, this resulted in different numbers of trials for each agent: 18937 for agent 1, 18921 for agent 2, 18647 for agent 3, and 19071 for agent 4. Below, we only present selected results obtained for agent 1 (with IF faulty perception) and agent 2 (with GN faulty perception).

```
public class TDLAgentArch extends AgArch {
    final String rootAgName = new String("tdlAgent");
    final int nAgents = 4;
    int[] perceptCount = new int[nAgents];
    final double stdDev = 0.1;
    final double mean = 0.0;
    Random r = new Random();

    // Agents' names are tdlAgent1, tdlAgen2, ...
    private int getAgId() {
        String agName = getAgName();
        String id = agName.replace(rootAgName,"");
        return (new Integer(id)).intValue();
    }

    public TDLAgentArch () {
        for (int i=0; i<nAgents; i++) {
            perceptCount[i] = 0;
        }
    }

    public List<Literal> perceive() {
        // Get the default perception
        List<Literal> per = super.perceive();
        // Alter percept
        int agId = getAgId();
        double v3 = 0.0;
        if (per != null) {
            Iterator<Literal> ip = per.iterator();
            if (ip.hasNext()) {
                perceptCount[agId-1]++;
                Literal l = ip.next();
                // Third argument of the percept per(Row,Col,Reward,TorN) is the reward
                NumberTerm t3 = (NumberTerm)(l.getTerm(2));
                if ((agId == 1) && // Agent with IF faulty perception.
                    (perceptCount[agId-1] >= 2000) && (perceptCount[agId-1] <= 2010)) {
                    // Alter percepts received between 2000th and 2010th perception.
                    try { v3 = t3.solve(); }
                    catch (NoValueException e) {}
                    v3 = v3+100.0;
                }
                else if (agId == 2) { // Agent with GN faulty perception
                    double noise = r.nextGaussian()*stdDev + mean;
                    try { v3 = t3.solve(); }
                    catch (NoValueException e) {}
                    v3 = v3+noise;
                }
                t3 = new NumberTermImpl(v3);
                l.setTerm(2,t3);
            }
        }
    }
    return per;
}
```

**Fig. 4.** Java code for simulating faulty perception.

Figure 5 presents values of utilities $u(1,1)$ and $u(2,3)$ for the agent with IF faulty perception. We can observe that sometime after the 2000-th iteration the utilities are severely increased (comparing to their actual value). However this effect being intermittent, it does not last too long. So, sometime before the 3000-th iteration the values of the utilities appear to converge to their correct values. Note that at this time the effect of the intermittent faulty perception was canceled. Actually (not shown on Fig. 5) $u(1,1)$ converges to a value close to 0.7, while $u(2,3)$ converges to a value close to 0.65. Note that Fig. 5 displays the values of utilities only up to the 9000-th iteration, although we ran in our experiment 100000 iterations, in order to better capture, in the figure, the effect of the intermittent fault.

Figure 6 presents the values of utilities $u(1,1)$ and $u(2,3)$ for the agent with GN faulty perception. The effect of the Gaussian noise is pretty obvious, being more accentuated at the start of the exploration process. As agent 2 is progressing, the effect of the noise is decreasing, and we can observe a convergence of the utilities to values that we found similar to those obtained by the other agents, either faulty or non-faulty.

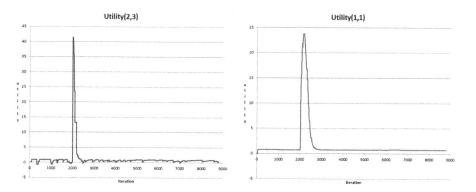

**Fig. 5.** Results for agents with IF faulty perception.

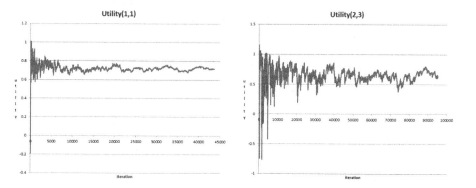

**Fig. 6.** Results for agents with GF faulty perception.

## 3.3   Experiments with Agents with Faulty Action

We also performed experiments with agents experiencing unsuccessful actions. In order to keep things simple, we have considered an agent for which the actions *left*, *right*, *up*, and *down* (but not *null* !) can fail. Failure is understood here as: (i) the action does not produce any effect in the environment; (ii) the result of the action reports failure to the agent, causing the corresponding agent plan to fail. Simulation of unsuccessful actions was achieved by overwriting method *act* of the *AgArch* class, as shown in Fig. 7.

There are already proposed solutions, in the literature, for dealing with plan failure [5]. In our experiment we adopted a simple solution, by using contingency plans.

```
public class TDLAgentArch extends AgArch { // ...
    public void act(ActionExec action, List<ActionExec> feedback) {
        int i = r.nextInt(2); // randomly set the flag to indicate faulty action
        String afunctor = action.getActionTerm().getFunctor();
        if (! afunctor.equals("null") && (i==0)) {
            action.setResult(false);
            feedback.add(action);
        }
        else { // calls the default implementation
            super.act(action,feedback);
        }
    }
}
```

**Fig. 7.** Script that defines the architecture of an agent that can perform faulty actions.

According to the model introduced in [2], TDL agents were defined as proactive agents with the goal *!keep_move* of continuously exploring the environment. Achievement of *!keep_move* assumes to update the utility function based on the current percept and to continue to explore the environment via goal *!continue_move*. Then, for the achievement of *!continue_move*, if the exploration was not terminated by reaching the upper bound of the number of iterations (i.e. when *below_limit(M)* context condition in Fig. 8 is true), there are two cases:

(i) a new trial was terminated by reaching a finals state (i.e. *non_terminal_state(St)* context condition from Fig. 8 is true); in this case the agent executes a *null* action that, according to our assumptions, cannot fail;

(ii) the last explored state is not terminal (i.e. *terminal_state(St)* context condition from Fig. 8 is true); in this case the agent selects a move according to its static policy. In this case the action can fail, producing a failure of the *!continue_move* goal.

Therefore, we have updated the Jason plan library, introduced in [2] for the implementation of TDL agents, by adding a contingency plan using the blind commitment strategy for the achievement of the *!continue_move* goal. This simply restates the *!continue_move* goal causing the failed action to be re-executed until it succeeds. The Jason code is shown in Fig. 8.

We ran an experiment by allowing all the agents (either perception faulty or perception non-faulty) to execute actions that can fail according to this model.

```
+!continue_move(M,St) : non_terminal_state(St) & below_limit(M) <-
    !do_one_move(St);
    !!keep_move.
+!continue_move(M,St) : below_limit(M) & terminal_state(St)  <-
    ?last_trial(N); N1 = N+1; -+last_trial(N1);
    ?check_trial(N1);
    null;
    -+last_action(null);
    !!keep_move.
+!continue_move(M,St) : not below_limit(M) <-
    ?last_trial(N);
    .print("END OF RUN. TRIALS: ",N," ITERATIONS: ",M);
    ?print_results.
-!continue_move(M,St) : below_limit(M) <-
    !continue_move(M,St).
```

**Fig. 8.** Plans associated to the *!continue_move* goal.

All the agents were able to finalize the experiment with success producing appropriate utility values. The only inconvenience that was added by introducing faulty actions (according to this model) was the increase of the learning time. This was caused by the necessity to re-execute failing actions until they were successful.

## 4   Conclusion

In this paper we show how multiple BDI agents enhanced with TDL capabilities learn their utility function, while they are concurrently exploring an uncertain environment. Our main results are related to the programming aspects of the agents using the Jason agent-oriented programming language and Java. We provide experimental results showing the behavior of different agents acting in a Markovian grid environment: agents with the perception function affected by intermittent faults and Gaussian noise, as well as agents for which their action function can fail. As future work we plan to expand these results in at least two directions: (i) by considering active learning strategies, for example Q-learning; (ii) by allowing teams of agents to cooperate by exchanging messages while they are exploring the environment, with the goal to either improve the learning process or to exclude faulty and/or malicious agents from the team.

## References

1. Bădică, C., Budimac, Z., Burkhard, H.-D., Ivanović, M.: Software agents: Languages, tools, platforms. Comput. Sci. Inf. Syst. **8**(2), 255–298 (2011). doi:10.2298/CSIS110214013B
2. Bădică, A., Bădică, C., Ivanović, M., Mitrović, D.: An approach of temporal difference learning using agent-oriented programming. In: Proceedings of the 20th International Conference on Control Systems and Computer Science (CSCS 2015), pp. 735–742. IEEE, (2015). 10.1109/CSCS.2015.71
3. Bellifemine, F.L., Caire, G., Greenwood, D.: Developing Multi-Agent Systems with JADE, ser. Wiley Series in Agent Technology. John Wiley & Sons Ltd (2007)

4. Bordini, R.H., Hübner, J.F., Wooldridge, M.: Programming Multi-Agent Systems in AgentSpeak using Jason, ser. Wiley Series in Agent Technology. Wiley (2007)
5. Hübner, J.F., Bordini, R.H., Wooldridge, M.J.: Programming declarative goals using plan patterns. In: Baldoni, M., Endriss, U. (eds.) DALT 2006. LNCS (LNAI), vol. 4327, pp. 123–140. Springer, Heidelberg (2006)
6. Jason: a Java-based interpreter for an extended version of AgentSpeak. http://jason.sourceforge.net//. Accessed February, 2016
7. Jennings, N.R., Wooldridge, M.: Applications of intelligent agents. In: Jennings, N.R., Wooldridge, M.J. (eds.) Agent Technology, pp. 3–28. Heidelberg (1998). http://dl.acm.org/citation.cfm?id=277789.277799
8. Rao, A.S.: AgentSpeak(L): BDI agents speak out in a logical computable language. In: Van de Velde, W., Perram, J.W. (eds.) Agents Breaking Away. LNCS, vol. 1038, pp. 42–45. Springer, Heidelberg (1996). doi:10.1007/BFb0031845
9. Russell, S., Norvig, P.: Artificial Intelligence: A Modern Approach. Prentice Hall Series in Artificial Intelligence, 3rd edn. Prentice Hall, Saddle River (2010)
10. Shoham, Y.: Agent-oriented programming. Artif. Intell. **60**(11), 51–92 (1993). doi:10.1016/0004-3702(93)90034-9
11. Sutton, R.S.: Learning to predict by the methods of temporal differences. Mach. Learn. **3**(1), 9–44 (1998). doi:10.1007/BF00115009

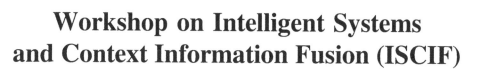

# Workshop on Intelligent Systems
# and Context Information Fusion (ISCIF)

# Measuring Heterogeneous User Behaviors During the Interaction with Dialog Systems

David Griol$^{(\boxtimes)}$ and José Manuel Molina

Computer Science Department, Carlos III University of Madrid,
Avda. de la Universidad, 30, 28911 Leganés, Spain
{david.griol,josemanuel.molina}@uc3m.es

**Abstract.** In this paper, we describe a technique to develop simulated user agents that are able to interact with dialog systems. By means of these agents, it is possible not only to automatically evaluate the overall operation of the dialog system, but also to assess the impact of the user responses on the decisions that are selected by the system. The selection of the user responses by the simulated user agent are based on a statistical model that is automatically learned from a dialog corpus. The complete history of the interaction is considered to carry out this selection. The paper describes the application of this technique to evaluate a practical dialog system providing tourist information and services.

**Keywords:** Dialog systems · Agent simulation · Human-machine interaction · User modeling · System evaluation · Statistical methodologies

## 1 Introduction

Research in techniques to generate simulated user agents has a long history within the fields of language processing and dialog systems. The main purpose of a simulated user agent in this field is to improve the usability of a dialog system by means of its interaction with the simulated user agent [11,14].

By means of simulated user agents, it is possible to reduce time and effort that would be required to complete the evaluation of a dialog system by means of real users. Moreover, each time changes are made to the system it is necessary to complete a new evaluation to assess the impact of these changes. Thus, the availability of a large number of dialogs acquired with a simulated user agent should contribute positively to the development of the dialog system [4,14].

Simulated user agents can be used to evaluate different aspects of a dialog system, particularly at the earlier stages of development, or to determine the effects of changes to the system's functionalities (e.g., evaluate confirmation strategies or introduce of errors or unpredicted answers in order to evaluate the capacity of the dialog manager to react to unexpected situations). A second usage is to support the automatic learning of optimal dialog strategies using statistical methodologies. Large amounts of data are required for a systematic

© Springer International Publishing Switzerland 2016
J. Bajo et al. (Eds.): PAAMS 2016 Workshops, CCIS 616, pp. 289–300, 2016.
DOI: 10.1007/978-3-319-39387-2_24

exploration of the dialog state space and corpora acquired with simulated users are extremely valuable for this purpose.

Two main approaches can be distinguished to the creation of simulated user agents: rule-based and data or corpus-based. In a rule-based simulated user, the defined rules determine the behavior of the agent [2,9,10]. This approach is particularly useful when the purpose of the research is to evaluate the effects of different dialog management strategies. In this way the researcher has complete control over the design of the evaluation study.

Corpus-based approaches are based on probabilistic methods to select the user responses, with the advantage that this uncertainty can better reflect the unexpected behaviors of users interacting with the system. Statistical models for modeling users behavior have been suggested as the solution to the lack of the data that is required for training and evaluating conversational interfaces [4]. Using this approach, the dialog system can explore the space of possible dialog situations and learn new potentially better strategies. A summary of corpus-based user modeling techniques for reinforcement learning of the dialog strategy can be found in [14].

In this paper, we describe a proposal for using simulated user agents to assess the different users' behaviors during the interaction with a dialog system. The proposed simulated user agents are based on a statistical user model, which is learned by means of a training dialog corpus. This model provides the probabilities of selecting each one of the user responses according to the previous dialog history and the objective of the dialog. This selection is carried out by means of a classification process that takes these information sources as input.

We have applied our proposal to evaluate the different users' behaviors interacting with a practical conversational agent that provides tourist information and services in Spanish. Our proposal has been used not only to evaluate the overall operation of the conversational agent, but also to detect the most important user's characteristics that have influence in the correct operation of the system and errors detected during the interaction.

The remainder of the paper is as follows. Section 2 describes our proposal to develop user simulated agents. Section 3 shows the application of our proposal for the evaluation of a practical dialog system providing tourist information and services. In Sect. 4 we discuss the results obtained after the overall evaluation of the simulated user agent and the influence of different user's features in these results. Finally, Sect. 5 presents our conclusions and future work guidelines.

## 2   Proposed User Modeling Technique

Usually, spoken dialog systems carry out five main tasks: Automatic Speech Recognition (ASR), Spoken Language Understanding (SLU), Dialog Management (DM), Natural Language Generation (NLG), and Text-To-Speech Synthesis (TTS). These tasks are typically implemented in different modules of the system's architecture.

The goal of speech recognition is to obtain the sequence of words uttered by a speaker [15]. It is a very complex task, as there can be a great deal of variation in the input the recognizer must analyze, for example, in terms of the linguistics of the utterance, inter and intra speaker variation, the interaction context and the transmission channel. Once the speech recognizer has provided an output, the system must understand what the user said. The goal of spoken language understanding is to obtain the semantics from the recognized sentence. This process generally requires morphological, lexical, syntactical, semantic, discourse and pragmatical knowledge [17].

The dialog manager decides the next action of the dialog system [16], interpreting the incoming semantic representation of the user input in the context of the dialog. In addition, it resolves ellipsis and anaphora, evaluates the relevance and completeness of user requests, identifies and recovers from recognition and understanding errors, retrieves information from data repositories, and decides about the next system's response. Natural language generation is the process of obtaining sentences in natural language from the non-linguistic, internal representation of information handled by the dialog system [8]. Finally, the TTS module transforms the generated sentences into synthesized speech [3].

The user modeling technique that we propose in this paper replaces real users in the interaction with the conversational agent. This technique simulates the user intention level, that is, the simulated user agent provides concepts and attributes that represent the intention of the user utterance. Therefore, this agent carries out the functions of the ASR and NLU modules, i.e., it generates the semantic interpretation of the user utterance in the same format defined for the output of the SLU module. Figure 1 shows the interaction of the real users and the simulated user agent user with the described architecture of a spoken conversational agent.

The methodology that we have developed for user modeling extends our work for developing a statistical methodology for dialog management [6]. The user responses are generated taking into account the information provided by the simulator throughout the history of the dialog, the last system turn, and the objective(s) predefined for the dialog.

In order to control the interaction, the simulated user agent uses the representation the dialogs as a sequence of pairs $(A_i, U_i)$, where $A_i$ is the output of the dialog system (the system answer) at time $i$, expressed in terms of dialog acts; and $U_i$ is the semantic representation of the user turn (the result of the understanding process of the user input) at time $i$, also expressed in terms of dialog acts. This way, each dialog is represented by $(A_1, U_1), \cdots, (A_i, U_i), \cdots, (A_n, U_n)$, where $A_1$ is the greeting turn of the system (the first turn of the dialog), and $U_n$ is the last user turn. We refer to a pair $(A_i, U_i)$ as $S_i$, the state of the dialog sequence at time $i$.

In this framework, we consider that, at time $i$, the objective of the simulated user agent is to find an appropriate user answer $U_i$. This selection is a local process for each time $i$ and takes into account the sequence of dialog states that

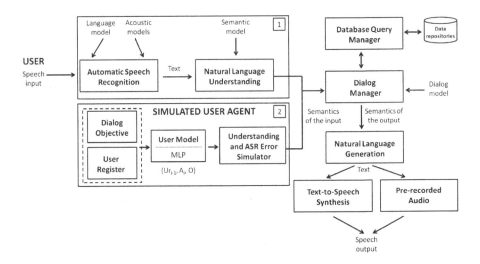

**Fig. 1.** Interaction of a conversational agent (1) with real users. (2) with the proposed user modeling technique

precede time $i$, the system answer at time $i$, and the objective of the dialog $\mathcal{O}$. If the most probable user answer $U_i$ is selected at each time $i$, the selection is made using the maximization:

$$\hat{U}_i = \arg\max_{U_i \in \mathcal{U}} P(U_i | S_1, \cdots, S_{i-1}, A_i, \mathcal{O})$$

where set $\mathcal{U}$ contains all the possible user answers.

As the number of possible sequences of states is very large, we establish a partition in this space (i.e., in the history of the dialog preceding time $i$).This data structure, that we call *User Register* $(UR)$, contains the information provided by the user agent throughout the previous history of the dialog. After applying the above considerations and establishing the equivalence relations in the histories of the dialogs, the selection of the best $U_i$ is given by:

$$\hat{U}_i = \arg\max_{U_i \in \mathcal{U}} P(U_i | UR_{i-1}, A_i, \mathcal{O})$$

As in our previous work on dialog management [6], we propose the use of a multilayer perceptron (MLP) [1,12] to make the determination of the next user response. The input layer receives the current situation of the dialog, which is represented by the term $(UR_{i-1}, A_i, \mathcal{O})$ in the previous equation. The values of the output layer can be viewed as the a posteriori probability of selecting the different user responses defined for the user agent given the current situation of the dialog. The choice of the most probable user answer of this probability distribution leads to the previous equation. In this case, the simulated user agent will always generate the same response for the same situation of the dialog. Since we want to provide a richer variability of users behaviors, we base our choice on the probability distribution supplied by the MLP on all the feasible user responses, not only selecting the most probable user response for each dialog situation.

For the simulated user agent to select the next response, we have assumed that the exact values provided by this agent are not significant. They are important for accessing the data repositories and for constructing the output sentences of the dialog system. However, the only information necessary to determine the next action by the simulated user agent is the presence or absence of specific information. Therefore, the information we used from the $UR$ is a codification of this data in terms of three values, $\{0, 1, 2\}$, for each field in the $UR$ according to the following criteria:

- **0**: The value of the specific position of the $UR$ has not been provided by the user agent.
- **1**: The value of the specific position of the $UR$ has been provided with a confidence score that is higher than a given threshold. Confidence scores are provided by the Understanding and ASR Error Simulator Agent, as it is explained in Sect. 2.1.
- **2**: The value of the specific position of the $UR$ has been provided with a confidence score that is lower than the given threshold.

### 2.1   The Understanding and ASR Error Simulator Agent

A real dialog corpus includes information about the errors that were introduced by the ASR and the SLU modules during the acquisition. This information also includes confidence measures, which are used by the conversational agent to evaluate the reliability of the concepts and attributes generated by the SLU module. This way, an error simulator agent has been designed to perform error generation. This agent modifies the dialog acts generated by the user simulator once the $UR$ is updated. In addition, the error simulator adds confidence scores to the semantic representation generated by the user simulator.

One of the main problems that must be considered during the interaction with a conversational agent is the propagation of errors through the different modules in the system. The ASR module must deal with the effects of spontaneous speech and with noisy environments; consequently, the sentence provided by this module could incorporate some errors. The SLU module could also add its own errors (which are mainly due to the lack of coverage of the semantic domain). Finally, the semantic representation provided to the dialog manager might also contain certain errors. Therefore, it is desirable to provide the dialog manager with information about what parts of the user utterance have been clearly recognized and understood and what parts have not.

In our proposal, the simulated user agent provides the dialog system with the dialog act representation associated to the user input together with its confidence scores [5]. To do this, an error simulation agent has also been incorporated to include semantic errors in the generation of dialogs. This agent modifies the dialog acts provided by the user model once it has selected the next user response.

In addition, the error simulation agent adds a confidence score to each concept and attribute in the semantic representation generated for each user turn.

For the study presented in this paper, we have improved this agent using a model for introducing errors based on the method presented in [13]. The generation of confidence scores is carried out separately from the model employed for error generation. This model is represented as a communication channel by means of a generative probabilistic model $P(c, a_u|\tilde{a}_u)$, where $a_u$ is the true incoming user dialog act $\tilde{a}_u$ is the recognized hypothesis, and $c$ is the confidence score associated with this hypothesis.

The probability $P(\tilde{a}_u|a_u)$ is obtained by Maximum-Likelihood using the initial labeled corpus acquired with real users and considers the recognized sequence of words $w_u$ and the actual sequence uttered by the user $\tilde{w}_u$. This probability is decomposed into a component that generates a word-level utterance from a given user dialog act, a model that simulates ASR confusions (learned from the reference transcriptions and the ASR outputs), and a component that models the semantic decoding process.

$$P(\tilde{a}_u|a_u) = \sum_{\tilde{w}_u} P(a_u|\tilde{w}_u) \sum_{w_u} P(\tilde{w}_u|w_u) P(w_u|a_u)$$

Confidence score generation is carried out by approximating $P(c|\tilde{a}_u, a_u)$ assuming that there are two distributions for $c$. These two distributions are handcrafted, generating confidence scores for correct and incorrect hypotheses by sampling from the distributions found in the training data corresponding to our initial corpus.

$$P(c|a_u, \tilde{a}_u) = \begin{cases} P_{corr}(c) & if \quad \tilde{a}_u = a_u \\ P_{incorr}(c) & if \quad \tilde{a}_u \neq a_u \end{cases}$$

During the automatic interaction of the simulated user agent and the dialog system, the dialog manager of the dialog system considers that a dialog is not successful when one of the following conditions takes place: (i) the dialog exceeds a maximum number of system turns, usually higher than the average number of turns of the dialogs acquired with real users; (ii) the answer selected by the dialog manager corresponds to a query not made by the simulated user agent; (iii) the database query module generates an error because the simulated user agent has not provided the mandatory data needed to carry out the query; (iv) the answer generator generates an error when the selected answer involves the use of a data item not provided by the user agent. A user request for closing the dialog is selected once the system has provided the information defined in its objective(s). The dialogs that fulfill this condition before the maximum number of turns are considered successful.

## 3   Practical Application

We have applied our proposal to develop and evaluate the *Enjoy Your City* spoken dialog system, which provides user-adapted tourist information in natural language in Spanish [7]. The information provided by the system includes places of interest, weather forecast, hotel booking, restaurants and bars, shopping, street guide and "how to get there" functionalities, cultural activities (cinema, theater, music, exhibitions, literature and science), sport activities, festivities, and public transportation. The information offered to the user is extracted from different web pages and several databases are also used to store this information and automatically update the data that is provided.

We have defined ten concepts to represent the different queries that the user can perform (*Places-Interest, Weather-Forecast, Hotel-Booking, Restaurants-Bars, Shopping, Street-how-to-get, Cultural, Sport, Festivities,* and *Public-Transport*). Three task-independent concepts have also been defined for the task (*Affirmation, Negation,* and *Not-Understood*). A total of 115 system actions (dialog acts) were defined taking into account the information that is required by the system to provide the requested information.

An example of the semantic interpretation of a user utterance is shown in Fig. 2.

| **Input sentence:** |
| [SPANISH] *Me gustaría conocer el horario de visita del Templo de Debod para mañana.* |
| [ENGLISH] *I would like to know the visit hours of the Temple of Debod for tomorrow.* |
| **Semantic interpretation:** |
| (*Places-Interest*) |
|     *Query-type*: Timetables |
|     *Place*: Temple of Debod |
|     *Date*: Tomorrow |

**Fig. 2.** An example of the labeling of a user turn in the *Enjoy Your City* system

The $UR$ defined for the task is a sequence of 128 fields, corresponding to:

- The 10 concepts defined for the dialog act representation.
- The total of 115 possible attributes for the concepts.
- The 3 task-independent concepts that users can provide (*Acceptance, Rejection* and *Not-Understood*).

## 4   Experiments and Results

A corpus of 300 dialogs was acquired by means of real users interacting with the *Enjoy Your City* system. In the acquisition of this corpus participated 60 recruited users at the Technical University of Valencia (Valencia, Spain), University of Granada (Granada, Spain), and Carlos III University of Madrid (Leganés, Spain).

A 5-fold cross-validation process was used to carry out the evaluation of the proposal to develop simulated user agents. The corpus was randomly split into five subsets (20 % of the corpus). Our experiment consisted of five trials. Each trial used a different subset taken from the five subsets as the test set, and the remaining 80 % of the corpus was used as the training set. A validation subset (20 %) was extracted from each training set.

In order to successfully use neural networks as classifiers, we firstly tested the influence of the topology of the MLP, by training different MLPs of increasing number of weights using the standard backpropagation algorithm (with a sigmoid activation function and a learning rate equal to 0.2), and selecting the best topology according to the mean square error (MSE) of the validation data. Different training algorithms were evaluated: the incremental version of the backpropagation algorithm (with and without momentum term) and the quickprop algorithm. The best result on the validation data was obtained using an MLP with one hidden layer of 32 units trained with the standard backpropagation algorithm and a value of LR equal to 0.3.

We defined three measures to compare the response automatically generated by the simulated user agent for each sample in the test partition with regard to the reference response annotated in the training corpus. This way, the evaluation is carried out turn by turn. These measures are:

- *Exact*: the percentage of responses provided by the simulated user agent that are exactly the same that the reference response annotated in the training corpus;
- *Coherent*: the percentage of responses provided by the simulated user agent that are coherent with the current state of the dialog although they are not exactly the same response annotated in the training corpus.
- *Error*: the percentage of responses provided by the user model that would cause the failure of the dialog;

Firstly, we evaluated the overall operation of the simulated user agent by carrying out a 5-fold cross validation process that considers only the semantic information provided by the SLU module for each user utterance, without considering any additional context information related to the user for the definition of the training and test partitions. The number of user turns in each partition considered users' location, gender, duration of the turns, and number of words provided in each turn. Table 1 shows the results of this evaluation.

**Table 1.** Results of the overall evaluation of the users modeling technique

| Exact | Coherent | Error |
|-------|----------|-------|
| 78.3% | 94.7%    | 5.3%  |

These results show the satisfactory operation of the proposed user modeling technique. The codification of the state of the dialog and the correct operation of the MLP classifier allow the simulated user agent to generate a response that is coherent with the current state of the dialog in a 94.7 % percentage. The user response also coincides exactly with the reference response in the corpus in 78.3 % of cases. Finally, the number of responses that can lead to system failure is only 5.3 %.

Secondly, we completed an evaluation of the user model taking into account the size of the training corpus. The same partitions described in the overall evaluation were employed, discarding training samples randomly to reduce the size of this partition. Three experiments were completed, using a 75 % of the training samples (3678 samples), 50 % of the training set (2452 samples) and 25 % (1226 samples). The test sets were the same described for the overall evaluation of the simulated user agent. Table 2 shows the results of this evaluation.

**Table 2.** Results of the evaluation of the users model according to the size of the training corpus

|        | Exact  | Coherent | Error  |
|--------|--------|----------|--------|
| 100 %  | 78.3 % | 94.7 %   | 5.3 %  |
| 75 %   | 75.9 % | 91.4 %   | 8.6 %  |
| 50 %   | 72.1 % | 88.3 %   | 11.7 % |
| 25 %   | 68.6 % | 82.6 %   | 17.4 % |

The results of this evaluation show the correct operation of the user model even if only used 50 % of the training corpus is used to learn the user model. Thus, the results obtained for the coherent measure are very similar if more than the 50 % of the training corpus is used. However, if only 25 % of the training corpus is used, the percentage of responses that can cause the failure of the dialog increases to 17.4 %. The good operation of the user modeling technique (even for a reduced size of the training corpus) can be explained because there are many dialog states that are very frequent in the corpus, or are similar to other states and then can be easily classified by the MLP.

Then, we evaluated our proposal considering the gender of the users as a parameter to be assessed. To do this, the corpus was divided into a set of partitions with equal number of samples of women and men. Table 3 shows the results of this evaluation, specifying the partitions used for training and test (Training/Test).

**Table 3.** Results of the evaluation of the user model taking into account the influence of gender

|               | Exact  | Coherent | Error   |
|---------------|--------|----------|---------|
| Women / Both  | 70.6 % | 89.1 %   | 10.9 %  |
| Men / Both    | 70.3 % | 93.1 %   | 6.9 %   |
| Both / Women  | 71.8 % | 92.5 %   | 7.5 %   |
| Both / Men    | 77.1 % | 93.4 %   | 6.6 %   |

The results of this evaluation show that there are not remarkable differences if the learning of the user model for the simulated user agent is completed using only samples of men or women (first two columns of results in Table 3). Higher differences are observed in the evaluation of the model considering the gender of the users in the test partitions (third and fourth column of this table). The differences obtained in these cases show a greater similarity in the samples of men.

Following, we evaluated the influence of the users' expertise level in the operation of the user modeling technique. Users were classified into three groups: Group 1 (users that employed the system 5 or less times), Group 2 (users that employed the system between 5 and 10 times), and Group 3 (users that employed the system more than 10 times). Table 4 shows the results of this experimentation, specifying the partitions used for training and test (Training/Test).

**Table 4.** Results of the evaluation of the user model taking into account the influence of age

|                   | Exact  | Coherent | Error  |
|-------------------|--------|----------|--------|
| Group 1 / Group 2 | 61.4 % | 66.2 %   | 33.8 % |
| Group 1 / Group 3 | 53.8 % | 59.1 %   | 40.9 % |
| Group 2 / Group 1 | 67.6 % | 75.9 %   | 24.1 % |
| Group 2 / Group 3 | 68.3 % | 78.3 %   | 21.7 % |
| Group 3 / Group 1 | 60.7 % | 69.3 %   | 30.7 % |
| Group 3 / Group 2 | 72.5 % | 80.8 %   | 19.2 % |

As the results of Table 4 show, the more significant differences were observed when novel users (Group 1) where employed for training the user model and the test partition included the rest of users. These differences are very important when users in Group 1 were used for training and users of Group 3 were employed to test the user model.

Finally, we have evaluated our proposal taking into account the influence of the origin of the dialogs. This evaluation starting with the same partitions defined for the overall evaluation of the proposal, training the simulated user agent with the samples coming from the specific location to be evaluated and using the same test partitions (samples from the three locations). Table 5 shows the results of this evaluation.

The results of this evaluation show the better operation of the proposal when the user model was learned with the dialogs acquired at Location 2. When the user model was learned using only the dialogs of the Location 1, the percentage of responses that follow the strategy is equivalent to the one obtained for the Location 3. With regard the dialog corpus acquired at Location 3, in addition of obtaining a percentage of exact responses of only 66.4 %, the number of user responses that can cause the failure of the dialog is also the highest. Therefore, considering the values obtained for the different measures, we can conclude a significant difference between the dialogs acquired at each location.

**Table 5.** Results of the evaluation of the user model taking into account the origin of the dialogs

|            | Exact  | Coherent | Error  |
|------------|--------|----------|--------|
| Location 1 | 71.9 % | 84.8 %   | 15.2 % |
| Location 2 | 77.2 % | 91.3 %   | 8.7 %  |
| Location 3 | 66.4 % | 82.6 %   | 17.4 % |

# 5 Conclusions and Future Work

In this paper, we have described a technique to generate simulated user agents to automatically evaluate spoken dialog systems. The simulated user agent is based on a statistical model which takes the complete history of the interaction into account to decide the next user response. This decision is modeled by a classification process in which a neural network is used. An additional statistical model has been introduced for errors introduction and confidence measures generation. This way, the dialog system can also be evaluated by considering different conditions in the communication channel.

The simulated user agent simulates the user intention level in terms of the semantic representation that would be generated by the ASR and NLU modules in the architecture of a dialog system. This way, dialogs are automatically labeled during the simulation using the semantics defined for the task. Thus, the interaction of the simulated user agent and a dialog system allows the generation of new dialogs with little effort and the adaptation of a the system to a new task can also simplified.

We have described the application of our proposal to evaluate both the overall operation of the user model and the main characteristics of a dialog corpus acquired with real users. This evaluation has allowed us to measure the influence of the most important user's features characteristics that affect the interaction of the simulated user agent with the dialog system. As a future work, we are adapting the proposed user modeling technique for its application in more difficult domains. We also want to extend our proposal for user modeling by means of the incorporation of additional features related to the user's emotional state and their personality.

**Acknowledgements.** This work was supported in part by Projects MINECO TEC2012-37832-C02-01, CICYT TEC2011-28626-C02-02, CAM CONTEXTS (S2009/ TIC-1485).

# References

1. Bishop, C.M.: Neural networks for pattern recognition. Oxford University Press, Bristol (1995)

2. Chung, G.: Developing a flexible spoken dialog system using simulation. In: Proceedings of 42nd Annual Meeting of the Association for Computational Linguistics (ACL 2004), pp. 63–70 (2004)

3. Dutoit, T.: An introduction to text-to-speech synthesis. Kluwer Academic Publishers (1996)

4. Engelbrecht, K.: Estimating Spoken Dialog System Quality with User Models. T-Labs Series in Telecommunication Services. Springer, Heidelberg (2012)

5. García, F., Hurtado, L.F., Sanchis, E., Segarra, E.: The incorporation of confidence measures to language understanding. In: Matoušek, V., Mautner, P. (eds.) TSD 2003. LNCS (LNAI), vol. 2807, pp. 165–172. Springer, Heidelberg (2003)

6. Griol, D., Callejas, Z., López-Cózar, R., Riccardi, G.: A domain-independent statistical methodology for dialog management in spoken dialog systems. Comput. Speech Lang. **28**(3), 743–768 (2014)

7. Griol, D., Molina, J.M.: Modeling users emotional state for an enhanced human-machine interaction. In: Onieva, E., Santos, I., Osaba, E., Quintian, H., Corchado, E. (eds.) HAIS 2015. LNCS, vol. 9121, pp. 357–368. Springer, Heidelberg (2015)

8. Lemon, O.: Learning what to say and how to say it: Joint optimisation of spoken dialogue management and natural language generation. Comput. Speech Lang. **25**, 210–221 (2011)

9. Lin, B., Lee, L.: Computer aided analysis and design for spoken dialogue systems based on quantitative simulations. IEEE Trans. Speech Audio Process. **9**(5), 534–548 (2001)

10. López-Cózar, R., de la Torre, A., Segura, J., Rubio, A.: Assessment of dialogue systems by means of a new simulation technique. Speech Commun. **40**, 387–407 (2003)

11. Möller, S., Englert, R., Engelbrecht, K., Hafner, V., Jameson, A., Oulasvirta,A., Raake, A., Reithinger, N.: MeMo: towards automatic usability evaluationof spoken dialogue services by user error simulations. In: Proceedings of the 9th International Conference on Spoken Language Processing (Interspeech/ICSLP), pp. 1786–1789. Pittsburgh, USA (2006)

12. Rumelhart, D.E., Hinton, G.E., Williams, R.J.: PDP: Computational models of cognition and perception, I, chap. Learning internal representations by error propagation, pp. 319–362. MIT Press, Cambridge (1986)

13. Schatzmann, J., Thomson, B., Young, S.: Error simulation for training statistical dialogue systems. In: Proceedings of IEEE Automatic Speech Recognition and Understanding Workshop (ASRU 2007), pp. 273–282. Kyoto, Japan (2007)

14. Schatzmann, J., Weilhammer, K., Stuttle, M., Young, S.: A survey of statistical user simulation techniques for reinforcement-learning of dialogue management strategies. Knowl. Eng. Rev. **21**(2), 97–126 (2006)

15. Tsilfidis, A., Mporas, I., Mourjopoulos, J., Fakotakis, N.: Automatic speech recognition performance in different room acoustic environments with and without dereverberation preprocessing. Comput. Speech Lang. **27**(1), 380–395 (2013)

16. Williams, J., Young, S.: Partially observable markov decision processes for spoken dialog systems. Comput. Speech Lang. **21**(2), 393–422 (2007)

17. Wu, W.L., Lu, R.Z., Duan, J.Y., Liu, H., Gao, F., Chen, Y.Q.: Spoken language understanding using weakly supervised learning. Comput. Speech Lang. **24**(2), 358–382 (2010)

# A Data Fusion Model for Ambient Assisted Living

Javier Jiménez Alemán[2], Nayat Sánchez-Pi[1(✉)], Luis Marti[2],
José Manuel Molina[3], and Ana Cristina Bicharra Garcia[2]

[1] Computer Science Department, Mathematics and Statistics Institute,
Rio de Janeiro State University (UERJ), Rio de Janeiro (RJ), Brazil
`nayat@ime.uerj.br`
[2] Institute of Computing, Fluminense Federal University (UFF), Niteroi (RJ), Brazil
`{jjimenezaleman,lmarti,bicharra}@ic.uff.br`
[3] Computer Science Department,
Carlos III University of Madrid (UC3M), Madrid, Spain
`molina@ia.uc3m.es`

**Abstract.** Ambient Assisted Living (AAL) is an emergent area that provides useful mechanisms that allows tracking elders through sensoring. For AAL systems, it is very important to provide information fusion techniques, which merge the information available in sensors available in different devices like the smartphones to infer possible risk situations for elders in outdoor environments. The Data Fusion Model is the most widely used method for categorizing data fusion-related functions. In previous works we have developed SafeRoute, an AAL system that pretends monitoring elders in their day-to-day daily living activities in outdoor environments. In this context, this paper presents a specific proposal of application of the JDL Data Fusion Model to tracking old persons in outdoor environments. We additionally present the social interaction model in the context of the SafeRoute system, showing the interactions between caregivers and elders and including new contextual elements to make more efficient the tracking process.

**Keywords:** JDL Data Fusion Model · Ambient Assisted Living · Interaction model

## 1 Introduction

Ubiquitous spaces are a common research field nowadays, mostly due to the increase in sensors installed on environments and the technological opportunity it presents. Ambient Intelligence (AmI) refers to a vision in which people are empowered by an electronic environment that is sensitive and responsive to their needs, and is aware of their presence. Its target is improving quality of life by creating the desired atmosphere and functionality through intelligent and inter-connected systems and services. Inside AmI, Ambient Assisted Living (AAL) is an emergent area that provides useful mechanisms that allows

© Springer International Publishing Switzerland 2016
J. Bajo et al. (Eds.): PAAMS 2016 Workshops, CCIS 616, pp. 301–312, 2016.
DOI: 10.1007/978-3-319-39387-2_25

tracking elders through sensoring, for example, using mobile devices, that not only work like communication devices, but also are equipped with several sensors like accelerometer, gyroscope, proximity sensors, microphones, GPS system and camera. Ambient Assisted Living (AAL) can be defined as the use of information and communication technologies (ICT) in a persons daily living and working environment to enable them to stay active longer, remain socially connected and live independently into old age [1].

Information fusion focused in sensors has become increasingly relevant during the last years due to its aim to combine observations from a number of different sensors to provide a solid and complete description of an environment or process of interest. The information fusion systems are characterized by its robustness, increased confidence, reduced ambiguity and uncertainty, and improved resolution. There are examples of applications of information fusion techniques that use sensors in different environments such as remote sensing, surveillance, home care, and so forth, but there are few applications using smartphones devices-blazquez.

The Data Fusion Model maintained by the JDL Data Fusion Group is the most widely used method for categorizing data fusion-related functions. They proposed a model of six levels, of which the first is related to information extraction, and the last with the extraction of knowledge. The JDL model was never intended to decide a concrete order on the data fusion levels. Levels are not alluded to be processed consecutively, and it can be executed concurrently [2]. Although the JD data fusion model has been criticized, still constitutes a reference to design and build systems to obtain information from the data in complex systems and generate knowledge from the extracted information.

Attending that, was created the SafeRoute project, a system able to assist elders with activities related to their day-to-day activities in outdoor environments that use geo-localization technologies built-in mobiles devices. The objective of SafeRoute is to monitor elders who follow predefined routes and to notify to their caregiver in case of emergencies (losses and falls). In recent works [3–5], we have considered the inclusion of new actors and other elements in our model that contribute to improve the monitoring process of elders and to reduce response time in case of emergencies. The purpose of this work is to describe the social interaction model in the context of the SafeRoute system, showing the interactions between caregivers and elders and including new contextual elements to make more efficient the tracking process. In addition, we describe our proposal of information fusion using the JDL Data Fusion Model to tracking old persons in outdoor environments.

The paper is ordered as follows: Sect. 2 depicts the actual state-of-art of some AAL studies that implements activity recognition techniques using smartphones and information fusion techniques. Section 3 aims to describe our proposed Interaction Model. Section 4 presents our proposed JDL Data Fusion Model application. In Sect. 5 we present in a Study Case the new functionalities of the SafeRoute system and we also show the results of some initial user-centered tests to evaluate our work. Finally, in the Sect. 6 shows the conclusions and future works.

## 2    Work Related

In the case of AAL systems, it is necessary to provide to elders the simplest way to interact with the systems, to minimize as much as possible the error product of this interaction. It is recommended limiting the possible options, dialogues has to be linear and parallel tasks must to be avoided. For example, Kopal [6] is a system, which provides a feedback mechanism based on speech, which helps people with dementia and their caregivers. The caregiver may use the own mobile for ask for information to the elder through the own mobile. OutCare [7] is an example of an AAL application that attempts to help people with Alzheimer's and their caregivers. In this case, the authors implemented a multi-agent system (MAS) that monitoring outdoor daily routines for people with Alzheimer, sending alerts to their caregivers in case of deviation via SMS, e-mail, and voice.

InContexto [2] is a distributed fusion of information architecture that uses smartphone to retrieve user and context information. This architecture provides guidelines for collecting information of users through sensors provided by smartphones, making differences between softsensors and hardsensors, and sharing the processes between the smartphone and a cloudserver. InContexto uses information fusion to integrate data from different softsensors and hardsensors to extract relevant information about users. Authors based his work on the JDL model and divided the fusion process in five levels. Regarding the distributed architecture of InContexto, it is composed by two components: a Web Service and a Smartphone Server. The main purpose to the InContexto architecture is to infer physical actions performed by users (walking, running, etc.) through an application developed for Android. The recognition module activity was tested, getting a very high overall (97 % accuracy) in the classification of this activities. Summarizing, [2] seems to be the most promising approach studied. However, the authors focus their work on the use of only the accelerometer smartphone and do not exploit the use of other hardsensores as the light sensor, temperature sensor, etc. to infer new user activities and situations in outdoor environments.

The main contributions of this paper is to describe our propose of data fusion using the JDL Data Fusion Model in a context that combine traditional elements of an AAL environment with new human actors and functionalities, finding to create a safety network around the city. This new social actors will act as sensors and actuators, to detect emergencies and reduce the response time in this cases. Furthermore, we describe the interaction model of this hybrid context.

## 3    Interaction Model

In [5] we considered the inclusion of new actors and other elements in our model. In this work, we define our interaction model, considering other elements and actors. In the studied context, our objective is to monitor the daily routines of elders in outdoors, and acting according the diagnostic product of the mentioned status. There are different people involved in the care for the elders. Relatives and health attendants will be monitoring constantly the elder status, doctors will be alerting in case of and medical emergency and stand workers will be receiving information about the status of elders in the proximity of their workplaces and will help elders in case of emergency. It is possible to infer a diagnostic of the elder status, for example, if elder falls, his health condition or his motor activity (walking, standing, etc.). We defined different kinds of actions that will act over the correspondent actuator, and depending the previous diagnostic, we divide actions in communication actions and human help actions. Other important aspect that we realized is concerning the different information sources that our system can consume to diagnose the elder status. We taking in consideration not only the sensor observations of sensor built-in the mobile devices, but also other external information (maps, environmental information located in the web, profile information of elder). An important aspect to take in consideration regards information sources is their reputation and uncertainty, which can influence significantly in the diagnostic of the elder status.

Additionally, we not only considered mobile devices as devices to sense the elder activity in our study, we also included ambient devices and wearable devices, but focused mainly in smartphones as main sensing tool. We consider smartphones as other sensor inside our Ambient Intelligence system. It may be possible to consider a smartphone like a non-intrusive device to obtain activity con text from people, in this case, elders. Indeed, smartphones experience almost the same physical forces, temperature, and noise of the person who carries them out. If we track their actions, we are tracking people actions (Fig. 1).

Summarizing, relatives and health assistants will form a safety network that will be monitoring the elder status in their daily activities; also, doctors would receive alerts in case of severe emergencies (cardiac problems, etc.). In addition, finding to reduce the risk of accidents, we include an innovative tracking system formed by stand workers who work in these newsstands that often are geographically distributed throughout cities in Brazil, these people will be aware of the elders circulating in the vicinity of their workplace, to provide quick help in case of emergency (Fig. 2).

## 4   JDL Model

In [3] we presented the problem to solve and we made an early design of the SafeRoute system, using mobile technologies. On the other hand, in [4] we included new functionalities in our system and we presented an initial strategy through the JDL Data Fusion Model to merge data sensors in mobiles to infer new knowledge about context information, finding to improve the decision making process. Furthermore, in [5] we made a first description of our interaction model, emphasizing the new actors to be taken into account in our context. In this work, we proposed a data fusion method based in the JDL Data Fusion Model, looking to infer possible risk situations to elders in outdoor environments in their day-to-day daily living activities.

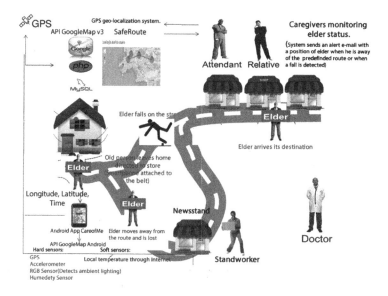

**Fig. 1.** Proposed social interaction model

## 4.1    Level 0: Data Collection

In order to provide an efficient description of the data, a pre-processing process is required to improve performance (noise removal and redundancy of measurements). We consider smartphones because they not only works as communication devices; they are also equipped with several powerful and economical sensors. We consider two kinds of sensors. Firstly, we use some of the hardsensors built-in smartphones such as the accelerometer, lux sensors, barometers, GPS, etc. In our case, we get the user localization in outdoor environments using mainly the GPS sensor and the Internet Services (Wi-Fi) like alternative method. We measure the different frequencies of the accelerometer sensor to develop a method of activity recognition through. On the other hand, accelerometer's frequencies are not fixes and depend on the operating system, and there is no control over it. In our case, we use the Android operating system, which provides four different sampling frequencies.

In the Fig. 3 we show our proposal method of fall detection using the measures of acceleration of the different axes (x, y and z) of the smartphone. Firstly, when the accelerometer records 1G (Earth's gravity) mean that the smartphone is stopped and we can infer that user is not walking. Otherwise, while acceleration values are between the upper and the lower threshold we can say that the smartphone has a constant oscillatory motion and therefore, user can be walking or running. When a suddenly acceleration values that exceeds the predefined thresholds (A, B) is detected, followed by a short-term increase in the acceleration that means a strong impact on the ground (C), we can infer that a fall is detected.

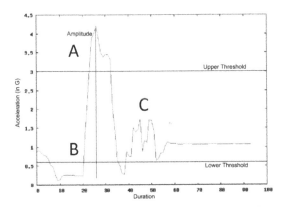

**Fig. 2.** Fall detection using the accelerometer sensor

Regarding ambient temperature, we face the problem that nowadays, most of smartphones has not integrated the ambient temperature sensor. For this reason we use as softsensor an Online Weather Service, in this case World Weather Online, a service that provide an API with several features to measure weather in a determinate localization.

## 4.2    Level 1: Object Assessment

In this level we proposed an Object-Oriented Design to identify and locate relevant objects based in the incomplete information provided by level 0 (Fig. 4). We defined some classes and their attributes. Firstly, the class Route represents a predefined route that the old person must to follow when he is outdoor. In addition, the localization class defines the features of a determinate spatial localization in time; the most important attributes are related to the geographic coordinates (latitude and longitude) and the type of location (fall, lost, confused, normal). On the other hand, class Sensor defines a generic measure in time; in this class, we stored sensors measure just like ambient temperature, luminosity level or relative humidity.

## 4.3    Level 2: Situational Assessment

In the last years, the interest in ontologies as symbolic models to acquire, represent, and exploit knowledge in context aware computing, has increased considerably. The amount of research projects using semantic technologies, like [8–11], can illustrate the importance of ontologies in the field of Ambient Intelligence and pervasive computing architectures. Typical AAL environments and ontological model represents entities such as target user, sensor, actuator, physical space, ubiquitous device, etc. However, we do not find examples when human actors were considers as sensors of user and environmental information and actuator at the same time. We believe that the studied ontological models do not

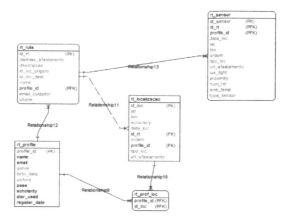

**Fig. 3.** Database design

cover all the elements of the context studied. In our case, we use an ontology for representing the contextual information of our interaction model, that represents the context-aware tracking for the elders using mainly mobile devices and being monitored by a network of caregivers to guarantee the safety of the elders in outdoor environments (Fig. 5).

In the studied context, the objective is to control the status of an elder located in an outdoor place, and acting according the diagnostic product of the mentioned status. There are different people involved in the care for the elders. Relatives and health attendants will be monitoring constantly the elder status, doctors will be alerting in case of and medical emergency and stand workers will be receiving information about the status of elders in the proximity of their workplaces with the objective to help them in case of necessity. We defined as Sensors in our context those elements that provide information about the elder status to make a diagnostic of their situation, for example, the stand worker, who sense constantly all elders near him and send constantly information about him to the web server. Moreover, Actuators will be those elements that receive an action derived from a diagnostic and directly helps to elder. Caregiver, Mobile Device, Doctor, Stand Worker, are actuators. We focused in four objectives to monitor the elder status: the elder activity, equilibrium, the elder health status and the environment status. Inside the elder activity, we analyzed the displacement in time to detect distancing for a predetermined route and the motor activity. For each predetermined route is defined the distancing allowed. The executed route representing those that are being executed in a specific moment by the elder. Depending the monitored objective will be inferred a diagnostic of the elder status. This way, for example, it is possible to know if elder falls, his health condition or his motor activity (walking, standing, etc.).

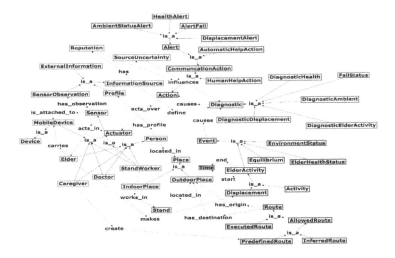

**Fig. 4.** Upper level ontology

We defined different kinds of actions that will act over the correspondent actuator, and depending the previous diagnostic, we divide actions in communication actions and human help actions. Other important aspect that we realized is concerning the different information sources that our system can consume to diagnose the elder status. Additionally, we not only considered mobile devices as devices to sense the elder activity in our study, we also included ambient devices and wearable devices, but focused mainly in smartphones as main sensing tool. We consider smartphones as other sensor inside our Ambient Intelligence system.

## 5 Study Case

In previous work, we defined the SafeRoute system, a distributed system composed by two components: the Android application CareofMe and the web system SafeRoute. Our solution scenario is as follows: Elder leaves home directed to an outdoor location with a smartphone attached to the belt, the smartphone has installed CareofMe (application for Android that constantly tracks the user's activity (running, walking, standing, sitting, fall) his position in geographical coordinates) and falls on the street or moves away from his predetermined route.

Regarding previous work, we include new functionalities to our system. For example, besides route tracing functionality we include the concept of safety net, defined as a set of known locations in the vicinity from which elder must not walk away. (Fig. 5). This new functionality will allow to locate to elder in a more specific way because we could know what is the closest point our safety to the elder's position in a certain time. We consider this functionality very important because it could be reduced the time of response in case of emergencies. We include an innovative element in our tracking system, in this case, we include the newsstand, an specific component of our safety network where is working

**Fig. 5.** Safety network

a stand worker, who sense constantly all elders near him and send constantly information about him to the web server. We include this element because in case that elder has an accident or lost in the street, an alert will be sent to the near stand of the elder position, this way, the stand worker who works there could assist very fast to elder, reducing the response time. Could happen that elder would be lost and would arrive to the stand, in this case, stand worker could check in the system installed in the stand and inform the route that elder must follow or ask him if prefer call for help some relative or other caregiver.

In addition, our system aims to facilitate the process of elder tracking by caregivers and relatives. Thus was created a panel of to control the state of the elder to enable to caregiver or relative to have a complete view of the elder's status (geographical position and environmental conditions).

**Fig. 6.** Predefined route

## 5.1    Evaluation

To evaluate our work we carried out a user-centered test with three elders. Our test consisted in that every elder followed a predefined route (Fig. 6) inside our safety network. We simulate falls (in a controlled environment) and intentional departures from the safety network. Our objective with this test was to compare localization accuracy using localization sensors provided by the Arduino platform with the geographic localization obtained by sensor embedded in the smartphone and used by the CareofMe application (GPS, Wi-fi).

Results showed in Figs. 7 and 8 showed a better accuracy for locations obtained by the CareofMe application in comparison with location sensors of Arduino. However, the results showed the necessity to implement calibration functionalities and to find alternatives to get localization, not only GPS and

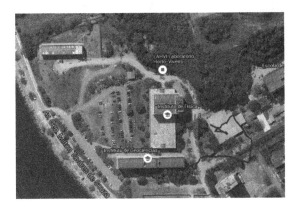

**Fig. 7.** Tracked route using Arduino sensors

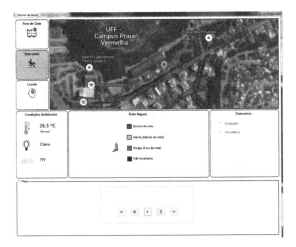

**Fig. 8.** Tracked route through the Control Panel and using the App CareofMe

localization through Internet, finding to improve the localization accuracy. In addition, the obtained results allowed us to measure a set of relevant values for our system, for example, we measured the average displacement speed of elders and the delay in alerting to the caregiver. We took these values in consideration to make corrections in our system, for example, we changed frequency, which our system sends the user's position to the web system, considering that a low frequency can affect the lifetime of the battery of cell and affect the proper functioning of the application.

# 6   Conclusions and Future Work

In this paper, we presented an application of the JDL Data Fusion Model to tracking old persons in outdoor environments as a continuation of previous works in the context of the develop of the SafeRoute system. We described the three first levels of our proposed model, considering different aspect of the involved technologies and contextual characteristics. In addition, we presented a social interaction model for represents the interaction between caregivers and elders that are being monitored in the context of the SafeRoute AAL system. We showed that it is possible helping elders better and to reduce the time response in case of emergency in this context with the inclusion of new social actors as the stand workers, who acts like sensors and actuators in our model. With our model, we described a hybrid context, when caregivers and embedded technologies work together to create a safety network for care elders in outdoors environments and how is it possible that using our system, the response time in case of emergencies could being reduced.

In addition, we showed the results of an initial user-center test that had the objective to compare the localization accuracy between our proposed localization method and an alternative method provided by the Arduino platform. We showed that with the fusion of some localization methods our system obtain a better accuracy that an alternative method that only use a simple localization sensor. However, we considered indispensable for validate our model, to make a more extensive experimental phase in our project. We aim to evaluate prototype through a technology evaluation consisting in some post-test questionnaires to measure the satisfaction level of users.

As part of our ongoing work and finding to improve the decision making process, we are developing inference rules through SWRL (Semantic Web Rule Language) to infer new knowledge about context information as part of the Level of Impact Assessment of the JDL Data Fusion Model. In this sense, with this new inferred knowledge, we plan to develop some new intelligent functionalities that respond automatically to user and to the environment behavior to allow a faster response in case of emergency. This new functionalities include other available sensors and other information sources (environmental sensors, location sensor, accelerometer, camera, microphone, etc.), for example, we pretend manipulate the camera for automatically taking photos of users in case of emergency.

**Acknowledgement.** This work was partially funded by CNPq BJT Project 407851/2012-7, FAPERJ APQ1 Project 211.500/2015, FAPERJ APQ1 Project 211.451/2015, CNPq PVE Project 314017/2013-5, CNPq PEC-PG 190428/2013-9 and by Projects MINECO TEC2012-37832-C02-01, CICYT TEC2011-28626-C02-02.

# References

1. Active Assisted Living Programme (2015). http://www.aal-europe.eu
2. Blázquez, G., Berlanga, A., Molina, J.: InContexto: multisensor architecture to obtain people context from smartphones. Int. J. Distrib. Sens. Netw. **2012**, 1 (2012)
3. Jiménez, J., Sánchez-Pi, N., Garcia, A.C.B.: Opportunistic sensing using mobiles for tracking users in ambient intelligence. In: Mohamed, A., Novais, P., Pereira, A., González, G.V., Fernández-Caballero, A. (eds.) Ambient Intelligence-Software and Applications. AISC, vol. 376, pp. 111–123. Springer, Switzerland (2015)
4. Alemán, J.J., Sanchez-Pi, N., Garcia, A.C.B.: SafeRoute: an example of multisensoring tracking for the elderly using mobiles on ambient intelligence. In: Bajo, J., Hallenborg, K., Pawlewski, P., Botti, V., Sánchez-Pi, N., Duque Méndez, N.D., Lopes, F., Vicente, J. (eds.) PAAMS 2015 Workshops. CCIS, vol. 524, pp. 201–212. Springer, Heidelberg (2015)
5. Jiménez, J., Sánchez-Pi, N., Garcia, A.C.B.: Modeling social interactions for multisensory tracking of elders in outdoor environments on ambient assisted living. In: Simpsio Brasiliero sobre Fatores Humanos em Sistemas Computacionais (IHC 2015) (2015)
6. Fudickar, S., Schnor, B.: KopALa mobile orientation system for dementia patients. In: Tavangarian, D., Kirste, T., Timmermann, D., Lucke, U., Versick, D. (eds.) Intelligent Interactive Assistance and Mobile Multimedia Computing. CCIS, vol. 53, pp. 109–118. Springer, Heidelberg (2009)
7. Wan, J., et al.: Orange alerts: lessons from an outdoor case study. In: 5th International Conference on Pervasive Computing Technologies for Healthcare, pp. 446–451 (2011)
8. Roussaki, I., et al.: Hybrid context modeling: a location-based scheme using ontologies. In: 4th Annual IEEE International Conference on Pervasive Computing and Communications Workshop (2006)
9. Wang, X., et al.: Ontology based context modeling and reasoning using OWL. In: Second IEEE Annual Conference on Pervasive Computing and Communications Workshops, pp. 18–22 (2004)
10. Akcay, O., Altan, O.: Ontology for context-aware visualization for spatial data in mobile devices. In: Joint Workshop Visualization and Exploration of Geospatial Data, vol. 36 (2007)
11. Hage, V., et al.: Design and use of the Simple Event Model (SEM). Web Semant. Sci. Serv. Agents World Wide Web **9**, 128–136 (2011)

# CIALCO: Alternative Marketing Channels

Washington R. Padilla[1] and H. Jesús García[2](✉)

[1] Research Group Ideia Geoca,
Salesian Polytechnic University of Quito-Ecuador Engineer Systems, Quito, Ecuador
wpadillaa@ups.edu.ec
[2] Applied Artificial Intelligence Group, Carlos III University, Madrid, Spain
jgherrer@inf.uc3m.es

**Abstract.** This research uses data mining techniques to establish data predicting consumption of products that are grown in areas of the Andean region of Ecuador by relatives and marketed in alternative circuits that prevent intermediary called Cialcos to improve their income groups.

**Keywords:** Time series · Predictive analysis · Alternative circuits of commercialization · Agro producers · Time series trend · Association rules

## 1 Introduction

This research is aimed at finding patterns in the behavior of consumption of agricultural products in the Andean region of Ecuador that will generate a support for decision-making, based on techniques of predictive data mining.

Using information from 2014, provided by the General Coordination Network Marketing Ministry of Agriculture, Livestock, Fisheries and Aquaculture of Ecuador detailing the behavior of sales of agricultural products made by small farmers located in Ecuador's central highlands specifically in provinces of Tungurahua and Chimborazo.

In Ecuador there are small family groups engaged in agricultural work especially in planting vegetables, product marketing becomes part of the income monthly support. They are associated with other producers of the same area and establish direct marketing channels with the consumer avoiding the presence of other actors, which are able to improve their income. The Cialco acronym comes from using the first two letters of the words in Spanish CIrcuitos ALternativos de COmercialización.

There are several types of marketing channels, this study is limited to information of groups involved in fair type circuits which are defined as specific places where agricultural producers meet periodically to conduct their business.

The file in Excel format provided, comprising information on quantity and volume of sales of products such as vegetables, legumes, meat, dairy, fruits, tubers and processed products, finding an average of 1,200 items per month divided on a weekly basis.

© Springer International Publishing Switzerland 2016
J. Bajo et al. (Eds.): PAAMS 2016 Workshops, CCIS 616, pp. 313–321, 2016.
DOI: 10.1007/978-3-319-39387-2_26

## 2   Methodology

This work is responsible for preparing the subset of vegetables data that is initially processed to generate a data file with CSV (Comma Separated Values) format. This sample can generate observations to establish different patterns of behavior such as building a ranking product offered (volume sales), establish relationships between products offered and agro producers, predict future behavior, establish partnerships between the products offered and purchased, number of producers involved in each Cialco and participatory frequency, once the geographic component would be added it can be extended to an analysis including physical areas for agro-ecological production.

The work presented here takes on two issues: establish time series to predict the future behavior of the largest consumer products, in a second section predictions presented in acquisition of products based on association rules.

Both the analysis in time series and rules of association has been performed using WEKA (Waikato Environment for Knowledge Analysis) is a GNU (General Public License) tool that contains a collection of libraries with machine learning algorithms oriented data mining.

## 3   Predicting Future Behavior

As a result of a preliminary analysis of the data is known that the products most widely accepted are Carrot, Tree Tomato and Broccoli, the vegetable called carrot (Fig. 1), is the one with the largest trading volume in the period 2014, so the particular analysis of this product is performed by applying a time series that allows us to analyze their behavior in the future.

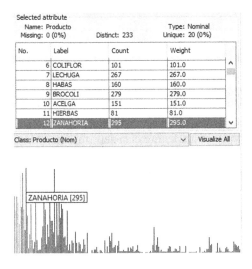

**Fig. 1.** Preliminary data analysis

## 3.1 Initial Data Preprocess

Extracting corresponding carrot vegetable for each month of 2014 information is made, the set also result verification is performed, eliminating incomplete information, and standardizing the word carrot (Fig. 2).

```
ArtificialTimeIndex*Lag_VOLUMEN DE PRODUCTO VENDIDO-9
ArtificialTimeIndex*Lag_VOLUMEN DE PRODUCTO VENDIDO-10
ArtificialTimeIndex*Lag_VOLUMEN DE PRODUCTO VENDIDO-11
ArtificialTimeIndex*Lag_VOLUMEN DE PRODUCTO VENDIDO-12

-------------------------------------------------------
The following training instances had missing values
imputed via interpolation. Check source data as
this may affect forecasting performance:

    51,98,99,111,131,153,155,157
-------------------------------------------------------

VOLUMEN DE PRODUCTO VENDIDO:
SMOreg

weights (not support vectors):
    -      0.0144 * (normalized) ArtificialTimeIndex
    +      0.0903 * (normalized) Lag_VOLUMEN DE PRODUCTO VENDIDO-1
    +      0.1504 * (normalized) Lag_VOLUMEN DE PRODUCTO VENDIDO-2
    -      0.0219 * (normalized) Lag_VOLUMEN DE PRODUCTO VENDIDO-3
    -      0.005  * (normalized) Lag_VOLUMEN DE PRODUCTO VENDIDO-4
```

**Fig. 2.** Data extraction for target variable

These consolidated monthly under the carrot conditioning, data are placed in a CSV type structure that allows recognition by the Weka software, however it is not possible to define a structure accepted date, which proceeds to generate a file with ".arff", own format of the tool directly manipulating its structure in defining attributes in Fig. 3.

```
 1   @relation consolidado2014zanahoria
 2
 3   @attribute Producto {Zanahoria}
 4   @attribute Mes date yyyy-MM-dd
 5   @attribute Valor numeric
 6
 7   @data
 8   Zanahoria,2014-01-01,156
 9   Zanahoria,2014-02-01,106
10   Zanahoria,2014-03-01,211
11   Zanahoria,2014-04-01,173.5
12   Zanahoria,2014-05-01,97
13   Zanahoria,2014-06-01,305.25
14   Zanahoria,2014-07-01,265.25
15   Zanahoria,2014-08-01,398.75
16   Zanahoria,2014-09-01,169.5
17   Zanahoria,2014-10-01,197
18   Zanahoria,2014-11-01,270.75
19   Zanahoria,2014-12-01,169.5
20
```

**Fig. 3.** Attributes in prepared data file

Applying the algorithms SMOReg (support vector machine for regression) of the Weka tool with default settings, are looking to find future behavior of this particular element, using data from January to December 2014 (Fig. 4).

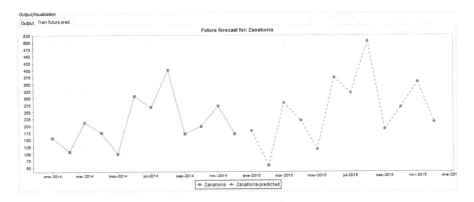

**Fig. 4.** Data series forecasging

Using the same methodology the .arff file is set for the three most required products Carrot Tree Tomato, Broccoli, making a projection under the same parameters of the previous case obtaining the following projections Fig. 5.

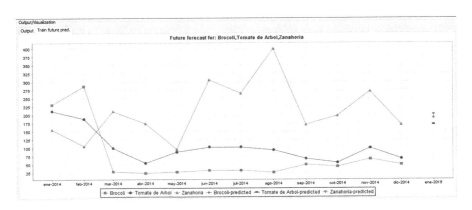

**Fig. 5.** Projections for the three products

## 3.2   Results Obtained

The data used in this study were collected sequentially throughout 2014, in Ecuador's Andean region of Chimborazo and Tunhuragua as a result of the direct marketing of agricultural producers in marketing circuits named as fairs, which are specific places where a group of producers usually meet once a week for marketing.

Selection was based on the number of occurrences of the sample elements, they are: carrot (Daucus carota), tree tomato (Solanum beta-Ceumar) and broccoli (Brassica oleracea italics).

When performing a linear projection of each element the obtained slopes are the following: For the sample of carrot slope of the straight line connecting the start point with the endpoint is 1.5, for the tree tomato the slope is -13.04 to -16.45 broccoli slope.

Therefore, the trend of the samples are positive for growing carrots and negative for other elements.

The amount of data analyzed does not allow clearly finding components of seasonality and randomness, even though the first two samples for elements tree tomato and broccoli can be a strong tendency for existing a random element that allows different behavior with respect to the rest of the samples in the following months.

Although the sample does not allow a conclusive view periodicity may be mentioned the hypothesis that for the period from March to October there is a seasonality in the marketing of all products.

Using the algorithm for predicting future behavior we can see that the original trend continues and for a projection to 12 months and a fall in demand for products such as tree tomatoes and broccoli could be anticipated (Fig. 6).

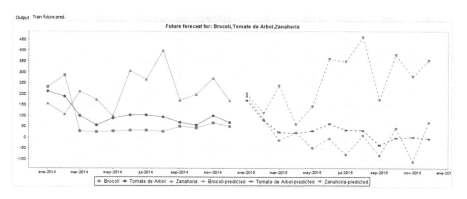

**Fig. 6.** Data prediction for all products

# 4    Products Association Rules

The second part of this research is related to the prediction of products to be marketed taking into account which products are purchased together.

To address this issue the association rules available in the Weka environment is used. The data set used corresponds to the months of January to June 2014.

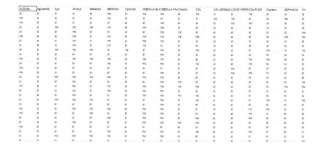

**Fig. 7.** Si/No data value

Initially the information is processed using variables 'si' ('yes') to identify a product sold and 'no' to the opposite case Fig. 7.

Each column identifies an item and each row indicates the transaction is done with this element.

The matrix on which testing is performed association had 63 items and 130 transactions, shown in Fig. 8 .

**Fig. 8.** Validated information

**Fig. 9.** Definition of parameters.

Using the characteristics of Apriori algorithm to find association rules between products using the 'Confidence' parameter with a minimum value of 0.9 the minsup (sup = number of times an item appears /number of transactions recorded) in 0.1 and in 1.0 maxsup (Fig. 9).

It was found that having a populated matrix with elements that indicate that the acquisition of an item was not completed, the rules that comply with the values set for minsup (support) most likely to find are related to the 'no' as it can be seen in Fig. 10.

**Fig. 10.** First Rules 'no' option

The result did not make a contribution to the task of finding interesting relationships between products purchased rules, so that a change is proposed in the structure of.arff file, using the unknown value ('?') property.

A new structure by first defining the file header, each of the items as a label that can support a value t if a product is purchased, otherwise the sign is used '?' is created to indicate that a product is not purchased, Fig. 11.

```
 1   @relation enerojuniotransraeng
 2
 3   @attribute 'ACELGA' { t}
 4   @attribute 'Aguacate' { t}
 5   @attribute 'Ajo' { t}
 6   @attribute 'Arveja' { t}
 7   @attribute 'Babacos' { t}
 8   @attribute 'BROCOLI' { t}
 9   @attribute 'Camote' { t}
10   @attribute 'CEBOLLA BLANCA' { t}
11   @attribute 'CEBOLLA PAITEÑA' { t}
12   @attribute 'Choclo' { t}
13   @attribute 'COL' { t}
14   @attribute 'COL MORADA' { t}
15   @attribute 'COLES VERDE' { t}
```

**Fig. 11.** New file structure

The above process is again running for Apriori association rules algorithm under the same parameters of minimum support finding interesting association rules for product sales Fig. 12.

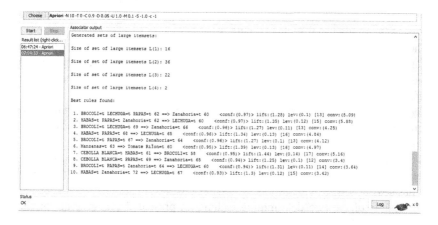

**Fig. 12.** Rules obtained using the variable 't'

Using the following values for Apriori algorithm metrics:

leverage = Probability (L, R) -Probability (L).Probability(R)

is advisable to use values greater than 0 which indicates the number of covered above expected cases and metrics lift use values greater than 1 indicates that the appearance of two products together in a transaction is due to a relationship and not by chance

Using lift > 2.7 are the following results (Fig. 13).

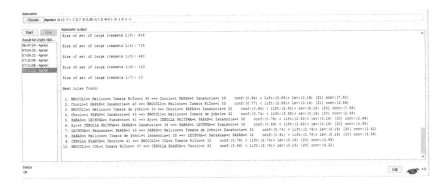

**Fig. 13.** Interesting rules generated

## 5 Conclusions

The information provided has an average level of quality, finding errors that can be easily removed using standardization in income through the development of an information system oriented to data capture.

The most important products found in the sample correspond to carrots, tomatoes and broccoli tree; that is related to the cultivation of products in small tracts of land, made by hand.

The linear trend obtained by joining the start and end point of the product carrot, calculating its slope coincides with the time series and the projections made using the libraries of the mining tool Weka 3.7 data.

The projections obtained allow establishing future behavioral trends for the specific case of the three products: carrots, broccoli and tree tomato. It is necessary to establish policies that help improving the process of production and marketing in the Ecuadorian Andes.

The sale of products that have a negative trend indicates that this would not be an attractive activity for profit considering risks. It would be convenient the design of policies to improve the quality of products and their marketing.

With the definition of association rules in marketing products, it has defined a set of interesting rules that can be used to improve marketing strategies and improve profitability in sales.

The results of the two data mining techniques presented can generate predictive information which can be used as support for marketing products using alternative marketing channels.

**Acknowledgements.** This work was supported in part by Project MINECO TEC2014-57022-C2-2-R and by Commercial Coordination Network, Ministry of Agriculture, Livestock, Aquaculture and Fisheries Ecuador.

# References

1. Hidalgo, F., Lacroix, P., Roman, P. (eds.): Comercialización y Soberanía Alimentaria. Taller Gráfico, Quito (2013)
2. Heifer International: La agroecología está presente. Fundación Heifer Ecuador, Quito (2014)
3. Nyéléni 2007: Foro para la Soberanía Alimentaría. 23–27 de Febrero de 2007, Sélingué. Mali, 27 de febrero de 2007 Obtenido de. http://www.nyeleni.org/spip.php?article291
4. Waikato, U. O.: From Machine Learning Group at the University of Waikato, 15 Jan 2016. http://www.cs.waikato.ac.nz/ml/weka/
5. Pérez, J. L.: La Estadística: Una orquesta hecha instrumento Curso de Estadística. From analisis-de-series-temporales, 15 de 01 de 2016
6. Análisis de Datos en WEKA, Obtenido de Análisis de Datos en WEKA: 2 de Marzo de 2016. http://isa.umh.es/asignaturas/crss/turorialWEKA.pdf
7. Carlos, C. J., Fernando, B.: Sistemas Inteligentes de Gestión, 2 de Marzo de 2016, Obtenido de. http://elvex.ugr.es/decsai/intelligent/workbook/D2%20Association.pdf
8. Claudia, J. R. (s.f.). Reglas de Asociacion, Obtenido de. https://tecaprendizajeest.wikispaces.com/file/view/reglas+de+asociaci%C3%B3n.pdf
9. Ramírez, J. H.: Introducción al Weka, Obtenido de. http://users.dsic.upv.es/~jorallo/docent/doctorat/weka.pdf, 02 de Marzo de 2016

# An Intelligent Agent-Based Journalism Platform

Alberto L. Barriuso[✉], Fernando de La Prieta, Álvaro Lozano Murciego,
Daniel Hernández, and Jorge Revuelta Herrero

Department of Computer Science and Automation Control, University of Salamanca,
Plaza de Los Caídos s/n, 37008 Salamanca, Spain
{albarriuso,fer,loza,danihiglesias,jrevuelta}@usal.es

**Abstract.** Internet upswing has entailed a structural change for journalism in general and the press in particular. The emergence of a new horizontal, low cost and accessible space for communication, has brought profound changes in journalism, both on the production and distribution. In this paper, we present a novel agent-based social platform which aims to improve the organization, management and distribution of the media contents through the application of artificial intelligence techniques.

**Keywords:** Journalism · Multi-agent systems · Cloud computing

## 1   Introduction

The concept of journalism, as well as the role of communicators, is rapidly changing due to the vertiginous progress of technology. By cause of this progress, this profession is being framed in a new context that integrates a novel set of elements that diametrically change the way of work. The tools which have been used by the media (online newspapers, television and radio websites, etc.) up to now, have a classical structure, which has been inherited from the last century. Usually, there are different levels of hierarchy in the treatment of information before it is published (collaborators, correspondents, writers, editors, etc.). However, these archaic procedures, which were effective time ago, do not allow to manage information in a flexible way, with the promptitude which is demanded by users.

In this situation, we must not forget that the traditional business model of communication is bound to its end due to the low demand of traditional media: online newspapers against the press, radios on the Internet at the expense of traditional radios, online television and digital terrestrial television, availability of information in real time through social networks, etc. Today, there is a change in the consumption patterns of printed newspapers, with a continuous reduction due to the introduction of new technologies. This fact joins other fact: online newspapers must not only compete with other web media, but also with other online news providers [10].

The main challenge for media groups is to put at the disposal of their employees the technical tools that enable newspaper industry professionals to address the new communication models, allowing them to response the low publication time requirements

© Springer International Publishing Switzerland 2016
J. Bajo et al. (Eds.): PAAMS 2016 Workshops, CCIS 616, pp. 322–332, 2016.
DOI: 10.1007/978-3-319-39387-2_27

demanded by society, and providing the tools that enable new business models to make the online media profitable.

Since there are currently no integral and dynamic multichannel information management tools, the main objective of this platform consists in responding to this demand in the telecommunications sector, by developing an effective platform to organize and manage with-held generating media (written information, photographs, videos, audio, graphics, etc.) holistically.

Thus, this platform is divided into three technological pillars: a new Communication model based on Social Computing, Cloud Computing and Artificial Intelligence. First, it is developed a model for effective communication, capable of receiving information from multiple heterogeneous sources, allow to the journalism to work in collaboration with the tools, and then publish on different platforms. Second, the deployment in a cloud computing environment that allows to address the needs of scalable computing (persistence, communication, etc.), offering applications through a web platform and multi-device environment, allowing to apply a pay per use business model. Finally, it makes use of Artificial Intelligence techniques, such as multi-agent systems to model and govern the platform, developing algorithms that can be used by these agents to manage and capture information from heterogeneous data sources.

Given the characteristics of dynamism on the platform environment, the use of organizational MAS (Multi-agent sytem) is proposed, following the approach proposed by the Virtual Organizations (VO) of agents. GORMAS (Guidelines for Organization-based MultiAgent Systems) [2] is chosen as the design methodology, allowing to model an open-MAS system. This agents include different techniques to improve the capabilities of the platform (recommendation, web mining, etc.). Regarding the Cloud Computing (CC) environment, it was decided to use an existing platform. In this sense, the OpenStack platform [9] is selected as the deployment environment. This platform allows both to display the set of components, as well as the integration of all the MAS components. In short, the combination of both the MAS technology and the Cloud Computing paradigm, allows to model an intelligent platform for journalism with advanced capabilities.

This paper is organized as follows. In the following section the main architecture concepts are described, and in Sect. 3 the proposed architecture model is described. In Sect. 4 the Case study is presented, and Sect. 5 presents the conclusions of this work.

# 2 Architecture Concepts

Throughout this section, we analyze the key technologies to be used in the platform. Starting from this analysis of the state of the art, it is necessary to take stock of the following steps on the development of the platform.

## 2.1 Artificial Societies and Virtual Organizations of Agents

Artificial societies and VO are closely related terms, along this section, the relationship between these concepts will be clarified, according to the existing literature. First, the concept of artificial society is introduced, which has been previously defined by a wide variety of authors [4]. For instance, [3] formally characterize an artificial society according a set of agents, restrictions in the society, a communication language, the roles that agents can develop, and the joint owners of the agents. Nevertheless, the most accurate definition, from our point of view, is the one proposed by Annunziato *et* Pierucci [1]: *An artificial society is defined as a set of interrelated and interacting artificial entities, which are governed by certain rules and conditions.*

Within literature, Davidsson et Johansson [4] propose a classification of artificial societies based on (i) openness, which is the possibility that an agent can join the society; (ii) flexibility, indicating the restriction degree that the agent has, regarding its behavior according to the rules of the society; (iii) stability, which is a measure of predictability of its actions and, finally, (iv) reliance, which measures the degree to which the agent can rely on the society.

Once the concept of artificial society has been defined, the organization concept can be seen as a set of entities which are regulated by social mechanisms, so this entities try to achieve common goals. As with corporations, there is a wide variety of literature on agent organizations [5] or [12]. However, from our point of view, the best way to define an organization of agents is attending to its characteristics [5]: (i) an organization is made up of agents (individual) who express their behavior; (ii) the organization can be divided into organizations that may be overlapped (sub-organizations or groups); (iii) the agents' behavior is functionally related to the organization as a whole, defining its functionality as a role to have within the organization; (iv) agents relate each other dynamically; (v) the types of behavior are related by links between roles, tasks and protocols.

Among these features, the key concept is role, which is an abstract description of the agents' behavior, including obligations, restrictions and skills. Likewise, the role must include a description of the interaction patterns between the different actors in the system.

## 2.2   Cloud Computing

The CC concept has been strengthening both at the enterprise level, as in the research field. For this reason, many definitions have emerged [ 6, 8, 11]. In each definition, authors try to highlight those features which, in his opinion, are most relevant. At the end of 2011, NIST (National Institute of Standards and Technology) [7], proposes a very accurate definition from a technical and functional point of view: *Cloud computing is a model for enabling ubiquitous, convenient, on-demand network access to a shared pool of configurable computing resources (e.g., networks, servers, storage, applications, and services) that can be rapidly provisioned and released with minimal management effort or service provider interaction. This cloud model is composed of five essential characteristics, three service models, and four deployment models.*

In addition, this definition includes 5 mandatory features that any CC environment should have: (i) **automatic on-demand services**, which must be provided automatically, according to the demand, without human interaction; (ii) **availability of services through the network**, customers must access services through the network, and therefore, suppliers must use this mean to provide their services; (iii) **availability of resources,** the provider must have the ability to offer services regardless the demand, reassigning physical or virtual hardware resources dynamically to each service according to demand; (iv) **elasticity,** different resources must be provided elastically and even automatically depending on demand; (v) **tailored services**, provided services must be fully monitored, being the control tasks performed automatically.

As stated above, a CC platform that provides computational support to deploy all the platform components is necessary. As a basis of this platform, we use OpenStack [9], a Project founded by Rackspace Hosting and NASA in July 2010, which aims to create a free and open-source software platform to create private and public Cloud infrastructures.

# 3   Proposed Platform

To design a platform with the proposed features using traditional software design techniques would be very complex, which would entail a lot of time, and would give uncertain results. Therefore, it was decided to use an innovative design model, based on VO of intelligent agents.

Overall, this platform aims to solve a wide variety of needs of the media: the dynamic and standardized management of information distributed in digital format, automatic layout and organization of the information, dissemination of information via web portals–accessible from any device, regardless of time and place–, agile content management, or 'pay-per-use' features.

In Sect. 3.1 we present the design and components of the MAS, and in Sect. 3.1, the design of the cloud computing platform is described.

## 3.1   The Proposed Multi-agent Model

As stated before, to design the MAS model, GORMAS has been chosen as methodology. Following the phases of GORMAS design methodology, an analysis of the motivation pursued by the organization is done, in order to define the organization (e.g. the reason for the existence of the organization). As the results that are expected to achieve, the environment in which the MAS exists, is defined, detailing the products and/or services which the organization offers, what the groups of interest are, as well as their location. We can see the result of analysis of the organization mission in Fig. 1.

The **mission** of the organization is to minimize the tasks to be performed by the users (in terms of management and production of the information) and maximize the quality of services offered to readers. Overall, the system offers two basic **products**: a *platform management* environment and *news*. The *platform management environment* includes a set of services which are aimed to be used by the workers of media companies, so they can manage the underlying platform as the content to be subsequently disseminated. The *news product* represents both the content and services that end users (readers) consume.

First, the interface agents that perform management tasks in the management environment platform, and tasks within the newspaper views and statistics tool are described:

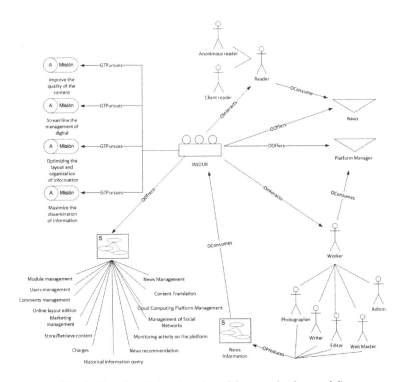

**Fig. 1.** Functional view (mission of the organization model)

- **Users Manager**: Manages the access to the platform, allowing to create and delete users, as well as defining different access levels to the services offered by the platform.
- **News Manager**: Is responsible to provide a range of services that allow you manage information relating to news, including searching, editing and deleting of news, and the inclusion of any additional content managed in other modules, such as videos, images, maps or comments.
- **Gallery Manager**: Manages galleries, which subsequently allows the inclusion of multimedia content in the news.
    Modules Manager: It allows you to manage additional content that may be associated with the news. It can be of different types, such as static HTML content, surveys, videos or maps.
- **News Archive Manager**: It is the role responsible for controlling the retrieval of information from the historical record news. This archive service will enable to retrieve news from two separate databases, a document-oriented one which keeps a record of the previous ten years, and another one with the latest news.
- **Payment Manager**: It is the role entrusted to manage payments of the reader's subscriptions. Every report has a specific value associated to it, and every access to this content by the user is recorded, so the calculation of the price to pay for the use of the platform is calculated based on this. Once calculated, the agent receives a payment order, so the payment can be performed through a gateway.

In addition to the above agents, we have developed a set of independent agents who make use of techniques, tools and advanced features. The design and development of these agents is the basis of the functional algorithms of the platform.

- **Comments Manager:** It provides the necessary services to manage the user's comments on the different news. It allows to certain users within the system to determine which comments are published, providing a supervised publishing process. Beside of this services, it also includes a service which will provide an automatic publishing process for the comments, as the result of the analysis of the comments polarity.
- **Content retrieval agent:** Agent in charge, on the one hand, to extract news from a predefined list of media, and on the other, to perform a recovery process of the extracted news. This is done with two objectives: the recommendation of news from other media, and the analysis of possible content that may be plagiarism of contents generated by the media.

  The news extraction process begins Reading the RSS feeds from the defined media, from which several features are extracted, as the deadline, date of publication or the URL of the full content. Since through the RSS, the body of the new is not available, it has been necessary to implement crawlers to extract this information from the URL.

  After getting the news, an XML document is generated for each news item and stored in a directory on which the index of the documents contained in the directory is created using Apache Lucene[1]. Any software agent may use a search service by specifying query terms to be searched using this index, obtaining a JSON response with all the information about the obtained news items.
- **Recommendation provider**: This role implements the web mining process through which content recommendations are made, in response to user interactions with the system. The development of this recommender system is based on **Apache Mahout**[2]. In this case, we do not have explicit ratings from the users. The used algorithm is within the group of user-based collaborative filtering algorithms, whose similarity model is based on a *Tanimoto coefficient ratio*,–**Eq.** (1)-., which, given two sets, A and B, with common elements, is expressed as ratio of items that match in both sets, and the total elements of both sets:

$$T_c = \frac{K_{11}}{(K_{01} + K_{10} + K_{11})} \tag{1}$$

Where $K_{11}$ is the total amount of elements which are shared by both sets, $K_{01}$ the number of elements which belong to B but not to A, and $K_{10}$ the number of elements which belong to A but not to B.

- **Marketing manager**: This agent is a component that offers its services to the Online Journal application, which can generate useful information for positioning the

---

[1] Apache Lucene library: https://lucene.apache.org/core/.
[2] Apache Mahout project: http://mahout.apache.org/.

different media websites. To do this, this agent makes use of rich snippets, a schema.org convention of the three major search engines (Google, Bing and Yahoo) to label the contents of the websites and facilitate search results.

The service offered by this agent allows digital publications pages to be indexed easily, thus presenting better quality search results, and making them better positioned and more attractive.

- **Translation provider:** It is the role responsible for providing translation services. Agents that use this services will indicate the text, the language of the text and the language that is to be translated, obtaining the translated text in response to the specified language. The process of translating the texts is done through to the Languaje Grid[3] project API, which builds on the concept of Language Grid [7]. As a result, the content generated by journalists will be automatically translated into different languages.

- **Storage Manager:** This role is responsible for integrating the persistent information with the cloud computing platform. The managed information may have a different nature, as it handles both content stored in the database as multimedia content.

  Data storage, both database and multimedia data, is distributed on different machines of the cloud computing platform, so this role will manage the distribution of these data in the corresponding machines, always offering the same communication methods to the other agents, so they can access transparently, regardless of possible changes in the way in which the information remains in the underlying infrastructure.

- **Cloud Manager:** This role is responsible for controlling the cloud computing infrastructure on which operates the platform, allowing: managing computing resources, establish a scalable, and redundant storage system, define the topology of the network through which the different nodes that make up the base infrastructure communicate, or managing cloud computing users who have access to the functionality offered by the cloud manager.

- **Monitoring agent:** This role examines the different behavior of the agents involved users on the platform in order to carry out an analysis of the processes taking place in the organization. It also provides a set of visualization tools to provide all this information to the cloud computing managers.

### 3.2  Cloud Computing Platform

This section describes the design of the cloud computing platform that will give computational and deployment support to the components of the platform. As a basis for this platform, an OpenStack based environment has been selected. The objective of this platform is:

- Developing an infrastructure that allows the deployment of virtual servers on demand.

---

[3] Language Grid project: http://langrid.org/en/index.html.

- Ensuring growth or scalability possibilities through the architectural design and the employed technologies. Thus, by increasing the hardware resources, more virtual machines can be supported, so that they make use of higher processing and storage possibilities.

The initial version of the platform will have four nodes: a controller node and three computing nodes. According to the design of the CC platform, Fig. 2 shows all the services or components that will are installed within each node of the cloud platform, as well as the network interfaces used by each node.

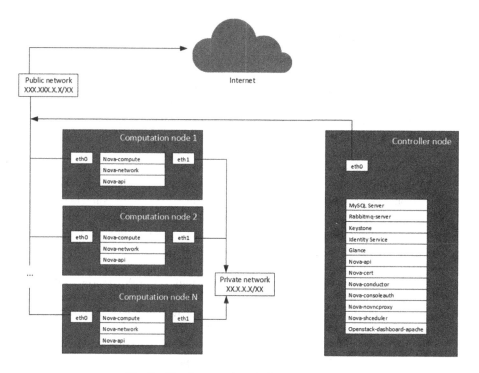

**Fig. 2.** Cloud computing platform components

In relation to the multi-agent system, the different agents that compose it are distributed in the three computation nodes:

- **Computation node 1–*database server*-:** storage manager and database manager.
- **Computation node 2–*backend server*-:** user manager, news archive manager, modules manager, content retrieval agent, news manager, gallery manager, monitoring agent and social media manager.
- **Computation node 3–*front-end server*-:** comments manager, payment manager, recommendation provider.

## 4   Case Study, Preliminary Results

The presented platform was tested on a Spanish media group, *Promecal*, which gathers various newspapers, both on printed and online editions, such as *Diario de Burgos, Diario Palentino.or Diario de Ávila*. This experimental phase aims to validate: (i) the proper operation of the platform; (ii) the ability of the VO to model a human organization, by defining roles, tasks and restrictions; (iii) the correct operation of the CC platform that supports the platform; (iv) the integration of the different components; (v) the scalability possibilities of the whole platform.

In order to perform this validation, an experimental deployment phase has been performed, dividing it into two stages.

- The first stage is a set-up of the platform for *Diario de Burgos* online edition, where a group of three journalists, two photographers, two editors, one webmaster and one administrator have used the different components of the management platform, which embraces the inclusion of new contents on the platform, the edition and layout of the news information, the publishing process, and the final generation of the online newspaper web content.
- Once the operation and integration of the different elements has been proved, a second stage of validation is performed. This stage is focused on validating the scalability of the platform. For that purpose, the number of computational nodes has been duplicated, from the three initial nodes, to a total amount of six. At this point, the platform gives support to the whole set of newspapers of the media group, including: *La Tribuna de Albacete, Diario de Ávila, Diario de Burgos, La Tribuna de Ciudad Real, Diario Palentino, El Adelantado de Segovia, La Tribuna de Cuenca, La Tribuna de Toledo and El Día de Valladolid.*

At this point, besides a tenfold increase of the number of workers who have access to the management tool, a set of users have also had access to the online newspaper edition, through the client user role, so the comments manager and the recommendation provider performance could also have been tested.

In the case of the recommendation system, we have used the activity registered on the production websites of the different newspapers, so we had a valid binary dataset to be used by the recommender system, where two user-based similitude metrics were compared: *Log Likelihood* and *Tanimoto,* being *Tanimoto* the one which presented a lower error when providing recommendations, as shown in Table 1, which presents the Mean Absolute Error (MAE) and Root Mean Square Error (RMSE).

**Table 1.**   Result of the errors: MAE and RMSE

| Algorithm | MAE | RMSE |
|---|---|---|
| UserBasedTanimotoCoefficient | 0.4836 | 0.6802 |
| UserBasedLogLikelihoodRatio | 0.5792 | 0.8373 |

# 5 Conclusions

Internet has been a structural change for journalism in general and the press in particular. The emergence of a new horizontal, low cost and accessible space for communication, has brought profound changes in journalism, not only on the production of information materials, distribution and management of companies, but also on how they are produced, edited and how they disseminate their own information.

In this context, and more particularly in the last decade, employers and workers have intensified efforts to adapt themselves to the new scenario, using Internet and the tools and applications that arise in their environment to improve his position and regain that space of privilege in the information context.

In conclusion at the development of platform, it has led to the development of an innovative functional prototype, with a high technological component that improves the operational capacities of the different companies of media, within the introduced context, that provides a technical solution which is very close to the needs of the media market.

**Acknowledgements.** This work is supported by the European Social Fund (Operational Programme 2014-2020 for Castilla y León, EDU/128/2015 BOCYL).

# References

1. Annunziato, M., Pierucci, P.: The emergence of social learning in artificial societies. In: Cagnoni, S. (ed.) AOSE 2008. LNCS, vol. 2611, pp. 467–478. Springer, Heidelberg (2003)
2. Argente, E., Julian, V., Botti, V.: MAS modeling based on organizations. In: Luck, M., Gomez-Sanz, J.J. (eds.) AOSE 2008. LNCS, vol. 5386, pp. 16–30. Springer, Heidelberg (2009)
3. Artikis, A., Kamara, L., Pitt, J.: Towards an open agent society model and animation. In: Proceedings of the Agent-Based Simulation II workshop, Passau, pp. 48–55 (2001)
4. Davidsson, P., Johansson, S.: On the potential of norm-governed behavior in different categories of artificial societies. Comput. Math. Organ. Theor. **12**(2–3), 169–180 (2006)
5. Ferber, J., Gutknecht, O., Michel, F.: From agents to organizations: an organizational view of multi-agent systems. In: Giorgini, P., Müller, J.P., Odell, J.J. (eds.) AOSE 2003. LNCS, vol. 2935, pp. 214–230. Springer, Heidelberg (2004)
6. Foster, I., Zhao, Y., Raicu, I., Lu, S.: Cloud computing and grid computing 360-degree compared. In: Grid Computing Environments Workshop, GCE 2008, pp. 1–10. IEEE (2008)
7. Ishida, T., Nadamoto, A., Murakami, Y., Inaba, R., Shigenobu, T., Matsubara, S., Tsunokawa, E.: A non-profit operation model for the language grid. In: International Conference on Global Interoperability for Language Resources, pp. 114–121 (2008)
8. Mell, P., Grance, T.: The NIST definition of cloud computing (draft). NIST special publication, 800(145), 7 (2011)
9. OpenStack documentation page. http://docs.openstack.org/ (Accessed on 20 January 2015)
10. Rubio, J.L.: La demanda de los periódicos impresos y online: un análisis económico. Ambitos: revista internacional de comunicación **18**, 29–39 (2009)

11. Vaquero, L.M., Rodero-Merino, L., Caceres, J., Lindner, M.: A break in the clouds: towards a cloud definition. ACM SIGCOMM Comput. Commun. Rev. **39**(1), 50–55 (2008)
12. Wooldridge, M., Jennings, N.R., Kinny, D.: The Gaia methodology for agent-oriented analysis and design. Auton. Agent. Multi-Agent Syst. **3**(3), 285–312 (2000)

# Belief-Based Argumentation in Intelligence Analysis and Decision Making

James Llinas[✉] and Galina Rogova

State University of New York at Buffalo, Buffalo, NY, USA
{llinas,rogova}@buffalo.edu

**Abstract.** This paper asserts that a multi-perspective viewpoint must be taken in the design of a computational system support capability for decision-making. We offer views from a Decision-Science slant, a Systemic Architectural view, and the need for technological support to realize improvements in analytical rigor. We have been researching and evolving the design of an analysis tool framework exploiting the hybrid concepts of a Belief-based Argumentation and Story-based subsystem. The notion of rigor, defined as a quality measure on the reasoning/analysis process, is one overarching principle of our approach, driven by the need for the associated analysis/decision-support product quality that complex modern problems demand. Our approach to the design of a mixed-initiative analysis tool is highly multidisciplinary and has taken account of an exhaustive review of the relevant literature along each viewpoint.

**Keywords:** Decision support · Transferable belief model · Defeasible argumentation · Sequential decision making · Story telling

## 1 Introduction

The fields of Intelligence Analysis and associated Decision-Making have, in the last twenty years, become extraordinarily more complicated and demanding. There are many reasons for this evolution in complexity, such as the nature of conflict that has become asymmetric and of a counterinsurgency and/or terrorism-based framework with no clearly identifiable adversaries and much higher risks of collateral damage. Additional complications arise from the clever employment of both sophisticated and consumer technologies, and importantly the considerably difficult issue of understanding a wide range of socio-political contexts.

Overall, we call these types of problems "weak knowledge" problems because the ability to construct procedural, dynamic models of expected adversarial behaviors based on prior knowledge is so difficult; even the utility of doing so can be questioned, since adversaries have demonstrated that they change their "TTP's" (Tactics, Techniques, and Procedures) at a high rate of frequency that can confound such attempts at modeling. In the face of these difficulties, many modern toolkits designed to provide system support for analysis and decision-making are made up of sets of disparate tools, each of some utility for helping to produce pointed, but limited-scope hypotheses (we call these "situational fragments"). However, such system support designs are of little help toward

© Springer International Publishing Switzerland 2016
J. Bajo et al. (Eds.): PAAMS 2016 Workshops, CCIS 616, pp. 333–340, 2016.
DOI: 10.1007/978-3-319-39387-2_28

supporting the formation of synthesized or fused hypotheses, leading to a holistic, situational or story/narrative type understanding that is usually required to aid in decision-making.

This paper presents a mixed initiative approach to hypothesis nomination and integration, aiding a decision maker in detecting and identifying potential and imminent threat situations with higher confidence and reduced cognitive workload. This data-fusion-based human-machine threat recognition approach described in this paper combines story-based argumentation [1], the Transferable Belief Model (TBM) [2] for belief management, decision fusion, and anytime decision making [3].

We combine the story and argumentation based approaches following the suggestions of Bex in [1]. This approach exploits the advantages of an argument-based approach that is: (1) based on simple principles of reasoning (2) makes the generalizations and the evidence explicit in the arguments, and (3) allows the reasoning from the evidence to a conclusion to be easy to follow. However, one disadvantage of the argument-based approach is that it does not provide a complete overview of the situation, as the narrative-type structure describing "what happened" is distributed among the specific conclusions of different arguments and counter-arguments. In the combined argument/story approach, the stories are represented as networks of causally linked events and provide a basis to form a more holistic understanding and a path to constructing an evidentially-grounded narrative understanding, which is the typical requirement for the product of intelligence analysis.

The TBM is a two-level model in which quantified beliefs in hypotheses about an object or state of the environment are represented and combined at the credal level while decisions are made based on probabilities obtained from the combined belief formed by the pignistic transformation [2]. We choose the TBM since it has several advantages for reasoning about threats in the uncertain environment. First, in the uncertain threat environment incoming information is usually unique and a probability function characterizing this information is rarely available. Second, unexpected or even unimaginable ("Black Swan") situations can arise and therefore a set of hypotheses under consideration may not be exhaustive. Beliefs represented in the TBM "do not ask for explicit underlying probability functions" [2]. They are sub-additive, which permits numerical expressions of uncertainty and ignorance. Within the TBM, the unnormalized Dempster rule can combine basic belief masses based on multiple pieces of evidence, and allow for incorporation of belief reliability. Importantly, the TBM works under the open world assumption, i.e. it does not assume that the set of hypotheses under consideration is exhaustive. These properties of the TBM have been successfully exploited in uncertain reasoning and are considered very appropriate for the open-world domain of intelligence analysis.

We see anytime decision making models as necessary because they allow the quality of results to improve gradually as more observations are available. They offer a tradeoff between time and decision quality [3] for those situations that require timely decisions and swift actions. Incorporation of the anytime decision making provides for the decision quality control by weighing time and hypothesis credibility.

Argumentation is recognized in the literature as a promising method for defeasible reasoning with vague, inconsistent, and incomplete knowledge and evidence, and has been used in multiple domains as a decision aid tool. It is based on the construction, combination and comparison of arguments for and against certain hypotheses. The majority of argumentation-based methods utilize a deterministic formal logic and theorem proof, and the notion of argument acceptance and attack (see, e.g. [4]). However this type of argumentation doesn't address the issue of finding/discovering arguments, identifying attacks, and exploiting premises shared by different arguments [5]. In general, abstract argumentation is "a tool for analyzing particular argumentation systems and for developing a meta-theory of such systems, and not a formalism for directly representing argumentation-based inference" [4]. An exhaustive review of the domain of computational support to argumentation showed that the logic-based automatic argumentation scheme has several drawbacks as applied to the problem of threat assessment. The authors of [5] introduced a probabilistic extension of Dung's argumentation framework by assigning probabilities to arguments and defeats. This framework enables deduction of a set of justified arguments and the computation of the likelihood of these arguments being compatible with respect to the other arguments, defeats and probabilities which make up the framework. This framework can be applied to the problem of coalition formation as well as incorporating considerations of trust and reputation but requires the knowledge of a priori probabilities of arguments and defeats. A combination of logic and belief theories for argumentation under uncertainty is also considered in [6, 7] but these models require a known knowledge base, which does not exist in an open world context of threat assessment.

While most pure argument-based approaches to analyzing an information stream are deductive and support or reject a certain hypothesis, a system supporting an analyst in threat detection and evaluation requires an understanding of "what happened" based on the evidence (abduction); that is, a robust approach must consider hypothetical situations. The most promising approach introduced in [1] is an abstract argumentation approach including stories, in which hypothetical "causal stories are hypothesized to explain the evidence, after which these stories can be supported and attacked using evidential arguments." However, the major drawback of this theory is that it does not explicitly incorporate credibility associated with the information representing these pieces of stories and reliability, nor are truthfulness or pedigree of the source of these data and information considered. The approach proposed in this research is an extension of [8], which represents a strategy to overcome these drawbacks of existing argumentation models and associated computational support prototypes by incorporating uncertainty and provenance into the story-based hybrid argumentation.

## 2 Perspectives on Design for System Support

An effective approach to architecting our proposed decision-support concept requires that we assert our views of the overall reasoning process from evidence to decisionmaking and decision enablement. Most traditional characterizations describe decision-making (DM) as contemplative, analytic, involving nomination and evaluation of options that are weighed in some context, eventually leading to a choice of a "course of action (COA)". This model, often labeled as the "System 2" model, can be seen in most descriptions of the "Military Decision-Making Process" or MDMP as for example in published military Field

Manuals such as in [9]. The literature also identifies a "System 1" or largely intuitive decision-making paradigm (IDM) that operates in conjunction with System 2 processes in what is argued to be an improved DM process model, often called the "Dual-Process Model". Most research in decision support however has focused on System 2 DM ideas since this model is quantitative and can be mathematically studied using notions of utility theory and other frameworks for mensuration. We intend however to factor the Dual-Process Model concept into our systemic design approach; the basis of this rationale cannot be elaborated here but we offer our references for the interested reader, e.g., [10, 11].

Furthermore, in our view of the System Support context for DM, we see what today are called Sensemaking processes, as lying between automated System Support capabilities such as Data Fusion processes and DM processes, in a stage wherein "final" situation assessments and understandings (in the human mind) are developed. Thus, our view of this meta-process is as a three-stage operation: System Support (SS) as an automated process that nominates algorithmically-formed situational hypotheses (such as from the combined operations of data fusion and argumentation). There is a substantive literature on Sensemaking, such as the three models of [12–14]. Our key thoughts on and rational for the meta-architecture for System Support have been summarized in [15]. Finally, in the face of significant production pressures [16] and rapidly proliferating data availability [17]—and the resulting data overload deluging the professional analyst—it is increasingly easy for analysts and decisionmakers to be trapped by shallow, low-rigor analysis. Zelik et al. [18] argue that rigor is a quality measure on the reasoning and analysis process and thus in turn they develop a viewpoint regarding the "sufficiency" of the process toward achieving rigor. In [18], eight characteristics or risks of analysis processes that exhibit poor or low rigor are defined, and by addressing each of these factors, Zelik et al. assert the analysis process properties by which the degree of rigor in analysis can be gauged. In our approach, we intend to consider these design factors such that the associated improvements are "embedded" in the SS design.

## 3   Threat Concept

The particular focus of analysis and DM chosen to motivate our work is the notion of threat detection; other analysis goals could be set but this goal is certainly related to a broad range of critical situations. Threat is a complex notion related to risk and vulnerability but most definitions/ontologies of threat define it as an integrated whole of three inter-related parts [19]: Intentions (plans, goals), Capabilities (capacities, capabilities), and Opportunities (spatio-temporal requirements to employ the Capabilities). For our purposes, we assert that the existence of three parts of threat as a whole constitutes an imminent threat, whereas the existence of any of two parts constitutes a potential threat; these are arguable but are notions acceptable to most analysts. Timely recognition of potential threats is very important since it permits appropriate action taking to prevent them from becoming imminent threats. This partitioning also allows for a straightforward design approach to argument partitioning and belief assignments, as well as belief integration.

## 4   Belief-Based Hybrid Argumentation

The argumentation-based approach proposed in this research is designed to provide the capability to support symbiotic human-machine dynamics, and defeasible abductive reasoning over uncertain heterogeneous information. The goal here is to help analysts in recognizing adversarial activity, and detecting and identifying potential and imminent threats with higher confidence and reduced cognitive workload. In evaluating arguments to corroborate or repudiate situational hypotheses, human experts need to perform real-time refinement of: (a) trust in regard to the source of information and (b) the quantitative degree of belief in arguments based on what the experts see and know. These operations may lead to the imaginative discovery of novel arguments. The decision-makers also support the process by framing queries, which gives context to the search for, and prioritization of, relevant hypotheses.

The approach presented here is a variation of the story-based model [8], in which pro and contra arguments are formed from uncertain transient information while seeing each piece of this information as an element of alternative stories (hypotheses based in part on "what might happen", i.e., on hypotheticals). Incoming information is produced by physical sensors (hard data) and/or by human sensors such as intelligence, social networks, opportunistic sensors (soft data) and may be uncertain, unreliable, or not trustworthy. The hypotheses about hypotheticals are evaluated within the framework of the TBM by assigning beliefs and reliability/trust to each evidentially based argument[1], combining these beliefs, and selecting a combined story based on the highest pignistic probability [2]. A functional diagram of this hybrid argumentation/story-based decision making process is shown in Fig. 1.

Figure 1 shows a high-level architectural depiction of our overall approach. As described earlier, this approach overtly considers the interdependencies among Data Fusion processes, Sensemaking processes, and Decision-making processes; these process-design interdependencies have been described in our paper [15]. Our approach to design also exploits our previous work in both design and prototyping of: (1) association and fusion of hard and soft data streams and named entity extraction and recognition [21], and Belief-based evidential reasoning [6]. In this approach, the Data Fusion processes that include a Relevance Filtering function and a Provenance Tracking function, yield an ensemble of validated multisource inputs that includes observational data, ("atomic") arguments (detected/extracted automatically), and named entities, among possibly other data that could include exploited contextual data. An analyst interface exists to allow analyst foraging over and interaction with the fusion process. These data and analyst-nominated stories form the foundation for assembly of belief-weighted nested arguments that collectively form the basis for narrative formation. The particular focus of this paper is in the Sensemaking process where we are currently studying and designing the prototype Story/Argumentation based analysis tool. We see the design of this tool evolving into a structure

---

[1] It is important to notice that uncertainty related to arguments based on soft and hard information are usually represented within the frameworks of the different uncertainty theories (probability, fuzzy, belief, etc.). One of the methods to deal with different uncertainty representations is to transform them to be expressed in terms of the TBM [20].

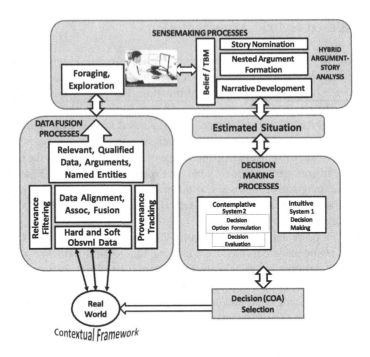

**Fig. 1.** Functional diagram of the argumentation-based decision making process

similar to the current-day CISpaces argumentation-support system, designed largely for multianalyst collaboration [22] but employing some features unique to our approach such as a Work Box that enables a mixed-initiative process for argument development and review. Most modern analysis tools are based on a design that mixes a Service Oriented Architecture (SOA) set of functional Services with an Agent-based design that executes supportive special operations such as algorithmic processes; our evolving design employs a similar approach. The result of all this processing is a situational interpretation in the form of a narrative, vetted in an evidential foundation. That situational understanding (an estimate) forms a basis for decision-making but also has to consider decision-making constraints [15]. We see the overall design approach as unique in taking this high-level view and integrating a variety of inter-process dependencies and constraints into the focal design of the Belief-based Hybrid Argumentation system.

All the processes (automatic and human-based) are supported by domain specific information, which includes, rules, statistical information, key words, arguments, a hypothesis and story library, etc. They are performed within a specific context [23] which offers expectations for hypothesis, relations, and stories as well as providing constraints for establishing relevance, thereby constraining the ontology of the domain, observations, rules, and statistics. An important part of the collection of automated processes is visualizations supporting decision makers by displaying argument and hypothesis diagrams and the verification process. The result of verification and discovery allows for augmentation of the set of supporting information.

# 5  Summary and Conclusions

We have wandered over a large, complex, and multidisciplinary landscape here, because we feel that the design of a System Support capability for Decision-Making must address the varying views of that capability as presented here. The paper has presented a mixed-initiative hybrid model of knowledge discovery capable of monitoring a dynamic environment, in which uncertain and unreliable inputs are reasoned over for recognizing human activities and predicting likely potential and imminent threats. The model is built on a hybrid framework of argumentation with stories, the Transferable Belief Models, Anytime decision making, and decision fusion. We envision a layered and phased approach toward developing a prototype of the design described here, a first version of which will still likely demand considerable human cognitive support. We are also in discussion with operational intelligence analysts and those in the operational community that are looking at realizable advanced System Support concepts so that we can strike a practical balance between long-term and mid-term prototyping goals.

**Acknowledgements.**  This paper results from research supported by the U.S. Naval Postgraduate School Assistance Grant No. N00244-15-1-0051 awarded by the NAVSUP Fleet Logistics Center SanDiego (NAVSUP FLC San Diego). The views expressed in written materials or publications, and/or made by speakers, moderators, and presenters, do not necessarily reflect the official policies of the Naval Postgraduate School nor does mention of trade names, commercial practices, or organizations imply endorsement by the U.S. Government.

# References

1. Bex, F.J.: Abductive argumentation with stories. In: ICAIL-2013 Workshop on Formal Aspects of Evidential Inference (2013)
2. Smets, P.: Data fusion in the transferable belief model. In: Proceeding of the FUSION 2000-Third Conference on Multisource- Multisensor Information Fusion, pp. 21–33 (2002)
3. Rogova, G., Hadrazagic, M., St-Hilaire, M.-O., Florea, M., Valin, P.: Context-based information quality for sequential decision making. In: Proceeding of the 2013 IEEE International Multi-Disciplinary Conference on Cognitive Methods in Situation Awareness and Decision Support (CogSIMA) (2013)
4. Simari, G., Rahwan, I.: Argumentation in Artificial Intelligence. Springer, New York (2009)
5. Li, H., Oren, N., Norman, T.J.: Probabilistic Argumentation Frameworks. In: Modgil, S., Oren, N., Toni, F. (eds.) TAFA 2011. LNCS, vol. 7132, pp. 1–16. Springer, Heidelberg (2012)
6. Rogova, G., Scott, P., Lollett, C., Mudiyanur, R.: Reasoning about situations in the early post-disaster response environment. In: Proceeding of the FUSION 2006-9th Conference on Multisource Information Fusion (2006)
7. Haenni, R., Kohlas, J., Lehmann, N.: Probabilistic Argumentation Systems. In: Kohlas, J., Moral, S. (eds.) Handbook of Defeasible Reasoning and Uncertainty Management Systems, vol. 5. Kluwer, Dordrecht (2001)
8. Rogova, G., Llinas, J., Gross, G.: Belief-based hybrid argumentation for threat assessment. In: Proceeding of the 2015 IEEE International Multi-Disciplinary Conference on Cognitive Methods in Situation Awareness and Decision Support (CogSIMA2015), March 2015
9. Headquarters, Dept of Army, Army Field Manual 5-0, The Operations Process, May 2010

10. Croskerry, P.: A universal model of diagnostic reasoning. Acad. Med. **84**(8), 1022–1028 (2009)
11. Djulbegovic, B., et al.: Dual processing model of medical decision-making. BMC Med. Inform. Decis. Mak. **12**, 94 (2012)
12. Piroli, P., Card, S.: The sensemaking process and leverage points for analyst as identified through cognitive task analysis. In: International Conference on Intelligence Analysis, McLean (2005)
13. Klein, G., Moon, B., Hoffman, R.R.: Making sense of sensemaking 2: a macrocognitive model. IEEE Intell. Syst. **21**(5), 88–92 (2006)
14. Kurtz, C.F., Snowden, D.J.: The new dynamics of strategy: Sense-making in a complex and complicated world. IBM Syst. J. **42**(3), 462–483 (2003)
15. Llinas, J.: Reexamining information fusion–decision making inter-dependencies. In: Proceeding of the IEEE Cognitive Methods in Situation Awareness and Decision Support (CogSIMA) Conference, San Antonio, March 2014
16. Johnson, R.: Analytic Culture in the US Intelligence Community: An Ethnographic Study. U.S. Government Printing Office, Washington, DC (2005)
17. Patterson, E.S., Roth, E.M., Woods, D.D.: Predicting vulnerabilities in computer-supported inferential analysis under data overload. Cogn. Technol. Work **3**, 224–237 (2001)
18. Zelik, D.J., Patterson, E.S., Woods, D.D.: Measuring attributes of rigor in information analysis. In: Patterson, E.S., Miller, J. (eds.) Macrocognition metrics and scenarios: Design and evaluation for real-world teams. Ashgate Publishers, UK (2010)
19. Little, E., Rogova, G.: An ontological analysis of threat and vulnerability. In: Proceeding of the FUSION 2006-9th Conference on Multisource Information Fusion (2006)
20. Rogova, G., Llinas, J., Yager, R.: Integration of Argumentation and fusion of soft-hard information for threat assessment. In: Proceeding of the NATO Joint Symposium on Information Fusion (Hard and Soft) For Intelligence, Surveillance & Reconnaissance (ISR)
21. Hall, D.L., Llinas, J., Nagi, R.: Information fusion and intelligence analysis with hard and soft data: findings from a five-year MURI research program. In: Proceedings of the NATO Symposium on "Information Fusion (*Hard* and *Soft*) for ISR" (IST-SET-126) (2015)
22. Toniolo, A., et al.: Supporting reasoning with different types of evidence in intelligence analysis. In: Proceedings of the 2015 International Conference on Autonomous Agents and Multiagent Systems, Istanbul, May 2015
23. Snidaro, L., Garcia, J., Llinas, J., Blasch, E., (eds.) Context-Enhanced Information Fusion. Springer, London (in press)

# Workshop on Multi-agent Based Applications for Energy Markets, Smart Grids and Sustainable Energy Systems (MASGES)

# Decentralized Coalition Formation in Agent-Based Smart Grid Applications

Jörg Bremer$^{(\boxtimes)}$ and Sebastian Lehnhoff

University of Oldenburg, 26129 Oldenburg, Germany
{joerg.bremer,sebastian.lehnhoff}@uni-oldenburg.de

**Abstract.** A steadily growing pervasion of the energy grid with communication technology is widely seen as an enabler for new computational coordination techniques for renewable, distributed generation as well as for controllable consumers. One important task is the ability to group together in order to jointly gain enough suitable flexibility and capacity to assume responsibility for a specific control task in the grid. We present a fully decentralized coalition formation approach based on an established heuristic for predictive scheduling with the additional advantage of keeping all information about local decision base and local operational constraints private. The approach is evaluated in several simulation scenarios with different type of established models for integrating distributed energy resources.

**Keywords:** Smart grid · Coalition formation · Coalition structure generation · Combinatorial heuristics

## 1 Introduction

Across Europe, especially in Germany where currently a financial security of guaranteed feed-in prices is given, the share of distributed energy resources (DER) is rapidly growing. Following the goal defined by the European Commission [11], a concept for integration into electricity markets is needed for both: active power provision and ancillary services [1,27] to reduce subsidy dependence. A well-known concept for aggregating DER to a jointly controllable entity is known as virtual power plant (VPP). Apart from controlling distributed electricity generation, e.g. combined heat and power (CHP), photovoltaic or wind power, controllable consumption like shiftable loads, heat pumps or air conditioning might also be included for planning active power schedules. Battery storages are discussed to complement such groups of DER.

Virtual power plants are a well-known means for aggregating and controlling DER [2] and integration into current market structures recently led to VPP systems that frequently re-configure themselves for a market and product-led alignment [28]. Based on the size of products from the order book (e. g. traded at a day-ahead market), coalitions of usually small energy resources have to be found that may apply for the product, as single units often do not have a sufficient power level nor the flexibility to fulfill the product alone. In scenarios

© Springer International Publishing Switzerland 2016
J. Bajo et al. (Eds.): PAAMS 2016 Workshops, CCIS 616, pp. 343–355, 2016.
DOI: 10.1007/978-3-319-39387-2_29

with self-dependently operated units that trade their power independently, consequentially self-organizing algorithms are required also for coalition formation to find potential partners specifically for the current product at hand.

In general, distributed control schemes based on multi-agent systems are considered advantageous for large-scale problems as expected in future smart grids due to the large number of distributed energy resources that take over control tasks from large-scale central power plants [27]. Some recent implementations are [15,20,33]. Distributed organization and self-organized control is also a special characteristic of dynamic virtual power plants [28] whereof efficient coalition formation is an essential requirement, but with hard combinatorial specifications.

We adapted an approach for decentralized predictive scheduling (COHDA) [16] that already rendered efficient for decentralized combinatorial problems and that provides the additional advantage of keeping all information about local decision base's and local operational constraints private and develop it further to decentralized coalition formation. The rest of the paper is organized as follows. As a start, a review of related approaches with focus on applications to the smart grid is given. We then briefly introduce the concept of basic COHDA and our extensions to the use case of coalition formation. Finally, a conclusion is drawn with results from several simulation runs that prove applicability.

## 2   Related Work

Grouping agents together so as to form coalitions is a major interaction concept within multi-agent systems. The usual reason for grouping is that a group of agents might achieve a goal better than a single agent [19,25]. Often, a group of agents is indispensable in the smart grid field because, a single DER usually has not the capability to achieve a goal. Nevertheless, it is possible to have different groups consisting of a different mixture of agents.

Clearly, each agent (or the associated real unit) possesses certain traits or benefits that contribute to the overall success of the coalition with different amount. In some use cases, the utility of the members of a coalition may be easily quantified. For example, [18] studies several examples from the transport sector; with numbers of drivers or trucks and costs expressed in dollar. In the use case studied in this paper, the utility has to be expressed as the contribution that eases a joint planning problem (jointly planning individual loads for gaining a desired aggregated schedule) that has to be expressed in terms of traits and size of individual search spaces of alternative schedules. The actually chosen schedule is not necessarily proportional to the utility, because the richness of offered opportunities (moreover in case of having backup capabilities for later re-scheduling) has to be considered, not the taken choice. The role of integrating whole flexibility considerations into decentralized value calculations has been studied in [7].

As opposed to the here scrutinized distribution of joint effort for value maximization, distributing joint cost is a long discussed topic [7,12]. The division of surplus has applications in production [12,36], electricity pricing [22], public goods [9,24], and other situations modeled by cooperative games. A survey of coalition games applied to several use cases in the smart grid can be found in [35]; e.g. some utility functions (analytically calculable) are given, but profit distribution is not discussed.

In recent years, researchers have investigated a variety of approaches to coalition structure generation as a major challenge in multi-agent systems [32]. An overview can for example be found in [31]. The main problems in all solutions arise with execution performance, solution quality or memory requirements [32]. Several algorithms have also been developed for coalition formation especially in the smart grid; e. g. [4,13,39]. The focus in this works lies on constructing stable, i. e. long term, coalitions whereas dynamic reconfigurations are hardly supported. Individual DER models for determining volatile, individual sets of situation-dependent flexibilities are not integrated. All approaches from the smart grid field are either not decentralized and thus do not fully comply with requirements resulting from the large number of decentralized energy resources [27], do not take into account individual flexibilities and operation constraints of individual units or rely on integrated models and thus on specific, restricted implementations. Other approaches specialize to sub use cases, e. g. electric vehicles [10], to ease computation.

A first formal model for a self-organized solution has been presented in [3]. In general, decentralized algorithms are considered advantageous in many fields of smart grid computation [27,34]. For the case of predictive scheduling, [16] developed a decentralized algorithm for constrained combinatorial problems. Combined with an appropriate abstraction from individual flexibilities [6], it has been successfully applied to dynamic day-ahead market scenarios [28] for intra coalition optimization. We will now extend this approach to the combinatorial problem of coalition formation.

# 3 Algorithm

## 3.1 COHDA

We start with a brief recap of the used base algorithm. The Combinatorial Optimization Heuristics for Distributed Agents (COHDA) was originally introduced in [16,17]. Since then it has been applied to a variety of smart grid applications [15,28,29,38]. With our explanations we follow [16] (Fig. 1).

Originally, COHDA has been designed as a fully distributed solution to the predictive scheduling problem (as distributed constraint optimization formulation) in smart grid management [17]. In this scenario, each agent in the multi-agent system is in charge of controlling exactly one distributed energy resource (generator or controllable consumer) with procuration for negotiating the energy. All energy resources are drawn together to a virtual power plant and the controlling agents form a coalition that has to control the VPP in a distributed way. It is the goal for the predictive scheduling problem to find exactly one schedule for each energy unit such that

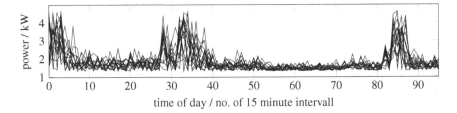

**Fig. 1.** Example for a discrete version of the search space for a co-generation plant. Usually, 2000 different, operable schedules to choose from are used in this contribution. A state-of-charge of 50 % at night and an increased thermal demand for showering in the morning and dish washing in the evening result in higher flexibilities during these periods.

1. each assigned schedule can be operated by the respective energy unit without violating any hard technical constraint, and
2. the difference between the sum of all targets and a desired given target schedule is minimized.

The target schedule usually comprises 96 time intervals of 15 min each with a given amount of energy (or equivalently mean active power) for each time interval, but might also be constituted for a shorter time frame by a given energy product that the coalition has to deliver.

An agent in COHDA does not represent a complete solution as it is the case for instance in population-based approaches [21,30]. Each agent represents a class within a multiple choice knapsack combinatorial problem [23]. Applied to predictive scheduling each class refers to the feasible region in the solution space of the respective energy unit. Each agent chooses schedules as solution candidate only from the set of feasible schedules that belongs to the DER controlled by this agent. Each agent is connected with a rather small subset of other agents from the multi-agent system and may only communicate with agents from this limited neighborhood. The neighborhood (communication network) is defined by a small world graph [40]. As long as this graph is at least simply connected, each agent collects information from the direct neighborhood and as each received message also contains (not necessarily up-to-date) information from the transitive neighborhood, each agent may accumulate information about the choices of other agents and thus gains his own local belief of the aggregated schedule that the other agents are going to operate. With this belief each agent may choose a schedule for the own controlled energy unit in a way that the coalition is put forward best while at the same time own constraints are obeyed and own interests are pursued.

All choices for own schedules are rooted in incomplete knowledge and beliefs in what other agents do; gathered from received messages. The taken choice (together with the basis for decision-making) is communicated to all neighbors and in this way knowledge is successively spread throughout the coalition without any central memory. This process is repeated. Because all spread information about schedule choices is labeled with an age, each agent may decide easily whether the own knowledge repository has to be updated. Any update results in recalculating of the own best schedule contribution and spreading it to the direct neighbors. By and by all agents accumulate complete information and as soon as no agent is capable of offering a schedule that results in a better solution, the algorithm converges and terminates. Convergence has been proved in [14].

More formally, each time an agent receives a message, three successive steps are conducted. First, during the perceive phase an agent $a_j$ updates its own working memory $\kappa_j$ with the received working memory $\kappa_i$ from agent $a_i$. From the foreign working memory the objective of the optimization (i. e. the target schedule) is imported (if not already known) as well as the configuration that constitutes the calculation base of neighboring agent $a_i$. An update is conducted if the received configuration is larger or has achieved a better objective value. In this way, schedules that reflect the so far best choices of other agents and that are not already known in the own working memory are imported from the received memory.

During the following decision phase agent $a_j$ has to decide on the best choice for his own schedule based on the updated belief about the system state $\gamma_k$. Index $k$ indicates the age of the system state information. The agent knows which schedules of a subset (or all) of other agents are going to operate. Thus, the schedule that fills the gap to the desired target schedule exactly can be easily identified. Due to operational constraints of the controlled DER, this optimal schedule can usually not be operated. In addition, other reasons might render some schedules largely unattractive due to high cost. Because of this reason, each agent is equipped with a so called decoder that automatically maps the identified optimal schedule to a nearby feasible schedule that is operable by the DER and thus feasible. Based on a set of feasible schedules sampled from an appropriate simulation model for flexibility prediction [8], a decoder can e. g. be based directly on this set (by linearly searching the schedule with the smallest deviation) or be built by learning a support vector model after the approach of [6]. Both approaches – with individual advantages and drawbacks regarding computational complexity, search space size and accuracy – have been tested here.

As the whole procedure is based exclusively on local decisions, each agent decides privately which schedules are taken. Private interest and preferences can be included and all information on the flexibility of the local DER is kept private.

If the objective value for the configuration with this new candidate is better, this new schedule is kept as selected one. Finally, if a new solution candidate has been found, the working memory with this new configuration is sent to all agents in the local neighborhood. The procedure terminates, as soon as all agents reach the same system state and no new messages are generated. Then all agents know the same final result.

## 3.2  Decentralized Coalition Formation

In general, a set of units has to be assigned to a given electricity product such that the assigned group is capable of jointly operating the target schedule defined by the product. If a set of products is given, the set of all available energy units has to be divided out to the different products in a way that the outcome (generated by product delivery) for the units and product fulfilment are maximized concurrently. The problem of partitioning a set of agents into several groups is a coalition structure generation problem [28]. Given is a set of products $\mathcal{P}$. Each product $P \in \mathcal{P}$ defines a schedule $P = (p_1, \ldots, p_d) \in \mathbb{R}^d$ that defines for each time interval $i$ a value $p_i$ of mean active power that is to be delivered as close as possible. Usually, 15 min time intervals for a given product horizon $d$ (up to 96 intervals) are considered. We do not consider the origin of the products. Energy products might be drawn from some energy market like active power or reserve control markets. In this contribution we restrict our simulations w.l.o.g. to day-ahead active power trading but take all products as already given from some earlier market phase. In addition to the product set $\mathcal{P}$ a set of agents $\mathcal{A}$ is given.

We want to find a coalition structure $CS = (\mathcal{A}_1, \ldots, \mathcal{A}_{|\mathcal{P}|})$ such that the following implication holds: $A_i \in \mathcal{A}_j \Rightarrow A_i \notin \bigcup_{k \neq j} \mathcal{A}_k$, i.e. each agent may only be part of exactly one coalition but does not necessarily have to join a coalition. Usually in coalition structure formation one wants to maximize the profit of the coalition structure. In our use case we want to equivalently minimize the deviation from the coalition's ability to fulfil their assigned energy product and thus define the value $v(CS)$ of a coalition structure $CS$ as

$$v(CS) = \sum_{j=1}^{|\mathcal{P}|} \delta \left( \sum_{A \in \mathcal{A}_j} x_A, P_j \right) \rightarrow \min \tag{1}$$

such that

$$x_{A_i} \in \mathcal{F}_{U_i}, \ \forall A_i \in CS. \tag{2}$$

Equation (1) defines the value $v(CS)$ as the sum of minimal deviations $\delta$ (w.l.o.g. the Euclidean distance has been used) between a coalition's best schedule choice and the respective target product. This means, each coalition gathers flexibilities from different DER such that each coalition can distribute the effort of jointly achieving the product to feasible schedules for the respective coalition members. As a constraint (2), schedules must be taken from the subset $\mathcal{F}_{U_i}$ of feasible schedules. Each unit $U_i$ defines its individual feasible region based on individual technical and economical restrictions and on current operational state and forecasts (e. g. weather, etc.).

COHDA can easily conduct different types of combinatorial optimization if the decision phase is appropriately adapted to the problem at hand. Some minor changes for objective evaluation and working memory content are additionally necessary. We adopted COHDA for solving the coalition formation problem as follows. The system configuration $\gamma_i$ denotes the assignment of each (so far known) agent to a coalition; i. e. each agent may assign itself to exactly one coalition (denoted by the index of the chosen product) or not be a member of any coalition (index 0). After receiving an updated system configuration with assignments from other agents, a decision has to be made on the best own assignment. To achieve this, the agent tests all possible assignments for its own DER for finding the one with the smallest error:

$$\arg \min_{0 \leq i \leq |\mathcal{P}|} v(CS_{a_j \in \mathcal{A}_i}). \tag{3}$$

$CS_{a_j \in \mathcal{A}_i}$ denotes a coalition structure with agent $a_j$ being a member of coalition $i$ (or not in a coalition if $i = 0$). The value of the coalition is given by the residual error Eq. (1). Thus, the better the ability of the coalitions to resemble the target schedules defined by the associated products, the better the coalition structure. In this way, evaluating the objective (3) comprises a number of inner optimization processes. Evaluating an assignment necessitates solving the optimization problem of finding best schedules for each coalition in order to calculate Eq. (1). This task is achieved by starting standard COHDA processes as described in [16] on the respective subset of agents (belonging to the coalition at question) and a respectively smaller communication overlay network. Figure 2 illustrates the overall process and the interaction between the different COHDA instances. These COHDA behaviours are interlaced with the main coalition formation COHDA behaviour. Thus, working memories $\kappa_{j,c}$ are distinguished by an additional identifying key $c$; cf. Fig. 2.

Two interlaced COHDA processes do the work (Fig. 2). One COHDA process (the outer) determines in its decision part the best assignment to a coalition by probing each possible one (left part of Fig. 2). Evaluating an assignment of one's own controlled energy resource to a coalition (a belief about the assignment of other agents is derived combining the information from received messages) incorporates a need for solving a predictive scheduling optimization problem for

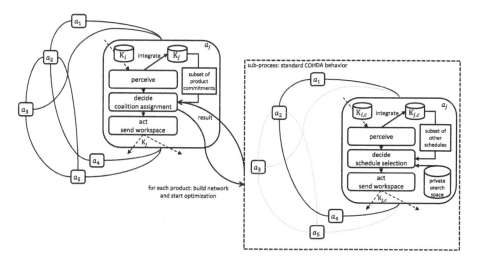

**Fig. 2.** Basic architecture and process of coalition formation as nested decentralized combinatorial optimization.

each assignment. In order to solve this (inner) optimization problem, the outer process is paused and a new COHDA process is initiated by emitting a message to an agent from the neighborhood. The inner process comprises only agents from the currently evaluated coalition and thus the neighborhood is smaller (right side of Fig. 2 that illustrates the internal of the decision stage of the outer process). When the inner optimization terminates with a value of the tested coalition, the next inner evaluation process is started. After all possible assignments have been tested, the best is chosen and the outer process continues.

## 4    Results

Evaluation was done by simulation. Each energy unit is associated with a controlling agent responsible for conducting local decisions and communication with other agents. For simulating distributed energy resources we used a model for co-generation plants that has already served in several studies and projects for evaluation [5,6,15,26,29]. This model comprises a micro CHP with 4.7 kW of rated electrical power (12.6 kW thermal power) bundled with a thermal buffer store. Constraints restrict power band, buffer charging, gradients, minimum runtime, and satisfaction of thermal demand. The relationship between electrical (active) power and thermal power was modeled after engine test benches. Thermal demand is determined by simulating a detached house (including hot water drawing) according to given weather profiles. In addition, we used models for heat pumps and boilers for hot water provision [37]. For each agent the model is individually (randomly) configured with state of charge, weather condition, temperature range, allowed operation gradients, and similar. From these model instances, the respective training sets for building the decoders have been generated with the sampling approach from [8].

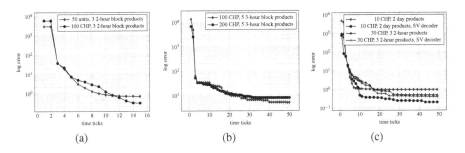

**Fig. 3.** Mean convergence behavior of several test runs (100 each) for different scenarios for the first execution steps of the outer combinatorics. The intermediate best solution quality was collected during executing the multi-agent system with the help of a global observer. This data collection is not part of the otherwise fully decentralized algorithm.

Figure 3 shows the results of some first convergence experiments with coalitions of co-generation plants. In order to ensure reproducibility of results and measurability of convergence, an event-based simulation of our multi agent system with a discrete time model and with asynchronous execution within each time step has been used. Shown are the achieved mean residual errors. Please note that in each of these time steps of the outer algorithm a different number of agents has to conduct the inner (predictive scheduling algorithm) several times in order to evaluate the value of each possible coalition structure during the decision phase. All simulations have been stopped early after 15 and accordingly 50 steps to demonstrate the fast convergence. The omitted improvements during later time steps are rather marginal.

Figure 3(a) shows the results of two easy problem instances with 50 and 100 units and 3 block products for a 2 h period (resolution: 15 min) as for example traded at the European Power Exchange[1]. The height of the load has been chosen with respect to the mean operated power of all CHP. Nevertheless, it is not guaranteed that a coalition can be found for each product such that it is possible to find a schedule for each unit in the coalition such that the aggregated schedule of all units in the coalition resembles the product exactly. As error measure, the mean absolute percentage (MAPE) measure

$$d_M = \frac{100}{d} \sum_{i=1}^{d} \left| \frac{p_i - x_i}{p_i} \right| \tag{4}$$

has been used for products over $d$ time periods with product power $p_i$ and joint coalition power $x_i$ at interval $i$. Scaled in this way, results with different number of units and power levels can be compared by the mean deviation in percent from the wanted power. MAPE allows comparing coalitions of different size. Please note that minimizing some error for the coalition structure is equivalent to maximizing some given revenue measure.

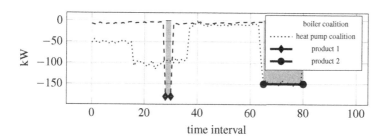

**Fig. 4.** Example result for a scenario with two block products. One (30 min in the morning) tailor made for the boilers in the agent set and one in the evening suitable for the heat pumps. Without knowing the unit under control the set of agents splits apart correctly and schedules are assigned (taking also into account the operation of the rest of the day) such that product fulfilment is maximized while all technical constraints are obeyed.

---

[1] http://www.epexspot.com.

Figure 3(b) shows results for more complex scenarios. Figure 3(c) takes into consideration products for a whole day and uses support vector decoder as search space model instead of the discrete model. Here an exact result was achievable if the right CHPs are in the right coalition and the schedules are chosen appropriately.

Figure 4 shows an example result for a scenario with two different block products: one tailor made for the heat pumps in the scenario and one suitable for the boilers (although again an exact solution was not achievable). The set of all agents is split up into two coalitions (not being in a coalition was again an allowed option for an agent) while flexibilities of all units for the whole day had to be kept in mind when calculating possible contributions to the shorter intra-day products. The figure shows the aggregated schedules for the whole day and the two products.

In Table 1 several scenarios are compared with regard to the achieved result quality and the used number of objective evaluations. The scenarios are:

**CHP:** A scenario with 10 agent controlled CHP with randomly chosen initial operation state regarding state of charge, weather condition and possible gradients. Two coalitions for two products covering a time range of 96 intervals of 15 min each are sought. Both products have been chosen such that an exact fulfilment (zero error) could be achieved. Support vector decoders have been used as search space models.

**HP:** This is basically the same scenario as for the CHPs but with 10 heat pumps. This time, the discrete model has been used as search space.

**Mixed 1:** This scenario consists of 5 CHP, 5 heat pumps, 5 boilers and 3 products. Each product was tailor made for one of the groups of units. Thus, an error of zero was achievable. For modeling the search space, the discrete model with 100 different possible schedules for each unit has been used.

**Mixed 2:** The setup for this scenario was the same as for Mixed 1. This time a discrete model with 200 schedules had been used for each unit; resulting in an increase in problem size.

**Table 1.** Results of different coalition formation scenarios. The residual error is given as MAPE $d_M$ Eq. (4). Evaluations are counted as number of decisions on coalition assignment (outer) and decision on optimal schedule choice (inner).

| Scenario | Error | Outer evaluations | Inner evaluations |
|----------|-------|-------------------|-------------------|
| CHP | $0.24971 \pm 0.23290$ | $2655.31 \pm 1450.40$ | $176539.42 \pm 101171.13$ |
| HP | $1.1545 \times 10^{-3} \pm 2.2155 \times 10^{-4}$ | $3864.07 \pm 1492.07$ | $299072.67 \pm 115364.16$ |
| Mixed 1 | $4.5084 \times 10^{-15} \pm 8.3635 \times 10^{-16}$ | $6494.50 \pm 3776.21$ | $663890.85 \pm 417128.31$ |
| Mixed 2 | $0.08572 \pm 0.34291$ | $9908.12 \pm 3157.91$ | $1115235.44 \pm 379695.34$ |

Table 1 shows the residual error (MAPE $d_M$) that has been achieved together with the number of conducted evaluations of the objective function distinguished in outer (agent decides on coalition assignment) and inner (agent decides on appropriateness of the schedule selection within a questioned coalition) objective.

## 5  Conclusion

We presented a fully decentralized approach to coalition formation based on the combinatorial heuristics COHDA. This approach fully relies on exchange of messages and local decisions and thus also allows for the integration of private interests. No information about the own flexibilities or any underlying models of private operation constraints have to be given away. A major contribution is the integration of dynamically changing flexibilities by decoders, allowing coalitions to valuate traits and size of individual search spaces for specific product fulfilment.

The results are promising and show an acceptably small computational footprint due to the fully decentralized, parallel calculations. With this approach, a further building block is available for fully decentralized energy management.

## References

1. Abarrategui, O., Marti, J., Gonzalez, A.: Constructing the active european power grid. In: Proceedings of WCPEE 2009, Cairo (2009)
2. Awerbuch, S., Preston, A.M. (eds.): The Virtual Utility: Accounting, Technology & Competitive Aspects of the Emerging Industry. Topics in Regulatory Economics and Policy, vol. 26. Kluwer Academic Publishers, Boston (1997)
3. Beer, S., Appelrath, H.J.: A formal model for agent-based coalition formation in electricity markets. In: Innovative Smart Grid Technologies Europe (IEEE ISGT EUROPE), pp. 1–5, October 2013
4. Bistaffa, F., Farinelli, A., Vinyals, M., Rogers, A.: Decentralised stable coalition formation among energy consumers in the smart grid (demonstration). In: Proceedings of the 11th International Conference on Autonomous Agents and Multiagent Systems, vol. 3, pp. 1461–1462. International Foundation for Autonomous Agents and Multiagent Systems, AAMAS 2012, Richland, SC (2012)
5. Bremer, J., Rapp, B., Sonnenschein, M.: Support vector based encoding of distributed energy resources' feasible load spaces. In: IEEE PES Conference on Innovative Smart Grid Technologies Europe. Chalmers Lindholmen, Gothenburg, Sweden (2010)
6. Bremer, J., Sonnenschein, M.: Constraint-handling for optimization with support vector surrogate models - a novel decoder approach. In: Filipe, J., Fred, A. (eds.) ICAART 2013 - Proceedings of the 5th International Conference on Agents and Artificial Intelligence, vol. 2, pp. 91–105. SciTePress, Barcelona, Spain (2013)
7. Bremer, J., Sonnenschein, M.: Estimating shapley values for fair profit distribution in power planning smart grid coalitions. In: Klusch, M., Thimm, M., Paprzycki, M. (eds.) MATES 2013. LNCS, vol. 8076, pp. 208–221. Springer, Heidelberg (2013)
8. Bremer, J., Sonnenschein, M.: Sampling the search space of energy resources for self-organized, agent-based planning of active power provision. In: Page, B., Fleischer, A.G., Göbel, J., Wohlgemuth, V. (eds.) 27th International Conference on Environmental Informatics for Environmental Protection, EnviroInfo 2013, pp. 214–222. Shaker (2013)

9. Champsaur, P.: How to share the cost of a public good? Int. J. Game Theory **4**, 113–129 (1975)

10. de O Ramos, G., Rial, J., Bazzan, A.: Self-adapting coalition formation among electric vehicles in smart grids. In: 2013 IEEE 7th International Conference on Self-Adaptive and Self-Organizing Systems (SASO), pp. 11–20, September 2013

11. European Parliament & Council: Directive 2009/28/ec of 23 on the promotion of the use of energy from renewable sources and amending and subsequently repealing directives 2001/77/ec and 2003/30/ec, April 2009

12. Friedman, E., Moulin, H.: Three methods to share joint costs or surplus. J. Econ. Theory **87**(2), 275–312 (1999)

13. Gensollen, N., Becker, M., Gauthier, V., Marot, M.: Coalition formation algorithm of prosumers in a smart grid environment. In: 2015 IEEE International Conference on Communications, ICC 2015, London, United Kingdom, June 8–12, 2015, pp. 5896–5902. IEEE (2015)

14. Hinrichs, C.: Selbstorganisierte Einsatzplanung dezentraler Akteure im Smart Grid. Ph.D. thesis, Carl von Ossietzky Universit Oldenburg (2014)

15. Hinrichs, C., Bremer, J., Sonnenschein, M.: Distributed hybrid constraint handling in large scale virtual power plants. In: IEEE PES Conference on Innovative Smart Grid Technologies Europe (ISGT Europe 2013). IEEE Power & Energy Society (2013)

16. Hinrichs, C., Lehnhoff, S., Sonnenschein, M.: A decentralized heuristic for multiple-choice combinatorial optimization problems. In: Helber, S., et al. (eds.) Operations Research Proceedings 2012, pp. 297–302. Springer, Heidelberg (2014)

17. Hinrichs, C., Sonnenschein, M., Lehnhoff, S.: Evaluation of a self-organizing heuristic for interdependent distributed search spaces. In: Filipe, J., Fred, A.L.N. (eds.) International Conference on Agents and Artificial Intelligence (ICAART 2013). vol. 1, pp. 25–34. SciTePress (2013)

18. Hsu, M.-C., Soo, V.-W.: Fairness in cooperating multi-agent systems – using profit sharing as an example. In: Lukose, D., Shi, Z. (eds.) PRIMA 2005. LNCS, vol. 4078, pp. 153–162. Springer, Heidelberg (2009)

19. Kahan, J., Rapoport, A.: Theories of Coalition Formation. Basic Studies in Human Behavior. L. Erlbaum Associates, Hillsdale (1984)

20. Kamphuis, R., Warmer, C., Hommelberg, M., Kok, K.: Massive coordination of dispersed generation using powermatcher based software agents. In: 19th International Conference on Electricity Distribution, May 2007

21. Karaboga, D., Basturk, B.: A powerful and efficient algorithm for numerical function optimization: artificial bee colony (ABC) algorithm. J. Global Optim. **39**(3), 459–471 (2007)

22. Lima, J., Pereira, M., Pereira, J.: An integrated framework for cost allocation in a multi-owned transmission-system. IEEE Trans. Power Syst. **10**(2), 971–977 (1995)

23. Lust, T., Teghem, J.: The multiobjective multidimensional knapsack problem: a survey and a new approach. CoRR abs/1007.4063 (2010)

24. Mas-Colell, A.: Remarks on the game-theoretic analysis of a simple distribution of surplus problem. Int. J. Game Theory **9**, 125–140 (1980)

25. Mas-Colell, A., Whinston, M.D., Green, J.R.: Microeconomic Theory. Oxford University Press, Oxford (1995)

26. Neugebauer, J., Kramer, O., Sonnenschein, M.: Classification cascades of overlapping feature ensembles for energy time series data. In: Aung, Z., et al. (eds.) DARE 2015. LNCS, vol. 9518, pp. 76–93. Springer, Heidelberg (2015). doi:10.1007/978-3-319-27430-0_6

27. Nie, A., Lehnhoff, S., Trchel, M., Uslar, M., Wissing, C., Appelrath, H.J., Sonnenschein, M.: Market-based self-organized provision of active power and ancillary services: An agent-based approach for smart distribution grids. In: 2012 Complexity in Engineering (COMPENG), pp. 1–5, June 2012

28. Nieße, A., Beer, S., Bremer, J., Hinrichs, C., Lünsdorf, O., Sonnenschein, M.: Conjoint dynamic aggregation and scheduling for dynamic virtual power plants. In: Ganzha, M., Maciaszek, L.A., Paprzycki, M. (eds.) Federated Conference on Computer Science and Information Systems - FedCSIS 2014, Warsaw, Poland, September 2014

29. Nieße, A., Sonnenschein, M.: A fully distributed continuous planning approach for decentralized energy units. In: Cunningham, D.W., Hofstedt, P., Meer, K., Schmitt, I. (eds.) Informatik 2015. GI-Edition - Lecture Notes in Informatics (LNI), vol. 246, pp. 151–165. Bonner Köllen Verlag (2015)

30. Poli, R., Kennedy, J., Blackwell, T.: Particle swarm optimization. Swarm Intell. **1**(1), 33–57 (2007)

31. Rahwan, T., Michalak, T.P., Wooldridge, M., Jennings, N.R.: Coalition structure generation: A survey. Artif. Intell. **229**, 139–174 (2015)

32. Rahwan, T., Ramchurn, S.D., Jennings, N.R., Giovannucci, A.: An anytime algorithm for optimal coalition structure generation. CoRR abs/1401.3466 (2014)

33. Ramchurn, S.D., Vytelingum, P., Rogers, A., Jennings, N.R.: Agent-based homeostatic control for green energy in the smart grid. ACM Trans. Intell. Syst. Technol. **2**(4), 35:1–35:28 (2011)

34. Ramchurn, S.D., Vytelingum, P., Rogers, A., Jennings, N.R.: Putting the 'smarts' into the smart grid: A grand challenge for artificial intelligence. Commun. ACM **55**(4), 86–97 (2012)

35. Saad, W., Han, Z., Poor, H.V., Basar, T.: Game theoretic methods for the smart grid. CoRR abs/1202.0452 (2012)

36. Sen, A.K.: Labour allocation in a cooperative enterprise. Rev. Econ. Stud. **33**(4), 361–371 (1966)

37. Sonnenschein, M., Appelrath, H.J., Canders, W.R., Henke, M., Uslar, M., Beer, S., Bremer, J., Lünsdorf, O., Nieße, A., Psola, J.H., et al.: Decentralized provision of active power. In: Smart Nord - Final Report. Hartmann GmbH, Hannover (2015)

38. Sonnenschein, M., Hinrichs, C., Nieße, A., Vogel, U.: Supporting renewable power supply through distributed coordination of energy resources. In: Hilty, L.M., Aebischer, B. (eds.) ICT Innovations for Sustainability. Advances in Intelligent Systems and Computing, vol. 310, pp. 387–404. Springer, Heidelberg (2015)

39. Vinyals, M., Bistaffa, A., Farinelli, A., Rogers, A.: Stable coalition formation among energy consumers in the smart grid. In: Proceedings of the 3th International Workshop on Agent Technologies for Energy Systems (ATES 2012), pp. 73–80, June 2012

40. Watts, D., Strogatz, S.: Collective dynamics of 'small-world' networks. Nature **393**(6684), 440–442 (1998)

# Agent-Based Modelling of Cost Efficient and Stable Transmission Grid Expansion Planning

Johannes Hiry[1(✉)], Jonas von Haebler[1], Ulf Häger[1],
Christian Rehtanz[1], Gerardo Blanco[2], and Aldo Martinez[2]

[1] Institute of Energy Systems, Energy Efficiency and Energy Economics (ie3),
Technical University Dortmund, Dortmund, Germany
johannes.hiry@tu-dortmund.de
[2] Grupo de Investigación en Sistemas Energéticos (GISE), Universidad Nacional
de Asunción, Asunción, Paraguay
gblanco@pol.una.py

**Abstract.** Due to politically defined goals to raise the share of renewable energy, the landscape of electricity production has changed in recent years. Normally, a decision to invest in new generation capacity by generation companies is often based on profit maximization criteria. Criteria considering the costs resulting from the required expansion or construction of new transmission capacity are only playing a minor role, if any. This paper introduces an integrated model based on a multi-agent system to simulate the investment and decision behavior of the relevant entities in the liberalized energy market and their impact on social welfare. The interaction between the modelled market entities is based on a non-cooperative game theoretic approach. Its functionality is demonstrated within a small application example.

**Keywords:** Multi-agent systems · Macroeconomics · Simulation · Transmission grid · Expansion planning

## 1 Introduction

Investments in new production capacity in a liberalized energy market have a huge impact on the transmission and distribution grid, as well as on the price structure of the supplied electrical energy. Whereas generation companies (GenCos) are normally allowed to select their investment in new generation capacity and power plants based on their own business criteria, transmission system operators (TSOs) are regulated by governmental institutions. The fact, that GenCos are allowed to freely choose their investment point can lead to necessary cost-intensive transmission grid expansion and consequently to a decrease in social welfare.

Agent-based modelling (ABM) or Multi-Agent based simulation (MABS) has become popular in recent years to model and simulate the electricity market behavior. Its flexibility allows a wide range of application like analyzing generation expansion decisions in electricity markets by simulating the decentralized decision making process of GenCos [1] or to improve the planning of distribution grids [2, 3].

© Springer International Publishing Switzerland 2016
J. Bajo et al. (Eds.): PAAMS 2016 Workshops, CCIS 616, pp. 356–368, 2016.
DOI: 10.1007/978-3-319-39387-2_30

Beside the use of MABS to improve planning of distribution grids, expansion planning of power grids in general has been and still is an important field of research. A good overview about the various economic and engineering issues and challenges on this field of research is given by Wu *et al.* in [4]. In the recent years, anticipative network planning models have been formulated to simulate the correlation between transmission grid expansion planning and investments in new generation capacity. While there is not yet many work related to this, already published work investigates the effects of transmission grid expansion strategies on investments of GenCos in new generation company.

Sauma and Oren [5, 6] propose and solve a three-stage approach for the investigation of the investment behavior of a transmission system operator (TSO) under the assumption that the TSO is anticipating the investment behavior of GenCos. Their proactive transmission expansion planning model includes the valuation of different grid expansion possibilities. In [7], Pozo *et al.* relate to this approach and continue its development. In their proposed approach, the transmission planner is able to consider the induced behavior by the GenCo investment and the electricity market equilibrium for new transmission grid expansion plans including demand uncertainty. A transmission grid expansion framework under consideration of the strategic behavior of GenCos is also proposed by Motamedi *et al.* in [8]. They propose an iterative, agent-based search algorithm to solve a multiple layer optimization problem. In [9], Yen *et al.* present a multi-agent based approach under the use of cooperative game theory and coalition forming. They investigate different outcomes of coalitions of different agents, which are responsible for the development of the transmission grid.

The approach presented in this paper differs from already existing work that a non-cooperative game is formulated as a framework for a MABS. The result is a MABS tool that is capable to simulate the strategic investment behavior of the electricity market participants while considering the regulation framework of the energy market. The goal is to find solutions for transmission grid planning considering the investment behavior of GenCos in a liberalized energy market. The main difference to existing work is that the market power of GenCos in a liberalized market with regulations is anticipated. To achieve this objective, the influence parameters of the individual market entities have been investigated and their objectives have been formulated. The modeled decision makers are interacting with each other in a predefined, non-cooperative game theoretic based simulation framework. The target of this approach is to propose a new simulation model to identify instruments and mechanisms, which are able to increase social welfare. One of the main objectives is to determine if there are any instruments in a regulated liberalized energy market to influence GenCos to invest in new generation capacity while reducing or avoid transmission capacity expansion. The combination of a MABS with the game theoretic framework creates a basic but highly expandable simulation tool.

The paper starts with a description of the assumptions and the theoretical concept of the model. Afterwards the developed MABS and its agents are introduced. To demonstrate its functionality, the results of a three node application case simulation are presented.

## 2   Assumptions and Theoretical Concept

The developed model assumes a general network topology with a DC power flow. Congestion or violation of the $(n-1)$-criterion on multiple lines are possible. The violation of the $(n-1)$-criterion is estimated as a branch usage equal or bigger than 70 % of its capacity [10]. It is assumed that all nodes are demand and generation nodes and that there is a constant load at every node over the whole simulation runtime. Furthermore, uncertainty is not included, which means that every market entity can exactly calculate the costs, revenue and any other parameters of an investment opportunity. For the sake of simplicity it is assumed that the electricity market is represented by an optimal power flow calculation.

In the simulation, the following sequence of events is assumed:

*Step 1* – The regulator evaluates different regulation options for a specific period
*Step 2* – The GenCo evaluates different investment projects and invests in the most profitable one while considering the resulting transmission grid expansion costs. The investment decreases its marginal cost of production.
*Step 3* – If necessary the TSO invests in new transmission capacity.
*Step 4* – Market operations are taking place.

The assumed sequence of events can be interpreted as a one-period investment cycle, whereas one period can be interpreted as one year. At the beginning of each year, the regulator evaluates its different regulation options for a specific period. Afterwards, every company evaluates the investments that are possible or have to be made during the year. If each company made their investment (or decided itself against to make an investment) the market operations are taking place until the end of the period. In the next period, the same sequence of events is taking place again while considering the results of the previous period.

The interactions between the different decision makers in electricity markets are modeled as a complete and perfect information leader-follower game. This includes that every player is able to observe the actions of the other players and to make its "rational" decision based on these decisions. The game consists of four players, representing the modeled market entities regulator, GenCo, TSO and a fictitious market operator (MO) which is responsible for market calculations. Due to the nature of non-cooperative game theory, every player has its own objectives and tries to maximize them. This intrinsic objective can be formulated in an objective function for each agent. To solve the game, a subgame perfect Nash equilibrium has to be found.

In the proposed approach, each round of the game represents one period (*e.g.* one year) and all actions are made sequentially. To simulate more than one period, the sequence of every player's action has to be repeated, considering the simulation results from the previous period.

Hence at the end of each year, respectively shortly before the end of each year, the regulator decides if it will change the regulations for the following year or not. After this step, the GenCo decides if it is going to invest in new generation capacity or not. Depending on the GenCo decision, the TSO has to invest in new transmission capacity to prevent congestion. It is assumed, that the TSO has to connect a new power plant of the GenCo and is also responsible for the stability of the transmission grid. Following the decision of the TSO, market operations are taking place. In this sequence of actions, every player tries to determine its best strategy anticipating the best strategy of the other players and vice versa. Thus, they choose a strategy that performs better against other strategies. The resulting strategy of each player is not necessarily a strategy that maximizes its payoff but a strategy that maximizes its payoff considering the reaction of the other players. If no player has an incentive anymore to pick another strategy, a subgame perfect Nash equilibrium is found. If such an equilibrium exists, it represents a specific strategy combination and determines the solution of the game.

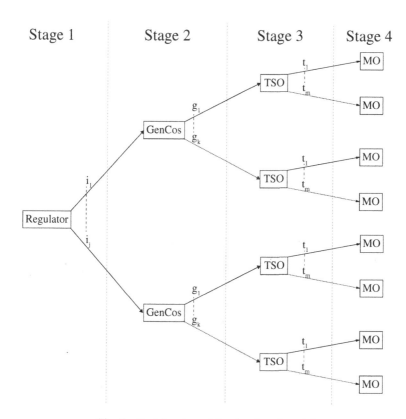

**Fig. 1.** Decision tree of the developed model

The tree in Fig. 1 corresponds to the previously introduced sequence of actions, it cannot be used to find the best solution for every player in the game. Hence, the concept of backward induction is used. This concept is based on the idea that one has to identify the "bottom-most" (here: stage 4) equilibria of the subgame trees and assume, that those equilibria will be played. In the next step, the equilibria of the subgames on the next higher stage (here: stage 3) have to be found. This procedure has to be done for every stage until the top of the tree is reached.

Figure 2 displays the schematic sequence of the backward induction solution process. As observable, the number of calculations and iterations to solve the game highly depends on the number of players and options of each player in the different stages. Additionally, the time for solving the game computationally depends on the complexity of the objective functions of each player on each stage, as well as the number of players on each stage and their number of options.

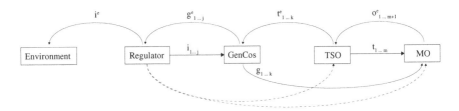

**Fig. 2.** Schematic sequence of the solution process via backward induction

For every of its $j$-options $(t_{1..j})$ the RegulatorAgent (stage one) informs the GenCoAgent(s) (stage two) about its regulation(s). Additionally, it is also possible but not obligatory to let the regulator inform the TSOAgent (stage three) as well as the MarketOperatorAgent (stage four) about their regulation(s). Then, the GenCoAgent informs the MarketOperator agent about its first of its $k$-options $(g_{1..k})$. The MarketOperatorAgent then reports its equilibrium option $o_1^e$ based on its objective function to the TSOAgent. The TSOAgent then selects its first option $t_1$ and sends this option to the MarketOperatorAgent which reports its equilibrium option $o_2^e$ based on $g_1$ and $t_1$. This process is repeated until $t_m$ is reached. The TSOAgent then selects the best result of the $m$ results and sends $t_1^e$ to the GenCoAgent. Then, the GenCoAgent selects $g_2$ and the whole optimization process through stage four and three takes place again. This process goes on until $g_k$ is reached. The GenCoAgent then reports its equilibrium $g_1^e$ to the RegulatorAgent. The RegulatorAgent then selects $i_2$ and the whole optimization process through stages four, three and two are taking place again. This activity is done until the RegulatorAgent reaches $i_j$. The RegulatorAgent then selects $i^e$ according to its objective function as the result of the optimization process for the specific period and sends it to the EnvironmentAgent. The selection of $i^e$ determines the selected option in all subsequent stages. This is because every agent on the subsequent stages select its option that performs best as a response to the options selected by the other agents. Hence, at this point, a Nash equilibrium through backward induction for the simulated period is found. It is important to take into account, that all the optimization steps explained above have to be made for every period that is simulated. That means in effect, playing the game several times can simulate a multi-period-optimization problem.

# 3    Agents

The proposed MABS in the game framework consists of five agents, whereas one agent, the EnvironmentAgent, can be considered as the "game master" (a non-player agent) and four player agents. It has been developed with the use of the Java Agent Development Framework (JADE) [11].

## 3.1    EnvironmentAgent

The EnvironmentAgent is necessary to ensure a stable synchronization between the player agents by providing them with all necessary information about the grid, generators, investment possibilities and investment costs. Furthermore, it ensures an orderly sequence of the simulation by sending a start signal to the player agents and settling each period and its specific simulation results. If required, it is able to provide the user with a GUI of the investigated grid.

## 3.2    MarketOperatorAgent

The MarketOperatorAgent simulates the market behavior. Its goal is to solve a DC optimal power flow calculation (DC OPF). Whereas this means that it has no objective function in the classical sense, the calculation of the DC OPF and the provision of the resulting data can be considered as its goal function. The optimal power flow calculation is based on work by Sun and Tesfatsion [12, 13]. The MarketOperatorAgent receives its initial data at the beginning of each period from the EnvironmentAgent. During the simulation, it receives its data from the GenCoAgent and the TSOAgent. The optimal generation dispatch, the prices and the branch usage are then calculated through the DC OPF calculation. The resulting data, like generator and branch usage and production costs, is assumed to represent the optimal market behavior. It is send to the TSOAgent for further calculation. Hence, the main objective of the MarketOperatorAgent can be described as "the provision of the result of an optimal market behavior".

## 3.3    TSOAgent

The TSOAgents objective is to minimize its overall costs while supplying power over the transmission grid to satisfy demand. The costs incurred resulting from investments to secure system stability and transmission grid expansion due to congestion or violation of the (n-1)-criterion. The high complexity of the transmission grid expansion cost calculation in reality requires a few assumptions and simplifications to model the behavior of a TSO. It is assumed that the TSO is obligated to provide a secure network. It does not consider any costs for maintenance of already existing transmission lines. Only investments in new transmission lines or upgrades of existing transmission lines are considered. Furthermore, it is assumed, that the TSOs investment options are limited to one possible investment material and that every investment and its costs take place in the contemplated period. Under these assumptions, the TSOAgent investigates the resulting grid data it receives from the MO. If there is any congestion or violation of the ($n$-1)-criterion it executes a grid optimization method to remedy the problem in the branch configuration.

### 3.4  GenCoAgent

The GenCoAgents objective is to maximize its revenue from the production and sale of electricity of a new power plant. For the sake of simplicity, it is assumed that already existing power plants that are owned by a specific GenCo are not taken into account. Hence, the GenCoAgent just considers the possible investment projects and their expected revenue.

To do so, the GenCoAgent solves the following objective function (The formula is based on [15].):

$$\max(\mathrm{Rev} - \mathrm{IC(PC)} - \mathrm{varCo}) \tag{1}$$

Whereby Rev is the expected revenue of an investment project, IC(PC) are the investment costs which depend on the production capacity of the new power plant and possible costs due to necessary transmission grid capacity expansion if given. VarCo are the expected variable costs during the expected lifetime of the power plant. The expected revenue is calculated using the expected utilization rate and the expected energy price provided by the DC OPF of the MarketOperatorAgent.

The GenCoAgent calculates the internal rate of return (IRR) to compare the different investment possibilities in power plants. It then selects the investment possibility with the highest IRR and compares the value with an individual, user-defined minimum accepted rate of return (MARR). If the IRR is higher or equal to the MARR, it selects the specific investment. If the IRR is lower than the MARR, the GenCoAgent will not invest in one of the available investment possibilities.

For the calculation of the generation costs during the optimal power flow calculation, the following generator total cost function for a generator $i$, presented in [14], is used.

$$\mathrm{TC}_i(\mathrm{p}_{Gi}) = \mathrm{a}_i * \mathrm{p}_{Gi} + \mathrm{b}_i * \mathrm{p}_{Gi}^2 + \mathrm{FCost}_i \tag{2}$$

Here $\mathrm{p}_{Gi}$ denotes real power produced by generator $i$, $a_i$ denotes costs that are proportional to the generated power, $b_i$ denotes a cost depending efficiency factor and $\mathrm{FCost}_i$ denotes fix costs that are independently from the power production.

**RegulatorAgent.** The RegulatorAgent is a player agent representing the behavior of the regulator in the real world. Furthermore, it is the leader for all players in the game. Its main objective is to increase social welfare. Social welfare in the context of the developed model is defined under the assumption, that there is a constant demand on every node of the grid independent of price changes. Hence, the objective function of the RegulatorAgent can be expressed as follows:[1]

$$\min\left(\sum_{i \in G} C_i(p_{Gi}) + \sum_{k \in TL_n} C_k\right) \tag{3}$$

Whereby $\sum_{i \in G} C_i(p_{Gi})$ is the sum of all electricity generation variable costs to satisfy the demand on every node and $\sum_{k \in TL_n} C_k$ is the sum of all costs for new transmission lines which are necessary due to investments in new power plants by the GenCo.

To fulfill its objective, the RegulatorAgent is interested in influencing the market participants to increase social welfare. In the developed approach, it has the ability to influence the GenCoAgent's investments by setting up a specific splitting ratio. This splitting ratio divides the costs for new transmission capacity investments between the GenCo and the TSO (respectively the consumer). In the base case, all costs for extending the transmission grid are worn by the TSO (or the consumer due to higher electricity prices). The RegulatorAgent then changes the ratio by splitting up the costs of transmission grid extension, whereby 10% of a new line due to an investment in a new power plant have to be paid by the GenCo and 90% have to be paid by the TSO (or the consumer). This process goes on until the RegulatorAgent found a splitting ratio, which leads to an equal or increased social welfare compared to the status quo.

## 4  Application Example

In the following an application example to demonstrate the functionality of the developed model is presented. The subject of investigation is a liberalized energy market that consists of a three-node grid. The existing configuration of the grid, the technical details of the branches, loads and power plants are presented in the following tables. Only one period is simulated and it is assumed, that every investment in transmission lines and generation capacity takes place at the beginning of the period. Furthermore, a constant demand at every node over the whole simulation period is assumed (Tables 1, 2, and 3).

**Table 1.** Sample case branch configuration

| Parameter | Element | | |
|---|---|---|---|
| | Branch 1 | Branch 2 | Branch 3 |
| Start node | 1 | 1 | 2 |
| End node | 2 | 3 | 3 |
| Length [km] | 20 | 20 | 20 |
| Reactance | 0,2 | 0,2 | 0,2 |
| Capacity [MW] | 400 | 450 | 600 |

---

[1] The formula is based on [16].

**Table 2.** Sample case load configuration

| Parameter | Element | | |
|---|---|---|---|
| | Load 1 | Load 2 | Load 3 |
| ID | L1 | L2 | L3 |
| Node | 1 | 2 | 3 |
| Load [MW] | 300 | 500 | 1000 |

**Table 3.** Sample case generator configuration

| Parameter | Element | | |
|---|---|---|---|
| | Generator 1 | Generator 2 | Generator 3 |
| ID | G1 | G2 | G3 |
| Node | 1 | 2 | 3 |
| Fix costs [€/h] | 0 | 0 | 0 |
| Cost coefficient a [€/MWh] | 13 | 60 | 40 |
| Cost coefficient b [€/MW²h] | 0.00001 | 0.00001 | 0.00001 |
| Minimum capacity [MW] | 0 | 0 | 0 |
| Maximum capacity [MW] | 770 | 1300 | 500 |
| Initial production [MW] | 0[a] | 0[a] | 0[a] |

[a]Set by the MarketOperatorAgent as part of the model initialization

After an initial DC OPF, the data presented above leads to the following graphical representation in the GUI of the EnvironmentAgent (Fig. 3).

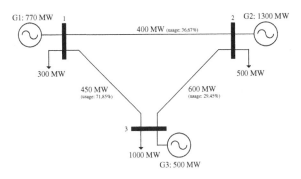

**Fig. 3.** Initial grid configuration of the sample case

Furthermore, it is assumed that the GenCo considers the following three investment options in new generation capacity whereby every investment option represents a new power plant. Furthermore, the GenCo assumes different parameters for each investment option (Table 4).

With the parameters for the different investment options given in Table 4, the GenCoAgent calculates the revenue and the rate of return of every investment. For the

**Table 4.** Sample case GenCo investment options

| Parameter | Option | | |
|---|---|---|---|
| | Investment Option 1 | Investment Option 2 | Investment Option 3 |
| ID | 1 | 2 | 3 |
| Node | 0 | 0 | 0 |
| Minimum capacity [MW] | 150 | 100 | 200 |
| Maximum capacity [MW] | 0 | 0 | 0 |
| Assumed freight costs | 0 | 0 | 0 |
| Assumed Fix costs [€/MW] | 5.190.000 | 4.000.000 | 4.000.000 |
| Assumed invest costs [€/MW] | 20 | 13,5 | 12,5 |
| Assumed runtime [years] | 1 | 2 | 3 |

sample case the best rate of return is given by the investment option 1 at node 1. Hence, without any regulations the GenCo tends to invest in 150 MW generation capacity at node 1.

In the following, only the options and the corresponding results of the RegulatorAgent calculations are displayed. This is because in its function as the game leader, its decision is crucial for the decisions of all subsequent game stages. In this application case, the RegulatorAgent has 11 different regulation options. Every option distributes the costs of new transmission capacity between the TSO ($tc_i$) and the GenCo ($gc_i$) whose investment in generation capacity requires the grid capacity expansion.

**Table 5.** Optimization results for the eleven regulator options of the application case

| Option configuration | Regulator option ($gc_i$, $tc_i$) | Overall system costs [Euro/period][a] |
|---|---|---|
| Regulator option 1–11 | (0,0; 1,0) | $4,7079*10^8$ |
| GenCo option* | (0,1; 0,9) | $4,7079*10^8$ |
| TSO option* | (0,2; 0,8) | $4,7079*10^8$ |
| Market option* | (0,3; 0,7) | $4,7079*10^8$ |
| | (0,4; 0,6) | $4,7079*10^8$ |
| | (0,5; 0,5) | $4,7079*10^8$ |
| | (0,6; 0,4) | $4,7079*10^8$ |
| | (0,7; 0,3) | $4,7079*10^8$ |
| | (0,8; 0,2) | $4.36509*10^8$ |
| | (0,9; 0,1) | $4.36509*10^8$ |
| | (1,0; 0,0) | $4.36509*10^8$ |

[a]All values rounded.

Table 5 displays the different results the RegulatorAgent receives from its subsequent stages. For the first eight options the overall system costs are constant, while for the last three options the value is quite smaller which implies a higher level of social welfare. According to its goal to increase social welfare (respectively minimize the overall system costs) while regulating as little as possible the RegulatorAgent selects the option with the splitting ratio (0,8; 0,2). This means in effect, that in the case in which the GenCo has to pay 80 % new transmission line costs due to its power plant investment at node 1, it tends to invest in another location and tries to avoid an investment that would need transmission grid expansion.

Since the RegulatorAgent made its decision, a result for the simulated sample case has been found. Now, every agent chooses its best option according to its objective function while anticipating the decision of the other agents. These decisions lead to the following changed graphical representation of the grid configuration in the EnvironmentAgent GUI which represents the static operation point after the DC OPF.

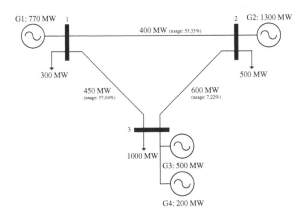

**Fig. 4.** Graphical grid representation of the final optimal grid of the sample case

There are two important things that have to be noted from the final result of the simulated period represented by Fig. 4. Firstly, in contrast to its best investment option, which is 150 MW at node 1, the final investment in new generation capacity of the GenCo is 200 MW at node 2. That is because at the point, where the GenCo is forced to pay 80 % of the transmission capacity extension costs, the break-even point for the investment at node 1 is exceeded. Secondly it is observable that no investment in new transmission capacity by the TSO has been made. While any other investment in new generation capacity would lead to necessary investments in transmission capacity by the TSO, the investment at node 2 reduces the power flow on branch 2. Due to this reduction of the branch usage an investment in new transmission capacity is not necessary anymore.

## 5 Analysis and Outlook

The application example above shows that depending on the grid configuration and transmission expansion planning scenarios a regulation of investments in new generation capacity can increase social welfare. Such a growth in social welfare depends mainly on the power that is granted to the regulator. If the regulator is restricted to the responsibility to guarantee free markets and if it has no instruments to regulate the market behavior of market entities directly, an increase is not taking place inevitably.

But if the regulator has the power to restrict the investment behavior of GenCos, social welfare could be increased. In the very simple application example, this fact is shown by giving the regulator the power to set up a "splitting ratio" which distributes the share of costs of transmission grid expansion to the transmission grid operator or the consumer and the investing generation company. In further works, the developed approach needs to be extended in different directions to consider the complex interdependencies of the electricity market and grid. First of all, the modeling of the market has to be extended to provide a realistic behavior of the power plant production including a model for an energy exchange. This also includes the consideration of a more realistic simulation of the grid by using time-series base power flow calculations considering a more fluctuating load and demand. Furthermore, a possible regulatory framework as well as different mechanisms to influence GenCos and TSOs has to be developed. In a second step, the evaluated grid has to be justified and extended to represent a more realistic grid. Consequently, the objectives of the agents have to be justified to consider the complex dependencies of a more challenging test grid.

# References

1. Botterud, A., Mahalik, M.R., Veselka, T.D., Heon-Su, R., Ki-Won, S.: Multi-agent simulation of generation expansion in electricity markets. In: Power Engineering Society General Meeting 2007, pp. 1–8. IEEE (2007)
2. Kays, J.: Agent-based simulation environment for improving the planning of distribution grids. Sierke Verlag, Göttingen (2014)
3. Kays, J., Seack, A., Rehtanz, C.: Agent-based modelling of regenerative energy sources for an efficient distribution power system design. In: Cigré Bologna 2011, pp. 1–9 (2011)
4. Wu, F.F., Zheng, F.L., Wen, F.S.: Transmission investment and expansion planning in a restructured electricity market. Energy 31(6–7), 954–966 (2006)
5. Sauma, E.E., Oren, S.S.: Proactive planning and valuation of transmission investments in restructured electricity markets. J. Regul. Econ. 30(3), 261–290 (2006)
6. Sauma, E.E., Oren, S.S.: Economic criteria for planning transmission investment in restructured electricity markets. IEEE Trans. Power Syst. 22(4), 1394–1405 (2007)
7. Pozo, D., Contreras, J., Sauma, E.: If you build it, he will come: anticipative power transmission planning. Energy Econ. 36, 135–146 (2013)
8. Motamedi, A., Zareipour, H., Buygi, M.O., Rosehart, W.D.: A transmission planning framework considering future generation expansions in electricity markets. IEEE Trans. Power Syst. 25(4), 1987–1995 (2010)
9. Yen, J., Yan, Y., Contreras, J., Ma, P.-C., Wu, F.F.: Multi-agent approach to the planning of power transmission expansion. Decis. Support Syst. 28, 279–290 (2000)
10. German Energy Agency (dena): dena Grid Study II - Integration of Renewable Energy Sources in the German Power Supply System from 2015–2020 with an Outlook to 2025. Berlin (2010)
11. Java Agent Development Framework (JADE) (2015). http://jade.tilab.com/, Accessed 05 Nov 2015
12. Sun, J., Tesfatsion, L.: DC optimal power flow formulation and solution using QuadProgJ. In: ISU Economics of Education Working Paper No. 06014, pp. 1–62, 1 March 2010 (2010)

13. Tesfatsion, L.: DCOPFJ Package: A Java DC-OPF Solver (Leigh Tesfatsion) (2015). http://www2.econ.iastate.edu/tesfatsi/DCOPFJHome.htm, Accessed 05 Nov 2015
14. Sun, J., Tesfatsion, L.: DC-OPF Formulation with Price-Sensitive Demand Bids (2008)
15. Kirschen, D., Strbac, G.: Fundamentals of Power System Economics. Wiley, Chichester (2004)
16. Swami, R.: Social welfare maximization in deregulated power system. Int. J. Power Syst. Oper. Energy Manage. 1(4), 4–8 (2012)

# Evaluation of Aggregated Systems in Smart Grids: An Example Use-Case for the Energy Option Model

Nils Loose[✉], Yudha Nurdin, Sajad Ghorbani, Christian Derksen, and Rainer Unland

DAWIS, ICB, University of Duisburg Essen, Essen, Germany
{nils.loose,yudha.nurdin,sajad.ghorbani,christian.derksen,
rainer.unland}@icb.uni-due.de

**Abstract.** As a result of fast growing share of renewable energy production in the energy market the management of power and its distribution becomes more and more complex. The here presented Energy Option Model (EOM) seems to be a promising solution to handle this newly arisen complexity. This paper will present the EOM and analyze its capabilities in centralized evaluation of aggregated systems. The example use-case will be the charging process of a fleet of electric vehicles. While the results support the potential of the EOM to implement coordination strategies for aggregations of systems, they also show the general limitations of centralized control solutions for larger groups of systems in the context of smart grids.

**Keywords:** Smart grids · EV charging · Central and decentral charging strategies · Energy agent · Energy option model

## 1 Introduction

Smart Grids are believed to be a key element for mastering the major challenges our energy supply system is currently facing. With an increasing market share of renewable energy sources, power generation becomes more volatile, more decentral and less plannable. Additionally, traditional producer and consumer roles start to dissolve, as more and more households and small businesses become "prosumers" that provide energy to the grid at times with high renewable generation but still need grid-based supply when it is low.

By enabling communication and, on this basis, the implementation of automated coordination processes between the involved flexible technical systems, smart grids can be a valuable tool for handling this growing complexity. One important question in this context is how coordination between the involved systems can be organized, i.e. how to decide about the behavior of every single system. This can be done in a centralized, decentralized, or in a hybrid manner, as for example in a hierarchical-decentralized way [1, 2]. In the centralized case, decisions for all involved systems are made by a central authority, which facilitates the organization of the decision making process, but probably raises performance issues. Especially, for larger numbers of involved systems the central authority might become a bottleneck. In the decentralized case, this problem can be avoided, as all decisions are made on the subsystem level. However, coordinating the

© Springer International Publishing Switzerland 2016
J. Bajo et al. (Eds.): PAAMS 2016 Workshops, CCIS 616, pp. 369–380, 2016.
DOI: 10.1007/978-3-319-39387-2_31

involved systems without any central instance will probably lead to additional complexity. Between these two extremes, a wide range of partly centralized solutions might also be feasible, like for example organizing critical parts centrally while leaving the uncritical parts to the responsibility of the subsystems.

With the approach of Energy Agents and their inherent Energy Option Model (EOM) [3–5], a concept for a unified on-site software system was developed at DAWIS. In this paper we will focus on how the EOM can be utilized for centralized and decentralized decision making processes, which makes it a valuable tool for developing, investigating and comparing coordination approaches for smart hybrid energy grids. For the centralized case, we will show the EOM's capabilities by exploring its limits along an example use case, namely the charging of a fleet of electric vehicles (EVs).

The paper is organized as follows: The next section will give a short introduction to the concepts of Energy Agents and EOM and classify different scenarios for EOM-based evaluation processes. Section 3 will provide some general information on the topic of EV charging, pointing out the challenges as well as the chances that arise from the integration of large EV fleets into current energy grids. Additionally, an overview on strategies for coordinated EV charging is given. In Sect. 4, we will describe how our example use-case was implemented in the EOM context, as well as the experiments we conducted and the results we generated. Finally, Sect. 5 will provide a summary and an outlook on future work.

## 2    Theoretical Background

### 2.1    Basic Concepts

At the DAWIS, an agent-based approach for modelling and controlling smart grids is currently being developed. The core of this approach is the concept of a unifying energy agent, which is defined as follows: "An Energy Agent is a specialized autonomous software system that represents and economically manages the capacitive abilities of the energy consumption, production, conversion and storing processes for a single technical system …" [4]. This software system is supposed to be applied during the whole life cycle of the system, which comprises specification and modelling, implementation, simulation, test-bed application and finally the deployment to real systems. Unlike most other agent-based smart grid approaches (e.g. [2, 6, 7]), the energy agent concept is not limited to electrical energy, but can take different energy carriers (natural gas, heat, …) into account, including conversion processes between them.

To be able to fulfil its task, the energy agent needs detailed knowledge about the behavior and flexibility of the underlying technical system. This knowledge is provided by the Energy Option Model (EOM), which can be seen as the internal reasoning model of the agent. Using the EOM, any kind of energy conversion process can be modelled and described. As this description is supposed to be used in a hybrid network context, it is focused on describing the energy flows at each system specific connection to a network and its corresponding energy carrier.

A general description of the system's behavior is given as a finite state machine, specifying all possible operating states and the transitions between them. For every state, a duration must be specified, which is mainly relevant as a discretization step size during evaluations (see below). Additionally, upper and lower bounds for the residence time in a state can be defined by a constant value or a mathematical function. An example for this kind of system description can be found in Fig. 3 in Sect. 4.1.

For every operating state and every network connection, the energy flows can be specified by defining either a constant value, a time series or a mathematical equation. For the latter case, so called system variables can also be taken into account, that can consist of static data models, external information (like measurements) or user- or agent-controlled set points. Additionally, storage capacities for all involved energy carriers can be defined.

As the EOM is, among others, based on the first law of thermodynamics, the sum of all energy flows will always be zero. This relation is described by Eq. (1)

$$\sum \dot{E}_i = \dot{E}_{in} + \dot{E}_{out} + \dot{E}_{stor} + \dot{E}_{loss} = 0 \tag{1}$$

where $\dot{E}_{in}$ describes the incoming, $\dot{E}_{out}$ the outgoing energy flow, while $\dot{E}_{stor}$ describes the change of the storage level and $\dot{E}_{loss}$ the losses of the actual energy conversion process.

For more complex applications, the EOM supports the modelling of aggregations of systems. While internally consisting of a number of subsystems an aggregation appears towards its surrounding as one unified technical system. It summarizes energy flows, interfaces and storage capacities by energy carriers and enables network calculations if required. Like the aggregation itself, subsystems can also be aggregations, so that complex, hierarchically structured systems of systems can be defined.

## 2.2  EOM-Based Evaluation of Systems

Based on the above described fundamental model, the behavior and flexibility of the system can be derived. Here, the EOM can be used to evaluate possible system states over time with the help of individual, so-called "evaluation strategies" that include the required algorithms.

Starting from an initially defined state, a number of possible successor states result from the operating state transitions and the set point variations that are defined in the base model. To distinguish from a systems operating state as described above, we will refer to the states in this context as "evaluation states". An evaluation state is defined by the current time, the current operating state and further individual parameters, like the battery state of charge (SoC) for the EV example used in this paper. Iteratively generating all possible evaluation states will consequently lead to a full description of the possible system behavior over time in a comprehensive variability graph. Every path through this graph is a possible execution schedule for the modelled system. To extract an execution schedule, a decision making algorithms can be implemented in an evaluation strategy that iteratively generates and selects one of the possible successor states. Figure 1 illustrates this method.

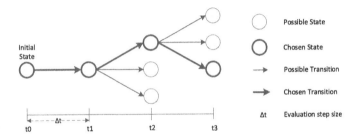

**Fig. 1.** Schedule generation

There is a wide range of possible application cases for this evaluation that can be classified as described in the following and depicted in Fig. 2. First, we can distinguish by the goal of the evaluation, which can be *constraint satisfaction*, i.e. finding feasible execution schedules within given technical limitations or *optimizations* for criteria like cost or efficiency. Further, the evaluation process can be focused on a *single energy carrier* or include *multiple energy carriers*, and possibly conversion processes between them. Another separation arises from the time of use: EOM evaluations can be used for *planning the system behavior in advance*, but also for *real time control* by an energy agent "in the field". As mentioned in Sect. 2.1, evaluations can be executed on *single technical systems* or on *aggregations of systems*.

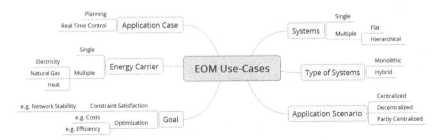

**Fig. 2.** Classification of EOM use-cases

For aggregations of systems, a number of further separations arises. The aggregation can be *monolithic*, like a fleet of identical EVs, or *hybrid*, like a number of devices in a smart house. Finally, the actual decision making process can be executed in a *centralized* way on the aggregation level, *decentralized* on the subsystem level, or *partly centralized*, for example by dealing with critical parts on the central aggregation level while leaving less critical parts to the responsibility of the subordinate systems.

## 3 Related Work

Depending on how it is organized, the increasing use of electric vehicles can either be a further problem or a chance for the stability of a distribution grid. Uncoordinated charging of large numbers of EVs can induce high peak loads and voltage deviations on the distribution grid level, in case that all EVs are charged at the same time [8–14]. On the other hand, if the charging is coordinated appropriately, the growing EV fleet might even help to stabilize the grid. As EV charging is usually not time critical, it can easily be shifted to times with high renewable generation or low power demand. Moreover, coordinated EV charging, along with the EV capability to quickly provide electric energy, may enable EVs to participate in electricity markets (e.g. by providing peak power, spinning reserves or contribute in the frequency regulation) [15, 16]. In recent years, researchers focused on various optimization technics for solving the above mentioned issues. Rahman et al. [17] gives an overview of the most recent studies about various optimization strategies and objective functions related to the EV charging integration. Various optimization methods being used in the literature are mentioned, namely Genetic Algorithms (GA) [18], Stochastic Optimization [19], Game Theory [20], Differential Evaluation (DE) [21], Linear programming [22] and others.

Regardless of the optimization methods used, the coordination process can basically be implemented in a centralized or decentralized way. As mentioned before, in a centralized approach there is a central authority that generates charging schedules for all involved EVs, while considering technical constraints as well as external influences or preferences of the EV users [10, 23, 24].

In a decentralized strategy there is no central authority, and each EV is responsible for its own charging schedule. A major challenge in this scenario is the collaboration between the involved EVs, as the sum of all schedules must still respect technical grid constraints. As mentioned in [25], due to the variety of local methods chosen by the individual EVs, the overall charging pattern is not necessarily optimal for a distribution network. Further examples for decentralized charging strategies can be found in [9, 14, 25, 26].

## 4 Application and Results

### 4.1 EV Modelling and Evaluation

The basic model for describing a single EV was taken from [5]. As shown in Fig. 3, it consists of three possible system states: Charge, Idle and Discharge. Here, we assume constant energy flows of 3.5 kW for charging, 0 kW for the idle state and –3.5 kW for discharging. As shown in the figure, transitions are possible from idle to charge or discharge state and back, but not directly between charge and discharge. Additionally, self-transitions (the repetition of the same state) are possible for all states, if the maximum residence time is not violated. The evaluation step size (10 s in the figure) was varied between 1 s and 10 min during our experiments. A minimum residence time of one minute was defined for all three states to avoid a rapidly fluctuating behavior. The maximum residence time for the charging and discharging states depends on the current SoC of the battery, as it can only be charged till full or discharged till empty. There is no upper bound for the idle state.

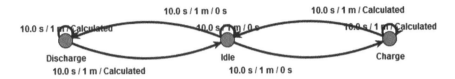

Fig. 3. EV basic model - system states and transitions

For running our experiments on group evaluations we defined a number of aggregations consisting of several instances of the above described EV. Here, the actual number of EVs was one of the parameters we varied during our experiments (see Sect. 4.2 for details). All EV models were located on the top level of the aggregation, without further hierarchical structuring.

The evaluation strategy we used for our experiments is rather simple, mainly a centralized group implementation of the price-optimal charging strategy already shown in [5]. In this context centralized means that the evaluation is done on the aggregation level. Thus, the execution schedules are generated for all subsystems. The strategy itself is based on a time-dependent electricity price model. The cost function we used during our experiments is shown in Fig. 4.

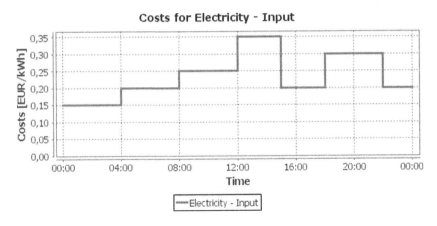

Fig. 4. Example cost function

For generating a price-optimal charging schedule the developed strategy selects and sorts time intervals according to increasing costs. Thus, for the example shown above, it would first use the cheapest time interval between 00:00 and 04:00 and, then, move to the next more expensive one if the desired charging amount is not yet reached. Of course with this greedy-like approach all EVs would charge at the same time, which will lead to high peak loads as described in Sect. 3. Consequently, this strategy should not be applied to charge bigger EV fleets in reality. Since the focus of this paper is not on developing smart charging strategies for an EV fleet that considers network issues, but exploring the capabilities of the EOM to implement centralized decision making processes, this simple strategy approach seems sufficient to us.

## 4.2 Experimental Design and Result

In order to investigate the evaluation capabilities of the EOM, we applied the evaluation strategy described above on a number of aggregations with different sizes, consisting of multiple instances of the base model described above. With the classification given in Sect. 2.2, this corresponds to an optimization use case, focusing on a single energy carrier. Additionally, it is executed for advance planning on a monolithic aggregation of systems in a centralized way.

To get an impression of the level of freedom for this use case, we measured the time that was required to generate all schedules for the aggregations. Since the evaluation process outlined in Sect. 2.2 can be summarized as a series of consecutive decisions, it is clear that, besides the performance of the hosting system, the overall number of decisions may have the main impact on the evaluation time. In detail, three relevant influencing factors for the overall number of decisions can be identified:

- the length of the evaluation period $\Delta t_E$,
- the decision density $d_D$, resulting from the length of the evaluation time steps, and
- the number of involved subsystems $n_S$.

Together with the performance $p$ of the hosting system, the evaluation time $t_E$ results to a function of the above parameters and can be written as:

$$t_E = f(\Delta t_e, d_D, n_s, p) \tag{2}$$

To explore the limitations of a centralized evaluation approach by using the EOM, in our main experiment we systematically measured the execution times for a number of evaluation runs with different combinations of $d_D$ and $n_s$, namely:

- $n_s \in \{1, 5, 10, 20, 30, 40, 50, 75, 100, 150, 200\}$
- $d_D \in \{0.1, 1, 6, 10, 20, 30, 60\}$ DPM (Decisions per minute and per system)

For the evaluation scenario we assumed all EVs to be connected to the grid in a partly discharged state at 8 pm in the evening and expected to be fully charged at 6 am the next morning, resulting in an evaluation period $\Delta t_E$ of 10 h for all subsystems. All runs have been executed on a machine with a performance $p$ of 1997 MFlops (average SciMark 2.0[1] benchmark result). The structure of the experiments is illustrated in Fig. 5. Additionally, we repeated some of this runs on different machines and with different evaluation periods to get an impression of the influence of $\Delta t_E$ and $p$ on the result.

For our main experiment and to minimize the influence of disrupting effects like background processes of the OS, every combination of parameters was evaluated 25 times. Table 1 summarizes the average execution times in seconds for all evaluation runs; a graphical representation is shown in Fig. 6.

The results confirm our assumption that the overall number of decisions has an important impact on the execution time. However, looking at the chart in Fig. 6, the correlation seems much weaker than expected, as the gradient of the curves is increasing with the

---

[1] http://math.nist.gov/scimark2/.

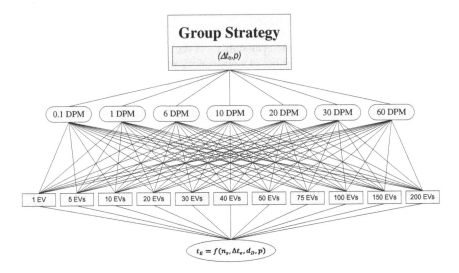

**Fig. 5.** The structure of our main experimental run

number of systems most of the time, but not always. Especially for the 10 and 20 DPM curves, there is a significant decrease of the gradient at 100 systems for 10 DPM and at 50 systems for 20 DPM. Further investigations are required to explain this effect.

If no time is given for an evaluation setup in Table 1, the system we used for evaluation (Core I7-5600, 16 GB of memory) was not able to deliver results within reasonable time. It can also be seen from Table 1 that the evaluation system reached its limits when evaluating 150 systems with each 20 DPM, as well as 75 systems with 30 DPM and 40 systems with 60 DPM. This supports our assumption that centralized decision making processes might become a bottleneck. Despite the higher complexity of organizing and implementing decentralized decision making processes, this seems to be necessary when evaluating larger setups with high decision densities or numbers of systems.

**Table 1.** Average evaluation runtimes

| No. systems | 1 | 5 | 10 | 20 | 30 | 40 | 50 | 75 | 100 | 150 | 200 |
|---|---|---|---|---|---|---|---|---|---|---|---|
| 60 DPM | 1.818 | 12.225 | 26.336 | 57.644 | 69.550 | N/A | N/A | N/A | N/A | N/A | N/A |
| 30 DPM | 0.575 | 2.843 | 8.454 | 17.456 | 29.499 | 37.682 | 72.251 | N/A | N/A | N/A | N/A |
| 20 DPM | 0.483 | 1.867 | 3.768 | 10.495 | 13.221 | 21.627 | 38.847 | 41.420 | 142.701 | N/A | N/A |
| 10 DPM | 0.235 | 1.013 | 1.589 | 5.461 | 10.585 | 12.815 | 15.848 | 16.865 | 35.592 | 38.024 | 120.664 |
| 6 DPM | 0.134 | 0.472 | 0.970 | 2.275 | 3.261 | 5.234 | 6.670 | 11.224 | 12.975 | 19.712 | 37.725 |
| 1 DPM | 0.057 | 0.104 | 0.222 | 0.365 | 0.593 | 0.784 | 0.969 | 1.429 | 2.840 | 3.174 | 4.734 |
| 0.1 DPM | 0.060 | 0.068 | 0.077 | 0.135 | 0.172 | 0.201 | 0.266 | 0.379 | 0.481 | 0.766 | 0.908 |

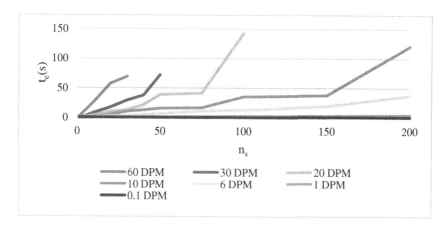

**Fig. 6.** Average evaluation runtimes

To get an impression of the impact of the length of the evaluation period $\Delta t_e$ on the runtime of the evaluation process $t_e$, another series of experiments was executed with a number of systems $n_s = 30$ and a decision density $d_D$ of 6 DPM, varying $\Delta t_e$ between 2 and 24 h in 2 h steps. Again, 25 evaluation runs were executed for every setup. Judging from the average runtimes depicted in Fig. 7, the relation between these factors seems to be roughly linear.

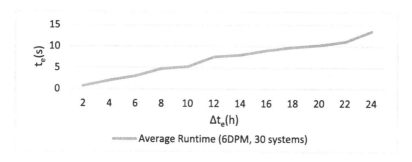

**Fig. 7.** Average evaluation runtimes for different $\Delta t_e$ ($d_D = 6$ DPM, $n_S = 30$)

Finally, we executed a number of evaluation runs on different computers, to explore the influence of the system's performance on the evaluation runtime. For this experiment, we chose a decision density of 6 DPM, the number of systems was varied between 1 and 200 like in our main experiment. Three different systems were used:

- CPU Intel Core i7-5600U, Memory 16 GB, 1996.97 MFlops
- CPU AMD Phenom II X2 555, Memory 4 GB, 1178.22 MFlops
- CPU Intel Core i3 M380, Memory 4 GB, 898.25 MFlops

The results are illustrated in Fig. 8. While the average evaluation times on the strongest machine where significantly shorter no significant differences between the two weaker systems could be seen, despite a difference of about 180 MFlops in their benchmark results. The only remarkable difference is that the 1178 MFlops system was able to calculate the 100 subsystems in reasonable time, while the 898 MFlops system reached its limits with 75 subsystems. Thus, the effect of smaller changes in the system performance seems rather limited, to achieve a significant acceleration of the evaluation process, a significantly stronger machine is required. Additional measurements with system performances between 898 and 1178 MFlops will be required to further investigate this relationship.

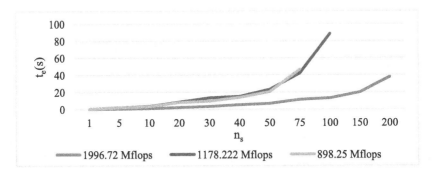

**Fig. 8.** Average evaluation runtimes on different systems ($d_D = 6$ DPM, different $n_S$)

## 5    Conclusion and Outlook

In this paper, we presented first experiments that describe the capabilities of the Energy Option Model (EOM) that, in principle, enables to aggregate and utilize the operational flexibility of any type of energy conversion process. Focusing on a monolithic system structure and the single energy carrier electricity, we investigated a centralized coordination or planning approach for an electric vehicle fleet. The experiments were executed several times on different machines with different performances and the results were compared. It could be shown that the length of the evaluation period, the decision density (number of decisions per time), and the number of involved subsystems have a major impact on the overall evaluation time.

Thus, this supports the assumption that pure centralized decision making processes might turn out to be a bottleneck, when coordinating larger numbers of systems. On the other hand, it leads to the subsequent question which discretization steps are possible, in order to still enable suitable centralized control approaches. Here we believe that such modelling decisions depend on the planning horizon and should carefully be balanced.

For the future, we will further investigate those issues, while also focusing on (partly) decentralized decision making processes. In all cases many questions are to be answered, in order to suggest a reliable future energy structure.

Overall, we believe that the chosen, system-egoistic approach that is provided by the Energy Option Model is the required base approach for a systematic investigation of the future structure of our energy supply. Since the EOM allows the comparison of centralized and decentralized control approaches, it represents a sustainable development that also can be used in the future and for a broad range of applications.

# References

1. Lehnhoff, S.: Dezentrales Vernetztes Energiemanagement: Ein Ansatz Auf Basis Eines Verteilten Adaptiven Realzeit-multiagentensystems. Vieweg + Teubner, Verlag (2010)
2. Linnenberg, T., Wior, I., Schreiber, S., Fay, A.: A market-based multi-agent-system for decentralized power and grid control. In: 2011 IEEE 16th Conference on Emerging Technologies Factory Automation (ETFA), pp. 1–8 (2011)
3. Derksen, C., Linnenberg, T., Unland, R., Fay, A.: Structure and classification of unified energy agents as a base for the systematic development of future energy grids. Eng. Appl. Artif. Intell. **41**, 310–324 (2015)
4. Derksen, C., Linnenberg, T., Unland, R., Fay, A.: Unified energy agents as a base for the systematic development of future energy grids. In: Klusch, M., Thimm, M., Paprzycki, M. (eds.) MATES 2013. LNCS, vol. 8076, pp. 236–249. Springer, Heidelberg (2013)
5. Derksen, C., Unland, R.: Energy agents - foundation for open future energy grids. In: Position Papers of the 2015 Federated Conference on Computer Science and Information Systems, vol. 6, pp. 259–264 (2015)
6. Kok, K., Warmer, C., Kamphuis, R., Mellstrand, P., Gustavsson, R.: Distributed control in the electricity infrastructure. In: 2005 International Conference on Future Power Systems, pp. 1–7 (2005)
7. Platt, G.: The decentralised control of electricity networks - intelligent and self-healing systems. In: Grid Interop 2007 Forum Proceedings (2007)
8. Das, R., Thirugnanam, K., Kumar, P., Lavudiya, R., Singh, M.: Mathematical modeling for economic evaluation of electric vehicle to smart grid interaction. IEEE Trans. Smart Grid **5**, 712–721 (2014)
9. Gan, L., Topcu, U., Low, S.: Optimal decentralized protocol for electric vehicle charging. In: 2011 50th IEEE Conference on Decision and Control and European Control Conference (CDC-ECC), pp. 5798–5804 (2011)
10. Kelly, L., Rowe, A., Wild, P.: Analyzing the impacts of plug-in electric vehicles on distribution networks in British Columbia. In: 2009 IEEE Electrical Power Energy Conference (EPEC), pp. 1–6 (2009)
11. Lopes, J.A.P., Soares, F.J., Almeida, P.M.R.: Integration of electric vehicles in the electric power system. Proc. IEEE **99**, 168–183 (2011)
12. Luo, Y., Zhu, T., Wan, S., Zhang, S., Li, K.: Optimal charging scheduling for large-scale EV (electric vehicle) deployment based on the interaction of the smart-grid and intelligent-transport systems. Energy **97**, 359–368 (2016)
13. Roe, C., Farantatos, E., Meisel, J., Meliopoulos, A.P., Overbye, T.: Power system level impacts of PHEVs. In: 42nd Hawaii International Conference on System Sciences, 2009. HICSS 2009, pp. 1–10 (2009)
14. Valogianni, K., Ketter, W., Collins, J., Zhdanov, D.: Effective management of electric vehicle storage using smart charging. In: Proceedings of 28th AAAI Conference on Artificial Intelligence, pp. 472–478 (2014)
15. Kahlen, M., Ketter, W.: Aggregating electric cars to sustainable virtual power plants: the value of flexibility in future electricity markets. In: Proceedings of the Twenty-Ninth AAAI Conference on Artificial Intelligence (AAAI-15) (2015)
16. Kempton, W., Tomic, J.: Vehicle-to-grid power fundamentals: calculating capacity and net revenue. J. Power Sources **144**, 268–279 (2005)
17. Rahman, I., Vasant, P.M., Singh, B.S.M., Abdullah-Al-Wadud, M., Adnan, N.: Review of recent trends in optimization techniques for plug-in hybrid, and electric vehicle charging infrastructures. Renew. Sustain. Energy Rev. **58**, 1039–1047 (2016)

18. Fazelpour, F., Vafaeipour, M., Rahbari, O., Rosen, M.A.: Intelligent optimization to integrate a plug-in hybrid electric vehicle smart parking lot with renewable energy resources and enhance grid characteristics. Energy Convers. Manag. **77**, 250–261 (2014)
19. Zhu, Z., Lambotharan, S., Chin, W.H., Fan, Z.: A stochastic optimization approach to aggregated electric vehicles charging in smart grids. In: 2014 IEEE Innovative Smart Grid Technologies - Asia (ISGT Asia), pp. 51–56 (2014)
20. Malandrino, F., Casetti, C., Chiasserini, C.-F., Reineri, M.: A game-theory analysis of charging stations selection by EV drivers. Perform. Eval. **83–84**, 16–31 (2015)
21. Tikader, R., Ganguly, S.: Energy management at municipal parking deck for charging of plug-in hybrid electric vehicles. In: 2014 IEEE Students' Conference on Electrical, Electronics and Computer Science (SCEECS), pp. 1–5 (2014)
22. Zheng, Y., Dong, Z.Y., Xu, Y., Meng, K., Zhao, J.H., Qiu, J.: Electric vehicle battery charging/swap stations in distribution systems: comparison study and optimal planning. IEEE Trans. Power Syst. **29**, 221–229 (2014)
23. Liu, C., Zhou, Q., Hu, J., Xu, H., Zhang, H.: Modelling and simulation of centralized electric vehicle charging station wireless communication networks. Procedia Eng. **31**, 746–750 (2012)
24. Quan-Do, V., Jeong-Hyo, B., Jae-Duck, L., Seong-Joon, L.: Monitoring of power allocation in centralized electric vehicle charging spot system. Energy Procedia **17**(Part B), 1542–1549 (2012)
25. Ma, Z., Callaway, D., Hiskens, I.: Decentralized charging control for large populations of plug-in electric vehicles. In: 2010 49th IEEE Conference on Decision and Control (CDC), pp. 206–212 (2010)
26. Liu, M., Crisostomi, E., Gu, Y., Shorten, R.: Optimal distributed consensus algorithm for fair V2G power dispatch in a microgrid. In: 2014 IEEE International Electric Vehicle Conference (IEVC), pp. 1–7 (2014)

# Network Operator Agent: Endowing MASCEM Simulator with Technical Validation

Ana Freitas, Isabel Praça, Tiago Pinto[✉], Tiago Sousa, and Zita Vale

GECAD – Knowledge Engineering and Decision-Support Research Center,
Institute of Engineering – Politechnic of Porto (ISEP/IPP), Porto, Portugal
{1080598,icp,tmcfp,tabsa,zav}@isep.ipp.pt

**Abstract.** The actual flexibility of the electricity sector, with a distributed nature and new players, such as the smart grid operator and several types of aggregators, brings new business models and introduces new challenges from the power systems technical operation point of view. In this context, the Network Operator Agent of the Multi-Agent Simulator of Competitive Electricity Markets (MASCEM) plays a crucial role, not only in the scope of the technical validation of the economic transactions established by the market, but also has an agent that can be supporting the grid operation under the scope of a smart grid. A set of new features has been added to the Network Operator making it a "new agent", bringing a more effective decision support, from the grid technical operation point of view, and achieving its usefulness beyond MASCEM. In this paper the new features are described. A case study is also included to better illustrate the approach and to highlight its usefulness under the scope of a smart grid scenario.

**Keywords:** Electricity markets · Multi-Agent simulation · Network operator

## 1 Introduction

Over the last decades the electricity sector has been suffering a deep restructuring that started with the privatization and liberalization of previously nationally owned systems [1]. This has bought the competition into the electricity markets, and a set of new mechanisms has been defined [2].

Some tools have emerged to better support electricity sector players to understand and take decisions under the new types of market negotiations. Some of the most well-known tools in this domain are AMES (Agent-based Modeling of Electricity Systems) [3], EMCAS (Electricity Market Complex Adaptive System) [4] and MASCEM (Multi-Agent Simulator of Competitive Electricity Markets) [5].

The present work was done and funded in the scope of EUREKA - ITEA2 Project SEAS with project number 12004; AVIGAE Project (P2020-3401); and UID/EEA/00760/2013 funded by FEDER Funds through COMPETE program and by National Funds through FCT.

© Springer International Publishing Switzerland 2016
J. Bajo et al. (Eds.): PAAMS 2016 Workshops, CCIS 616, pp. 381–392, 2016.
DOI: 10.1007/978-3-319-39387-2_32

The optimal power flow analysis is not a recent subject; there are several tools in this domain, such as: PowerWorld [6], CymPower [7] and MatPower [8], a Matlab package. But, the new market rules and the increasing penetration of renewable sources of energy, deeply encouraged by the European environmental policies, that actually are also headline targets of the Europe 2020 strategy for smart, sustainable and inclusive growth [9] imposes the need for a straightforward cooperation between market and power system operators. A way to realize the emerging potential of renewable sources usually distributed and near the consumption sites, is to take an approach that manages these resources as a subsystem according to the new paradigm of Smart Grids [10, 11].

MASCEM is one of the most flexible and comprehensive tools that allows the simulation of the market transactions as well as technical analysis of competitive markets under the scope of a smart grid, at a country level and also at an European level [11]. This is achieved by the completeness of its multi-agent model, which includes a strong cooperation between the Market Operator agent and the actual System Operator agent.

This paper addresses recent MASCEM improvements, which led to a restructuring of the System Operator. This agent now becomes a Network operator in the sense that it is not just a Distribution or Transmission System operator, but may also be considered at the smart grid level. Section 2 describes MASCEM multi-agent model, comparing the previous and the new structure of the agent assuring the system technical validation. Section 3 focuses on the description of the Network Operator, its interface and capabilities. In Sect. 4 a smart grid case study is used to highlight the decision support provided by the Network Operator. Finally in Sect. 5 some conclusions are elicited.

## 2    MASCEM Multi-agent Model

MASCEM is a multi-agent simulator of competitive electricity markets and it was developed with the purpose of studying the complex and restructured electricity markets. Since its first version in 2003 [5] MASCEM has undergone several improvements [12, 13] to become an increasingly comprehensive tool and to accommodate new management models of electricity markets.

MASCEM model includes agents that represent the entities involved in the electricity markets including their interactions, collecting data in the medium and long term to support the decisions of these entities according to their characteristics and objectives, thus allowing better understanding of the behavior, the development of trade relations and the mechanisms of these markets. The simulator uses game theory, learning techniques, scenario analysis and optimization techniques for modeling and supporting market actors in their decisions [13]. Figure 1 illustrates the multi-agent model and market structure of MASCEM.

MASCEM went through a restructuring process, having adopted the JADE (Java Agent Development Framework) [14] framework, mainly due to its support to agents' communications. JADE is a developing environment for agent-based applications, according to the specifications of FIPA (Foundation for Intelligent Physical Agents) [15] and fully implemented in JAVA. It ensures a standard of interoperability between multi-agent systems through a comprehensive set of system services, which enable

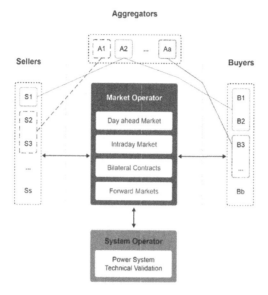

**Fig. 1.** MASCEM's agents [13]

communication between agents. This interoperability brings a lot of further possibilities for MASCEM and for its agents. From the agents point of view it is now possible that they be also part of other models and tools. It also brings MASCEM a new dimension as it may consider in the same simulation bids coming from external agents or tools.

Electricity markets are quite different from other types of markets as the stability of the power system must be assured, thus economical transactions have a strong dependency on the results of the optimal power flow of the electrical grid. In MASCEM the technical analysis of the power flow was assured by the System Operator agent, as mentioned in Fig. 1.

The role of the System Operator assumes, in the most recent version of MASCEM, a broader role. It becomes a Network Operator (NO) in the sense that it is not only linked to the Transmission System Operator (TSO) or Distribution System Operator (DSO), but may accomplish the technical operation of electrical grids on the scope, for example, of a smart grid. Figure 2 highlights the current MASCEM multi-agent model, enhancing the NO modules and the links with the Market Operator as well as its usefulness abroad MASCEM. NO core modules are the "OPF Algorithms", the environment for the grid definition "Virtual and Geo-location Grids" and a User Interface to make it also useful outside the simulation environment. The "OPF Algorithms" module contains a set of algorithms for the optimal power flow, used to analyze the viability of the economic transactions established at the wholesale market, and communicated by the Market Operator (MO). The economic dispatch may result in unacceptable flows or voltages in the network, so, NO may need to remove some of the previewed power injection to avoid unacceptable flows.

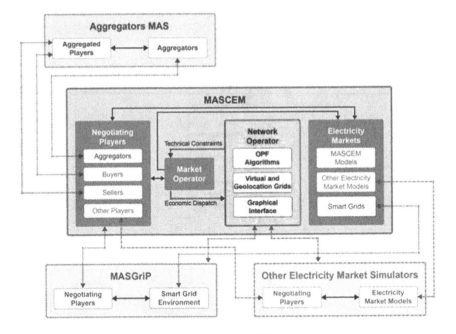

**Fig. 2.** MASCEM and NO structure

The scenarios that can be tested with this tool can be related to a real power grid, and thus, based on the geo-location of the grid elements (bus, lines, etc.), or based on virtual grids, this means, scenarios based on grids for test cases. Grids under test may be defined by means of input files or through the user interface, which is quite friendly and easily manipulated. It is worth mentioning that although NO is an agent from MASCEM, it may be used to perform power flow analysis under the scope of other tools, as long as they have communication capability with JADE and respect FIPA regulations.

In Fig. 2, both the link to other simulators and to MASGriP (Multi-agent Smart Grid Simulation Platform) [16] highlights this flexibility. MASGriP is a tool that simulates a smart grid environment, modeling the main involved entities and their interconnections. It was also developed in JADE and it can easily benefit from the NO features at the smart grid level. In this paper we address this "independency" of the actual NO by highlighting the Graphical Interface capabilities and describing the usefulness of this agent in a smart grid scenario.

## 3    Network Operator Agent

Network Operator Agent (NO) allows the definition and analysis of real and virtual grids. Real grids are those based on the geo-location within a terrestrial map, like the Portuguese transmission grid, while virtual networks aimed at the study of test cases, usually defined to simplify real networks, as those provided, for example, by the IEEE [17]. The NO agent is able not only to create the network to work with, but also to analyze it, and give the instructions to the user of where are the problems in the network.

NO has a clean interface, with the main area for the grid map. Figure 3 shows the interface. The top selected area shows the application menu and a tab bar. The tab bar contains two options: Real Map (the one selected in Fig. 3) and Virtual Network. The Real Network option allows the user to create a network on a map based in real geo-location coordinates. The Virtual Network option allows the user to create a network without geo-location coordinates, mainly to allow the analysis of case studies based on simplified grids or case studies based on hypothetical scenarios.

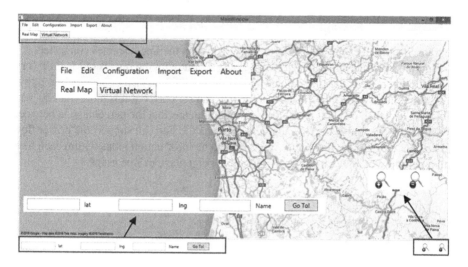

**Fig. 3.** NO interface for Real networks

The options on menu bar are:

- File
  - Exit Application;
- Edit
  - Clear Power Grid – Deletes all buses, transmission lines and players defined;
- Configuration
  - New Type Of Player – Types of Players (such as Seller, Buyer, VPP…) are managed by the user. This options allows the user to create new types of Player;
  - Delete Type Of Player – Based on all the types the user has created in the NO, the user can delete one or more types of Player;
- Import
  - Import Grid – Import a network previously created;
  - Import Player Results – To get the market transactions;
  - Import Results – To get Optimal Power Flow (OPF) results;
- Export
  - Export Grid – Export grid to allow testing different market scenarios without the need to create it again;

The second selected area, on the left bottom, is the navigation area. The user can select geographical coordinates and navigate to them or, for example, search by name of city, country, village, etc. This makes the use of the NO user friendly in defining networks from all over the globe. The third selected area, on the right bottom, contains the zoom controllers. To define a grid, the buses, transmission lines and each player location needs to be specified. After this definition, or by loading a previously defined network, the interface shows all the specified elements. When using the import feature, it is still possible to add new buses, transmission lines and players.

Before the OPF analysis of market transactions, the transmission lines are shown in blue. After, transmission lines will be colored according with the OPF results, based on the transmission lines flow, with red being used when the line becomes congested.

Figure 4 illustrates the same network as Fig. 3, but with the results of the OPF for a negotiation period. If the line color is red, it means the line cannot support the power flow. If the line is yellow, it means that the line can support, but it is more than 30 % of usage and less than 60 %. If the color is orange it means that the percentage is between 60 % and 100 %. And if the line is green, it means the line can support the power flow and it is not close to the maximum. There are some information icons within each line, with a pop-up window that shows the effective percentage of line usage.

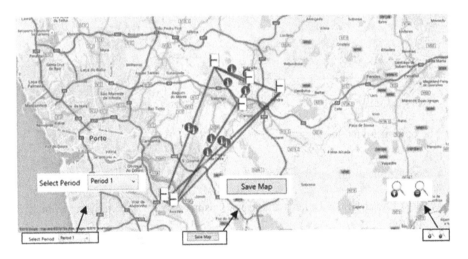

**Fig. 4.** OPF results for one hour

In Fig. 4 the three "small areas" at the bottom allow: the left one is to be used to change between periods; the centered one is used for saving the image of the network; and the right one represents the zoom controllers.

## 4    Case Study

The objective of this case study is to validate the role of MASCEM's NO agent in electricity market simulations. With this aim a simulated smart grid scenario is considered, including several agents that represent consumers and producers based on real data from Portugal. A smart grid internal market is simulated using MASCEM, which results in a set of purchase and sale amounts of power, referring to each seller and buyer player. The internal smart grid market results are then communicated to MASCEM's NO agent, so that it validates the power flow in the network lines.

## 4.1 Characterization

The considered smart grid power network is the 14 bus IEEE test system network [18]. This network is connected to the main grid through a MV/LV transformer. Table 1 shows the characteristics of the 20 considered power network lines, where each table line represents a network line: the first and second columns are the buses connected by the line; the third column (R p.u.) is the resistance of the line in series; the fourth column (X p.u.) is the inductive impedance in series; the fifth column (B p.u.) is the capacitive impedance in parallel; and the last column (Smax p.u.) is the line maximum capacity.

**Table 1.** Characteristics of the considered power network lines

| Bus I | Bus J | R (p.u) | X (p.u.) | B (p.u.) | Smax (p.u.) |
|-------|-------|---------|----------|----------|-------------|
| 1  | 2  | 0,01938 | 0,05917 | 0,0528 | 5  |
| 1  | 5  | 0,05403 | 0,22304 | 0,0492 | 10 |
| 2  | 3  | 0,04699 | 0,19797 | 0,0438 | 5  |
| 2  | 4  | 0,05811 | 0,17632 | 0,034  | 10 |
| 2  | 5  | 0,05695 | 0,17388 | 0,0346 | 10 |
| 3  | 4  | 0,06701 | 0,17103 | 0,0128 | 10 |
| 4  | 5  | 0,01335 | 0,04211 | 0      | 10 |
| 4  | 7  | 0       | 0,20912 | 0      | 11 |
| 4  | 9  | 0       | 0,55618 | 0      | 10 |
| 5  | 6  | 0       | 0,25202 | 0      | 10 |
| 6  | 11 | 0,09498 | 0,1989  | 0      | 10 |
| 6  | 12 | 0,12291 | 0,25581 | 0      | 10 |
| 6  | 13 | 0,06615 | 0,13027 | 0      | 10 |
| 7  | 8  | 0       | 0,17615 | 0      | 10 |
| 7  | 9  | 0       | 0,11001 | 0      | 10 |
| 9  | 10 | 0,03181 | 0,0845  | 0      | 10 |
| 9  | 14 | 0,12711 | 0,27038 | 0      | 10 |
| 10 | 11 | 0,08205 | 0,19207 | 0      | 5  |
| 12 | 13 | 0,22092 | 0,19988 | 0      | 5  |
| 13 | 14 | 0,17093 | 0,34802 | 0      | 5  |

The considered smart grid accommodates distributed generation (photovoltaic and coal based generation), provided by 22 producers: 17 are solar based and 5 based on coal generation; and 82 consumers (8 residential houses, 8 residential buildings, each with 8 residential apartments and a common place, and 2 commercial buildings (a bar, which works at night, and a self-service laundry). Each consumer is represented by an independent software agent. Further details on the considered scenario can be consulted in [20].

### 4.2 Results

The smart grid internal market is simulated in MASCEM, including sale and purchase bids from all the involved players (buyers and sellers) for each of the 24 hourly periods of a simulated day: January 21st 2015, a business day during the winter. Figure 5 presents the total amount of transacted power in each hour, resulting from the market execution of the considered simulation day.

**Fig. 5.** Hourly market results

From Fig. 5 it is visible that, as expected, the smart grid internal market results in a balance between generation and consumption in each hour of the considered day. It can also be seen that in this case the larger amounts of traded power occur during the night, mostly due to the high consumption values of the commercial buildings (especially the bar), as can be seen by Fig. 6, which represents bought power of each of the 82 consumers in each hour of the considered simulation day.

From Fig. 6 one can clearly distinguish the consumption amount of the two commercial buildings, which is much higher than the residential consumers. It is also visible that the huge amount of consumption of the commercial buildings occurs during the night (the bar is represented by the blue line, and the laundry by the red line). The residential consumers present rather similar consumption profiles.

Figure 7 shows that the 17 solar based agents present similar generation profiles, as they dependent on the solar intensity in the smart grid location. Therefore the generation of these players achieves higher values during the hours of the day where the sun in more intense, and the production during the night in null. On the other hand, the amount sold by the 5 coal based sellers varies according to the needs in each moment. These 5 players have a maximum generation capacity of 3, 5, 10, 15 and 20 p.u., and the sale prices are lower for the players with lower capacity, and increase as the maximum

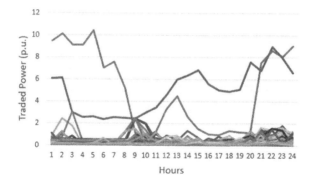

**Fig. 6.** Consumers profile

capacity increases. This means that, in order to meet the demand, the smaller coal based sellers are used first, and the larger ones are only used when the required amount of power increases. For this reason, the larger coal based sellers, purple and green lines in Fig. 7, do not sell any power during many hours of the day.

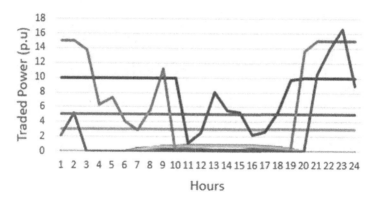

**Fig. 7.** Generation profiles

In order to analyze MASCEM's NO role in validating the market transactions through a technical validation of the network, the periods that present the lower and huge amounts of traded power are shown, which are respectively, hour 11 and hour 23, as presented in Fig. 5. MASCEM's market results are sent to the NO, which uses the created network to execute the power flow and validate the technical feasibility of the market results. The NO displays the network with an information marker in each line, and changes the color of the line depending on the percentage of the line capacity that is being used, as shown in Fig. 8 for the 11th period.

As can be seen from Fig. 8, the power flow analyses indicates that there was no congestion in this hour, as can be seen by the line colours. Five lines out of twenty have less than 30 % of use (green lines), and all the remaining can support the required power. The information markers shows the percentage of use of the line in two directions: Bus I to Bus J and from Bus J to Bus I.

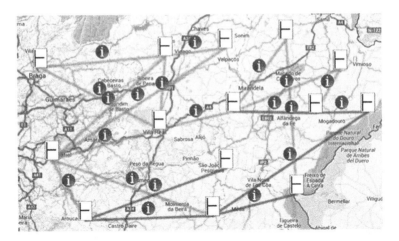

**Fig. 8.** Results of the 11<sup>th</sup> period

Figure 9 shows the power flow results, achieved by the NO, regarding the market results of period 23. As shown, in this period, five out of twenty lines become congested. This occurs because the traded amount of power is bigger than the amount the lines can support, which happens because of the huge amount of transacted power verified in the 23<sup>rd</sup> period (see Fig. 5). MASCEM's market operator can use the feedback from the NO to validate and close the market session, or, as in this later case, re-execute the market in order to reach a market solution that respects the network constraints. This is usually done by separating the network into several zones, in order to avoid an excessive amount of power from being sent through critical lines.

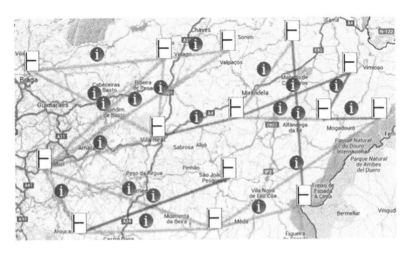

**Fig. 9.** Results for the 23<sup>rd</sup> period

## 5  Conclusions

This paper presents MASCEM improvements, regarding the introduction of a flexible and independent Network Operator agent, able to perform the optimal power flow of real or virtual networks. The independency of NO brings the possibility of being used by other simulation tools or even in the analysis of power flow without the market.

A case study based on a smart grid scenario with 82 consumers and 22 producers is presented. Two periods power flow have been analyzed: one for the $11^{th}$ period, the one with the lower amount of traded power, and another for $23^{rd}$ period, the one with the huge amount of traded power. Results show that the NO is able to perform the technical validation of the network lines considering the market results, and show this information in a user-friendly way, to ease the interaction with the users. Indeed, these two extreme periods analysis illustrate NO graphical user interface usefulness in understanding what is happening in the simulated scenario. The network technical validation results are also useful information for MASCEM's market operator, so that it can validate the feasibility of the established transactions, or reschedule the market in order to guarantee the viability of the market trades.

## References

1. Shahidehpour, M., Yamin, H., Li, Z.: Market Operations in Electric Power Systems: Forecasting, Scheduling, and Risk Management, pp. 233–274. Wiley-IEEE Press, New York (2002)
2. Meeus, L., Purchalaa, K., Belmans, R.: Development of the internal electricity market in Europe. Electr. J. **18**(6), 25–35 (2005)
3. Li, H., Tesfatsion, L.: Development of open source software for power market research: the AMES test bed. J. Energy Markets **2**(2), 111–128 (2009)
4. Koritarov, V.: Real-world market representation with agents: modeling the electricity market as a complex adaptive system with an agent-based approach. IEEE Power Energy **2**, 39–46 (2004)
5. Praça, I., Ramos, C., Vale, Z., Cordeiro, M.: MASCEM: a multi-agent system that simulates competitive electricity markets. IEEE Intel. Syst. **18**(6), 54–60 (2003). doi:10.1109/MIS.2003.1249170. Special Issue on Agents and Markets
6. Power World. http://www.powerworld.com/. Accessed on Jan 2016
7. CYME Power Engineering Software. http://www.cyme.com/software/. Accessed on Jan 2016
8. Zimmerman, R.D., et al.: MATPOWER - A MATLAB Power System Simulation Package. http://www.pserc.cornell.edu/matpower/. Accessed on Jan 2016
9. European Commission: The 2020 climate and energy package. http://ec.europa.eu/clima/policies/strategies/2020/index_en.htm. Accessed on Jan 2016
10. Electricity Advisory Committee: Smart Grid: Enabler of the New Energy Economy, December 2008
11. Buchholz, B.M., Styczynski, Z.: Smart Grids - Fundamentals and Technologies in Electricity Networks. Springer, Heidelberg (2014)

12. Pinto, T., Silva, H., Vale, Z., Santos, G., Praça, I.: Pan-European electricity market simulation considering the European power network capacities. In: Fourth International Workshop on Artificial Intelligence Techniques for Power Systems and Energy Markets (IATEM 2015), 26th International Conference on Database and Expert Systems Applications (DEXA 2015), Valencia, Spain, pp. 1–4, September 2015

13. Pinto, T., Morais, H., Oliveira, P., Vale, Z., Praça, I., Ramos, C.: A new approach for multi-agent coalition formation and management in the scope of eletricity markets. Energy **36**(8), 5004–5015 (2011). doi:10.1016/j.energy.2011.05.045

14. Santos, G., Pinto, T., Morais, H., Sousa, T.M., Pereira, I.F., Fernandes, R., Praça, I., Vale, Z.: Multi-agent simulation of competitive electricity markets: autonomous systems cooperation for European market modeling. Energy Conver. Manag. **99**, 387–399 (2015). doi:10.1016/j.enconman.2015.04.042

15. JADE - Java Agent DEvelopment Framework. http://jade.tilab.com/. Accessed on Jan 2016

16. Foundation for Intelligent Physical Agents (FIPA), Agent Management Specification (2002). http://www.fipa.org/specs/fipa00023/SC00023J.html. Accessed on Jan 2016

17. Oliveira, P., Pinto, T., Morais, H., Vale, Z.: MASGriP – a multi-agent smart grid simulation platform. In: IEEE Power and Energy Society General Meeting 2012, 22–26 July 2012, San Diego CA, USA (2012). doi:10.1109/PESGM.2012.6345649

18. Power Flow Cases. http://publish.illinois.edu/smartergrid/. Accessed on Jan 2016

19. 14 bus IEEE test system network. https://www.ee.washington.edu/research/pstca/. Accessed on Jan 2016

20. Canizes, B., et al.: Resource scheduling in residential microgrids considering energy selling to external players. In: Power Systems Conference (PSC 2015), 10–13 March 2015, South Carolina, USA (2012)

# Electricity Markets Ontology to Support MASCEM's Simulations

Gabriel Santos[1], Tiago Pinto[1(✉)], Zita Vale[1], Isabel Praça[1],
and Hugo Morais[2]

[1] GECAD – Research Group on Intelligent Engineering and Computing
for Advanced Innovation and Development, Institute of Engineering,
Polytechnic of Porto (ISEP/IPP), Porto, Portugal
{gajls,tmcfp,zav,icp}@isep.ipp.pt
[2] AUTomation and Control Group – Department of Electrical Engineering,
Technical University of Denmark (DTU),
Elektrovej, Building 326, 2800 Kongens Lyngby, Denmark
morais@elektro.dtu.dk

**Abstract.** Power systems worldwide are complex and challenging environments. The increasing necessity for an adequate integration of renewable energy sources is resulting in a rising complexity in power systems operation. Multi-agent based simulation platforms have proven to be a good option to study the several issues related to these systems, including the involved players that act in this domain. To take better advantage of these systems, their integration is mandatory. The main contribution of this paper is the development of the *Electricity Markets Ontology,* which integrates the essential concepts necessary to interpret all the available information related to electricity markets, while enabling an easier cooperation and adequate communication between related systems. Additionally, the concepts and rules defined by this ontology can be extended and complemented according to the needs of other simulation and real systems in this area. Each system's particular ontology must import the proposed ontology, thus enabling the effective interoperability between independent systems.

**Keywords:** Electricity markets · Multi-agent simulation · Ontologies

## 1 Introduction

The power sector business has been completely revolutionized by the emergence of liberalized Electricity Markets (EM). The sector's restructuring process brought out several challenges, requiring the transformation of the conceptual models that previously dominated the power sector [1]. This restructuring made the market more competitive, but also more complex, posing new challenges to its participants. Therefore, the involved entities are forced to rethink their behavior and market strategies.

The present work was done and funded in the scope of the following projects: H2020 DREAM-GO Project (Marie Sklodowska-Curie grant agreement No 641794); EUREKA - ITEA2 Project SEAS with project number 12004; AVIGAE Project (P2020-3401); and UID/EEA/00760/2013 funded by FEDER Funds through COMPETE program and by National Funds through FCT.

© Springer International Publishing Switzerland 2016
J. Bajo et al. (Eds.): PAAMS 2016 Workshops, CCIS 616, pp. 393–404, 2016.
DOI: 10.1007/978-3-319-39387-2_33

To give entities decision support to address the new challenges, the use of simulation tools becomes decisive in order to study, analyze, and test different alternatives for markets' structure and evolution. For market participants it is important to anticipate scenarios and define strategies, while for the operators it is essential to test new market architectures. The main purpose of these tools is to deal with the constantly evolving reality of EM and grant actors with appropriate solutions to adapt themselves to the new reality, gaining experience to act in the context of a changing economic, financial, and regulatory environment. Market players aim to optimize their results (minimize costs if buying; or maximize profits if selling) and operators must ensure a competitive and transparent market in which no entity has significant market power [2].

EM simulators must be flexible in order to handle this complex and evolving reality, providing players with proper tools to adapt themselves to this dynamic reality and learn from experience. Several studies sustain that multi-agent systems (MAS) with the adequate simulation capabilities are suitable for the simulation of EM, considering the complex interactions of the involved players [3–5]. Some of the main advantages that multi-agent approaches provide are the facilitated inclusion of new models, market mechanisms, player types, and different types of interactions [6]. In this domain some reference modelling tools have emerged, such as AMES (Agent-based Modelling of Electricity Systems) [4], EMCAS (Electricity Market Complex Adaptive System) [3] and MASCEM (Multi-Agent Simulator of Competitive Electricity Markets) [6, 7].

MASCEM [6–8] is a modeling and simulation tool developed for studying complex restructured EM. It provides players with competitive advantage in the market by supplying them with simulation and decision-support resources.

Current tools are directed to the study of different EM mechanisms and to the analysis of the relationships between market entities, but they do not enable the interoperability with external systems. Simulators could gain significant added value by sharing their knowledge and market models with other agent societies. Such tools would provide the means for an actual improvement in current EM studies and development.

This paper introduces the *Electricity Markets Ontology* (EMO) designed to provide the means to achieve interoperability between EM simulation platforms. After this introductory section, an overview of MASCEM is presented in Sect. 2. Section 3 presents the proposed EMO, while Sect. 4 features a case study based on real data from several European EM operators. Finally, the conclusions are presented in Sect. 5.

## 2  MASCEM Overview

MASCEM – Multi-Agent Simulator of Competitive Electricity Markets [6–9] is a modelling and simulation tool which has been developed aiming at studying the operation of complex and competitive restructured EM. It models the main complex and dynamic market entities and their interactions. To support players' decisions in accordance with their characteristics and goals, medium/long-term gathering of data and experience is also considered.

Software agents in MASCEM represent the main entities and players involved in EM, such as: market operator, system operator, buyer and seller agents (consumers, producers and/or prosumers), and the aggregators. Figure 1 shows a general overview of MASCEM's multi-agent model.

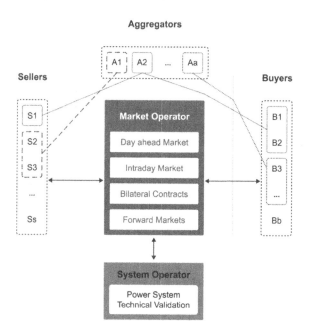

**Fig. 1.** MASCEM's multi-agent model, adapted from [6]

The market operator agent is responsible for coordinating and regulating the pool markets operation. It informs buyer and seller agents when the pool is open, receives their proposals, validates and analyses them, and determines the clearing market price, accepted and refused bids for each trading period.

The system operator agent is responsible for the system's security and ensures that all constraints are satisfied within the system. It is always present during the simulations. After being informed by the market operator of the market's outcome, it examines the technical feasibility from the power system point of view and solves congestion problems that may arise.

Buyer and seller agents – the market players – are the key elements of EM. Buyer agents represent the demand side entities, while generation units are represented by seller agents. On one hand, sellers compete with each other trying to increase their profits; on the other, they may also cooperate with buyer agents trying to reach agreements that are advantageous for both parties.

The aggregators represent alliances of small independent players. The meaningful increase of small independent producers and consumers participating in the market, brought the need to make such alliances to enable them competing with big producers.

They manage their aggregates' information and are seen in the market as buyer or seller agents. Each aggregator is modelled as an independent MAS, allowing agents to be installed on different machines while maintaining the high performance as possible.

MASCEM includes the main types of negotiations normally present in EM, such as: day-ahead and intraday pool (symmetric or asymmetric, with or without complex conditions) markets; bilateral contracts and forward markets. By selecting a combination of these market models, it's also possible to perform hybrid simulations.

The user defines each scenario by inputting the market and market type to simulate, the number of simulation days, the number of participating players and their strategies considering each type of agent, with their own decision-support resources, assuring them competitive advantage in the market.

Communications between agents are carried out through the exchange of messages. The Foundation for Intelligent Physical Agents (FIPA) suggests Agent Communication Language (ACL) as a standard for communications between agents [10]. Its content includes the content language, specifying the syntax, and the ontology which provides the semantics of the message assuring the correct interpretation [11]. MASCEM agents use the *Electricity Markets Ontology* (EMO) to enable the interoperability with other MAS or agent-based simulators that intend to participate in MASCEM's simulations.

## 3   Electricity Markets Ontology

Currently, MAS in the power system's domain are developed with their own specific ontologies. These systems share common concepts that are differently represented between the independently developed ontologies, and translating these concepts automatically is not as straightforward as it may seem. In order to take full advantage of the functionalities of those systems, there is a growing need for knowledge exchange between them.

FIPA suggests the use of an Ontology Agent (OA), which provides some related services, to solve the problem of multiple ontologies [12]. This is still an experimental standard and mappings between ontologies must still be performed by ontologies' designers, which increases the human effort required and costs of implementation. In alternative, Catterson [13] proposes the use of an upper ontology representing the general concepts of the domain, ensuring a common basis for the representation of those concepts and their relationships between systems while reducing the complexity of ontology mapping.

Inspired by this last approach, this paper proposed the use of EMO for the interoperability of EM multi-agent simulation platforms, which can be extended in a way to enable the full interoperability between those systems.

To reuse existing ontologies is usually a requirement for systems' interoperability. It is possible to find in the literature some ontologies developed for the field of energy markets, namely electricity and natural gas [14–16]. Unfortunately none is publicly available for reuse and/or extension, which led to the development from scratch of the proposed ontology.

In [14] a very extensive and interesting work has been developed, although the authors decided to take in mind only the domain of the ontology, leaving aside its application scenario. It is also important to note that the developed ontology is aimed at the Greek EM, not having been extended to any other European EM. If this ontology was publicly available, its reuse would be considered, given the extensity and accuracy of the knowledge already represented. In any case, ELMO ontology [14], as it is, is not suitable for EM multi-agent simulators.

## 3.1 EMO Specification

The EMO incorporates abstract concepts and axioms referring to the main existing EM. This ontology aims to be as inclusive as possible so that it can be extended and reused in the development of (lower level) market-specific ontologies, such as the MIBEL [17], EPEX [18], Nord Pool [19] or any other EM ontology. It was kept as simple as possible in order to facilitate its reuse and extension independently of the market's features and/or rules. However, given that the suggested ontologies were developed considering its use by agent based simulation tools, some markets' constraints were also defined in EMO. Figure 2 illustrates EMO's relations between the identified classes and object and data properties.

From Fig. 2 it is possible to see the object properties represented in blue and the data properties defined within each class with the respective data types. The orange relations represent the inferred object properties, which are inverse properties of the ones defined in blue in the opposite direction.

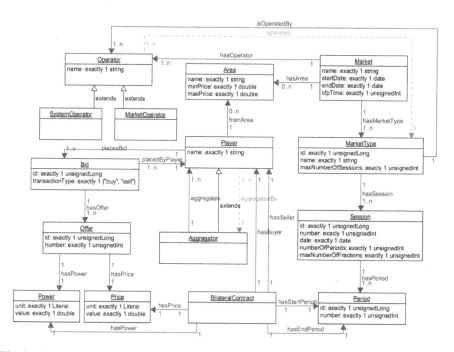

**Fig. 2.** *Electricity Markets Ontology* (EMO) (Available online: http://www.mascem.gecad.isep. ipp.pt/ontologies/imgs/fig.2.png)

It should be noticed that three object properties defined in this ontology are not present in the UML diagram, namely: *hasBilateralContract*, *placedInPeriod* and *placedInSinglePeriod*. These are important properties that are introduced in EMO to be reused by the ontologies defined by each EM's domain.

EMO has expressivity *ALCHIQ(D)*. The *AL* (*Attributive Language*) is the base language allowing: (i) atomic negation, *i.e.* the negation of concept names that do not appear on the left side of axioms; (ii) concept intersection; (iii) universal restrictions; and (iv) limited existential quantification. *C* is the *Complex concept negation* extension. The *H* extension is related with the *role Hierarchy* (e.g. the sub properties). The *I* extension represents the *Inverse properties*. The *Q* extension are the *Qualified cardinality restrictions*, *i.e.* cardinality restrictions with fillers other than ⊤. And finally, the *(D)* refers to the use of datatype properties, data values or data types.

The definition of an **Area** includes a string *name*, a double *minPrice* and a double *maxPrice*. All the three data properties are defined as *Functional*. A functional property is a property that only relates the same subject to one single object/value. Each EM area has an identifying name and its minimum and maximum prices are usually defined in its market rules.

An **Operator** includes only a *name*, while the **MarketOperator** and **SystemOperator** classes are extended from **Operator**. Other types of operators may be present in different EM, which can be defined is each market's ontology after importing the EMO.

A **Period** is here identified only with an *id* and (period) *number*. These two properties are both *Functional* as well, and it has been found important to include them in this ontology due to simulation and data storage purposes. It is certain that a period (of time) can also be defined with a start and end instants, but that terminology was left open so that, if required, one can always extend its definition in the ontology by importing EMO.

Both **Price** and **Power** are defined as a set of a *unit* (e.g. EUR and MW respectively) and a *value* in double, being these two data properties *Functional* as well. An **Offer**, in turn, includes an *id*, a *number* and exactly a **Power** and a **Price** set by the object properties *hasPower* and *hasPrice* respectively. These two object properties are also *Functional*.

A **Bid** also includes an *id*, in addition to a *transactionType* ("*buy*" and "*sell*" only), a single **Player** (set with the *Functional* object property *placedByPlayer*) and **Offer**s (set by the *hasOffer* object property).

A **Player** includes a *name*, and identifies its **Area** and placed **Bid**s with the respective object properties *fromArea* and *placesBid*. The *placesBid* object property is the *inverse of placedByPlayer*, being also *Inverse Functional*, *i.e.* this property only relates the same object/value to a single subject. An **Aggregator**, on the other hand, is a subclass of **Player**, which *aggregates* other **Player**s. The *aggregates* object property is *inverse of* the *aggregatedBy* object property, being this last inferred by the reasoner when active.

A **Session** includes an *id*, a *number*, a *date*, the *numberOfPeriods* and the *maxNumberOfFractions* data properties, and also the **Period**s. The *date* data property is *Functional*, the *numberOfPeriods* identifies the number of periods to consider in the simulation, while the *maxNumberOfFractions* determines the maximum number of fractions (**Offer**s) per **Bid**. The **Period**s are set with the *hasPeriod* object property, which is *Inverse Functional*.

The **MarketType** is defined by an *id*, a *name*, the *maxNumberOfSessions*, including its **Session**s and **Operator**s. The *maxNumberOfSessions* determines the maximum number of sessions to consider in the simulation. The **Session**s and **Operator**s are set with the *hasSession* and *isOperatedBy* object properties respectively. The *hasSession* property is *Inverse Functional* and the *isOperatedBy* is the inverse of *operates* object property, which is inferred by the reasoner.

A **Market** comprises a *name*, a *startDate*, an *endDate*, a *cfpTime*, and its **Area**(s), **MarketType**(s) and **Operator**(s). The *startDate*, *endDate* and *cfpTime* properties are *Functional*. The *startDate* and *endDate* describe the simulation start and end dates, from which are also determined the number of simulation days. The *cfpTime* sets the call for proposal time limit a **MarketOperator** will wait to receive the players' proposals. The **Area**(s) are set through the *hasArea* property, the **MarketType**(s) by the *hasMarketType* property and the **Operator**(s) via the *hasOperator* object property.

A **BilateralContract** includes a buyer and a seller **Player**, a start and an end **Period**, a **Power** amount and a **Price** offer. The players are set by the *hasBuyer* and *hasSeller Functional* object properties. The start and end periods by the *hasStartPeriod* and *hasEndPeriod* properties respectively, where both are also *Functional*. And the *hasPower* and *hasPrice* properties set the **Power** and **Price** respectively.

Finally, the **Area**, the **Operator**, the **Period**, the **Power**, the **Price**, the **Offer**, the **Player**, the **Bid**, the **Session**, the **Market**, the **MarketType** and the **BilateralContract** classes are all *Disjoint Classes*, meaning that none of these classes has members in common. In other words, an element cannot be an instance of more than one of these classes, or else it makes the ontology inconsistent.

EMO was formulated in OWL DL, using Protégé[1] tool, and its representation is in RDF/XML. It is publicly available[2] so it can be used by third-party developers who wish to integrate their agent-based simulators with MASCEM, taking advantage of its simulation capabilities and market models. On the other hand, EMO may also be reused and extended for the development of new multi-agent simulation tools in the context of wholesale EM.

## 3.2 Additional Modules

To enable semantic communication between the market operator and player agents, two additional modules have been developed separately from EMO. These are: (i) the *Call For Proposal Ontology* (CFP) and (ii) the *Electricity Markets Results Ontology* (EMR). Although these are not detailed in this paper, are also publicly available[3].

---

[1] http://protege.stanford.edu/.

[2] http://www.mascem.gecad.isep.ipp.pt/ontologies/electricity-markets.owl.

[3] http://www.mascem.gecad.isep.ipp.pt/ontologies/call-for-proposal.owl,http://www.mascem.gecad.isep.ipp.pt/ontologies/electricity-markets-results.owl.

The CFP has the purpose of being used by the market operator agents to ask player agents for bids to be placed in the market, and for players to send their proposals to the respective market operators. In turn, the EMR is the ontology used by market operator agents to inform player agents about their results and outcomes in the market.

Both modules have expressivity *ALCHIQ(D)*, similarly to EMO, and have also been formulated in OWL DL, being represented in RDF/XML as well.

## 4   Case Study

This case study intends to demonstrate the usefulness and advantage of using EMO to support players' participation in the market. The simulation scenario was created with the intention of representing the European reality through a summarized group of players, representing buyer and seller entities of each area of each regional market. It includes two agents (buyer and seller) per area, practicing the average prices and negotiating the total amount of power that have been transacted in each of these areas in the reality, for the day 16<sup>th</sup> January, 2013 (Wednesday).

Forty one areas are considered, *i.e.* 41 buyers and 41 sellers, resulting in a total of 82 players for this simulation. The selected market type is the symmetrical day-ahead pool without considering any complex offer or condition.

As the simulation starts, the market operator sends a call for proposal (CfP) to each registered player. Figure 3 presents a snippet of the CfP sent by the market operator. The full version can be found online[4].

```
35      <rdf:Description rdf:about="mibel.owl#iM-MIBEL">
36          <emo:hasMarketType rdf:resource="mibel.owl#iMT-SPOT"/>
37          <emo:name>MIBEL</emo:name>
38          <rdf:type rdf:resource="mibel.owl#MIBEL"/>
39      </rdf:Description>
40      <rdf:Description rdf:about="call-for-proposal.owl#iCFP-DayAheadSession2013-01-16-0">
41          <cfp:forElectricityMarket rdf:resource="mibel.owl#iM-MIBEL"/>
42          <rdf:type rdf:resource="call-for-proposal.owl#CallForProposal"/>
43      </rdf:Description>
```

**Fig. 3.** CfP RDF snippet

Analyzing Fig. 3, it is possible to observe the definition of a *CallForProposal* (from line 40 to line 43) for the EM named "*MIBEL*" (defined from line 35 to 39).

After receiving the CfP, each player queries its knowledge base in order to send its proposal to the respective market operator. Figure 4 presents a snip of the *Proposal* sent by agent Seller 38. The complete version is available online[5].

---

[4] http://www.mascem.gecad.isep.ipp.pt/ontologies/paper/paams/16/CfP.rdf.

[5] http://www.mascem.gecad.isep.ipp.pt/ontologies/paper/paams/16/Proposal.rdf.

```
567    <rdf:Description rdf:about="mibel.owl#iPrice1-P19-DayAheadSession2013-01-16-0">
568      <emo:value rdf:datatype="http://www.w3.org/2001/XMLSchema#double">60.04</emo:value>
569      <emo:unit>EUR</emo:unit>
570      <rdf:type rdf:resource="electricity-markets.owl#Price"/>
571    </rdf:Description>
572    <rdf:Description rdf:about="mibel.owl#iOffer1-P19-DayAheadSession2013-01-16-0">
573      <emo:hasPrice rdf:resource="mibel.owl#iPrice1-P19-DayAheadSession2013-01-16-0"/>
574      <emo:hasPower rdf:resource="mibel.owl#iPower1-P19-DayAheadSession2013-01-16-0"/>
575      <emo:number rdf:datatype="http://www.w3.org/2001/XMLSchema#unsignedInt">1</emo:number>
576      <emo:id rdf:datatype="http://www.w3.org/2001/XMLSchema#unsignedLong">3468251671864012524</emo:id>
577      <rdf:type rdf:resource="electricity-markets.owl#Offer"/>
578    </rdf:Description>
```

**Fig. 4.** Seller 38's Proposal RDF snippet

Observing Fig. 4, it is noticeable the definition of an *Offer* for period 19 (between lines 572 and 578). The *Price* proposed for this offer is defined from line 567 to 571.

After receiving the proposals and validating all incoming offers, the market operator analyses the bids, and generates the RDF results to be sent to the participating players. An excerpt of the RDF result achieved by Seller 38 is illustrated in Fig. 5. The full version of this RDF can be found online[6], where the results may be observed with better insight.

```
67    <rdf:Description rdf:about="electricity-markets-results.owl#iTradedPower-HourlyResult-19">
68      <emo:unit>MW</emo:unit>
69      <emo:value rdf:datatype="http://www.w3.org/2001/XMLSchema#double">11364.2</emo:value>
70      <rdf:type rdf:resource="electricity-markets-results.owl#TradedPower"/>
71    </rdf:Description>
72    <rdf:Description rdf:about="electricity-markets-results.owl#iTradedPower-HourlyResult-8">
73      <emo:unit>MW</emo:unit>
74      <emo:value rdf:datatype="http://www.w3.org/2001/XMLSchema#double">11351.9</emo:value>
75      <rdf:type rdf:resource="electricity-markets-results.owl#TradedPower"/>
76    </rdf:Description>
77    <rdf:Description rdf:about="electricity-markets-results.owl#iMarketPrice-HourlyResult-19">
78      <emo:unit>EUR</emo:unit>
79      <emo:value rdf:datatype="http://www.w3.org/2001/XMLSchema#double">61.52</emo:value>
80      <rdf:type rdf:resource="electricity-markets-results.owl#MarketPrice"/>
81    </rdf:Description>
```

**Fig. 5.** Seller 38's Result RDF snippet

By the analysis of Fig. 5 it is possible to observe the traded power of Seller 38 (between lines 67 and 71) and market clearing price (from line 77 to line 81) of period 19.

Figure 6 presents the results achieved by Seller 38 for each hourly period of the considered day.

As it is possible to notice, Seller 38 sold almost all its available power for the 24 hourly periods of the day. In periods 4 and 6 Seller 38 was not able to sell any of the offered power. In turn, in period 5, this agent is the one who determines the market price, being only able to sell less than ¼ of its available power.

It is also possible to observe that the market prices vary approximately between €38 (period 4) and €75 (period 10).

---

[6] http://www.mascem.gecad.isep.ipp.pt/ontologies/paper/paams/16/Result.rdf.

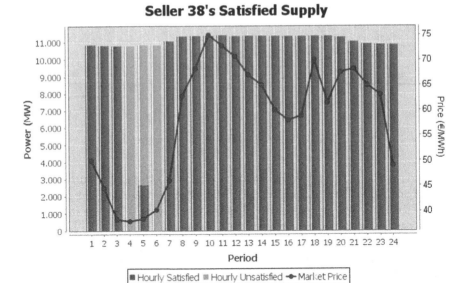

**Fig. 6.** Seller 38's satisfied supply

## 5  Conclusions

In order to disseminate the development of interoperable MAS within power engineering, interconnection issues must be addressed. To take full advantage of these systems, there is a growing need for knowledge exchange with the aim at providing full interoperability between different systems. With the objective of overcoming these issues, the *Electricity Markets Ontology* (EMO) is proposed, gathering the EM main concepts, enabling the interoperability of independently developed multi-agent based simulation platforms.

Additionally, particular modules conceived to deal with the different communications between market operators and market players have also been developed, namely: (i) the *Call For Proposal Ontology* (CFP) and (ii) the *Electricity Markets Results Ontology* (EMR).

Using EMO, different types of agents are able to communicate with each other, understanding a common language, while providing the means for any agent from external systems to do the same, simply by importing the developed ontologies. By "speaking the same language", agents from different communities can understand each other and communicate efficiently, without the need for spending unnecessary computational resources and execution time (which is an essential issue in a simulation process) in translating messages.

The developed ontology is publicly available online so it can be easily accessed, reused and extended by Ontology Engineers or MAS developers in the scope of EM. This is a relevant contribution, not only to provide the participation in joint simulations with MASCEM, but also to give the basis for the development of other systems specific ontologies. The comparison of the system's performance with and without the use of ontologies is considered as future work, as well as the conversion of RDF messages to JSON-LD[7] in order to reduce the computational weight of the communications.

The presented case study has proven the usefulness and advantages of using the proposed ontology in the scope of the wholesale EM. The new EM simulator resulting from the integration of the proposed ontology in MASCEM provides a solid platform to study and explore the implications and consequences of new and already existing approaches in EM. Researchers of the power systems area consider tools with this type of capabilities essential in order to be prepared to deal with the constant changes in the EM environment. It is important to point out that it was used real EM players' data in the simulation, extracted from the market operator's website.

# References

1. Sioshansi, F.: Evolution of Global Electricity Markets – New paradigms, New Challenges, New Approaches. Academic Press, Waltham (2013)
2. Shahidehpour, M., Yamin, H., Li, Z.: Market Operations in Electric Power Systems: Forecasting, Scheduling, and Risk Management, pp. 233–274. Wiley-IEEE Press, New York (2002)
3. Koritarov, V.: Real-world market representation with agents: modeling the electricity market as a complex adaptive system with an agent-based approach. IEEE Power Energy Mag. **2**, 39–46 (2004)
4. Li, H., Tesfatsion, L.: Development of open source software for power market research: the AMES test bed. J. Energy Markets 2(2), 111–128 (2009)
5. Migliavacca, G.: SREMS: a short-medium run electricity market simulator based on game theory and incorporating network constraints. IEEE Power Tech, Lausanne, Swiss (2007)
6. Santos, G., et al.: Multi-agent simulation of competitive electricity markets: autonomous systems cooperation for european market modelling. Energy Conv. Manage. **99**, 387–399 (2015)
7. Praça, I., Ramos, C., Vale, Z., Cordeiro, M.: MASCEM: a multi-agent system that simulates competitive electricity markets. IEEE Intell. Syst. **18**(6), 54–60 (2003). Special Issue on Agents and Markets
8. Pinto, T., Praça, I., Vale, Z., Morais, H., Sousa, T.: Strategic Bidding in Electricity Markets: An agent-based simulator with game theory for scenario analysis. Integr. Comput. Aided Eng. **20**(4), 335–346 (2013). IOS Press
9. Vale, Z., Pinto, T., Praça, I., Morais, H.: MASCEM - Electricity markets simulation with strategic players. IEEE Intell. Syst. **26**(2), 54–60 (2011). Special Issue on AI in Power Systems and Energy Markets
10. Foundation for Intelligent Physical Agents (FIPA), FIPA Agent Management Specification (2004). http://fipa.org/specs/fipa00023/. Accessed January 2016
11. Foundation for Intelligent Physical Agents (FIPA), ACL Message Structure Specification (2002). http://www.fipa.org/specs/fipa00061/. Accessed on January 2016

---

[7] http://json-ld.org/.

12. Foundation for Intelligent Physical Agents (FIPA), FIPA Ontology Service Specification (2001). http://www.fipa.org/specs/fipa00086/ Accessed on January 2016
13. Catterson, V. et al.: An upper ontology for power engineering applications, April 2010. http://sites.ieee.org/pes-mas/. Accessed on January 2016
14. Alexopoulos, P., Kafentzis, K., Zoumas, C.: ELMO: an interoperability ontology for the electricity market. In: Proceedings of the International Conference on e-Business, Milan, Italy, July 7–10, 2009
15. Dam, K., Chapping, E.: Coupling agent-based models of natural gas and electricity markets. In: Proceedings of the First International Workshop on Agent Technologies for Energy Systems (ATES 2010), pp. 45–52, 11 May 2010
16. Dam, K., Keirstead, J.: Re-use of an ontology for modelling urban energy systems. In: Proceedings of the 3rd International Conference on Infrastructure Systems and Services: Next Generation Infrastructure Systems for Eco-Cities (INFRA), Shenzhen, China, 11–13 November 2010
17. MIBEL - Mercado Ibérico de Electricidade (2016). http://www.mibel.com/. Accessed on January 2016
18. EPEXSPOT - European Power Exchange (2016). https://www.epexspot.com/. Accessed on January 2016
19. Nord Pool Spot (2016). http://www.nordpoolspot.com/. Accessed on January 2016

# Workshop on Multiagent System Based Learning Environments (MASLE)

# A Proposal to Integrate Context-Awareness Services to Enhance CSCL Environments Based on Intelligent Agents

Santiago Álvarez, Oscar M. Salazar, and Demetrio A. Ovalle[✉]

Universidad Nacional de Colombia - Sede Medellín, Medellín, Colombia
{salvarezl,omsalazaro,dovalle}@unal.edu.co

**Abstract.** Computer Supported Collaborative Learning (CSCL) is a computational approach allowing students—being organized into groups— to work together for a common goal and discuss from different points of view always seeking to improve learning processes. The context-awareness concept, which is inherent to humans when performing any learning activity, becomes the main component for monitoring activities in virtual learning environments. The aim of this paper is to integrate context-awareness services to enhance CSCL environments supported by Multi-Agent Systems. The awareness-group-agent that composes the system architecture provides the coordination of several agents responsible of handling each of the 11 context-awareness services proposed. This characteristic allows both students and teachers at a given time be aware of their teamwork progress status during execution of the CSCL-MAS environment. In order to validate the incorporation of context-aware services a prototype was built and tested through a case study. Results obtained demonstrate the effectiveness of using this kind of approaches in collaborative learning environments which constitutes an attempt to improve learning processes.

**Keywords:** Computer supported collaborative learning · Adaptive virtual courses · Awareness services · Ontologies · Multi-agent learning environments

## 1 Introduction

Teamwork has been extensively used into the classrooms over the past years by teachers in order to improve the learning process effectiveness. This work methodology, better known as collaborative learning, is looking for that students within each group work together for a common goal, and allows them to discuss from different points of view during the acquisition of knowledge process. These advantages added with the increase of the interaction capabilities between students, enables the dynamic learning and makes it the possibility to become in collaborative and social [1].

Despite this work methodology has many advantages, it is common to find out difficulties when the teacher wants to identify which students performed better within the group, who reach the learning objectives completely and properly, or it is even more difficult to measure the acquired knowledge percentage by the whole group.

© Springer International Publishing Switzerland 2016
J. Bajo et al. (Eds.): PAAMS 2016 Workshops, CCIS 616, pp. 407–418, 2016.
DOI: 10.1007/978-3-319-39387-2_34

In order to face these problems we propose a model based on the integration of several approaches such as: user-centered multi-agent systems, adaptive and recommender systems, ontologies, among others. In fact, the model implements an evaluation mechanism using awareness services with the aim of providing solution for evaluation of the working groups, in this way is further enhanced the implementation of the proposed model.

The rest of the paper is organized as follows: Sect. 2 outlines main concepts involved in this research concerning Awareness Services, Computer Supported Collaborative Learning, Ontologies, among others. Section 3 shows some related works according to the model proposed. Section 4 shows the prototype implementation, and validation of the features related to context-awareness services are presented in Sect. 5. Finally, Sect. 6 presents conclusions and future work.

## 2    Conceptual Framework

Following are the main concepts and fields related with this research.

The concept of Awareness Services is used in collaborative learning environments the reason is that if two students are using distributed schemes of computer-supported collaborative work (CSCW) they generally cannot see or hear, and neither feel the presence and perceive each other actions. In this kind of CSCW environments, these awareness skills are quite limited. The context-awareness has thus become one of major issues when designing pedagogical computer systems in order to reduce the need of meta-cognitive efforts for collaborating on distributed computer environments [2]. Gaver highlights the importance of providing context-awareness information with the purpose of help people to change the individually work role to work in groups [3]. In this fashion, Dourish and Bellotti [4] apply this characteristic within shared learning environments and define the awareness as a shared understanding of each other activities, thus providing a context for their own activity.

According to Tim Berners-Lee [5] "The Semantic Web is an extension of the current Web in which information has a well-defined meaning, it is understandable by computers and where people can work cooperatively and collaboratively". From this new paradigm, ontologies appear as the means to represent knowledge on the Web in a way that is made readable and usable by computers. "An ontology is the result of selecting a domain and apply the same method to obtain a formal representation containing the concepts and relationships that exist among them" [6].

Adaptive Virtual Courses (AVC) are educational computing tools capable of guiding students along a particular domain of knowledge for learning purposes. During this process some solving tasks should be performed such as the development of a planning strategy concerning learning activities, adaptation of educational content, and the performance evaluation of students during the development of an online course process [7].

According to Diaz [8], Computer Supported Collaborative Learning (CSCL) is defined as a research field aiming at "constructing knowledge or solving problems through mutual engagement of two or more learners in a coordinated effort using the

Internet and electronic communications for their interactions". When considering the three metaphors of learning, i.e., 'learning as acquisition', 'learning as participation' and 'learning as knowledge creation' [9], collaborative learning (CL) is one of the main approaches to gain knowledge creation [10]. CL can positively affect the student learning process in developing countries. Among the four types of interactions such as learner-learner, learner-instructor, learner-content, learner-interface [11], in CL learner-learner and learner-instructor interactions are considered. Collaborative learning includes problem-based learning, case-based learning, group works, discussions, reflection and other ways in which students are active participants in the learning process [12].

## 3   Related Works

This section presents some related works with the research field, and compares them in order to identify their strengths and weaknesses.

Kanaganayagam and Fernando [13] made a research about the awareness of the effectiveness of CSCL instructional models used in the Sri Lankan university education. The study was conducted by interviews, phone calls and email among the participants in order to categorize the most important variables that affect CSCL. Finally the research showed that, electronic tools and resources related factors, students' attitude-related factors and the availability of non-electronic resources related factors are the most critical factors affecting CSCL. Furthermore, the findings reveal that the most used production tools are presentation tools, simulation tools, and content management systems. The most widely used learning tools are Moodle, wiki (except from Moodle) and online sources.

Ovalle et al. [14] use awareness services to support collaborative activities in the classroom assisted by a knowledge management system named KnowCat built at Universidad Autónoma de Madrid [1]. The proposed awareness services in this research are the following: (1) registered-students, (2) online-students, (3) radar-view, (4) historical-view, (5) participation-level, and (6) annotation-graph.

Ovalle et al. [15, 16] present the implementation of a personalized recommendation ubiquitous MAS model using mobile devices, which is in agreement with current requirements on virtual teaching-learning methods. This model incorporates the concept of intelligent agents which uses mechanisms that allows searching and recommendation of educational resources being adapted to the students' preferences and characteristics. In addition, the model incorporates several awareness services that enable to the learners generate a context of their own activities. Those services consider the student as an individual entity and they are not based on group interaction.

Luna et al. [17] presents an ontology-based approach for representing the interaction process between the user profile and its context (e.g. locations such as government offices, schools, or restaurants) for collaborative learning environments. Since the user profile represents faithfully the interests and preferences of the user hence it plays a significant role in improving adaptive searches for educational recommendation processes. For doing this, authors analyze the role assignments, permissions, restrictions, and the definition of rules that are applied to the user, particularly in the collaborative learning context where the subject is involved. In addition, authors establish that since ontologies reflect changes in domains of real world, ontologies should represent changes in the conceptualized domain. A methodology consisting of following three stages is proposed: the first stage, Handshake, corresponds to the presentation of the user profile into the current context; the second named Interaction stage represents the process of the interaction between the user and their context (e.g. the role that the user acquires, permissions and restrictions); and the last and third stage, named Farewell stage, corresponds to the user's context farewell. A case study related to the context of a school as well as two different user profiles represented in the user profiling ontology is proposed. In this case, the user's characteristics and preferences and the context models in order to find the relationships generated, when a person interacts in a defined context are analyzed.

Considering the research works previously reviewed one of the improvements proposed in this paper in order to enhance CSCL systems based on MAS is the integration of awareness services specifically created for monitoring teamwork processes. These features concerning context-monitoring, group interaction, and alerts offered by the learning environment allow students and teachers to become conscious of the advancement status of learning activities proposed for collaborative learning. In this way, the system gives the students, student groups, and teachers the opportunity to maintain updated information that helps them to improve their performance during their collaborative learning process.

## 4    Model Proposed

The Multi-Agent model proposed was designed to provide 11 different awareness services, which allow groups of students to be aware of their activities within the virtual learning environment. Similarly, some services are designed so that the teacher can monitor group of students' progress, and in this way, attempt to improve the support for group learning activities development. This section describes the model from three different perspectives: firstly, awareness services offered by the system will be presented and detailed. Second, each detail of the software agents considered within the system and the interactions among them will be explained. Third and last, we explain how the information of educational resources is structured and stored within the database.

### 4.1   Awareness Services

The considered awareness services allowing students, groups, and teachers at a given time to be aware of their status during MAS execution. It is important to highlight that the information regarding students' learning activities is constantly updated and thus the fact to be aware of these changes might surely improve the performance on their learning process. The awareness services offered by the system are the following:

- Participation-level: it is a statistical view that allows identifying a student's participation level within the group related to AVC topics, getting well an activity level measure associated with learning process.

- Group-progress-graph: it presents a group's state overview within the AVC and pending topics to be reviewed by the group, keeping in this way the teacher informed about the progress and the difficulties of the group in its learning process.
- Learning-assistant-group-interaction-graph: this graph exhibits the interaction between the group of students and learning assistants, showing if the student has received learning advice sessions. In addition, the graph detects the learning assistants that are the best recommended by group of students.
- Historical-group-learning-activity-view: it presents to both teachers and groups recent learning activities that have been performed within an AVC, in this fashion, the teacher has the ability to continuously monitor the group of students learning process.
- Alarms: this service exhibits proactivity features since it is on charge of generating learning activity expiration alarms concerning AVC without student intervention. This fact can generate an awareness state in group of students of the activities that need to be performed and prevents the desertion of students within the groups.
- Online-assistants: this service deploys online learning assistants associated with each AVC. In addition, it presents the contact details and features of each learning assistant such as knowledge areas, previous grades, proximity, and availability. As an additional functionality the CSCL-MAS allows the group of students to contact in real time the assistant and to know its schedule availability.
- Accessed-educational-resources: this service enumerates the educational resources that the CSCL-MAS has recommended to the group of students and emphasizes on previous resources that have been accessed by the group.
- Practice-community: given that the practice community is a space for sharing ideas and resources among registered group of students in the AVC, this service deploys it to groups of students. The community idea is that teachers and group of students may raise issues about topics of the AVC, in order to generate a feedback from all of the students.
- Group-brainstorming-wall: this service provides a space that allows the development of new ideas by students of the same group associated with the specific domain of the AVC.
- Group-schedules-manager: this service allows viewing and overlapping academic activities present in the schedules of each one of the students in the group. The above in order to find free spaces for activities allocation.
- Group-resource-sharing: this service allows sharing an academic resource at any time, either to all members of the group or one specific.

### 4.2 Multi-agent System Architecture

As shown in Fig. 1, the system resource agent has two knowledge sources, the first one stores the data and knowledge necessary for operation (i.e. user profiles, Adaptive Virtual Course (AVC) structure, etc.), and the second consists of a specific domain ontology. Using this ontology the MAS can makes inferences concerning, students, and group of students, and can represent AVC domain structures. In addition, the system consists of 10 typology of agents that are described below:

- Student Agent: it is responsible to represent each student within the platform, aims to acquire, store, and handle the student profile information.
- Awareness Group Agent: it represents the group within the platform and interacts with other agents in order to attend the service request.
- Alarm Agent: it is in charge of keeping user informed at any time, about the execution alarms service and its administration.
- Historical Agent: it is responsible for managing services that require historical activities within the platform, i.e., the Participation-level services, Group-progress-graph and Historical-group-learning-activity-view.
- Assistant Agent: It provides services related to information assistants for courses, services such as Learning-assistant-group-interaction-graph and the Online-assistants.
- Learning Resource Agent: it is in charge of managing services related to educational resources, i.e., Accessed-educational-resources and Group-resource-sharing.
- Schedule Agent: it deploys the group-schedules-manager service in order to display the overlapping schedules.
- Practice Community Agent: it is in charge of managing practice community service within the platform.
- Brainstorm Wall Agent: it manages and presents the new ideas that are generated into the group using the Group-brainstorming-wall service.
- System Resource Agent: This agent is responsible for managing the system information sources, that is, both the central database and the ontology. When we talk about central database we mean to the data layer (queries, insert, update and delete). However when we speak about the ontology, we refer to both the information generation as generate inferences from this. The next section will detail the sources information structure mentioned.

### 4.3   Information Resource Structure

As mentioned above, the first information source is the central database of the system. In this database the information about the AVC, user profiles (schedules, historical activities and academic history) and awareness services are stored.

Figure 2 shows the relational structure for the representation of the AVC. It is important to clarify that any entity that supports the learning process by students is considered in this system as an educational resource. The user entity contains basic information about each one of these, and from there unfolds a profile according to the role it has within the MAS. The data contained in the profile varies depending on the role, just as a student may belong to a single group. The hierarchical structure of the general model of the AVC, comprises the users involved in collaborative learning. The AVC breaks down into topics which contain a range of activities proposed by the teacher (workshops, lectures, presentations, examinations, etc.). These activities are assessed at group level, based on this evaluation weaknesses are detected in the learning process; this in order to recommend assistants and improve performance.

The activities are associated with the AVC topics; this activities may be lectures, workshops, presentations and/or other activities that may be developed at the group

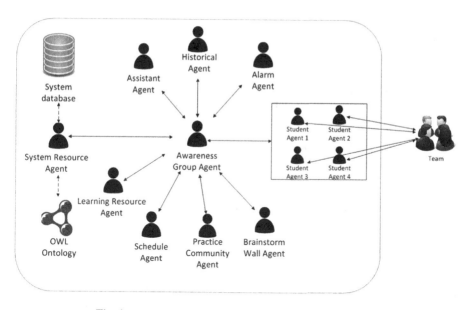

**Fig. 1.** Awareness services in a CSCL multi-agent system.

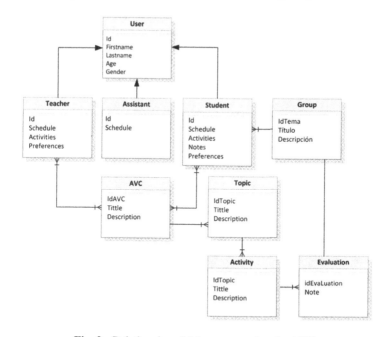

**Fig. 2.** Relational model for representing the AVC.

level. Similarly, the user entity contains the description of each of the profiles, which in turn contain information about the academic record, historical activity (past activities, notes, visualizations of resources, etc.) and the students' schedules.

The second information source is the ontology, which is also handled by the system resource agent. This is responsible for extracting the information contained in the profiles database and map it within the ontology. From this, the ontology is empowered to make inferences such as recent activities, overlapping of schedules, smart alarm generation, and progress within the AVC activities. The following section describes the tools used to implement both the data layer and the MAS prototype.

## 5    Model Implementation and Validation

The MAS was implemented using the JADE Framework [18] that is oriented to the development of MAS according to the FIPA standards (Foundation for intelligent Physical Agents) of the IEEE. This feature provides interoperability to the platform, thus allowing systems that are governed by the same communication protocols to easily exchange messages. Another advantage is that JADE is developed under JAVA language that facilitates the integration of other tools in our database and ontologies case. For installation and deployment of the central database was used MySQL database engine, which for purposes of system meets all requirements about relational models. For the ontological integration was used JENA framework [19]. It is important to highlight that the ontology was mapped to OWL language by Protégé framework. As a result, SPARQL query language was used as reasoning engine from the ontology. This language is supported by the W3C to perform queries on RDF and OWL graphs, thus enhancing the information search and selection on the semantic Web. Finally, the graphical user interfaces were developed using the Java Swing library, this library allows to generate user friendly interfaces.

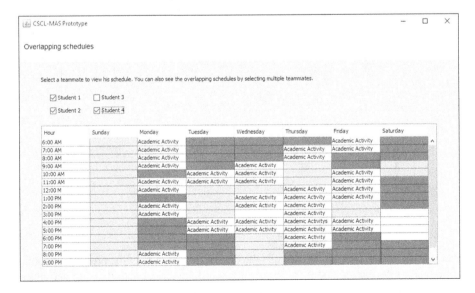

**Fig. 3.**  Group-schedules-manager service.

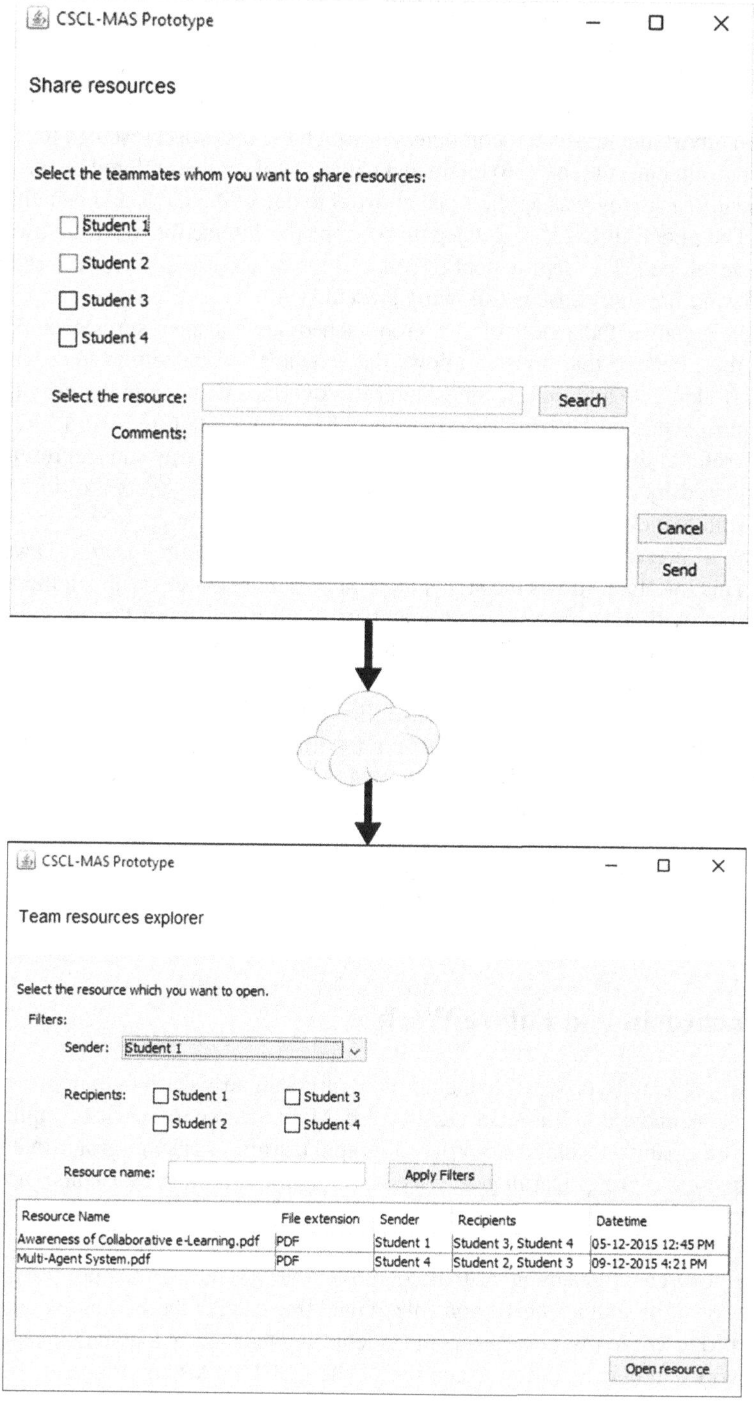

**Fig. 4.** Group-resource-sharing service interfaces.

In order to validate the model proposed a case study is developed to illustrate each of the functionalities of the MAS learning environment. Is worth mentioning that, the case study deployment and validation considered a controlled environment associated with the course of Artificial Intelligence at the National University of Colombia. In this controlled environment, several computers in which the tool was presented to students. In this environment, students (36) interacted with several services offered by the system. Subsequently, a survey was applied that allowed to detect the flaws and benefits of the system. The above in order to get feedback from the interaction with the awareness services developed. The deployment of some of the awareness services offered by the system during the study case is following presented.

Figure 3 shows the result of the group-schedules-manager service deployment wherein the interface that appears allows the schedules visualization for each of the group of students. In addition, it can generate an overlap, showing in this way the time periods during the week shared by students. Slots that contain the word "Academic Activity" refer to time periods that students do not share, light gray slots represents time periods shared by some of the students, and finally, dark gray slots are time periods shared by all team members.

Figure 4 presents the deployment result of group-resource-sharing awareness service. This interface allows the student to either share resources with another student in the group, with a number of group members or all members of the group. The top interface in Fig. 4 allows visualizing how the student can select those groupmates with which he wants to share the educational resource. In addition, he can attach the resource and send any comments about the attached file. Subsequently, the attachment resource is stored in the cloud so that it is available at the time you want to be accessed.

Furthermore, it can be noted at the bottom of Fig. 4 the graphic user interface showing the functionality to the students that were shared resource. In this interface shared files are presented in a table detailing the resource name, extension, sender, recipient and the date on which the resource was shared. In addition, the student can apply filters: sender, recipient and/or name of the resource. Finally, the "Open resource" button allows the user to download or select educational resources on the table.

## 6   Conclusions and Future Work

This paper presented a proposal to include context-awareness services to improve CSCL environments under a multi-agent architecture. Main awareness services implemented such as participation-level, group-progress-graph, learning-assistant-group-interaction-graph, historical-group-learning-activity-view, alarms, online-assistants, accessed-educational-resources, group-schedules-manager, group-resource-sharing, among others provides relevant support to CSCL tasks in order to monitor collaborative activities. The awareness-group-agent that composes the system architecture provides the coordination of several agents responsible of handling each of the 11 context-awareness services proposed. In this way, group of students and teachers at a given time are aware of teamworks' progress during execution of the CSCL-MAS environment. Based on results from validation of awareness services it is demonstrated that the use of them along with adaptive Multi-Agent Systems can be relevant and effective in order to provide a significant solution for collaborative learning processes.

As future work we attempt to integrate the awareness services implemented to a multi-agent system that considers collaborative learning course planning, topics evaluation, student-centered recommendation of resources and activities, among other features in this way to provide a more robust and dynamic collaborative learning environment. In addition, we pretend to improve ontological modeling concerning group of student's profiles in order to consider dynamic role assignments, heterogeneous and homogeneous group formations, among others. Also, we consider to migrate awareness services to web technologies to access these functionalities from any computer. Another important future work is to develop a robust evaluation and apply it to the model proposed, defining what are the goals of the evaluation and establish a plan for it. Finally, in order to improve ubiquitous system functionality we seek to allow not only awareness services but also temporal and spatial information of groups of students to be accessed from mobile devices.

**Acknowledgments.** The research was developed with the aid of the master grant offered to Oscar M. Salazar by COLCIENCIAS through "Convocatoria 645 de 2014. Capítulo 1 Semilleros-Jóvenes Investigadores".

# References

1. Peña, J.: El aprendizaje cooperativo y las competencias. Rev. d'Innovació Docent Univ. **2**, 1–9 (2010)
2. Palfreyman, K., Rodden, T.: A protocol for users awareness on the world wide web. In: Proceedings of CSCW 1996, pp. 130–139. USA (1996)
3. Gaver, W.: Sound support for collaboration. In: Proceedings of the ESCW 1991, pp. 293–308 (1991)
4. Dourish, P., Bellotti, V.: Awareness and coordination in shared workspaces. In: Proceedings of the ACM Conference on Computer Supported Cooperative Work (CSCW 1992), ACM Press, Toronto (1992)
5. Berners-Lee, T., Hendler, J.: Publishing on the semantic web. Nature **410**(6832), 1023–1024 (2001)
6. Tramullas, J., Sánchez-Casabón, J., Garrido-Picazo, P.: An evaluation based on the digital library user: an experience with greenstone software. Procedia Soc. Behav. Sci. **73**, 167–174 (2013)
7. Duque, N.D., Ovalle, D.A.: Artificial Intelligence planning techniques for adaptive virtual course construction. Rev. DYNA **78**(170), 70–78 (2011). 0012-7353
8. Diaz, V., Brown, M., Salmons, J.: Assessment of collaborative learning project outcomes, pp. 1–11. Educause (2010)
9. Hong, H.-Y., Sullivan, F.R.: An idea-centered, principle-based design approach to support learning as knowledge creation. In: ICLS 2008, Utrecht, (2008)
10. Sing, C.C., Wei-Ying, L., Hyo-Jeong, S., Mun, C.H.: Advancing collaborative learning with ICT: conception, cases and design. Ministry of Education, North Buona Vista Drive (2011)
11. Rovai, A.A.P.: A preliminary look at the structural differences of higher education classroom communities in traditional and ALN courses. Virginia, Rodriguez (2002)
12. Larsen, A.K., Hole, G.O.: Collaborative learning in e-learning. Bergen (2009)

13. Kanaganayagam, I., Fernando, S.: Analysis of the awareness of collaborative e-Learning (CeL) in sri lankan university education, pp. 253–260 (2013)

14. Ovalle, D., Jiménez, J., Collazos, C., Claros, I., Pantoja, L., Cobos, R., Moreno-Llorena, J., Pifarré, M., Argelagos, E.: Guía metodológica para el seguimiento y evaluación de aprendizaje colaborativo asistido por el sistema KNOWCAT. In: Congreso de Facultades de Ingeniería, ACOFI– Asoc. Colombiana de Facultades de Ingeniería, pp. 1–9 (2009)

15. Ovalle, D., Salazar, O.Y., Duque, N.: Modelo de recomendación personalizada en cursos virtuales basado en computación ubicua y agentes inteligentes. Rev. Inf. Tecnol. **25**(6), 131–142 (2014)

16. Salazar, O.M., Ovalle, D.A., Duque, N.D.: Adaptive and personalized educational ubiquitous multi-agent system using context-awareness services and mobile devices. In: Zaphiris, P., Ioannou, A. (eds.) LCT 2015. LNCS, vol. 9192, pp. 301–312. Springer, Heidelberg (2015)

17. Luna, V., Quintero, R., Torres, M., Moreno-Ibarra, M., Guzmán, G., Escamilla, I.: An ontology-based approach for representing the interaction process between user profile and its context for collaborative learning environments. Comput. Human Behav. **51**, 1387–1394 (2015)

18. Bellifemine, F., Poggi, A., Rimassa, G.: JADE–A FIPA-compliant agent framework. In: Artículo científico en congreso, Proceedings of PAAM, pp. 97–108 (1999)

19. Ameen, A., Khan, K., Rani, B.: Extracting knowledge from ontology using Jena for semantic web. In: International Conference for Convergence for Technology-2014, pp. 1–5. IEEE (2014)

# Recommendation System of Educational Resources for a Student Group

Paula Rodríguez[1,2(✉)], Mauricio Giraldo[1], Valentina Tabares[2],
Néstor Duque[2], and Demetrio Ovalle[1]

[1] Universidad Nacional de Colombia Sede Medellín, Medellín, Colombia
{parodriguezma,maugiraldooca,dovalle}@unal.edu.co
[2] Universidad Nacional de Colombia Sede Manizales, Manizales, Colombia
{vtabaresm,ndduqueme}@unal.edu.co

**Abstract.** In a face-class, where the student group is heterogeneous, it is necessary to select the most appropriate educational resources that support learning for all. In this sense, multi-agent system (MAS) can be used to simulate the features of the students in the group, including their learning style, in order to help the professor find the best resources for your class. In this paper, we present MAS to recommendation educational resources for group students, simulating their profiles and selecting resources that best fit. Obtained promising results show that proposed MAS is able to delivered educational resources for a student group.

**Keywords:** Educational resources · Metadata · Multi-agent systems · Recommendation systems · Student group · User profile

## 1 Introduction

In the classroom education, the teacher is facing a heterogeneous group of students. This group there are students with different features, preferences and ways of learning [1]. The UNESCO in 2011 defined educational resource how any type of resource (including curricula, course materials, textbooks, video, multimedia applications, streaming audio, and other material that is designed for use in the teaching and learning process) that are available for use by teachers and students, without the need for any payment for rights or licenses for use.

Likewise, a Recommendation Systems (RS) is defined as a piece of software that facilitates users to discern more relevant and interesting learning information [2]. RS are a tool aims at providing users with useful information results searched and recovered according to their needs, making predictions about matching them to their preferences and delivering those items that could be closer than expected [3]. In the case of educational resources, the system should be able to recommend resources adapted to one or more user's profile characteristics using metadata [4].

Students and teachers need a starting place for thinking about, and understanding, how they learn. In addition, a learning style is a description of a process, or of preferences. Any inventory that encourages a learner to think about the way that he or she learns is a useful step towards understanding and hence improving, learning [5].

© Springer International Publishing Switzerland 2016
J. Bajo et al. (Eds.): PAAMS 2016 Workshops, CCIS 616, pp. 419–427, 2016.
DOI: 10.1007/978-3-319-39387-2_35

Besides, is necessary that students "learn to learn" and teachers should recognize the individual differences of their students to customize their education. Is important highlights that teaching styles do not influence the learning styles of the students [6].

Similarly, teachers should give classes using teaching strategies that strengthen learning styles. That is teach the classes first with a style after another so that all students feel cared for according to their preferences in the way they learn [7].

Currently, the group recommender systems have been extended and are increasingly popular. Some works make recommendations using hybrid approach combining content-based and collaborative strategies. It is used in cases where groups are heterogeneous and can only recommend a small amount of items in a given period [1, 8].

This type of recommendation is mainly applied in various contexts where people gather to perform a specific activity. These contexts are associated with the use of multimedia such as movies, TV content, music selections resources and educational resources [9]. Also, consider learning styles in the classroom to deliver tailored materials is increasing.

An alternative to the selection of the most suitable educational resources for each learning style is a mapping between metadata and every learning style. Several proposals have been made in this regard, using different models of learning styles and metadata standards [10–12].

Multi-agent Systems (MAS)-being emergent computing approaches- are widely spread in several e-learning areas providing solutions for complex and restrictive systems. In contrast with conventional computing approaches, MAS has special features such as customization, intelligence, accessibility, safety, task distribution, decision making, among others [13].

In this paper, we propose a recommender system of educational resources for a student group, taking account the learning style of each student of the group. The aim is delivering, for the teacher, educational resources to supporting the face class.

Experiments are done using Repository Federation of Learning Objects Colombia-FROAC (available at: http://froac.manizales.unal.edu.co/froac/). For quantifying the retrieval quality, a precision metric is used.

The rest of the paper is organized as follows: Sect. 2 describes the proposed model the recommender for group student and the proposed MAS. Section 3 explains the model validation and the results of the proposed model, through a case study. Finally, the main conclusions and future research directions are shown in Sect. 4.

## 2  Proposed Model

This work proposes a multi-agent system for adaptive educational resources recommendation for a student group. The search resources are recommended according to learning style of each student. The learning style are built according to VARK model proposed by Fleming and Baume [5]. The students answer the test to kwon the learning style own, this is the main input of the recommender system. Fleming and Mills suggested four modalities that seemed to reflect the experiences of the students and teachers (Visual, Aural, Read/write, and Kinesthetic). This is sensory modalities that are used for learning information [5].

The test alerts people to the variety of different approaches to learning. It supports those who have been having difficulties with their learning and has particular applications in business, sport, training and education.

In order to select the most suitable educational resources for each learning style is performed a mapping between metadata and every learning style. Similar to the proposal in [10], this paper presents a mapping between the scores in the VARK test for each simulated student and the metadata "Educational Resource Type" included in the LOM metadata standard.

Table 1 shows the mapping performed, where indicated with "1" if the Resource Type is relevant or not for each learning style. For example, if the Educational Resource Type of a LO is "Diagram", this will be convenient for a student with a 'Visual' learning style.

**Table 1.** LOM metadata vs. VARK learning styles

|  | V | A | R | K |
|---|---|---|---|---|
| Exercise |  |  |  | 1 |
| Simulation | 1 |  |  | 1 |
| Questionnaire |  |  |  |  |
| Diagram | 1 |  |  |  |
| Figure | 1 |  |  |  |
| Graph | 1 |  |  |  |
| Slide |  | 1 | 1 |  |
| Table | 1 |  |  |  |
| Narrative text |  | 1 | 1 |  |
| Exam |  |  | 1 | 1 |
| Experiment |  |  |  | 1 |
| Problem statement |  |  | 1 | 1 |
| Self assessment | 1 |  |  | 1 |
| Lecture |  | 1 | 1 |  |

Likewise, the agents of MAS can assume different roles within the system and can be created following a template. Each student is represented through an agent and it behaves autonomously, this ensure that the realized evaluation to each resource is independent. Once created the agents that representing students with their respective profiles, the evaluation process of educational resources begins.

The proposed model assisting teacher in the selecting educational resources for students group, because the system simulates the resource evaluation depending on their characteristics. After the evaluation, the scores assigned to educational resource for each simulated student are aggregated, and the educational resource with more points are best suited to the group average. This ensures greater efficiency and effectiveness against individual recommendation.

Figure 1 presents the architecture of the MAS proposed. Then explains the behavior of each agents in this work.

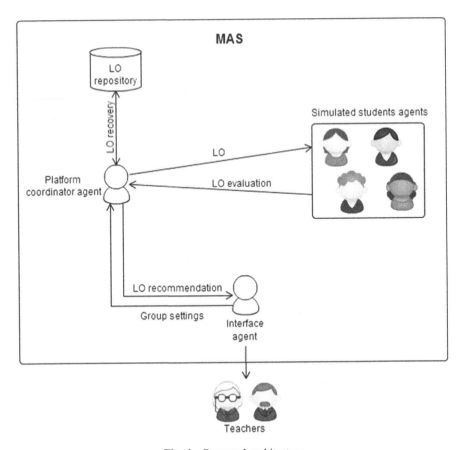

**Fig. 1.** Proposed architecture

**Interface agent:** It is responsible for presenting two interfaces to the teachers. A first interface allows entry the characteristics of a group. The data can be entered to the platform using a plain text that contains the id of the students and the results of the scores for each learning style. In addition to the above, the teacher can enter keywords related to the central theme of the course and with these perform the initial search of the LO in the repository. Other data that help to refine the amount of resources to be evaluated are: the education level to which is this course, learning time than is available for the course and the age range of students.

**Coordinator agent:** responsible for creating agents that simulate each of the members of the student group, which are created with the profile of learning according to the VARK model, admitted by the teacher together with the configuration data of the group. This agent also makes consulting LO in the repository and sends these to each of the simulated students so that they make their respective evaluation. Finally received the assessments made during the simulation and totals the results for the overall rating for each LO and recommend the LO with the higher qualifications.

**Generic student agent:** This generic agent is the basis for creating the simulation of each student. Each simulation must be different, receiving the configuration data of individually profile, where the complete classification of each learning style is present being as the profile contains not only data of the predominant style, but also takes the calcification obtained in the other styles available in the model. This allows a weighted score of each LO. Once completion the LO classification, these come back to the Coordinator agent who totalizes the obtained data.

## 3 Case Study

To validate the model proposed we make two different experiments apply to case study. We use the educational resources stored in Repository Federation of Learning Objects Colombia-FROAC (available at: http://froac.manizales.unal.edu.co/froac/), in the aim to delivered metadata resources to initialized process.

The JADE (Java Agent Development Environment) framework was used to perform the prototype implementation, that offers a suite of resources to supply the development and implementation of MAS. For this work, we have chosen JADE-LEAP (http://jade. tilab.com/), a FIPA-compliant agent platform that follows agent international communication standards.

Figure 2 shows the configuration interface for the group, where the specifics of each student and the general characteristics of the group are entered.

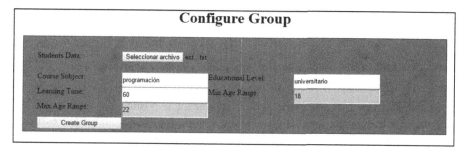

**Fig. 2.** Configure group interface

Figure 3 shows the interface to display LOs that are recommended to the teacher.

The aim the first experiment is to validate the discriminating among different groups. If two groups have the different predominant learning style, presumably the recommender result are different for these groups, although the search string are equals.

For this experiment, we have two student groups, in the Fig. 4 show learning style for each student in these groups.

Students group 1, the learning style predominant is Reader/Write; this means that the preference for learning are the narrative text, slide, exam, problem statement, and lecture.

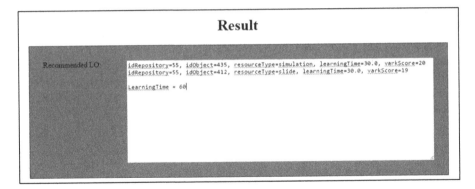

**Fig. 3.** Results interface

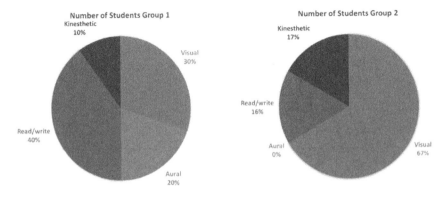

**Fig. 4.** Distribution of groups in learning styles in experiment 1

Students group 2, the learning style predominant is Visual; this means that the preference for learning are simulation, diagram, figure, graph, table, and self assessment.

In the experiment, the results are different in both cases; the searching string is "programación". The Table 2 show the educational type resources result.

**Table 2.** Educational type results for each group

| Group 1 | Group 2 |
|---------|------------|
| Text | Simulation |
| Lecture | Graph |
| Lecture | |

With this experiment concludes that the proposed recommendation system discriminates and delivers different results for each group of students, according to the learning style of the majority.

The second experiment want to measure the level of satisfaction of the recommendation. Formula 1 is the metric of precision that is commonly used to measure the quality of information retrieval. The relevance is understood as the importance of LO delivered for carrying out a learning process. For that students of Computer/Management Information Systems, Universidad Nacional de Colombia, Manizales, belonging to the research group on adapted and intelligent environment-GAIA, were selected to rank the relevance of the recommendation outcomes.

$$Precision = \frac{Relevant\ LOs}{Relevant\ LOs + Retrieved\ LOs} \tag{1}$$

A precision metric was applied for performing the LO relevance evaluation. The Table 3 and 4 show the results for precision metric for each group.

**Table 3.** Precision metric results with recommender

| Group | Relevant LO | Recommended LO | Precision |
|---|---|---|---|
| Group 1 | 4 | 5 | 0,8 |
| Group 2 | 2 | 3 | 0,67 |
| Average | 3 | 4 | **0,75** |

**Table 4.** Precision metric results without recommender

| Group | Relevant LO | Recommended LO | Precision |
|---|---|---|---|
| Group 1 | 1 | 7 | 0,14 |
| Group 2 | 1 | 3 | 0,33 |
| Average | **1** | 5 | **0,2** |

On average, recommendation system recovered around four LO for each student group and on average, three were relevant, therefore the result of precision was 0.75 on average for this experiment. If delivered to the student group random LO about theme (without recommender), the number of results are five LO, on average only 1 which is relevant LO, then precision is 0.2., and can be concluded that recommendations adapted to the student groups are delivered supports the teaching process on the face classroom.

## 4   Conclusions and Future Work

This paper proposes a model for recommendation of educational resources for a student group, which is based on the MAS paradigm using repository federations. Such a model takes advantage of simulating.

This proposal can support the teacher in the difficult task of selecting educational resources for use in the teaching of large groups of students. The suggestions are based on the characteristics of the students and how they learn best.

The results of the case study show that there is differentiation between the recommended educational resources for each group of students, who are relevant and can support the learning process.

Experiments are carried out over Repository Federation of Learning Objects Colombia- FROAC (http://froac.manizales.unal.edu.co/froac/). Our model not only slightly improves the precision rate but optimizes the amount and quality of delivered LOs.

As a future work, we are aiming at exploring and incorporating more student characteristic and other recommendation techniques. Also, expand the validation of the system. As well, the model performance is to be improved from an adequate agent behavior configuration.

**Acknowledgments.** The research presented in this paper was partially funded by the COLCIENCIAS project entitled: "RAIM: Implementación de un framework apoyado en tecnologías móviles y de realidad aumentada para entornos educativos ubicuos, adaptativos, accesibles e interactivos para todos" of the Universidad Nacional de Colombia, with code 1119-569-34172. It was also developed with the support of the grant from "Programa Nacional de Formación de Investigadores– COLCIENCIAS".

# References

1. Kaššák, O., Kompan, M., Bieliková, M.: Personalized hybrid recommendation for group of users: top-N multimedia recommender. Inf. Process. Manag. **52**, 459 (2015)
2. Sikka, R., Dhankhar, A., Rana, C.: A survey paper on E-learning recommender system. Int. J. Comput. Appl. **47**, 27–30 (2012)
3. Mizhquero, K., Barrera, J.: Análisis, Diseño e Implementación de un Sistema Adaptivo de Recomendación de Información Basado en Mashups. Rev. Tecnológica ESPOL-RTE (2009)
4. Li, J.Z.: Quality, evaluation and recommendation for learning object. In: International Conference on Educational and Information Technology, pp. 533–537 (2010)
5. Fleming, N., Baume, D.: Learning styles again: VARKing up the right tree! Educational Development (2006)
6. Alonso, C., Gallego, D., Honey, P.: Los Estilos de Aprendizaje. Procedimientos de diagnostico y mejora. Bilbao (1997)
7. Othman, N., Amiruddin, M.H.: Different perspectives of learning styles from VARK model. Procedia-Soc. Behav. Sci. **7**, 652–660 (2010)
8. Elahi, M., Ricci, F., Massimo, D.: Interactive Food Recommendation for Groups, pp. 6–7 (2014)
9. Boratto, L., Carta, S.: State-of-the-art in group recommendation and new approaches for automatic identification of groups. Stud. Comput. Intell. **324**, 1–20 (2010)
10. Duque, N., Tabares, V., Vicari, R.: Mapeo de Metadatos de Objetos de Arendizaje con Estilos de Aprendizaje como Estrategia para Mejorar la Usabilidad de Repositorios de Recursos Educativos. VAEP-RITA **3**, 107–113 (2015)
11. Peña, C.I., Marzo, J., De la Rosa, J.L., Fabregat, R.: Un sistema de tutoría inteligente adaptativo considerando estilos de aprendizaje. Univ. Girona, España (2002)

12. Rodriguez, P., Tabares, V., Duque, N., Ovalle, D., Vicari, R.: BROA: an agent-based model to recommend relevant learning objects from repository federations adapted to learner profile. Int. J. Interact. Multimed. Artif. Intell. **2**, 6 (2013)
13. Ahmad, S., Bokhari, M.: A new approach to multi agent based architecture for secure and effective E-learning. Int. J. Comput. Appl. **46**, 26–29 (2012)

# ILOMAS: An Intelligent Learning Objects Implementation Study Case

João de Amorim Jr. and Ricardo Azambuja Silveira[✉]

PPGCC – UFSC, Florianópolis, Brazil
joao.amorim.jr@gmail.com,
ricardo.silveira@ufsc.br

**Abstract.** This paper presents the implementation and evaluation of ILOMAS, an architectural model designed to select Learning Objects (LO) for e-learning, based on multi-agent systems. The proposed model extends the Intelligent Learning Objects approach through the use of a BDI agent architecture, allowing the communication with the instructional resources that constitute the LO according to the SCORM standard. A prototype implementation is presented to evaluate the proposed model.

**Keywords:** Dynamic learning experience · LO · LMS · BDI · Multi-agent system

## 1 Introduction

The Intelligent Learning Objects Multi-Agent Systems (ILOMAS) is a dynamic virtual learning environment, based on the Multi-agent systems (MAS) approach, integrated to a Learning Management System (LMS), which aims to include Learning Objects (LO) dynamically, adding intelligent behavior to LMS. The proposed model improves reusability by the combination of LOs available in some LO repositories and adaptability by selecting new Learning Objects from the repository according to the student's performance and behavior. This paper presents the implementation details of the ILOMAS prototype. The detailed description of the conceptual model, the design of the proposed architecture, the theoretical background and a discussion of related works was previously presented in [11, 12].

To produce more intelligent LO, previous works [2, 3] proposed the convergence between the LO and MAS technologies, called Intelligent Learning Objects (ILO). This approach makes possible to offer more adaptive, reusable and complete learning experiences. An ILO is an agent capable to play the role of a LO, which can acquire new knowledge by the interaction with students and other ILO (agents' information exchange), raising the potential of student's understanding.

This new version of the model called Intelligent Learning Object Multi-Agent System (ILOMAS) is composed by agents with specific goals, and capable of communicating and offering learning experiences to students in an LMS course, according to the interaction with these students.

© Springer International Publishing Switzerland 2016
J. Bajo et al. (Eds.): PAAMS 2016 Workshops, CCIS 616, pp. 428–434, 2016.
DOI: 10.1007/978-3-319-39387-2_36

## 2 Design and Implementation

The ILOMAS framework was implemented according to the architecture proposed by De Amorin and Silveira [10, 11] as a prototype aiming to validate the proposed model. The JADEX framework [5, 6] was chosen to implement the agents based on the BDI architecture [1, 4]. The JADEX platform supports the creation of active components which is an approach that gets benefits from the association of two distinct technologies: Agents e SCA. The SCA model was proposed by IT companies (i.e.: IBM, ORACLE) with the intention of promoting the interoperability among distributed applications, according to concepts of components and service oriented architecture (SOA) [5, 6].

The interaction interface between the student and the agents' environment was implemented based on the Java Servlets and JSP technologies, getting benefits of the JADEX BDI V3 services communication structure. The Servlets technology allows the execution of services and Java classes at the server side from Web requests.

On the prototype, the servlet layer delegates the handle of the student browser request to a Java class (non-agent) based on the Facade design pattern. This pattern provides a unified and simplified interface to a sub-system, promoting low coupling [7]. The ILOMASFacade class offers to the servlet classes and the access to agents' services (the agents' capabilities, plans, etc.) keeping the separation between the MAS layer and the external items (front-end and servlets), avoiding unnecessary coupling (Fig. 1) [8].

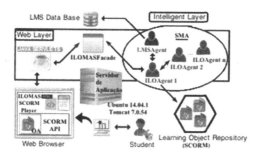

**Fig. 1.** ILOMAS web prototype architecture

## 3 Evaluation

Two different prototypes of the proposed model were implemented. The very first prototype was deployed to run over the Apache Tomcat Server (7.0.57) to perform the first simple tests of the proposed model. In this version of the prototype, it was built a scenario which, while the system runs, a student accesses the system and the LMSAgent identify that the student needs to study Photosynthesis. After that, the student ask for the learning experience leading to a new servlet requesting. This servlet forward it to ILOMASFacade, which waits for the ILOAgentBDI's deliberation. Then, this agent identifies some LO related to this subject matter within the repository. Finally, this LO was shown to the student successfully.

Besides, during this test it was simulated a student's request for a complementary learning experience (by pressing the corresponding button). As result, a new ILOAgentBDI instance was created in the system, which searched for and found a different LO related to the same subject (photosynthesis) within the repository. It was not explicitly defined in the database that the student should have watched this new LO (only the subject was required, any specific LO), so the MAS obtained the related LO dynamically by itself.

Further, it was simulated a student's request for a complementary learning experience (by pressing the corresponding button). As result, a new ILOAgentBDI instance was created on the system, which searched for and found a different LO related to the same subject (photosynthesis) within the repository. It was not explicitly defined in the database that the student should have watched this new specific LO (only the subject was required, no specific LO), so the MAS obtained the related LO dynamically.

### 3.1    ILOIR: Moodle Plug-in

The next step to evaluate the proposed model was, to integrate the environment ILOMAS with the LMS Moodle in a transparent manner, so that the student does not need to leave the virtual environment neither access any other system, preventing possible loss of attention. We developed a Moodle plug-in as an interface resource to the Intelligent Learning Objects, called ILOIR (Intelligent Learning Object's Resource interface). This resource allows the teacher to define: the subject matter (theme) and the learning objective of the instructional unit; and the address where the ILOMAS platform is available (Fig. 2). Furthermore, the ILOIR plug-in provides access to the functionality of ILOMAS system for the student, within the Moodle. The developed extension engages the ILOMAS the web layer (SCORM player, container HTML and JavaScript library) in the LMS structure, allowing the access to these features in Moodle and establishing (indirect) communication to the learning environment with the agents.

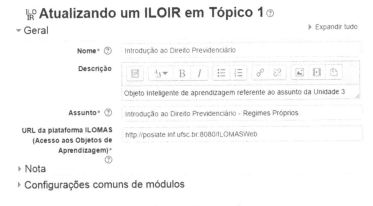

**Fig. 2.** ILOIR screenshot

**Fig. 3.** Structure of the course with Scorm

**Fig. 4.** Structure of the course with ILOIR

## 3.2 Experiments

The second experiments to evaluate the proposed architecture is to use the model for the creation of an introductory course in Social Security Law, offered by a school of government of a public agency statewide. The evaluation model aimed to compare two types of scenarios: one is a course set normally in a conventional way and another one set dynamically according to the student interaction using the ILOIR features. For that, we performed some comparisons between two courses created in Moodle (Fig. 3 and 4).

The first course was built with three LOs about Social Security Law (available in the repository) included as SCORM objects resources (native in Moodle). The second course was set just including only one ILOIR type resource (usin the ILOIR new developed plug-in), whose subject refers to the subject of the first SCORM object inserted in the course mentioned above. In order to facilitate the description, hereinafter the course with SCORM objects will be called "Course 1" and the course with ILOIR feature is called "Course 2".

**Table 1.** LMS configuration course

|  | Included resources | Included OAs | Time to configure | Total time to configure | Available OAs |
|---|---|---|---|---|---|
| Course 1 | 3 | 3 | 00:02:18 | 00:08:30 | 1 |
| Course 2 | 1 | 0 | 00:00:58 | 00:04:30 | Total amount of OAS available on the repository |

Tables 1 and 2 compare the two mentioned courses set in Moodle. While the course 1uses the explicitly included LOs, the course 2 presented several different OA to the student during the experiment, related to the object matter theme set by the teacher using the ILOIR feature. This feature offered by the plug-in facilitates the reuse of OA. It is important point to observe that only one object was included by the teacher in the course 2.

**Table 2.** ILOIR students interaction

| Student | Partial concept | Number of subjects demonstrated | Student's attention time | Number of wrong answers | Extra OAs (reinforcement) |
|---|---|---|---|---|---|
| 1 | Good | 1 | 00:09:46 | 0 | 0 |
| 2 | Regular | 2 | 00:21:13 | 3 | 1 |
| 3 | Bad | 3 | 00:34:19 | 6 | 3 |

With regard to student interaction scenarios with the plug-in ILOIR, we evaluated the access of three students with different degrees of understanding of Social Security Law (concepts: poor, fair and good), according to results of Table 2.

To note that, depending on the student's performance (the amount of errors in the assessment test in OA, or the delay in interacting with the object), additional new LOs are displayed to the student the same learning session. Is therefore the adaptation of dynamically OA content, as resolved by the agents (intelligent system layer), according to student performance (Figs. 5 and 6).

**Fig. 5.** Diagnosis and signaling new LO to the student 3, during OA display related to Unit2

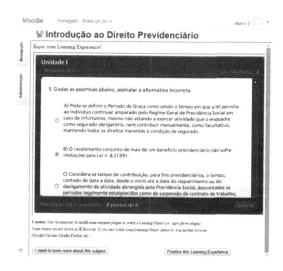

**Fig. 6.** Provision of prerequisite LA (Unit1).

## 4    Conclusions and Future Work

This paper presented the prototype implemented to evaluate a model to build more adaptive and reusable educational experiences, using learning objects. The ILOMAS framework was designed to allow the dynamic LO selection on LMS courses, as an improvement of ILO's previous approach. The agents are modeled based on the practical reasoning paradigm (towards goal achievement). The MAS was developed following the JADEX BDI V3 framework, which permits that the agents' functionalities can be accessed as services. The use of Servlet technology provides the integration of front-end and intelligent layer.

The prototype was implemented to verify the proposed model, and some evaluation tests were executed. As result, the ILOMAS has received the learning experience requested by the student, and has identified dynamically a LO associated with the subject that the student must have learned about (according to the LMS database information).

We are aware that this is just very small observation of the system's performance and the validation performed is still small to affirm the success of the proposed model. New tests will be done with the system with more objects and more students. As future work, the ILOMAS framework will be extended to supply the integration with LO recommendation systems based on ontologies in order to raise reuse, dynamic sequencing, and interoperability. Moreover, the model will be tested with different learning situations and real students.

# References

1. Wooldridge, M.: An Introduction to MultiAgent Systems, 2nd edn. Wiley, Chichester (2009)
2. Silveira, R., Gomes, E., Vicari, R.: Intelligent Learning Objects: An Agent-Based Approach of Learning Objects. In: IFIP – International Federation for Information Processing, vol. 182, pp. 103–110. Springer-Verlag (2006)
3. Silva, J., Silveira, R.: The development of intelligent learning objects with an ontology based on SCORM standard. In: Seventh International Conference on Intelligent Systems Design and Applications, pp. 211–216. IEEE (2007)
4. Pokahr, A., Braubach, L., Haubeck, C., Ladiges, J.: Programming BDI agents with pure Java. In: Müller, J.P., Weyrich, M., Bazzan, A.L. (eds.) MATES 2014. LNCS, vol. 8732, pp. 216–233. Springer, Heidelberg (2014)
5. Pokahr, A., Braubach, L., Jander, K.: The Jadex project: programming model. In: Distributed Systems and Information Systems, Chap. 1, pp. 1–34. University of Hamburg (2012)
6. JADEX. http://www.activecomponents.org/bin/view/About/Features
7. Prometheus Design Tool (Eclipse Plug-in). https://code.google.com/p/pdt-plugin/
8. Braubach, L., Pokahr, A.: Jadex Active Components Framework – BDI Agents for Disaster Rescue Coordination. University of Hamburg (2011)
9. Braubach, L., Pokahr, A.: Developing Distributed Systems with Active Components and JADEX. University of Hamburg (2012)
10. SCORM 2004. Advanced Distributed Learning. http://www.adlnet.org/scorm
11. de Amorim Jr., J., Silveira, R.A.: Dynamic selection of learning objects based on SCORM communication. In: Pereira, F., Machado, P., Costa, E., Cardoso, A. (eds.) EPIA 2015. LNCS, vol. 9273, pp. 658–663. Springer, Heidelberg (2015)
12. de Amorim Jr., J., Gelaim, T.Â., Silveira, R.A.: Dynamic e-learning content selection with BDI agents. In: Bajo, J., Hallenborg, K., Pawlewski, P., Botti, V., Sánchez-Pi, N., Duque Méndez, N.D., Lopes, F., Vicente, J. (eds.) PAAMS 2015 Workshops. CCIS, vol. 524, pp. 299–308. Springer, Heidelberg (2015)

# The Teaching Evaluation Model: A Web Application Framework

Ida Verna[1], Edgardo Bucciarelli[2(✉)], Gianfranco Giulioni[2],
and Marcello Silvestri[2]

[1] Department of Management and Business Administration,
University of Chieti-Pescara,
Viale Pindaro 42, 65127 Pescara, Italy
ida.verna@unich.it
[2] Department PPEQS – Economics and Quantitative Methods,
University of Chieti-Pescara,
Viale Pindaro 42, 65127 Pescara, Italy
{e.bucciarelli,g.giulioni,
marcello.silvestri}@unich.it

**Abstract.** The paper proposes a model for the continuous improvement of academic teaching aimed at delivering a programmed excellent learning in perspective. The proposed Teaching Evaluation Model (TEM) is a dynamic and open system based on the Deming Cycle (PLAN-DO-CHECK-ACT). The objective pursued by the model is to match the expected learning with real learning. The results of this work are intended to highlight the field application of the TEM approach. Specifically, the application consists of a web-based tool conceived and designed to allow teachers and institutions to build a continuous improvement of the teaching and learning processes. By enhancing the interior design education and hence the profession itself, the model reveals that technology-enhanced assessment may deliver tangible benefits for learners, teachers and institutions.

**Keywords:** Learner-centered-teaching · PDCA cycle · Graphical User Interface · Technology-enhanced assessment

## 1 Introduction

The Teaching Evaluation Model (TEM) is a working method developed for teachers and aimed at reducing the gap between learning objectives (quality promised, ideal learning) and learning outcomes (real quality, real learning). The method is represented by the PLAN-DO-CHECK-ACT (PDCA) cycle conceived by W. Edwards Deming [3]. Therefore, the TEM approach is proposed as an integrated system of design, implementation, evaluation/self-evaluation and improvement in order to implement a university course evaluation system. The aim is to offer the teacher the possibility to act on real learning and work toward an ideal one, right when this process is being realized on the field, giving rise to a dynamic system. The TEM model is proposed also as an open system that "learns" through classroom exams. Thus, learning which results is then fed

© Springer International Publishing Switzerland 2016
J. Bajo et al. (Eds.): PAAMS 2016 Workshops, CCIS 616, pp. 435–443, 2016.
DOI: 10.1007/978-3-319-39387-2_37

back to the teacher in the form of a sort of "guidelines for improvement". These guidelines are created when one or more teachers implement the model on the field. In this sense, in order to have a concrete possibility of operating in an effective way on training progress, the TEM approach has been developed in a software application (evaluation management system). The research contents of this paper are discussed in Sects. 3 and 4. Section 3 presents the TEM framework, its operational method, and its purposes. We emphasize how the TEM model has been transformed into an evaluation management system giving rise to an enforceable application. Section 4 introduces the first results of the work that are expressed highlighting the peculiarities of this management system, the advantages and limitations that distinguish it and its numerous potential further applications.

## 2 Theoretical Background

The TEM is part of a context of consolidated studies with a particular tradition in the North European and Australian studies [4, 8] in which teaching and learning are considered in close relation. In this sense, Biggs distinguishes three levels of thinking about teaching where the responsibility (success/failure) can be taken by students (first level), teachers (second level) or both (teaching and learning, third level) [1]. In the latter case, the author identifies the good teacher in the one who is able to stimulate learning activities and to lead students to become independent lifelong learners. In this line, the TEM proposes a novel approach to teaching in which teaching and learning are inseparable parts of a system of continuous improvement centered on learner and directed by the teacher. The TEM approach bases its operational logic on the Biggs's theory of the constructive alignment in outcomes-based teaching and learning [1]. Ultimately, teaching modalities and strategies as well as evaluation practices are aligned to education and training objectives. Therefore, a coincidence between what is taught, learned and assessed must be realized. On this basis, the TEM takes its steps towards the continuous improvement and enhancement of the educational processes in progress. The aim is to reduce the gap between "ideal learning" and "real learning". Thus, the TEM builds its bases on a continuous process of reflection and self-assessment [2] that integrates into a specific working model and leads to teachers' professional growth by stimulating their innovative behaviors. There is a plenty of studies focusing on the opportunities arising from processes of teachers' self-evaluation in the international literature [5, 7]. However, although an extensive discussion on the topic of self-evaluation has well-founded [6, 9], the international literature related to the teachers' self-evaluation and in the perspective of the teaching quality is very limited. In that regard, the TEM is placed in this particular research area. Far from being a complete answer and without limits, the proposed model offers the teacher the opportunity to observe and evaluate its own teaching and learning path, through a self-evaluation and self-training process that leads to the inescapable virtuous horizon of the continuous improvement.

# 3   The TEM Methodology

The TEM approach is a system that incorporates the PDCA phases. The subdivision in phases is presented in the following sub-sections.

## 3.1   The PLAN Phase

The first phase of the process of continuous improvement is embodied in the design of a specific course. The teacher divides the course into several modules, defining every learning goals in a specific designing pattern. Each module, in turn, consists of a number of classes (defined by the teacher). Initially, the teacher defines only the macro objectives to be achieved within the different modules - that at a later phase will be articulated into classes and related objectives. The PLAN phase includes the organization by the teacher of an entrance exam/test to be administered to students on the first class day. The model is centered on learners and their full satisfaction tending, therefore, to an excellent learning outcome and teaching experience. To this purpose, the PLAN phase must be based on competences (knowledge and skills) that students demonstrate at the beginning of each course. The aim is to make the course design effective and efficient, adapting "the production cycle" (training) to the "technical characteristics of the raw material to be processed" (students). In this sense, the items composing the exam should be defined for a perfect adherence to the objectives of the course modules. The entrance exam/test results will highlight the level of skills possessed by the learners at the beginning of the course. Compared to these skills, the results may show a homogeneity in the class of learners (upward or downward) or a heterogeneity. This information is necessary to achieve a design which is able to lead the educational process towards a high quality learning environment. These results will then be reported in the outline design scheme (see first column under Outcomes in Fig. 1). After having become aware of the learning level, and hence the learning needs, shown by the class (entrance exam) teachers have to:

1. Articulate the objectives of each module into sub-goals defined in terms of precise actions that learners have to be able to know and carry out at the end of each lesson;
2. Define the teaching strategies most appropriate to the level of knowledge/skills shown by the class (an effective method of identification of the teaching strategies is represented by the QFD) [10];
3. Organize the exam/test at the end of each module (one for each module of the course) in which each exam/test item (one or more) contributes to verify the achievement of a specific objective. The items are addressed to test the skills possessed by learners (defined in the learning objectives) at the end of the lectures – that compose the module under evaluation. There will be as many items as many specific objectives defined in each lectures composing each module. The scores of each item have to be predefined. The main goal is to foster the DO and CHECK phases.

| Lectures | | Objectives | Strategies | | | Outcomes | | | |
|---|---|---|---|---|---|---|---|---|---|
| module | lecture | specific educational objective | subject | methods | tools | entrance exam | end-of-module exam | improvement | end-of-course exam |
| 1 | 1 | | | | | | | | |
| | 2 | | | | | | | | |
| | 3 | | | | | | | | |
| | 4 | | | | | | | | |

**Fig. 1.** The PLAN phase - Course design scheme to be filled by the teacher. Source: our own elaboration.

### 3.2    The DO Phase

The PLAN phase fosters the DO phase in which the teacher conducts lectures as planned, starting with the first module. After having doing her/his job, the teacher will go down in the delicate phase of the learning check.

### 3.3    The CHECK 1 Phase

At this stage, the teacher administers the students' end-of-module exam, designed in the PLAN phase and given to learners in the last lecture of each module. These results merge in the designing pattern of the course in the column of outcomes (end-of-module exam) indicating whether there was an effective learning and at what level. A critical threshold establishes the acceptable level of learning beneath which the second check phase has to start, that is the CHECK 2 (teacher's self-evaluation). Ultimately, the objectives not achieved in terms of "learning-awaited" (evaluation below the critical threshold) become the subject of a critical analysis to be carried out by the teacher, who will delve into the possible causes of this unattained learning (see CHECK 2 phase). The objectives not achieved may be more than one, regardless of their number, and they may indicate a problem with a specific educational objective (skill, knowledge or expertise) not acquired by the learner. The CHECK 1 phase ends with the identification of the objectives not achieved. This identification fosters the CHECK 2 phase. If all objectives are achieved, the teacher can continue the most ideal process skipping CHECK 2 and ACT phases.

### 3.4    The CHECK 2 Phase

Once the objective/s not achieved are identified in the CHECK 1 phase, teachers have to reflect on the possible causes which determined the failure in achieving the learning objective/s with a self-assessment questionnaire (CHECK 2) [10]. Two types of levels are included in the questionnaire. The first level is aimed at those novice teachers in the use of the TEM approach. The second one is aimed at those teachers who have already demonstrated their ability to effectively master the model, understanding the conditions required to design a course and/or to govern a classroom. In the latter case, teachers will use a shorter but more technical version of the questionnaire. In the first level, two areas of analysis are highlighted: "what to do" and "how to do it". The teachers begin their search for the possible causes through a gradual widening of the first area of analysis investigating the PLAN phase (thing). The first level also includes "the identification of the right things to do". The teachers are encouraged to reflect on some aspects: learners' knowledge/skills, learning objectives, topics included in each class and definition of the teaching strategies. In this kind of analysis, the teachers have to trace out the fundamentals of the course design and assessing if they were properly defined. The self-assessment questionnaire, therefore, offers the teacher a gradual analysis of the key aspects of the course design where each "point of deepening" allows the teacher to show or to discard the possible causes of the problems encountered by the learners. In the second area of analysis, the teacher proceeds in the same way, but focusing on the "how". The latter sticks to "do well the right things". Indeed, it is not enough to identify "the right thing to do", it is necessary to do them well. And how to do them well? The points highlighted in the questionnaire suggest to the teacher some critical aspects to be carefully considered during the lectures. The objectives to be achieved are at stake. The problem may lie in the ability to master the methods and/or educational tools and/or methods of presentation of a lecture. Ultimately, the teacher could have defined the best teaching strategies (combination of methods, tools and scheduling) mastering them in the best possible manner. At the same time, the teacher could have not considered how her/his communication and presentation skills and the quality of relationships may affect students' learning. Even in this case, each "in-depth study point" allows the teacher to highlight or discard the possible causes of the problems emerged during the CHECK 1 phase. The self-assessment questionnaire allows the teacher to evaluate both the aspects defined in the PLAN phase (objectives, topics, educational strategies – section titled "thing" in the questionnaire) and those that cannot be defined in that phase as relating to the teacher's skills and expressed during the DO phase – section titled "how" in the questionnaire. Subsequently, the entire CHECK phase allows the teacher to reflect on aspects that s/he may have considered irrelevant or predictable as well simply never considered and that can enrich the teacher's experience and training in a continuous virtuous improvement (self-training). In this sense, the teacher performs a process of analysis, evaluation and selection of the possible causes of the problems encountered by the students (self-assessment, CHECK 2) that boosts the significance of the next ACT phase. The second level of the questionnaire provides a much more streamlined and technical workflow mainly focused on how the teaching strategies have been implemented. In both cases, first and second level, the analysis requires that the teacher recognizes the possible cause/s (more likely occurred in the failure of one or more learning educational objectives) and highlights it/them in the designing scheme and, in particular, within the section dedicated to the improvement, in the corresponding line/s of the target/s not achieved. The ACT phase is going to start.

## 3.5   The ACT Phase

The teacher after having identified the possible causes of the problems encountered by the students (CHECK 2 phase) defines the actions to be taken to overcome the problems identified so that to achieve the learning objective/s unattained. More specifically, in the line/s that show/s the objectives not achieved – in which the teacher has reported the points highlighted in the self-assessment questionnaire – the teacher writes the corrective actions to be implemented in the next course module (see column improvement under Outcomes in Fig. 1). These corrective actions are defined by the teacher on the basis of her/his reflections made in the CHECK 2 phase. Ultimately, the teacher has to redesign the modalities for pursuing the unattained objectives, to be experienced in the next module - with specific lectures. These corrective actions will, therefore, integrate one or more classes of the next course module. In this way, the ACT phase has been completed.

At this point, the PDCA cycle will be repeated again with the implementation of the lectures of the new course module (DO phase). At the end of this new module, the CHECK 1 phase will allow the teacher to check if all the educational objectives of the module have been achieved, in particular those including the "corrective actions". If one or more objectives previously not achieved still persist in the module, the teacher will proceed in the manner illustrated in the PDCA cycle. With regard to the case of objectives subject to corrective actions, if the exam shows the achievement of an acceptable level of learning (threshold exceeded), the line corresponding to these objectives will be highlighted with a specific color (green). This color highlights a best practice that will be reported in the self-assessment questionnaire (for example) if the end-of-course exam will confirm a positive outcome. The purpose is to foster the self-assessment questionnaire only by standardizing the best practices resulting from the application of the TEM in an ongoing course. The best teachers' experiences will be gathered in the self-assessment questionnaire (in terms of the example of "good practice"). The questionnaire is now taking its most important functions: to organize, manage and share knowledge and skills (best practices) with the users of the model - teachers [10]. In this sense, the self-assessment questionnaire is an instrument of self-training, a sort of "guidelines" that leads the teacher in the process of continuous teaching improvement: "ideal learning" towards "real learning". The PDCA cycle will be concluded at the end of the last module of the course. At this point, the teacher will administer a final test (end-of-course exam) to verify the achievement of the main objectives of all the modules. The results thus obtained will enable the teacher to assess their own teaching, particularly in terms of effective learning by students. From the teacher's point of view, the TEM emphasizes the difference between "ideal and real" learning, constituting a starting point not a finishing point. In this sense, a last CHECK phase, will be implemented by the teacher in order to change the overall design of the course for the new academic semester, if necessary.

## 4   A Web Application Framework

The structure of the TEM approach can be easily implemented by the HTML, PHP and MySQL programming languages giving teachers an user-friendly application to project their educational activity. On the one hand, as it is well known, the HTML and PHP codes are a programming languages to build dynamics web pages where users interact and make decisions. The HTML code is the standard language to create visually web pages, while the PHP code is an object-oriented language particular useful in building Graphical User Interfaces (GUIs). The GUI allows users to interact with computer devices and are now a cornerstone in developing modern teaching methods and strengthening the learning process as a whole. On the other hand, MySQL is an open-source relational database management system that works together with the PHP code and stores knowledge (data) created by users who make their decisions in the GUI. To this end, we have built a GUI to let the TEM framework feasible and usable to any teacher (users) interested to improve the evaluation of their teaching courses. In what follow, we briefly highlights basic mechanisms on the functioning of the GUI we conceived and developed:

1. Any teacher points her/his browser to the URL http://erre.unich.it/ees/teacheval and has to fulfil the registration form before using the GUI;
2. The application is now ready to use. Figure 2 shows the possibility of managing the teaching plan according to the TEM approach. At this stage the teacher choices objectives of her/his lectures and then s/he edits the teaching plan by pressing the virtual button dedicated to this function. The teacher follows the PDCA process as shown in Sect. 3 (TEM methodology) and, therefore, s/he sets up the number of modules and lectures. S/he specifies her/his teaching strategy (topic, method and tool). Finally, s/he has to insert the outcomes. The outcomes are at the heart of the teacher self-evaluation. The teacher finds the solution to the problem/s emerged when learners do not reach the minimum threshold of learning.

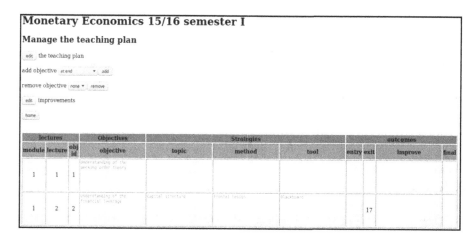

**Fig. 2.** The web page for managing the teaching plan (*e.g.* the course of Monetary Economics). Source: our own elaboration.

3. Suppose that the class has not reached the standard requirement: in this case, the teacher has to press the button to edit improvements, and the application goes to the improvement page as shown in Fig. 3. Here, the teacher has to press the edit button and the application jumps to the self-evaluation page where the teacher is guided by an evaluation survey list in order to check off the selected item that s/he believes can

be helpful to improve the students' performances. The self evaluation points identified by the teacher are given in the checkbox "improve" where the new teaching strategy shall be specified. The teacher will use the selected strategy in the next module in order to overcome the problem emerged.

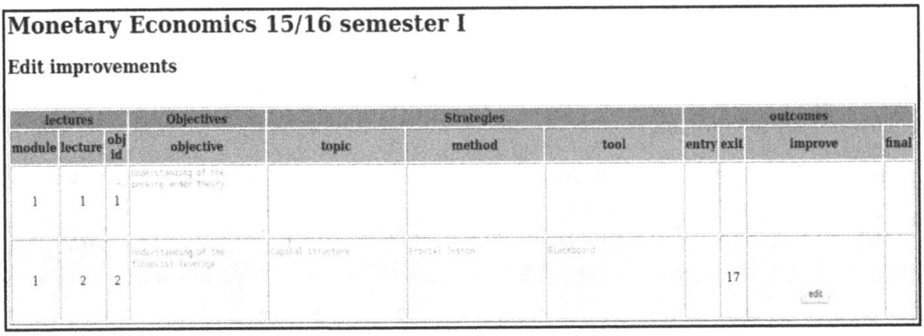

| **Monetary Economics 15/16 semester I** | | | | | | | | | | |
|---|---|---|---|---|---|---|---|---|---|---|
| **Edit improvements** | | | | | | | | | | |
| lectures | | | Objectives | Strategies | | | | | outcomes | |
| module | lecture | obj id | objective | topic | method | tool | entry | exit | improve | final |
| 1 | 1 | 1 | understanding of the pecking order theory | | | | | | | |
| 1 | 2 | 2 | Understanding of the financial leverage | Capital structure | financial leverage | Blackboard | | 17 | edit | |

**Fig. 3.** The web page for improving the teaching plan (*e.g.* the course of Monetary Economics). Source: our own elaboration.

## 5   Concluding Remarks

The TEM approach is a novel method to think, plan, manage and evaluate the university teaching process in view of the continuous improvement of education and training. The benefits are numerous and may be more useful for more subjects: learners, teachers, and institutions. Although the TEM approach is not exempt from limitations, it may offer a new approach to raise awareness of how to work towards learner-centered practices, whilst managing major educational change. Indeed, the authors of this paper are currently administering a pilot program in the University of Chieti-Pescara (Italy) working on developing a standard and guidelines for an international accreditation procedure.

## References

1. Biggs, J.: Teaching for Quality Learning at University. Open University Press, Buckingham (2007)
2. Cooper, K., Olson, M.R.: The Multiple Is of Teacher Identity. The Falmer Press, London (1996)
3. Deming, W.: Elementary Principles of the Statistical Control of Quality. Nippon Kagaku Gijutsu Renmei, Tokyo (1950)
4. Entwistle, N., Ramsden, P.: Understanding Student Learning. Croom Helm, London (1983)
5. Kyriakides, L., Campell, R.J.: School self evaluation and school improvement: a critique of values and procedures. Stud. Educ. Eval. **30**, 23–36 (2004)
6. Lyons, N.: With Portfolio in Hand. Validating the New Teacher Professionalism. Teachers College Press, New York (1998)

7. MacBeath, J.: Schools Must Speak for Themselves. The Case for School Self Evaluation. Routledge, London (1999)
8. Prosser, M., Ramsden, P., Trigwell, K., Martin, E.: Dissonance in experience of teaching and its relation to the quality 2003 of student learning. Stud. High. Educ. **28**(1), 37–48 (2003)
9. Selding, P.: Changing Practices in Evaluating Teaching. Anker Publishing Company, Bolton (1999)
10. Verna, I., Perozzi, D.: Applying TEM model (teaching evaluation model) in an academic course in accounting: a comparison across five years. Eur. Sci. J. **1**, 1–15 (2014)

# Author Index